BUILDING BRIDGES

INTERPERSONAL SKILLS FOR A CHANGING WORLD

BUILDING BRIDGES

INTERPERSONAL SKILLS FOR A CHANGING WORLD

William B. Gudykunst
California State University at Fullerton

Stella Ting-Toomey
California State University at Fullerton

Sandra Sudweeks
Golden West College

Lea P. Stewart
Rutgers University

Houghton Mifflin Company Boston Toronto
Geneva, Illinois Palo Alto Princeton, New Jersey

Sponsoring Editor: Margaret Seawell
Senior Project Editor: Susan Westendorf
Senior Production/Design Coordinator: Jill Haber
Senior Manufacturing Coordinator: Marie Barnes
Marketing Manager: George Kane

CREDITS

Cover design by Ron Kosciak, Dragonfly Design
Illustration: Shelburne Museum, Shelburne, Vermont. Photography by Ken Burris.

Printed in the U.S.A.

Library of Congress Catalog Card Number: 94-76504

Student Edition
ISBN: 0-395-63707-4

Examination Copy ISBN: 0-395-71894-5

123456789-DH-98 97 96 95 94

Contents in Brief

Contents

Part Two Skill Resourcefulness

Preface

Our purpose in writing this book is to help readers improve their ability to communicate effectively. We have tried to systematically incorporate suggestions for improving the quality of communication throughout the book and the accompanying instructor's resource manual. To help instructors and readers understand why we use the approach we do, we outline the philosophy we used in writing the book and overview the organization of the book in this preface.

Our Philosophy and Approach to Pedagogy

We believe that people can improve their ability to communicate effectively. Improving the effectiveness of communication requires that individuals understand how they generally communicate (that is, understand their implicit theories of communication) and consciously think about how they want to communicate in the situations in which they find themselves (that is, become mindful of their communication). Throughout the book, therefore, we emphasize the importance of understanding implicit theories and making mindful choices about how to communicate.

We include *questions* to stimulate readers to think about the content of their implicit theories of communication throughout the text and provide space on the page for readers to answer those questions. To illustrate, we present questions designed to get readers to think about how they conceptualize communication in Chapter 1. So that readers can get an idea of where they stand with respect to the concepts being discussed, we present *self-assessment questionnaires* in most chapters. In Chapter 3, for example, we present questionnaires designed to help readers assess their communication apprehension, verbal aggressiveness, empathy, and moral inclusiveness.

We believe that one of the reasons that people often do not use new skills of which they are made aware is that using new skills is awkward at first. Several components of the book, therefore, are designed to help readers overcome this awkwardness. Throughout the book, we present written *skill exercises* designed to help readers think about their current communication practices and develop new scripts for communication in the situations in which they will use the skills discussed. By completing the written Skill Exercises readers begin to cognitively develop new scripts they can use when they practice the skills. In the instructor's resource manual, we present ways that instructors can help students in their classes practice the new skills. We also suggest *journal reflections* at the end of each chapter. Some of the suggested journal reflections at the end of each chapter are designed to use the skills practiced in class in everyday communication. Other journal reflections are designed to help readers develop new cognitive, affective, or ethical resources for communication.

We believe that when individuals communicate with others, their communication is influenced by their personal identities (based on being unique individuals) and social identities (based on group memberships or roles). Stated differently, all communication between individuals is influenced by interpersonal and intergroup factors. Intergroup factors may be based on any group membership (such as our culture, ethnicity, gender, social class, disability status, age, membership in social groups such as fraternities or sororities) or the roles individuals play in society (such as professor, student, spouse, parent, supervisor, subordinate). We, therefore, systematically discuss how both interpersonal and intergroup factors influence communication.

Other pedagogical features include:

- Boxed *readings,* from magazines, newspapers, or books, that reinforce the concepts or skills presented in the chapter.
- *Key terms* in italics and *key ideas* in boldface.
- Photographs and cartoons that visually render the concepts in the text.
- Chapter *summary, study questions,* and annotated *suggested readings* at the end of each chapter.
- Glossary at the end of the text.

Overview of the Text

We divide the text into three parts. In Part I (Chapters 1-6), we examine the nature of interpersonal communication and the factors that influence the way people communicate. We examine how messages are interpreted and transmitted in Part II (Chapters 7–11). In Part III (Chapters 12–15), we look at how communication is used in interpersonal relationships. To illustrate how this book is similar to and different from other books, we will briefly overview the chapters.

In Chapter 1, we begin by pointing out that communication is guided by implicit theories of communication, and we point out that understanding implicit theories is critical to experiential learning. Also in this chapter we overview interpersonal communication and present a model that guides the analysis throughout the book. We examine the major identities that influence our communication (such as personal and social identities in general and cultural, ethnic, gender, age, social class, and disability status in particular) in Chapter 2. In Chapter 3, we discuss how individuals' orientations toward communication (such as motivation, assertiveness, communication apprehension, empathy, and ethical orientations) affect their interpersonal communication. We look at how cognitive processes (such as uncertainty and attributions) influence communication in Chapter 4. Also in this chapter, we present the major cognitive resources individuals can use to improve the effectiveness of their communication (skills such as being mindful, understanding alternative interpretations, and overcoming cognitive distortions are presented). In Chapter 5, we focus on the influence of emotions on communication, and discuss the major affective resources individuals can use to improve the effectiveness of their communication (skills such as managing anxiety and anger, tolerating ambiguity, and forgiving others). We conclude Part I with a discussion of structural factors (such as rules, roles, networks) and situational factors that influence interpersonal communication.

We begin Part II with a discussion of how the perceptual process and expectations for others influences the way individuals interpret messages. We extend the discussion of perception in Chapter 8 where we examine listening and feedback. We present skills useful in listening responsively, as well as skills in giving and receiving critical feedback. In Chapter 9, we examine how language and verbal communication styles (including cultural/ethnic and gender styles) influence communication. Also in this chapter we discuss the role of language in holding conversations (that is, opening conversations, turn taking, and closing conversations are discussed). In Chapter 10 we look at how individuals exchange information through asking questions and self-disclosing, seeking affinity from others, and influence others in conversations. We conclude Part II in Chapter 11 by examining the nature of nonverbal communication, how individuals respond to violations of their nonverbal expectations, and the role of culture and gender in nonverbal communication.

We begin Part III by looking at the factors that contribute to the formation of relationships with others, the stages of relationship development and deterioration, as well as the dialectics that operate in relationships in Chapter 12. We also discuss how relationships between people from different groups form and change over time in this chapter. In Chapter 13, we overview communication in friendships, romantic relationships, marital relationships, and the family. We discuss strategies for maintaining, rejuvenating, and transforming interpersonal relationships in Chapter 14. We extend the analysis of maintaining relationships in Chapter 15 when we look at ways to manage conflict constructively.

A Note to Instructors

The material presented in the book and in the instructor's resource manual is designed to help students complete the experiential learning cycle (described in Chapter 1). We believe that completing the experiential cycle is necessary for new skills to be incorporated into the communication repertoires students use in their everyday lives. We hope that you incorporate skill practice as a portion of your class when you use this book. Skill practice is different from experiential exercises. Experiential exercises are designed to help students see how concepts operate in their communication. While experiential exercises are valuable, they do not provide practice using specific skills. Learning new skills requires practice transmitting and interpreting messages involved in the skill, and receiving feedback on the skill practice. Without practicing skills in class and discussing their practice, students will be hesitant to use the skills presented in their everyday communication.

In writing the book we have tried to be thorough and cover most topics taught in interpersonal communication courses. In addition, we have incorporated several topics that we think are important but may not typically be included in many courses. It is possible that there is more material in this book than you include in the course you teach. In this case you can easily omit some material. We suggest that you *not* omit material from Part I. This material is used as building blocks for the discussion in Parts II and III. If you must omit some material, we suggest you consider omitting the portions of Parts II or III that you do not typically include in your course.

A Note to Students

One of our goals in writing this book is to help you understand the choices you can make about the ways that you communicate. The ways that you currently communicate with others are not the only alternatives available. You may not be aware of other alternatives because you probably have not consciously thought much about the ways that you communicate. Throughout the book we ask you to think about how you currently communicate, present alternatives that you can use if you choose, and ask you to think about how you want to communicate in the future.

There is a direct association between what you will learn from reading this book and your effort. It is possible to read the text and cognitively master the concepts presented without practicing the skills. Although this approach may yield high scores on exams, it will *not* help you improve the effectiveness of your communication. If you want to increase your ability to communicate effectively, you must think about the ways you currently communicate, practice the skills presented in your everyday communication, and analyze why the skills you use work or do not work when you practice them. The skills presented in the book are not only useful during the term you use this book; they are skills you can use the remainder of your life! Although your instructor can facilitate your learning and practicing the skills, making the skills part of the resources you use throughout your life is up to you.

You can practice the skills presented in the book even if your instructor does not focus on skill improvement in the class you are taking. By answering the questions posed in the text, completing the questionnaires presented, and doing the written skill exercises you will become aware of your current communication practices and the alternatives available to you. By completing the journal reflections at the end of each of the chapters you will see how the skills presented apply in your everyday communication. We urge you to do as many of the journal reflections as you can. The more you do, the more opportunity you have to learn new skills. In practicing the skills presented it is important to keep in mind that using new skills feels awkward at first. The fact that it feels awkward does *not* mean that the skill is useless; rather, it means that you have not engaged in these behaviors before. The more you use the skills presented, the less awkward they will feel, and eventually they will become habits. That is, you will use the skills without thinking about them.

Ancillaries to Accompany the Text

The following are available to users of *Building Bridges: Interpersonal Skills for a Changing World:*

- *Instructor's Resource Manual with Test Items,* written by Sandra Sudweeks, of Golden West College, and Ruth Guzley, of California State University at Chico.

  Part I of the manual includes the following sections: "How the Instructor's Manual Can Help"; "Philosophy Guiding the Skill-based Course"; a skill practice observation form; sample syllabi for a sixteen-week semester and a ten-week quarter; "Using Media Resources," which describes videos, films, slide shows, and television programs appropriate for the classroom as well as guidelines for using transparencies and overhead projectors; and "Teacher Tips," which offers suggestions for handling issues of content, methods, and student/teacher relationships.

  Part II contains for each chapter an overview, a discussion linking the chapter to the previous one (except for Chapter 1, which is discussed in relation to the following chapters), objectives, a detailed outline, discussion questions and classroom resources, activities and exercises, video resources, transparency masters (overheads), and examination questions.
- *Computerized Instructor's Resource Manual,* in ASCII format, contains all the information from the print version (except for the test items, available separately). The disk allows instructors to adapt and customize the IRM materials for lectures and other classroom activities.
- *Computerized test bank* is available in IBM and Macintosh versions.
- *Transparencies* serve as concept summaries or reminders during skill practice or subsequent lectures.

Acknowledgements

To begin, we want to thank our colleagues who served as reviewers for their thoughtful suggestions:

Judith Anderson
University of Rhode Island

Njoku E. Awa
Cornell University

Jin Brown
University of Alaska—Fairbanks

Jensen Chung
San Francisco State University

Sheryl L. Dowlin
Mankato State University

Mary Anne Fitzpatrick
University of Wisconsin—Madison

Karla Kay Jensen
University of Kansas

Nan J. Peck
Northern Virginia Community College

Dora E. García Saavedra
University of Texas—Pan American

Chris Segrin
University of Kansas

Dick Stine
Johnson County Community College

Edwina Stoll
DeAnza College

Lynn H. Turner
Marquette University

Steve Wilson
Michigan State University

Melinda S. Womack
Rancho Santiago College

Sonia Zamanou
Southern Illinois University at Edwardsville

In writing the book we have adapted some material from our other writing. We especially want to thank Sage publications for permission to use the self-assessments and to adapt material on intergroup communication from Gudykunst's *Bridging Differences.*

We were fortunate to work with an excellent group of editors at Houghton Mifflin. Margaret H. Seawell, sponsoring editor for communication, encouraged us to write the book and provided support throughout the writing process. Her knowledge and sensitivity were valuable resources in completing the book. We are grateful for Margaret's professional and personal concern for the book and us as authors. Doug Gordon, our developmental editor, facilitated the review process in a professional manner and helped us decide what to incorporate from the reviews. We benefited greatly from Doug's editorial expertise. We also want to thank Susan Westendorf, our project editor. Susan was responsible for seeing that the production of the book went smoothly. She also made sure that the book was accurate and aesthetically pleasing.

We also want to thank the students in our interpersonal communication courses over the years. They have helped us understand how to present the concepts and skills incorporated in the book in an effective manner, and served as an inspiration for writing the book. Finally, we want to thank the students at California State University, Fullerton (CSUF) who read different drafts of the book in class and provided suggestions on improving readability and clarity of presentation. Their contribution was more valuable than they will ever know.

Completion of the book was facilitated by a Senior Faculty Research Grant from CSUF to the first author. The book was finalized while the first author was on sabbatical leave from CSUF.

Bill Gudykunst Laguna Beach, CA
Stella Ting-Toomey Fullerton, CA
Sandy Sudweeks Huntington Beach, CA
Lea Stewart Somerset, NJ

Part One

Conceptual Foundations

1

THE NATURE OF INTERPERSONAL COMMUNICATION

We all spend a great deal of time communicating with others. The average person, for example, spends between one-half and three-quarters of the time awake talking and listening to other people. Because we communicate all the time, we tend to assume that we know a lot about communication. We assume that we know how to communicate effectively, what the problems of communication are, and how to solve these problems when they occur. We also tend to assume that we can communicate effectively without effort. Most of us, however, fail to recognize many misunderstandings that occur when we communicate with others.

We actually know less about communication than we think we do, and many of us communicate less effectively than we think we do. One reason for this is that, as children, we learned a very limited set of skills for communicating. The ways we learned to communicate as children, however, are not the only alternatives available to us. There are many different skills we can use to communicate more effectively. In addition to learning new skills, we also need to be able to recognize misunderstandings when they occur, to communicate more effectively. This requires that we understand how misunderstandings occur.

The two general goals for this book are designed to help you learn to communicate more effectively. The first goal is to introduce the concepts and theories used to explain interpersonal communication. Theories and research help us understand the process of communication and recognize when misunderstandings occur. The second goal is to help you learn new skills for communicating with others. New skills are necessary so that we are not limited to the ways we learned to communicate as children.

These two goals may appear unrelated. They are, however, highly interrelated because "there is nothing so practical as a good

People communicate all the time and we assume we know a lot about communication. But to improve the quality of the communication, we have to recognize that we are making a choice and that we can consciously choose to behave in ways different from those in which our implicit personal theories lead us to behave.

theory" (Lewin quoted by Morrow, 1969, p. ix). Good theories not only explain how we communicate, they also provide guidelines for how to improve the effectiveness of our communication. The problem is that most of us are not taught how to use theories to modify our behavior. Theories, therefore, are described in everyday language throughout the book in order to derive suggestions for how we can improve the quality of our communication. To improve our communication, we not only need to understand the theories used to explain communication, we also need to understand our implicit personal theories of communication.

Implicit Personal Theories of Communication

Much of our everyday communication is based on the implicit personal theories we learned as children. Our *implicit personal theories of interpersonal communication* are our unconscious, taken-for-granted assumptions about communication. As human beings, we "construct theories about social reality. [Our] theories have all of the features of the formal theories constructed by scientists. They employ concepts and relationships derived from observation; they provide a structure through which social reality is observed; they enable [us] to make predictions" about how other people will communicate with us (Wegner & Vallacher, 1977, p. 21).

Our implicit theories tell us with whom we should communicate, when we should communicate with others, what we should communicate, how we should communicate with others, how we should present ourselves when we communicate, what effective communication is, and how to interpret other people's communication behavior. Because we learn our implicit personal theories of communication as we grow up and live our lives, they are based on the culture in which we were raised, our ethnic background, our gender, our social class, the region of the country in which we were raised, as well as on our unique individual experiences.

When we do not consciously think about how we want to communicate with others, our behavior is based on our implicit personal theories of communication. By not thinking about our communication, we are making a choice to follow our implicit personal theories. The choice, however, tends to be made unconsciously because we are not aware that there is another alternative. To improve the quality of our communication, we have to recognize that we are making a choice and that we can *consciously* choose to behave in ways different from those in which our implicit personal theories lead us to behave.

Since we are not aware that we are using implicit, unconscious theories to guide our behavior, we do not question our theories or think about how they can be modified. Not questioning our implicit theories leads us to assume that the predictions we make about other people's behavior (based on our implicit theories) are accurate. The predictions we make based on our implicit theories, however, are not always accurate. To be able to improve our accuracy in predicting other people's behavior, we must become aware of the implicit theories we use to guide our behavior and think about how they can be improved.

To help you begin to think about your implicit personal theory of communication, several scenarios follow. Read each scenario and think about how you might communicate with the other person if you found yourself in the situation described, and write your response in the space provided. (The authors realize that some of you may not like to write in your books, but they hope you will make an exception in this book. Taking the time to complete all of the questions and exercises posed in the text will help you to better understand the material and improve the quality of your communication.)

Scenario 1 You are at a party, and your best friend introduces you to a friend of his or hers whom you have not previously met. Before the party, your best friend told you a great deal about this person. You have wanted to meet this person for some time. What will you do to get to know her or him?

In this situation, I would ______________

____

____

____

Scenario 2 You are in the student center, and an international student approaches you. You have not met this student before and have never visited her or his native culture. The international student tells you that he or she needs your help to complete a class assignment. The assignment is to get to know an American. How would you respond to the student?

In this situation, I would ______________

____

____

Scenario 3 You are in a restaurant and have just finished dinner with your romantic partner. You are making plans for what you two will do for the remainder of the evening. How would you convince your romantic partner to do what you want to do?

In this situation, I would ______________

____

____

Scenario 4 You are assigned to work with a person from a different ethnic group on a specific task, such as writing a report. You have never met this person before, and you have a negative view of some people from this person's ethnic group. How would you communicate with this person in order to do a good job on the task?

In this situation, I would ______________

____

____

Scenario 5 You are at a social gathering and see a person to whom you are physically attracted. Would you approach this person? If so, how would you communicate in order to make arrangements to meet him or her again?

In this situation, I would ______________

____

____

You will be asked to look at these scenarios again later in the chapter, but for now it is necessary only to recognize that the characteristics of the other person and the situation in which the communication takes place influence our communication behavior. We usually are not highly aware, however, of how these factors affect the way we communicate because we tend to react unconsciously, basing our communication on our implicit theories of communication. To illustrate, consider our interactions with members of the opposite sex. We all have unconscious stereotypes, or mental images, of males and females which are part of our implicit personal theories of communication. If we do not think about our communication when we communicate with members of the opposite sex, our stereotypes guide our communication behavior. Our stereotypes, however, may be inaccurate, or the person with whom we are communicating may not be a typical member of the group stereotyped. When we understand our implicit theories of communication and we are conscious of our communication behavior, we can choose not to use our stereotypes of males and females to guide our communication.

There is nothing wrong with following our implicit theories, but at times doing so inhibits our ability to communicate effectively. To illustrate, the way we learned to express or not to express anger as children may damage our relationships with others. If, for example, we learned to express our anger immediately, we may fly off the handle at people at inappropriate times. Alternatively, if we never learned to express our anger, we will constantly have problems in our relationships with others because they will never know that we are upset at their behavior. We can, however, learn new resources for dealing with our anger, which can help us be more effective in our interpersonal relationships.

As previously mentioned, any time we communicate, we have made a choice whether or not to follow our implicit theories, our choice may not have been a conscious one. Our choice nevertheless has consequences for our communication with others. **Many of the things we take for granted in our implicit personal theories may not be appropriate in some situations or may actually be incorrect.** We may, for example, assume that we are unable to change the way we communicate, but **we are capable of changing the way we communicate if we want to change.**

Before proceeding, think about your implicit theory of communication. Below are several questions designed to help you start to bring your implicit theory of communication into awareness. Answer each question before continuing to read:

1. Do other people usually interpret what you say the way you intended it? Why or why not? ______________________________
____
____

2. Do you have to intentionally send messages to others for communication to take place? Why or why not? ______________
____
____

3. Can you communicate with yourself? Why or why not? ______________
____
____

4. When you communicate with others, how do you want them to view you?
____
____
____

5. To what extent are you usually aware of your communication behavior? Are you more aware of your communication in some situations than in others? In what situations are you most aware of your communication behavior? ______________
____
____

6. How is your communication with members of your own groups, such as your ethnic group or your age group, similar to and different from your communication with members of other groups, such as other ethnic groups or other age groups?
____
____

7. How do you know if you have communicated effectively with others? __________
____
____

Your answers to these questions should help you begin to understand the content of your implicit personal theory of communication. The answers you give to the other questions posed throughout the book and your answers to the Skill Exercises will also help you understand the content of your implicit theory. Keep your answers to these questions in mind as you read the remainder of this chapter and compare your implicit personal theory with the conceptualization of communication presented in the book.

To communicate effectively, we need to understand the nature of interpersonal communication. This involves making our implicit personal theories explicit (conscious) *and* integrating our personal theories with existing knowledge about interpersonal communication. Comparing your implicit theory and the material presented throughout the remainder of this book will help you develop more effective plans for communicating in the future.

An Approach to Interpersonal Communication

As indicated earlier, one of the major goals of this book is to provide an introduction to theory and research in interpersonal communication. The theories used to explain interpersonal communication and the research conducted provide models against which we can compare our implicit personal theories of communication. If there are inconsistencies between our personal theories and the scien-

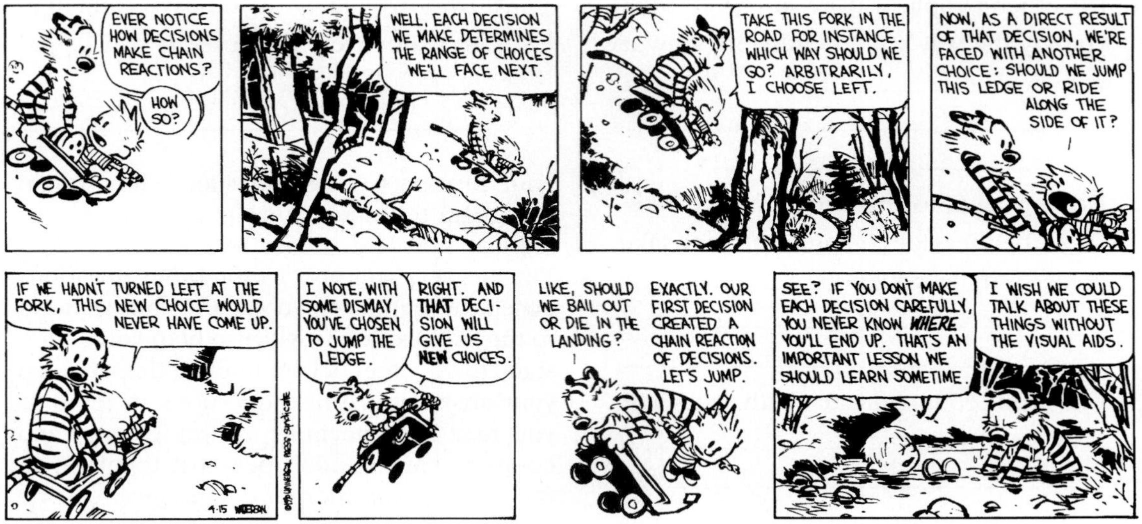

CALVIN AND HOBBES © Watterson. Reprinted with permission of UNIVERSAL PRESS SYNDICATE. All rights reserved.

tific theories and research, it does not mean we must reject either our implicit personal theories or existing knowledge. It does suggest, however, that we should try to understand *why* our implicit personal theories are different from existing knowledge and, whenever possible, to integrate our implicit theories with existing knowledge. Remember, theory and research can be used to improve the quality of our communication.

This book should help you understand the consequences of the unconscious choices you make when you communicate based on your implicit personal theories. Throughout the book, typical patterns of communication are described, and the consequences of communicating in these ways are presented. Alternative choices we can make when we communicate and the consequences of these choices are also discussed.

The focus of the book is on helping you to understand and increase the cognitive (thoughts), affective (feelings), behavioral (interpersonal communication skills), and ethical (moral) resources you have available when you communicate. Additional resources that can be used to accomplish your goals are provided throughout the book. Reading this book should help you make choices that increase the effectiveness of your communication, your satisfaction in communicating with others, and the quality of your interpersonal relationships.

Throughout the book, activities you can use to improve your communication are presented. In this chapter, for example, you have been asked to think about your implicit personal theory of communication and write down your responses. Doing these activities as you read will help you understand the material. Do *not* skip the questions asked in the text or the written Skill Exercises presented throughout the book. Thinking about the material and writing down your answers will help you crystallize new plans for how you want to communicate in the future.

Short questionnaires are included in most chapters to help you assess your communication behavior in various situations. To illustrate, when the concept of communication apprehension (anxiety about communicating) is discussed, there is a questionnaire to help you understand how apprehensive you are when you communicate. Completing these questionnaires will help you understand the concepts under discussion and help you assess your own communication.

Further, Journal Reflections are included at the end of each chapter. The purpose of these reflections is to help you apply the material being studied to your everyday life. You will get the most out of reading this book if you choose to actively participate and complete the activities suggested.

Each of the components included in this book has a purpose. Taken together, they are designed to be part of the experiential learning cycle (see Figure 1.1). Improving our skills requires experiential learning; that is, learning based at least in part on reflecting on our experiences (Johnson & Johnson, 1982). We can start anywhere in the experiential learning cycle, but for true learning to take place, we must complete the cycle and return to where we started. To illustrate the experiential learning cycle, let's begin with communication behavior. When we engage in communication behavior, we usually do not think much about it; it is based on our implicit personal theories. For experiential learning to occur, we must *reflect* on our behavior. We can, for example, ask ourselves questions like, "Was our communication effective?" or "Why was our communication ineffective?" If we stop at reflection, however, our learning is incomplete. We need to see how our reflections are consistent or inconsistent with what is known about interpersonal communication. Are there things we could do to improve the effectiveness of our communication? Once we have compared our reflections with existing knowledge, we can better understand our personal theories of communication and consciously choose to revise them if we think this will increase the quality of our communication.

An example may help clarify the nature of experiential learning. Assume that as children we learned that we should express our

FIGURE 1.1 The Experiential Learning Cycle

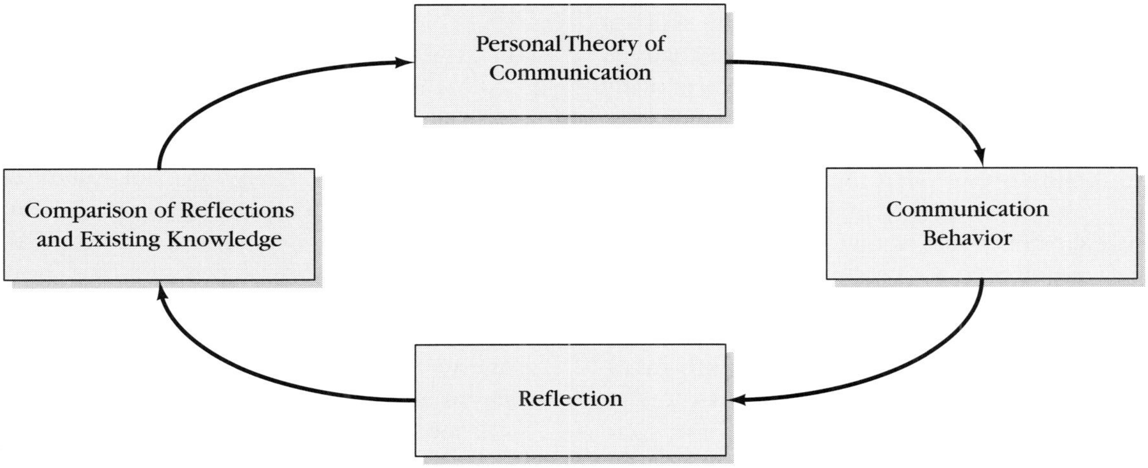

anger when we are feeling it (one small piece of our implicit theory). One time when we are angry and express it immediately to someone else, we stop and reflect on our communication in order to begin the experiential learning cycle. We ask ourselves what the effect of expressing our anger was. Did we feel better after expressing our anger? The answer is probably "no." How did expressing our anger affect our relationship with the person to whom we expressed it? The answer is probably that it had a negative effect on our relationship, such as that the relationship became strained. After reflecting on our communication, we compare our experience with existing knowledge on the expression of anger.

Expressing anger is discussed in Chapter 5, but for the purpose of this example, it is sufficient to point out that generally we should wait until we have calmed down to discuss with others the reasons why we are angry. Given this, we might decide to tentatively revise our implicit theories. We might, for example, decide to calm down the next time we are angry before talking to the person with whom we are angry. After trying out this behavior, we would reflect on our experience again. If it worked well, we might decide to permanently change our implicit theories. If the new behavior did not work well, we would have to analyze why. Did we use the skill appropriately? Was this one of the few situations in which it would have been better to actually express our anger? Once we have answered these questions, we can decide how we want to modify our implicit theories regarding the expression of anger. It is important to recognize, however, that changing our implicit theories requires that we be conscious of our communication behavior. In the previous example, if we decide that we want to calm down before telling others why we are angry, we have to consciously remind ourselves to do this when we get angry until we have done it sufficient times that we do it unconsciously.

As indicated earlier, we generally are not highly aware of our personal theories of communication; they are implicit or unconscious. To improve our communication, we need to make our theories explicit by bringing them into our awareness. Once we are aware of our personal theories of communication, we can consciously choose to change them. We can then consciously use our modified personal theories to guide our behavior when we communicate. The following discussion of the characteristics of interpersonal communication provide areas where we can compare our implicit theories with current conceptualizations of communication.

Characteristics of Interpersonal Communication

Interpersonal communication shares many characteristics with other forms of communication. There are also characteristics that differentiate it from other forms of communication. Let's begin by looking at the role of symbols in interpersonal communication.

Interpersonal Communication Involves the Use of Symbols

Language often is equated with speech and communication. There are, however, important differences. *Language* is a system of rules regarding how sounds are combined to form words, how meanings are assigned to words or combinations of words, and how sentences are formed. Language is a medium of communication. When the rules of language are translated into a channel of communication using symbols, messages are created.

There are several *channels* of communication through which messages can be transmitted. We can transmit messages using the spoken word, nonverbal cues, or writing. If a person cannot speak or hear, sign language may be used. Alternatively, messages can be transmitted through mathematics or through artistic forms of expression, such as painting or photography. Only when the spoken word is used does speech occur. Speech is a uniquely human phenomenon, and it is the human ability to engage in speech that allows us to use symbols (Dance, 1982).

Communication involves the use of symbols. A *symbol* is a thing conventionally used to represent something else. Virtually anything can be a symbol—written words, spoken words, gestures, facial expressions, flags, and so forth. Symbols have referents; that is, the things they symbolize. A red light at an intersection, for example, symbolizes "stop."

The referents for symbols can be objects, ideas, or behaviors. If we did not use symbols to communicate, we would have to have the referent with us every time we wanted to talk about it, to make our messages clear. If the word *mother* were not symbolic of our female parent, we would have to have our mother present every time we wanted to talk about her. Our names are symbols for us, and they allow others to talk about us without our being present.

We learn the meanings of symbols through the process of socialization, the process of learning to be a member of our culture. Symbols may take on different meanings in different situations. In this respect, symbols differ from signs. *Signs* are concrete and fixed regardless of context (Dance, 1982). When we show a dog the palm of our hand, for example, it means "stay" regardless of where we use this gesture.

In most cases, there is *not* a natural connection between a symbol and its referent. **Symbols are symbols because a group of people have agreed on their common usage.** One of the defining characteristics of a culture is agreement among the people who share a culture on the general meaning of symbols. This does not imply, however, that all members of a culture share a common meaning for any given symbol. The meaning we attach to a symbol is a function of our culture, our ethnic group, our family, and our unique individual experiences. No two people *ever* attach the same meaning to a specific symbol. Within a culture, nevertheless, there is sufficient agreement that people can communicate with relative clarity on most topics of communication.

While there is not a natural, direct relationship between a symbol and its referent, there are direct connections between our thoughts and a symbol and between our thoughts and the symbol's referent (Ogden & Richards, 1923). This is diagrammed in Figure 1.2. If we think of the referent, the symbol comes to mind; if we think of the symbol, the referent comes to mind. To illustrate this point, consider the symbol "mother." If we think of our female parent (the referent), the symbol "mother" comes to mind. If we think of the symbol "mother," we automatically think of our female parent. It is important, however, to remember that the symbol (or word) is not the thing (or referent); it is only used to represent the thing (Ogden & Richards, 1923).

Interpersonal Communication Is a Process Involving the Exchange of Messages

We combine symbols to create messages. We transmit messages to others, and we interpret the messages others transmit to us. *Transmitting messages* involves putting our thoughts, feelings, emotions, and/or attitudes into a form recognizable by others. We transmit messages using different channels of communication, including spoken words, written words, and

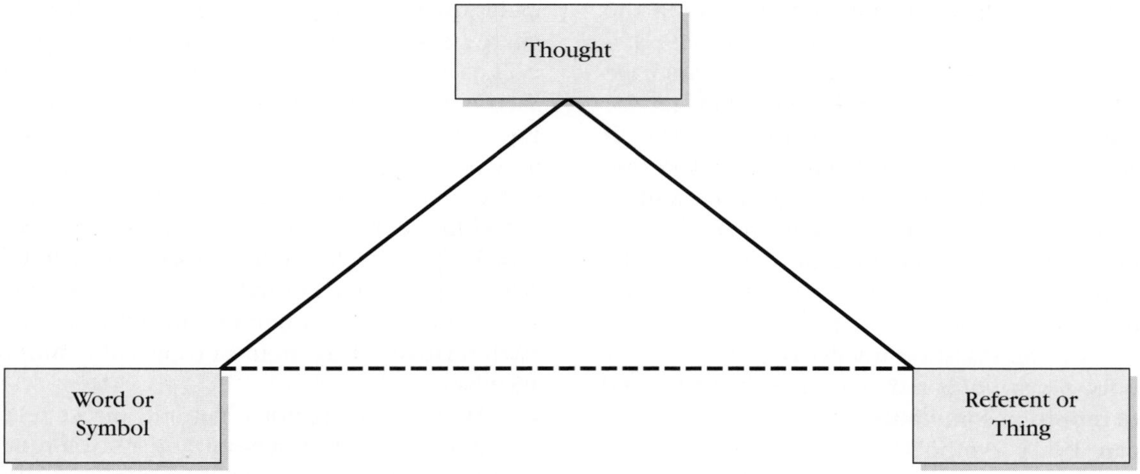

FIGURE 1.2 The Triangle of Meaning

nonverbal behaviors (which include facial expressions, gestures, vocal pitch, and so forth), to name only three channels. *Interpreting messages* is the process of perceiving messages using our senses (seeing, hearing, touching, smelling, and tasting) and attaching meaning to them.

When we transmit a message, one of four things can happen. The message may not get through at all; that is, the other person may not perceive that we transmitted a message. If the message gets through, one of three things can happen. The message may not mean anything to the person interpreting it. In this case, the other person will likely ignore the message. Alternatively, the message may mean about the same thing to the person interpreting it as it did to us when we transmitted it. In this case, communication will be relatively effective. The final thing that can happen is that our message will mean something different to the person interpreting it than we intended. **Misunderstandings arise when we do not recognize that the meaning the other person attaches to the message is different from our intended meaning.** To communicate effectively, we have to learn to negotiate and clarify meanings with others.

The way that we transmit and interpret messages is influenced by our background—our culture, our ethnicity, our family upbringing—and our unique individual experiences (including our experiences with others and the emotions we have felt). Since no two people have exactly the same background or individual experiences, **no two people transmit or interpret messages the same way.**

The transmission and interpretation of messages are not static activities. **We transmit and interpret messages at the same time.** We interpret other people's messages at the same time we transmit messages to them. We may change what we are saying because of our interpretation of other people's messages while we are talking. If, for example, we are talking with others and they have their arms crossed and are not making eye contact, we may interpret this nonverbal behavior to mean that they are bored with what we are saying. We might then try to change the subject based on our interpretation of the message. (Whether others intended to indicate boredom is an important issue, discussed later in this chapter.)

The fact that we transmit and interpret messages at the same time suggests that communication is a *process.* If we recognize that interpersonal communication is a process, "we view events and relationships as dynamic, ongoing, ever changing, continuous . . . we also mean that it does not have a beginning, an end, a fixed sequence of events. It is not static, at rest. It is moving. The ingredients within a process interact: each affects all of the others" (Berlo, 1960, p. 24). Viewing communication as a process forces us to recognize that it is a complex phenomenon that occurs continually and cannot be reversed.

Since interpersonal communication has neither a fixed beginning nor an end, there is no one cause for our communication behavior in any particular situation. Our communication behavior influences the people with whom we are communicating, and the other people's communication behavior influences us. A husband may, for example, believe that he drinks too much because his wife works late. The wife, in contrast, may believe that she works late because her husband drinks to much. In actuality, each person is influencing the other, and there is *not* one cause for either person's behavior.

Interpersonal Communication Involves the Creation of Meaning

When we communicate, we exchange messages and create meanings. *Meaning* is the significance we attach to messages or our translations of messages. As pointed out earlier, no two people attach the same meaning to symbols. Communication, therefore, is effective to the extent that we can maximize the overlap in the meanings communicators attach to messages. Stated differently, **effective communication involves minimizing misunderstandings.**

Messages can be transmitted from one person to another; meanings cannot. The meaning attached to a message is a function of the message itself, such as what is said and how it is said; the channel used, such as whether the message was spoken or written; the situation in which the message is transmitted, as in an office or a home; the people who transmit and interpret it; and the interaction that is taking place between those individuals.

There are two aspects of the message itself that influence the meanings attached to it. We can distinguish between the content and the relationship dimensions of a message (Watzlawick, Beavin, & Jackson, 1967). *Content* refers to the information in the message;

SUBURBAN COWGIRLS. Reprinted by permission: Tribune Media Services Inc.

that is, what is said. The *relationship* component is inferred from how the message is transmitted (including the specific words used in the message); it deals with how the participants relate to each other. A student, for example, may tell a professor, "I want to discuss my grade," but the tone of voice will tell the professor whether this is going to be a friendly discussion or a hostile encounter. The *way* we communicate with others offers a definition of the relationship between us.

To further illustrate this process, consider the following brief dialogue. The words that two individuals say to each other are provided, and there is space for you to indicate how different ways of saying the words might lead to different definitions of the relationship between the two people. After reading the dialogue, reread it and think about how different ways of saying the words might be interpreted differently. The situation involves a student and a professor discussing the student's paper:

STUDENT: What did you think of the way I defined communication?

Possible interpretations: ________________

____

PROFESSOR: Well, I wouldn't define it that way.

Possible interpretations: ________________

____

STUDENT: How would you define it?

Possible interpretations: ________________

____

Depending on how the professor says "that way," the student may perceive the relationship to be defined very differently. To illustrate, saying "that way" without a change in pitch might suggest that the professor has a different definition, while emphasizing "that way" might be interpreted as meaning that the student's definition is not very sound. Similarly, the way the student says "How would you define it?" can lead to very different relational definitions. Emphasizing "you," for example, might lead the professor to become defensive.

The children's saying "Sticks and stones will break my bones, but names will never hurt me" is not accurate. **The words we use and the way we say them affect our relationships with others.**

In addition to the content and relationship components of messages, the channel used to transmit a message also can influence how we interpret the message. A message transmitted face to face using the spoken word may be interpreted differently if it is said exactly the same way on a telephone answering machine. An order from our boss written in memo form will be interpreted differently from the same words given in person in a pleasant tone of voice. Similarly, messages transmitted over computer-mediated networks may be expressed differently from messages in a handwritten letter or those transmitted face-to-face. Computer-mediated messages, for example, make it easier to express anger. To illustrate, one manager reports, "Before [computers], if I was really angry, it took time to find the person and vent my anger. A lot of the times I cooled down. . . . Now, I can just hit a button and in a matter of 30 seconds, send hate mail to dozens of people" (Scott, 1993, p. A33).

The situation in which a message is transmitted also influences its interpretation. The same message transmitted in two different locations might be interpreted very differently. To illustrate, if we have a friend who is a physician and she or he says, "How are you?" we will interpret the message one way at a party and another in the physician's office. The situation also influences the degree to which we must elaborate our messages in order to be understood. Sometimes we must use concrete language and complete sentences to be understood. At other times, this type of elaboration is not necessary. In communicating with close friends in an informal situation, for example, we may use shorthand speech and slang. We would not, however, use the same speech patterns at work, talking to our supervisor. At work we would use formal language.

The people involved in any particular encounter also influence the interpretation of the messages exchanged. If we know other people, we use our knowledge of them in interpreting their messages. If we do not know others, we use our stereotypes of their group memberships (our mental images of the groups) in interpreting their messages. The culture, ethnicity group, social and gender classes, and age of the people involved influence how we interpret their messages.

Meanings also emerge out of the interaction that occurs. We always interpret other people's messages in terms of the messages they have transmitted to us during the same encounter and in terms of the messages we have transmitted to them during the same encounter. If it appears that we are attaching meanings to messages different from the person with whom we are communicating, we can negotiate a new meaning with that person. To illustrate, suppose we are having a conversation with a friend, and we say something like, "My partner thinks that we should take a short trip over the weekend." We use the word *partner* to refer to our romantic partner. If our friend says, "I didn't know you had a business," we would know there was a misunderstanding, and we could correct the problem by telling our friend that "partner" referred to the person we are dating.

To decrease our chance of misinterpreting other people's messages, we must be aware of how misinterpretations occur. Misinterpretations occur because:

> (1) We can never know the state of mind—the attitudes, thoughts, and feelings—of other people.
> (2) We depend on [messages], which are frequently ambiguous, to inform us about the attitudes and wishes of other people.
> (3) We use our own coding system, which may be defective, to decipher these [messages].
> (4) Depending on our state of mind at a particular time, we may be biased in our method of interpreting other people's behavior . . .
> (5) The degree to which we believe that we are correct in divining another person's motives and attitudes is not related to the actual accuracy of our belief. (Beck, 1988, p. 18)

Many of the resources discussed throughout this book are designed to help us improve the accuracy of our interpretations and in turn improve the quality of our communication.

Interpersonal Communication Takes Place Within a System

A *system* is an interdependent set of elements that constitutes a whole (Fisher, 1982).[1] A system can involve two people, a group, an organization, or a society. A family, for example, is a system. A mother, father, and child are the basic elements of the system. Two friends are also a communication system. Several characteristics of communication systems are important to understanding interpersonal communication.

The first characteristic of human communication systems is *interdependence* (Fisher, 1982). All elements of a system are dependent on one another, and all elements in a system influence one another. To continue our family example, the mother influences and is influ-

Interpersonal communication involves the use of personal information about the party with whom we are communicating. Our implicit personal theory tells us how we should present ourselves when we communicate and how to interpret others' communication behavior.

enced by the father and the child. Each family member influences and is influenced by the other family members. We cannot understand family members' communication in the family without looking at their interactions with other members of the family. This does *not* imply that one member of the family causes the behavior of another. Rather, each person's behavior influences all of the other family members' behavior and is influenced by the behavior of each other member of the family.

The second characteristic of a human communication system is *wholeness and nonsummativity* (Fisher, 1982). Because the elements of a system interact, the whole of a system is different from the sum of the parts.[2] We cannot understand a family by looking at the father, mother, or child in isolation. If we understand each individual separately, we will not understand the family as a unit. Understanding the family requires that we also understand the interactions among the mother, father, and child.

All systems are *open* to some degree (Fisher, 1982). Saying that a system is open means that the boundaries of the system are permeable and the system exchanges information with its environment. A family, for example, does not exist in isolation. Families live in a community, the parents work, and the children go to school. The parents' work, for example, influences what goes on in the family, and what goes on in the family influences the parents' work. Understanding the communication that occurs within one system, therefore, requires looking at how this system interacts with other systems.

Interpersonal Communication Involves Predicting Other People's Behavior

The nature of the predictions we make about other people's behavior can be used to distinguish interpersonal communication from other forms of communication. To explain this distinction, it is necessary to begin with the idea of making predictions. **Any time we communicate we make predictions about our own and other people's behavior** (Miller & Steinberg, 1975). Sometimes we are very conscious of the predictions we make, and sometimes we are not highly aware of them. When we meet someone we find attractive, for example, we may think of alternative ways to arrange a next meeting or date, and then select the communication strategy we think will work best to accomplish this goal. Under conditions like this, we are aware of the predictions we make.

When we meet someone we know for the first time in a day, we might say, "Hi. How are you?" Although we are not highly aware of it, we are making an unconscious prediction; namely, that the other person will respond with something like, "Hi. I'm fine, and you?" Assuming that the other person responds in this way, we would not be highly aware of having made a prediction. If, in contrast, the other person says, "Hi. I'm horrible. I've really been feeling bad today," we would have to stop and think about what to say since our unconscious prediction was not confirmed. The degree to which we are conscious of our communication, therefore, depends on the circumstances in which we find ourselves and the responses we receive from others.

When we communicate with others, we try to develop explanations for their behavior so we can understand why they communicate with us the way they do (Miller & Steinberg, 1975). Our explanations for why people behave the way they do affect the predictions we make. If, in the above example, we assume that our acquaintance is feeling bad because he or she is physically ill, we will make one set of predictions. If we assume, in contrast, that she or he is feeling bad because of some emotional reason, we will make other predictions.

Predictions Based on Group Memberships. We use three different types of data or information when making predictions about others: cultural, sociological, and psychological (Miller & Steinberg, 1975). When we use cultural or sociological data, our predictions are based on the category in which we place other people, such as "member of my culture" or "not a member of my culture." We choose the category in which we place others through the process of social categorization. *Social categorization* refers to the way we order our social environment and the people with whom we come in contact by grouping people in a way that makes sense to us (Tajfel, 1978). We may, for example, divide people into women and men, professors and students, "Americans" and foreigners, to name only a few of the sets of categories we use. In categorizing others and ourselves, we emphasize our memberships in social groups. A *social group* can be thought of as two or more people who define themselves as sharing a common bond (Turner, 1982). The role of categories in everyday life is examined in Reading 1.1. Take a moment and read this now.

People in any culture generally behave in a consistent way because they follow the norms, rules, and values of their culture. This consistency allows us to use *cultural data* to make predictions. Our "knowledge about another person's culture—its language, beliefs, and prevailing ideology—often permits predictions of the person's probable response to messages" (Miller & Sunnafrank, 1982, p. 226). Assuming that we are in the United States, if we are introduced to others from the United States,[3] we can make certain assumptions about their understanding of introduction rituals. We unconsciously predict, for example, that if we stick out our right hand to shake hands, they will do the same.

Sociological predictions are based on memberships in or aspirations to particular

Reading 1.1 MAKING DISTINCTIONS IN EVERYDAY LIFE/EVIATAR ZERUBAVEL

Separating entities from their surroundings is what allows us to perceive them in the first place. In order to discern any "thing," we must distinguish that which we attend from that which we ignore. Such an inevitable link between differentiation and perception is most apparent in color-blindness tests or camouflage, whereby entities that are not clearly differentiated from their surroundings are practically invisible. It is the fact that it is differentiated from other entities that provides an entity with a distinctive meaning as well as with a distinctive identity that sets it apart from everything else.

The way we cut up the world clearly affects the way we organize our everyday life. The way we divide our surroundings, for example, determines what we notice and what we ignore, what we eat and what we avoid eating. By the same token, the way we classify people determines whom we trust and whom we fear, whom we marry and whom we consider sexually off limits. The way we partition time and space likewise determines when we work and when we rest, where we live and where we never set foot.

Indeed, our entire social order is a product of the ways in which we separate kin from nonkin, moral from immoral, serious from merely playful, and what is ours from what is not. Every class system presupposes a fundamental distinction between personal features that are relevant for placing one in a particular social stratum (for example, occupation, color of skin, amount of formal education) and those that are not (for example, sexual attractiveness, height, intelligence), and any society that wishes to implement a welfare or retirement policy must first distinguish the well-to-do from the needy and those who are fully competent to work from those who are "too old." By the same token, membership in particular social categories qualifies us for, or disqualifies us from, various benefits, exemptions, and jobs. It is the need to distinguish "us" from "them" that likewise generates laws against intermarriage, and the wish to separate mentally the "masculine" from the "feminine" that leads to the genderization of professions and sports.

social groups or social roles. *Sociological data* are the principal kind used to predict behavior of people from our culture (Miller & Steinberg, 1975). When sociological data are used, group memberships based on ethnicity,[4] gender, religion, disabilities, gender orientation, and so forth provide the basis for our predictions of others' behavior. Roles such as professor, physician, clerk, supervisor, and so forth also provide a basis for the sociological predictions we make.

Predictions Based on Personal Information. When we base our predictions on cultural or sociological information, we assume that the people within the category, such as the culture or ethnic group, are similar. While individuals within a category share similarities (there are similarities shared by people born and raised in the United States), individuals within each category also differ. When we are able to discriminate how individuals are similar to and different from other members of

In making predictions about others, we may use sociological data. The roles we play, our gender, or ethnicity, among other characteristics, provide the basis for our predictions of others' behavior.

the same category, we are using psychological data to make predictions. The use of *psychological data* involves taking into consideration the specific person with whom we are communicating and how she or he will respond to our messages when we make our predictions (Miller & Steinberg, 1975). **Interpersonal communication takes place when our predictions about other people's behavior are based on psychological data.**

Psychological information is important when we communicate frequently with someone in a specific role relationship. Physicians who treat all patients alike by using only sociological data, such as categorizing them as patients who need treatment, will not be very effective. Successfully treating patients requires knowledge of them both as patients and as individuals, specific information about them, and how they are similar to and different from other patients. To communicate effectively with others, it is necessary to differentiate individuals from the groups of which they are members. Relying completely on cultural and/or sociological data when communicating with others over an extended period of time inevitably leads to misunderstandings. Using psychological data facilitates effective communication and developing interpersonal relationships with others.

We rely on cultural and sociological data in the vast majority of our interactions (Miller & Steinberg, 1975). There is nothing wrong with this. It is natural, and it is necessary to allow us to deal with the complexity of our social environment. Imagine going into a restaurant and having to get to know your server in order to make psychological predictions about his or her behavior before you could place your order. This would complicate every interaction and is not necessary. We can communicate effectively with a server in a restaurant without using psychological data. Sociological data are all that are necessary to get our order correct. The same is true for most other role relationships that do not involve interaction over an extended period of time, such as our interaction with store clerks or mechanics.

Application. To apply the ideas in this section, take a minute to reread the scenarios at the beginning of this chapter. For each scenario try to determine the types of data you would be using to predict the other person's behavior, and write your answers in the space provided below:

Scenario	Types of Data Being Used
1. Friend of best friend	____________
2. International student	____________
3. Romantic partner	____________
4. Person from different ethnic group	____________
5. Person to whom you are physically attracted	____________

In Scenario 1, all three types of data are available when you are introduced to your best friend's friend. You know cultural and sociological information (the person's gender and ethnicity), and you have psychological information (what your best friend told you about the person). In Scenario 2, you have only cultural and sociological information (you would know the student's gender) available to predict the international student's behavior. In Scenario 3, you have all three types of information about your romantic partner. In Scenario 4, you would have cultural (he or she is from your culture) and sociological information (his or her ethnicity and gender) about the person from the other ethnic group. Finally, in Scenario 5, you also would have only cultural and sociological information about the other person. Since you have not met the person, you do not have information about the specific person to use in making predictions. Note that, if you are basing your predictions on the other person's appearance, the information you are using is based on your stereotype of a group with a certain type of appearance, such as people who are attractive.

Interpersonal and Intergroup Communication Occur at the Same Time

As indicated earlier, the term *interpersonal communication* refers to communication in those encounters in which most of the predictions we make about others are based on psychological data (Miller & Steinberg, 1975). When most of our predictions about another person are based on cultural or sociological data (using social categorizations), we are engaging in "noninterpersonal communication." Another way of thinking about this is to say that we are engaging in intergroup communication. The distinction between these two types of communication is important and deserves further discussion.

Our communication can be seen as varying on a continuum from purely intergroup to purely interpersonal (Tajfel & Turner, 1979). Intergroup communication occurs when we base most of our predictions of other people's behavior on the categories in which we place them. Interpersonal communication occurs when we use mostly psychological data to predict other people's behavior. We can never base all of our predictions on psychological data. Group memberships influence even the most intimate forms of communication. Consider the communication between two lovers. While it might seem that group memberships and social identities do not influence this form of communication, they do. Whether we define ourselves as heterosexual, homosexual, or bisexual, for example, influences the gender of the partners we select and the way we communicate with them.

Thinking of interpersonal and intergroup communication as varying along a continuum oversimplifies the nature of the communication process. In actuality, **we use cultural, sociological, and psychological data at the same time to predict other people's behavior.** In other words, both interpersonal and intergroup communication occur at the same time. While both occur at the same time, our encounters with others tend to be either predominantly interpersonal or predominantly intergroup. Since both operate simultaneously, however, interpersonal and intergroup factors are integrated whenever possible throughout the discussion in the book. Information and skills are presented that can be used to increase the quality of our interpersonal *and* intergroup communication.

Functions and Sources of Communication Behavior

There are many reasons why we communicate with others. We communicate to inform someone about something, to entertain another person, to change another person's attitudes or behavior, and to reinforce our view of ourselves, to name only a few possibilities. Whether or not we accomplish our goals, however, may be influenced by the source of our communication behavior.

Functions of Communication

We have three basic objectives in communication situations (Clark & Delia, 1979). First, we have *instrumental objectives* that we try to meet. Our instrumental objectives are the goals we have in the situation. Second, we have *interpersonal objectives.* Our interpersonal objectives deal with developing and maintaining relationships with others. Third, we have *identity objectives* when we communicate. Our identity objectives deal with the image we want to present to others. To illustrate, our instrumental objective in a situation may be to convince our friends that we should see a particular movie. At the same time, we may have the interpersonal objective of maintaining our relationships with our friends and the identity objective of having our friends see us as cooperative.

To achieve our objectives and communicate effectively, we must manage the uncertainty and anxiety we experience when communicating with others. If uncertainty and anxiety are too high or too low, we cannot accomplish our instrumental, interpersonal, or identity objectives.

Uncertainty is a cognitive inability to predict and/or explain our own and other people's attitudes, feelings, values, and behavior (Berger & Calabrese, 1975). Prediction involves projecting what will happen in a particular situation; explanation involves stating why something occurred. *Anxiety* is an affective response involving the feeling of being uneasy, tense, worried, or apprehensive about what might happen. Our "anxiety stems from the anticipation of negative consequences" (Stephan & Stephan, 1985, p. 159).

Uncertainty and anxiety often are highest when we find ourselves in new situations interacting with members of other groups, but they can be high any time we enter new situations. To deal with the ambiguity of new situations, we usually seek information to manage our uncertainty, and we try to manage our anxiety by reducing our tension. It is necessary for our uncertainty and anxiety to be in our comfort range in order for us to communicate effectively with others.

We do not, however, want to totally reduce our uncertainty or anxiety when we communicate with others. If uncertainty is too low we become bored, and if anxiety is too low we are not motivated to communicate.

Sources of Communication Behavior

Our communication behavior can be based on one of three sources: habits/scripts, intentions, or emotions. First, **we engage in much of our communication behavior out of habit.** We have learned habits which we enact in particular situations. Habits are behaviors in which we engage without thinking about them. Our habits can be unique to us as individuals, but there also is habitual behavior in which we engage with other group members without thinking. *Scripts* are habitual patterns of communication that are shared by a group of people (Abelson, 1976). Scripts provide predictions of our own and other people's behavior in specific situations. When we first encounter a new situation, we seek out clues to guide our behavior (Langer, 1978). As we have repeated experiences with the same type of situation, there is less need to consciously think about our behavior, and we tend to rely on our scripts.

To illustrate the idea of scripts, consider the greeting ritual. In every culture, the ritual for greeting others provides a script for interacting with others when we first see them during the day. The rules of the greeting ritual provide us with guidelines on how to communicate with others and how others will respond in the situation. The rules of the greeting ritual reduce to manageable proportions the uncertainty and anxiety present in initial interactions with strangers and allow us to interact with them without high levels of uncertainty and anxiety.

When someone deviates from a script, we cannot fall back on the script's predictions. Under these circumstances, we have to actively reduce our uncertainty and anxiety before we can make accurate predictions and communicate effectively. To illustrate, if Chris and Pat are greeting each other, a typical scripted interaction might go as follows:

CHRIS: Hi Pat, how are you today?

PAT: Hello. Fine. How are you?

CHRIS: Okay.

In this situation, both Chris and Pat are following the greeting script. But what if Pat deviates from the script and, instead of saying, "Fine," Pat says, "Not so good. I just found out my father has cancer"? Since Pat deviated from the script, Chris will experience an increase in uncertainty and/or anxiety. If the anxiety and/or uncertainty becomes too high and is outside Chris' comfort range, Chris will have to actively try to manage this anxiety and uncertainty in order to communicate effectively with Pat.

Our communication behavior also can be based on the intentions we form. *Intentions* are instructions we give ourselves about how to behave in a specific situation (Triandis, 1977). When we think about what we want to do in a particular situation, we form intentions. Our intentions are our plans for how to communicate.

We are not always highly aware of our intentions. When we get dressed in the morning, for example, we do not always stop and consciously think about the messages we want to transmit to others through our dress. When we purchased the clothes, however, we probably thought about the image they would project when we wore them.

Misunderstandings often occur when we do not intend to transmit a message and others perceive that a message was transmitted and react based on their interpretation of the message. Misunderstandings also occur when we intend to transmit a message and others do not perceive that a message was transmitted and therefore do not respond to the message.

Our communication behavior also can be based on our emotions, feelings, or affect. We often react on a strictly emotional basis to messages others transmit. We do not follow a script or think about our communication and form intentions. If we feel criticized, for example, we may become defensive and strike out at the other person without thinking. We can, however, manage our emotional reactions cognitively. In fact, it is suggested later in this chapter that this is necessary for us to communicate effectively.

Any time we interact with others, our communication is based on our habits, our emotions, *or* our intentions. When our behavior is based on our habits or our emotions, we are not highly aware of our communication. We are, however, more aware of our communication when it is based on our intentions.

To summarize, interpersonal communication is a process involving the use of symbols to exchange messages and create meaning. While interpersonal communication involves the use of personal information about others, group-based information also is used every time we communicate. Given this overview of the characteristics of interpersonal communication, let's look at a model of interpersonal communication that can be used to guide our communication when we want to improve its effectiveness.

A Model of Interpersonal Communication

Models are useful because they can help us to isolate and identify the factors important in understanding interpersonal communication. Of course, any model simplifies the process. The one presented here is no exception. The model presented, nevertheless, helps visualize the process of interpersonal communication and provides suggestions on how we can improve the quality of our interpersonal communication. The material that follows provides an overview of the model. All elements in the model are discussed in detail in the chapters that follow.

An Overview of the Model

Communication between two people is diagrammed in Figure 1.3. Person A is represented by a rectangle and Person B, by a circle. Different symbols are used to indicate that the two people are unique in some respect. The differences may be due to culture, ethnicity, gender, or life experiences, to name only a few of the possible ways two people may differ.

In the figure, the dynamic, processual nature of communication is illustrated by showing the interrelationships among the elements. Of course, the processes depicted take place within seconds. In order to discuss these processes, however, each element in the model must be discussed separately. Throughout the following discussion, keep in mind that these processes occur almost instantaneously.

To begin, each person engages in *communication behavior.* This involves the transmission of messages to the other person using verbal and/or nonverbal channels of communication. Communication behavior is drawn as outside each person to indicate that it occurs *between* people. Communication behavior does not take place within a person.

The communication behavior in which each person engages is one aspect of the *relational processes* occurring when two people communicate. There are several other relational processes taking place when we com-

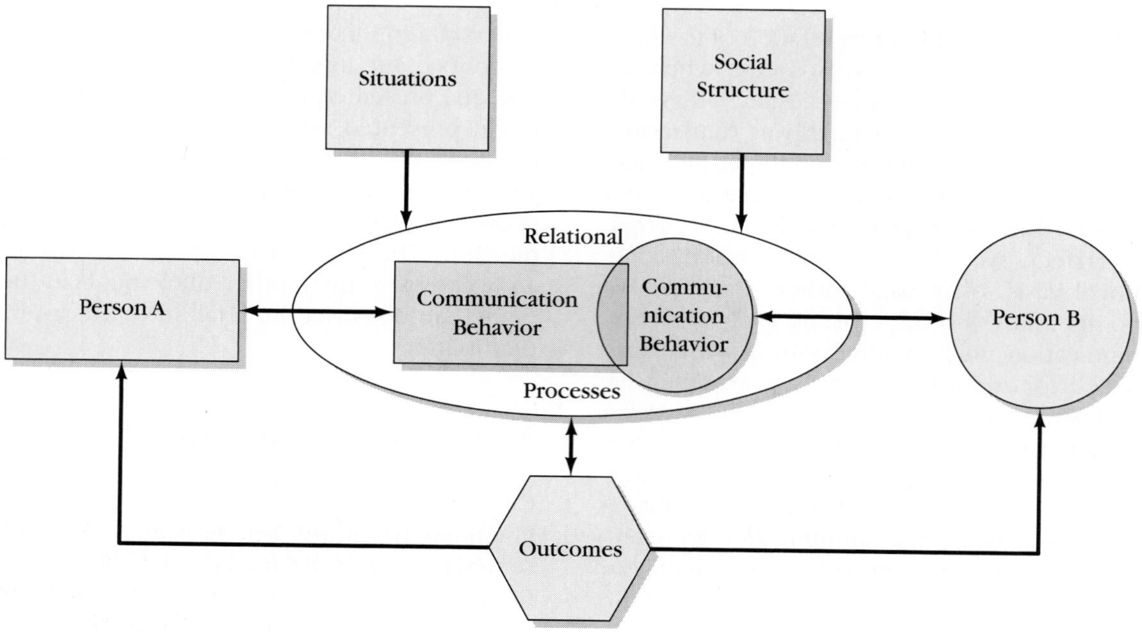

FIGURE 1.3 The Communication Process

municate. When we communicate, for example, we usually try to coordinate our behavior with the other person. Part of this coordination involves negotiating how we view the other person and how the other person views us (the identity objective of communication discussed earlier). We may see ourselves as cooperative and helpful, while other people see us as being obstructive. When the two views are inconsistent, we try to negotiate how other people see us by the ways in which we communicate. Our communication behavior, the degree of coordination, and our perceptions influence the outcomes of the communication that takes place between us and another person.

The relational processes that take place when we communicate are influenced by the *situation* in which we are communicating. The situation involves the physical setting; the social roles we are filling, such as professor or student, boss or subordinate; the communication rules guiding our behavior; and the degree to which the situation facilitates interpersonal communication. There are several aspects of situations that facilitate interpersonal communication. Interpersonal communication can take place more easily in informal situations, for example, than in formal situations. In formal situations, the roles individuals fill influence their communication. Similarly, situations in which the individuals have equal status facilitate communication more than situations in which people are unequal. Further, people can communicate interpersonally more easily when they are working on cooperative tasks than when working on competitive tasks.

The *social structure* in which the individuals are involved also influences the relational processes that take place when they communicate. Social structure refers to social influences on communication. Our location within the class structure of our society (such as a member of the middle class), for example, influences our communication. The relative power we have because of our personal position or our membership in social groups also affects our communication. The overall relationship between the groups of which we are members also affects the communication. To illustrate, if a European American (a person whose heritage is derived from Europe) and an African American are communicating, the relations between these two ethnic groups in the United States affect the nature of the communication that takes place between the two individuals.

Another aspect of the social structure influencing our communication is the *networks* in which we are involved. If Person A and Person B both know Person C, for example, the three people are involved in a communication network. If Person A and Person B do not have any acquaintances in common, on the other hand, they are not involved in a common network. In general, shared networks facilitate effective interpersonal communication.

The relational processes that occur between individuals influence communication. If we successfully negotiate the identities we want to present in a particular encounter, for example, we will be able to communicate more effectively. Relational processes also influence the outcomes that can occur as the result of two people communicating. *Outcomes* include, but are not limited to, the degree to which we accomplish our goals (the instrumental objective discussed earlier), the degree to which we understand each other, our satisfaction with the communication episode, the degree to which we perceive each other as communicating appropriately and effectively, and the development of a relationship (the interpersonal objective of communication discussed earlier). These outcomes, in turn, influence the individual communicators and the relational processes taking place. To illustrate, if Person B communicates in a way that suggests to Person A that he or she is not competent, this will influence person A's view of her or himself.

The Individual Communicator

Figure 1.4 isolates the central processes taking place within individuals that influence the quality of their communication. Let's begin by looking at identity.

Identity. Our *self-concept,* how we define ourselves, consists of three components—our human identities, our social identities, and our personal identities (J. C. Turner, 1987).[5] Our human identities involve those characteristics we share with all other humans. Our social identities are derived from our shared memberships in social groups.[6] We have social identities for each group in which we claim membership and for the important roles we play. We have social identities based on our culture, our ethnicity, our gender, our religion, our sexual orientation, and our profession, to name only a few of our potential social identities. Our personal identities include those aspects of our self-definitions that we believe make us unique individuals. Our personal identities are derived from our unique individual experiences and how we differ from other members of our groups.

Our communication behavior can be based on our human, social, or personal identities. In a particular situation, we may choose (either consciously or unconsciously) to define ourselves communicatively as unique persons or as members of groups. When our communication behavior is based mostly on our own and other people's personal identi-

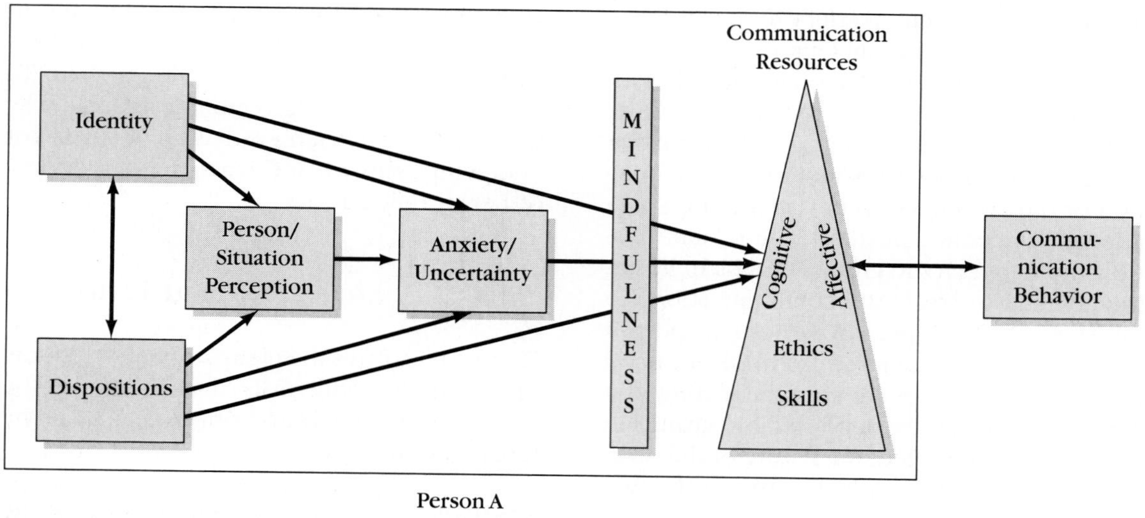

FIGURE 1.4 The Individual in the Communication Process

ties, we tend to make predictions based on psychological data, and interpersonal communication takes place. When we define ourselves and other people mostly in terms of our social identities (including our cultural and ethnic identities), we tend to make predictions based on cultural or sociological data, and intergroup communication occurs.

Any time we communicate, one or more of our identities influences our communication behavior. If we meet a member of the opposite sex for the first time, for example, our gender identity (one of our social identities) influences our communication. Our personal identities, however, also influences how we communicate in this situation.

Dispositions. Our dispositions toward communication influence our communication behavior. Our *dispositions* are our prevailing tendencies or inclinations toward communication. Our dispositions include our general tendencies toward communication such as whether we are introverts or extroverts, our motivation to communicate, and the ethical principles on which our communication is based.

Our motivation is influenced by the degree to which our needs, such as our need for other people's behavior to be predictable, are met. If our needs are met and we feel motivated to communicate with other people, we approach them with a positive attitude. If, on the other hand, our needs are not met and we are not motivated to communicate with other people, we may go out of our way to avoid them. To illustrate, we tend to avoid interacting with other people whose behavior is unpredictable. The extent to which we are motivated to communicate with other people is, in part, a function of the identities that are guiding our behavior. If we are considering interacting with a person from another ethnic group and our insecure ethnic identity is guiding our behavior, for example, we will probably choose, either consciously or unconsciously, to avoid the other person. Our motivation also influences which identity gets activated in a particular situation. If we are physically attracted to others and are motivated to communicate with them, it may activate our "dating" personal identity.

Person/Situation Perception. Our identity and our dispositions toward communication influence how we perceive the person and the situation in which the communication takes place. If we are motivated to communicate with another person and our gender identity (our male or female identity) is activated, for example, we interpret the other person's behavior and define the situation differently than if we are not motivated to communicate and our gender identity is not activated. Objective characteristics of situations (such as the location or the number of people present) are different from our perceptions of situations. It is our perceptions of situations that affect our communication. We may view a situation as involving competition and act accordingly, while other people in the situation may see it as a situation calling for cooperation and act accordingly.

Anxiety/Uncertainty. Our identities, dispositions, and perceptions influence the amount of anxiety and uncertainty we experience in any particular communication episode. If our perceptions of the other person are not clear, if we feel insecure in our identities, or if we are not motivated to communicate, we will probably experience high anxiety and high uncertainty. If our perceptions are clear, if we feel secure, and if we are motivated to communicate, on the other hand, our anxiety and uncertainty will be within our comfort range.

If our anxiety and uncertainty are too high or too low, it is not possible to communicate effectively in nonscripted situations or in situations that call for more than an automatic response. To communicate effectively in nonscripted situations, we must be able to manage our anxiety and uncertainty. This requires that we be mindful.

Mindfulness. When we first encounter a new situation, we consciously seek cues to guide our behavior. As we have repeated experiences with the same event, we have less need to consciously think about our behavior; "the more often we engage in the activity, the more likely it is that we rely on scripts for the completion of the activity and the less likely there will be any correspondence between our actions and those thoughts of ours that occur simultaneously" (Langer, 1978, p. 39).

When we are engaging in habitual or scripted behavior or our behavior is based on our emotions, we are not highly aware of what we are doing or saying. To borrow an analogy from flying an airplane, we are on automatic pilot. Stated differently, we are "mindless" (Langer, 1989). *Mindfulness,* in contrast, involves being aware of our own and other people's behavior in the situation, and paying attention to the *process* of communication taking place between us and them.

There are three characteristics of mindfulness (Langer, 1989). First, mindfulness involves *creating new categories.* If we rely on our old categories, we are mindless. To illustrate creating new categories, consider meeting a person who is using crutches. Most of us do not regularly place people in the category "person on crutches"; rather, we probably use a broad category, such as "cripple" or "disabled." If we create the new category "person on crutches," we will not automatically assume that the person is unable to walk, type, use a telephone, and so forth, as we might if we used the broader category "cripple" or "disabled." Second, to be mindful, we must be *open to new information* when we are communicating with others. Finally, to be mindful, we must be *aware of more than one perspective.*

BALLARD STREET by Jerry Van Amerongen. By permission of Jerry Van Amerongen and Creators Syndicate.

Stated differently, we need to understand how others are interpreting the messages being exchanged.

When we are mindful, we need to focus on the *way* we are communicating, not on the outcome. If we focus on the outcome, such as whether we will make fools of ourselves, we miss important cues that will help us increase the accuracy of our interpretations of others' messages. Reading 1.2 illustrates the need to be mindful using Napoleon's invasion of Russia as an example. Take a moment to read this before continuing.

When we are on automatic pilot, our anxiety and uncertainty are a function of our identities, dispositions, and perceptions of the other person and the situation. We cannot manage our anxiety and uncertainty when we are in this state. Rather, when we are on automatic pilot, high anxiety and/or high uncertainty affects our communication behavior. To manage our anxiety and uncertainty, we must be mindful. If we are not mindful, we have made an unconscious choice to allow our uncertainty and anxiety to influence our behavior. When we are mindful, we can consciously manage our anxiety and uncertainty when they are too high or too low to bring them within our comfort range. We can then consciously choose how we want to communicate. It is important here to recognize that our actions have consequences, whether we make a conscious decision or not.

Communication Resources. Our identities, dispositions, levels of anxiety and uncertainty, and whether we are mindful influence the communication resources available to us. Communication resources are the ways of thinking, feeling, behaving, and judging others that can help us communicate more effectively. We use four types of resources when we communicate: cognitive (thinking), affective (emotional), behavioral skills, and ethical dispositions. In general, when we communicate on automatic pilot and high levels of anxiety and/or uncertainty are present, our communication resources are limited to those we learned as we were growing up. When we are mindful of our communication, however, we can manage our anxiety and uncertainty and increase the communication resources available to help us communicate effectively. One purpose of this book is to help you increase the resources you can use to communicate when you are mindful.

Reading 1.2 NAPOLEON'S INVASION OF RUSSIA/ELLEN LANGER

When Napoleon invaded Russia, he appeared to the world as a brilliant conquering hero, yet again proving his military genius by daring to march against a giant. But behind the proud banners and eagles, he carried a dangerous mindset, a determination to have Russia, to have Russia no matter what the cost in human life. As Tolstoy describes him in *War and Peace,* Napoleon had no use for alternatives; his determination was absolute.

Opposite Napoleon stood the old Russian bear of a general, Kutuzov, a mellowed veteran who liked his vodka and had a habit of falling asleep at state occasions. An uneven match, or so it would appear.

As Napoleon's army advanced, Kutuzov let his army fall back, and then fall back some more. Napoleon kept coming, deeper into Russia, farther from his supply lines. Finally, as Kutuzov knew would happen, a powerful ally intervened: the Russian winter. The French army found itself fighting the cold, the wind, the snow, and the ice.

When Napoleon at least achieved his single, obsessive goal—Moscow—there was no one there for him to conquer. Everyone had left. The Russians had set their holy city on fire to greet the invader. Once more Kutuzov played the seeming loser. . . .

At that moment, when Napoleon had no choice but to retreat—from the burned city, from the winter—the mindful old general attacked. He appealed to Mother Russia, an appeal that Stalin was to use with similar success years later. He appealed to the people to save their land, and that appeal revived all of Russia. The French had everything against them, including the Cossacks, who rode down off the winter steppes. Mother Russia prevailed, just as she would when Hitler was to repeat Napoleon's mistake.

In the character of Kutuzov we can find portrayed the key qualities of a mindful state of being: (1) creation of new categories; (2) openness to new information; and (3) awareness of more than one perspective.

In each case, Napoleon's blind obsession provides a vivid mirror image, a portrait of mindlessness. First of all, Kutuzov was flexible: Evacuating a city would usually fall under the category of defeat, but for him it became the act of setting a trap. Second, his strategy was responsive to the news of Napoleon's advance, while Napoleon did not seem to be taking in information about Kutuzov's moves. Finally, while Napoleon saw his rapid advance and march on Moscow only from the point of view of conquering enemy terrain, Kutuzov could also see that an "invasion" in the context of winter and distance from supplies could be turned into a bitter rout.

Our *cognitive resources* involve the ways we think about others and our communication with them. The way we define situations and the expectations we have for our own and other people's behavior are examples of cognitive resources we use when we are communicating. To illustrate, our attitudes, including our prejudices, biases, and stereotypes (our mental images of other groups), create expectations for how to communicate with others. If we are prejudiced against members of specific ethnic groups, we will expect them to behave negatively toward us.

The way we feel, our emotions, and our ability to empathize are our *affective resources* for communication. If we feel hurt, we communicate one way. If we feel happy, in contrast, we communicate differently. Similarly, if our emotional response is anger, we communicate differently than if our emotional response is caring. Communication based on emotions such as hurt and anger generally is not effective. To communicate effectively, we must be able to manage our emotional responses so that they do not automatically lead us to behave in ways we do not want to behave.

If we are on automatic pilot, our emotional responses, such as anger, tend to lead to high levels of anxiety and/or uncertainty. If, for example, our romantic partner indicates, "I want to be alone this weekend," we might feel hurt and our anxiety/uncertainty might increase so that they are higher than our comfort level. The high anxiety/uncertainty would trigger an automatic emotional response based on the responses we learned as children; for example, feeling that there is something wrong with us. Effective communication under these conditions is difficult. If we are mindful, on the other hand, we can manage our anxiety/uncertainty and try to determine what our partner meant when he or she said, "I want to be alone this weekend." When mindful, we can choose another emotional response, such as that our partner needs "space" and it has nothing to do with his or her feelings for us.

Our *behavioral skills* also provide resources for communication. Our ability to gather information about others and our ability to adapt our communication behavior to other people are examples of skills that influence the effectiveness of our communication. To illustrate, if we cannot adapt our behavior to other people, we probably will not be able to communicate effectively. When we are on automatic pilot, the way we accommodate our behavior may not facilitate effective communication. When we are mindful, however, we can consciously choose the skills we want to use to maximize the effectiveness of our communication.

The final resource we use in communication is our *ethical dispositions.* Do we focus on the means (the ways we try to reach our goals) or the ends (our goals)? Do we treat others with dignity and respect? Do we take others' views into consideration when we communicate? Do we define morality as justice or as caring? Are we morally inclusive or morally exclusive (do we put some people in a category that does not require us to behave in a moral fashion toward them)? Do we judge other people's behavior using our own standards or try to understand their behavior from their point of view? When we are mindless, for example, we tend to automatically judge other people's behavior based on the ethical standards we learned as children. The problem is that other people may have learned different ethical standards. If we want to understand other people, we must suspend our ethical judgments. This requires that we be mindful. Ethical judgments, however, must still be made when we are mindful. This issue is discussed in more detail in Chapter 3.

Summary

Our communication with others is based on implicit personal theories that we learned both as children and as we have communicated with others over the years. When we communicate on automatic pilot, we unconsciously choose to let our implicit personal theories of communication guide our behavior. This works reasonably well in a large number of situations, but our implicit theories often do not provide accurate predictions of other people's behavior. To communicate more effectively in these situations, we need to make conscious decisions about how we want to communicate.

Interpersonal communication involves the use of symbols, the exchange of messages, and the creation of meanings. Interpersonal communication takes place within a system. It involves the use of personal information about the person with whom we are communicating, and it is inseparable from intergroup communication.

Our communication behavior can be based on habits/scripts, on the intentions we form, or on our emotions. When it is based on habits/scripts or emotions, we are not highly aware of our communication. Levels of anxiety and uncertainty that are either too high or too low can lead to ineffective communication when we are not highly aware of our communication. We can, however, manage our anxiety and uncertainty and increase the effectiveness of our communication. When we are on automatic pilot, the communication resources available to us are limited to those we learned as children. When we are mindful, we can choose to communicate differently.

Notes

1. We draw our discussion of systems from Fisher (1982).
2. Systems theorists usually say that the whole is greater than the sum of the parts. It is possible, however, for the whole to be less than the sum of the parts. To illustrate, when people work in groups, the final group product is often of lower quality than any of the individuals would have produced alone. In this case, the whole is less than the sum of the parts.
3. You will notice that, throughout this book, we talk about people from the United States rather than "Americans." The reason for this is that use of the term *Americans* to refer to people from the United States often is considered offensive by people from Mexico and Latin and South America who are also Americans. Where possible, we will use *North Americans,* but this term also can be problematic.
4. Ethnicity may be based on race, religion, culture, or national origin. We differentiate culture and ethnicity in Chapter 2.
5. This discussion is drawn from social identity theory (e.g., Tajfel, 1978; Tajfel & Turner, 1979) and ethnolinguistic identity theory (e.g., Giles & Johnson, 1987).
6. Douglas (1986) also points out that we derive social identities from the institutions (such as schools, clubs, or places of worship) with which we are associated.

Journal Reflections

A large part of improving communication skills involves reflecting on current communication behavior in order to understand why we communicate the way we do. For skills learned in this book (and in class) to transfer to interactions outside the classroom, it is important to practice new skills in everyday interactions with others and to reflect on the outcomes that result from these new skills. It is therefore recommended that you keep an Interpersonal Communication Journal while reading the book. The purpose of this journal is to keep a log of interpersonal communication that takes place both inside and outside the classroom during the class.

You should plan to do the Journal Reflections as you read *every* chapter. Your entries should address your responses to the exercises discussed in the chapter (there were no specific Skill Exercises discussed in Chapter 1, but they will be presented in other chapters); when you think it would be appropriate to use the skills discussed in the chapter in your everyday communication; and what adaptations (if any) you think are necessary for you to feel comfortable using the skill in everyday communication.

In addition, specific reflections are provided at the end of each chapter to help you use the information presented in the chapter. Ideally, you should do each of the reflections to get the most out of the book.

1. *Identifying Misinterpretations.* We inevitably misinterpret other people's verbal and nonverbal messages at times when we communicate. During the next week, try to pay attention to how you are interpreting other people's messages. If you think there is a possibility that you might have misinterpreted someone's messages, stop and think about alternative interpretations. Try to determine which interpretation you think the other person might have meant when he or she transmitted the message. If you are comfortable doing so, ask the other person if your interpretation is what she or he meant. Describe the situation and not the outcome in your journal.
2. *Identifying Intentions.* In this chapter, it was pointed out that our communication can be based on our intentions, on our habits/scripts, or on our emotional responses to situations. Based on the discussion of intentions, reflect on your intentions (or lack of intentions) in at least five communication encounters this week. Answer the following questions in your journal: Does your communication behavior differ when you have specific intentions and when you do not? How does it differ? How do different intentions influence the way you communicate?
3. *Being Mindful.* As suggested earlier, we communicate on automatic pilot a large part of the time. During the next week, pay attention to how mindful you are when you communicate. At random, stop after four or five conversations every day and ask yourself how mindful you were when you were talking. Keep track of whether there are particular circumstances in which you are more mindful than others. A later journal assignment will return to mindfulness to ask you to try to be more mindful; at this point, just keep track of when you are mindful. Describe in your journal the situations in which you are mindful and the situations in which you are not mindful.

Study Questions

1. Why can messages, but not meanings, be transmitted from one person to another?
2. Are symbols limited to words? Why or why not?
3. How can recognizing that no two people attach the same meaning to a symbol help us communicate more effectively?
4. What is the difference between interpersonal and intergroup communication? Can communication situations be classified as mainly interpersonal or intergroup? Why or why not?
5. Is interpersonal communication limited to two people? Why?
6. Why is it important to manage our anxiety and uncertainty when we communicate with others?
7. How can we become mindful in communication situations?
8. How do the communication resources we learned as children limit our ability to communicate effectively?
9. How does being mindful increase the communication resources available to improve the quality of our communication?

Suggested Readings

Beck, A. (1988). *Love is Never Enough.* New York: Harper & Row. Aaron Beck's book introduces cognitive therapy and its use in improving the quality of romantic relationships. Beck discusses the factors that lead us to misinterpret others' messages and provides suggestions for increasing the accuracy of our interpretations.

Fisher, B. A. (1978). *Perspectives on Human Communication.* New York: Macmillan. B. Aubrey Fisher's book contains an excellent discussion of several of the concepts (e.g., intentions, process, messages) discussed in this chapter. Fisher also provides a good introduction to the different ways communication is conceptualized.

Langer, E. (1989). *Mindfulness.* Reading, MA: Addison-Wesley. Ellen Langer's book is the single best introduction to the idea of mindfulness. She discusses mindfulness, ways to achieve mindful communication, and the benefits of mindfulness in various situations. This book is a valuable resource for improving the quality of communication.

2

Identity and Communication

We want the people with whom we interact to view us in particular ways. The way we communicate with others defines who we are. We may, for example, want our friends to see us as friendly, cooperative, and sure of ourselves. We therefore communicate in particular ways so that our friends will see us in this way. How we view ourselves also affects the way we communicate with others. If we are sure of ourselves, we communicate one way; if we are unsure of ourselves, we communicate differently. How we define ourselves as men and women also affects the way we communicate with members of the opposite sex. Our views of ourselves and the ways that we communicate are highly interrelated.

The way we view ourselves is developed socially and is influenced by the society in which we live. Our views of ourselves, in turn, are the "prime determinant" of our behavior (Stryker, 1987). To improve the quality of our communication with others, we need to understand the various aspects of ourselves and how they affect our communication. We need to understand our general self-conceptions, as well as our social identities, such as our cultural, ethnic, and gender identities. We also need to understand how our self-esteem affects our communication. Let's begin by looking at our self-conceptions.

Self-Conceptions and Identities

The way we view ourselves in general, our personal and social identities, and our self-esteem affect the way we communicate with others. We'll begin examining how these self-related factors influence our communication by looking at the self and self-concept.

The Self and Self-Concept

The term *self* refers to ourselves as we really are (Westen, 1991). We act differently in various situations and play different roles, but we often are not aware of how the different aspects of ourselves fit together. The various aspects of ourselves, nevertheless, do fit together to form a whole.

Our *self-concepts* are our views of ourselves when we think about ourselves (Westen, 1991). Three principles affect the development of our self-concepts (Rosenberg, 1979).[1] First, our self-concepts are based on *reflected appraisals* from other people. As we are growing up, we are influenced by the attitudes other people express toward us, and over time we start to view ourselves as other people see us. Second, we learn about ourselves through the process of *social comparisons.* By comparing ourselves with other people, we learn how to define ourselves. One of the outcomes of the social comparison process is that we form positive, neutral, and negative evaluations of ourselves. Third, our self-concepts are influenced by our self-attributions. *Self-attributions* are the inferences we make about our motives, or the causes that lead us to behave the way we do. We may, for example, think we did not get a good grade in a class because we were lazy. The conclusions we draw about our motives for behaving in a particular way influence the way we see ourselves. It is important to recognize that we are not highly aware of these processes when they operate.

How we view ourselves has a tremendous influence on how we feel and how we behave. Our self-concepts can create self-fulfilling prophecies. *Self-fulfilling prophecies* occur when we think something is true and act accordingly; it then tends to come true, whether it was originally true or not. If we think we are attractive to others, for example, we dress attractively and behave in a way that others perceive to be attractive, and these behaviors affect how others see us. Other people will perceive us as more attractive if we think we are attractive and behave accordingly than if we do not think we are attractive and behave accordingly.

Identity

Our self-concepts are made up of the different ways we think about ourselves in various situations. These different ways of thinking about ourselves are our *identities.* In any particular situation, we may or may not be conscious of the identities influencing our behavior. **Even though we may not always be highly aware of the identity influencing our behavior, we act as if there is a clear identity guiding our behavior** (R. H. Turner, 1987).

The self is a structure of identities that are organized in a rank ordering of importance (Stryker, 1987). We have *master identities* that influence our other identities. Master identities influence how we view the other identities we have. Our master identities include our cultural identities, ethnic identities, gender identities, and age identities. Our identities as parents, for example, are influenced by our cultural, ethnic, and gender identities. How important our identities are to us also influences the degree to which our specific identities operate in various situations (Stryker, 1987). If an identity is very important to us, we define more interactions based on that identity, and that identity influences our behavior in more situations than identities that are not important to us.

As pointed out in Chapter 1, our identities can be grouped under three broad categories: human, social, and personal (J. C. Turner, 1987). Our *human identities* involve those views of ourselves that we believe we share with all other humans. It is important to recognize that "people and their cultures perish in isolation, but they are born or reborn in contact with other men and women, with men and women of another culture, another creed, another race. If we do not recognize our humanity in others, we shall not recognize it in ourselves" (Fuentes, 1992, back cover). To understand our human identities, we have to look for those things we share in common with all other humans.

Our *social identities* involve those views of ourselves that we assume we share with other members of our ingroups. *Ingroups* are "groups of people about whose welfare [we are] concerned, with whom [we are] willing to cooperate without demanding equitable returns, and separation from whom leads to discomfort or even pain" (Triandis, 1988, p. 75). Our social identities may be based on the roles we play, such as student, professor, or parent; the demographic categories in which we are categorized, such as our nationality, ethnicity, gender, or age; and our memberships in formal/informal organizations, such as political parties, organizations, or social clubs.

Our *personal identities* involve those views of ourselves that differentiate us from other members of our ingroups—those characteristics that define us as unique individuals. Our personality characteristics, for example, are part of our personal identities. Our personal identities may involve viewing ourselves as intelligent, attractive, caring, and so forth.

Before proceeding, take a few minutes to think about the identities that influence your behavior. In the spaces provided, list the identities that you think influence the way you communicate:

________ ( )   ________ ( )
________ ( )   ________ ( )
________ ( )   ________ ( )
________ ( )   ________ ( )
________ ( )   ________ ( )
________ ( )   ________ ( )
________ ( )   ________ ( )
________ ( )   ________ ( )

Look back at the identities you listed. Which are social identities (S), and which are personal identities (P)? Put an S or a P in the parentheses after the identities to indicate which you think they are. The ones you marked as social identities should involve

shared group memberships, including, but not limited to, culture, ethnicity, gender, age, sexual orientation, political party; roles you play, such as father/mother, son/daughter, student, or occupation; and other group memberships you share with others, such as smoker, religion, alcoholic, feminist, or liberal/conservative. Personal identities should include characteristics that separate you from others. Virtually all personality characteristics, such as open- or closed-minded and introverted or extroverted, are personal identities. Examples of personal identities include being a sociable person (extrovert), a caring person, patient, irritable, or intelligent (but being a member of MENSA, a club for people with high IQs, is a social identity).

We are less aware of how our social identities influence our communication than we are of how our personal identities influence our communication. To improve the quality of our communication, we need to better understand how our social identities affect how we behave and how we interpret other people's messages.

Social Identities

Social identities differ on two dimensions: voluntary-involuntary and desirable-undesirable (Deaux, 1991). A *voluntary identity* is one that we can choose, while an *involuntary identity* is one in which we do not necessarily have free choice (others may categorize us in an involuntary identity). *Desirable identities* are those we think are positive, and *undesirable identities* are those we think are negative. Table 2.1 displays *one group* of people's perceptions of various social identities on these dimensions. Your perceptions of the identities in Table 2.1 may be different from those listed. The voluntary nature of identity influences the amount of effort we need to maintain the identity; voluntary identities require more effort and work than involuntary identities. The desirability dimension influences the degree to which we express our identities or hide them (Deaux, 1991). This dimension, therefore, influences the degree to which we feel pride or shame from expressing our identities. We feel pride expressing desirable identities and shame expressing identities that we perceive to be undesirable.

There is not widespread agreement on the desirability of some social identities. Gay/lesbian, for example, is one of the social identities listed as undesirable in Table 2.1.[2] Obviously, not everyone would agree that gay/lesbian is an undesirable social identity. One consequence of viewing gay/lesbian as an undesirable social identity, however, is that gay-bashing has become widespread in the United States in recent years. Viewing other people's social identities as undesirable is communicated to them in the way we transmit our messages. **If we want to communicate effectively and if we want to develop relationships with other people, we must be aware of our biases and mindfully manage them when we transmit our messages and interpret other people's messages.**

There often is a difference between our subjective social identities (those we use to define ourselves) and our objective characteristics (the groups into which others might categorize us; Deaux, 1991). We therefore need to keep in mind that **other people may not see groups into which we categorize them as important aspects of their identities, and other people may categorize us in ways we do not consider important.**

Our social identities are relatively consistent over time (Deaux, 1991). In any given interaction and at any given time, one of our social identities tends to predominate to influence our behavior.[3] The importance of our identities, our background, and the situational characteristics influence which identity guides our behavior. To illustrate, "the individ-

Table 2.1

One Group's Perceptions of Social Identities

	Desirable Identities	Undesirable Identities
Voluntary	Catholic Club member Democrat/Republican Feminist Friend Husband/wife Mother/father Student	Alcoholic [Drug addict] Gay/lesbian Smoker
Involuntary	African American Daughter/son Hispanic [Chicano/Chicana] Jew Man Woman	[Blind] Deaf [Disabled] Old person

Adapted from Deaux and Ethier (1990) as reported in Deaux (1991). The perceptions presented here are those of one group of people. Your perceptions of the identities may be different. The identities in brackets [ ] have been added to further illustrate how other identities tend to be perceived.

ual entering a classroom brings out the professor or student identity; the individual moving into an operating room takes on the identity of surgeon, nurse, or patient" (Deaux, 1991, p. 85).

The characteristics of the situation are also important in influencing the importance we place on our social identities. If we find ourselves in a situation where people sharing our identity are in a numerical minority, that identity becomes important to us. To illustrate, most people in the United States do not think much about being an "American," but when they travel to another country, this identity becomes important. Finally, other people's actions can influence the identity we choose to guide our behavior. If someone communicates with us based on one of our identities, we will probably use that identity to guide our behavior.

Issues of social identity have been overviewed in this section. Several important social identities—cultural, ethnic, gender, disability, age, and social class—are discussed in more detail later in this chapter. Before examining specific social identities, another aspect of the self—self-esteem—needs to be examined.

Self-Esteem

Self-esteem is our positive or negative orientation toward ourselves (Rosenberg, 1979). A person with high self-esteem "considers himself [or herself] a person of worth. Appreciating his [or her] own merits, he [or she] nonetheless recognizes his [or her] faults, faults that he [or she] expects to overcome" (Rosenberg, 1979, p. 54). When we have high self-esteem, we do not necessarily consider ourselves better than other people, but we do not consider ourselves worse than other people either. When we have low self-esteem, however, we consider ourselves unworthy and lack respect for ourselves.

The Nature of Self-Esteem

Before reading further, think about your self-esteem and how it influences your behavior. Take a moment to answer the questions listed below:

> In general, do you have positive feelings about yourself? Are there particular situations in which you do *not* feel good about yourself? What are they? ____________
>
> ______________________________
>
> ______________________________
>
> ______________________________
>
> How do you communicate differently when you are feeling good about yourself from when you are not feeling good about yourself? Try to list specific behaviors.
>
> ______________________________
>
> ______________________________
>
> ______________________________

Your answers to these questions should provide some insight into how self-esteem fits into your implicit personal theory of communication. Keep your answers to these questions in mind as you read the remainder of this section.

Our self-esteem is an overall positive or negative view of ourselves, which is relatively stable over time. Our self-esteem affects all aspects of our lives. Low self-esteem is associated with many psychological problems, such as depression, anxiety, and maladjustment (Rosenberg, 1979). Reading 2.1 contains a summary of research on people with negative self-concepts. Take a moment to read it now.

High self-esteem is associated with happiness, satisfaction with life, and positive mental health (Rosenberg, 1979). People with high self-esteem tend to be open to criticism because they are able to acknowledge their mistakes (Branden, 1992). People with high self-esteem are flexible in the way they respond to situations and challenges. They are relaxed and accept themselves as they are, even with their shortcomings.

Self-esteem is culturally based. Our culture provides us with the criteria by which we judge our self-worth (Greenberg, Pyszczynski, & Solomon, 1986). **We have a sense of self-esteem to the extent that we think we have met our culture's criteria for being a good or worthwhile people.** In the United States, children learn that positive self-esteem is associated with warmth and security, and negative self-esteem is associated with anxiety and exclusion.

Personal self-esteem is useful in explaining our interpersonal behavior, but it does not explain how we behave in intergroup contexts. *Collective self-esteem,* the degree to which we generally evaluate our social groups positively, must be taken into consideration to understand our intergroup behavior (Crocker & Luhtanen, 1990). Our self-esteem is a combination of personal and collective self-esteem. Part of our self-esteem "is based on fitting in, being accepted, pleasing others, and gaining approval for meeting the expectations of others" (collective self-esteem). The other part of our self-esteem "is based on realizing [our] unique potentialities; being an indi-

Reading 2.1 **Mired In Misery**

Of all the problems with low self-esteem, this may be the worst: people who have it create relationships that tend to perpetuate it. For them, the need for positive feedback takes a sad second to the need for a stable identity.

It's terrible but true, says William B. Swann, Jr., Ph.D., professor of psychology at the University of Texas. People with negative self-views prefer people—even seek them out—who also evaluate them negatively. To the extent their spouses see them as they see themselves, no matter how poorly, the more committed they are to marriage.

Negative evaluations bolster their belief that "they are in touch with social reality, however harsh that reality may be." It allows them to predict—and thus control—the responses of others. Should they find themselves with spouses who appraise them favorably, they tend to withdraw from the relationship.

Swann's studies show that for those with positive self-views, there is no discrepancy between the need for positive feedback and the need for self-verification. But if a partner rates us negatively, our commitment to the relationship diminishes. . . .

Among the most astonishing of Swann's findings is that people with negative self-views never recognize their partner's disenchantment. Obeying the rules of social decorum, their partners maintain "a facade of kind words"—but leak their disdain in such nonverbal cues as tone of voice.

So, to add injury to insult, those with negative self-views don't have the skills to recognize the kind of feedback that would let them know what they're doing wrong.

vidual in [our] own right; and having others recognize, respect, affirm, support, and encourage [our] personal talents and individual uniqueness" (personal self-esteem; Josephs, 1991, pp. 8–9). When self-esteem is based only on fitting in, it can lead to mindless conformity. When self-esteem is based only on uniqueness, in contrast, it can lead to social alienation. We need to find a balance "between fitting in and being an individual in [our] own right" (p. 9).

Assessing Your Personal Self-Esteem

Before proceeding, it is important for you to have an idea of your relative level of personal self-esteem. Assessment 2.1 contains a self-esteem questionnaire. Take a moment to complete it.

Generally speaking, the higher your score on Assessment 2.1, the more secure you will feel when communicating with others. Keep in mind that our level of self-esteem affects all of our behavior. It is easier, for example, for people with high self-esteem to be mindful of their communication than it is for people with low self-esteem. Mindfulness, however, is a very important resource for people with low self-esteem. To the extent that people with low self-esteem can be mindful, they can make conscious choices about how they want to communicate rather than allowing their low levels of self-esteem to guide their behavior. (Branden, 1992, provides excellent suggestions on how people with low self-esteem can build self-esteem.)

Assessment 2.1 *Assessing Your Self-Esteem*

The purpose of this questionnaire is to assess your self-esteem. Respond to each statement by indicating the degree to which you agree or disagree with each of the items: Strongly Disagree (1), Disagree (2), Agree (3), and (4) Strongly Agree (5).

_______ 1. On the whole, I am satisfied with myself.

_______ 2. At times, I think I am no good at all.

_______ 3. I feel that I have a number of good qualities.

_______ 4. I am able to do things as well as most other people.

_______ 5. I feel I do not have much to be proud of.

_______ 6. I feel useless at times.

_______ 7. I feel that I am a person of worth.

_______ 8. I wish I could have more respect for myself.

_______ 9. All in all, I'm inclined to feel that I am a failure.

_______ 10. I take a positive attitude toward myself.

To find your score, first reverse your answers to items 2, 5, 6, 8, and 9 (if you wrote 4 make it 1; if you wrote 3, make it 2; if you wrote 2, make it 3; if you wrote 1, make it 4). Next, add the numbers next to each statement. Scores range from 10 to 50. The higher your score, the greater your self-esteem.

If you want to get an idea of your collective self-esteem regarding a particular social identity, you can complete Assessment 2.1 again, thinking of a particular group membership. To illustrate, if you want to know your collective self-esteem regarding your occupational social identity, answer the questions in Assessment 2.1 thinking of your occupational identity instead of your personal identity. In answering item 1, for example, you would read the statement as if it said, "On the whole, I am satisfied with myself *in my occupation.*" You could calculate a collective self-esteem score for each of your social identities.

As indicated earlier, our self-esteem is culturally based. Our culture defines what a worthwhile person is and does. All other aspects of our self-concepts are affected by our culture. To better understand our self-concepts, we need to understand the nature of culture and our cultural identities.

Cultural Identity

One of the important social identities that influences our communication behavior is our *cultural identities*—the social identities associated with being members of our cultures. We all have a sense of being members of our cultures. To illustrate, everyone born and/or raised in the United States has a sense of being an "American." Before reading further, take a moment to think about what it means to you to be a member of your culture. Think of being a member of your culture, such as being an "American," rather than being a member of your ethnic group, such as Irish American or African American.

> What are your initial thoughts about being a member of your culture? ______________
> ____________________________________
> ____________________________________
> ____________________________________
>
> How does being a member of your culture influence your communication? __________
> ____________________________________
> ____________________________________
> ____________________________________
>
> Are there situations in which your culture influences your communication more than in other situations? ______________
> ____________________________________
> ____________________________________
> ____________________________________

Your answers to these questions should provide some insight into how your cultural identity fits into your implicit personal theory of communication. Keep your responses to these questions in mind as you read the remainder of this section.

Culture

Culture is our theory of the "game being played" in our society (Keesing, 1974). We use our theory of the game being played in interacting with the other people we encounter. It tells us how to communicate with others and how to interpret their behavior. We generally are not highly aware of the rules of the game being played, but we behave as though there is general agreement on the rules. To illustrate, if we met a person from Mars and the Martian asked us to explain the rules of our culture, we probably would not be able to describe many of the rules because we are not highly aware of them.

We learn to be members of our culture from our parents, from teachers in school, from religious institutions, from our peers, and from the mass media. Originally, we learn about our culture from our parents. Our parents begin to teach us the norms and communication rules that guide behavior in our culture. *Norms* are socially shared guidelines for how we should or should not behave, which have a basis in morality. *Rules,* in contrast, are guidelines for the ways we are expected to communicate. Rules are not based in morality (Olsen, 1978). Our parents do *not* explicitly tell us the norms and rules of our culture. They do not, for example, tell us that, when we meet someone for the first time, we should stick out our right hands and shake three times. Rather, they teach us the norms and rules by modeling how to behave and correcting us when we violate a norm or rule.

Once we are old enough to interact with other children, they reinforce the norms and rules we learned from our parents. We also learn additional norms and rules of our culture from them. We learn from our peers, for example, how to be cooperative and how to compete with others. When we attend religious services or school, we learn other norms and rules of our culture. The other way we learn about our culture is through the mass media, especially television. Television teaches us many of the day-to-day norms of our culture and provides us with a view of reality. Television has become the medium through which most of us learn what others' expectations are for our behavior. It appears that the more television we watch, the more our views of reality overlap with other people's views (Gerbner, Gross, Morgan, & Signorielli, 1980).

Not all members of a culture share exactly the same view of their culture (Keesing, 1974). **No one member of a culture knows all aspects of the culture, and all members of a culture have a unique view of their culture.** The theories that members of a culture share, however, overlap sufficiently so that they can coordinate their behavior in everyday life. Since people developed their individual implicit theories of communication while learning to be members of their cultures, there is some overlap of all the implicit personal theories of communication that members of the same culture use to guide their behavior.

Our culture provides us with a system of knowledge that allows us to know how to communicate with other people and how to interpret their behavior (Keesing, 1974). The term *culture* usually is reserved to refer to the systems of knowledge used by relatively large numbers of people. The boundaries between cultures *usually* coincide with political, or national, boundaries between countries. To illustrate, we can speak of the culture of the United States, the Mexican culture, the Japanese culture, and so forth.

Cultures are *not* uniform, and the members are not all alike. The members of all cultures are different to some degree. The differences are due, at least in part, to the existence of subcultures within the larger culture. *Subcultures* are groups within a culture whose members share many of the values of the culture but that also have some values that differ from those of the larger culture. We can talk about a student subculture, a business subculture, a medical subculture (people who work in medicine), a homosexual subculture, and so forth. Subcultures also can be based on ethnicity (discussed in the next section of this chapter) or social class (discussed later in this chapter). The subcultures of which we are members influence the implicit personal theories of communication we use to guide our behavior.

As indicated earlier, the implicit theories that individuals use to guide their communication overlap to some extent in every culture. If they did not overlap, people would not be able to coordinate their actions. The more individuals' implicit theories overlap, the more homogeneous the culture. Although the United States is not highly homogeneous, there is sufficient homogeneity for most people to know how to behave and how to coordinate their communication in most situations.

Assessing the Strength of Your Cultural Identity

Being a member of our culture influences the way we communicate. The extent to which our culture influences our behavior is dependent in part on how strongly we identify with our culture. Assessment 2.2 is designed to help you determine how strongly you identify with your culture. Take a moment to complete it now. In completing it, think of the culture with which you identify, *not* your subculture or ethnic group. For most readers this will be the "American" culture, but for some (such as international students studying in the United States) it will be another culture.

The higher your score on Assessment 2.2, the more you probably follow the rules of your culture, and the more your culture is likely to influence your interactions with people from other cultures. Also, the higher your score, the more likely you are to expect other people from your culture to follow the norms and rules of your culture when you communicate with them.

Assessment 2.2 *Assessing the Strength of Your Cultural Identity*

The purpose of this questionnaire is to help you think about the degree to which you identify with your national culture. Respond to each statement by indicating the degree to which the statement is true regarding the way you typically think about yourself. When you think about yourself is the statement "Always False" (answer 1), "Mostly False" (answer 2), "Sometimes True and Sometimes False" (answer 3), "Mostly True" (answer 4), or "Always True" (answer 5)?

_______ 1. Being a member of my culture is important to me.

_______ 2. Thinking about myself as a member of my culture is not central to how I define myself.

_______ 3. I have a positive view of my culture.

_______ 4. I rarely think about being a member of my culture.

_______ 5. Being a member of my culture plays a large role in my life.

_______ 6. It does not bother me if others do not recognize me as a member of my culture.

_______ 7. I enjoy being a member of my culture.

_______ 8. I rarely choose to express my culture in the way I communicate.

_______ 9. I like the things that make me a member of my culture and different from people in other cultures.

_______ 10. If I were born again, I would want to be born as a member of a different culture.

To find your score, first reverse the responses for all the *even-numbered* items (if you wrote 1, make it 5; if you wrote 2, make it 4; if you wrote 3, leave it as 3; if you wrote 4, make it 2; if you wrote 5, make it 1). Next, add the numbers next to each of the statements. Scores range from 10 to 50. The higher your score, the more you identify with your group.

There is one additional thing to keep in mind about your scores on Assessment 2.2. When you travel to another culture or interact with a person from a different culture, the degree to which you identify with your own culture will increase when you are on automatic pilot. Even if your score here is relatively low, it will be higher when you are in another culture or interacting with a person from a different culture. You may not, however, be highly aware of the influence of your cultural identity on your behavior when you communicate on automatic pilot. When you are mindful of your communication, on the other hand, you will be able to recognize how your cultural identity is influencing your behavior.

Individualism-Collectivism

In order to understand similarities and differences in communication across cultures and to better understand the implicit theories guiding our behavior, it is necessary to have a way of talking about how cultures differ. Saying that "Yuko communicates indirectly because she is Japanese" or that "Kimberly communicates directly because she is from the United States" does not tell us why there are differences between the ways people communicate in the United States and in Japan. There has to be some aspect of the cultures in Japan and the United States that is different, and this difference in turn explains why Japanese communicate indirectly and people from the United States communicate directly. In other words, there are dimensions on which cultures can be different or similar that can be used to explain communication across cultures.

Individualism-collectivism is a broad dimension that is used widely to explain cross-cultural differences in behavior. In *individualistic cultures,* individuals' goals are emphasized over group goals, and self-realization is promoted. In individualistic cultures, "each person is viewed as having a unique set of talents and potentials. The translation of these potentials into actuality is considered the highest purpose to which one can devote one's life. The striving for self-realization is accompanied by a subjective sense of rightness and personal well-being" (Waterman, 1984, pp. 4–5).

In *collectivistic cultures,* group goals take precedence over individuals' goals. Collectivistic cultures require that individuals fit into the group. To illustrate, in Kenya "nobody is an isolated individual. Rather, his [or her] uniqueness is a secondary fact. . . . First, and foremost, he [or she] is several people's contemporary. . . . group activities are dominant, responsibility is shared and accountability is collective" (Saleh & Gufwoli, 1982, p. 327). Ingroup memberships are critical in determining how people in collectivistic cultures behave.

Importance of Ingroups. The relative importance of ingroups is one of the major factors that differentiates individualistic and collectivistic cultures (Triandis, 1988; recall the definition of ingroups earlier in the chapter). Members of individualistic cultures have many specific ingroups, such as family, religion, social clubs, and profession, to name only a few that might influence behavior in any particular social situation. Since people are members of many ingroups in individualistic cultures, individual ingroups have very little influence on people's behavior. In collectivistic cultures, there are only a few general ingroups, such as work group, university, and family, the major ingroups that influence behavior in collectivistic cultures, which have a strong influence on behavior across situations.

While the ingroup may be the same in individualistic and collectivistic cultures, the degree to which it influences behavior is different. The ingroup affects behavior in very specific circumstances in individualistic cultures, while the sphere of influence in a collectivistic culture is very broad (the ingroup affects behavior in many different aspects of a person's life). To illustrate, in an individualistic culture like the United States, the company for which people work is an ingroup, but it does not have a broad influence on behavior. The influence is generally limited to the hours of 9 to 5, Monday through Friday (or whatever hours a person works). In the collectivistic culture of Japan, in contrast, the company for which a man works influences all aspects of his and his family's life.

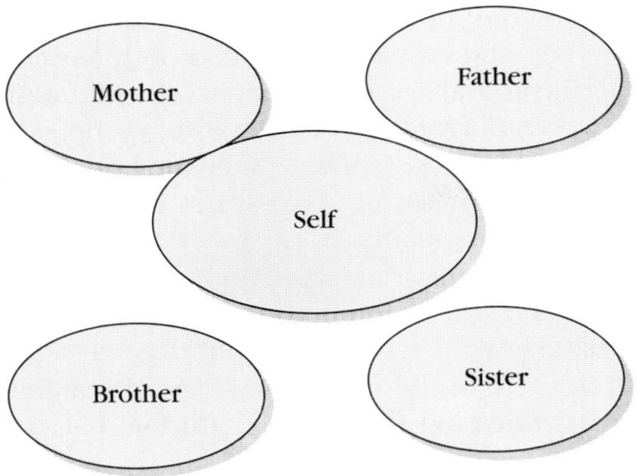

FIGURE 2.1 An Independent Construal of Self with Respect to Family

Ingroups have different rank-orders of importance in collectivistic cultures. People in some collectivistic cultures, for example, put family ahead of all other ingroups, while people in other cultures put their companies ahead of other ingroups (Triandis, 1988). To illustrate, the company often is considered the primary ingroup in Japan (Nakane, 1970), while the family is the primary ingroup in most other collectivistic cultures, such as cultures in Africa, Asia, Latin America, and the Middle East.

Independent and Interdependent Self-construals. The second way to differentiate individualistic and collectivistic cultures is to look at how people view themselves (their self-concepts). The self-conception that predominates in individualistic cultures is an independent construal of self, and the self-conception that predominates in collectivistic cultures is an interdependent construal of self.

When an *independent construal of self* predominates, we view ourselves as unique individuals with clear boundaries that separate us from others (Markus & Kitayama, 1991). Figure 2.1 illustrates how this self-construal might be manifested with respect to our family. In the figure, the self represents a unique individual who is separate from the other members of the family. The self-construal may involve close ties with members of the family. The circle representing the mother, for example, is touching the circle representing the self, and the circle representing the father is closer than the circles representing the brother and sister. When the independent construal of self predominates, we see ourselves as unique individuals who can decide how to behave on our own. To illustrate, in the United States, for example, European Americans generally assume that they can decide how to behave in any situation without worrying about how their behavior reflects on others.

When an *interdependent construal of self* predominates, we view ourselves as part of a social relationship (Markus & Kitayama, 1991). Our view of the self is not separate from others, but interlinked with others. Figure 2.2 illustrates how an interdependent construal of the self might be represented for a family. Notice that the circles representing all family members overlap with the self. In this situation, we would *not* view ourselves as separate from other members of the family. Rather, we would see ourselves as connected to others and define ourselves in terms of our relation-

FIGURE 2.2 An Interdependent Construal of Self with Respect to Family

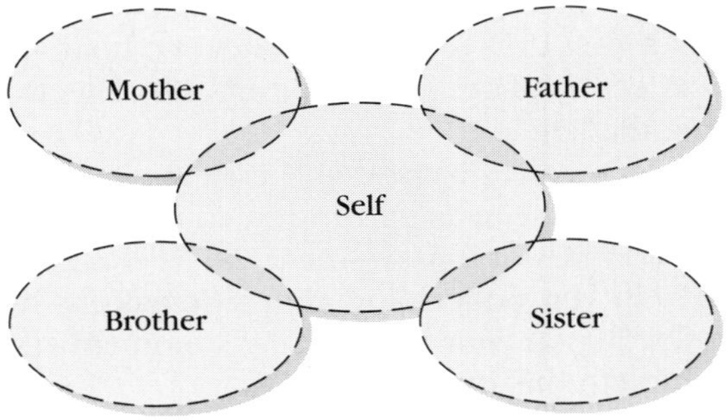

ships within the family. When an interdependent construal of the self hpredominates, we take others involved in our self-conception into consideration in deciding how we should behave. To illustrate, a Japanese businessman would consider how his behavior reflects on his company before deciding how to behave in public.

We can use an independent or interdependent self-construal when we think about ourselves. One of the two self-construals, however, tends to predominate any time we think about ourselves. The independent self-construal tends to predominate in the way people in the United States think about themselves. There are, however, gender differences. Males, for example, tend to be socialized to separate themselves from others, whereas females tend to be socialized to define themselves in terms of their connections to others (an interdependent self-construal; Gilligan, 1982). Both males and females, nevertheless, have both independent and interdependent self-construals.

Assessing Your Individualistic and Collectivistic Cultural Identities. The individualistic and collectivistic tendencies in our culture influence the values we hold. *Values* "have to do with modes of conduct and end-states of existence. To say that a person 'has a value' is to say that he [or she] has an enduring belief that a specific mode of conduct or end-state of existence is personally and socially preferable to alternative modes of conduct or end-states of existence" (Rokeach, 1972, pp. 159–160). The values we hold are a reflection of our individualistic and collectivistic tendencies.

Our individualistic and collectivistic values can be seen as part of the content of our cultural identity. Assessment 2.3 is designed to help you understand your orientations by reflecting on your values. Take a moment and complete this questionnaire.

In computing your scores on Assessment 2.3, you should have computed both an individualism and a collectivism score. Although it is possible for you to receive high scores on both scales, most people will tend to score higher on one of the two scales than on the other. Most people born and raised in the United States tend to score higher on the individualism scale than on the collectivism scale. Whatever your scores are, keep them in mind as the role of cultural identity in influencing communication is discussed throughout the book.

It is important to recognize that our individualistic and collectivistic orientations guide our communication when we are on automatic pilot. They affect how we define ourselves, the messages we transmit, and how we interpret other people's messages. To become aware of how our orientations affect our communication, we must be mindful of our communication.

Low- and High-Context Communication. The types of messages people use when they communicate on automatic pilot differ across cultures (Hall, 1976). A *high-context message* is one in which "most of the information is either in the physical context or internalized in the person, while very little is in the coded, explicit, transmitted part of the message" (p. 79). A *low-context message,* in contrast, is one in which "the mass of information is vested in the explicit code" (p. 70). **Members of individualistic cultures tend to communicate in a low-context, direct fashion, while members of collectivistic cultures tend to communicate in a high-context, indirect fashion** (Gudykunst & Ting-Toomey, 1988).

People using high-context messages expect other people to know what is on their minds and are not specific when they talk. Rather, they talk around the main point and

Assessment 2.3 *Assessing Your Individualistic and Collectivistic Tendencies*

The purpose of this questionnaire is to help you assess your individualistic and collectivistic tendencies. Respond by indicating the degree to which the values reflected in each phrase are important to you: "Opposed to my Values" (answer 1), "Not Important to Me" (answer 2), "Somewhat Important to Me" (answer 3), "Important to Me" (answer 4), or "Very Important to Me" (answer 5).

_______ 1. Obtaining pleasure or sensuous gratification

_______ 2. Preserving the welfare of others

_______ 3. Being successful by demonstrating my individual competency

_______ 4. Restraining my behavior if it is going to harm others

_______ 5. Being independent in thought and action

_______ 6. Having safety and stability of people with whom I identify

_______ 7. Obtaining status and prestige

_______ 8. Having harmony in my relations with others

_______ 9. Having an exciting and challenging life

_______ 10. Accepting cultural and religious traditions

_______ 11. Being recognized for my individual work

_______ 12. Avoiding the violation of social norms

_______ 13. Leading a comfortable life

_______ 14. Living in a stable society

_______ 15. Being logical in my approach to work

_______ 16. Being polite to others

_______ 17. Being ambitious

_______ 18. Being self-controlled

_______ 19. Being able to choose what I do

_______ 20. Enhancing the welfare of others

To find your individualism score, add your responses to the *odd-numbered* items. To find your collectivism score, add your responses to the *even-numbered* items. Both scores will range from 10 to 50. The higher your scores, the more individualistic and/or collectivistic you are.

expect the person listening to figure out what is happening. High-context communication in the Amhara culture in Ethiopia (a collectivistic culture) "is indirect, often secretive. Amharic conversation abounds with general, evasive remarks" (Levine, 1985, p. 25). High-context communication tends to be indirect and vague. Low-context communication in the United States (an individualistic culture), in contrast, "affords little room for the cultivation of ambiguity. The dominant [North] American temper calls for clear and direct communication. It expresses itself in such common injunctions as 'Say what you mean,' 'Don't beat around the bush,' and 'Get to the point' " (Levine, 1985, p. 28). Although low-context messages are used most frequently in individualistic cultures like the United States, people in individualistic cultures also use high-context messages. Similarly, high-context messages are used most frequently in collectivistic cultures, but low-context messages also are used.

To communicate effectively with others, we must interpret their messages the way they were intended. Obviously, there will be misunderstandings when one person transmits a high-context message and another tries to interpret it as a low-context message. Misunderstandings also occur when one person transmits a low-context message and another tries to interpret it as a high-context message. This is what happens when we communicate on automatic pilot. Consider a conversation between a husband (a nonnative speaker [NNS] of English who uses high-context communication) and a wife (native speaker [NS] using low-context communication) that illustrates the problems:

NS (wife):	Bob's having a party. Wanna go?
NNS (husband):	OK.
NS:	(later) Are you sure you wanna go?
NNS:	OK, let's not go. I'm tired anyway. (Tannen, 1975)

In this conversation the husband interpreted the wife's question ("Are you sure you wanna go?") as an indirect indication that she did not want to go. Her intent, however, was to find out what her husband wanted to do. For effective communication to occur in this situation, one or both parties must become mindful of the communication taking place and check out whether they are accurately interpreting the other person's message.

Characteristics of Individualistic and Collectivistic Cultures. Table 2.2 contains a summary of the major characteristics of individualistic and collectivistic cultures. Also included in this table are examples of individualistic and collectivistic cultures.

Understanding how individualistic and collectivistic cultural identities influence communication can help us communicate more effectively with members of other cultures without having specific information about the other cultures. If we are from an individualistic culture, for example, and we are communicating with someone from a collectivistic culture, we can use our knowledge of collectivistic cultures to interpret and to make predictions about the other person's behavior. This idea is illustrated throughout the book when specific issues of interpersonal communication are discussed.

Ethnic Identity

Cultural identity is not the only social identity that influences our communication. Our ethnic identities also have a tremendous effect on the way we communicate. *Ethnic identity* is "a person's subjective orientation toward his or her ethnic origins" (Alba, 1990, p. 25). **Ethnicity can be based on national origin,**

Table 2.2
INDIVIDUALISTIC AND COLLECTIVISTIC CULTURES

Major Characteristics	
Individualistic	**Collectivistic**
Emphasis on individual's goals	Emphasis on ingroup's goals
Self-realization	Fitting into the ingroup
Independent self-construal	Interdependent self-construal
"I" identity	"We" identity
Say what you are thinking	Avoid confrontations in ingroup
Low-context communication	High-context communication

Example Cultures*			
Australia	Israel	Brazil	Mexico
Belgium	Italy	China	Nigeria
Canada	Netherlands	Colombia	Panama
Denmark	New Zealand	Egypt	Pakistan
Finland	Norway	Greece	Peru
France	South Africa	India	Saudi Arabia
Germany	Sweden	Japan	Thailand
Great Britain	Switzerland	Kenya	Venezuela
Ireland	United States	Korea	Vietnam

*The cultures listed are based on the *predominant* tendencies in the cultures.

race, or religion (Gordon, 1964). For people in the United States, ethnicity is based on the countries from which their ancestors came, their religious heritage, such as Jewish, or their race. Most whites in the United States, for example, can trace their ethnic heritage to a European country.

Before reading further, take a moment and think about what it means to you to be a member of your ethnic group.

What are your initial thoughts about being a member of your ethnic group? ______
____
____
____

How does your ethnicity influence your communication? ______________
____
____
____

Are there situations in which your ethnicity influences your communication more than other situations? What differences are there in these types of situations? ______________
____
____
____

Your answers to these questions should provide some insight into the role of your ethnic identity in your implicit personal theory of communication. Keep your responses to these questions in mind as you read the remainder of this section.

Ethnic Identity in the United States

Our ethnic identities are one of the major social identities influencing our communication. Our ethnicity provides us with

> commonality in language, a series of customs and symbols, a style, rituals, and appearance, and so forth, which can penetrate life in many ways. These trappings of ethnicity are particularly attractive when one is continually confronted by others who live differently . . . If I see and experience myself as a member of an ethnic category or group, and others—fellow members and outsiders—recognize me as such, "ways of being" become possible for me that set me apart from the outsiders. These ways of being contribute to the *content* of my self-perceptions. In this sense, I *become* my ethnic allegiance; I experience any attack on the symbols, emblems, or values (cultural elements) that define my ethnicity as an attack on myself. (Roosens, 1989, pp. 17–18)

Asserting our ethnic identities, therefore, helps us define who we are.

In recent years, there has been a transformation regarding how ethnic identities are expressed by whites in the United States. Ethnic distinctions based on ancestry from specific European countries are fading, and these identities are being replaced by a "new" ethnic group, "one based on ancestry from *anywhere* on the European continent" (Alba, 1990, p. 3)—a group called *European Americans* throughout the book. Marriage partners who

For people in the United States, ethnicity is based on the countries from which their ancestors came, their religious heritage, or race. Assessing our ethnic identities helps us define who we are.

trace their origins to different European countries, for example, do not perceive their partners to be from different ethnic groups (Alba, 1990).

Not all European Americans see themselves as similar. There are big cities in the United States, like New York, Boston, or Chicago, where some European Americans still have strong ethnic identities based on their country of origin. The number of places where people draw strong distinctions, however, is consistently decreasing over time (Alba, 1990). Distinctions among European Americans also are drawn on the basis of religious background (for example, Jewish Americans often are viewed as different from other European Americans).[4] Although there are some differences in how European Americans communicate, there are many similarities. There are sufficient similarities that European Americans can be viewed as a distinct social group. This becomes clear when we compare European Americans with non-European Americans.

One important aspect of ethnicity for European Americans is that **European Americans can choose when to express their ethnic identities.** Ethnicity among European Americans today tends to be symbolic. *Symbolic ethnicity* refers to "the desire to retain a sense of being ethnic, but without any deep commitment to the ethnic social ties and behavior" (Alba, 1990, p. 306). European Americans "have a lot more choice and room for maneuver than they themselves think they do. The situation is very different for members of racial minorities, whose lives are strongly influenced by their race or national origin regardless of how much they choose not to identify themselves in ethnic or racial terms" (Waters, 1990, p. 157). Some European Americans, however, do not recognize the differences between their experience of ethnicity and the way non-European Americans experience it (Waters, 1990). The voluntary aspect of European Americans' asserting their ethnicity and the enjoyment they receive from their ethnicity make it difficult for some European Americans to understand the way ethnicity affects non-European Americans.

Generally, ethnic identities are more important for non-European Americans than for European Americans. The influence of ethnic identities for non-European Americans is illustrated by the way a Japanese American playwright describes his experiences. The playwright was raised in the United States but lived in Japan. His time in Japan helped him understand his ethnicity:

> After I'd been living in Japan for about a year, I had an extraordinary experience. . . . I was walking down the street and I looked over to my left and I saw a bank of televisions all lined up, and they were filled with a Japanese newscaster. I looked up at the billboard and there was a Japanese face, I looked at the magazines on display and they were filled with Asian faces; I looked ahead and I saw a sea of people coming toward me, all about my same height, with black hair, with skin that looked exactly like mine. . . . What I experienced for the first time was this extraordinary thing called anonymity—the sense of being able to be part of a group, of everything around me reinforcing what I was. I didn't have to second guess my obviousness, to be constantly aware that I was different. . . . in that instant in Tokyo something lifted from me, and I was able to move freely. . . . Of course, the longer I was in Japan the more I became aware of the fact that I wasn't strictly Japanese either, that I would never be Japanese Japanese—that I was Japanese-American. (Gotanda, 1991, pp. 9–10)

"Flesh color, please, Dolly."
"WHICH flesh color?"

FAMILY CIRCUS. Reprinted with special permission of King Features Syndicate.

This experience clearly illustrates that ethnicity is not "symbolic" for non-European Americans in the United States. Generally, non-European Americans cannot choose when to express their ethnic identities or when they will be treated as a member of their ethnic group.

Assessing the Strength of Your Ethnic Identity

Assessment 2.4 allows you to determine how strongly you identify with your ethnic group. Take a moment and complete this questionnaire now.

The higher your score on Assessment 2.4, the more strongly you identify with your ethnic group. People who strongly identify with their ethnic groups tend to engage in ethnic behavior (such as speak the ethnic dialect), evaluate their group positively, have an interest in and knowledge about their group, and are committed to belonging to the group. People who do not identify strongly with their ethnic groups, in contrast, tend not to engage in ethnic behaviors, may evaluate their group negatively, tend not to be interested in knowing about their group, and are not committed to being a group member.

There is nothing wrong with low *or* high scores on Assessment 2.4. What is important to remember is that, the higher your score, the more likely your ethnicity will influence your interactions with members of other ethnic groups. It is important to remember, however, that, even if your score is low, members of other ethnic groups may define your ethnicity as important when they communicate with you and treat you as a member of your ethnic group. Also, the degree to which you identify with your ethnic group is influenced by the numbers of people from your group who are present. When your group is in a numerical minority, your ethnic identity will be more important than when your group is in a numerical majority.

Language and Ethnic Identity

Skin color and national origin are only two of the markers we use to define our own and other people's ethnicity. We also use the language or dialect spoken to mark boundaries between our ethnic groups and other ethnic groups. This is true in informal conversations with strangers, acquaintances, and friends, as well as in formal communication situations, such as when we talk to our supervisors at work. The importance of language is illustrated by a Mexican American writer's description of the effect, when he was growing up, of

Assessment 2.4 *Assessing the Strength of Your Ethnic Identity*

The purpose of this questionnaire is to help you think about the degree to which you identify with your ethnic group. Respond to each statement by indicating the degree to which the statement is true regarding the way you typically think about yourself. When you think about yourself is the statement "Always False" (answer 1), "Mostly False" (answer 2), "Sometimes True and Sometimes False" (answer 3), "Mostly True" (answer 4), or "Always True" (answer 5)?

_______ 1. If I were born again, I would want to be born as a member of a different ethnic group.

_______ 2. Being a member of my ethnic group is important to me.

_______ 3. I rarely think about being a member of my ethnic group.

_______ 4. Being a member of my ethnic group plays a large role in my life.

_______ 5. Thinking about myself as a member of my ethnic group is not central to how I define myself.

_______ 6. I like the things that make me a member of my ethnic group and different from people in other ethnic groups.

_______ 7. I rarely choose to express my ethnicity in the way I communicate.

_______ 8. I have a positive view of my ethnic group.

_______ 9. I do not enjoy being a member of my ethnic group.

_______ 10. If others do not recognize me as a member of my ethnic group, it upsets me.

To find your score, first reverse the responses for the *odd-numbered* items (if you wrote 1, make it 5; if you wrote 2, make it 4; if you wrote 3, leave it as 3; if you wrote 4, make it 2; if you wrote 5, make it 1). Next, add the numbers next to each of the statements. Scores range from 10 to 50. The higher your score, the more you identify with your ethic group.

hearing his father speak English to a European American gas station attendant:

> I cannot forget the sounds my father made as he spoke. At one point his words slid together to form one word—sounds as confused as the threads of blue and green oil in the puddle next to my shoes. His voice rushed through what he had left to say. And, toward the

> end, reached falsetto notes, appealing to his listeners' understanding. I looked away to the lights of passing automobiles. I tried not to hear anymore. (Rodriguez, 1982, p. 15)

In contrast to the alienation he felt when he heard his father speaking English, the writer felt comfort when members of his family spoke to him in Spanish:

> A family member would say something to me and I would feel specially recognized. My parents would say something to me and I would feel embraced by the sounds of their words. Those words said: I am speaking with ease in Spanish. I am addressing you in words I never use with los gringos. I recognize you as someone special, close, like no one outside. You belong with us. In the family. (Rodriguez, 1982, p. 15)

This example illustrates how language provides a way for non-European Americans to express solidarity with each other.

Another way language affects our identities is through the labels we use to define ourselves. Today it appears that the majority of blacks prefer to use the label African American when they refer to themselves (Larkey, Hecht, & Martin, 1993; a CNN/*Time* poll in February 1994 indicates that a majority prefer this term). Two individuals provide the reasons for the use of this term:

> I grew up in a time when "black" was the accepted term. It was used on application forms and among family and friends. I changed to African American because it seemed more accurate and more enduring to our culture.
>
> [In the past] I didn't prefer "black," it was just used. However, when I began to realize that the term "black" was just making us be seen in terms of skin color (and not including our ethnic heritage), I embraced the term African American. After all, a "white, American, Irish person" is Irish American. We've done just as much for the country, and we have a heritage from *our* mother land, so why not express it! (Larkey et al., 1993, p. 312)

Note that there is *not* a hyphen in the label "African American." In fact, most non-European Americans no longer use a hyphen for their ethnicity; for example, Japanese American and Mexican American are written without hyphens. While it may seem like a minor point, omitting or including a hyphen may be interpreted by members of those groups as providing support for their self-concepts (omitting) or denying their self-concepts (including it). We therefore need to pay attention to the labels others use to refer to themselves if we want to support their self-concepts when we communicate with them.

Concern over the use of ethnic labels is not limited to African Americans. Many people born in Mexico, Puerto Rico, and Cuba find *Hispanic,* a term used for all of these cultures combined, archaic and offensive. Participants in a recent Latino Political Survey (summarized in Gonzalez, 1992) report that they prefer the term *Latino* over Hispanic. Even the pronunciation of the term can be a statement of identity (the preferred pronunciation is lah-TEEN-oh). Some argue that "to say Latino is to say you came to my culture in a manner of respect" (Cisneros quoted by Gonzalez, 1992). People who prefer the term Hispanic tend to want to fit into the mainstream culture (that is, give up their original culture), rather than retain their ethnicity, while people who use the term Latino appear to want to maintain their ethnicity (though they may also want to fit into the mainstream culture; Cisneros).

All terms used to refer to groups of cultures are misleading because they imply similarity across the cultures included under the term. People who come from Mexico, Cuba, and Puerto Rico, for example, share some similarities based on a common language, but there are many cultural differences among the three groups which cannot be ignored. Respondents in the Latino Political Survey indicate that they prefer labels based on their country of origin, such as "Mexican American" or "Cuban American," rather than terms like *Latino* (Gonzalez, 1992). Similarly, first-generation Asian Americans may share a collectivistic upbringing, but there are many differences among Chinese Americans, Japanese Americans, and Vietnamese Americans, to name only a few of the Asian groups often combined under the term Asian American.

The labels individuals use regarding their ethnic group memberships can tell us a lot about them. People who trace their heritage to Mexico, for example, might use several different terms to refer to themselves. To illustrate, a person who labels himself a "Chicano" or herself "Chicana" defines himself or herself differently from a person who uses the label "Mexican American." The person who defines himself as a Chicano or herself as a Chicana probably has political goals, such as promoting "La Raza" and community solidarity, that the person who defines herself or himself as a Mexican American may not.

The labels individuals use to define themselves may not tell us how strongly they identify with their ethnic groups. It appears that "self-identification (that is, choice of group name such as 'Chicano' or 'Mexican American') is more closely tied to cultural knowledge rather than to ethnic identify, which is linked to pride in cultural heritage" (Keefe & Padilla, 1987, p. 9). We, therefore, need to understand what members of other ethnic groups want to be called and how strongly they identify with their ethnic groups to communicate effectively.

If we do not mindfully try to understand how other people define themselves, we will use our own ethnic labels for them when we communicate on automatic pilot. To communicate effectively with others, it is important to know that they prefer one label or another. This is important, as indicated earlier, because **effective communication requires that we support others' self-concepts, including their preferred ethnic identities.**

Gender Identity

In addition to our cultural and ethnic identities, our gender identities also influence our communication. We all have a sense of ourselves as males or females. Before reading further, take a moment and think about what it means to you to be a female or a male.

What are your initial thoughts on how you feel about being a man or a woman?

____

____

____

How does your view of yourself as a male or a female affect the way you communicate? ______________________________

____

____

Are there situations in which you define yourself as a woman or a man more than

We all have a sense of ourselves as males or females. Females tend to relate to one another one on one; males tend to prefer group relationships.

other situations? What characteristics do these situations share in common? ______

____

____

____

Your answers to these questions should provide some insight into the role of your gender identity in your implicit personal theory of communication. Keep your responses in mind as you read the remainder of this section.

Gender and Moral Development

Males and females learn to behave differently. In the United States, males learn to see themselves as separate individuals, and they tend to see their relationships with others as involving *reciprocity* between separate individuals (Gilligan, 1982). Males' concern for others is based on considering others as they want to be considered. Males see relationships as guided by rules that maintain *fairness* in the relationships. **Relationships for males are based on autonomy and are grounded in roles that involve obligation and commitment.**

In the United States, females learn to view themselves as *connected to others* (Gilligan, 1982). Their concern for others is based on what is good for others. Females see relationships as guided by the activity of *caring* for others. **Relationships for females are grounded in interdependence and recognizing the interconnections between people.**

Given the way they learn to view themselves, males and females develop different conceptions of morality (Gilligan, 1982). Males tend to use a morality of *justice and fairness* that is based on reciprocity between separate individuals. Males learn to define moral problems as decisions that need to be made and to resolve them by using a set of impartial standards they have learned. The main criteria used to resolve moral problems are obligations and commitments inherent in the roles being played, as well as what is considered fair. Judging fairness toward others is based on how they would want to be treated if they were in the same situation.

Females learn to use a morality of *response and care* that is based on seeing themselves as connected to others (Gilligan, 1982). Females define moral problems as issues of the relationship that need to be resolved through the activity of care. The main criteria

CATHY © Cathy Guisewite. Reprinted with permission of UNIVERSAL PRESS SYNDICATE. All rights reserved.

used to resolve moral problems are maintaining their connections to others, as well as promoting other people's welfare and/or preventing them from experiencing harm.

Psychological Sex Roles

Psychological sex roles are one specific way that we can think about our gender identities. They are the traits and behaviors that traditionally are called masculine or feminine. They are "the psychological traits and the social responsibilities that individuals have and feel are appropriate for them because they are male or female" (Pleck, 1977, p. 182). The traits and behaviors we associate with being female or male are based on stereotypes we learned as we were growing up. Females, for example, are viewed as more nurturing than males. Some males, however, are nurturing. The stereotype nevertheless persists that females are more nurturing than males. Traits typically stereotyped as masculine and feminine in the United States are listed in Table 2.3.

Traditionally, sex roles have been explained based on biological differences between males and females (Pleck, 1977). Current explanations of sex roles recognize that biological differences do exist, but they emphasize that the social environment (including the culture) plays a large role in teaching us our sex roles. The focus of many explanations is on the development of *psychological sex role identities.* They explain why we learn to be masculine or feminine (rather than male or female) and why some of us exhibit *psychological androgyny* (a blend of masculine and feminine traits).

Masculinity and femininity are *not* opposite ends of a continuum; both males and females exhibit masculine and feminine traits (Bem, 1974). Four psychological sex role orientations can be isolated. First, we have a *masculine sex role* if we exhibit a high degree of masculine traits and behaviors, and a low degree of feminine traits and behaviors. Second, we have a *feminine sex role* if we exhibit a high degree of feminine traits and behaviors, and a low degree of masculine traits and behaviors. Third, we have an *androgynous sex role* if we exhibit a high degree of both masculine

Table 2.3

MASCULINE AND FEMININE SEX ROLE STEREOTYPES IN THE UNITED STATES

Masculine Traits	Feminine Traits
Acts as a leader	Affectionate
Aggressive	Cheerful
Ambitious	Childlike
Analytical	Compassionate
Assertive	Does not use harsh language
Athletic	Eager to soothe hurt feelings
Competitive	Feminine
Defends own beliefs	Flatterable
Dominant	Gentle
Forceful	Gullible
Independent	Loves children
Individualistic	Loyal
Leadership abilities	Sensitive to others' needs
Makes decisions easily	Shy
Masculine	Soft-spoken
Self-reliant	Sympathetic
Self-sufficient	Tender
Strong personality	Understanding
Willing to take a stand	Warm
Willing to take risks	Yielding

Based on Bem (1974).

and feminine traits and behaviors. Finally, we have an *undifferentiated sex role* if we exhibit a low degree of both masculine and feminine traits and behaviors.

Assessment 2.5 is designed to help you determine your sex role orientation. Take a moment to complete it now.

You should have calculated three scores for Assessment 2.5: a masculinity score, a femininity score, and an androgyny score. The higher each of these scores is, the more you exhibit that quality. The higher our androgyny scores, the more flexible our sex roles and the better we can adapt our behavior to different situations (Bem, 1974).

Our psychological sex roles are a reflection of the "gender lenses" we learned as children. Our gender lenses influence the way we look at the world and the way we communicate with others. **Traditionally sex role oriented individuals (highly masculine men and highly feminine women) tend to organize and recall information on the basis of gender** (Bem, 1993). Masculine males and feminine women, for example, tend to remember information about people

Assessment 2.5 *Assessing Your Sex Role Identity*

The purpose of this questionnaire is to assess your sex role identity. Rate the degree to which the 20 adjectives listed apply to you. If the adjective is never true of you, answer 1; if it is almost never true of you, answer 2; if it is true of you a little of the time, answer 3; if it is true of you about half the time, answer 4; if it is true of you most of the time, answer 5; if it is true of you almost all of the time, answer 6; if it is true of you all of the time, answer 7.

______	1. Helpful	______	11. Eager to soothe hurt feelings
______	2. Independent	______	12. Dominant
______	3. Assertive	______	13. Warm
______	4. Has a strong personality	______	14. Willing to take a stand
______	5. Forceful	______	15. Tender
______	6. Has leadership abilities	______	16. Friendly
______	7. Sensitive to needs of others	______	17. Aggressive
______	8. Understanding	______	18. Acts as a leader
______	9. Compassionate	______	19. Competitive
______	10. Sincere	______	20. Gentle

To find your femininity score (*F*), add the numbers you wrote next to items 1, 7, 8, 9, 10, 11, 13, 15, 16, and 20; $F =$ ______ (your score should range between 10 and 70). To find your masculinity score (*M*), add the numbers you wrote next to items 2, 3, 4, 5, 6, 12, 14, 17, 18, and 19; $M =$ ______ (your score should range between 10 and 70). To find your androgyny score, use the following formula: $2(M + F) + (F - M)$. The higher each of your scores is, the more you have this quality.

that fits their sex role stereotypes, such as those described in Table 2.3. Traditionally sex role oriented individuals also tend to follow the cultural definitions of culturally appropriate behavior. To illustrate, "conventionally masculine men [are] independent but not nurturant, and conventionally feminine women [are] nurturant but not independent"

Reading 2.2 GENDER WARS

Ask not what the essential differences are between men and women. Ask why American culture focuses on what small differences there are and imposes the view that the male form is the standard and the female is other and inferior (androcentrism). And why it divides up virtually every object and variety of experience into masculine and feminine (gender polarization).

Society does this so early and so thoroughly by constructing whole social institutions around it—say, a workplace that has no equal coverage for female medical conditions—that we mistake female disadvantage for neutrality and assume it is the way things must be. We fail to notice, says Cornell University psychologist Sandra Bem, Ph.D., that we're looking through a lens, hidden but distorting, long ago implanted in our individual psyches.

The gendered classification of social reality is all-pervasive but at its most profound in dictating how we experience sexual desire. In a new book, *The Lenses of Gender* (Yale University Press), Bem argues that polarization mistakenly lumps all men together and all women together, obliterating the true diversity of impulses that "naturally exists within each sex and the overlap that naturally exists between the two sexes." Among them: erotic interest in people of both sexes, the wish to don vibrant colors and silky textures, feelings of nurturance toward a child.

Gender polarization also becomes the single most important dimension around which personality and individual identity is organized. But by expanding the meaning of what it is to be male or female beyond the biological, it generates deep insecurity about one's maleness or femaleness. It becomes something that must constantly be worked on, protected from loss.

This burden falls disproportionately on men, since androcentrism devalues feelings or behaviors culturally defined as female and punishes men who have them. So they wind up becoming gender caricatures. And homophobes, deeming homosexual impulses unnatural and abhorrent because they so threaten the shaky enterprise of male identity.

Not everyone accepts the "presumed naturalness of the link between the sex of the body and the gender of the psyche," however. There are "gender subversives," primarily homosexuals, who manage to escape the distorting lenses of the culture. If Bem is right, they are the leaders of a necessary psychological revolution.

(Bem, 1993, p. 157). Our gender identities are created in part by our self-definitions, but they are supported by the structural and situational forces operating in our culture. Reading 2.2 contains a discussion of how our gender lenses affect us. Take a moment to read it.

The gender identities we learned as children affect our communication when we communicate on automatic pilot. They affect how we define ourselves, how we transmit messages, and how we interpret other people's messages. We are not, however, prisoners of our gender identities. We can choose to behave differently when we are mindful of our communication.

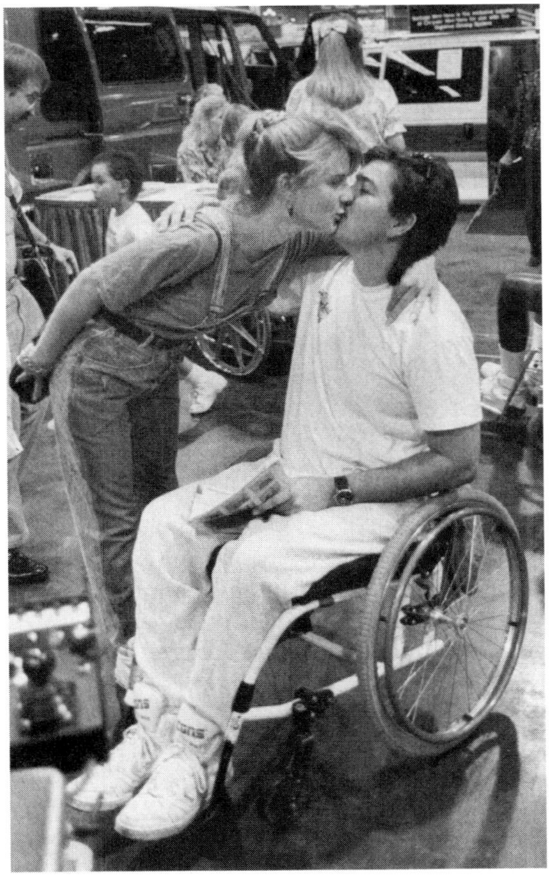

Our identities as disabled or nondisabled people influence our communication when we interact with members of the other group. Many disabled people want their friends to appreciate and accept them with their disabilities.

SOCIAL IDENTITIES BASED ON DISABILITY, AGE, AND SOCIAL CLASS

In addition to our cultural, ethnic, and gender identities, there are many other social identities that influence our communication. Three social identities are particularly important in everyday interactions in the United States: social identities based on disabilities, age, and social class. Let's begin by looking at identities based on disabilities.

Disability

We categorize others based on their physical appearance, and we often evaluate novel appearances negatively (McArthur, 1982). When nondisabled people communicate with people who are visibly disabled in some way, they tend to experience uncertainty and anxiety, and avoid interaction when possible.[5] Nondisabled people communicating with people using wheelchairs, for example, predict more negative outcomes than when communicating with other nondisabled individuals (Grove & Werkman, 1991). Similar observations can be made about interactions with other people viewed as stigmatized, such as people who are blind, deaf, AIDS patients, or mentally ill (Goffman, 1963). Nondisabled people prefer to interact with other nondisabled people. Disabled people, in contrast, prefer to interact with other disabled people and can even be biased against disabled people who act like nondisabled people. To illustrate, there is a sign in the American Sign Language with the right index finger circling forward in front of the forehead which indicates a deaf person who thinks like a hearing person. This sign is *not* meant as a compliment, and its use demonstrates a negative bias toward people who can hear (Barringer, 1993).

Both nondisabled and disabled individuals contribute to miscommunication when they interact (Coleman & De Paulo, 1991). The nondisabled, for example, often have negative stereotypes of disabled people. Disabled people often are seen as "dependent, socially introverted, emotionally unstable, or depressed, hypersensitive, and easily offended, especially with regard to their disability" (p. 69). Nondisabled people may expect that disabled people will view them as prejudiced against disabled people. When nondisabled people interact with disabled people, they may experience anxiety, fear, and surprise. These reactions often are displayed nonverbally in the voice or on the face, even though the nondisabled may try to control their reactions.

Disabled people also contribute negative expectations to their interactions with nondisabled individuals. Disabled people, for example, may be "bitter and resentful about their disability" (Coleman & De Paulo, 1991, p. 75), or they may expect to be perceived negatively by nondisabled individuals; "for example, blind people think that sighted persons perceive them as slightly retarded and hard of hearing" (p. 75). Disabled people's disabilities may affect their communication with nondisabled people. To illustrate, blind people cannot make eye contact, and hearing-impaired people who read lips cannot pick up nuances of communication in the tone of voice.

There are idioms in English such as "the blind leading the blind" and "that's a lame excuse" to which disabled individuals react negatively (Pogrebin, 1987). Also, the labels that nondisabled people use to refer to disabled people can cause problems in communication. To illustrate, a man who wears leg braces says, "I'm not handicapped, people's attitudes about me handicap me" (Pogrebin, 1987, p. 218). "Differently abled" and "physically challenged" also do not appear to be labels accepted widely by disabled individuals. A psychotherapist with cerebral palsy says:

> Friends who care most sometimes think they're doing you a favor by using euphemisms or saying "I never think of you as disabled." The reason they don't want to acknowledge my disability is that they think it is so negative. Meanwhile, I'm trying to recognize it as a valued part of me. I'm more complex than my disability and I don't want my friends to be obsessed by it. But it's clearly there, like my eye color, and I want my friends to appreciate and accept me with it. (Rousso quoted in Pogrebin, 1987, p. 219)

Some disabled people prefer the label "cripple" or "gimp" because they are not euphemisms (an "agreeable" term that is substituted for a "disagreeable" term) and recognize the realities facing disabled people.

As with members of different ethnic groups, it is important that we know what the individuals with whom we are communicating want to be called. (Note that "disabled people" is used here, but some may prefer "people with disabilities.") We tend to use our own labels for members of other groups when we communicate on automatic pilot. This can cause problems in our communication if our labels do not support other people's self-concepts.

Age

Members of other groups do not have to be visually disabled for us to experience uncertainty and anxiety and want to avoid communicating with them; for example, young people often avoid communicating with old people, and old people often avoid communicating with young people. We categorize others based on age when we guess their age based on their physical appearance; when they tell us their age; when they make references to age categories, such as indicating they are retired; and when others talk about experiences in the past that give us cues to their age, to name only a few of the ways we categorize others based on age. Age-based identities can take place at the beginning of our interactions with others or emerge during our communication with others (Coupland, Nussbaum, & Coupland, 1991).

The development of age-based identities in the United States is a result of the growing number of old people, the development of retirement communities which segregate old people, the increase in retirement which decreases interaction between young and old on the job, the amount of money available to older people, and the emergence of groups and organizations exclusively for old people (Rose, 1965). Older people demonstrate "all of the signs of group identification. There is a desire to associate with fellow-agers, especially in formal associations, and to exclude younger adults from these associations. There are expressions of group pride. . . . There are manifestations of a feeling of resentment at 'the way older people are being mistreated' " (Rose, 1965, p. 14). Intergenerational interaction, therefore, is clearly a form of intergroup communication.

Young people often view elderly people as less desirable interaction partners than other young people or middle-aged people (Tamir, 1984). When young people are communicating with the elderly there are several things they do that contribute to misunderstandings (Coupland et al., 1988). First, young people may adapt their behavior by overaccommodating to the elderly because they assume the elderly are handicapped, such as being hard of hearing. Second, young people may communicate with the elderly in ways that reflect the attitude that the elderly are dependent on the young. This allows young people to control the elderly. Third, young people may speak differently from elderly people to establish their identity as young people, such as using slang the elderly do not understand. Fourth, young people may overaccommodate to the elderly to nurture them. To illustrate, young people might use baby talk when talking to the elderly. Fifth, young people may not adapt their behavior to the elderly. The elderly, in turn, may perceive this as lack of interest in them.

The elderly contribute to misunderstandings when they communicate with young people (Coupland et al., 1988). First, the elderly may not accommodate their behavior to the young. One reason for this is that they may have little contact with young people and thus may not know how to adapt their behavior. Second, the elderly may try to protect themselves because they anticipate negative interactions with young people. Third, the elderly may anticipate that they will not perform well when they communicate with young people. Fourth, the elderly may have negative stereotypes of being old. Fifth, the elderly may speak differently from young people because they want to establish their social identity.

Self-concept support is necessary for effective intergenerational communication. One of the major concerns of older people is maintaining healthy self-concepts. Older people's self-concepts are threatened by the process of aging and the cultural attitudes toward old people in the United States (Tamir, 1984). When older people's self-concepts are threatened, "lack of self-affirmation by others can lead to a vicious circle of decreasing self-worth and continued negative and self-effacing encounters (Tamir, 1984, p. 36). Older people will find interactions with younger people who support the older people's self-concepts more satisfying than interactions with younger people who do not support their self-concepts. Supporting other people's self-concepts requires mindfulness.

Social Class

We all identify with a social class whether or not we are aware of it. Social class

> is much more than a convenient pigeonhole or merely arbitrary divisional unit—like minutes, ounces, I.Q. points or inches—along a linear continuum. It is a distinct reality which embraces the fact that people live, eat, play, mate, dress, work, and think at contrasting and dissimilar levels. These levels—social classes—are the blended product of shared and analogous occupational orientations, educational backgrounds, economic wherewithal, and life experiences. Persons occupying a given level need not be conscious of their class identity. But because of their approximately uniform backgrounds and experiences and because they grew up perceiving or "looking at things" in similar ways, they will share comparable values, attitudes, and lifestyles. (Hodges, 1964, p. 13)

The social class to which we belong may be the class with which we identify if we are satisfied with our position in society. Alternatively, if we are seeking upward mobility, our class identity may be based on the social class to which we aspire.

Sociologists tend to divide the social classes in the United States into upper class, upper middle class, middle class, lower middle class, and lower class. No matter how we divide up the class structure, we sort ourselves and others into social classes when we interact. The criteria we use for sorting ourselves and others are usually based on income, occupation, education, beliefs/attitudes, and style of life (Jackman & Jackman, 1983). We also can tell people's social class by their home town, their houses, their yards, and the decorations in their houses, as well as the clothes people wear and the cars they drive (Fussell, 1983).

Our class identities influence the way we communicate. We can tell other people's class background from the way they speak. Using the standard dialect, the dialect used by newscasters on national broadcasts, is perceived to be of higher social status than using a nonstandard dialect, such as a regional or ethnic dialect. The use of double negatives, such as "I can't get no satisfaction," and nongrammatical use of numbers, such as "He don't" or "I wants it," clearly distinguish lower-class speakers from middle-class speakers. The way we pronounce words and the vocabulary we use distinguish between middle-class and upper-middle/upper-class speakers (Fussell, 1983).

Lower- and middle-class speakers learn to emphasize different communication codes, and these codes reinforce class identity (Bernstein, 1973).[6] Middle-class speakers are taught to speak using an elaborated code. An *elaborated code* involves the use of verbal explicitness and direct messages, being verbally elaborate, focusing on the verbal aspects of messages, being oriented toward individual persons, and planning messages in advance. Lower-class speakers, in contrast, are socialized to speak using restricted codes. A *restricted code* involves using metaphors and indirectness, not being verbally elaborate, stressing nonverbal aspects of communication, being oriented toward the group, and not planning messages in advance. Class differences in the use of these codes is one of frequency. Middle-class speakers use elaborated codes more than restricted codes, but they do use restricted codes. Similarly, lower-class speakers use restricted codes more than elaborated codes, but they can use elaborated codes.

Our class identities and our status in particular communication situations—such as whether we are superiors or subordinates, teachers or students, physicians or patients—influence our communication. Class identification tends to be stronger in lower classes than in middle or upper classes (Jackman & Jackman, 1983). Our communication in particular situations, in turn, influences how we define these situations and the social identities we choose to emphasize in these situations. In thinking about how our class identities influence our communication, it is important to keep in mind that our class identities interact with other identities, particularly ethnicity. There are, for example, few differences between the ways middle-class European Americans and middle-class African Americans communicate in organizations. There are, however, significant differences between the ways middle-class European Americans and lower-class African Americans communicate (Gudykunst & Lim, 1985).

Summary

We define ourselves in terms of our human, social, and personal identities. Our human identities involve the characteristics we share with all other humans. Our social identities are based on our membership in social groups and the roles we play. Our personal identities are those characteristics that make us unique individuals.

Although we often are not highly aware of them, several of our social identities influence our communication behavior in most situations. Our cultural identities are based on the culture in which we live. Our ethnic identities are based on our national origin, race, religion, or some combination of these three characteristics. Our gender identities involve how we define ourselves as male or female. Our cultural, ethnic, and gender identities are master identities that influence our other social identities. When our social identities guide our communication, we tend to engage in intergroup communication. When our personal identities guide our communication, we tend to communicate in interpersonal communication.

Our cultural identities influence our communication when we communicate with members of other cultural groups, while our ethnic identities affect our behavior when we communicate with members of other ethnic groups. Our gender identities influence our communication any time we are communicating with members of the opposite sex, or anytime we are talking about members of the opposite sex with members of the same sex. Other social identities also affect our communication, too. To illustrate, our identities as disabled or nondisabled people influence our communication when we interact with members of the other group. Our age-based identities affect our communication with members of other age groups, and our social class identities influence our communication with members of other social classes.

Notes

1. Rosenberg also isolates a fourth factor: psychological centrality. This factor, however, appears to focus on why selected aspects of our self-concepts influence our behavior rather than on self-concept formation.
2. It should be noted that there is some medical evidence that homosexuality is *not* a voluntary identity, but it tends to be perceived as voluntary.
3. Burke and Franzoi (1988) clearly demonstrate that different situations activate different identities.
4. People of Jewish heritage also draw distinctions based on national origin; for example, Jews from Russia and Jews from Germany.
5. For a review of this research, see Dahnke (1983). See Schearer (1984) for disabled persons' views of their communication with nondisabled. There is a problem with selecting terms to refer to this group. *Disabled people* is used because there is a parallel term to refer to nondisabled people. Some people in this group might prefer the term *people with disa-*

bilities because it emphasizes that they are people first and have disabilities second.

6. Bernstein's distinction is similar to Hall's low- and high-context messages discussed earlier in this chapter: low-context messages are similar to elaborate codes, and high-context messages are similar to restricted codes. See Haslett (1990) for a summary of research supporting Bernstein's distinction.

Journal Reflections

1. *Identifying When Your Identities Influence Your Communication.* In the next week, note when your various identities are influencing your communication. At several points each day, make a note of conversations you have with others (note with whom you were communicating and where it took place) and the identity or identities you think are guiding your behavior. At the end of the week, go back over your list to look for commonalities. Are there particular types of situations or people where specific identities influenced your behavior? Write your conclusions in your journal.
2. *Identifying How Self-Esteem Influences Communication.* In your communication in the next week, think about how your self-esteem and self-evaluations influence your communication. How do you behave differently when you feel good about yourself and when you do not feel good about yourself? When looking at how your self-esteem influences your communication, keep in mind that it has positive influences on behavior (it may help us feel good about ourselves) and negative influences (it may cause us to distort our interpretations of what we do). In your journal, describe how you behave differently when you feel good about yourself and when you do not.

Study Questions

1. What is the difference between self and self-concept?
2. How do our human, social, and personal identities differ?
3. How does self-esteem have positive and negative consequences on behavior?
4. What is the difference between personal and collective self-esteem?
5. How are individualistic and collectivistic cultural identities different?
6. What are the differences between low- and high-context communication?
7. How does language influence our ethnic identity?
8. How are males' and females' moral orientations different?
9. What are the differences among masculine, feminine, and androgynous sex role orientations?
10. How do disabilities, age, and social class create social identities?

Suggested Readings

Davis, F. (1992). *Fashion, Culture, and Identity.* Chicago: University of Chicago Press. Fred Davis discusses what our clothes say about the identities we want to project to others. His analysis explains how our clothes indicate who we are and who we want to be.

Dittmar, H. (1992). *The Social Psychology of Material Possessions: To Have Is To Be.* New York: St. Martin's. Helga Dittmar examines how our material possessions serve as symbols of our identity.

Gudykunst, W. B., & Kim, Y. Y. (1992). *Communicating With Strangers* (2nd ed.). New York: McGraw-Hill. This book is an introduction to intercultural communication. It focuses on how culture and ethnicity influence the way people communicate.

Rodriguez, R. (1982). *Hunger Of Memory.* New York: Bantam Books. Richard Rodriguez discusses growing up Mexican American in the United States. His book clearly illustrates issues of language and ethnic identity for people of color.

Stewart, L. P., Stewart, A. D., Friedley, S. A., & Cooper, P. J. (1990). *Communication Between The Sexes: Sex Differences and Sex-role Stereotypes* (2nd ed.). Scottsdale, AZ: Gorsuch Scarsbrick. In this book, Lea Stewart and her colleagues discuss the major approaches to the study of gender and communication. It explains how males and females communicate similarly and differently across contexts (e.g., in language usage, in the workplace).

3

DISPOSITIONS TOWARD INTERPERSONAL COMMUNICATION

Motivation to Communicate
- Need for a Sense of Predictability
- Need for Group Inclusion
- Need to Manage Anxiety
- Need to Sustain Our Self-Conceptions

Communication Dispositions
- Communication Apprehension
- Verbal Aggressiveness
- Empathy

Ethical Dispositions Toward Communication
- We Are All Moral Agents
- Dignity and Integrity
- Moral Inclusion-Exclusion
- Dialogue-Monologue

No two people communicate in exactly the same way. Although there is a great deal of similarity in the way people in a culture communicate, each person's way of communicating is somewhat unique. Each of us has slightly different inclinations toward when we should communicate, with whom we should communicate, how we should communicate (such as the words and the tone of voice we should use), where we should communicate, and why we communicate. Our inclinations toward communication are part of our implicit personal theories of communication.

Although our communication may appear to be a totally automatic process, as you have seen in the previous chapters it is much more complicated. In many situations, we behave on automatic pilot, but there are many situations in which we consciously choose to communicate or not to communicate, and when we choose to communicate we also choose how to communicate. The choices we make are affected by our dispositions toward communication. As indicated in Chapter 1, our dispositions are our general inclinations or orientations toward communication.

Several dispositions influence how we choose to communicate with others. Our motivation to communicate, for example, is influenced by our needs and the degree to which they are being met. Our general inclinations toward communication also influence our communication. To illustrate, people who see themselves as extroverts generally prefer to communicate with others more than do people who see themselves as introverts. Our ethical dispositions, such as our dignity or moral integrity, also affect our general approaches to communication.

Our dispositions toward communication are derived from our motivation to communicate with others, our personal identities, and our ethical orientations. Our personal dispositions toward communication are part of our implicit personal theories of communication. To understand our personal dispositions and how they influence our communication, we must understand how our dispositions fit into our implicit theories. Questions, therefore, are posed at the beginning of each section in this chapter to encourage you to think about your dispositions and how they fit into your implicit personal theory. Where appropriate, self-assessment questionnaires are presented for you to complete. Let's begin our analysis of dispositions by looking at our motivation to communicate.

Motivation To Communicate

The degree to which we meet our basic needs provides the motivational energy necessary for us to interact with others (Turner, 1988).[1] *Needs* are "fundamental states of being that create feelings of deprivation and that mobilize [people] to act on their environment in ways to eliminate this sense of deprivation" (p. 59). The needs that influence our motivation to interact with others include our need for a sense of security, our need for a sense of trust or predictability, our need for a sense of group inclusion, our need to manage anxiety, our need for a sense of a common shared world, our need for symbolic and material gratification, and our need to sustain our self-conceptions. We are not equally aware of all of our needs. We are the least conscious of our needs for security, predictability, and group inclusion, moderately conscious of our need to manage anxiety, and most conscious of our needs for a shared world view, for gratification, and to sustain our self-concepts.

The extent to which we have met our needs, separately and in combination, influences how we present ourselves to others, the intentions we form, and the feelings we have. The needs also influence one another. Anxiety, for example, occurs when our needs for group inclusion, predictability, security, or sustaining our self-concepts are not met. Our overall motivational energy to interact with others is a function of the level of anxiety produced by these four needs (Turner, 1988). To understand our motivation to communicate with others, it is critical that we understand our needs. Four needs are particularly important in understanding our communication: our need for predictability, our need for inclusion, our need to manage anxiety, and our need to sustain our self-conceptions. Let's begin by looking at our need for predictability.

Need for a Sense of Predictability

We "need to 'trust' others in the sense that, for the purposes of a given interaction, others are 'reliable' and their responses 'predictable' " (Turner, 1988, p. 56).[2] If we see other people's behavior as reliable and predictable, it helps confirm our self-concepts and helps us to feel included.

Think about how the need for predictability fits in your implicit personal theory of communication. Take a moment to answer the following questions:

> What influences whether you see other people's behavior as predictable and reliable or as unpredictable and unreliable? ____________________
> ____________________
> ____________________

> How does your communication differ when you see other people's behavior as predictable and reliable and when you see it as unpredictable and unreliable? ______
> ____________________
> ____________________

Your answers to these questions should provide some insight into how your need for predictability fits into your implicit personal theory of communication. Keep your answers to these questions in mind as you read the remainder of this section.

We need to feel that there is a "rhythm" to our interactions with others (Turner, 1988). **To perceive there is rhythm in our interactions with others, we must view other people's behavior as predictable and reliable.** The rhythm we expect to take place varies depending on the context of our interaction. We expect one kind of predictability when we interact with a server in a restaurant and another when we are talking with a close friend. When other people's behavior is not predictable, we feel anxiety.

If we do not feel a part of the interaction taking place, we will have a difficult time seeing other people's behavior as predictable. Our cultural, ethnic, and gender identities provide us with implicit predictions about other people's behavior. The categories in which we place others also provide us with implicit predictions of their behaviors. When we categorize others, our stereotypes of the groups in which we categorize them are activated. Our stereotypes provide predictions of other people's behavior, and our interactions will appear to have rhythm if other people conform to our stereotypes. If other people do not follow our stereotypes, our interactions with them will seem to lack rhythm.

Our ability to predict other people's behavior tends to increase as relationships become more intimate (we have greater ability to predict our friends' behavior than our acquaintances' behavior), but even within a specific relationship, uncertainty fluctuates over time. There is a *dialectic,* or dynamic opposition, between predictability and novelty. In other words, we need both predictability *and* novelty to maintain our relationships. Predictability is necessary to know how to expect other people to behave, but novelty is needed to keep our relationships interesting. When we communicate on automatic pilot, however, we may focus exclusively on our need for predictability and ignore our need for novelty.

There are three features of dialectics that are important: dialectics involve oppositions, there is a unity to the opposites involved, and there is a dynamic relationship between the opposites (Altman, Vinsel, & Brown, 1981). **The elements in a dialectic process exhibit opposition, but at the same time, they complement and define each other; both elements are necessary to be human.** Predictability, for example, is defined in part by being the opposite of novelty. Understanding the idea of predictability would be impossible if the idea of novelty did not exist. The idea of oppositions is part of many different views of human beings. To illustrate, the Chinese represent human nature as involving *yin* and *yang. Yin* involves our feminine side, which is characterized as cool, soft, and weak. *Yang* involves our masculine side, which is characterized as hot, hard, and strong. *Yin* and *yang* must be balanced for us to be human.

Need for Group Inclusion

Our need for group inclusion results from *not* feeling involved in or part of social relationships with others (Turner, 1988). The meaning of inclusion depends on the situation, but clearly we know when we do not feel included. When we do not feel included, we experience anxiety.

The need for inclusion is related directly to how we see our social identities. Our social identities are derived from a tension between our need to be seen as similar to and to fit in with others and our need to be seen as unique people (Brewer, 1991). The need to be seen as similar allows us to identify with different groups and involves the general process of *inclusion,* or the degree to which we fit in with others. The need to be seen as unique is expressed in the general process of *differentiation,* making ourselves stand out from oth-

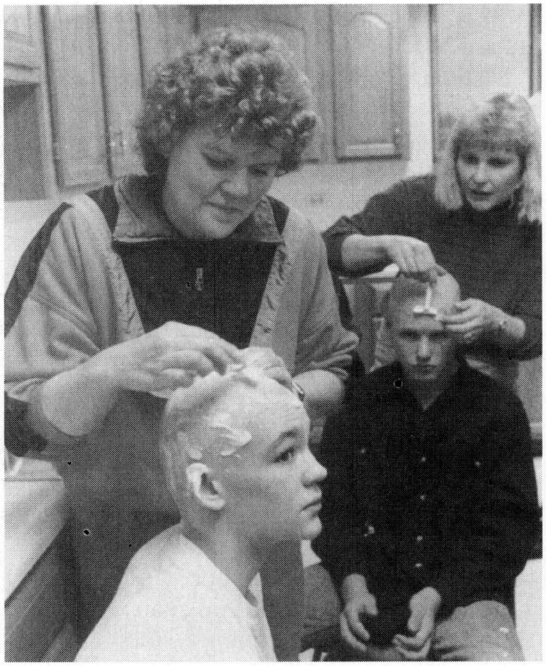

Everyone experiences the need for group inclusion. By having their heads shaved, these boys are helping a classmate who will lose his hair due to cancer treatment meet his need for group inclusion.

ers. **We need to be seen as similar to and different from others.**

Before reading further, stop and think about your needs for inclusion and differentiation. When do you feel the need for inclusion, and when do you feel the need for differentiation? Do they vary in different situations? How do these needs influence the way you communicate? Take a moment and answer the questions below:

When do you feel a need for inclusion?

____

____

____

How does your need for inclusion influence the way you communicate with others? ______________________________

____

____

When do you feel a need for differentiation? ______________________________

____

____

How does your need for differentiation influence the way you communicate with others? ______________________________

____

____

Your answers to these questions should provide insight into how inclusion and differentiation fit into your implicit personal theory of communication. Keep your answers to these questions in mind as you read the remainder of this section.

The processes of inclusion and differentiation are not end points of a single continuum. We do *not* have *either* a need for inclusion *or* a need for differentiation. We have *both* a need for inclusion *and* a need for differentiation at the same time. Inclusion-differentiation is a dialectic like the predictability-novelty dialectic discussed earlier.[3]

In the United States, people strive to compromise between inclusion and differentiation. If there is too much differentiation or inclusiveness, "the person's sense of security and self-worth is threatened. Being highly [differentiated] leaves one vulnerable to isolation . . . total [inclusion] provides no basis for comparative appraisal or self-definition. As a consequence, [people in the United States] are uncomfortable in social contexts in which

FOR BETTER OR FOR WORSE © Lynn Johnston Prod., Inc. Reprinted with permission of UNIVERSAL PRESS SYNDICATE. All rights reserved.

we are either too distinctive or too undistinctive" (Brewer, 1991, p. 478).

Our preferred balance between inclusion and differentiation is a function of our culture, our individual socialization, and our recent experiences. **Effective communication in interpersonal relationships requires that we recognize that we have a need for inclusion and a need for differentiation at the same time.** When we communicate on automatic pilot, however, we may focus on one need over the other. People who use an independent self-construal, for example, tend to focus on differentiation when they communicate on automatic pilot. People who use an interdependent self-construal, in contrast, tend to focus on inclusion when communicating on automatic pilot.

If we assume that inclusion and differentiation are opposite ends of a continuum (a person feels either one or the other, but not both), then we may misinterpret other people's intentions. To illustrate, consider the following short dialogue:

PARTNER 1: Do you want to get together this weekend and do something?

PARTNER 2: Well, we just went out on Tuesday—let's skip this weekend. I could really use some time alone.

If partner 1 sees inclusion and differentiation as opposite ends of a continuum, he or she might interpret partner 2's statement as not wanting to be in the relationship (low inclusion). Partner 2, however, may only be expressing a need for more differentiation and *not* be indicating lack of interest in the relationship.

Need to Manage Anxiety

Anxiety is a "generalized or unspecified sense of disequilibrium," or imbalance (Turner, 1988, p. 61). It stems from feeling uneasy, tense, worried, or apprehensive about what might happen. **Anxiety is an emotional (affective) response to situations based on the anticipation of negative consequences** (Stephan & Stephan, 1985). Anxiety is one of the fundamental problems with which all humans must cope (Lazarus, 1991; May, 1977).

Think about your anxiety and how it influences your communication. Take a few minutes to answer the following questions:

When do you feel most anxious about communicating with others? ____________

____

____

How does your anxiety influence the way you communicate? ____________________

____

____

Your answers to these questions should provide some insight into the role of anxiety in your implicit personal theory of communication. Keep your answers to these questions in mind as you read the remainder of this section.

We feel anxious when our need for security, predictability, group inclusion, and self-confirmation (discussed below) are not met (Turner, 1988). If our needs for security, predictability, and group inclusion are not met, we try to deal with the anxiety associated with these unmet needs. Because we are not highly aware of our needs for security, predictability, and group inclusion, we will have a hard time pinpointing the source of the anxiety. The net result is that "considerable interpersonal energy can be devoted to meeting these needs as individuals grope around for a solution to their often vague feelings of discomfort" (p. 63). The feelings of discomfort may lead us to question our self-concepts.

Need to Sustain Our Self-Conceptions

We try to maintain our self-conceptions, and we may even go to the point of using defense mechanisms such as denial to maintain our views of ourselves (Turner, 1988). Our need for self-concept support directly influences our communication. We are attracted to other people who support our self-concepts (Cushman, Valentinsen, & Dietrich, 1982). Our perceptions of other people's support of our self-concept and their perception that we support their self-concepts is critical if we are going to form an interpersonal relationship with them.

Think about your need to confirm your self-concept. Take a moment to answer the questions below:

In which situations do you try to confirm your self-concept, and in which situations do you not try to confirm your self-concept? ____________________

____

How do you communicate differently when you try to confirm your self-concept and when you are not worried about confirming your self-concept? ____________

____

____

Your answers to these questions should provide some insight into the role of self-concept support in your implicit personal theory of communication. Keep your answers to these questions in mind as you read the remainder of the section.

We try to verify our self-conceptions in our interactions with others (Swann, 1990). **We want consistency and stability in our views of ourselves because this helps us predict and control our environment.** Our stable self-conceptions provide anchors in a rapidly changing world. We also want to ensure that the impressions that others form about us are ones that we want them to form and ones we are able to enact.

We use different techniques to verify our self-conceptions (Swann, 1990). First, we prefer to communicate with people who verify our self-concepts. This frequently involves seeking out people who are similar to us as opposed to people who are different from us. Second, we display *identity cues* that tell others how we want to be viewed. The identity cues may include the clothes we wear, the car we drive, the way we speak, and the titles we use. Consider, for example, two professors—one who insists on being called "Dr." and the other who uses his or her first name. These two professors clearly are sending different identity cues to students. Third, we communicate in ways that are designed to get others to behave toward us as we want them to. To illustrate, if we want to be seen as extroverted, we will act outgoing when we meet new people at a party.

We selectively look for feedback from other people and selectively interpret other people's behavior so that it confirms our views of ourselves (Swann, 1990). We try to verify those views of ourselves of which we are most certain. We engage in self-verification more in long-term relationships such as a marriage than in short-term relationships such as a dating relationship. We seek to verify our self-concepts even if they are negative (see Reading 2.1 in the previous chapter). If we view ourselves negatively, we prefer to interact with others who share this view, because they support our self-concepts. We, therefore, tend to associate with people who share our views of ourselves.

There are two processes operating simultaneously. We try to verify our self-concepts in interactions with others (Swann, 1990), but at the same time, we engage in self-enhancing behaviors. *Self-enhancement* involves attempts to build or maintain our self-esteem. The degree to which we seek self-enhancement, however, is dependent on our ability to confirm our self-concepts. If we are not able to sustain a minimal level of self-confirmation, we will not try to engage in self-enhancement.

To communicate effectively, we have to support the identities others claim when we interact with them, especially those they view as important. This is particularly critical in interethnic communication. One of the major factors predicting the satisfaction non-European Americans feel in their communication with European Americans is the degree to which the non-European Americans perceive that their identities are supported (Hecht, Ribeau, & Alberts, 1989). We do not have to agree that the identities are desirable, but we do need to understand and accept people as they choose to define themselves if we want to communicate effectively and develop relationships with them. This requires that we are mindful of our communication.

Reading 3.1 illustrates some of the processes discussed in this section. Take a moment to read it before continuing.

The author in the reading in Reading 3.1 initially had a low opinion of herself. Her communication with her boyfriend verified her self-conception. Since her self-esteem was low, she accepted verification of a negative self-conception. As she developed a higher level of self-esteem, however, she no longer accepted this negative view of herself. She realized that acceptance is necessary for a healthy interpersonal relationship.

To conclude, our needs influence our motivation to communicate. Our needs, however, are not the only dispositions that influence the way we communicate. Our general dispositions toward communication also affect how we communicate with others.

Communication Dispositions

We all have dispositions toward communication. *Dispositions* are our enduring tendencies or inclinations to think, feel, or behave in a particular way (Daly, 1987). Our dispositions are based on the traits we have. A *trait* is "any distinguishable, relatively enduring way in

Reading 3.1 'We Are Not Colors; We Are People'/Anna Songco

He wasn't Filipino—he was white. Oh, God, he was so perfect—he was rich, smart, funny . . . white—he was perfect. But I was stupid. What had I done to myself? Lied. I lied to myself. You see, for a moment, I felt equal—I felt white. I was glorious! No one could take me off my pedestal—I was white—I had a white boyfriend. Didn't that make me perfect, too? . . .

I used him. And he used me. We used each other. I wanted a white boyfriend—it comes with the territory of being a banana, an Oreo, a coconut, a-shamed. Yeah, that's right, I'm embarrassed. I'm ashamed of all those Filipino gangsters . . . of all those FOBs [fresh off the boat] . . . of Tagalog . . . of the country I was born in . . . of my culture . . . of myself. I'm ashamed of my blood—of the ethnicity that burns through my veins, stains my skin, and molds my face! I denied myself and rejected every other Filipino in America! I was stupid. . . . Why didn't I defend myself when he belittled me? Why? Because I agreed with him. . . . But I was also stupid. Who was he to say all that to me? He was American—full *pledged* red, blue and WHITE. And I was a foreigner in his God-gracious, perfect land.

Do you know why I'm like this? No, how can you, when I don't even know myself? How can anyone know what it feels like to live somewhere that you don't belong? Only those who have experienced what I have can relate. I don't belong anywhere—I don't feel comfortable with white people, with brown people, with yellow people, with black people. I'm sorry, but I don't fit in with any color.

Why? Because I am not a color. And Martin Luther King Jr. is not a color. And Connie Chung is not a color. And George Bush is not a color. We are not colors. We are people. We don't resemble white walls, or brown trees or yellow suns. We're human beings—we're beyond color. . . .

I'm not stupid. I used to be . . . I lacked knowledge. I lacked the knowledge of my culture . . . I lacked the respect of myself. But I taught myself to love myself—my true, Filipina self. But for what? Did I teach myself in vain, only to live with your ignorance? I broke through my ignorance because I couldn't live a lie. Are you going to break through yours, or are we both going to live lies?

Anna Songco, 16, is an 11th-grader at Immaculate Heart High School in Los Angeles. She is a first-generation Filipino-American.

Songco, Anna, "We Are Not Colors; We are People" *The Los Angeles Times,* October 5, 1992. Used by permission of the author.

which one individual differs from others" (Guilford, 1959, p. 6). Our personality traits are part of our personal identities.[4] Like other aspects of our personal identities, our communication dispositions are a function of our upbringing in our culture, ethnic group, social class, and family, as well as our unique individual experiences.

Although our traits are relatively enduring, we can choose to manage and/or modify them. Stated differently, our personality traits or personal identities influence our tendencies toward communication when we communicate on automatic pilot. When we are mindful of our communication, however, we can choose to use other communication resources that are available to us (other dispositions toward communication).

There are many dispositions that influence the way we communicate. Three that will help you understand your implicit theory of communication and improve the quality of your communication are communication apprehension, aggressiveness, and empathy. Let's begin with communication apprehension.

Communication Apprehension

Communication apprehension is "a relatively stable predisposition toward experiencing fear and/or anxiety in a variety of communication contexts" (McCroskey & Richmond, 1987, p. 143). Think about the degree to which you are apprehensive about communicating with others. Take a minute to answer the following questions:

> To what extent do you feel apprehensive about communicating with others? Are there situations in which you feel more anxious than in others? ____________
> ______________________________
> ______________________________
>
> How does your apprehension influence your communication? ____________
> ______________________________
> ______________________________

Your answers to these questions should provide some insight into the role of communication apprehension in your implicit personal theory of communication. Keep your answers to these questions in mind as you read the remainder of this section.

The Nature of Communication Apprehension. We become communication apprehensive because we experience anxiety in a variety of communication situations as we are growing up (McCroskey & Richmond, 1987). As we grow up, we develop expectations for how other people will behave. We also develop expectations for possible outcomes of the different behaviors in which we engage, such as talking. If our expectations are met when we interact with others, we develop confidence. If our expectations are not met in our interactions with others, however, we experience anxiety. When we develop expectations that involve negative outcomes associated with talking to others, fear is produced. **The greater our negative expectations associated with talking to others, the greater our communication apprehension.**

We all have a general tendency toward communication apprehension, and the amount

SINGLE SLICES © Peter Kohlsaat, October 30, 1992, Los Angeles Times Syndicate. Reprinted with permission.

Fred finally comes face to face with a supermodel.

of apprehension we experience can be different in different situations. We might, for example, be highly apprehensive about giving a speech in public or talking at a large meeting, but less apprehensive in a small group discussion. We also can experience different levels of apprehension depending on the person with whom we are communicating. We might be highly apprehensive about communicating with strangers and acquaintances but feel relatively comfortable communicating with friends.

There are four general ways individuals with high levels of communication apprehension respond to others: communication avoidance, communication withdrawal, communication disruption, and excessive communication (McCroskey & Richmond, 1987). When people experience high levels of communication apprehension, they may choose to *avoid* communicating as much as possible, so that they will not feel uncomfortable. Avoiding talking to others is not always possible, however. When forced to communicate unexpect-

Assessment 3.1 *Assessing Your Communication Apprehension*

This instrument is composed of 24 statements concerning your feelings about communication with other people. Please indicate in the space provided the degree to which each statement applies to you by marking whether you (1) strongly agree, (2) agree, (3) are undecided, (4) disagree, or (5) strongly disagree with each statement. There are no right or wrong answers. Many of the questions are similar to other statements. Do not be concerned about this. Work quickly, just record your first impressions.

_______ 1. When talking in a small group of acquaintances, I am tense and nervous.

_______ 2. When presenting a talk to a group of strangers, I am tense and nervous.

_______ 3. When conversing with a friend, I am calm and relaxed.

_______ 4. When talking in a large group of acquaintances, I am calm and relaxed.

_______ 5. When presenting a talk to a group of friends, I am tense and nervous.

_______ 6. When conversing with an acquaintance, I am calm and relaxed.

_______ 7. When talking in a large meeting of strangers, I am tense and nervous.

_______ 8. When talking in a small group of strangers, I am tense and nervous.

_______ 9. When talking in a small group of friends, I am calm and relaxed.

_______ 10. When presenting a talk to a group of acquaintances, I am calm and relaxed.

_______ 11. When I am conversing with a stranger, I am calm and relaxed.

_______ 12. When talking in a large meeting of friends, I am tense and nervous.

_______ 13. When presenting a talk to a group of strangers, I am tense and nervous.

_______ 14. When conversing with a friend, I am tense and nervous.

_______ 15. When talking in a large meeting of acquaintances, I am tense and nervous.

_______ 16. When talking in a small group of acquaintances, I am calm and relaxed.

_______ 17. When talking in a small group of strangers, I am calm and relaxed.

_______ 18. When presenting a talk to a group of friends, I am calm and relaxed.

_______ 19. When conversing with an acquaintance, I am tense and nervous.

_______ 20. When talking in a large group of strangers, I am calm and relaxed.

_______ 21. When presenting a talk to a group of acquaintances, I am tense and nervous.

_______ 22. When conversing with a stranger, I am tense and nervous.

_______ 23. When talking in a large meeting of friends, I am calm and relaxed.

_______ 24. When talking in a small group of friends, I am tense and nervous.

To compute the subscores, begin with the constant noted (the first number in the formula is a constant; the number you use to begin your calculations) and then add or subtract the number you answered for each item as indicated: *public* = 18 − (2) − (5) + (10) + (13) + (18) − (21); *meeting* = 18 + (4) − (7) − (12) − (15) + (20) + (23); *group* = 18 − (1) − (8) + (9) + (16) + (17) − (24); *dyad* = 18 + (3) + (6) + (11) − (14) − (19) − (22); *stranger* = 24 − (2) − (7) − (8) + (11) + (13) + (17) + (20) − (22); *acquaintance* = 24 − (1) + (4) +(6) + (10) − (15) + (16) − (19) − (21); *friend* = 24 + (3) − (5) + (9) − (12) − (14) + (18) + (23) − (24); *total PRCA* (Personal Report of Communication Apprehension) = *stranger* + *acquaintance* + *friend.* Subscores range from 6 to 30. The higher your subscores or total scores, the greater your communication apprehension. Scores above 18 on the subscales suggest some degree of apprehension.

From McCroskey, J. C. (1986). *An introduction to rhetorical communication* (5th ed.). Englewood Cliffs, NJ:Prentice-Hall. Printed by permission of Dr. James C. McCroskey, West Virginia University.

edly, people with high levels of communication apprehension may choose to *withdraw* from the situation as soon as they can.

If people with high levels of apprehension find themselves in situations where they are forced to communicate and cannot withdraw, one of two responses is likely. The most likely response is *communication disruption.* When this occurs, they will not be fluent in their verbal communication—such as using a lot of "ahs," "ums," and "you knows"—or they will select inappropriate strategies for communication—such as using big words to impress others or being passive when assertiveness is needed. Alternatively, some people with high levels of communication apprehension engage in *excessive communication,* such as not being able to stop talking. The responses that people with high communication apprehension choose in these situations are based, at least in part, on the assumption that they do not have the skills necessary for effective communication.

Assessing Your Communication Apprehension. Assessment 3.1 contains a questionnaire designed to help you assess your level of communication apprehension. Take a few minutes to complete it now.

As indicated, a score above 18 on any one of the subscales suggests some degree of apprehension regarding that subscale. It is important to keep in mind that your level of communication apprehension influences your communication with others when you are communicating on automatic pilot; that is, when you are *not* mindful of your communication. You can choose to mindfully manage your apprehension and use other communication resources available to you. This procedure is discussed in more detail in Chapter 5 when the ways to manage our anxiety are examined.

Cultural Identity and Communication Apprehension. Our individualistic and collectivistic cultural identities influence our view of communication apprehension. In individualistic cultures like the United States, talk is valued highly. People who are able to express themselves well in individualistic cultures are perceived to be competent. In collectivistic cultures, talk is not valued in the same way as in individualistic cultures. Members of collectivistic cultures tend to be attracted to people who do *not* engage in a lot of verbal activity, rather than people who talk a great deal (Elliot et al., 1982). In collectivistic cultures, verbal communication, or talk, is viewed as only one aspect of communication. Nonverbal aspects of communication are important in interpreting the high-context or indirect messages that predominate in collectivistic cultures.

When people in individualistic cultures like the United States and Australia are compared with people in collectivistic cultures like Japan and Korea using Assessment 3.1, the people in collectivistic cultures score higher on communication apprehension than the people in individualistic cultures.[5] These differences may also hold for different ethnic groups in the United States. Japanese Americans, Korean Americans, Chinese Americans, and Vietnamese Americans who hold collectivistic values, for example, may not highly value verbal communication and may appear communication apprehensive to European Americans.

The cultural or ethnic differences in communication apprehension are *not* important when we are communicating with members of our own culture or ethnic group. When we communicate with people from different cultures, however, cultural differences in communication apprehension can be problematic. People from collectivistic cultures who do not value talk, for example, will interpret high levels of verbal communication negatively. Similarly, people in individualistic cultures who value talk will view people from collectivistic cultures who do not talk a lot negatively. **To communicate effectively with people from other cultures, we must try to understand what the behavior means to the other person. This requires that we be mindful and not interpret their behavior using our own frame of reference.**

Verbal Aggressiveness

Communication apprehension focuses on our general tendencies to communicate or not. Now let's turn to the ways we communicate with others. One way that we communicate that is problematic and that decreases our effectiveness involves verbal aggressiveness.

Verbal aggressiveness is "the tendency to attack the self-concepts of individuals instead of, or in addition to, their positions on topics of communication" (Infante, 1987, p. 164). All verbal aggressiveness involves a hostile response to others, but not all hostility involves

Verbal aggressiveness is not an effective means of communication because it attacks an individual's self concept. Verbal assertiveness, on the other hand, is effective because it involves standing up for our own rights and at the same time respecting the rights of others.

attacking other people's self-concepts. Before proceeding, think about how aggressive you are when you communicate. Take a few moments to answer the following questions:

> To what extent are you verbally aggressive when you communicate with others? Are there situations in which you are more aggressive than others? ______________
>
> ____________________________________
>
> How does your verbal aggressiveness influence the way others respond to you? ____________________________
>
> ____________________________________

Your answers to these questions should provide insight into the role of aggressiveness in your implicit personal theory of communication. Keep your responses to these questions in mind as you read the remainder of this section.

The Nature of Verbal Aggressiveness. A verbally aggressive message is one that intentionally or unintentionally causes others pain or leads them to think less favorably about themselves. We sometimes refer to these messages as "put-downs." We are not necessarily conscious of our intention to put down other people when we are verbally aggressive. To illustrate, consider the following conversation:

HUSBAND: I'm looking forward to a vacation this summer.

WIFE: Me too. Let's do something exciting.

HUSBAND: I want to do what we always do, take our boat to Lake Erie for two weeks. . . .

WIFE: That's stupid! You never want to do anything different. It's always the same boring thing, year after year.

HUSBAND: Well, I think there is something wrong with you! All you want is excitement. (Infante, 1988, pp. 17–18)

Clearly, the last two comments involve attacking the partner's self-concept and, therefore, are verbally aggressive.

What is considered verbally aggressive depends on the individuals involved, who is observing, and the culture in which the interaction takes place (Infante, 1988). We may not intend to be verbally aggressive, but the people with whom we are communicating may feel like they are being attacked. Alternatively, we may intend to be verbally aggressive, but the people with whom we are communicating may not perceive our message to be aggressive.

We are verbally aggressive toward other people when we attack their character, attack their competence, attack their background or physical appearance, insult them, speak evil of them, tease or ridicule them, use profanity, threaten them, and or use nonverbal indicators such as shaking a clenched fist or giving "the finger" (Infante, 1988). **Engaging in verbal aggressiveness can lead to damaged self-concepts, hurt feelings, anger, irritation, embarrassment, relationship deterioration, relationship termination, and physical violence** (Infante, 1988).

There are gender differences in how aggressiveness is interpreted (Campbell, 1993). Women, for example, tend to see aggression as a failure of the people engaging in aggressive behavior to control themselves. Men, in contrast, see aggressive behavior as an attempt to control others.

Assessing Your Verbal Aggressiveness. Assessment 3.2 contains a questionnaire designed to help you assess your verbal aggres-

Assessment 3.2 *Assessing Your Verbal Aggressiveness*

This survey is concerned with how we try to get people to comply with our wishes. Indicate how often each statement is true for you personally when you try to influence other persons. Use the following scale: 1—almost never true; 2—rarely true; 3—occasionally true; 4—often true; 5—almost always true.

______ 1. I am extremely careful to avoid attacking individuals' intelligence when I attack their ideas.

______ 2. When individuals are very stubborn, I use insults to soften the stubbornness.

______ 3. I try very hard to avoid having other people feel bad about themselves when I try to influence them.

______ 4. When people refuse to do a task I know is important, without good reason, I tell them they are unreasonable.

______ 5. When others do things I regard as stupid, I try to be extremely gentle with them.

______ 6. If individuals I am trying to influence really deserve it, I attack their character.

______ 7. When people behave in ways that are in very poor taste, I insult them in order to shock them into proper behavior.

_______ 8. I try to make people feel good about themselves even when their ideas are stupid.

_______ 9. When people simply will not budge on a matter of importance I lose my temper and say rather strong things to them.

_______ 10. When people criticize my shortcomings, I take it in good humor and do not try to get back at them.

_______ 11. When individuals insult me, I get a lot of pleasure out of really telling them off.

_______ 12. When I dislike individuals greatly, I try not to show it in what I say or how I say it.

_______ 13. I like poking fun at people who do things which are very stupid in order to stimulate their intelligence.

_______ 14. When I attack a person's ideas, I try not to damage their self-concepts.

_______ 15. When I try to influence people, I make a great effort not to offend them.

_______ 16. When people do things which are mean or cruel, I attack their character in order to help correct their behavior.

_______ 17. I refuse to participate in arguments when they involve personal attacks.

_______ 18. When nothing seems to work in trying to influence others, I yell and scream in order to get some movement from them.

_______ 19. When I am not able to refute others' positions, I try to make them feel defensive in order to weaken their positions.

_______ 20. When an argument shifts to personal attacks, I try very hard to change the subject.

To find your score:

1. Add your scores on items 2, 4, 6, 7, 9, 11, 13, 16, 18, 19.
2. Add your scores on items 1, 3, 5, 8, 10, 12, 14, 15, 17, 20.
3. Subtract the sum obtained in step 2 from 60.
4. To compute your verbal aggressiveness score, add the total obtained in step 1 to the result obtained in step 3.

Interpretation:
59–100 = High in verbal aggressiveness
39–58 = Moderate in verbal aggressiveness
20–38 = Low in verbal aggressiveness

"Verbal Aggressiveness: An Interpersonal Model and Measure," D.J. Infante and C.J. Wigley, *Communication Monographs*, Vol. 53, p. 61–69. Used by permission of the Speech Communication Association.

siveness. Take a few minutes to complete it now.

The higher your score on Assessment 3.2, the greater your verbal aggressiveness. High levels of verbal aggressiveness are not conducive to effective communication. Effective communication requires that we take other people's perspectives into consideration. This requires verbal assertiveness, not verbal aggressiveness.

Assertiveness. The opposite of aggressiveness in nonassertiveness. When we are *nonassertive,* we do not take our own rights into consideration. Nonassertive behavior denies our rights and allows other people to choose. Letting others choose for us often leads to our feeling hurt when the others do not choose what we want. When we are unassertive, we deny our right to express ourselves and inhibited from telling others our feelings. When we are nonassertive, we generally do not accomplish our goals (Alberti & Emmons, 1990).

The middle ground between aggressiveness and nonassertiveness is assertiveness. *Assertiveness* involves communicating in a way that indicates that we are standing up for our rights but at the same time respecting the rights of others. Assertive communicators state their opinions and express their feelings directly and honestly. They express themselves in a way that does not put the other person down. Verbally, assertiveness involves stating our wants, honestly expressing our feelings, using objective words (such as describing other people's behavior, not evaluating it), using direct statements of what we mean, and using "I messages" (such as "I felt angry," not "You made me angry"; Bloom, Coburn, & Pearlman, 1975). Nonverbally, assertiveness involves attentive listening behavior and communicating care for the other person (Bloom et al., 1975).

The value placed on assertiveness in the United States is based on the notion of individual rights. Assertive behavior is viewed positively because everyone's rights are protected (Heimberg et al., 1977). Nonassertive and aggressive behavior are viewed negatively because other people's rights (aggressive) or our own rights (nonassertive) are not taken into consideration. Nonassertive behavior, however, is valued in collectivistic cultures.

Before proceeding, there are several things to keep in mind about assertiveness. First, it is important to recognize that what is perceived as assertiveness depends on the person perceiving the behavior. To illustrate, a woman and a man may engage in the same behavior in an organization. Even when the behavior is the same, the man's behavior might be perceived as being assertive and the woman's behavior perceived as being aggressive because of the perceiver's sex-role stereotypes. Second, we may have to adapt how we are assertive depending on the person with whom we are communicating. If individualists are communicating with collectivists, for example, they may not want to be totally direct since collectivists tend to emphasize indirect communication. Individualists, nevertheless, can be assertive while being somewhat indirect. Third, it is important to remember that we do not always have to be assertive. We should be assertive when we think it is appropriate given the situation and our relationship with the other person. There are times when unassertive behavior is appropriate (such as times when we truly do not care what happens or when we think we might suffer negative consequences if we are assertive). Aggressive behavior, however, is never justified.

Skill Exercise 3.1 provides an opportunity for you to begin developing assertiveness skills. Take a few minutes to complete it now.

After completing Skill Exercise 3.1, you should understand how nonassertive, assert-

Skill Exercise 3.1 *Being Assertive*

Being assertive requires that we stand up for our rights and at the same time respect others' rights. Indicate how you would typically respond and how you might respond assertively in each situation given below. Also, indicate why you think this is an assertive and not an aggressive response.

1. An acquaintance has borrowed one of your books. You want her or him to return the book to you.

   How would you typically respond?

   ____

   ____

   ____

   How would you respond assertively?

   ____

   ____

   ____

   Why is this assertive and not aggressive or unassertive? ______________

   ____

   ____

   ____

2. Your friend is angry with you and is not speaking with you. You want your friend to speak with you so that you can try to resolve the problem.

   How would you typically respond?

   ____

   ____

   ____

   How would you respond assertively?

   ____

   ____

   ____

   Why is this assertive and not aggressive or unassertive? ______________

   ____

   ____

3. Your romantic partner has been late for three dates in a row. You want your partner to stop being late for dates.

   How would you typically respond?

   ____

   ____

   ____

   How would you respond assertively?

   ____

   ____

   ____

   Why is this assertive and not aggressive or unassertive? ______________

   ____

   ____

ive, and aggressive messages differ. Your responses are nonassertive if you do not stand up for your own rights in the situations presented. To illustrate, your response in the first scenario would be nonassertive if you did not ask the other person to return your book. Your typical behavior is aggressive if you trample on other people's rights to get your way. Your response in the first scenario, for example, is aggressive if you put the other person down when you asked for your book back. An assertive response in the first scenario might be something like, "I need the book I loaned you. Would you please return it as soon as possible?"

If all of your typical responses in Skill Exercise 3.1 are assertive, then you may not have to develop new skills. If your typical responses are nonassertive or aggressive, however, you'll want to practice being assertive. One important aspect of assertiveness is that it involves taking other people's perspectives into consideration. This requires that we be empathic.

Empathy

Sympathy involves "the imaginative placing of ourselves in another person's position" (Bennett, 1979, p. 411). When we are sympathetic, we imagine how *we* would think or feel in a particular situation. Sympathy involves a heightened awareness of another person's suffering (Wispe, 1986). *Empathy,* in contrast, involves "the imaginative intellectual and emotional participation in another person's experience" (Bennett, 1979, p. 418). When we empathize, we imagine how the *other person* thinks or feels in the situation. Empathy involves trying to nonjudgmentally understand other people's experiences (Wispe, 1986).

Before proceeding, think about your tendency to empathize or sympathize with others. Take a minute to answer the following questions:

> To what extent can you imagine how other people think and feel in a particular situation (not imagine how *you* would think or feel in the same situation)? Are there times when you are better able to this than others? ______________________
>
> ____________________________________
>
> How does being able to imagine how other people feel in a situation influence the way you communicate with them?
>
> ____________________________________
>
> ____________________________________

Your answers to these questions should provide some insight into the role of empathy and sympathy in your implicit personal theory of communication. Keep your responses to these questions in mind as you read the remainder of this section.

The Nature of Empathy. We all have a general tendency to be empathic or sympathetic in our interactions with others. Empathy involves cognitive, affective, and communication components (Bell, 1987). Cognitively, we try to take other people's perspectives when we are empathic. We try to see the situation from other people's points of view. When we are sympathetic, we use our point of view to think about other people's situations. Affectively, we try to understand the emotions other people are experiencing. When we are sympathetic, we imagine how we would feel in the other person's situation. When we are empathic, we also try to signal to other people that we understand them by the way we transmit our verbal and nonverbal messages. The cognitive, affective, and communication components of empathy all must be present for others to perceive that we are being empathic. When we are empathic, we frequently check with other people to make sure we are accurately understanding their feelings, and we modify our behavior toward them based on their response to us (Rogers, 1975).

Being empathic is associated with perceived communication effectiveness across cultures. Characteristics of empathy include "listening carefully to what people say," understanding "how other people are feeling," being "interested in what others have to say," being "sensitive to the needs of other people," and understanding "another's point of view" (Hwang, Chase, & Kelley, 1980, p. 74). Although these indicators of empathy include verbal components, we tend to rely on nonverbal behavior more than verbal behavior when we interpret other people's behavior as empathic (Bell, 1987). The greater our empathy, the more we are able to *accurately* predict and explain other people's behavior.

Assessing Your Empathy. Assessment 3.3 contains a questionnaire designed to help you assess your level of empathy. Take a few minutes and complete it now.

The higher your score on Assessment 3.3, the greater your empathy. The greater your empathy, the better you will be at understanding how others are interpreting your messages and, therefore, the more effective your communication will be.

Skill Exercise 3.2 is designed to help you see the difference between these two ways of understanding other people's thoughts and feelings. Take a few minutes to complete it now.

Your answers to the sympathetic responses in Skill Exercise 3.2 should be based on how the person responding would feel in the situation. To illustrate, in the first scenario, Kim's sympathetic response to Pat would be based on how he, Kim, would feel in this situation. An empathic response, in contrast, would be based on imagining how the person having the experience feels (how Pat feels). The response to the first scenario, therefore, would be based on how Kim imagines that Pat feels losing someone very close to her. Since Kim was not close to his grandmother, his sympathetic response may not take into consideration the depth of Pat's grief over losing a grandmother who raised her.

It is important to keep in mind that, when our behavior is based on our implicit theories of communication, we probably tend to respond to others with sympathy, not empathy. When we use our implicit theories to guide our behavior, we tend to interpret other people's behavior from our own frame of reference. To overcome this tendency, we need to be mindful of our communication and try to understand other people's perspectives.

As indicated throughout this section, our general dispositions toward communication, including our communication apprehension, verbal assertiveness, and empathy, affect our communication with others. We also have general orientations toward morality that influence the way we communicate.

Ethical Dispositions Toward Communication

As indicated in the model of communication presented in Chapter 1, ethical dispositions are an important aspect of interpersonal communication. Our ethical dispositions include the extent to which we see ourselves as accountable for our behavior (moral agency), what we see as necessary for people to have dignity, our tendency to be morally inclusive or exclusive, and our tendency to engage in monologues or dialogues. Let's begin by looking at how we are all moral agents.

We Are All Moral Agents

In all communication situations, we make choices about how we want to communicate. Many of these choices have to do with whether to behave morally or ethically. As

Assessment 3.3 *Assessing Your Empathy*

The purpose of this questionnaire is to help you assess your ability to empathize. Respond to each statement by indicating the degree to which the statement is true regarding the way you typically communicate with others. When you think of your communication, is the statement "Always False" (answer 1), "Usually False" (answer 2), "Sometimes False and Sometimes True" (answer 3), "Usually True" (answer 4), or "Always True" (answer 5).

_______ 1. I try to understand others' experiences from their perspectives.

_______ 2. I follow the Golden Rule ("Do unto others as you would have them do unto you") when communicating with others.

_______ 3. I can "tune in" to the emotions others are experiencing when we communicate.

_______ 4. When trying to understand how others feel, I imagine how I would feel in their situation.

_______ 5. I am able to tell what others are feeling without being told.

_______ 6. Others experience the same feelings I do in any given situation.

_______ 7. When others are having problems, I can imagine how they feel.

_______ 8. I find it hard to understand the emotions others experience.

_______ 9. I try to see others as they want me to.

_______ 10. I never seem to know what others are thinking when we communicate.

To find your score, first reverse the responses for the *even-numbered* items (if you wrote 1, make it 5; if you wrote 2, make it 4; if you wrote 3, leave it as 3; if you wrote 4, make it 2; if you wrote 5, make it 1). Next, add the numbers next to each statement. Scores range from 10 to 50. The higher your score, the more you are able to empathize.

moral agents, we make moral choices and decisions about whether to restrain our appetites and passions when necessary. One of the reasons we restrain ourselves is that "we regard ourselves as generally accountable for our conduct, and even to some extent, for our attitudes and character" (Pritchard, 1991, p. 39). If we do not meet our minimal standards for moral behavior, we hold ourselves accountable and blame ourselves.

We are living in a time of "moral skepticism." Many people today, for example, are not sure that it is valid to make moral judgments, because morality is assumed to be relative (Taylor, 1992). To illustrate, moral standards differ across cultures and among ethnic groups in the United States. Also, as indicated in Chapter 2, males and females learn different standards of morality. Even if we recognize the relativity of moral standards, we must still

Skill Exercise 3.2 *Sympathy and Empathy*

The purpose of this skill exercise is to help you begin to differentiate sympathy and empathy. Read the scenarios provided and answer the questions for each scenario.

1. Pat tells Kim that her grandmother passed away yesterday. Assume that Kim had very little contact with his grandmothers (Kim met them only a few times). Pat's grandmother, however, lived with her for the last ten years after Pat's mother died.

   How would Kim respond to Pat using sympathy? ______________________

   ____

   ____

   ____

   How would Kim respond to Pat using empathy? ______________________

   ____

   ____

   ____

   Why does this involve empathy and not sympathy? ______________________

   ____

   ____

2. Scott tells his friend Maria that he found out yesterday that his parents are getting a divorce. No one in Scott's family has ever been divorced before. Maria's parents were divorced several years ago, and her aunt and uncle were divorced a few years earlier.

   How would Maria respond to Scott using sympathy? ______________________

   ____

   ____

   How would Maria respond to Scott using empathy? ______________________

   ____

   ____

   Why does this involve empathy and not sympathy? ______________________

   ____

   ____

make ethical judgments. **We cannot avoid making ethical judgments.** We must, however, understand others and their groups before we judge them. In making moral judgments, we have to balance individual and community needs (Taylor, 1992).

To understand how our ethical standards influence our communication, we must recognize the ethical principles guiding our behavior. Before proceeding, think about the following questions and write your responses in the space provided.

What ethical principles do you follow in your life? ______________________

____

____

How do you use these principles in judging other people's behavior? ____________

____

____

____

Your answers to these questions should provide some insight into the role of morality in your implicit personal theory of communication. Keep your answers to these questions in mind as you read the remainder of this section.

Dignity and Integrity

Dignity and integrity are central to ethical behavior. *Dignity* involves having a minimal level of self-respect (Pritchard, 1991). It refers to feeling worthy, honored, or respected as a person. **Being moral involves maintaining our own sense of dignity and maintaining other people's sense of dignity as well.** When we uphold a set of principles for the right reasons, even under adverse circumstances, we have *personal integrity* (McFall, 1987). We do not have to agree with the principles other people hold to say that they have integrity. For people to have personal integrity, the principles that they uphold must be "ones that a reasonable person might take to be of great importance" (McFall, 1987, p. 11).

Personal integrity reflects our view of what is important, and it is linked closely to moral integrity. *Moral integrity* requires "a somewhat unified moral stance. . . . Those with moral integrity can be expected to refuse to compromise moral standards for the sake of personal expediency" (Pritchard, 1991, p. 90). Our moral standards are learned in our culture, our ethnic group, our family, and religious institutions. One potential set of moral standards is suggested by the Aspen Declaration on Character Education, which specifies six core values that make up a unified moral stance: respect, responsibility, trustworthiness, caring, justice and fairness, and civic virtue and citizenship.[6]

Morality should always prevail in guiding our behavior; "one should not choose immoral or morally objectionable courses of action over those that are morally acceptable" (Pritchard, 1991, pp. 225–226). Cheating, for example, is not morally acceptable under any circumstances. Morality must be a major concern any time we communicate with others.

Behaving morally requires that we respect other people and their moral views (Gutmann, 1992). We do not have to agree with other people's views of morality to respect them; we only have to see their views as based on a unified moral stance. Those who disregard other people's views are not worthy of respect (Gutmann, 1992). This has clear implications for what often is referred to as *hate speech,* speech that puts down others

because of their membership in a group. There is "no virtue in misogyny [hatred of women], racial or ethnic hatred" (p. 22). Racist and anti-Semitic remarks are not defensible on moral grounds, because "hate speech violates the most elementary moral injunction, to respect the dignity of all human beings" (p. 23).[7] Many of us make racist or anti-Semitic remarks when we communicate on automatic pilot. Saying we are sorry after we make these kinds of remarks does not excuse us (see Reading 3.2). Stopping this practice requires that we mindfully decide to change the way we communicate. When we are mindful, we need to pay attention to what we say and what other people say. We have a moral obligation to respond when we hear others engage in hate speech. If we do not, we are being morally exclusive.

Moral Inclusion-Exclusion

We are engaging in *moral exclusion* when we see individuals or groups "as *outside the boundary in which moral values, rules, and considerations of fairness apply.* Those who are morally excluded are perceived as nonentities, expendable, or undeserving; consequently, harming them appears acceptable, appropriate, or just" (Optow, 1990, p. 1). Before proceeding, think about the extent to which you are morally inclusive or morally

Reading 3.2 'Sorry Doesn't Excuse Politicians Who Utter Ethnic Slurs

Well, one thing you can say about some politicians in multicultural California: they manage to offend on an equal-opportunity basis.

The lates chapter in the saga, "Politicians with Foot-in-Mouth Disease,* belongs to Assemblywoman Kathleen M. Honeycutt (R-Hesperia). Honeycutt, seeking to explain during a televised legilative hearing how a negotiator might gain financial advantage over another, said, "It gives the contractor great leverage to kind of Jew down the subcontractor if he is going to have to wait for the money."

Honeycutt paused, but completed her remarks. After she finished Assemblyman Byron D. Sher (D-Palo Alto) told her he found the term "Jew down" offensive. She apologized. But how easily stereotypes take hold and become part of everyday thought and speech.

Recall that there seems to be a disturbing pattern among elected officials who do or say something hurtful and foolish first, think later and then all insist they didn't mean it the way it came out. Earlier this year Assemblyman William J. (Pete) Knight (R-Palmdale) circulated a racist poem from a constituent about Latino illegal immigrants. Later a San Jose city councilwoman referred to Latinos as "pit bulls" and used her fingers to pull her eyes into slits while referring to Asians.

The latest offense by Honeycutt prompted a letter signed by about a dozen lawmakers. The letter appropriately asked: "How can we expect the people of our state to act to end the evil of racism and hate crimes when leaders are guilty of promoting racism?"

How indeed. In the case of Knight, San Jose City Councilwoman Kathy Cole and now Honeycutt, apologies were issued after the fact. But "sorry" somehow doesn't quite take back the insidious effects of uttering racist poems and ethnic slurs.

exclusive. Take a moment to answer the following questions:

> Are there people you think do not have to be treated in a "moral" way? If yes, who? ______________________________
> ______________________________
> ______________________________
>
> Are there situations in which you do not think about the morality of your behavior? If yes, what situations? ______________
> ______________________________
> ______________________________
>
> How does your communication differ when you are aware of the need to act in a moral fashion and when you are not aware of it? ______________________
> ______________________________
> ______________________________
> ______________________________

Your answers to these questions should provide some insight into the role of moral exclusion in your implicit personal theory of communication. Keep your answers to these questions in mind as you read the remainder of this section.

The Nature of Moral Inclusion/Exclusion. Two major factors lead us to behave in a morally exclusive fashion (Optow, 1990). When we are engaged in group *conflict,* for example, we feel close to other members of our ingroups, but at the same time our concern for fairness to members of outgroups is low. Another factor that contributes to moral exclusiveness is *feeling unconnected* to other people or groups. We feel unconnected from others when we see them as totally separate from ourselves. When we feel connected to others in any way, we feel attraction and empathy and engage in helpful behavior. When we do not feel connected to others, we treat them in a morally exclusive fashion when we communicate on automatic pilot.

Moral exclusion can take many forms. It can range from slavery, genocide, political repression, and violations of human rights to failing to recognize undeserved suffering in others. The Holocaust in Germany and the My Lai massacre incident during the Vietnam War are examples of severe moral exclusion. Moral exclusion, however, occurs in everyday interactions, too. If we distance ourselves from other people psychologically, displace our responsibility to others, or glorify violence, we are being morally exclusive. Table 3.1 presents

Table 3.1
Some Characteristics of Moral Exclusiveness

Making unflattering comparisons of outgroups with our ingroup.
Regarding others as a lower form of life.
Seeing contact with others as threatening.
Accepting a moral code that allows harm to others.
Harming others.
Seeing our ingroup as better than outgroups (regarding outgroups as inferior).
Perceiving others as objects.
Having different moral codes for different people.
Accepting violent behavior as normal.
Perceiving our harmful behavior as an isolated incident (we just harmed others this one time).

Based on Optow's (1990) description of moral exclusion.

some of the major characteristics associated with moral exclusiveness.

When we see someone within our moral community (those we believe should be treated morally) harmed, we perceive an injustice to have taken place. If we harm others in our moral community, we feel shame, guilt, remorse, or self-blame. When we see someone outside our moral community harmed, however, we may not perceive that their rights have been violated and therefore may not be concerned. To be morally inclusive, we need to consciously change the boundaries of our moral community to include everyone. This requires that we make a conscious decision and mindfully modify our behavior.

Assessing Your Moral Inclusiveness. Assessment 3.4 contains a questionnaire designed to help you determine how morally inclusive you are. Take a few minutes to complete it before you continue reading.

The higher your score on Assessment 3.4, the more morally inclusive you are. The "ideal"

Assessment 3.4 *Assessing Your Moral Inclusiveness*

The purpose of this questionnaire is to assess your moral inclusiveness. Respond to each statement indicating the degree to which you agree or disagree: "Strongly Disagree" (answer 1), "Disagree" (answer 2), "Sometimes Disagree and Sometimes Agree" (answer 3), "Agree" (answer 4), and "Strongly Agree" (answer 5).

_______ 1. Everyone should be treated fairly.

_______ 2. There are people who do not deserve my respect.

_______ 3. All people have a right to be treated with dignity.

_______ 4. I do not make sacrifices to foster others' well-being.

_______ 5. Moral values apply equally to everyone.

_______ 6. I am not morally obligated to treat everyone with respect.

_______ 7. I apply the same rules to my friends and enemies.

_______ 8. It is not my responsibility to help those who need assistance.

_______ 9. All forms of life should be treated with reverence.

_______ 10. There are conditions (other than in a declared war) under which it is acceptable to harm others.

To find your score, first reverse your responses for the *even-numbered* items (if you wrote 1, make it 5; if you wrote 2, make it 4; if you wrote 3, leave it as 3; if you wrote 4, make it 2; if you wrote 5, make it 1). Next, add the numbers next to each statement. Scores range from 10 to 50. The higher your score, the more morally inclusive you are.

score on this questionnaire is 50. Very few people, however, score this high. We, nevertheless, can choose to increase our moral inclusiveness. This requires that we be mindful when we find ourselves making judgments of others.

Dialogue-Monologue

Often, when we communicate with others, we only wait for them to finish talking so that we can say what we want to say. In these cases, what we say often has little to do with what other people say to us. Think about how you engage in this type of behavior. Take a minute to answer the following questions:

> To what extent do you usually adjust what you say to other people based on what they have just said to you? Are there situations when you do this more than others? ______________________
> ______________________________________
> ______________________________________

> How does the effectiveness of your communication differ when you adjust your communication to what other people say, and when you do not adjust what you say to what other people say? ____________
> ______________________________________
> ______________________________________

Your answers to these questions should provide insight into the role played by adjusting your communication to others in your implicit personal theory of communication. Keep your responses to these questions in mind as you read the remainder of this section.

The Nature of Dialogue. There are three types of conversations we have with others: monologues, technical dialogues, and dialogues (Buber, 1958). *Monologues* are self-centered conversations in which other people are treated as objects. When we engage in monologues, we do *not* see others as unique people or take their needs into consideration. We are engaging in monologues any time we focus on ourselves and do *not* take the other person into consideration or adjust what we say and do to what the other person says and does.

Often when we engage in monologues we are being conversational narcissists. *Conversational narcissism* is the "way conversationalists turn the topics of ordinary conversations to themselves without sustained interest in others' topics" (Derber, 1979, p. 5). *Narcissism* involves a focus on the self. Narcissistic communication occurs when we emphasize our self-importance by boasting or using terms others do not understand, when we exploit others by shifting responses to ourselves or talking for long periods, when we engage in exhibitionism by using exaggerated facial expressions or making ourselves the focal point of conversations, and when we are nonresponsive to others by "glazing over" or being impatient when they are talking (Vangelisti, Knapp, & Daly, 1990).

Technical dialogues are information-centered conversations. The purpose of the conversation is to exchange information with the other person, *not* make a connection with the other person. Monologues and technical dialogues are necessary and appropriate at times, but problems emerge when they are used too frequently, because this leads to a lack of connection between the participants.

In *dialogues,* other people are not treated as objects. Rather, they are seen as unique humans. The goal of dialogue is *not* to use or change other people, but to understand them.

In a dialogue, there is a search for mutuality (Buber, 1958). Goals and expectations do not come between the two people. Rather, what goes on between the two people is the focus. Participants in a dialogue adjust their goals and messages depending on what is taking place in the conversation. Each participant's feeling of control and ownership is minimized. Each participant confirms the other, even when conflict occurs. It is this mutual confirmation that allows us to be human (Buber, 1958). In a dialogue, "answers emerge in the relationship, not from one party or the other" (Arnett, 1986, p. 164). The focus in a dialogue is on the interchange between the people communicating, not on the individual communicators.

When we communicate on automatic pilot, much of our communication involves monologues and technical dialogues. Engaging in only monologues and technical dialogues does not allow us to make contact with others as unique humans. To make contact, we must engage in dialogue. To engage in dialogue, we need to make a conscious decision to change the way we communicate and mindfully change the way we behave. When we are mindful, we want to walk a narrow ridge.

Walking a Narrow Ridge. The key to engaging in dialogue is for us to walk a narrow ridge in our interactions with other people. The concept of *narrow ridge* involves taking both our own and other people's viewpoints into consideration in our dealings with them. The metaphor of a tightrope walker can be used to illustrate the narrow ridge concept (Arnett, 1986). If tightrope walkers lean too much in one direction, they begin to lose their balance. To regain their balance, tightrope walkers must compensate by leaning in the other direction. The same is true of walking the narrow ridge in our dealings with others. If we give our own opinions too much weight in a conversation, we must compensate by considering other people's opinions to be of equal weight if we are going to walk a narrow ridge.

In walking the narrow ridge, we must try to understand other people's points of view. We should not, however, take a nonjudgmental attitude toward others (Buber, 1958). Rather, we should openly listen to others, but if we are not persuaded by their arguments, we should maintain our original position; if we are persuaded, we should modify our opinions. There is a subtle difference between listening openly and not changing our minds when confronted with a sound reason, and being closed-minded. The difference depends on our intentions. If our intentions are to seriously consider other people's opinions, we are walking the narrow ridge; if we do *not* intend to consider other people's opinions, then we are closed-minded. To illustrate, if we walk the narrow ridge, we listen to what other people have to say and then make up our minds. If we are closed-minded, in contrast, we have made up our minds before we listen to others. While we may lead others to think that we are listening to them, we are really not considering what they have to say. It is the dual concern for self and other in walking the narrow ridge that stops polarized communication: assuming that we are right and others are wrong (Arnett, 1986).

In walking the narrow ridge, we also should avoid giving in and accepting other people's opinions just for the sake of peace (Buber, 1958). Rather, we should accept other people's opinions or compromise if it is the way to the best solution. Our commitment must be to principles, not to false peace. We also should not unquestioningly accept everything others say. Suspicion is sometimes warranted, but problems occur when suspicion becomes a norm of communication.

Summary

Our dispositions influence the ways that we communicate with others. Some of our dispositions toward communication are based on our motivation. If our need for other people's behavior to be predictable is not met, we are not motivated to communicate with them. Also, if our need for group inclusion is not met, we are not motivated to communicate with others. Similarly, if other people do not support our self concept, we are not motivated to communicate with them. If our needs for predictability, inclusion, and sustaining our self-concepts are not met, we experience anxiety. When our anxiety is too high, we focus on the anxiety and avoid communicating with others.

Several of our dispositions are directly related to our inclination to communicate. The more apprehensive we are and the lower our willingness to communicate, the less we are likely to communicate with others. Our verbal aggressiveness is related directly to our communication effectiveness. Being aggressive or unassertive are not effective strategies. Being assertive, in contrast, is an effective communication strategy.

Sympathy also is not an effective strategy for communication. When we are sympathetic, we base our predictions of other people's thoughts and feelings on how we would feel in their situation. When we are empathic, on the other hand, we try to imagine how other people are feeling or what they are thinking. This allows us to understand them.

It is important to keep in mind that, whatever our dispositions are when we communicate on automatic pilot, we can choose to behave differently when we are mindful of our communication. If, for example, we tend to be aggressive when we are on automatic pilot, we can choose to behave assertively when we are mindful.

Our ethical dispositions also affect our communication. Our communication needs to be based on a set of moral principles, and morality should be an overriding concern any time we communicate. We cannot focus only on our own concerns. We must take other people and their concerns into consideration when we communicate with them. This means we must treat other people in a morally inclusive fashion. We cannot, however, avoid making ethical judgments of other people's behavior. When we make ethical judgments of members of other groups, however, we need to try to understand the group and its moral principles before we make a judgment.

Notes

1. Schutz (1966) isolated three basic needs: inclusion, control, and affection. More recently, Rubin, Perse, and Barbato (1988) isolated six interpersonal communication motives: pleasure, escape, relaxation, inclusion, affection, and control. This work builds on Schutz's earlier work, but it is based on an extension of research on the uses and gratifications received from the mass media, and it is not linked theoretically to self-conceptions in any way. We have chosen to use Turner's (1988) theory because it is theoretically based and directly linked to issues of identity discussed in the preceding chapter.
2. Turner draws heavily on Giddens (1984).
3. The inclusion-differentiation dialectic is similar to other dialectics in the interpersonal communication: freedom to be independent–freedom to be dependent (Rawlins, 1983), intimacy-detachment (Masheter & Harris, 1986), and autonomy-connection (Baxter, 1988).
4. Another way of thinking about this is that the sum total of our traits is our *personality.* We use the term *personal identities* rather than *personality* to maintain a consistent line of thinking throughout the book.

5. See Gudykunst and Ting-Toomey (1988) for a summary of the research leading to this conclusion.
6. Reported in *World Monitor,* October 1992, pp. 6–7.
7. We are not arguing that racist remarks violate free speech; rather, that they violate standards of morality.

Journal Reflections

1. *Identifying Your Needs.* During the next week, stop after your conversations to identify the needs influencing your communication with the other person. You may not initially be aware of your needs (remember, our awareness of them varies). Reflect on which needs might have been influencing your communication. Keep a list of the conversations you have (list day, topic, person, and other information on how you communicated) and the needs that you think were influencing your communication. After you have completed your list, go over the list to see if any patterns emerge. Did particular needs lead you to communicate in particular ways?
2. *Identifying How Your Dispositions Influence Your Communication.* In the next week, look at how your dispositions toward communication (communication apprehension, assertiveness) influence the way you communicate. Isolate any patterns that you would like to change (for instance, not allowing your apprehensiveness to influence your communication in some situation). Write out a plan for how you might change this pattern. Plan on trying out the new behavior during the following week.
3. *Identifying Your Ethical Principles.* During the next week, look at the ethical choices you make when you communicate. We usually are not highly aware of our ethical principles. During your conversations this week, try to isolate the ethical principles you use to guide your communication with others, and note them in your journal.
4. *Being Assertive.* Being assertive implies standing up for our rights and at the same time taking the other person's rights into consideration (when we ignore the other person's rights, we are being aggressive). In the next week, try being assertive in at least one situation where you normally would not be. In your journal, describe the situation, how you were assertive (and why your behavior was assertive and not aggressive or unassertive), and analyze the influence of your use of the skill on your communication.

Study Questions

1. How do our needs influence the way we communicate? Which needs have the greatest influence? Why?
2. How do we try to verify our self-conceptions when we communicate?
3. Why is predictability important in communication?
4. Why does avoiding anxiety motivate us to communicate with others?
5. How does communication apprehension influence the way we communicate?
6. How is communication apprehension viewed in individualistic and collectivistic cultures?
7. How do verbal aggressiveness and verbal assertiveness differ? Which leads to more effective communication? Why?
8. Why is morality an overriding concern any time we communicate?
9. What are the consequences of being morally exclusive?
10. How do dialogues differ from monologues? Why should we engage in dialogue?

Suggested Readings

Infante, D. A. (1988). *Arguing constructively.* Prospect Heights, IL: Waveland Press. Dominic Infante discusses verbal aggressiveness and argumentativeness. He offers strategies for learning to argue constructively rather than being verbally aggressive.

McCroskey, J. C., & Daly, J. A. (Eds.). (1987). *Personality and interpersonal communication.* Newbury Park, CA: Sage. This edited book is the only volume on personality and communication. It contains chapters on willingness to communicate (including communication apprehension), aggressiveness, social involvement (including empathy), and social styles (including sex roles).

Pritchard, M. S. (1991). *On becoming responsible.* Lawrence: University of Kansas Press. Michael Pritchard discusses issues of dignity, personal integrity, accountability, and moral integrity. He incorporates the work of Carol Gilligan discussed in Chapter 2.

Wilson, K., & Gallois, C. (1993). *Assertion and its social context.* New York: Pergamon Press. Keithia Wilson and Cynthia Gallois examine how perceptions of assertiveness vary as a function of the context in which we communicate. They discuss when assertiveness facilitates our goal achievement and when it can hinder it. Wilson and Gallois also look at differential outcomes when males and females are assertive.

Zimbardo, P. G. (1972). *Shyness: What it is and what to do about it.* Reading, MA: Addison-Wesley. This is the classic work on shyness. Shyness is related closely to anxiety and communication apprehension. Philip Zimbardo provides clear suggestions on how individuals can "overcome" their shyness.

4

Social Cognition and Communication

In the previous chapters, some of the problems that occur when our communication is based on the habits or scripts we learned as children were examined. Imagine the difficulties we would have interacting with other people if our communication were limited to habits and scripts. If we were limited to following scripts, our interactions with others would become boring, and we would gain little pleasure from interpersonal communication. Fortunately, there are other alternatives available to us. Although we often communicate on automatic pilot, we also think about our communication with others. We can think about how other people are communicating with us, and we can consciously choose how we want to communicate with others.

Social cognition refers to our thought processes that are focused on human interaction. It involves how our knowledge about people is acquired and processed. Understanding how we acquire social information about others and the ways in which it is used when we explain their behavior is critical for communicating effectively. The cognitive resources available to us can help us improve the quality of our communication with others. The major cognitive factor that affects how and when we acquire the information about others that we need in order to communicate effectively is the amount of uncertainty we experience. Let's begin with that uncertainty.

UNCERTAINTY AND COMMUNICATION

The concept of uncertainty was introduced in Chapter 1. There are two distinct types of uncertainty present in our interactions with other people (Berger & Calabrese, 1975). First, there is the uncertainty we have about *predicting* other people's attitudes, feelings, beliefs, values, and behavior. We need to be able, for example, to predict which of several alternative behavior patterns others will choose to employ. Imagine meeting a person you find attractive at a party. Assuming you want to see this person again after the party, you try to think about different ways you can approach this person in order to convince him or her to see you again. The different approaches you consider using are the predictions of alternative behaviors that you could use to reduce your uncertainty.

The second type of uncertainty involves our inability to *explain* other people's behavior. Whenever we try to figure out why others behave the way they do, we are engaging in explanatory uncertainty reduction. The problem we are addressing is one of reducing the number of possible explanations for the other people's behavior (the issue here is making attributions; attributions are discussed in detail in this chapter). This is necessary if we are to understand their behavior and, thus, be able to increase our ability to predict their behavior in the future.

Before proceeding, think about what causes uncertainty in your interactions with other people. Answer the following questions:

> What type of information do you need to know in order to be able to predict other people's behavior? ________________
> ________________________________
> ________________________________
> ________________________________

> What type of information do you use to explain other people's behavior? ______
> ________________________________
> ________________________________
> ________________________________

> How do you typically gather the information you need to predict and explain other people's behavior? ________________
> ________________________________
> ________________________________
> ________________________________

Your answers to these questions should provide insight into the role of uncertainty in your implicit personal theory of communication. Keep your answers to these questions in mind as you read the remainder of the discussion of uncertainty.

Uncertainty and Predictability

Often when we meet people in our own culture for the first time, the norms and rules guiding our behavior in the situation provide sufficient information for us to be able to *generally* predict their behavior. Even though we do not know the people, we expect them to behave in a particular way. In these situations, we do not necessarily have to reduce uncertainty in order to interact with others. When there are not clear norms or rules telling us how to behave, we have to reduce our uncertainty to be able to generally predict other people's behavior. There also are situations in which we want to increase our ability to predict other people's behavior. **If we expect to see others in the future, if they can provide us with rewards such as status or affection, or if they act in a way we do not expect, we will try to gather information so that we can predict their behavior better** (Berger, 1979).

We experience different levels of uncertainty in different types of interactions. There is greater uncertainty in our initial interactions with people from other groups, such as cultural or ethnic groups, for example, than in our initial interactions with people from our

As he checks out his new cabinmates, Benji Rushwald tries to predict how the other boys will behave. For many, meeting people for the first time can be intimidating.

own groups (Gudykunst, 1991). This does not, however, mean that we are more motivated to actively reduce uncertainty when we communicate with members of other groups than when we communicate with members of our own groups. Although members of other groups may behave in a deviant fashion by not following the norms or communication rules we are using in the situation, they rarely are seen as sources of rewards, and we may not anticipate seeing them again in the future. When we do not actively try to reduce our uncertainty regarding other people's individual behavior, we rely on our stereotypes of other people's groups to reduce our uncertainty and guide our predictions. This often leads to misunderstandings because our stereotypes are inaccurate or do not apply to the people whose behavior we are trying to predict.

When we try to predict or explain other people's behavior, we have a certain degree of confidence in our predictions and explanations. We may, for example, be highly confident that our predictions and explanations are correct. Alternatively, in some instances we may not be very confident that our predictions and explanations are correct. It is important to keep in mind that our confidence in our predictions and explanations does *not* mean they are accurate. **We can be very confident about our predictions and explanations, but they may be highly inaccurate.** When we communicate on automatic pilot, we operate on the basis of our confidence in our predictions and explanations, and we *assume* they are accurate. It is only when we are mindful that we can assess the accuracy of our predictions and explanations.

Minimum and Maximum Thresholds

Some degree of uncertainty exists in all relationships. We can never totally predict or explain other people's behavior. We all have maximum and minimum thresholds for uncertainty (Gudykunst, 1993). If our uncertainty is above the maximum thresholds or below the minimum thresholds, we feel uncomfortable and we will have difficulty communicating effectively.

If our uncertainty is above our maximum thresholds, we do not think we have enough information to predict or explain other people's behavior. When uncertainty is above our maximum thresholds, we do not have confidence in our predictions and explanations of other people's behavior. When there are norms or rules guiding behavior in a particular situation, the norms or rules allow us to unconsciously predict how others will behave, and our uncertainty therefore will be below our maximum thresholds. Also, when we have some information about others so that we feel comfortable predicting how they will behave in the situation, our uncertainty will be below our maximum thresholds. When our uncertainty is below our maximum thresholds, we have sufficient confidence in the information we have to predict and explain other people's behavior.

If our uncertainty is below our minimum thresholds, we think other people's behavior is highly predictable; we have a high level of confidence in our ability to predict other people's behavior. High levels of predictability, however, often are associated with boredom. When this occurs, there may not be sufficient novelty in our relationships for us to sustain interest in interacting with the other people, and we may not be motivated to communicate. It also is important to remember that confidence in our predictions does not mean that our predictions are accurate. **When we see other people's behavior as highly predictable, we also are likely to misinterpret their messages because we do not consider the possibility that our interpretations of their messages are wrong.** In other words, overconfidence can breed misinterpretations.

Communicating effectively requires that our uncertainty be between our minimum and maximum thresholds (Gudykunst, 1993). If our uncertainty is above our maximum thresholds or below our minimum thresholds, we need to consciously manage our uncertainty to improve the effectiveness of our communication. How we can accomplish this is discussed in the section of this chapter focusing on cognitive resources for effective communication.

Uncertainty over Time

Generally, as we get to know others, our uncertainty regarding their behavior tends to decrease. Uncertainty, however, does not always decrease as relationships change over time. It also can increase. Figure 4.1 illustrates how uncertainty might vary over the course of a relationship. When we first meet other people, our uncertainty tends to be above our maximum thresholds, because we do not feel comfortable predicting their behavior. Once we meet other people and see that they "follow the rules" of interacting, our uncertainty will drop below our maximum thresholds. We will assume that we can use cultural rules to predict their behavior. As we get to know other people in the United States, we gather information about their attitudes, values, and beliefs to further reduce our uncertainty and be able to predict and explain their behavior (cultural differences in uncertainty reduction are discussed below).

Although uncertainty tends to decrease as we get to know others, events may occur in our established relationships or other people might do something we do not expect that increases our uncertainty. To illustrate, when we find out that others are engaged in competing relationships, when we lose closeness in

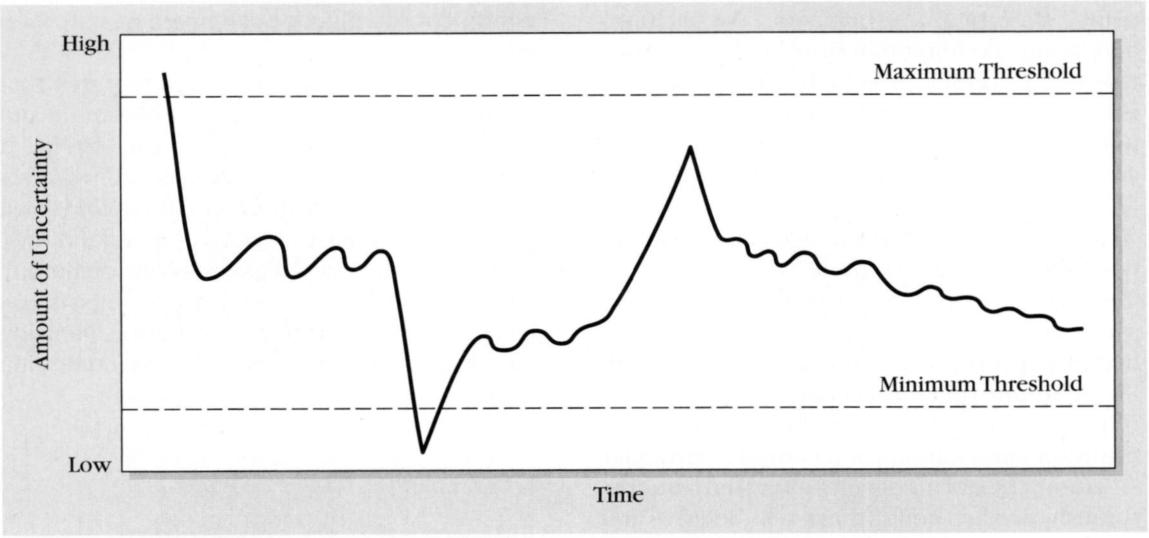

FIGURE 4.1 Uncertainty over Time

a relationship, or when we find out that others have deceived or betrayed us, our uncertainty may increase (Planalp, Rutherford, & Honeycutt, 1988). The more surprised we are, the more our uncertainty is likely to increase. It is possible that our uncertainty may increase so much that it rises above our maximum thresholds. If this occurs, we must reduce our uncertainty to feel comfortable interacting with other people. We can do this by seeking information, such as asking why they behaved the way they did.

Depending on the nature of the event that increases our uncertainty and how we manage the uncertainty, increases in uncertainty can have positive or negative consequences for our relationships with others. To illustrate, finding out that our romantic partner is seeing someone else will probably increase our uncertainty above our maximum thresholds. Depending on our partner's explanation, we may or may not be able to reduce our uncertainty about our partner's future behavior below our maximum threshold. If we cannot reduce our uncertainty, it might signal the end of the relationship. If we can reduce our uncertainty and we are confident that our romantic partner will not see others in the future, in contrast, our uncertainty probably will return to our comfort range.

Assessing Your Uncertainty

Before proceeding, think about your uncertainty in communicating for the first time with someone. Take a moment to complete Assessment 4.1 now.

Most of us experience some degree of uncertainty in communicating with new people. If our level of uncertainty is above our maximum threshold, we need to try to reduce it in order to feel comfortable interacting with them. There are several strategies we can use to reduce uncertainty in these situations.

Assessment 4.1 *Assessing Your Uncertainty in Communicating with Strangers*

The purpose of this questionnaire is to help you assess the amount of uncertainty you generally experience when you communicate with strangers. (*Note:* You can determine the amount of uncertainty you experience communicating with a specific person by substituting the person's name for "strangers" in each of the statements.) Respond to each statement by indicating the degree to which the adjectives are applicable when you interact with strangers. If you never have the experience, answer 1 in the space provided; if you almost never have the experience, answer 2; if you sometimes have the experience and sometimes do not, answer 3; if you almost always have the experience, answer 4; if you always have the experience, answer 5.

_______ 1. I am not confident when I communicate with strangers.

_______ 2. I can interpret strangers' behavior when we communicate.

_______ 3. I am indecisive when I communicate with strangers.

_______ 4. I can explain strangers' behavior when we communicate.

_______ 5. I am not able to understand strangers when we communicate.

_______ 6. I know what to do when I communicate with strangers.

_______ 7. I am uncertain how to behave when I communicate with strangers.

_______ 8. I can comprehend strangers' behavior when we communicate.

_______ 9. I am not able to predict strangers' behavior when we communicate.

_______ 10. I can describe strangers' behavior when we communicate.

To find your scores, first reverse the responses for the *even-numbered* items (if you wrote 1, make it 5; if you wrote 2, make it 4; if you wrote 3, leave it as 3; if you wrote 4, make it 2; if you wrote 5, make it 1). Next, add the numbers next to each of the items. Scores range from 10 to 50. The higher your score, the more uncertainty you experience when interacting with others.

Uncertainty Reduction Strategies

If we choose to reduce our uncertainty about other people, there are three general strategies we can use: passive, active, and interactive (Berger, 1979). When we use *passive strategies,* we take the role of unobtrusive observers and do not participate in the situations we are observing. To illustrate this process, assume that we want to find out about Yuko, a Japanese American to whom we have just been introduced.[1]

Obviously, the type of situation in which we observe Yuko influences the amount of information we can gain about her (Berger, 1979). If we observe Yuko in a situation in which she does not have to interact with others, we will not gain much information about her. Situations in which she is interacting with several people at once, in contrast, allow us to make comparisons of how Yuko interacts with the different people present in the situation.

If we know any of the people with whom Yuko is interacting, we can compare how she interacts with them and how she might interact with us (Berger, 1979). If other Japanese Americans are present in the situation, we can compare Yuko's behavior with theirs to try to determine how she is similar to and different from other Japanese Americans.

The formality of the situation will influence the amount of information we obtain about Yuko's behavior (Berger, 1979). Behavior is highly scripted in formal situations, and people's behavior is inhibited. If the situation is a formal one, Yuko's behavior is likely to be a function of the role she is filling in the situation. We, therefore, will not learn much about Yuko as an individual. Situations in which behavior is not guided by roles or social protocol, on the other hand, will provide useful information on Yuko's behavior because her behavior is not inhibited.

The preceding examples involve taking the role of an observer. *Active strategies* for reducing uncertainty require us to do something more than merely observing Yuko to acquire information about her. We must actively seek out information about her (Berger, 1979). One thing we could do to get information about Yuko is to ask questions about her of someone who knows her. When we ask others about someone, we need to keep in mind that the information we receive may not be accurate. The other person may not really know Yuko very well or may intentionally give us wrong information about her.

We can also gather information about Yuko by asking people who have had contact with her ethnic group or by gathering information from the library. In this example, we could gather information on Japanese Americans by questioning someone we know who has many Japanese American friends or by reading a book on Japanese Americans. This would give us information about Yuko's ethnic background that would allow us to make group-based predictions about her behavior. We would, of course, want to try to make sure that the information we gather is accurate.

When we use active strategies to gather information, we do not actually interact with the people about whom we are trying to gather information. The *interactive strategies* of verbal interrogation (asking questions), self-disclosure, and deception detection, in contrast, are used when we communicate directly with the person about whom we are trying to gather information (Berger, 1979). The strategies are overviewed here, and the specific verbal messages associated with these strategies in conversations are discussed in Chapter 10.

One obvious way we can gather information about others is by *verbal interrogation.* When we verbally interrogate others, we ask them questions about themselves. There are limitations to this strategy that have to be kept in mind. First, we can ask only so many questions. There is not a specific number that is too many, but we can tell when we have asked too many. Second, our questions must be appropriate to the nature of the interaction we are having and the relationship we have with the other person. Third, we must be willing to reciprocate and answer questions others ask us.

The second way we can gather information about other people when interacting with them is through *self-disclosure*—telling other people information about ourselves that they

FOR BETTER OR FOR WORSE © Lynn Johnston Prod., Inc. Reprinted with permission of UNIVERSAL PRESS SYNDICATE. All rights reserved.

do not already know (Berger, 1979). Self-disclosure works as an information-gathering strategy because of the reciprocity norm (Gouldner, 1960). Essentially, the reciprocity norm states that, if one person does something for another, the second person will reciprocate and do something for the first. In other words, if we self-disclose to other people, they will self-disclose to us. In conversations between people who are not close, such as acquaintances or people we meet for the first time, we tend to reciprocate and tell each other the same information about ourselves that the other person tells us. If we disclose our opinion on a topic to Yuko, she will probably tell us her opinion on the same topic. We have to recognize, however, that any self-disclosure involves a risk. When we tell others information about ourselves, we are making ourselves vulnerable.

The reciprocity norm changes as relationships become more intimate (Altman & Taylor, 1973). In intimate relationships, we do not necessarily reciprocate self-disclosures within specific conversations. Over the course of the relationships, however, we are expected to reciprocate. Friendships where only one person self-discloses, for example, probably will not last long. In friendships, both people are expected to reciprocate and disclose information about themselves, but not necessarily in the same interaction.

The third interactive strategy we can use to gather information is *deception detection* (Berger, 1979). Using verbal interrogation and self-disclosure as uncertainty reduction strategies is based on the assumption that the other person will tell us the truth. We also can try to determine if the other person is deceiving us. If we think the other person is agreeing with us to ingratiate him or herself with us, we would change our opinion and see how the person responds. To illustrate, in interacting with Yuko, she might have agreed with most things we said. We might, for example, have indicated early in the conversation that we liked sushi, and she might have agreed that she liked it, too. If we suspect that Yuko does not really agree with us, but is showing agreement to ingratiate herself or is just trying to be polite, we could change our opinion later in the conversation and say we do not really like sushi very much and see how she responds. If she agrees that she does not like sushi very much either, after having said earlier that she liked it, we would suspect that she is trying to ingratiate herself with us. Before using this strategy, however, we should consider whether it is ethical to express a dishonest opinion (lie) to test another person's honesty.

Skill Exercise 4.1 is designed to help you practice using the uncertainty reduction strategies discussed here. Take a few minutes to complete it before you continue reading.

Skill Exercise 4.1 is designed to help you see the different strategies that can be used to gather information about others. The various strategies yield different types of information. The information gathered by each strategy is useful in helping us better predict and explain other people's behavior.

Cultural Differences in Uncertainty

The type of information that people seek to reduce uncertainty varies across cultures. **In individualistic cultures like the United States, the focus tends to be on gathering personal information about others.**

Skill Exercise 4.1 *Gathering Information to Reduce Uncertainty*

Assume that you have been introduced to Chris, a person you find attractive. You only met him or her and did not get a chance to talk. You think you might want to date this person, so you want to gather additional information about him or her. You know several people who know this person. You also know that you will see this person at a club meeting and a party you are both attending later this week.

1. *Passive Strategies.* How could you gather information about Chris at the club meeting and party by observing him or her? How would the information you get at the club meeting and party differ?

____

____

____

____

2. *Active Strategies.* Since you and Chris know some of the same people, you can gather information about Chris by talking with the people you both know. How might you approach the people you know to gather information about Chris? How will you know if the information you gather in this way is accurate? ______

____

____

____

____

____

3. *Interactive Strategies.* You can gather information about Chris the next time you interact with him or her. What types of questions would you ask him or her? Are there any types of questions you would avoid? What information would you tell Chris about yourself? Is there any type of information you would *not* tell him or her about yourself? ______

____

____

____

____

____

Speaking an unfamiliar language is a small issue compared to the uncertainty and unpredictability that comes from immersing yourself in a foreign culture. The communication styles of the Rabari, an Indian nomadic tribe, differ greatly from that of the Australian woman who travels with the tribe.

Knowing other people's attitudes, beliefs, and values, for example, can be used to predict their behavior. In collectivistic cultures, in contrast, personal information is not necessarily useful in predicting other people's behavior. Rather, group-based information is needed. **Members of collectivistic cultures need to know whether other people are members of one of their own ingroups, other people's social status, other people's age, and other information that allows them to be placed in the web of group affiliations.** Person-based information does not lead to uncertainty reduction about strangers in collectivistic cultures, as it does in individualistic cultures. Personal information, however, is used in close relationships with members of the ingroup.

To illustrate the differences, consider a story told by a Japanese sociologist who taught at the University of Tokyo (Nakane, 1974). The professor was invited to give a talk at another university. She did not know the professor who invited her, and this person was meeting her at the lecture hall. Prior to her arrival, she was apprehensive about interacting with the person meeting her. When she arrived at the lecture hall, an elderly man approached her and bowed. Before he said anything else, the man said, "I am from the University of Tokyo," indicating that he had attended the University of Tokyo and that he shared an ingroup membership with her. The man then went on to give his name and present his business card. Once she knew that she shared an ingroup membership (the University of Tokyo) with the other professor, she relaxed because she knew that his behavior was predictable. There is no one comparable piece of information that would reduce uncertainty to the same degree in individualistic cultures like the United States.

Cultural differences in the types of information needed to reduce uncertainty can lead to interesting exchanges when individualists and collectivists meet for the first time. Individualists inevitably tell others personal information about themselves and seek this type of information from others, while collectivists tell others information about their group memberships and seek the same type of information from others. If we ask individualists what they do for a living, they will probably tell us their occupation. If we ask collectivists the same question, they will probably tell us the company for which they work. Collectivists might ask individualists their age so that they can determine who is older (an indicator of status). Many individualists will take offense at being asked their age by people they do not know. Individualists, in contrast, might ask collectivists about their feelings or attitudes when they first meet. The collectivists will tend to answer questions about their feelings or attitudes indirectly and avoid directly answering the individualists' questions because they see these questions as too personal. Both parties will be frustrated—the collectivists because the individualists asked personal questions, the individualists because the collectivists did not answer their questions.

It was pointed out earlier that there are two types of uncertainty. The focus of this section has been on predictive uncertainty. Reducing explanatory uncertainty involves making attributions.

Making Attributions

When we observe other people's behavior, we try to make sense out of it. We act as naive or intuitive scientists when we try to make sense of other people's behavior (Heider, 1958). We make attributions about their behavior. *Attributions* are our explanations for why other people behave the way they do or for what causes them to behave the way they do. We'll begin the discussion of attributions by looking at the nature of the attribution process.

The Nature of Attributions

Our attempts to explain other people's behavior are based on our knowledge of ourselves, others, and the situation in which the behavior occurs. In explaining other people's behavior, we can focus on their individual characteristics—such as their intelligence, their motivation, or their membership in social groups—or on situational factors. When we try to explain other people's behavior, we try to sort out the factors that caused them to behave the way they did (Heider, 1958). If we attribute the cause of other people's behavior to individual characteristics, we tend to hold them responsible for their behavior. Alternatively, if we decide that other people behaved the way they did because of situational factors, we do not hold them responsible for their behavior. Our interpretations and explanations of other

CURTIS. Reprinted with special permission of King Features Syndicate.

people's behavior affect our view of our reality.

When we try to explain other people's behavior, we often do not have sufficient information. In the presence of incomplete information, we fill in the missing information by inferring meaning based on our implicit personal theories of communication. Our implicit theories tell us how specific causes are associated with specific effects (Kelley, 1972). We may assume, for example, that the way people dress influences the money they spend when shopping. To illustrate, a store clerk may assume that people who are not dressed neatly are less likely to spend money in the store than people dressed neatly. A clerk who makes this assumption is likely to miss many sales. Our implicit theories permit "economical and fast attributional analysis, by providing a framework within which bits and pieces of information can be fitted in order to draw reasonably good inferences" (p. 152).

There are differences in how we tend to explain our own behavior and how people observing our behavior explain our behavior (Jones & Nisbett, 1972). The general tendency is for us to attribute our own behavior to situational factors, whereas people observing our behavior tend to attribute it to stable individual characteristics, such as our personality, gender, or ethnicity. The difference is particularly important regarding conflicts. When we have conflicts with others, we tend to assume that their behavior is driven by their individual characteristics (we are observing their behavior) and that our own behavior is a function of the situation. Obviously, they will assume that our behavior is due to our personal characteristics and their own behavior is due to the situation.

Once we have made attributions regarding other people's behavior, we tend to have confidence in our explanations (Sillars, 1982). We often make extreme attributions and assume we are accurate. We may, for example, be sure that our romantic partners' behavior during a conflict is due to their motivation (they do not care about us) and not consider alternative explanations. Our partners, however, may actually care for us a great deal and be basing their behavior on other factors, such as how they see the situation. It, therefore, is important to remember that **there is no association between the confidence we have in our attributions and their accuracy.**

Errors in Attributions

The attributions we make about other people's behavior are often inaccurate. Our errors in explaining other people's behavior occur because there are several biases that affect our attributional processes. **We tend to see our own behavior as normal and appropriate** (*egocentric bias;* Kelley, 1967). We therefore explain other people's behavior that is different from ours as a function of their personal characteristics. The specific personal characteristics we use to explain other people's behavior depends on how we are thinking about ourselves and the other people.

Sometimes we think about ourselves and others as unique individuals, and sometimes we think of ourselves and others as members of social groups. How we think about ourselves and others influences the characteristics we use to explain other people's behavior. When we think about ourselves and others in individual terms and when our behavior is guided by our personal identities, we tend to make person-based attributions (Hewstone & Brown, 1986). When we see a member of an outgroup as not typical of her or his group, we also make person-based attributions. When making person-based attributions, we focus on characteristics of other people as unique individuals in explaining their behavior. We might, for example, use other people's intelligence or personalities as explanations for their behavior. When we perceive ourselves and other people as members of groups and our behavior is guided by our social identities, we tend to make group-based attributions. When we make group-based attributions, we focus on other people's membership in social groups as explanations for their behavior.

We have a tendency to overestimate the influence of personal characteristics and to underestimate the influence of situational factors when we explain other people's behavior (*fundamental attribution error;* Ross, 1977). We are most likely to make the fundamental attribution error when we are explaining other people's behavior that we perceive to be negative. Often, when other people engage in behavior that we perceive to be positive, we explain their behavior as a function of the situation. We tend to think that other people behave positively because they have to, because of situational demands.

The opposite pattern occurs when we are trying to explain our own behavior. **We tend to explain our positive behavior or successes using our personal characteristics, and our negative behavior or failures by situational factors** (*ego-protective bias;* Kelley, 1967). When we act in a positive fashion, we explain it by thinking that we are "good people," but when we do something negative, such as yelling at another person, we do not think we are "bad" people. Rather, we think that it was necessary given the situation.

We have a tendency to stop looking for explanations for our own or other people's behavior once we have found a relevant and reasonable explanation for the behavior (*premature closure;* Taylor & Fiske, 1978). When we communicate on automatic pilot, we do not think about a large number of alternative explanations for our own or other people's behavior. Rather, we tend to stop searching for explanations once we have found a reasonable one.

We also have a tendency to overemphasize negative information about other people's behavior (*principle of negativity;* Kanouse & Hanson, 1972). When we try to explain other people's behavior while communicating on automatic pilot we tend to focus on those aspects of their behavior we perceive to be negative. We therefore often interpret other people's behavior more negatively than it actually is.

The *ultimate attribution error* is "a systematic patterning of intergroup misattributions shaped in part by prejudice" (Pettrigrew, 1979, p. 464). Our tendency to attribute other people's behavior to personal characteristics rather than to situational characteristics increases when members of other groups are perceived to engage in negative behavior. When members of other groups engage in negative behavior, we tend to use their group memberships to explain their behavior. When members of other groups engage in what is perceived to be positive behavior, in contrast, our tendency is to treat them as an exception to the rule and to discount explanations for the behavior based on personal characteristics. We therefore attribute their behavior to situational factors or to their individual motivation.

Most of us make the ultimate attribution error more than we think we do when we communicate on automatic pilot. To reduce the possibility of this error when making attributions about the behavior of members of other groups, we must be mindful. When we are mindful, we must recognize that behavior we interpret as negative may not be due to group memberships; it may be due to situational demands.

Skill Exercise 4.2 is designed to help you understand the attribution errors you typically make when trying to explain other people's behavior. Take a few minutes to complete it.

We all make errors in our attributions. Our

Skill Exercise 4.2 ***Identifying Attribution Errors***

We all make errors when we unconsciously create explanations for others' behavior. Think about the situations described below and answer each of the questions.

1. Pat, an acquaintance of yours, is always late when the two of you plan to get together.

   How might you explain Pat's behavior? ____________________

   What other causes might there be for Pat's behavior? ____________________

   How might you determine which explanation is most accurate? ____________________

2. Chris is a person from another culture. Whenever you and Chris talk, Chris never expresses her or his opinions directly.

   How might you explain Chris' behavior? ____________________

   What other causes might there be for Chris' behavior? ____________________

   How might you determine which explanation is most accurate? ____________________

3. Kim, a close friend of yours, is usually very outgoing. For the last week or so, Kim has been quiet when you have seen him or her.

   How might you explain his or her behavior? ____________________

   What other causes might there be for his or her behavior? ____________________

   How might you determine which explanation is most accurate? ____________________

errors are problematic when we communicate on automatic pilot, because we do not consider the possibility that our attributions are in error. We can decrease our attribution errors when we consciously think about our attributions about other people's behavior and understand the errors we tend to make. To accomplish this, we need to search for possible alternative explanations for the other person's behavior. Once we have isolated alternative explanations, we

Collectivist cultures, such as the Amish, are sensitive to situational features and explanations. In order for a collectivist and an individualist to communicate effectively, one of the speakers must recognize the differences in style and shift her or his style of speech.

can try to decide which explanation is most plausible.

Cultural Differences in Attributions

The types of attributions people make in individualistic and collectivistic cultures differ. Members of collectivistic cultures are highly sensitive to situational features and explanations, and tend to attribute other people's behavior to the context, situation, or other factors external to the individual. Members of individualistic cultures, in contrast, are highly sensitive to personal characteristics and tend to attribute other people's behavior to characteristics internal to the individual, such as personality.

If we do not understand cultural differences in individualism-collectivism and their influence on our communication, we can easily misinterpret the behavior of people from other cultures. A member of a collectivistic culture who identifies with the group, for example, may offer personal opinions by using the pronoun *we*. A member of an individualistic culture would perceive such a statement as something that the group may do or believe, but not necessarily interpret the statement as the speaker's opinion. This misinterpretation can result in misunderstanding if the cultural difference in use of personal pronouns is ignored.

To illustrate how attributions differ across cultures, consider the example in Reading 4.1. This example involves a segment of interaction between a male supervisor from the United States and a male subordinate from Greece. In the segment, the supervisor wants the employee to participate in decisions (a norm in the United States), while the subordinate expects to be told what to do (a norm in Greece). Take a minute to review Reading 4.1 now.

The different cultural expectations held by the supervisor and the subordinate in Reading 4.1 clearly led to miscommunication. Greeks (collectivists) tend to employ an indirect style of speech and interpret other people's behavior based on the assumption that they are using the same style (Tannen, 1979). North Americans (individualists), in contrast,

Reading 4.1 An Example of Misattributions in Intercultural Encounters

Behavior	Attribution
American: How long will it take you to finish this report?	American: I asked him to participate. Greek: His behavior makes no sense. He is the boss. Why doesn't he tell me?
Greek: I do not know. How long should it take?	American: He refuses to take responsibility. Greek: I asked him for an order.
American: You are in the best position to analyze time requirements.	American: I press him to take responsibility for his own actions. Greek: What nonsense! I better give him an answer.
Greek: 10 days.	American: He lacks the ability to estimate time; this estimate is totally inadequate.
American: Take 15. It is agreed you will do it in 15 days?	American: I offer a contract. Greek: These are my orders. 15 days.

In fact the report needed 30 days of regular work. So the Greek worked day and night, but at the end of the 15th day, he still needed one more day's work.

Behavior	Attribution
American: Where is my report?	American: I am making sure he fulfills his contract. Greek: He is asking for the report.
Greek: It will be ready tomorrow.	(Both attribute that it is not ready.)
American: But we agreed that it would be ready today.	American: I must teach him to fulfill a contract. Greek: The stupid, incompetent boss! Not only did he give me wrong orders, but he does not appreciate that I did a 30-day job in 16 days.
The Greek hands in his resignation.	The American is surprised. Greek: I can't work for such a man.

The example is drawn from the files of George Vassiliou, a Greek psychiatrist. It is reported by Triandis (1975, pp. 42–43). R. Brislin & S. Bochner (Eds.), *Cross-Cultural Perspectives on Learning,* pp. 42–43,

use a direct style of speech and assume that others are using the same style. When Greeks and North Americans communicate, there often are misunderstandings due to these differences in style of speech. Overcoming misunderstandings due to direct-indirect style differences is difficult because, "in seeking to clarify, each speaker continues to use the very strategy which confused the other in the first place" (Tannen, 1979, p. 5). To resolve the misunderstanding, obviously one of the people involved must recognize that the differences in style are creating the problem, try to accurately interpret the other person's messages, and then shift her or his style of speech. This requires that the person be mindful and use the cognitive resources for effective communication.

Cognitive Resources for Effective Communication

Our cognitive resources for effective communication are the ways we can think about others that will help us better understand them and their messages when we communicate. All of the cognitive resources we can use to improve the quality of our communication require that we be mindful of our communication.

Mindfulness

As indicated in Chapter 1, mindfulness involves: "(1) creation of new categories; (2) openness to new information; and (3) awareness of more than one perspective" (Langer, 1989, p. 62). There are, however, some conditions under which we tend to be mindful of our behavior. Let's begin by looking at the characteristics of mindfulness.

Characteristics of Mindfulness. Since "categorizing is a fundamental and natural human activity . . . Any attempt to eliminate bias by attempting to eliminate the perception of differences is doomed to failure" (p. 154). **Being mindful involves making more, not fewer, distinctions.** To illustrate, when we are on automatic pilot, we tend to use broad categories to predict other people's behavior; for example, other people's culture, ethnicity, sex, or the role they are playing. When we are mindful, we can create new categories that are more specific. Rather than using the broad category "professor," for instance, students can subcategorize professors into "male-female," "professors who are formal-professors who are informal," "professors who call me by my name-professors who do not call me by my name," and so forth. **The more subcategories we use, the more personalized the information we use to make predictions.**

Mindfulness also involves being open to new information. When we behave on automatic pilot in a particular situation, we tend to see the same thing occurring in the situation as we saw the previous time we were in the same situation. If we are consciously open to new information, we see the subtle differences in our own and other people's behavior that may take place. We can only be open to new information when we focus on what is going on in the present. If we think about the past or future, we will not be open to new information.

Being open to new information involves focusing on the *process* of communication that is taking place, not the *outcome* of our interactions with others:

> An outcome orientation in social situations can induce mindlessness. If we think we know how to handle a situation, we don't feel a need to pay attention. If we respond to the situation as very familiar (as a result, for example, of overlearning), we notice only minimal cues necessary to carry out the proper scenarios. If, on the other hand, the situation is strange, we might be so preoccupied with the thought of failure ("what if I make a fool of myself?") that we miss nuances of our own and others' behavior. In this sense, we are mindless with respect to the immediate situation, although we may be thinking quite actively about outcome related issues. (Langer, 1989, p. 34)

When we focus on the outcome, we miss subtle cues in our interactions with others, which often leads to misunderstandings. Focusing on the process of communication forces us to be mindful of our behavior and pay attention to the situations in which we find ourselves (Langer, 1989).

To be mindful, we must also recognize that there are different perspectives that can be used to understand or explain our interaction with others (Langer, 1989). Suppose a friend sprained her or his ankle and asked you to go to the local pharmacy for an Ace bandage. What would you do if the local pharmacy was out of Ace bandages (and there was only the one pharmacy open)? If we were acting on automatic pilot, most of us would probably return and tell our friend that the pharmacy was out of Ace bandages (Langer, 1989). If we were mindful, however, we might think to ask the pharmacist if there are alternatives to using an Ace bandage on a sprained ankle.

When we communicate on automatic pilot, we do not recognize alternative perspectives. The mindset we bring to communication situations limits our ability to see the choices we actually have about how to behave in most situations (Langer, 1989). When we communicate mindfully, however, we can use all of the communication resources available to us to look for new options and not be limited by only those that come to mind in the situation or those in our implicit personal theories of communication.

Recognizing alternative perspectives is critical to effective communication. Effective communication requires recognizing that other people use their own perspectives to interpret our messages and may not interpret our messages the way we intended them. The problem is that, **when we communicate on automatic pilot, we assume that everyone uses the same perspective we do.** It is only when we are mindful of the process of our communication that we can determine how our interpretations of messages differ from other people's interpretations of those messages.

NON SEQUITUR © 1994, The Washington Post Writers Group. Reprinted with permission.

Conditions Under Which We Tend to be Mindful. We often communicate on automatic pilot. There are, however, several conditions under which we tend to be mindful of our behavior (Berger & Douglas, 1982). We tend to be mindful when we find ourselves in new situations for which we do not have a script. We also are mindful when we start interacting with others and are following a script, but are not able to complete the script. To illustrate, if we are following the script for ordering food in a coffee shop and someone comes up and starts talking to our server, our script will be interrupted and we will become mindful.

We become mindful when we have to engage in a great deal more of a scripted behavior than usual (Berger & Douglas, 1982). When we are at a party, for example, and meet a lot of new people, we may become mindful of the way we are interacting with the people we meet because we are using our "getting to know you" script more than usual.

We also tend to become mindful when something happens that we do not expect. To illustrate, when we ask someone we do not know well, "How are you?" and she or he responds, "Not well. My spouse just asked for a divorce," the person responded in an unexpected fashion and we will become mindful. Further, we are mindful in situations in which there are several different scripts that we could follow. When students and professors meet in a grocery store, there may be conflicting scripts that could be used. The professor and student could follow their university roles and engage in a class discussion script or they could invoke the script for acquaintances who accidentally meet. Selecting the script that will be used leads to some degree of mindfulness.

We often are mindful of our behavior when we communicate with people from other groups, because they may act in an unexpected fashion or because we do not have a script to guide our communication with them. The problem is that we usually are mindful of the outcome, not the process. That is, we tend to think about how others perceive us or whether we will get what we want. Since we tend to interpret other people's behavior based on our own frame of reference, to communicate effectively we may need to become mindful of the process of communication, even when we are engaging in habitual behavior. We should not necessarily try to be mindful at all times. This would be impossible. Rather, **when there is a high potential for misunderstanding, we need to be mindful and consciously aware of the process of communication that is taking place.**

Assessing Your Mindfulness. Before proceeding, take a moment to assess your tendency to be mindful when communicating. Complete Assessment 4.2 now.

Scores on Assessment 4.2 range from 10 to 50. No matter what your score on this assessment, it is probably higher than your actual level of mindfulness. To complete the assessment, you had to become mindful of your behavior.

Even if we are not highly mindful of our communication, we can learn to be mindful. If we want to increase our mindfulness when communicating with others, we must create new categories and stop using general categories to understand other people's behavior, be open to new information, and recognize that there is more than one perspective for interpreting behavior. Engaging in these behaviors requires practice, practice in being mentally flexible. Mindfulness can help us improve the quality of our communication with others. It is not, however, a panacea for all of our communication problems. When we are mindful, we must practice the other skills discussed throughout the book.

Most of the cognitive resources for effec-

Assessment 4.2 *Assessing Your Mindfulness*

The purpose of this questionnaire is to help you assess your ability to be mindful when you communicate. Respond to each statement by indicating the degree to which it is true regarding the way you normally communicate: "Always False" (answer 1), "Usually False" (answer 2), "Sometimes False and Sometimes True" (answer 3), "Usually True" (answer 4), or "Always True" (answer 5).

_______ 1. I pay attention to the situation and context when I communicate.

_______ 2. I think about how I will look to others when I communicate with them.

_______ 3. I seek out new information about the people with whom I communicate.

_______ 4. I ignore inconsistent signals I receive from others when we communicate.

_______ 5. I recognize that the person with whom I am communicating has a different point of view than I do.

_______ 6. I use the categories in which I place others to predict their behavior.

_______ 7. I can describe others with whom I communicate in great detail.

_______ 8. I am concerned about the outcomes of my encounters with others.

_______ 9. I try to find rational reasons why others may behave in a way I perceive negatively.

_______ 10. I have a hard time telling when others do not understand me.

To find your score, first reverse the responses for the *even-numbered* items (if you wrote 1, make it 5; if you wrote 2, make it 4; if you wrote 3, leave it as 3; if you wrote 4, make it 2; if you wrote 5, make it 1). Next, add the numbers next to each statement. Scores range from 10 to 50. The higher your score, the more mindful you are when you communicate.

tive communication discussed below are related to mindfulness. Suggestions provided for each of these resources, therefore, can help us become more mindful.

Uncertainty Orientation

People differ in their orientation toward uncertainty. *Uncertainty-oriented* people are interested in seeking out information to reduce uncertainty when they experience it, while *certainty-oriented* people are not interested in seeking information to reduce the uncertainty they experience (Sorrentino & Short, 1986).

Characteristics of Uncertainty Orientation. Certainty-oriented people do not try to find out about themselves (Sorrentino &

Short, 1986). They do not try to figure out why they behave the way they do, and they do not try to reconcile inconsistencies in their behavior. Certainty-oriented people tend not to compare themselves with other people, hold traditional beliefs, and have a tendency to reject ideas that are different from their own. Overall, certainty-oriented people maintain a sense of self by not examining themselves or their behavior.

Uncertainty-oriented people integrate new and old ideas and change their belief systems accordingly (Sorrentino & Short, 1986). They evaluate ideas and thoughts on their own merit and do not necessarily compare them with those of others. Uncertainty-oriented people want to understand themselves and their environment. **Uncertainty-oriented people recognize that their expectations of other people's behavior are not necessarily accurate and, therefore, are more likely to try to reduce their uncertainty about other people by seeking new information than are certainty-oriented people.**

Assessing Your Uncertainty Orientation. Before proceeding, take a minute to assess your uncertainty orientation. Complete Assessment 4.3 now.

Scores on Assessment 4.3 range from 10 to 50. The higher your score, the greater your uncertainty orientation. Recall that uncertainty-oriented people (those with higher scores) are more likely than certainty-oriented people (those with low scores) to recognize that their interpretations of other people's behavior may be inaccurate and are more likely to seek out further information before drawing conclusions about others' behavior. If your score is lower than you want it to be, you can decide to consciously seek out new information about yourself and others. This requires that you be mindful.

Cognitive Complexity

The complexity of our cognitive systems also affects the way we perceive other people and interpret their messages (Applegate & Sypher, 1983). We use constructs to differentiate others when we communicate (Kelly, 1955). *Constructs* are perceptual categories we use to organize our thoughts. A panhandler, for example, might use the construct "looks generous–does not look generous" in deciding whom to approach for money. When communicating with others, we might use constructs such as "empathic–not empathic," "extroverted–introverted," "honest–dishonest," "trustworthy–not trustworthy," and so forth in trying to understand their behavior. Cognitively complex people use more constructs to understand other people than cognitively simple people.

It is not just the complexity of our cognitive system, however, that is important to how we communicate. The quality of the constructs we use in understanding others also is important (Clark & Delia, 1977). Quality is based on the relevance of the constructs to the situation in which we use them. If, for example, we are trying to improve the effectiveness of our communication with other people, assessing whether they are "generous–not generous" will not be very useful and, therefore, the quality of our construct will be low. Assessing the degree to which other people are "trustworthy–not trustworthy," in contrast, will be useful in improving the quality of our communication, because this construct is related directly to communication.

Think about the constructs you use to understand other people's communication. Take a few minutes to think about the following question and write your answer:

> What constructs do you use when you think about how your friends and ac-

Assessment 4.3 *Assessing Your Uncertainty Orientation*

The purpose of this questionnaire is to help you assess your orientation toward uncertainty. Respond to each statement indicating the degree to which it is true regarding the way you typically respond: "Always False" (answer 1), "Usually False" (answer 2), "Sometimes False and Sometimes True" (answer 3), "Usually True" (answer 4), or "Always True" (answer 5).

_______ 1. I do not compare myself with others.

_______ 2. If given a choice, I prefer to go somewhere new rather than somewhere I've been before.

_______ 3. I reject ideas that are different from mine.

_______ 4. I try to resolve inconsistencies in beliefs I hold.

_______ 5. I am not interested in finding out information about myself.

_______ 6. When I obtain new information, I try to integrate it with information I already have.

_______ 7. I hold traditional beliefs.

_______ 8. I evaluate people on their own merit without comparing them to others.

_______ 9. I hold inconsistent views of myself.

_______ 10. If someone suggests an opinion that is different from mine, I do not reject it before I consider it.

To find your score, first reverse the responses for the *odd-numbered* items (if you wrote 1, make it 5; if you wrote 2, make it 4; if you wrote 3, leave it as 3; if you wrote 4, make it 2; if you wrote 5, make it 1). Next, add the numbers next to each statement. Scores range from 10 to 50. The higher your score, the greater your uncertainty orientation.

quaintances communicate with you? List the constructs you use. ______________
____
____
____
____
____

Look over the constructs you listed. The first thing you should think about is whether there are a large number of additional constructs that you *could* use when you think about other people's communication with you. If there are, your construct system is not as complex as it could be (in other words, you may tend to be cognitively simple). Now go back over the list and think about how relevant each of the constructs you listed is to the quality of your communication with other people. If the constructs are not directly relevant to communication, you may want to reconsider their use in the way you think about other people's communication. To illustrate, the construct "agreeable–disagreeable" is not directly relevant to the effectiveness of our communication with others. People do not have to agree with us for us to communicate effectively with them.

Our cognitive complexity affects our communication with others. Cognitively complex people form impressions of others that are more extensive and better represent the behaviors of others than do cognitively simple people (O'Keefe & Sypher, 1981). Cognitively complex people seek out unique features of their environments more than cognitively simple people do (Honess, 1976). Cognitively simple people, in contrast, tend to seek information that is consistent with their prior beliefs. Cognitively simple people tend to use their own framework for interpreting other people's behavior. Cognitively complex people, on the other hand, use multiple frameworks for understanding other people's behavior (Davidson, 1975). Cognitively complex individuals, therefore, are better able to reduce uncertainty and anxiety regarding other people's behavior than are cognitively simple individuals (Gudykunst, 1988). **The more complex our cognitive systems, the more we are able to adapt our messages to other people and the more accurately we can interpret their messages.**

We all have a tendency to process information in a cognitively complex or cognitively simple fashion. When we communicate on automatic pilot, our tendency influences the way we interpret and create messages. If we are cognitively simple, we can be mindful and choose to process information in a more complex fashion.[2] We can decide to use more constructs than we typically do, and we can think about which constructs are most important in the situation. Many ideas that can be used to understand other people's communication are discussed throughout the book. When you see an idea that appears useful to you, try to mindfully add it to your construct system for understanding interpersonal communication.

Knowledge of Alternative Interpretations

There are three interrelated cognitive processes involved when we try to understand other people's behavior: description, interpretation, and evaluation. To communicate effectively, it is necessary to be able to distinguish among these three processes. *Description* is an actual report of what we have observed, with a minimum of distortion and without attributing social significance to the behavior. Description includes what we see and hear and is accomplished by counting and/or recording observations.

In order to clarify these processes, consider the following example:

Description
Kim stood six inches away from me when we talked.

This statement is descriptive in nature. It does not attribute social significance; it merely tells what the observer saw. If we attribute social significance to this statement or make an inference about what we saw, we would be engaged in *interpretation.* In other words, interpretation is what we think about what we see and hear. The important thing to keep in mind is that there can be multiple interpretations for any particular description of behavior, and we tend to stop searching for interpretations once we have found a reasonable one. Returning to our example:

Description
Kim stood six inches away from me when we talked.
Interpretations
Kim is aggressive.
Kim violated my personal space.
Kim likes me.

When we communicate on automatic pilot, we automatically use one interpretation when we observe the behavior in question. This is usually the first reasonable interpretation that comes to mind. The problem is that our interpretation may not be the same as that of the person engaging in the behavior.

Each of the interpretations listed can have several different evaluations. *Evaluations* are positive or negative judgments concerning the social significance we attribute to behavior; whether we like it or not. To illustrate this, consider the first interpretation given:

Interpretation
Kim is aggressive.
Evaluations
I like that; Kim stands up for her or himself.
I don't like that; Kim should not violate my rights by standing so close.

Of course, several other evaluations could be made, but these two are sufficient to illustrate potential differences in the evaluations for any one interpretation.

When we communicate on automatic pilot, we do not distinguish among description, interpretation, and evaluation. Skipping the descriptive process and jumping immediately to either interpretation or evaluation when confronted with different patterns of behavior often leads to misattributions of meaning and ineffective communication. Being able to distinguish among the three processes, on the other hand, increases the likelihood that we will be able to see alternative interpretations and select interpretations appropriate for the person with whom we are communicating. This will increase our ability to communicate effectively.

When we think there is a potential misunderstanding, we need to become mindful, describe the behavior in question, and recognize our interpretation of the behavior. If the other person is present, we can check our interpretation by asking what the other person meant by the behavior (we also can use the perception-checking skill presented in Chapter 7). If the other person is not present, we need to search for alternative interpretations of the behavior. Once we have isolated some alternatives, we can try to figure out which we think the other person meant.

Skill Exercise 4.3 provides an opportunity to practice differentiating descriptions, interpretations, and evaluations. Take a moment to complete it now.

With respect to Skill Exercise 4.3, it is important to note that, if someone does not look other people in the eye in the European American middle-class subculture, it frequently is interpreted as lying. There are, however, numerous alternative interpretations for why others do not look us in the eyes when we talk. That they might be shy or highly introverted or ashamed are alternative interpretations in the European American culture. Members of some ethnic groups, such as African Americans or Native Americans, however, might interpret this behavior as showing respect.

Overcoming Cognitive Distortions

When we interpret our own and other people's behavior on automatic pilot, our perceptions often are distorted because of the ways that we think about our feelings and behavior. Our cognitive distortions lead us to communicate ineffectively. There are several ways that

Skill Exercise 4.3 *Separating Descriptions, Interpretations, and Evaluations*

Descriptions of behavior involve a report of what was observed without attributing meaning to, or interpreting, the behavior. An interpretation is the meaning or social significance attached to the behavior. There are always multiple interpretations of any specific behavior. Evaluations involve passing judgments, making comparisons, accepting, or rejecting. Each interpretation, in turn, can be evaluated differently based on the person's values, attitudes, and beliefs.

A description of a behavior is listed below. There are many potential interpretations of this behavior. One potential interpretation of the behavior is given. Try to think of at least three alternative interpretations for the behavior and write these in the spaces provided. Once you have listed alternative interpretations, look at the possible evaluations of the interpretations. List at least two evaluations for the interpretation provided. Once you have completed this step, select one of your interpretations and list at least two potential evaluations for it.

Description

Pat did not look me in the eye when we communicated.

Possible Interpretations

1. Pat is lying.
2. ______
3. ______
4. ______
5. ______

Possible Evaluations

Interpretation 1: Pat is lying.

Alternative Evaluations:

1. I do not like people who are dishonest.
2. ______
3. ______

Interpretation __: ______

Alternative Evaluations:

1. ______
2. ______
3. ______

our interpretations of our own and other people's behavior can be distorted: all-or-nothing thinking, overgeneralization, mental filters, discounting the positive, jumping to conclusions, magnification, emotional reasoning, "should statements," labeling, and personalization and blame (Burns, 1989).

All-or-nothing thinking involves seeing things based on dichotomies (it is sometimes also referred to as polarized thinking; Burns, 1989). If we are not perfect, for example, we think that we are a total failure. When we use this type of thought process, we do not see the possibility of alternative outcomes between being perfect and failing. This form of twisted thinking often leads us to see other people as either friends or enemies.

Overgeneralization involves generalizing from one negative event to a "never ending pattern of defeat" (Burns, 1989). We tend to assume that negative events always happen to us and that positive events never occur. If a person turns us down for a date, for example, we tend to think that we will *always* be turned down for dates if we are overgeneralizing. This form of twisted thinking also might lead us to believe that, if other people misunderstood us once, they *never* understand us.

We use *mental filters* when we focus on specific negative details, and the negative details affect the way we look at the world (Burns, 1989). Consider our boss's telling us that there was one error in the report we wrote, but that in general the report was excellent. Our mental filter causes us to focus on the error, and this one negative comment affects the rest of our day.

When we ignore positive experiences, we are *discounting the positive* (Burns, 1989). Discounting the positive leads us to focus on negative aspects of our interactions with others. If we discount the positive and we have a positive interaction with another person, we think that the experience does not count. Discounting the positive "takes the joy out of life" (Burns, 1989, p. 8) and leads to low self-esteem.

We *jump to conclusions* when we interpret events negatively even though the facts do not support our conclusions (Burns, 1989). There are two ways we jump to conclusions: *mind reading,* which involves concluding (without checking it out) that others are reacting to us negatively; and *fortune telling,* which involves predicting that things will turn out negatively. When communicating with our romantic partner, for example, we might predict that he or she will not tell us what we want to hear.

Magnification occurs when we exaggerate our negative qualities and minimize our positive qualities (Burns, 1989). We may, for example, assume that no one will like us because we are shy. When we magnify our problems, we let little problems that should not get in the way of our communication become major barriers to communication.

Emotional reasoning involves assuming that our negative emotions reflect who we really are. If we experience anger, for example, we see ourselves as angry people. Alternatively, we might think, "I feel guilty. I must be a rotten person" (Burns, 1989, p. 9).

When we assume that things "should" be the way we want them to be, we are using *should statements* (Burns, 1989). To illustrate, when communicating with others, we want to speak fluently. If we use "you know" a few times when communicating with someone we want to impress, we might get very frustrated because we think we should always be fluent. When we direct should statements at ourselves and do not live up to them, we get frustrated or feel guilty. When we direct should statements at others and they do not live up to them, we become frustrated or angry.

Labeling involves using a negative label for ourselves based on something we did. If we are not fluent when we communicate with someone, for example, we might label ourselves as an incompetent communicator. "Labeling is quite irrational because you are not the same as what you do" (Burns, 1989, p. 10). We can label ourselves or others. To illustrate, if someone does or says something we do not like, we might label the person a "jerk."

When we hold ourselves responsible for things that are not under our control, we are engaging in *personalization and blame* (Burns, 1989). If, for example, our romantic partner gets mad at us, we assume that we are to blame. Blaming ourselves leads to feeling guilt, shame, and low self-esteem. Instead of blaming ourselves, we blame others. This also is problematic because, if we blame others, they may turn around and blame us.

Cognitive distortions occur when we communicate on automatic pilot and when we are consciously thinking about the *outcomes* of our interactions with others. **To overcome our cognitive distortions, we must learn to replace our distorted automatic thoughts with rational responses.**

Reading 4.2 THE DAILY MOOD LOG

Describe the upsetting event—I feel inhibited about flirting with Tom at the swimming pool.

Negative feelings—Record your emotions and rate each one on a scale from 0 (the least) to 100 (the most). Include feelings such as sad, anxious, angry, guilty, lonely, hopeless, frustrated, etc.

Rating Emotion (0–100)	Rating Emotion (0–100)	Rating Emotion (0–100)
1. Anxious 99%	3.	5.
2.	4.	6.

Automatic Thoughts Write down your negative thoughts and number them consecutively.	*Distortions* Identify the distortions in each "Automatic Thought."	*Rational Responses* Substitute more realistic and positive thoughts.
1. What if I carry it too far or say something stupid?	1. Fortune telling.	1. I can only learn through practice. Eventually I'll get better at it.
2. What kind of impression will he get of me? He might think I'm "a flirt."	2. Mind reading: labeling.	2. He might be attracted to me. There's no such thing as "a flirt," but it might be a good thing if I was a little more flirtatious.
3. What are the other guys at the pool going to think of me?	3. Mind reading.	3. They may feel jealous and wish I was flirting with them!
4. They may have a low opinion of me.	4. Mind reading.	4. That's always possible, but it wouldn't be the end of the world. I'm pretty lonely as it is, so what do I really have to lose?
5. If I make a fool of myself it would mean there was something wrong with me and I'd never learn.	5. All-or-nothing thinking.	5. No, it would just show I wasn't very good at flirting yet. If I work at it, I'll get better at it.

OUTCOME—Review your "Rational Responses" and put a check in the box that describes how you now feel:

☐ not at all better; ☐ somewhat better;

☐ quite a bit better; ☑ a lot better.

This requires that we become mindful of the *process* of our communication and not focus on the outcome. A technique that is useful in overcoming our cognitive distortions is outlined in Reading 4.2. This technique is useful any time we have a negative feeling that is influencing our behavior or when we want to try out new behaviors.

In the example, the person completing the Daily Mood Log is experiencing anxiety about flirting with Tom. By listing her automatic thoughts, looking at how these thoughts are distorted, and thinking of a rational response that can replace the automatic thought, she was able to manage her anxiety. Her list of rational responses provides interpretations of her own and other people's behavior that should allow her to communicate more effectively in these types of situations in the future.

Skill Exercise 4.4 is designed to help you practice overcoming cognitive distortions. Think of a recent upsetting event or an instance when you thought you did not commu-

Skill Exercise 4.4 ***Overcoming Cognitive Distortions***

Reading 4.2 presents an example of how the Burns Daily Mood Log is used. Review the reading before completing this exercise. The purpose of this exercise is to use the Daily Mood Log to overcome cognitive distortions about an upsetting event in your life. Select a recent upsetting event with your romantic partner or a friend which caused you to communicate ineffectively. Complete the Daily Mood Log regarding your reaction to this event.

The Daily Mood Log

Describe the Upsetting Event—__________

____

____

____

____

____

____

Negative Feelings—Record your emotions and rate each one on a scale from 0 (the least) to 10 (the most). Include feeling such as sad, anxious, angry, guilty, lonely, hopeless, frustrated, etc.

Rating (0–100) Emotion	Rating (0–100) Emotion	Rating (0–100) Emotion
1.	3.	5.
2.	4.	6.

Automatic Thoughts Write down your negative thoughts and number them consecutively.	*Distortions* Identify the distortions in each "Automatic Thought."	*Rational Response* Substitute more realistic and positive thoughts.

Outcome—Review your "Rational Responses" and put a check that describes how you now feel:

☐ not at all better; ☐ somewhat better;
☐ quite a bit better; ☐ a lot better.

nicate very effectively. Complete the Daily Mood Log for this event.

The Daily Mood Log is a valuable tool we can use to overcome cognitive distortions and manage negative emotions when we are mindful. You can construct your own version of the Daily Mood Log and complete it *any time* you find yourself using cognitive distortions or experiencing negative emotions.

Summary

To communicate effectively with others we have to manage our level of uncertainty. If our uncertainty is above our maximum threshold, we do not have sufficient information to feel comfortable predicting other people's behavior. If our uncertainty is below our maximum threshold, we may not experience sufficient novelty to maintain our interest in the relationship, or we may become overconfident in our ability to predict other people's behavior.

We try to reduce uncertainty about other people when we think we will interact with them in the future, when they can provide us with rewards, or when they violate our expectations. We can use these general strategies to reduce our uncertainty about other people: passive, active, and interactive strategies. Our uncertainty regarding other people's behavior tends to decrease as we get to know them. Within any interaction or stage of relationship (such as acquaintance relationship or friendship), however, our uncertainty fluctuates and we must balance the dialectic between predictability and novelty. When other people do something that surprises us, our uncertainty tends to increase. If our uncertainty rises above our maximum thresholds, we must bring it down before we will feel comfortable interacting with them.

When we communicate with other people, we develop attributions about, or explanations for their behavior. Our attributions can be based on their individual characteristics, such as intelligence, motivation, or group memberships. When we communicate on automatic pilot, our attributions often are in error. To illustrate, we tend to overestimate the effect of other people's group memberships on their behavior and overestimate the influence of situational demands on our own behavior.

Our cognitive processing of information and the emotions we experience influence our communication with others. To increase the effectiveness of our communication, we need to be mindful of our interactions with others. When we are mindful, we need to focus on the process of communication, not the outcomes of our interactions. When we are mindful, we can increase our effectiveness by being uncertainty oriented and engaging in complex information processing. To increase the effectiveness of our communication, we also can separate descriptions, interpretations, and evaluations in order to understand how other people are interpreting our messages and to more accurately interpret their messages. To communicate more effectively, we also can overcome the cognitive distortions that influence the ways we think about our feelings and behavior.

Notes

1. We are using an example involving ethnicity to illustrate the full range of strategies we can use to reduce our uncertainty.
2. Some writers would disagree with our position because they see cognitive complexity as a stable trait. We believe that our dispositions and traits are relatively stable when we communicate on automatic pilot, but that we can choose to alter them when we are mindful.

Journal Reflections

1. *Gathering Information to Reduce Uncertainty.* There are three general strategies we can use to gather information about others: passive, active, and interactive. In the next week, use each of these strategies to gather information about someone. How does the information obtained using the three different strategies differ?
2. *Identifying Errors in Attributions.* We frequently make errors in attributing causes to others' behavior (such as attributing their behavior to their personal traits such as group memberships when their behavior was based on situational demands). In the next week, try to identify at least two errors you make in attributing causes to others' behavior. In your journal, describe the situations, the cause to which you initially attributed the others' behavior, and why you think you might have been in error.
3. *Separating Descriptions, Interpretations, and Evaluations.* When we communicate with others, we generally interpret and/or evaluate their behavior without first describing it. This often leads to misinterpretations (we may, for example, interpret others' behavior differently than they intended). In the next week, use this skill in at least two interactions where you think there might have been a misunderstanding between yourself and another person. In your journal, describe the situation, how you initially interpreted the other person's message, the potential interpretations the other person may have used, and the one you think she or he intended. What influence did your misinterpretation (if any) have on the quality of your communication?
4. *Overcoming Your Cognitive Distortions.* We all have cognitive distortions in the way we think about ourselves and others. In the next week, use David Burns' Daily Mood Log to keep track of your cognitive distortions. In your journal, discuss how your cognitive distortions influenced your response to the people involved. How do you plan to respond differently in the future, given your understanding of your cognitive distortions?

Study Questions

1. Why is it important to reduce uncertainty in our interactions with others? How is our communication affected when our uncertainty is above our maximum thresholds? When is it below our minimum thresholds?
2. How does self-disclosure help us reduce our uncertainty about others?
3. How does uncertainty differ across cultures?
4. How are attributions social?
5. Why is it important to recognize the attributional errors we make? What is involved when we commit the ultimate attribution error?
6. Under what conditions do we tend to be most mindful when we communicate?
7. Why do we need to be mindful of the process of communication rather than the outcome in order to increase the effectiveness of our communication?
8. Why are uncertainty-oriented individuals likely to be more effective communicators than certainty-oriented ones?
9. How are cognitively complex and cognitively simple people different? Why does cognitive complexity facilitate effective communication?
10. Why is the statement "Pat violated my personal space" an interpretation and not a description?
11. How do our cognitive distortions lead us to experience negative emotions?

Suggested Readings

Berger, C. R., & Bradac, J. (1982). *Language and social knowledge.* London: Edward Arnold. Charles Berger and James Bradac discuss the relationship between language and social knowledge. They examine how language influences the ways we reduce uncertainty.

Burns, D. D. (1989). *The feeling good handbook.* New York: William Morrow. Davis Burns presents techniques for managing our negative emotions in everyday life. If you found the Daily Mood Log useful, you'll enjoy this book.

Prather, H. (1986). *Notes on how to live in the world . . . and still be happy.* Garden City, NY: Doubleday. Hugh Prather presents a systematic program for cognitively managing our view of the world. He presents many exercises that can be used to manage anxiety and let go of old hurts.

5

EMOTION AND COMMUNICATION

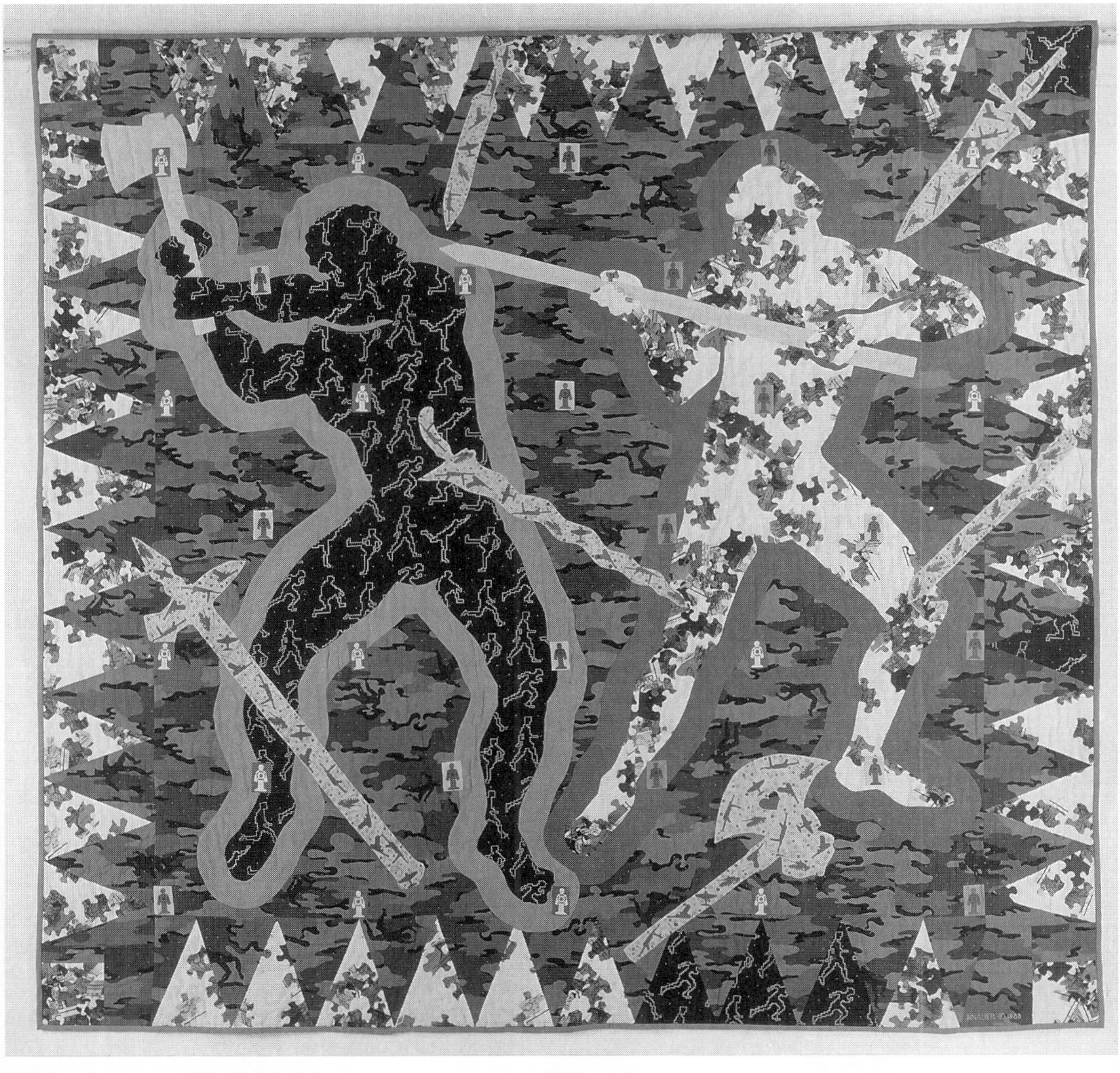

Our lives would be very limited if all we could do is think about interactions with other people. We are not, however, limited to cognitive processing of our interactions. We also have feelings and react emotionally to our interactions with others. We look forward to some emotional experiences, such as happiness and love, while we may try to avoid other emotional experiences, such as anxiety and shame. We nevertheless experience both types of emotions every day.

Emotions are our affective responses to changing relationships between ourselves and our environment (Lazarus, 1991). We do not directly experience emotions. We have experiences in a situation, and we label the physiological feelings we have. The labels we give our physiological feelings are our emotions. How we label our feelings is based on our interpretations of the situations in which we find ourselves. Our interpretations are based on subtle cognitive processes. These automatic cognitive processes are in turn necessary for us to interpret the feelings (Beck, 1976). The specific emotions we experience result from our interpretations of the situations in which we find ourselves.

Our emotions change over time because our interpretations of situations do not remain static; they change (Lazarus, 1991). One of the reasons why our emotions change is that we constantly receive new information, which we must evaluate. Our evaluations influence how we interpret the physiological feelings we have and how we label the emotions. To illustrate, if we feel demeaned and initially blame another person for demeaning us, we may label the feelings we experience as anger (directed at the other person). We may, however, receive new information indicating that this person was not responsible for what happened. When we receive this new information, we have to reevaluate the situation and relabel our feelings. In this situation, we might relabel the feelings as anxiety.

Experiencing and expressing diverse emotions is part of being human. We all experience emotions every day. The critical issue for effective communication is *not* the emotions we experience, but how we manage and express them. **We do not necessarily have to express all the emotions we experience. Also, we can choose how we express our emotions to others when we are mindful of our communication.** In other words, we have a choice about how to cope with our emotions.

Coping involves our cognitive and behavioral efforts to manage our emotions (Lazarus, 1991). There are two ways of coping with emotions. One way to cope is to remove the problem. This form of coping is not highly successful in interpersonal communication, because we usually cannot remove the problem. If, for example, someone is doing something that we do not like and we become angry, we cannot remove the other person. Another way to cope involves changing the way we interpret situations and our emotional responses to them. This method of coping can be very effective in interpersonal communication; it underlies much of the discussion of affective resources for communication later in this section.

Goal-Congruent and Goal-Incongruent Emotions

How we interpret our feelings when we have an experience depends on our appraisal of the situation. If we perceive that what has happened contributes to our well-being or our ability to accomplish our goals, we interpret our feelings as *goal-congruent emotions* (these often are called *positive emotions*) (Lazarus, 1991). There are at least six goal-congruent emotions: compassion, happiness, hope, love, pride, and relief (Lazarus, 1991). If we perceive that what has happened does *not* contribute to our well-being or does *not* contribute to our ability to achieve our goals, we interpret our feelings as *goal-incongruent emotions* (these often are called *negative emotions*). There are at least nine goal-incongruent emotions: anger, anxiety, disgust, envy, fright, guilt, jealousy, sadness, and shame (Lazarus, 1991).

Understanding the role emotions play in our implicit personal theories of communication is important to effective communication. In order to improve the effectiveness of our communication, we need to understand how we typically express our emotions. If we do not understand how we typically express our emotions and the alternatives available to us, we cannot make informed choices about how we *want* to express our emotions. Let's begin with the goal-incongruent emotions.

Goal-Incongruent Emotions

As indicated earlier, goal-incongruent emotions are those that interfere with our accomplishing our goals. They often are referred to as negative emotions. They are negative in that they can inhibit our ability to accomplish our goals or to function effectively. It is important that we understand how we typically respond when experiencing these emotions and learn ways to cope with them. If we do not understand how we typically express goal-incongruent emotions, we will not be able to manage them successfully or increase our ability to accomplish our goals. We'll begin by looking at anger.

We experience *anger* when we perceive that someone has committed a demeaning offense against us or people close to us (Lazarus, 1991). Behavior is interpreted as demeaning when we think that it is arbitrary, inconsiderate, or malevolent. When we get angry, we consciously or unconsciously think that other

Emotion and communication are inseparable. Situations and events sometimes provoke goal-incongruent emotions. In order to communicate effectively during these times we need to successfully manage these negative emotions.

people have threatened our identities. Anger is a very powerful emotion. It affects the person experiencing it, as well as the person to whom it is directed when it is expressed. Since anger is so important, it is discussed in more detail below.

Anxiety is experienced when we think that we are facing an uncertain threat (Lazarus, 1991). Anxiety is a response to ambiguity of information. We experience anxiety because we are not able to make sense out of the situation in which we find ourselves. Generally, we do not know why we are anxious. Managing anxiety is one of the major problems with which all humans must cope (Lazarus, 1991). Since anxiety is so central to human existence and has such a profound effect on our communication, it is discussed in more detail below.

We experience *disgust* when we want to avoid or get away from something we find offensive (Lazarus, 1991). Disgust often is associated with our responses to food, but it is not limited to food. We can experience disgust with respect to many different aspects of other people's behavior. When someone passes gas in public, for example, some people will experience disgust.

Envy is experienced when we want something that someone else has (Lazarus, 1991). We can envy anything that we consider desirable. The source of our envy could be a relationship with another person or other people's possessions, looks, personalities, and so forth.

Fright occurs when we face an immediate physical danger (Lazarus, 1991). Fright is based on the immediate prospect of harm to ourselves. The main way we cope with fright is by trying to escape or avoid the situation if possible.

Guilt occurs when we have done something or want to do something that we find morally wrong (Lazarus, 1991). We do not have to actually do anything morally wrong to experience guilt. We can experience guilt from thinking about it. We tend to feel guilt when we perceive that someone is experiencing distress and we think that we are responsible for their distress (Hoffman, 1983). Guilt often is based on a concern for others (Hoffman, 1983). The concern for others tends to lead us to engage in constructive behavior or to behave with other people's interests in mind. There are at least three ways we can try to deal with our feelings of guilt (Lazarus, 1991). One way we might cope when we feel guilty is to try to "make it up" to the person we think we harmed. We also may choose to cope with our guilt feelings by not thinking about the person we think we harmed. Alternatively, we may deny that we are to blame and instead blame the other person.

We experience *jealousy* when we hold a third party responsible for a threat to or the loss of someone's affection (Lazarus, 1991). Jealousy always involves the perception that there are three people involved, as in a "love triangle." When we experience jealousy, we often respond with anger or the impulse to attack the third party.

Sadness occurs when we think that we have experienced an irrevocable loss (Lazarus, 1991). When we experience sadness, we feel helpless to restore the loss. Sadness can result from the death of a loved one or pet, from failure at something that is important to us, or from thinking that we have lost the respect of someone important to us. Sadness is related to, but different from, depression. Sadness is a temporary state, which goes away when the loss has been accepted. Depression, in contrast, is more long term and does not include an acceptance of the loss (Lazarus, 1991).

Shame occurs when we perceive that we fail to live up to our expectations in someone else's eyes (Lazarus, 1991). When we feel disgraced or humiliated in the eyes of people important to us, we experience shame. It does not matter whether the other people think that we disgraced ourselves, only that we think we disgraced ourselves in their eyes. We often feel shame about feeling shame. Shame is such an undesirable emotion that we tend to use other labels for feelings of shame. We might, for example, say we are "feeling foolish, stupid, ridiculous, inadequate, defective, incompetent, low self-esteem, awkward, exposed, vulnerable, insecure, and so on" (Scheff, 1990, p. 86), rather than admit to ourselves that we are feeling shame.

Skill Exercise 5.1 is designed to help you think about how you tend to express goal-incongruent emotions. Take a few minutes to complete it now.

Skill Exercise 5.1 *Expressing Goal-Incongruent Emotions*

The purpose of this exercise is to help you become aware of how you express your goal-incongruent (negative) emotions. For each of the situations listed, indicate how you typically respond.

1. How do you usually express feeling anxiety verbally? ____________

   ____

   nonverbally? ____________

   ____

   ____

   Is there anything about how you express feeling anxiety that you would like to change in the future? If so, what? ____

   ____

2. How do you usually express feeling shame verbally? ____________

   ____

   nonverbally? ____________

   ____

   Is there anything about how you express feeling shame that you would like to change in the future? If so, what? ____

   ____

Skill Exercise 5.1 *Continued*

3. How do you usually express feeling disgusted with something someone else has done verbally? ______

______

nonverbally? ______

______

Is there anything about how you express feeling disgusted that you would like to change in the future? If so, what? ______

______

4. How do you usually express feeling sad verbally? ______

______

nonverbally? ______

______

Is there anything about how you express feeling sad that you would like to change in the future? If so, what? ______

______

5. How do you usually express feeling jealousy toward someone else verbally? ______

______

nonverbally? ______

______

Is there anything about how you express feeling jealousy that you would like to change in the future? If so, what? ______

______

______

6. How do you usually express feeling anger toward someone else verbally? ______

______

nonverbally? ______

______

Is there anything about how you express feeling anger that you would like to change in the future? If so, what? ______

______

______

7. How do you usually express feeling fright verbally? ______

______

nonverbally? ______

______

Is there anything about how you express feeling fright that you would like to change in the future? If so, what? ______

______

______

8. How do you usually express feeling envy verbally? ______

______

nonverbally? ______

______

Is there anything about how you express feeling envy that you would like to change in the future? If so, what? ______

______

______

9. How do you usually express feeling guilt verbally? ______

______

nonverbally? ______

______

Is there anything about how you express feeling guilt that you would like to change in the future? If so, what? ______

______

______

Skill Exercise 5.1 should help you understand your typical ways of expressing goal-incongruent emotions and ways of responding that you might want to change in the future. The way you express your emotions when you communicate on automatic pilot is based on the scripts you learned as a child. It is important, however, to remember that you have many options for how you express your emotions. You do not have to "act out" the scripts you learned as a child. If you mindfully plan how you want to express goal-incongruent emotions in the future, you are beginning to develop a new script for expressing these emotions. Having a new script helps you increase the likelihood that you will be able to express them constructively. Two of the goal-incongruent emotions, anxiety and anger, are discussed in more detail below.

Goal-Congruent Emotions

Goal-congruent emotions are those that facilitate our accomplishing our goals. Because they can facilitate accomplishing goals, they often are referred to as positive emotions. Although goal-congruent emotions tend to lead to positive feelings, they can inhibit our ability to communicate effectively. To illustrate, if we are happy, it can lead to positive illusions about the world. These positive illusions could lead to our misinterpreting other people's intentions. Others, for example, may intend to hurt us, but we do not recognize this because we look at the world through "rose-colored glasses." It is important that we understand how goal-congruent emotions fit into our implicit personal theories. Let's begin with compassion.

Compassion is experienced when we are moved by other people's suffering and want to help them (Lazarus, 1991). When we experience compassion, we want to help other people solve their problems and, at the same time, remain sufficiently detached so that we are not overwhelmed by their plight. Service to others makes us feel good. If our efforts to be compassionate are not perceived as "authentic" or we are clumsy in our attempt to be compassionate, however, it can make the other people feel worse (Lazarus, 1991).

We experience *happiness* when are making progress toward our goals (Lazarus, 1991).

Goal-congruent emotions can have positive effects on our relationships with others because people like to share their happiness with others.

Happiness is not a goal in and of itself, but it is a by-product of making progress toward other goals. Joy is closely related to happiness. Joy is an intense reaction to a specific event. When we are happy we feel secure and experience pleasure. Having these feelings usually leads us to be outgoing. Happiness has positive effects on our relationships with others because "we want to be with happy people and avoid being with unhappy people" (Lazarus, 1991, p. 269).

We feel *hope* when we think something bad is going to happen, but we want something better to happen (Lazarus, 1991). We fear the worst but want something better. Hope leads us to make constructive efforts toward accomplishing our goals.

Love is experienced when we have affection for other people (Lazarus, 1991). Our affection for other people may or may not be reciprocated. There are many different types of love. Romantic love, for example, involves a combination of intimacy, passion, and commitment (Sternberg, 1986). Companionate love, in contrast, involves intimacy and commitment, but there is no passion. When we experience romantic love, we desire social intimacy and physical affection from the person we love (Lazarus, 1991). The types of love are discussed in more detail in Chapter 13 on communication in close relationships.

We experience *pride* when we are able to enhance our self-esteem by taking credit for something that we did or something we obtained (Lazarus, 1991). We also can experience pride when the groups with which we identify have similar accomplishments. When we feel pride, we frequently want to tell other people about our accomplishments. "Showing off," however, can create problems in our relationships with other people if it appears that we are putting them down.

Relief occurs when we have been experiencing a goal-incongruent emotion and the situation changes for the better (Lazarus, 1991). Relief can only occur when something stopping us from reaching a goal has been eliminated. One of the main reactions we have when we are relieved is that tension is relieved and we feel relaxed.

ZIGGY © 1991 Ziggy and Friends, Inc. Reprinted with permission of UNIVERSAL PRESS SYNDICATE. All rights reserved.

Skill Exercise 5.2 is designed to help you think about how you express goal-congruent emotions. Take a few minutes to complete it now.

Skill Exercise 5.2 should help you understand the ways you express goal-congruent emotions when you communicate on automatic pilot and ways of responding that you might want to change in the future. If you mindfully plan how you want to express goal-congruent emotions in the future, you can increase the likelihood that you will be able to express them constructively.

To be able to express our emotions to others, we need to be aware of the affective experiences we have. Rather than "acting-out"

Skill Exercise 5.2 *Expressing Goal-Congruent Emotions*

The purpose of this exercise is to help you become aware of how you express your goal-congruent (positive) emotions. For each of the situations listed, indicate how you typically respond.

1. How do you usually express feeling pride in something you have done verbally? ____________________

   ____

   nonverbally? ____________________

   ____

   Is there anything about how you express feeling pride that you would like to change in the future? If so, what? ____

   ____

2. How do you usually express feeling happiness verbally? ____________________

   ____

   nonverbally? ____________________

   ____

   Is there anything about how you express feeling happiness that you would like to change in the future? If so, what? ____

   ____

3. How do you usually express feeling relief verbally? ____________________

   ____

   nonverbally? ____________________

   ____

   Is there anything about how you express feeling relief that you would like to change in the future? If so, what? ____

   ____

4. How do you usually express feeling love verbally? ____________________

   ____

   nonverbally? ____________________

   ____

   Is there anything about how you express feeling love that you would like to change in the future? If so, what? ____

   ____

5. How do you usually express feeling hope verbally? ____________________

   ____

   nonverbally? ____________________

   ____

   Is there anything about how you express feeling hope that you would like to change in the future? If so, what? ____

   ____

6. How do you usually express feeling compassion toward others verbally? ______

   ____

   nonverbally? ____________________

   ____

   Is there anything about how you express feeling compassion that you would like to change in the future? If so, what? _

   ____

our emotions, we can make conscious decisions about how we want to express them. When we express our emotions to others, we need to be assertive, not aggressive. We need to take responsibility for our own emotions and not blame our emotions on others. In individualistic cultures like the United States, emotions generally are expressed directly. Indirect expression of emotions, however, is necessary when being direct will lead to negative consequences (Bavelas et al., 1990). As discussed below, directly expressing anger generally has negative consequences for our relationships with others. We therefore may want to consider appropriate indirect expressions.

Given this overview of the major emotions, the two goal-incongruent emotions that have the greatest influence on our communication, anxiety and anger, will be discussed in more detail. Let's begin with anxiety.

ANXIETY AND COMMUNICATION

The amount of anxiety we experience influences our motivation to communicate with others (Turner, 1988), as pointed out in Chapter 3. If our anxiety is too high, we are not motivated to communicate with others. If our anxiety is too low, we do not have the energy to communicate with others.

We experience some amount of anxiety any time we communicate with other people. Before proceeding, think about what causes you to experience anxiety. Answer the following questions:

> In which types of communication situations do you experience the greatest anxiety? ______________________
> ______________________
> ______________________

> In which types of communication situations do you experience the least anxiety? ______________________
> ______________________
> ______________________

> How is your anxiety manifested when you experience it (sweaty palms, stomach ache, and so forth)? ______________________
> ______________________
> ______________________

Your answers to these questions should provide insight into the role of anxiety in your implicit personal theory of communication. Keep your answers to these questions in mind as you read the remainder of the discussion on anxiety.

Minimum and Maximum Thresholds

We have maximum and minimum thresholds for anxiety (Gudykunst, 1993). If our anxiety is above our maximum threshold, we are so uneasy that we do not want to communicate with others. If our anxiety is below our minimum threshold, there is not enough adrenalin running through our system to motivate us to communicate with others. For us to be motivated to communicate with others, our anxiety has to be below our maximum thresholds and above our minimum thresholds. The role of anxiety in interpersonal communication is similar to its role in our performance on tests. If we are too anxious, we do not perform well on tests. Similarly, if we are not at all anxious, we do not perform well. There is an optimal level of anxiety that facilitates our experiencing "flow" or having optimal experiences (Csikszentmihalyi, 1990).

To communicate effectively with others, our anxiety needs to be below our maximum threshold and above our minimum threshold. **When anxiety is above our maximum or below our minimum threshold, we tend to process information in a very simplistic fashion.** To illustrate, when our anxiety is too high, we only use our stereotypes to predict other people's behavior. Since stereotypes are never accurate when applied to an individual, our predictions are inaccurate, and our communication, therefore, is likely to be ineffective.

Individuals' minimum and maximum thresholds differ. One way that we can tell if our anxiety is above our maximum threshold is by paying attention to our "gut reaction." If we feel *a few* butterflies in our stomach, our anxiety probably is not above our maximum threshold. A few butterflies probably indicate a normal amount of anxiety, an amount between our minimum and maximum thresholds. When we do not feel *any* butterflies or nervousness, our anxiety is probably below our minimum threshold. If, however, we have a stomach ache and the palms of our hands are sweating, our anxiety is probably above our maximum threshold. The physical indicators will differ for each of us. By paying attention to our reactions, we can figure out when our anxiety is so high that we do not feel comfortable communicating, and when it is so low that we do not care what happens. Once we know where these points are, we can cognitively manage our anxiety. Anxiety management is discussed below in the section on affective resources for effective communication.

Anxiety over Time

Generally, as we get to know others, the anxiety we experience in interacting with them tends to decrease. This does not imply, however, that anxiety continually decreases. Although there is a general tendency for our anxiety to decrease the more we get to know others, our anxiety can increase or decrease at any particular point in a relationship depending on what is going on in the relationship and how we interpret it.

Figure 5.1 illustrates how anxiety might vary as a relationship develops. When we first meet someone new, our anxiety might be above our maximum threshold, especially if we see the other person as attractive in some way or as a member of a different group. After talking with the other person, our anxiety probably decreases somewhat, assuming that we see that the other person is not a threat to us. As our relationship with the other person becomes more intimate, our overall level of anxiety tends to decrease. As we get to know the other person, however, our anxiety fluctuates depending on the specific circumstances of our interaction. The first time we kiss a date, for example, our anxiety increases.

If we become extremely comfortable with the other person, our anxiety may drop below our minimum threshold. If this occurs, our motivation to communicate with the other person decreases and we may not make the effort to communicate effectively. It is also possible, however, that something may occur in our relationship and our anxiety will increase dramatically, possibly rising above our maximum threshold. If we are involved in a romantic relationship, think that the relationship is going well, and want it to continue, our anxiety might increase dramatically if our partner told us that he or she wanted to break off the relationship.

Assessing Your Anxiety

Before proceeding, think about your anxiety when communicating with strangers for the first time. Take a minute to complete Assessment 5.1 now.

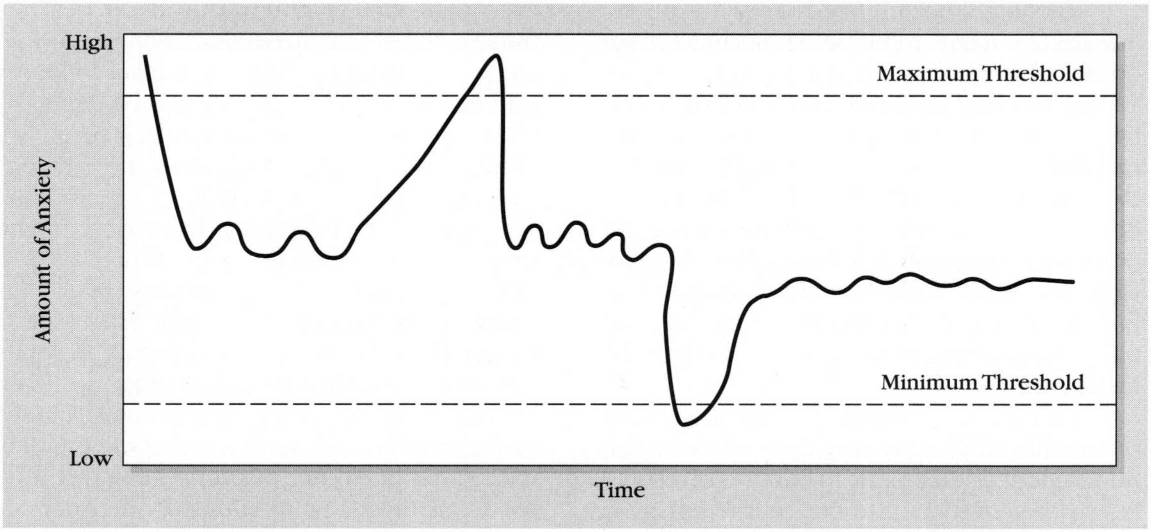

FIGURE 5.1 Anxiety over Time

Scores on Assessment 5.1 range from 10 to 50. There are not specific scores which we can use to indicate minimum and maximum thresholds. As indicated earlier, these are different for each of us. Very low scores, such as 10 to 20, would suggest little motivation to communicate with others. Similarly, very high scores, such as 40 to 50, probably suggest that we would avoid communicating with others.

Anxiety in Intergroup Communication

When we communicate with members of other groups, we not only have a high level of uncertainty, we also have a high level of anxiety. **The anxiety we experience when we communicate with members of other groups usually is based on negative expectations.** Actual or anticipated interaction with a member of a different ethnic group, for example, leads to anxiety (Stephan & Stephan, 1985). It is important to keep in mind that all of us are members of "another" group to the people with whom we are communicating. No other person shares all of our group memberships. The fears discussed here, as well as other material on intergroup interaction throughout the book, potentially applies to our interactions with anyone. We fear four types of negative consequences when interacting with members of other groups (Stephan & Stephan, 1985).

First, **we may fear negative consequences for our self-concepts.** In interacting with members of other groups, we worry "about feeling incompetent, confused, and not in control. . . . anticipate discomfort, frustration, and irritation due to the awkwardness of intergroup interactions" (Stephan & Stephan, 1985, p. 159). We also may fear the loss of self-esteem, that our social identities will be threatened, or that we will feel guilty if we behave in ways that offend members of other groups.

Assessment 5.1 *Assessing Your Anxiety in Communicating with Strangers*

The purpose of this questionnaire is to help you assess the amount of general anxiety you experience when you communicate with strangers. (*Note:* You can determine the amount of anxiety you experience communicating with a specific person by substituting the person's name for "strangers" in each of the statements.) Respond to each statement by indicating the degree to which the adjectives are applicable when you interact with strangers. If you never have the experience, answer 1 in the space provided; if you almost never have the experience, answer 2; if you sometimes have the experience and sometimes do not, answer 3; if you almost always have the experience, answer 4; if you always have the experience, answer 5.

_______ 1. I feel calm when I communicate with strangers.

_______ 2. I get frustrated when I communicate with strangers.

_______ 3. I do not get ruffled when I communicate with strangers.

_______ 4. I am insecure when I communicate with strangers.

_______ 5. I feel composed when I communicate with strangers.

_______ 6. I feel anxious when I communicate with strangers.

_______ 7. I do not get excited when I have to communicate with strangers.

_______ 8. I feel stress when I communicate with strangers.

_______ 9. I feel relaxed when I communicate with strangers.

_______ 10. I am worried when I communicate with strangers.

To find your score, first reverse the responses for the *odd-numbered* items (i.e., if you wrote 1, make it 5; if you wrote 2, make it 4; if you wrote 3, leave it as 3; if you wrote 4, make it 2; if you wrote 5, make it 1). Next, add the numbers next to each of the items. Scores range from 10 to 50. The higher your score, the more anxiety you experience when interacting with others.

Second, **we may fear that negative behavioral consequences will result from our communication with members of other groups.** We may feel that members of other groups will exploit us, take advantage of us, or try to dominate us. We also may worry about performing poorly in the presence of members of other groups or worry that physical harm or verbal conflict will occur.

Third, **we may fear negative evaluations by members of other groups.** We may fear rejection, ridicule, disapproval, and being stereotyped negatively. These negative evaluations, in turn, can be seen as threats to our social identities. We perceive communication with members of our ingroups as more agreeable and less abrasive than communication with members of outgroups (Hoyle, Pinkley, & Insko, 1989).

Finally, **we may fear negative evaluations by members of our ingroups.** If we interact with members of outgroups, members of our ingroups may disapprove. We may fear that "ingroup members will reject" us, "apply other sanctions," or identify us "with the outgroup" (Stephan & Stephan, 1985, p. 160).

One of the *behavioral consequences* of anxiety is avoidance (Stephan & Stephan, 1985). We avoid members of other groups because it reduces our anxiety. When we are experiencing anxiety and cannot avoid members of other groups, we often terminate the interaction as soon as we can. If there are norms for how to interact with members of other groups, anxiety intensifies our responses; that is, we follow the norms more rigidly. To illustrate, "if the norm prescribes or condones politeness, then individuals will be more polite as they become more anxious" (Stephan & Stephan, 1985, p. 166).

Cognitively, anxiety leads to biases in how we process information. The more anxious we are, the more likely we will focus on the behaviors we expect to see, such as those based on our stereotypes, and the more likely we are to confirm these expectations and not recognize behavior that is inconsistent with our expectations (Stephan & Stephan, 1985). The greater our anxiety, the more we are self-aware and concerned with our self-esteem. When we are highly anxious, we try to make our own group look good in comparison to other groups.

The anxiety we experience when communicating with members of other groups transfers to other *emotions* we experience in the particular situation. Intergroup anxiety amplifies our evaluative reactions to members of other groups; for example, the more anxious we are, the more likely we are to evaluate members of other groups negatively.

We can manage the amount of anxiety we experience when we communicate with members of other groups. Thinking about the behavior in which we need to engage when communicating with members of other groups, for example, can reduce our anxiety about interacting with them (Janis & Mann, 1977). Further, if we focus on finding out as much as we can and forming accurate impressions of members of other groups, the biases we have based on our anxiety and negative expectations are reduced (Neuberg, 1989).

Anger and Communication

We all experience anger at some point in our relationships with others. Experiencing and/or expressing anger can have profound effects on our relationships with other people. To improve our communication and the quality of our relationships with others, we need to understand how we respond when we feel anger. Before proceeding, think about when you experience anger. Answer the following questions:

Under what conditions do you experience anger the most? ________________

____

____

Under what conditions do you experience anger the least? ________________

____

____

How do you respond when you get angry? ________________________

____

____

Your answers to these questions can provide insight into the role of anger in your implicit personal theories of communication. Keep your answers to these questions in mind as you read the remainder of this section.

Defining Anger

As indicated earlier, the provocation that leads to anger is "*a demeaning offense against me or mine*" (Lazarus, 1991, p. 222). The offense involves some slight or injury to our identity, but "even a mere frustration may carry with it the implication that we are less significant or worthy of self-esteem than we would claim or wish" (p. 222). If identity issues are not involved in the situation, we will interpret our feelings as some other goal-incongruent emotion. To illustrate, if we are frustrated and do not perceive that we have been demeaned, we label our feeling as anxiety or shame.

Another aspect of anger is blame. We will see someone as accountable for the threat to our identity. If we see someone else as responsible for the event, we can blame them, and this blame might lead to anger. If we see ourselves as accountable, we will label the feelings as anger, shame, or guilt. Blame alone, however, is not sufficient for us to experience anger. We must also see the person we have blamed for the offense (someone else or ourself) as in control. If we blame someone else for the injury to our identity, we must also see that person as able to control what happened for us to be angry. If the person was not able to control what happened, we will view the situation differently and label the feelings as another emotion, such as sadness.

What makes us angry is a function of our upbringing, but our culture also provides guidelines about anger:

> People everywhere get angry, but they get angry in the service of their culture's rules. Sometimes these rules are explicit ("Thou shalt not covet thy neighbor's wife"); more often they are implicit, disguised in the countless daily actions performed because "That's the way we do things around here." These unstated rules are often not apparent until someone breaks them, and anger is the sign that someone has broken them. It announces that someone is not behaving as (you think) she or he *ought*. (Tavris, 1982, p. 47)

When we feel anger, we assume that people are responsible for their behavior and should behave differently. The expression of anger helps us maintain social control over our own and other people's behavior (Tavris, 1982).

Myths About Anger

There are two major myths regarding anger (Tavris, 1982). **The first myth about anger is that aggression is the instinctive response when we feel angry.** Aggression is a *learned* response to anger; it is not instinctive. Males tend to learn to respond aggressively to anger, while females tend to learn to respond to anger with friendliness. Females, however, can and do learn to respond to anger with aggression. Aggression is not an effective strategy for dealing with anger because it just makes the other person angry or upset.

The second myth about anger is that verbally expressing our anger gets rid of it or makes us feel better. Talking about our anger can make us more angry (Tavris, 1982). Expressing our anger to someone else can lead us to like them less than if we do not express our anger to them. Talking to friends about our anger toward someone else may help us blow off steam, but it does not help us get rid of our anger. Talking with friends may actually make us more angry. This does not imply that we should *not* express our anger when we experience it. Rather, we need to allow the initial intense feelings to pass and think about the consequences of expressing our anger (Skill Exercise 5.4 below is designed to help you do this). There may be times when we need to express our anger to resolve issues with others. The advice "if you can't say something nice about a person, don't say anything at all—at least if you want your anger to dissipate and your associations to remain congenial," however, is worth following (Tavris, 1982, p. 135). Expressing anger puts a damper on our interactions with others (see the "Ballard Street" cartoon).

Factors Influencing Our Tendency to Get Angry

Many different stimuli can arouse us, and if we ignore these stimuli, they can eventually lead us to experience anger over something that normally would not make us angry (Tavris, 1982). If we spend a lot of time in a noisy environment, for example, we become aroused. Similarly, feeling crowded or being held up in traffic leads to arousal. These background stimulants frequently provoke us without our recognizing it. If the provocation goes unrecognized, it will influence our responses to others. If we have experienced background stimulants and then someone does something we do not like, we are likely to blame the other person for our feelings, rather than the stimulants in our environment (Tavris, 1982).

To illustrate the processes being discussed here, consider the following situation. You have just finished driving to school through heavy traffic in a construction area that was very noisy. You meet your friend on the way to class. Your friend starts a conversation with you. You tell your friend that you are running late and want to make it to class on time. Your friend says, "You never have time to talk anymore." As you walk away, you begin to feel upset about your friend's comment. Your tendency when you are on automatic pilot will probably be to blame your friend for your feelings of anger. You might decide that your friend was being aggressive in making the comment. If you are mindful, however, you can recognize that your anger may be due to the tension you experienced driving to school. You, therefore, probably would not react negatively to your friend's

BALLARD STREET by Jerry Van Amerongen. By permission of Jerry Van Amerongen and Creators Syndicate.

comment and respond in a more constructive fashion when you see her or him later.

There are ways we can manage our anger constructively. These are discussed in the next section of this chapter, when our affective resources for effective communication are presented.

Affective Resources for Effective Communication

Our affective resources for effective communication are those emotional orientations that help us to mindfully manage our goal-incongruent emotions when we communicate. Our ability to tolerate ambiguity influences the amount of anxiety we experience in different situations. Our ability to manage our anxiety is critical for improving the quality of our communication. Our ability to manage our anger and our ability to forgive others affects our ability to maintain quality interpersonal relationships. Let's begin the discussion of affective resources for effective communication by looking at tolerance for ambiguity.

Ability to Tolerate Ambiguity

Tolerance for ambiguity is the ability to deal successfully with situations, even when a great deal of information needed to interact effectively is unknown. When we are not able to understand what is taking place in a given situation and we are able to withstand the emotional arousal that occurs, we have tolerance for ambiguity. Those who are able to tolerate ambiguity know that, if they search for additional information, they will be able to figure out what to do.

Our ability to tolerate ambiguity is related to our ability to adjust in new situations:

> The ability to react to new and ambiguous situations with minimal discomfort [or anxiety] has long been thought to be an important asset when adjusting to a new [environment]. . . . Excessive discomfort resulting from being placed in a new or different environment—or from finding the familiar environment altered in some critical ways—can lead to confusion, frustration, and interpersonal hostility. Some people seem better able to adapt well in new environments and adjust quickly to the demands of a changing milieu. (Ruben & Kealey, 1979, p. 19)

People who have a high tolerance for ambiguity are more effective in completing task assignments in new environments than are people with low tolerance for ambiguity. The higher our tolerance for ambiguity, the more we can use all of the communication resources available to us in ambiguous situations, and the more effectively we can communicate.

Tolerance for ambiguity allows us to be emotionally creative in how we respond to others. Emotional creativity involves developing "new and different responses" when we have unfamiliar experiences (Averill & Nunley, 1992, p. 115). When we are emotionally creative, we are able to respond constructively to others and enhance our relationships with them.

Before continuing, think about your tolerance for ambiguity. Take a few minutes to complete Assessment 5.2 now.

Scores on Assessment 5.2 range from 10 to 50. The higher your score, the greater your ability to tolerate ambiguity. If your score is low, you can increase your ability to tolerate ambiguity. When you are mindful of your behavior, you can recognize that you have the ability to gather the information you need to decide how to behave in the situation. Recognizing that you have the ability will make the ambiguous situation less threatening.

Assessment 5.2 *Assessing Your Tolerance for Ambiguity*

The purpose of this questionnaire is to help you assess your orientation toward ambiguity. Respond to each statement indicating the degree to which it is true regarding the way you typically respond: "Always False" (answer 1), "Usually False" (answer 2), "Sometimes False and Sometimes True" (answer 3), "Usually True" (answer 4), or "Always True" (answer 5).

_______ 1. I am not comfortable in new situations.

_______ 2. I deal with unforeseen problems successfully.

_______ 3. I experience discomfort in ambiguous situations.

_______ 4. I am comfortable working on problems when I do not have all of the necessary information.

_______ 5. I am frustrated when things do not go the way I expected.

_______ 6. It is easy for me to adjust in new environments.

_______ 7. I become anxious when I find myself in situations where I am not sure what to do.

_______ 8. I am relaxed in unfamiliar situations.

_______ 9. I am not frustrated when my surroundings are changed without my knowledge.

_______ 10. I am comfortable in situations without clear norms to guide my behavior.

To find your score, first reverse the responses for the *odd-numbered* items (if you wrote 1, make it 5; if you wrote 2, make it 4; if you wrote 3, leave it as 3; if you wrote 4, make it 2; if you wrote 5, make it 1). Next, add the numbers next to each statement. Scores range from 10 to 50. The higher your score, the greater your tolerance for ambiguity.

Ability to Manage Anxiety

Ideally, we want to maintain our anxiety between our minimum and maximum thresholds. To the extent that we can keep our anxiety between the two thresholds, it will facilitate our ability to communicate effectively. Being able to recognize when our anxiety is approaching our thresholds and manage it before it crosses the thresholds, therefore, is an important resource for effective communication. We can begin to recognize where our thresholds are if we pay attention to the physiological feelings associated with our anxiety. To illustrate, if we get sweaty palms when our anxiety is above our maximum threshold, we can use the initial wetness of our palms as a sign that we need to manage our anxiety. It is much easier to manage our anxiety before it goes above our maximum threshold than after it has risen above the threshold.

Whether our anxiety is above or below

We cope in many ways with anger and anxiety. One point is universal, we need to mindfully do something that will restore our calm. Techniques used to accomplish this vary from breathing exercises to hypnotism to yoga.

our thresholds, there are two general issues in managing our anxiety: controlling our bodily symptoms and controlling our worrying thoughts (Kennerley, 1990). There are several physical symptoms associated with anxiety. When we are highly anxious, we might experience respiratory problems, such as difficulty breathing, heart palpitations, dry mouth, muscular tension, or a tension headache.

To manage our anxiety, the most important thing we can do is mindfully break from the situation in which we feel anxious (Prather, 1986). This might mean excusing ourself to leave the room (going to the bathroom is always a viable alternative), or mentally withdrawing for a short period of time. Once we are alone or have mentally withdrawn, we need to calm ourselves and remember that our anxiety is not going to harm us. We can allow our anxious feelings to pass and then return to the situation. To do this, we need to be mindful of our behavior.

Once we break from the situation or have mentally withdrawn, we need to mindfully do something that will restore our calm. We might, for example, just sit still and meditate for a moment or use controlled breathing. One way to practice controlled breathing is to sit up straight and concentrate on our breathing. Mindfully draw in a long breath and focus on inhaling. Then let out the breath, focusing on exhaling. Other techniques we can use to control the physical symptoms associated with anxiety include exercise, yoga, hypnotism, meditation, and progressive muscular relaxation (relaxing the various muscle groups in our bodies in a systematic fashion). The suggestions for defusing panic attacks presented in Reading 5.1 also can be used.

We can control our worrying thoughts (number 4 in Reading 5.1) by using the techniques for overcoming cognitive distortion discussed in Chapter 4. Unless we stop distorting our thought processes, we will not be able to manage our anxiety consistently over long periods of time.

Skill Exercise 5.3 is designed to help you develop a plan for managing your anxiety. Take a few minutes to complete it now.

In completing Skill Exercise 5.3, you had to think about how you would manage your anxiety in particular situations. One thing should be clear from the exercise: thinking about the situation in rational terms leads to developing plans that will allow you to perform effectively in almost any situation. If we

Reading 5.1 TEN WAYS TO DEFUSE PANIC ATTACKS/Ann Landers

1. Remember that although your feelings and symptoms are frightening, they are neither dangerous nor harmful.

2. Understand that what you are experiencing is merely an exaggeration of your normal reactions to stress.

3. Do not fight your feelings or try to wish them away. The more willing you are to face them, the less intense they will become.

4. Don't add to your panic by thinking about what "might happen." If you find yourself asking, "What if?" tell yourself, "So what!"

5. Stay in the present. Be aware of what is happening to you rather than concern yourself with how much worse it might get.

6. Label your fear level from zero to 10 and watch it go up and down. Notice that it doesn't stay at a very high level for more than a few seconds.

7. When you find yourself thinking about fear, change your "what if" thinking. Focus on and perform some simple, manageable task.

8. Notice that when you stop thinking frightening thoughts your anxiety fades.

9. When fear comes, accept it, don't fight it. Wait and give it time to pass. Don't try to escape from it.

10. Be proud of the progress you've made. Think about how good you will feel when the anxiety has passed and you are in total control and at peace.

are not able to manage our anxiety, our anxiety guides our behavior. When we are able to behave mindfully, we can choose how we want to behave and not let our anxiety guide our behavior.

Ability to Manage Anger

The inappropriate expression of anger hinders our conversations and has a destructive influence on our relationships. As indicated earlier, expressing our anger to others is generally not an effective strategy. **Rather than expressing our anger, we need to learn to manage it.** We need to develop new ways we can deal with our anger when we are mindful of our communication.

There are several guidelines that are useful in managing anger (Alberty & Emmons, 1990). First, it is important to recognize that anger is a natural emotion and we do not need to fear experiencing it. Second, we need to remember that we are responsible for our feeling angry. The other person did not make us feel angry. We chose to feel angry. Sometimes other people do things to which anger is an appropriate response, but we still choose to feel angry. Third, we need to recognize that feeling anger and aggressive behavior are not the same thing. We can respond in an assertive fashion, rather than an aggressive fashion. We need to work toward a resolution, not a victory. Fourth, we need to know ourselves and what makes us angry. When we know what makes us angry, we can avoid the situation or

Skill Exercise 5.3 *Managing Anxiety*

When we feel highly anxious, we need to manage our anxiety in order to communicate effectively. Think about how you might manage your anxiety in the situations listed below. In the space provided, describe the concrete steps you could use to manage your anxiety and communicate effectively.

1. You are invited to a party, and you know in advance that you will not know anyone there. You've wanted to get to know some of the people who are attending, but you are afraid that you will not fit into the group attending the party. What can you do to manage the anxiety you experience and create a positive impression on the people at the party? ______

2. Your romantic partner tells you that she or he is concerned about your relationship. You think your partner is going to tell you that she or he wants to break off the relationship, but you want it to continue. What can you do to manage the anxiety you experience? ______

3. You met a person from a different ethnic group. You do not have much experience in interacting with people from this ethnic group. You have a negative stereotype of this person's group but generally see yourself as a nonprejudiced person. You are anxious about how you will communicate with this person. What can you do to manage your anxiety? ______

make sure that we are mindful in such situations.

Skill Exercise 5.4 is designed to help you find out more about how you manage your anger. Take a few minutes to complete it now.

There are many strategies that we can use to manage our anger. **The ability to step back from the situation is an important skill in dealing with our anger.** When we step back from the situation, we need to become mindful and not let the anger guide our response. When we are mindful, we need to remember that, when we "feel provoked, count to ten; and when [we] are also hot, hungry, exercising, walking along a noisy street, booing the opposition in a crowded stadium, driving a car to (or from) work, or disturbed for the forty-fifth time when [we] have a deadline tomorrow, count to a hundred" (Tavris, 1982, p. 177). If we cannot step back from the situation, we can try to relax when we experience anger (Alberty & Em-

Skill Exercise 5.4 ***Managing Anger***

Think of a situation in which you were angry in the past where your response did *not* lead to effective communication.

Briefly describe this situation. ____________

How did you respond in this situation verbally? ____________

nonverbally? ____________

What was the outcome? ____________

What could you have done to manage your anger and communicate more effectively in this situation? ____________

In the future, how might you manage your anger or express it in a more constructive fashion? ____________

mons, 1990). Any of the relaxation techniques discussed under "Ability to Manage Anxiety" can be used.

We also can avoid setting ourselves up to get angry. If we know that we get angry in a certain situation, such as freeway traffic or long lines, we can try to avoid these situations (Alberty & Emmons, 1990). We can "walk around" those situations that we know take away from our peace of mind (Prather, 1986). We also can walk around interactions with specific people if we know that interacting with them takes away from our peace of mind.

Up to this point, the focus has been on managing our anger. We also can help others manage their anger and manage the way that we respond to other people's anger. To help other people deal with their anger, we need to be able to allow them to vent their anger. This is not always easy, but if we realize that it is *their* anger, we can step back and listen to what they say. When others are angry, we need to respond by accepting the fact that they are angry, even if we do not think the anger is warranted. We could say something like, "I realize that you are angry." Responding in this way may require that we take a deep breath and remain calm (this may also be the first thing we need to do before allowing others to vent). We cannot deal with our own or other people's anger when one of us is experiencing intense feelings. We can offer to discuss the situation later, when we are both calm. We should set an exact time and place to discuss it, but this may not always be possible. When we sit down to discuss the other per-

CALVIN AND HOBBES © Watterson. Reprinted with permission of UNIVERSAL PRESS SYNDICATE.

son's anger, we need to use constructive conflict resolution skills (discussed in Chapter 15). In dealing with our own and other people's anger, we need to be able to forgive.

Ability to Forgive and Let Go

We are told that "to err is human, to forgive divine." We may believe in our hearts that forgiveness is the morally correct thing to do, but most of us have a difficult time forgiving those who we think have hurt us. If we hold on to old hurts and do not forgive others, however, the old hurts influence our communication in our current relationships.

To forgive others, we need to recognize that forgiveness "*is an act of the heart, not the body.* And genuine forgiveness contains not even a hint of the supposed necessity to force the mind to reason dishonestly" (Prather, 1986, p. 23). The root of the verb "to forgive" is "to let go, to give up, to cease to harbor" (Prather, 1986). Forgiveness is not forgetting, condoning, absolution, a form of self-sacrifice, or a one-time decision (Simon & Simon, 1991). We cannot forget what others have done, and we should not try. When we forgive, we do not condone or say what others did was acceptable. Forgiving does not involve letting others off the hook for what they have done, nor does it involve our "grinning and bearing it." Finally, forgiveness is not something we do once and forget about. Forgiveness occurs over time as we confront the pain.

Forgiveness is a by-product of the natural healing process. It takes place within us (Simon & Simon, 1991). Forgiveness is a sign of positive self-esteem, because we no longer make things that happened in the past a central aspect of our identity. *Forgiveness* means letting go of the strong emotions attached to past experiences with others. We still remember what happened, but we do not feel strong emotions about it. When we forgive, we recognize that we do not need to hold on to negative feelings, such as grudges, resentments, hatred, or self-pity. We also recognize that we do not need to punish others in order to experience inner peace—nothing we do to punish others will make us feel better about ourselves.

Forgiveness often is necessary to maintain high-quality close relationships with others:

> When wronged by those we love, we seem to devalue years of a relationship—a relationship that may have brought us many joys and which required much intel-

lectual and emotional energy to have lasted so long. Still, with a single harsh statement, a thoughtless act, an unfeeling criticism, we are capable of destroying even the closest of our relationships. . . . We ignore the possibility that in the act of forgiving and showing compassion we are very likely to discover new depths in ourselves and new possibilities for relating in the future. We are too proud. We engage rather in self-defeating activities which keep us from forgiving; beliefs that if we withdraw and run from the situation we will hurt the other and absence will heal us; the fantasy that in avoidance there can be closure; the naive hope that in hurting, shaming, blaming and condemning we will be made to feel better. We fail to realize that when we refuse to engage in forgiving behaviors, it is we who assume the useless weight of hate, pain and vengeance which is never ending, and, instead, weighs upon us rather than the wrongdoer. (Buscaglia, 1984, pp. 96–97)

The importance of forgiveness is illustrated further by the discussion of "Forgiveness Week" in Reading 5.2. Take a moment to read it now.

As suggested in Reading 5.2, we all have people we need to forgive. Failure to forgive these people negatively influences our communication with them *and* our communication with everyone else in our life. Another way to increase our willingness to forgive is to recite the Loving Kindness Meditation:

> If anyone has hurt me or harmed me knowingly or unknowingly in thought, word, or deed, I freely forgive them.
> And I too ask forgiveness if I have hurt anyone or harmed anyone knowingly or unknowingly in thought, word, or deed.
>
> May I be happy
> May I be peaceful
> May I be free
>
> May my friends be happy
> May my friends be peaceful
> May my friends be free
>
> May my enemies be happy
> May my enemies be peaceful
> May my enemies be free
>
> May all beings be happy
> May all beings be peaceful
> May all beings be free.[1]

Skill Exercise 5.5 is designed to help you think about the advantages and disadvantages of forgiving others. Take a few minutes to complete it now.

After completing Skill Exercise 5.5, it should be clear that *not* forgiving others harms us. All grievances that we hold against others influence our peace of mind and ultimately come out in how we communicate with others. When we do not forgive others, it affects us and our relationships with the people we have not forgiven, as well as our relationships with others. If we do not forgive others, we still want to hold their behavior against them. Usually we do not forgive because we are not ready to forgive (Prather, 1986). Forgiveness takes time and a commitment to forgive. To forgive we must let go of our resentments and learn to find peace within ourselves.

Summary

We experience emotions that are congruent with our goals and emotions that are incongruent with our goals. Goal-incongruent emotions are compatible with our achieving our goals

Reading 5.2 FORGIVENESS/Abigail Van Buren

DEAR READERS: Did you know there is an International Forgiveness Week? Well, neither did I until three years ago, when Alice Parenti of Fresno, Calif., wrote to tell me about it. . . .

If you are a card-carrying member of the human race, there is at least one person in your life who needs your forgiveness. Or perhaps it's you who needs to be forgiven, so hop aboard the *mea culpa* bandwagon, let go of those grudges and give your ulcer a chance to heal.

Robert Muller, former assistant secretary general of the United Nations, wrote this lovely piece especially for International Forgiveness Week:

DECIDE TO FORGIVE

Decide to forgive
For resentment is negative
Resentment is poisonous
Resentment diminishes and devours the self.
Be the first to forgive,
To smile and to take the first step.
And you will see happiness bloom
On the face of your human brother or sister.
Be always the first
Do not wait for others to forgive
For by forgiving
You become the master of fate
The fashioner of life
The doer of miracles.
To forgive is the highest,
Most beautiful form of love.
In return you will receive
Untold peace and happiness.

Here is the program for achieving a truly forgiving heart:
Sunday: Forgive yourself.
Monday: Forgive your family.
Tuesday: Forgive your friends and associates.
Wednesday: Forgive across economic lines within your own nation.
Thursday: Forgive across cultural lines within your own nation.
Friday: Forgive across political lines within your own nation.
Saturday: Forgive other nations.
Only the brave know how to forgive. A coward never forgives.
It is not in his [her] nature.

Skill Exercise 5.5 *Forgiveness*

The purpose of this exercise is to help you understand the process of forgiveness. Answer each of the following questions.

Think of a person who you feel has done you harm in the past. Briefly describe what you think this person did to you.

____

____

How did what happened influence the way you think about yourself? __________

____

____

What emotions did you experience when this event happened? __________

____

____

How would "punishing" the other person change the way you think about yourself or make you feel better? __________

____

____

What are the disadvantages of forgiving this person? __________

____

____

What are the advantages of forgiving this person? __________

____

____

What do you need to let go of in order to forgive this person?

____

____

What can you do to forgive this person today? __________

____

____

and goal-incongruent emotions are incompatible with accomplishing our goals. Goal-incongruent emotions include anger, anxiety, disgust, envy, fright, jealousy, sadness, and shame. Goal-congruent emotions include compassion, happiness, hope, love, pride, and relief.

If we express the goal-incongruent emotions we experience without thinking, it often inhibits the effectiveness of our communication with other people. If we do not recognize how we have learned to express our emotions, we are limited in our ways to respond when we experience the various emotions. Once we understand how we typically express our emotions, however, we can consciously choose whether we want to continue to express them this way in the future, or whether we want to express our emotions differently. We do *not* have to express all of the emotions we experience.

We experience some amount of anxiety any time we communicate with others. If our anxiety is above our maximum threshold or below our minimum threshold, we cannot communicate effectively. Effective communication requires that we manage our anxiety so that it is below our maximum threshold and above our minimum threshold. Our anxiety tends to be higher when we communicate with members of other groups than when we communicate with members of our own groups. Our anxiety is high when we communicate with members of other groups because we fear negative consequences.

To communicate effectively, we need to be mindful of our behavior and use the affective resources for communication that are available to us. To deal with our anxiety, we must develop a tolerance for ambiguity and learn techniques to lower the tension associated with anxiety. To deal with our anger we need to learn how to manage it and learn constructive ways to express it. Our ability to forgive also facilitates managing our anger and building healthy relationships with others.

Notes

1. There are many versions of this meditation. This one appeared in *Chop Wood, Carry Water* (Fields, 1984, p. 192).

Journal Reflections

1. *Managing Your Anxiety.* In the next week, try to manage your anxiety in at least two interactions in which you feel that your anxiety is above your threshold for effective communication. In your journal, describe the situations and discuss how your ability to manage your anxiety influenced your level of anxiety.
2. *Managing Your Anger.* Every other day during the next week, stop and count to ten (or a hundred) when you experience anger. On the other days, respond as you typically do if you feel angry. Each time you feel angry, describe the situation and how you behaved in your journal. At the end of the week, review what you wrote in your journal. Which way of responding was most effective? Why?
3. *Forgiving Others.* Think of someone in your life you want to forgive. Using the resources discussed in this chapter, try to forgive the person (keep in mind you do not have to tell the other person what you're doing). How does forgiving the other person affect the way you feel about him or her? How does it affect the way you communicate with him or her?

Study Questions

1. Why is changing the way we interpret situations a successful way of coping with emotions?
2. What differentiates goal-congruent and goal-incongruent emotions?
3. Why does anxiety above our maximum threshold or below our minimum threshold inhibit effective communication?
4. Why do we experience more anxiety when we communicate with people from other groups than when we communicate with people from our own group?
5. What are the consequences of our anxiety for the way we behave in intergroup situations?
6. Why do high levels of anxiety lead to simple information processing?
7. How do our everyday experiences, such as driving on the freeway, influence our emotional responses to others, such as the anger we experience?
8. How can we manage the physical symptoms associated with anxiety?
9. How can we control the worrying thoughts associated with anxiety?
10. How can we manage our anger effectively?
11. How can we respond effectively when others are angry with us?
12. Why do we need to forgive others to communicate effectively?

Suggested Readings

Burns, D. D. (1989). *The feeling good handbook.* New York: William Morrow. David Burns presents techniques for managing our negative emotions in everyday life.

Kennerley, H. (1990). *Managing anxiety: A training manual.* New York: Oxford University

Press. Helen Kennerley describes various techniques for managing anxiety. Among the techniques discussed are progressive relaxation, controlled breathing, and managing panic attacks.

Lazarus, R. S. (1991). *Emotion and adaptation.* New York: Oxford University Press. Richard Lazarus presents a theory of emotion. He discusses how emotions are based on individuals' appraisals of their relationship to their environment. He examines both positive and negative emotions in detail, linking these emotions to individuals' health and adaptation.

Tavris, C. (1982). *Anger: The misunderstood emotion.* New York: Simon & Schuster. Carol Tavris discusses the nature of anger and the cultural rules of anger, as well as the myths of suppressed and unsuppressed anger. She also examines how anger is expressed, differences between males and females, and anger in marriage.

6

STRUCTURAL AND SITUATIONAL INFLUENCES ON COMMUNICATION

In the preceding four chapters, the focus was on individual factors that influence the ways we communicate. Of course, other factors also influence our communication in daily life. Our communication, for example, is affected by structural factors in our society, such as the norms and rules of our culture. To illustrate, when other people ask us how we are, they expect us to say something like "fine" or "okay" without going into details. We know how to respond because of the communication rules we learned as children. Where we are when other people ask us how we are and who the other people are can influence how we answer the question. We answer differently if we are in our physician's office than if we are meeting a friend in the student center. The situation in which we communicate, therefore, influences our communication.

The concept of structure is related closely to the concept of system introduced in Chapter 1. All interpersonal communication takes place within a communication system, such as an interpersonal relationship, a family, or an organization. Systems are dynamic and constantly changing, but at the same time they strive for equilibrium or balance. If we could stop time and look at a system at one point in time, we would be looking at the structure underlying the system. When we talk about *structure* we are focusing on the pattern of relationships among the positions in the system. The *positions* are the relatively stable elements of the structure (Stryker, 1981). The positions in a family, for example, include father (also a husband) and mother (also a wife), as well as daughter and son (also siblings). Attached to each position is a set of shared behavioral expectations for the individuals filling the positions. This set of behavioral expectations is called a role. *Role* is "a term borrowed directly from the theater, [it] is a metaphor intended to denote that conduct adheres to certain 'parts' (or positions) rather than the players who read or recite them" (Sarbin & Allen, 1968, p. 489).

The various positions in a system are linked by communication networks. *Communication networks* are our personal ties with others through which we exchange information, express affect (emotions), and help each other (Albrecht & Adelman, 1984). Our communication networks can be based on the positions we fill, or they can emerge out of our informal interactions with others. In an organization, for example, the formal communication networks are based on the organizational positions workers fill, while the informal communication networks are based on informal interactions among workers in the organization, such as interactions around the coffee machine or over drinks after work.

Communication systems and the structure of those systems influence our communication with others. Our communication, however, also is influenced by the situation in which we are communicating. A *social situation* involves "two or more individuals interacting within a physical setting, in which the interaction has an observable beginning and ending" (Cody & McLaughlin, 1985, p. 264). Knowledge of situations helps us in several ways when we communicate (Cody & McLaughlin, 1985). We use our knowledge of situations as a framework for evaluating other people's behavior. Given our understanding of the roles other people are playing in a situation, we evaluate whether other people perform their roles competently. We use our purpose for being in the situation to interpret other people's behavior. We interpret other people's messages differently, for example, if we are in a situation to complete a task or in a situation to socialize. We make decisions about whether to enter situations based on our understanding of the situation and our perceptions of our competence to interact in the situation. If we do not think that we understand a situation or we think we are not competent to interact in a particular situation, we will try to avoid those situations. We also use our knowledge of situations as guides for how to behave. Our knowledge of situations tells us how we are expected to behave.

Both structural and situational factors affect our communication with others. Let's begin by looking at the structural influences on our communication.

Structural Influences on Communication

When we look at the structural influences on communication, we are concerned with the patterned regularities that influence the ways in which we communicate. The positions we fill and their corresponding roles, as well as our communication networks, influence our communication. There are also structural influences on our communication, which are linked to neither the roles we fill nor the networks in which we are embedded. Cultural norms and rules, for example, help us coordinate our behavior with others. Since norms and rules are the structural factors that have the broadest influence on our communication, we'll begin with them.

Norms and Rules

We know how to interact in the various situations in which we find ourselves because we have learned norms and rules that we can use to guide our behavior. Norms are "blueprints for behavior," and "cultural expectations." *Norms* can be defined as socially shared guidelines for expected and accepted behaviors, violation of which leads to some form of sanction (Gibbs, 1965). The sanctions can vary from a disapproving look to ostracism from a group or even to death. Norms are based in our moral codes.

Rules differ from norms in that rules do not have moral or ethical connotations. Rules are statements of "expected or intended behavior and its outcome. . . . Rules provide a set of mutual expectations, thus rendering the behavior of each person predictable and understandable to the other. . . . The rules partly serve to define the meaning a situation has, and to define the meaning that any given action has within a situation" (Noesjirwan, 1978, pp. 305–306). Rules help us coordinate our behavior with others. We negotiate the rules we use within particular relationships with others, but we are not usually aware of the process.

Norms and rules provide information about what our rights and obligations are in different situations. Norms and rules also provide us with interpretive schemes that are useful in understanding our own and other people's behavior (Giddens, 1984). When we coordinate our behavior with that of others in given situations, we draw on our understanding of the norms and rules to guide our behavior in those situations. The norms and rules provide information that we use to predict other people's behavior. Understanding the norms and rules guiding behavior in a situation usually brings our uncertainty and anxiety within our comfort range (between our minimum and maximum thresholds).

We learn the communication rules of our culture through a variety of sources. We learn them from observing our parents, through our interactions with our peers, from our teachers in school, from religious institutions, and from watching television and movies. Once we have learned communication rules, we tend to follow them without thinking about it when we are communicating on automatic pilot:

> Most people are aware that rules exist in all areas of life and take them into account when engaged in or anticipating interaction with other people. This awareness is part of the organized character of social life. . . . even when people dislike or reject a rule, it may be extremely difficult for them not to obey it, for much everyday life involves opportunities to demonstrate social competency, a factor that may override the will to disobey. Often obedience to the rule is simply reflexive, whereas transgression is effortful. (Birenbaum & Sagarin, 1976, p. 4)

Following a communication rule is only automatic if we grow up in the culture where the rule exists and follow it from a very early age.

If a member of one culture is living in or visiting another culture, obedience to the rules of the new culture takes effort, and violating the rules of the new culture may be automatic. Even though following the rules of our culture tends to be automatic, we can choose whether to follow communication rules. When we are mindfully choosing how to communicate, we can decide which rules we want to follow and which we want to violate in order to accomplish our objectives.

Before proceeding, think about the communication rules you follow and those you choose to violate. Answer the following questions:

> What are some of the rules you follow without thinking about it when you interact with new people? Be as specific as possible. ______________________
>
> ____________________________________
>
> ____________________________________
>
> Are there communication rules that you choose to violate? What rules do you vio-

late frequently? Why do you choose to violate these rules? ______________________

____

____

What effect does violating communication rules have on the way other people respond to you? ______________________

____

____

Your answers to these questions should provide some insight into the role of rules in your implicit personal theory of communication. Keep your answers to these questions in mind as you read the remainder of this section.

People in any culture are aware of some of the rules guiding their behavior, but they are unaware of many others. Even if they are aware that a rule exists, however, they probably cannot articulate all of the specific behavioral expectations associated with the rule. This lack of awareness can be illustrated by something as simple as a handshake. Shaking hands usually takes place when greeting people for the first time in the United States, but what are the rules for shaking hands? Can you tell a person who has never shaken hands before all of the rules necessary to shake hands "correctly"? Many people would say that you grip the other person's extended hand and pump up and down. But is it that simple? What would you do if you met a person for the first time and she or he extended the left hand? That obviously isn't appropriate, because we shake hands with the right hand. What if the other person extends the right hand but does not hold on to your hand and uses a "limp" grip? Is this acceptable? No, probably not. What if the person uses the "correct" grip with the right hand but doesn't stop when you shake hands, continuing to pump up and down, up and down? How would you feel? Comfortable? Uncomfortable? You would probably feel uncomfortable, because the rule is that we pump hands a few (one to three) times and then stop. By now you get the point that shaking hands is not as simple as it may initially seem. It is a complex process with many subtle expectations. We may not be able to explain all of the expectations, but we know when they are violated.

We become aware of the communication rules guiding our behavior when they are violated. When we interact with people from our own groups, such as our culture, our ethnic group, or our social class, our expectations are not violated frequently because people of the same group share relatively similar expectations. When we communicate with people from other groups, however, our behavioral expectations may be violated because people from other groups may have learned a different set of rules. When our expectations are violated, we may react to the other person negatively. There also is the possibility of positive outcomes. When our expectations are violated, for example, we can gain tremendous insight into the rules of our culture and how they influence our behavior. In addition, we come to see alternative behavioral patterns, which we might prefer. In other words, confronting cultural differences offers the possibility of personal growth and cultural change.

Communication rules vary systematically across cultures (Noesjirwan, 1978). To illustrate, in Indonesia (a collectivistic culture) and Australia (an individualistic culture), there is little variation in how people respond to rules within each culture. There are, however, many variations between cultures in the rules guiding communication. Different rules, for example, exist for dealing with other people in waiting rooms and at bus stops. The rule in Indonesia requires individuals to talk to any other person present. The rule for Australians requires individuals to ignore any other person present.

Roles

Rules involve expectations for our behavior in specific situations, while roles are the behavioral expectations attached to the various positions we hold. The roles we play also can be social identities if we consider them important. Not all roles, however, become social identities—only those we consider important in how we define ourselves. Before reading further, take a moment to think about the various roles you play. List the ten most important roles that come to mind in the spaces provided:

1. ____________ 6. ____________
2. ____________ 7. ____________
3. ____________ 8. ____________
4. ____________ 9. ____________
5. ____________ 10. ____________

Now look back at the list you made. Which of these roles was one of the social identities you listed in Chapter 2?

Role Expectations. We learn our role expectations through the same processes whereby we learn the norms and rules of our culture. Like understanding norms and rules, understanding our own and other people's role expectations usually brings our uncertainty and anxiety within our comfort range. **Once we learn the role expectations associated with the positions we hold, we try to conform to these expectations when we communicate on automatic pilot.** Our tendency to conform to a role is a function of how clearly the role is defined and how much consensus there is on how people are expected to behave in that role. The greater the clarity of the role definition and the greater the consensus on the role expectations, the more we tend to conform to role expectations (Stryker & Statham, 1985). Our tendency to conform is due to the fact that role expectations are taken for granted (Bem, 1970). Since we take the behavioral ex-

CATHY © Cathy Guisewite. Reprinted with permission of UNIVERSAL PRESS SYNDICATE. All rights reserved.

pectations for granted, we often assume that our roles cannot be redefined. We can, however, choose to redefine our roles when we are mindful of our communication.

Other people do not always share our role expectations; they may have different expectations for our roles than we do. We may fulfill our own role expectations and not the expectations other people have for us, or we may fulfill other people's expectations and not our own. Failure to live up to role expectations is traumatic to some degree. The trauma we experience when we do not meet role expectations is partly due to other people's responses to our performance (Stryker & Statham, 1985). We want to perform our roles adequately so that other people will view us as competent. It is important, however, to recognize that cooperation from other people is necessary for us to perform our roles adequately. To illustrate, for instructors to perform their roles adequately, the students in the class must cooperate and meet student role expectations, too. If instructors try to hold a discussion in class and the students do not participate, the instructors will not be able to meet their role expectations.

Conflict Among Roles. We play many roles at the same time. A woman who is married, has children, and works, for example, fills the roles of wife and mother in the family, as well as the roles of subordinate and superior at work. She may also fill roles in voluntary organizations such as the PTA, the Chamber of Commerce, and a local political party. There may be conflicts in the behaviors we are expected to perform for one of our roles or there may be expectations for different roles that are in conflict.

The behavioral expectations attached to one position (the behaviors that a person filling one role has to perform) may conflict with each other (Merton, 1957). *Role-set conflict,* therefore, is the conflict that occurs when we are expected to engage in contradictory behavior in the same role. A student, for example, is expected to take several classes at the same time. At times, the behaviors students must perform to fill their role expectations in different classes may not mesh. To illustrate, students often need to study for an exam for one class during the time they should be attending another class.

We also experience conflict between the expectations associated with the different roles we play (Merton, 1957). *Role conflict* exists when we are expected to behave one way based on one of our roles and differently based on another role in a particular situation.

Having it all—family, spouse, career—can cause role conflict. Defining the expectations of each role and prioritizing them is one way we can resolve our role conflicts.

Judges who must sentence their children or physicians who treat members of their family experience role conflict. Many women experience role conflict between their family roles and work roles. If they are expected to take care of household chores like housecleaning and cooking, they will experience role conflict at those points where they have to work late and are also expected to do work around the house. Students who are married and have children may experience role conflict when they try to adequately perform their various roles, such as student, husband/wife, mother/father, and worker.

There are many ways that we can try to resolve our role conflicts. We could, for example, choose to give up one of the roles in conflict. Alternatively, we could modify our expectations for one of the roles and choose to perform it differently. This strategy usually requires that we renegotiate our role with someone else. We can set priorities among the roles in conflict, or we can rotate attention among the roles in conflict. To illustrate, "establishing priorities for roles is common among women who experience conflict between family and work. The problem is often solved by reducing involvement in one role or another. . . . Working women also renegotiate household responsibilities with children . . . as well as spouse" (Stryker & Statham, 1985, p. 338).

Bargaining over role expectations appears to be the preferred way of resolving most role conflicts. This is especially true in intimate relationships, but it also is an effective strategy in work relationships. In bargaining, we are able to define what is important to us and deemphasize what is not important. We can create our roles as we want them to be, rather than having the roles define who we are (Stryker & Statham, 1985).

Before proceeding, look back at the roles you listed earlier. Are any of these roles in conflict? What specific expectations are in conflict? How do you typically try to handle the conflict between these roles? Are there other strategies that you could use to better manage these role conflicts in the future? In order to help you work through these issues, take a few minutes to complete Skill Exercise 6.1 now.

Communication Networks

The positions we fill are linked by communication networks. Communication networks connect individuals to each other through communication (Rogers & Kincaid, 1981). Before proceeding, think about the people with whom you are linked through communication. Answer the following questions:

List the initials of the people with whom you have the closest relationships in the left column, then answer the questions in columns two and three for each person:

Initials	How frequently do you talk with this person?	In what ways are you similar to this person?
____	__________	__________
____	__________	__________
____	__________	__________
____	__________	__________
____	__________	__________

The people you listed are probably those with whom you communicate frequently and with whom you are similar. The people listed are probably central members of your communication network.

When we look at the communication networks in which we are involved, our focus is not on the individuals who are communicating, but on the linkages or social bonds be-

Skill Exercise 6.1 ***Managing Role Conflicts***

The purpose of this exercise is to help you begin to develop a strategy for managing role conflicts. To begin, think of two roles you fill that involve role conflict. That is, two roles where the behavioral expectations for the two roles conflict.

1. What is the first role? ______________
2. What are the behavioral expectations for this role? ______________________________
3. What is the second role? ______________
4. What are the behavioral expectations for this role? ______________________________
5. How do the behavioral expectations listed in questions 2 and 4 conflict? ______________________________
6. How can you best resolve the conflicts in these two roles? ______________________________
7. If your answer to question 6 involved renegotiating one of the roles, how can you renegotiate the role with your role partners (the others involved in your role performance)? List specific communication strategies you can use. ______________________________

tween ourselves and others. We are connected to our society "through relations with other individuals: with kin, friends, coworkers, fellow club members, and so on. We are each the center of a web of social bonds that radiates outward to the people we know intimately, those whom we know well, those whom we know casually, and to the wider society beyond" (Fisher et al., 1977, p. vii). The number of people in our personal networks varies tremendously. The differences in the size of our personal networks is a function of factors such as education, occupation, income, physical attractiveness, social skills, and stage of dating or family life cycle (Milardo, 1986).

Communication Networks Influence Our Behavior. We tend to form communication networks with people who are similar to us in terms of culture, ethnicity, age, social class, beliefs, attitudes, education, and so forth. Our networks with people who are similar to us and with whom we communicate frequently tend to be relatively strong. We rarely obtain new information, however, from individuals who are highly similar to us. Rather, we tend to exchange the same type of information over time with these people. We tend to gain new information from people with whom our ties are relatively weak, such as people we know who are different from us, including those from other cultures or ethnic groups or people with whom we have infrequent contact (people we see every once in a while socially or people we meet every once in a while doing business). Job seekers, for example, find out about possible jobs through their weak ties, not their strong ties (Granovetter, 1973). This phenomenon is referred to as the *strength of weak ties.*

The *size* of our communication networks is an indicator of our degree of interpersonal connectedness (Rogers & Kincaid, 1981). **The more the people in our communication networks know each other, the more integrated our communication networks are.** Figure 6.1 illustrates the difference between an integrated network and a nonintegrated network. The more integrated our communication networks are, the more they influence how we behave. In highly integrated networks, informal norms and communication rules develop, and the members of the networks put informal pressure on one another to conform to these norms and rules.

You can get an idea of how integrated your networks are if you think of the people with whom you communicate most frequently. Put the names of these people in the circles in Figure 6.2. Once you have listed the people, think about who communicates with whom. Draw lines in Figure 6.2 linking the people who normally talk to each other. The more the people with whom you communicate talk to each other, the more integrated your communication networks are.

The communication networks in which we are involved influence our behavior. Being an *isolate* (a person not involved in a network), for example, can have negative consequences, such as suicide, not recovering from illnesses and disabilities, and not being satis-

FIGURE 6.1 Integrated and Nonintegrated Communication Networks

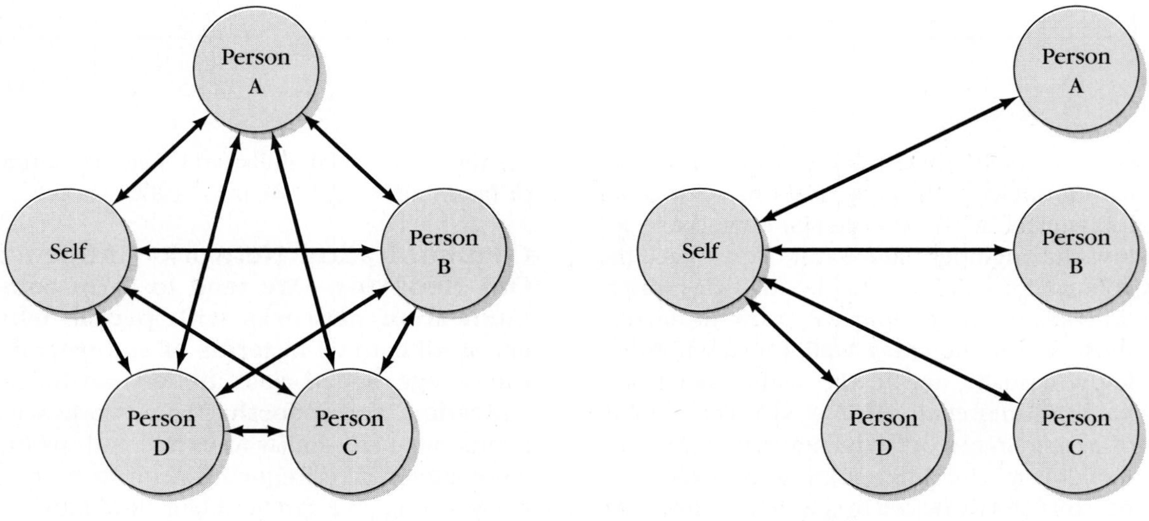

(a) Integrated Network

(b) Nonintegrated Network

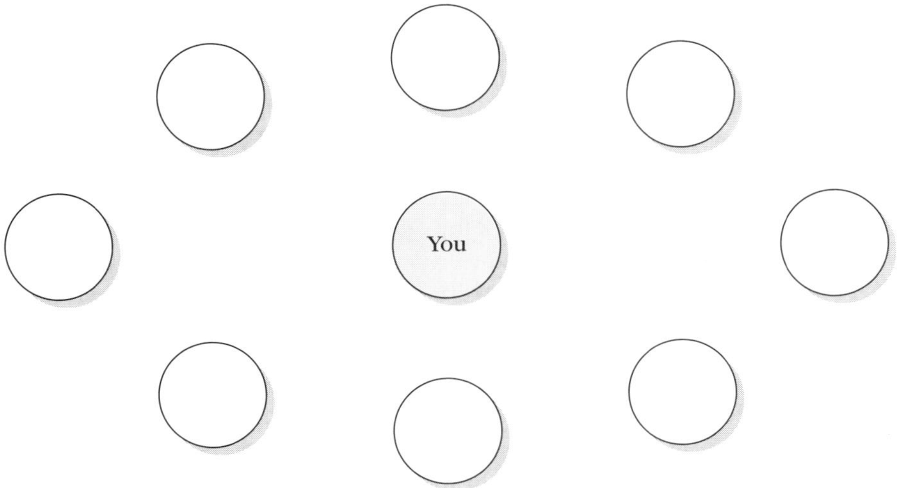

FIGURE 6.2 How Integrated Are Your Communication Networks?

fied with a job. Integrating individuals into communication networks, in contrast, is used frequently as a method to help individuals overcome problems. Examples of this approach include Alcoholics Anonymous and Overeaters Anonymous.

Our involvement in communication networks influences the people with whom we form relationships. Two people often become friends "because they each have many friends in common who know one another. . . . The network members may introduce the two individuals and encourage them to become friends" (Milardo, 1986, p. 156). Involvement in a romantic partner's communication network and perceiving that the members of this network support the relationship also helps us manage our uncertainty and contributes to the development of romantic relationships (Parks & Adelman, 1983). The number of people known in the partner's network appears to be the most important predictor of the de-

JUMP START reprinted by permission of UFS, Inc.

velopment of relationships (Kim & Stiff, 1991). As romantic relationships develop, there is a corresponding increase in the overlap of the partners' communication networks (Milardo, 1982). If there are problems with a partner's networks, it can create problems in the relationship (see Reading 6.1).

Communication Networks and Intergroup Communication. The type of contact we have with members of other groups depends on the structural conditions of the environment (Jaspars & Warnaen, 1982). To illustrate, **feeling "different" depends on the relative numbers of people present** (Kanter, 1977). If there are a large number of people like us present, we do not feel different. If there are only a few other people like us in a large group, in contrast, we probably feel different. In organizations, for example, when there are "tokens," or only a few people who are not part of the majority group, such as women or non-European Americans, these people feel pressure to conform to the numerical majority at the same time they feel different. Because of this pressure, members of the numerical minority may unconsciously try to become invisible and not communicate with the members of the numerical majority.

Our group memberships place constraints on our establishing intergroup relationships (Blau & Schwartz, 1984). The size of our ingroup influences the amount of contact we have with members of outgroups; as the size of our ingroup increases, the likelihood of contact with members of the outgroup decreases and the more likely we are to interact with members of our own group (Blau & Schwartz, 1984). The more members of different groups are present in the environment, the more intergroup contact we have.

The structural conditions discussed to this point influence our communication in all situations. The specific situations in which we communicate also affect our communication.

Reading 6.1 YOU NEVER JUST MARRY EACH OTHER/Dr. Joyce Brothers

DEAR DR. BROTHERS: Both my husband and I deliberately waited until we were "mature" before marrying. My spouse was 35 and I was 34 when we tied that legal knot. Foolish person that I am, I thought we were just marrying each other. I didn't realize I was also marrying his family—and the whole religious and cultural tradition that comes with it. Why didn't someone warn me? I don't happen to share a lot of my in-laws' views, and it is causing trouble.

—D. C.

DEAR D. C.: Most of us need to be reminded now and then that it isn't ever just two people who walk down that aisle and marry. It's more likely to be six, but it can even be eight, 10 or 20, depending on how large the families and how close the clans.

Without question, there's a close connection between how a couple gets along and how each partner relates to his or her family of origin.

One point to remember, however, is that just as couples don't always have to agree with each other or accept each other's point of view, spouses don't necessarily have to accept all the beliefs of the extended family. Each family member needs to develop a spirit of tolerance and respect for diversity.

Situational Influences on Communication

One approach we could use to understand how situations influence our communication is to examine the objective characteristics of the situation, such as the physical location (whether it is a classroom or a living room) and its characteristics. The objective characteristics of situations, however, are not good predictors of our behavior (Cody & McLaughlin, 1985). A better predictor of how people behave in a particular situation is how they perceive the situation.

Situations can be divided into two broad components: the scene and the participants (Brown & Fraser, 1979). These components are further divided to make finer distinctions that can help us understand what happens in specific situations, as indicated in Figure 6.3.

The *scene* tells us the setting and the purpose of the interaction (Brown & Fraser, 1979). The *setting* includes the locale of the interaction, the time of the interaction, and the bystanders observing the interaction. The *purpose* of the interaction focuses on the type of activity in which the individuals are engaged and the subject matter of the conversation. The *type of activity* involves the individuals' goals for the interaction and the roles they are filling, such as professor or student, clerk or customer, and friend. The *subject matter* includes the task being completed and the specific topic of conversation.

The *participants* are divided into two components: the individual participants and the relationships between the participants (Brown & Fraser, 1979). There are two aspects of the *individual participants* that are relevant. People act as individuals based on their personality, physical appearance, moods, or attitudes and also as members of social groups, such as culture, ethnicity, class, sex, and age. There also are two aspects of the *relationships between participants* that influence their behavior: the interpersonal relations between the people communicating (such as whether they like each other or whether they know each other) and the role and category relations (such as the relative difference in power and status between the people).

The participants' perceptions of the situation are critical to understanding their behavior in any situation (Brown & Fraser, 1979). Understanding how perceptions of situations influence our communication behavior is important in improving the quality of our communication. Let's begin by looking at the setting.

Setting

The setting for communication involves the locale of the interaction with others, the bystanders who observe our interaction, and the time of our interaction. We'll begin by looking at locale.

Locale. The physical space in which interaction occurs and the "props" that are present influence the way we communicate. Large spaces provide different opportunities for communication than small spaces. Space divided into many regions, such as offices or hallways, leads to different types of communication than open spaces. The physical appearance of the locale also affects our communication. When we find ourselves in a room we think is ugly, for example, we may experience "discontent, irritability, [and] hostility," whereas being in a room we think is attractive brings about "feelings of comfort, pleasure, [and] enjoyment" (Mintz, 1956, p. 466).

Where interactions take place "offers a host of cues that tell people how to orient themselves" (Turner, 1988, p. 156). **The cues provided by the locale of our interaction**

FIGURE 6.3 Components of Situations *Source:* Adapted from *Social Markers in Speech* by K. Scherer & H. Giles, Speech as a Marker of Situation by P. Brown & C. Fraser. Copyright © 1979 by Cambridge University Press. Reprinted with permission of Cambridge University Press.

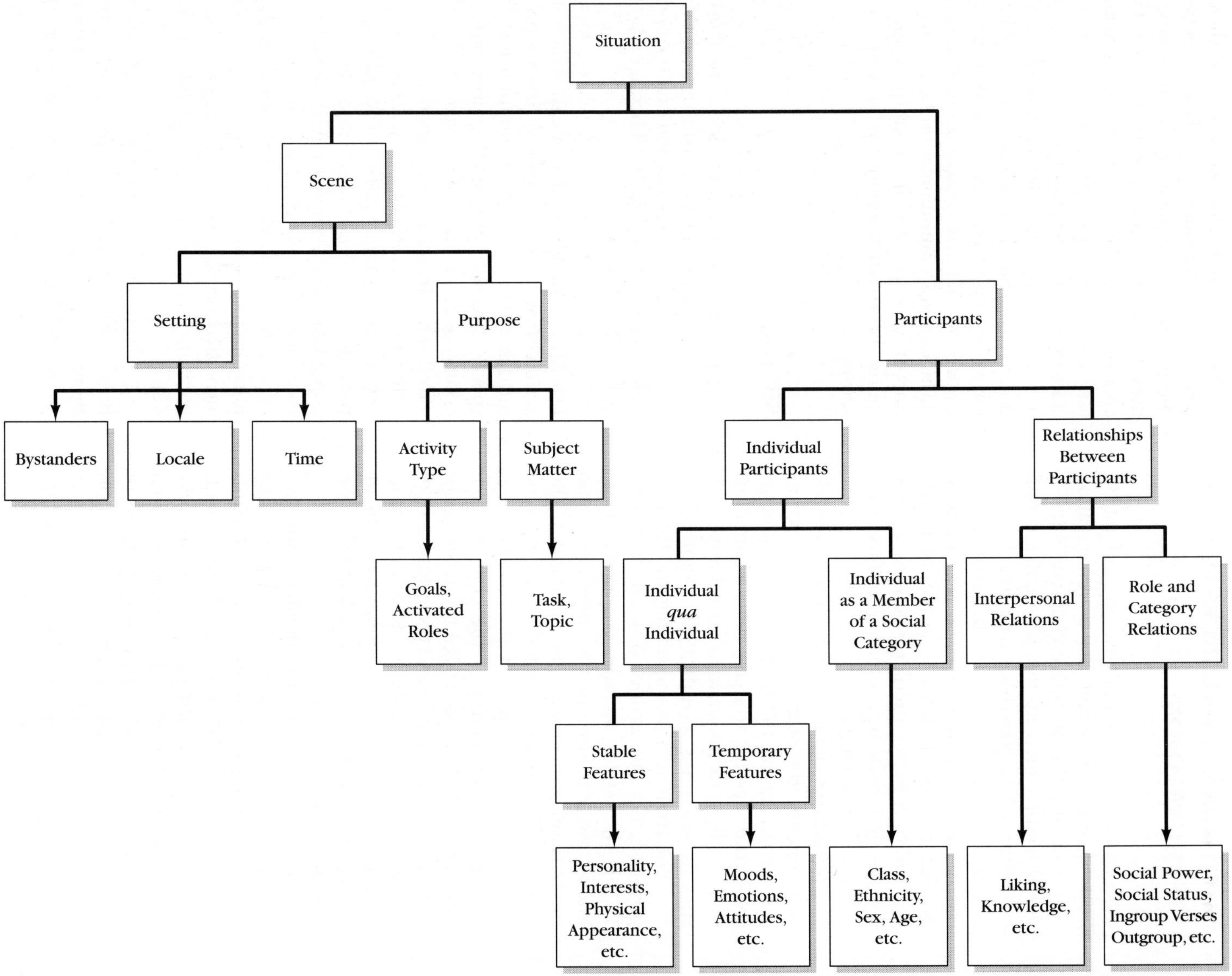

make coordination of our behavior easier and allow for smoother interaction. Without the cues that are provided by the locale, we would have to seek information to know how to expect others to act in different situations. To illustrate, the cues provided by an office tell us how to interact with the people working there. We know, for example, that the person sitting behind the desk as we enter the office is the receptionist. Without this knowledge, we would have to talk with the person in order to figure out what his or her function is in order to know how to talk to her or him.

Bystanders. Who is present in the situation (bystanders) also influences our communication. The status of the people who are observing our behavior influences how we present ourselves (Goffman, 1959). We tend to be more concerned with how we present ourselves if there are high-status bystanders than if the bystanders are low in status. We try to gain other people's favor and use self-enhancing statements more when there are high-status bystanders than when low-status bystanders are present (Ralston, 1985).

The degree to which we are familiar with bystanders also influences how we present ourselves in particular situations. Since people with whom we are familiar already have an impression of us, we tend to be more concerned about the impression we make on unfamiliar bystanders than on familiar bystanders.

The familiarity of the bystanders also influences the way we explain our behavior in situations. The more familiar the people are, the more likely we are to provide justifications for our behavior (try to explain our internal states and how they affected our behavior; Cody & McLaughlin, 1985). Justifications of our behavior, however, do not appear to work well with people we do not know.

Time. The time of our interactions also influences the communication that takes place.

Communication is influenced by the participants, even a bystander. In the presence of an adult, children may present themselves differently than if the adult were not present. High-status bystanders cause us to present ourselves in a more favorable light.

The day of the week influences our mood, and our mood in turn influences the way we communicate. Our moods are more positive on weekends than on weekdays (Stone et al., 1985). The quality of our communication appears to be highest on weekends and lowest on Tuesdays and Fridays (Duck et al., 1991). Conflict tends to be highest on Wednesdays, and the value we attach to our interactions is lowest on Mondays. While there are no clear explanations for this phenomenon, it is apparent that the time of our interactions influences our communication.

Purpose

The purpose of our interaction with others is based on the type of activity in which we are engaged and the subject matter we are discussing. Let's begin with type of activity.

Type of Activity. The type of activity in which we are engaged influences the scripts we use to guide our behavior. **The more we engage in particular activities, the more likely we are to learn scripts for them.** A *script* is as "a coherent sequence of events expected by the individual, involving him [or her] either as a participant or an observer" (Abelson, 1976, p. 33). Scripts are cognitive structures that help us to understand the situations in which we find ourselves. Scripts therefore help us reduce the uncertainty we have about various situations (Berger & Bradac, 1982). We learn scripts by participating in the situation or by observing others participating (Abelson, 1976). We have learned both task-oriented and nontask-oriented scripts. To illustrate, we learned the task-oriented script for ordering in a restaurant by observing our parents do it when we were young children, and we learned the nontask-oriented script of getting to know others by participating in it as children and watching our peers get to know others. We have learned thousands of different scripts.

In a situation, we have to figure out whether we have a script for the situation and what our role in the script is. This process, however, takes place at relatively low levels of awareness. Once we recognize the script, we know basically how we are expected to behave in the situation, and we can communicate on automatic pilot. Scripts provide guides for the conversations we have in different scenes. Although our conversations around different activities such as getting to know someone are routine, they are also flexible and adaptive (Kellermann, 1991). We use small, learned "chunks" of conversational behavior to adapt to topic changes in conversations (these chunks are called *memory organization packets*). To illustrate, when we meet someone for the first time, we might discuss the situation in which we find ourselves, the reason we are there, the weather, where we live, where we were born, and people we know in common. There is no strict order in which we discuss these things, but the six topics all occur early in "getting to know you" scripts.

Memory organization packets tend to be discussed in the order of the clusters shown in Figure 6.4 (Kellermann, 1991). The topics in cluster 1 tend to be discussed before those in cluster 2, cluster 2 before cluster 3, and so forth. Some topics fit in more than one cluster. These topics allow the conversation to stay at one level or move to the next. To illustrate how memory organization packets are used in conversations, consider one side of two conversations:

Conversation 1
Hi. (greeting)
How are you? (health)
Isn't the Bay Area expensive? (present situation)
Where do you live? (where live)
What do you do? (what do you do)
What do you like to do for fun? (interests)
Do you have any brothers or sisters? (family)
You sound like you're doing well. (compliments)
Well, I've got to go. (reason for terminating)
Bye. (good-byes)

Conversation 2
Hi. (greeting)
My name is Kathy. (introduction)
How are you? (health)
Where are you from? (hometown)
Do you know John Doe? (persons known in common)

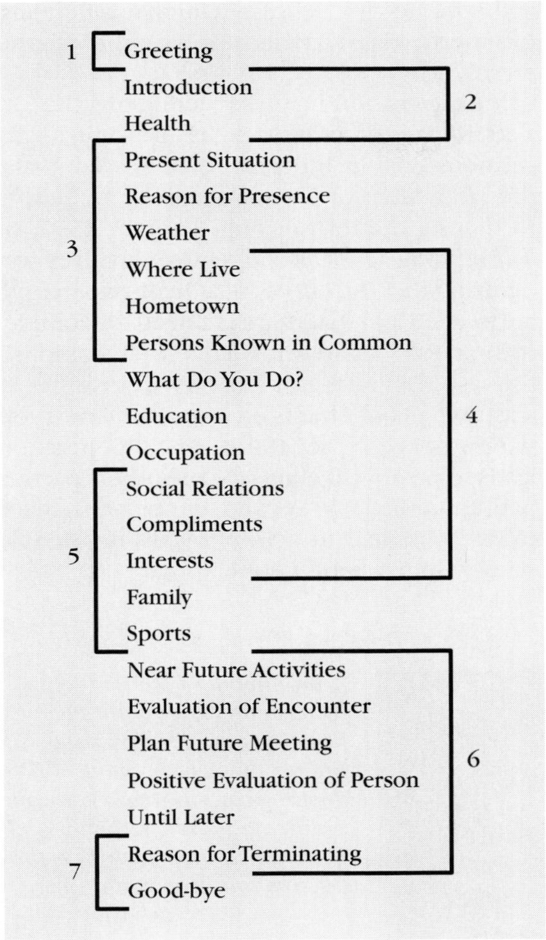

FIGURE 6.4 Memory Organization Packets for Initial Interactions *Source:* Adapted from *Human Communication Research,* Vol. 17 from The Conversational Mop II by K. Kellerman, p. 385–414. Copyright © 1991 by Sage Publications. Reprinted with permission.

> What are you majoring in? (education)
> Do you like to play tennis? (sports)
> Maybe we could get together sometime. (future activity)
> It was nice to meet you. (positive evaluation)
> Catch you later. (until later)
> Bye. (good-byes)
> (Kellermann, 1991, p. 389)

Although the two conversations are different, each generally follows the ordering of topics for initial interactions outlined in Figure 6.4.

Memory organization packets help us predict how other people will behave and therefore help us reduce uncertainty. If someone violates our expectations based on our memory organization packets, we may not know how to respond, and our uncertainty may increase. When this occurs, we have to consciously think about how to respond to the other person. If the other person consistently deviates, we may see his or her behavior as too unpredictable and decide not to pursue forming a relationship with her or him. This is an important issue in the development of interpersonal relationships, which is discussed in more detail in Chapter 12.

We have memory organization packets not only for initial interactions, but also for many other routine forms of conversations. Our memory organization packets are divided

SINGLE SLICES © Peter Kohlsaat, October 22, 1992, Los Angeles Times Syndicate. Reprinted with permission.

Having just broken up with her boyfriend, Sal isn't yet quite ready for small talk.

into two general categories: task oriented and nontask oriented. How we initially define the situation on this dimension influences which memory organization packet we use. It is important to keep in mind, however, that two individuals may define the situation differently on this dimension and select different memory organization packets. When this occurs, the individuals must negotiate how to define the situation. It also is necessary to recognize that cultural values and norms influence the content and ordering of memory organization packets.

Subject Matter. The task on which we are working and the topic being discussed affect our communication in any situation. Whether we define situations as cooperative or competitive influences our perceptions of the task, and whether we define situations as intimate or superficial influences how we approach the topic.

Cooperation involves "acting together, in a coordinated way at work, leisure, or in social relationships, in the pursuit of shared goals, the enjoyment of the joint activity, or simply furthering the relationship" (Argyle, 1991, p. 4). Defining a task as cooperative involves recognizing that the efforts of at least two people are needed and that there is a need for complementary skills and knowledge to accomplish the task. Defining tasks as cooperative has at least two major effects on our communication with others (Argyle, 1991). First, cooperation leads to positive feelings for the others participating on the task. Second, cooperation leads to interpersonal attraction toward the people with whom we are cooperating.

A product development team brings employees from various functions together. By cooperating on the development of a greeting card the team can communicate more effectively and accomplish their task in a productive and timely manner.

Our individualistic and collectivistic cultural identities influence the degree to which we perceive situations as cooperative or competitive. Collectivists in Hong Kong, for example, perceive situations as more cooperative than individualists in Australia. Individualists in Australia, in contrast, perceive the same situations as more competitive than collectivists in Hong Kong (Forgas & Bond, 1985).

How we perceive the topic of conversations varies on the intimate-superficial dimension of situations. Some topics are perceived to be more intimate than others. In the United States, for example, telling someone where we were born, what we do for a living, our political party affiliation, and so forth is considered relatively superficial. Telling someone about our love life, in contrast, is considered intimate. There appears to be consistency in the topics considered to be intimate and superficial across cultures. To illustrate, tastes and opinions are viewed as most appropriate topics for conversation, while physical attributes and personality traits are the least preferred topics for conversation, in Japan and the United States (Barnlund, 1975).

Individual Participants

We perceive the people with whom we interact as members of social groups and as individuals. Let's begin by looking at individuals as unique people.

Individuals as Individuals. Stable characteristics of individuals, such as their personality, physical appearance, and interests, influence how they respond to us and how we respond to them in specific situations (Brown & Fraser, 1979). One personality characteristic that influences the way we behave in particular situations is self-monitoring. *Self-monitoring* involves "self-observations and self-control guided by situational cues to social appropriateness" (Snyder, 1974, p. 526). High self-monitors are people "who, out of a concern for social appropriateness, [are] particularly sensitive to the expression and self-presentation of others in social situations and [use] those cues as guidelines for monitoring" the way they present themselves (p. 528). High self-monitors deliberately behave in a manner they believe is required in a social situation. Low self-monitors, in contrast, do not try to meet situational demands, but rather behave in a manner consistent with their values, attitudes, and beliefs.

High self-monitors prefer to interact in situations that provide clear cues as to how they are expected to behave, while low self-monitors prefer situations in which they can be themselves (Snyder & Gangestad, 1982). High self-monitors prefer situations in which they can engage in particular activities with specific people (Snyder, Gangestad, & Simpson, 1983). Low self-monitors, in contrast, prefer situations in which they can be with friends who are like themselves.

Other personality characteristics also influence how we approach situations. Recall, for example, the discussion of communication apprehension in Chapter 3. To illustrate, we may be apprehensive about communicating in public or in meetings, but not apprehensive about communicating in dyadic (two-person) situations. Personality characteristics, such as loneliness and shyness, influence the plans we make for dealing with different social situations. The less lonely and the less shy we are, for example, the more effective are our plans for getting to know a new roommate (Berger & Bell, 1988).

In addition to stable characteristics such as our personalities, our moods, attitudes, and emotions influence how we respond in situations and how others respond to them (Brown & Fraser, 1979). These characteristics differ from our personality in that our moods, emotions, and attitudes are temporary. Reading 6.2 indicates how our moods and emotions influence other people's impressions of us and how they respond to us in different situations.

Our moods, emotions, and attitudes are not the only temporary aspects of our behavior that influence how others respond to us in different situations. Our speech patterns also influence the impressions others form of us and the ways they respond to us. "Standard [dialect] speakers are more positively perceived and judged than nonstandard [dialect] speakers" (Haslett, 1990, p. 332).

Individuals as Members of Groups. Our group memberships and the group memberships of those with whom we are interacting influence how we define various situations. The ways that we are socialized into the various groups of which we are members tell us how to define situations and how to expect others to behave in these situations. Other people's group memberships influence whether we define situations as interpersonal or intergroup in nature. When we define situations as interpersonal, our personal identities influence our behavior more than our social identities, and our predictions of their behavior are based mainly on other people's unique characteristics (psychological data). When we define situations as mainly intergroup, our so-

Reading 6.2 GOOD VIBES VS. BIG BRAINS

What impresses a new boss more: attitude or ability? If your answer is ability, think again. Attitude—especially a negative one—might be the determining factor in your relationship with a new employer.

"We found that supervisors were able to pick up on negative traits such as anger, hostility, or irritability early in the relationship," reports David V. Day, Ph.D., assistant professor of psychology at Penn State. "These traits can destroy a good working relationship almost before it begins."

Even if a new employee has considerable ability, a negative attitude is what may stick in the employer's mind. And once that first impression is formed, it's hard to change. "Negative personality traits make a more powerful and long-lasting impression than positive ones," notes Day. "And even the most gifted employees are unlikely to join the supervisor's inner circle if they are perceived as angry, irritable, or depressed."

In his study, co-authored with Elona C. Crain, of Tulane University, undergraduate student "leaders" had to pick who they wanted to work with in an exercise. Their choices were based both on results from a mental-ability test and a questionnaire measuring positive and negative feelings and emotions. The results: the leaders favored good vibes over big brains.

Can you suppress negative feelings and fool the boss? Attitudes, especially negative ones, are often revealed through facial expressions and body language.

Day found that these hard-and-fast first impressions are part of an effort by the boss to find his own group within the employee pool. The "in" group gets choice assignments and more flexibility in how they work; the "outs" are saddled with more structure and drudgework. This herding happens quickly—forget about the three-month probationary period—and it's hard to change once you've been branded.

cial identities influence our behavior more than our personal identities, and our predictions of other people's behavior are based on their group memberships or the roles they fill (cultural or sociological data).

There are many specific group memberships that influence how we communicate in the situations in which we find ourselves. Group memberships such as age, sex, occupation, social class, religion, and income provide markers of individuals' status in different situations (Haslett, 1990). These status makers in turn are related to the power individuals have in those situations.

Some of the groups into which we categorize others involve some degree of stigmatization. *Stigmatization* involves discounting others because they are different (Goffman, 1963). Our expectations for how people we perceive to be stigmatized will behave in a situation are different from our expectations for those we do not perceive to be stigmatized. People who are disabled, for example, often are perceived to be stigmatized by nondisabled people. Whether or not we perceive a person to be disabled influences how we communicate with her or him. A blind person describes how a taxi driver's communication changed when the taxi driver found out that he was blind:

> I could tell at first that the taxi driver didn't know that I was blind because for a while there he was quite a conversationalist. Then he asked me what these sticks were for (a collapsible cane). I told him it was a cane, and then he got so different. . . . He didn't talk about the same things as he did at first. (Davis, 1977, p. 85)

It appears that the taxi driver initially defined the situation as interpersonal in nature, and when he discovered that the passenger was blind, he redefined the situation as intergroup in nature.

Relationships between Participants

The relationships between the participants in situations influence their communication. Both the interpersonal relations and the roles and categories the individuals are filling affect the way people behave in situations. Let's begin by looking at interpersonal relations.

Interpersonal Relations. One of the major factors influencing the interpersonal relations between participants as individuals is the degree to which they are attracted to each other. Probably the most important factors influencing the attraction between participants as individuals is the degree to which they *perceive* themselves to be similar. When we are free to choose the people with whom we communicate, we tend to select people like us (Rogers & Bhowmik, 1971). It often is assumed that communication between people who are similar is more effective than communication between dissimilar people. Although this is accepted widely, **moderate dissimilarities between communicators who are generally similar may bring about the most effective communication** (Simons, Berkowitz, & Moyer, 1970). One reason is that the similarities motivate the participants to want to communicate effectively, while the dissimilarities lead the participants to be sufficiently aware of differences that they watch out for misinterpretations.

Dissimilarity "is enjoyable when the interaction is brief, when the differences are few and on peripheral beliefs, and when the chance of rejection is small, that is, when the costs of pursuing dissimilar relations are negligible relative to the rewards" (Knapp cited in

Crockett & Friedman, 1980, p. 91). Perceived dissimilarities can be overcome if people have a chance to interact (Sunnafrank & Miller, 1981).

Role and Category Relations. The roles we are filling influence our communication in terms of the degree to which we define situations as formal or informal. In the United States, for example, if we perceive that we are interacting with our boss in a work situation, we probably define the situation as formal. If we are interacting with our boss at a party, on the other hand, we might define the situation as informal. At the party, we may assume that our boss is filling the role of friend and therefore define the situation as informal rather than formal.

The extent to which we define a situation as formal or informal influences many aspects of our behavior. When we define situations as formal, we tend to use standard speech patterns (Furnham, 1986). When we view the situation as informal, in contrast, we may use a nonstandard dialect, such as a speech dialect based on our ethnicity or the region of the country in which we live. When talking in formal situations we also speak slowly and attempt to use correct grammar. In informal situations we may speak rapidly and not worry much about our grammar.

How we categorize other people influences our communication in terms of the degree to which we define situations as between people who are equal or unequal. When the participants in a social situation are not equal in status, the higher-status people can define the situation by the speech patterns they use (Giles & Hewstone, 1982). Respect and authority often are established by using standard, formal speech patterns rather than using nonstandard dialects (such as a regional or ethnic dialect) and informal speech patterns. Once status is established using formal language, for example, people can switch to using informal language to foster a relaxed atmosphere. If the higher-status people begin using a speech pattern designed to define the situation as informal and their authority is questioned, they are likely to switch to more formal speech patterns. If the lower-status people perceive that they are being treated unfairly in a particular situation, they can choose to redefine the situation with the speech patterns they use. To illustrate, the lower-status people might use their ingroup speech patterns to change the definition of the situation from being based on status factors to defining the situation in terms of demonstrating solidarity with members of the ingroup.

SUMMARY

Structural and situational factors influence how we communicate with others. Structural factors include the norms and communication rules of our culture, the roles we play, and the communication networks in which we are involved. The communication rules of our culture provide mutual expectations that help us predict and understand each other. We are not highly aware of the rules guiding our behavior, but we become aware of rules when other people violate them. Although we tend to follow communication rules automatically, we can choose to violate these rules when we are mindful of our communication.

Our roles provide guidelines for how we are expected to communicate when we are filling various positions in society, such as professor, student, wife, or father. We tend to take our role expectations for granted and assume that other people have the same expectations that we do. Other people's expectations, however, often are different from ours. We may experience conflict in the behavioral expectations associated with one of our roles (role-set conflict) or the behavioral expectations for the different roles we play may conflict (role conflict).

The communication networks in which we are involved influence who we meet, the relationships we form, and the communication in our relationships. We tend to form communication networks with people who are similar to us. The more integrated our communication networks are, the more they influence our behavior. Our networks with members of our own groups tend to be more integrated than our networks with members of other groups.

Situations are multifaceted phenomena. The scene and the participants affect our communication. The scene includes the setting (locale, time, bystanders) and the purpose of the interaction (type of activity, subject matter). The participants include the individuals themselves (as individuals, as members of groups) and the relations between the participants (interpersonal relations, roles and categories). Objective characteristics of situations are not good predictors of other people's behavior, but their perceptions of situations can be used to predict their behavior.

Journal Reflections

1. *Understanding Your Role Expectations.* We fill many different roles every day. We are more aware of what is expected of us in some of these roles than in others. Over the next week, pay attention to the various roles you fill. When you recognize a role you fill, try to isolate the behavioral expectations associated with the role. What expectations do you have for filling the role? What expectations do others have for you in this role? Are there important inconsistencies in your expectations and others' expectations? In addition to paying attention to the various roles you fill, pay attention to conflicts that arise among the various roles. How did you manage these conflicts? Is there something you want to do differently in the future to better manage role conflicts?
2. *Understanding Your Communication Networks.* Over the next week, pay attention to your communication networks. Which of these networks are strong links and which are weak links? What types of information do you obtain from the various members of your communication networks? To what extent are your communication networks integrated (see Figure 6.1)?
3. *Understanding How Situations Influence Your Communication.* In the next week, pay attention to how your behavior varies as a function of different situations. What dimensions do you personally use to understand situations? Are there particular situations in which you feel more comfortable than others? How do you adapt your communication to the situations in which you find yourselves?

Study Questions

1. How are norms and communication rules similar and different?
2. Why is following rules automatic?
3. What is the difference between positions and roles?
4. How is role conflict different from role-set conflict?
5. What strategies can we use to manage role conflicts?
6. How do our communication networks influence our communication?
7. How does the status of the bystanders influence our communication?
8. How do memory organization packets operate in conversations?
9. What are the effects of cooperation on interpersonal communication?
10. How do high and low self-monitors approach situations differently?
11. What is the relationship between similarity and attraction?
12. How do status differences influence our definitions of situations?

Suggested Readings

Argyle, M., Furnham, A., & Graham, J. (1981). *Social situations.* Cambridge: Cambridge University Press. In this book, Michael Argyle and his associates summarize research on social situations. They examine how we define situations and how overt behavior varies across situations.

Edgerton, R. B. (1985). *Rules, exceptions, and social order.* Berkeley: University of California Press. Roger Edgerton examines how rules emerge in culture. Edgerton points out that most rules have exceptions. He discusses how an individual's status can exempt him or her from following a rule and how we are exempted from following some rules in particular social settings.

Forgas, J. P. (Ed.). (1985). *Language and social situations.* New York: Springer-Verlag. This is an edited book on the use of language in social situations. The authors address issues such as how situations influence the production of discourse, how the requests we make vary across situations, how situations influence our perceptions of others' language, and how situations influence our lack of fluency.

Rogers, E., & Kincaid, D. L. (1981). *Communication networks.* New York: Free Press. This is one of the few books devoted to communication networks. Rogers and Kincaid outline the various methods for studying communication networks and summarize the major research finding on communication networks.

Part Two

Skill Resourcefulness

7

PERCEPTION AND EXPECTATIONS

Any time we interact with other people, we have expectations for how they will behave. Our expectations influence the way that we perceive and interpret other people's behavior. Our relations with other people are based on our expectations for how they will behave, as well as on our perceptions and interpretations of their behavior, not on the actual behavior in which other people engage. Other people's reactions to us also are based on their expectations, perceptions, and interpretations of our behavior, not on our actual behavior. Many of the misunderstandings that occur when we communicate with others are a result of not recognizing that our behavior is based on our expectations, perceptions, and interpretations, not on actual behavior.

Perception is the process of selecting cues from the environment, organizing these cues into some coherent pattern, and interpreting the pattern. Our perceptions of other people's behavior are highly biased, and we generally are not aware of these biases or how they affect our communication. If we do not understand how our perceptions are biased, we cannot communicate effectively. There is one skill, perception checking, that we can use to determine the accuracy of our perceptions and improve the quality of our communication. To communicate effectively, we also need to understand what our expectations for other people's behavior are. Our expectations are based on our stereotypes and our attitudes, such as our ethnocentrism, prejudice, sexism, and ageism. Let's begin by looking at the general process of perception.

The Perception Process

If we had to pay attention to *all* of the stimuli in our environment, we would experience information overload. To avoid overloading ourselves, we pay attention only to those aspects of other people or the situation that are essential to what we are doing (Bruner, 1958). We might, for example, pay attention to the color of a person's skin, but not notice its texture; or we might pay attention to what others say, but not what they are wearing. Our perceptions of others, therefore, are highly selective, and generally we are not aware of how we select information from our environment.

Our Perceptions Are Biased

Selecting information from our environment and forming images takes place unconsciously; we do not consciously decide on the things to which we pay attention (Bateson, 1979). We are conscious of the results of our perceptions (what we "see"), but what we "see" is manufactured in our brain. What we see does not exist as we see it because "all experience is subjective" (Bateson, 1979, p. 31). Two people looking at the same article of clothing, for example, "see" it somewhat differently. The way they see the article of clothing is influenced by their personal tastes in clothing. Our presuppositions and expectations influence the information that we select from the environment and what we see (expectations are discussed in detail below).

Our perceptions are always a function of our interactions with specific people in specific situations (Ittelson & Cantril, 1954). We would perceive the same message spoken by Person A and Person B in the same situation differently. We also would interpret the same message said by the same person in Situation 1 and Situation 2 slightly differently. The difference in our perceptions may not be large, but there would be a difference. Our perceptions are influenced by many factors, including our culture, our ethnicity, our sex, our background experiences, and our needs. The "Cathy" cartoon, for example, illustrates how males and females might perceive the same situation differently. Our perceptions overlap with those of others only to the extent that we share common experiences. Although our perceptions are based on our interactions with others, we mistakenly assume that our perceptions are real and exist outside of our minds.

Difficulties in communication with other people may arise because we mistakenly assume that we perceive and observe other people in an unbiased way. This, however, is not the case. Our perceptions are highly selective and, often, biased. Our past experiences are one source of bias in our perceptions. If, for example, your mother was quiet before she got angry and exploded at you, you may perceive that other people are getting angry when they are quiet. Our previous experiences with particular people also can bias our perception of their current behavior. To illustrate, early in your relationship with another person he or she may not have self-disclosed her or his feelings to you. You perceived the person as closed. If the other person tells you that he or she is angry at a later stage of the relationship, you may not perceive this as personal information because of your assumption.

Our emotional states also bias our perceptions. **Our moods provide a lens through which we interpret our own and other people's behavior.** When we are feeling irritable or discouraged, for example, we perceive other people's behavior differently than when we are feeling calm or happy. Other biases in our perceptions are a function of how we categorize events and people and our expectations about how they will behave.

Perceptions Involve Categorizations. To make sense of situations, we select information from our environment and organize it in some way. We try to find meaningful patterns.

CATHY © Cathy Guisewite. Reprinted with permission of UNIVERSAL PRESS SYNDICATE. All rights reserved.

We do this by putting things or people into categories. Categorization allows "us to structure and give coherence to our general knowledge about people and the social world, providing typical patterns of behavior and the range of likely variation between types of people and their characteristic actions and attributes" (Cantor, Mischel, & Schwartz, 1982, p. 34).

When we categorize something, we group people or events on the basis of characteristics they have in common and ignore aspects they do not have in common. Since we cannot deal with massive amounts of information, our categorizations are based only on selected characteristics of the person or event. In categorizing, we ignore some characteristics in order to classify people or events. Once we have created the category, we assume that things within the category are similar and that things in different categories are different. To illustrate, we can classify photographic film as black and white or color, but in doing this we ignore another important quality of film—its speed of exposure. With respect to people, we might classify them as hostile, but in so doing we ignore other qualities they have, such as being helpful to others in need. Once formed, however, we take the category for granted, and it influences how we respond to other people. We therefore might never consider asking people we have categorized as hostile for help.

Events and people "assume a distinctive identity only through being differentiated from other things, and their meaning is always a function of the particular mental compartment in which we place them" (Zerubavel, 1991, p. 3). Once we have created the categories, we assume there are gaps between them. When we communicate on automatic pilot, these gaps reinforce our belief that the categories are separate and distinct. It is important to keep in mind, however, that we created the categories in the first place and that the gaps or differences between the categories are a result of the way we created the categories. To illustrate, to create the categories "talkative people" and "quiet people," we must use some criteria to determine talkativeness, such as the amount of time people talk. Once we form these categories, we assume, when we communicate on automatic pilot, that there are significant differences between talkative and quiet people, such as talkative people are friendly and shy people are not. We can nevertheless recognize similarities between talkative people and quiet people when we are mindful of our communication.

Rigid Categories Inhibit Effective Communication. Creating categories is a natural part of the perceptual process. Problems in communication emerge when we rigidly maintain the boundaries between categories. People with rigid categories try to classify everything and everyone into specific categories (Zerubavel, 1991). When something does not clearly fit one category, it threatens the thought processes of people with rigid category systems. People with rigid category systems experience anxiety or fear when confronted with something or someone that cannot be categorized (Zerubavel, 1991). People with rigid categories also tend to make inaccurate predictions and explanations of other people's behavior.

Forcing events or people into mutually exclusive categories biases our perceptions. **If our categories are held rigidly, we do not recognize any differences between people within our categories and have difficulty recategorizing people based on new information we learn about them.** If our categories are rigid, we may categorize someone as blind, for example, and see *all* blind people as alike. All blind people, however, are not alike. To communicate effectively with someone who is blind, we must be able to recognize how he or she is like other blind people *and* how she or he is different from other blind people. Similarly, if our categories are rigid, we might categorize people as untrustworthy and refuse to consider reclassifying them, even when confronted with consistent evidence that they are behaving positively toward us.

If our mental structures are flexible and elastic, we can "break away from the mental cages in which we so often lock ourselves" (Zerubavel, 1991, p. 122). **Having flexible categories facilitates effective communication.** If we recognize that we tend to have rigid categories, we can consciously choose to be more flexible when we are mindful of our communication. Only when we are mindful can we draw on new resources for effective communication.

When we are mindful, one thing we can do to overcome the biases in our perceptions is to look for exceptions. Once we recognize a single exception, it helps us to stop cognitive distortions that may be due to the either/or thinking that we use when we communicate on automatic pilot (Weiner-Davis, 1992). To illustrate, if we categorize our romantic partners as shy, we should try to think of times when they are talkative. When we recognize that there are times when they are talkative, we will not view them as always shy. This simple change in perceptions will lead to more accurate perceptions.

Perception Checking

When two people are talking, it is common for them to perceive the communication somewhat differently. Much of the time when we communicate, small differences in perceptions are not problematic. At times, however, even small differences in perceptions can lead to ineffective communication and negative consequences for our relationships. If others do not directly tell us what they are thinking or feeling, our perceptions can be inaccurate. When this occurs, perception checking is a valuable skill to have among our communication resources. To illustrate, imagine seeing your romantic partner walking in the park with someone, close together and laughing. In this situation, many of us would think that there is something going on between our partner and the other person. We might become jealous and confront our partner the next time we see her or him. Our jealousy could lead to a major conflict. There are, however, many reasons why our partner might be walking close to someone in a park and laughing. Rather than confronting our partner and creating a major uproar, we could use the perception checking skill to find out if our perceptions are correct. If our perceptions are not accurate, perception checking will help us avoid a major conflict.

The Process of Perception Checking. The purpose of perception checking is to make sure that our perceptions of other people's thoughts and feelings are accurate. If we assume that we understand other people's thoughts and feelings when they are not totally clear, misunderstandings will occur. This is particularly true when the thoughts or

As an android from television's Star Trek: The Next Generation, *Lieutenant Commander Data is to be free of judgment and incapable of emotion. Still, Data uses his perception processes to assess the feelings of his crew mates. We use perception processes, too. But as humans our communication is affected by our biases and we must be aware and keep them in check.*

feelings are not expressed directly. Perception checking sends the relational message that we want to understand other people. Perception checking provides us with an opportunity to make sure, before we act, that our interpretations of other people's behavior are what they meant. Perception checking helps reduce uncertainty for the person doing the perception checking. Checking perceptions also can reduce anxiety for both people involved, because it helps each recognize that their need for a common, shared view of the world is being met. Perception checking therefore increases the likelihood that we will communicate effectively.

Perception checking involves three processes. First, we have to describe other people's behavior. Second, we have to give our interpretation of other people's thoughts and/or feelings. In doing this, we *must* refrain from evaluating or judging other people's thoughts or feelings. Recall the difference between description, interpretation, and evaluation discussed in Chapter 4. Third, we need to ask other people if our perceptions are accurate. To illustrate, suppose you see someone enter a room and slam the door. You assume that the other person is angry. To check your perception in this situation, you could say something like, "I heard you slam the door. I guess you're angry. Are you?" This comment describes your observation of the other person's behavior, gives your interpretation of the other person's feelings without any evaluation, and asks the other person if your perception is correct. If in this situation you had said, "Why on earth are you mad?" or "You shouldn't slam the door," you would *not* be checking your perceptions. Rather, you would be judging the other person's feelings and implying that they are inappropriate.

If we are not sure what another person feels, we can still check our perceptions. The statement, "I'm not sure from your facial expression whether you are hurt or angry. Which is it?" is a form of perception checking. Alternatively, we can use the skill exercise for recognizing interpretations presented in Chapter 4 to try to figure out how the other person is interpreting the situation before we check our perceptions.

Sometimes we may think we are checking our perceptions when we actually are not. If we do not describe other people's behavior, give our interpretation, and ask if our interpretation is correct, we are not checking our perceptions. Just asking a question is not perception checking. "Are you angry with me?" and "Why are you mad at me?" are not perception checks. These questions send the relational message that the person doing the perception check knows what the other person is thinking or feeling. Asking someone, "Why are you mad at me?" also has an influence on the person asking the question. If we ask a question like this, we are not likely to consider that the other person is not mad at us. Speaking for the other person also is not checking our perceptions. If we say, "You're always depressed," we are not checking our perception. If we say, "You seem to be tired a lot lately, and you don't smile much. I assume you're depressed. Are you?" we would be checking our perceptions.

There are several important things to keep in mind about perception checking. If the person doing the perception checking does not change his or her perceptions after the other person says, "No. I'm not feeling . . . ," then the perception check will not improve the quality of communication. Rather, it will inhibit the possibility of effective communication. The other person will interpret the message from the person doing the perception checking as not believing what he or she said and really not wanting to understand her or his feelings.

The person responding to the perception check also has a responsibility for the quality of the communication taking place. For communication to be effective, the person responding to the perception check needs to tell the truth. If someone says to us, "You're yelling at me. I guess you're angry. Are you?" we need to tell the truth. If we are angry and say "no," then our anger will still influence the way we communicate, and the other person will not be able to respond appropriately. If we say "no," we have a responsibility to manage our anger for communication to be effective. If we do not manage our anger so that it does not influence our communication, we have lied to the other person, and it will affect our relationship.

Skill Practice. Skill Exercise 7.1 is designed to help you practice perception check-

Skill Exercise 7.1 *Perception Checking*

Perception checking involves (1) telling another person what you perceived, (2) how you interpreted what you perceived, and (3) soliciting feedback on your interpretation. Most people do not engage in perception checking when they communicate on automatic pilot. For each of the following situations, indicate what your typical response might be if you are on automatic pilot, and how you might check your perceptions if you are mindful of your communication.

1. You and your romantic partner go to a party where you do not know anyone. After you arrive at the party, your partner goes off to talk with someone else, and he or she does not talk with you again for almost two hours. In fact, your partner ignores you the one time you approach him or her to talk. You feel uncomfortable being left alone for this length of time. You interpret your partner's behavior as indicating that she or he is mad at you.

   How would you typically respond? ____
   ____
   ____
   ____

   How would you use perception checking to discuss why your partner did not talk with you for so long? ____________
   ____
   ____
   ____
   ____

2. You see a friend in the student center and walk toward the person. You think the other person sees you, but she or he turns around and walks the other way. You interpret the other person's behavior as indicating that he or she does not want to talk with you.

   How would you typically respond next time you see this person? ____________
   ____
   ____
   ____

   How could you use perception checking to find out why your friend walked away the last time you saw her or him?
   ____
   ____
   ____
   ____

ing. Take a few minutes to complete the exercise now.

Checking our perceptions is *not* something most of us do frequently in our everyday communication. Using this skill in your everyday communication with others may feel awkward at first. The more you use it, however, the more natural it will become because you will develop a perception checking script. Also, the more you engage in perception checking, the more likely it will become one of your resources for communication when you are on automatic pilot.

Perception checking is one of the simplest and most powerful techniques we can use to improve the quality of our communication. Of course, we should not use perception checking all the time. It is appropriate to use perception checking when we think that there is a chance that our perceptions may not be accurate or when it is important that we base our behavior on accurate perceptions. Keep in mind that our perceptions are inaccurate much more than we think they are. Also, it is important to keep in mind that perception checking involves direct communication, and therefore, it is more comfortable for individualists than for collectivists to do perception checking. If you are an individualist communicating with a collectivist, it is important to keep in mind that collectivists may not feel comfortable answering direct questions. You may have to check your perceptions indirectly by asking for information or looking for other clues about the person's feelings.

Expectations for Other People's Behavior

Our perceptions of others are influenced by our expectations for their behavior. Our *expectations* are our anticipations of future events or of how others will behave or communicate with us. Our expectations are derived in large part from the social norms and communication rules we learned as children. They also emerge from our experiences with others, observations of our own behavior, the mass media, and our ingroups.

When we communicate with others, expectations also emerge from the attitudes and the stereotypes we hold of other people's groups. *Attitudes* are learned predispositions "to respond in an evaluative (from extremely favorable to extremely unfavorable) manner toward some attitude object" (Davidson & Thompson, 1980, p. 27). In other words, our attitudes predispose us to perceive others in a positive or negative way, and to behave in a positive or negative manner toward them. *Stereotypes* are "pictures in our heads" of people in a particular category (Lippman, 1936). Our stereotypes, like our attitudes, predispose us to perceive others and to behave in certain ways. Stereotypes are discussed in more detail later in this chapter. Let's begin by looking at the nature of expectations.

The Nature of Expectations

When we interact with others, we "develop expectations about each other's behavior, not only in the sense that [we] are able to predict the regularities, but also in the sense that [we] develop preferences about how others *should* behave" (Jackson, 1964, p. 225). Our culture and ethnicity provide guidelines for appropriate behavior and for the expectations we use to judge other people's communication. To illustrate, in the European American middle-class subculture in the United States,

> one expects normal speakers to be reasonably fluent and coherent in their discourse, to refrain from erratic movements or emotional outbursts, and to adhere to

> politeness norms. Generally, normative behaviors are positively valued. If one keeps a polite distance and shows an appropriate level of interest in one's conversational partner, for instance, such behavior should be favorably received. (Burgoon & Hale, 1988, p. 61)

The problem is that the rules for what is a polite distance and what constitutes an emotional outburst vary across cultures and subcultures within a culture.

We can have positive or negative expectations for other people's behavior. Our expectations can create self-fulfilling prophecies. We expect other people to behave positively or negatively toward us, and we, therefore, behave toward them in a way consistent with our expectations. Our behavior, in turn, leads them to behave as we expected them to behave. To illustrate, if we have a negative expectation of how other people will behave, we will behave in a negative way toward them when we are communicating on automatic pilot. Because we behave negatively toward them, they behave negatively toward us when they are communicating on automatic pilot, even if they initially intended to behave positively toward us. Our expectation, therefore, is fulfilled.

When we have negative expectations, we tend to evaluate other people negatively, and when we have positive expectations, we tend to evaluate them positively (Burgoon & LePoire, 1993). Negative expectations lead to uncertainty and anxiety, especially in intergroup interactions (Gudykunst, 1993). Positive expectations, in contrast, tend to lead to reductions in uncertainty and anxiety.

If other people violate our expectations sufficiently, we become aware of the violations and have to assess the situation (Burgoon & Hale, 1988). In other words, violations of our expectations lead to some degree of mindfulness. The degree to which other people provide us with rewards affects how we evaluate the violation and the person committing it (Burgoon & Hale, 1988). As used here, "rewards" do not refer to money (although it might be a consideration if the other person is our boss or a client). Rather, rewards include the benefits, such as prestige or affection, that we obtain from our interactions with other people. When other people provide us with rewards, we tend to choose the most positive of the possible interpretations of violations of our expectations; "for example, increased proximity during conversation may be taken as a sign of affiliation if committed by a high reward person but as a sign of aggressiveness if committed by a low reward person" (Burgoon & Hale, 1988, p. 63). To illustrate, if a friend stands close to us, we may interpret the behavior as indicating that the person likes us. If someone we dislike stands close to us, we may interpret the behavior as an attempt to intimidate us.

Positively evaluated violations of our expectations have positive consequences for our communication, such as fewer misinterpretations or increases in the intimacy of our relationships (Burgoon & Hale, 1988). Negatively evaluated violations, in contrast, generally lead to negative outcomes, such as misinterpretations or decreases in the intimacy of our relationships.

Our expectations for other people's behavior are the result of many factors. Our attitudes, such as ethnocentrism, prejudice, sexism, and ageism, and the stereotypes we have of others create expectations when we communicate. Let's begin by looking at stereotypes.

Stereotypes

Stereotypes, as defined previously, are our mental pictures of the people we have placed in a particular social category. Stereotyping is

The social norms and communication rules we learn as children influence the expectations we hold throughout our lives. Stereotypes, though, can lead to wrong predictions about other people's behavior. As we communicate we must be aware of our stereotypes so we can compensate for the assumptions we draw.

the natural result of the communication process. **We cannot communicate with people we do not know without using stereotypes.** Our initial predictions about other people's behavior must, out of necessity, be based on the stereotypes we have about their culture, ethnic group, gender, or any other group of which they are a member until we get to know them as individuals.

Stereotyping involves three processes (Hewstone & Brown, 1986). First, we categorize other people based on observable characteristics such as their ethnicity, disability, and gender. Second, we assume that a set of characteristics applies to all (or most) of the members of the group in which we categorize other people. We assume that people within the group are similar to one another and different from people who are not members of the group. Third, when we communicate on automatic pilot, we assume that the characteristics associated with the group apply to individuals we categorize in the group.

We learn our stereotypes from many sources, such as our parents, the way members of our ingroups talk about other groups, our interactions with members of other groups, the mass media (newspapers, television, radio), and books we read. Our stereotypes can be positive or negative. Before proceeding, think about the different groups with which you have contact, such as cultural groups, ethnic groups, gender groups, disability groups, occupations, fraternities/sororities, and so forth. Answer the following questions:

> Of the groups with which you have contact, about which groups do you have stereotypes you consider to be positive? (List specific groups.) ____________________
>
> ____________________________________
>
> ____________________________________
>
> To what extent do you think that the members of these various groups would

agree that the traits you associate with them are positive? ________________

____

____

Of the groups with which you have contact, about which groups do you have stereotypes that you consider to be negative? (List specific groups.) ________________

____

____

Your answers to these questions should provide insight into the role of stereotypes in your implicit personal theory of communication. Keep your answers to these questions in mind as you read the remainder of this section.

Negative stereotypes create anxiety and lead to inaccurate predictions and explanations of other people's behavior (Gudykunst, 1993). The problem for effective communication is not that we have stereotypes, but rather that we make predictions of other people's behavior and act based on our stereotypes when we communicate on automatic pilot. When we are mindful, we can choose to recognize that individuals may not fit our stereotypes, and we can therefore make more accurate predictions of their behavior.

Stereotypes and Communication. We all place others in social categories and have stereotypes of people in those categories. Our stereotypes influence our perception of what people in a particular category are like. Stereotyping results from overestimating the association between group membership and psychological attributes (Hewstone & Giles, 1986). Although there may be some relationship between group membership and the psychological characteristics of members, it is much smaller than we assume when we communicate on automatic pilot.

Stereotypes influence the way we process information (Hewstone & Giles, 1986). We tend to remember favorable information about our ingroups and unfavorable information about outgroups. This, in turn, affects the way

NON SEQUITUR © 1994, The Washington Post Writers Group. Reprinted with permission.

we interpret incoming messages from members of ingroups and outgroups. We interpret incoming messages in a way that is consistent with our stereotypes when we are not mindful. Sorority and fraternity members, for example, know how much money they raise for charity, but nonmembers may not recall this information even after reading it in the student newspaper because it is inconsistent with their stereotypes of fraternities and sororities.

Stereotypes create expectations regarding how members of other groups will behave (Hewstone & Giles, 1986). Stereotypes are activated automatically when we categorize others (Devine, 1989). Unconsciously, we assume that our expectations are correct, and we behave as though they are. We also unconsciously try to confirm our expectations when we communicate with members of other groups. Reading 7.1 illustrates how stereotypes of the elderly create expectations for their behavior.

Our stereotypes constrain other people's patterns of communication and lead to stereotype-confirming communication. Stated differently, stereotypes create self-fulfilling prophecies. We tend to see behavior that confirms our expectations, even when it is absent. We ignore disconfirming evidence when we communicate on automatic pilot. If we assume other people are unfriendly, for example, and communicate with them based on this assumption, they will appear unfriendly to us even if they are actually friendly.

Stereotypes, in and of themselves, do not lead to miscommunication and/or communication breakdowns. **If stereotypes are held rigidly, we will make inaccurate predictions of other people's behavior, and**

Reading 7.1 OLD AGE SHOULDN'T SLOW HER DOWN/Dr. Joyce Brothers

DEAR DR. BROTHERS: I adore my 75-year-old grandmother, but I'm concerned because she doesn't seem to know, or accept, how old she is.

She wants to go around the world, not first class, but third class, and this is dangerous. She's been a widow for 10 years, but she always seems to have a man around, and I worry about this because I don't think she's cautious enough.

How can I get her to slow down a bit and act her age?

—J.O.

DEAR J.O.: I don't think you should. It sounds to me as if what she's doing is right for her. She probably has always needed more stimulation. Sitting at home trying to be the stereotypical senior citizen probably would bore her.

There are many myths about old age and the aging process that still dominate our thinking. Studies indicate that older people who shatter the stereotype not only live longer but also enjoy themselves more. Nonconformists tend to grow into healthier old people.

While I'm sure you love your grandmother and want what you think is best for her, it's important to remember that added years do not make one less of an individual. Your grandmother may be much more adept at protecting herself than you think. I strongly suspect that if she weren't, she wouldn't be where she is today.

There's really no such thing as "acting one's age" after adolescence. Age isn't necessarily related to how people think, feel or act.

misunderstandings will occur. Simple stereotypes of other groups also can lead to misunderstandings. Simple stereotypes are stereotypes involving only a few traits associated with the group. In order to increase our effectiveness in communicating with members of other groups, we need to increase the complexity of our stereotypes. Increasing the complexity of our stereotypes involves associating more traits with the group being stereotyped and creating subcategories within the group. We also need to question our unconscious assumption that most or all members of a group fit a single stereotype (Stephan & Rosenfield, 1982). In other words, we need to be willing to modify the content of our stereotypes and hold them flexibly.

Assessing your Stereotypes. Assessment 7.1 is designed to help you understand

Assessment 7.1 *Assessing Your Stereotypes*

The purpose of this questionnaire is to help you understand what your stereotypes of your own and other groups are. Several adjectives are listed below and there is space for you to add adjectives if the one you want to use is not listed. Since stereotypes are specific to particular groups, you will have to think of specific groups. Think of one group of which you are a member (e.g., your cultural or ethnic group) and an outgroup (e.g., another culture or ethnic group). Put a check mark in the column "My Group" next to the adjectives that apply to your group. Put a check mark in the column marked "Other Group" next to the adjectives that apply to the outgroup you have selected. After you put your check marks down, go back through the list and rate each adjective you checked in terms of how favorable a quality the adjective is: 1 = very unfavorable, 2 = moderately unfavorable, 3 = neither favorable nor unfavorable, 4 = moderately favorable, and 5 = very favorable. Put these ratings in the column to the right of the adjectives.

My Group	Other Group		Favorableness
________	________	Intelligent	________
________	________	Materialistic	________
________	________	Ambitious	________
________	________	Industrious	________
________	________	Compassionate	________
________	________	Deceitful	________
________	________	Conservative	________
________	________	Practical	________
________	________	Shrewd	________
________	________	Arrogant	________
________	________	Aggressive	________
________	________	Warm	________
________	________	Sophisticated	________
________	________	Conceited	________
________	________	Neat	________
________	________	Alert	________

Assessment 7.1 *Continued*

My Group	Other Group		Favorableness
______	______	Friendly	______
______	______	Cooperative	______
______	______	Impulsive	______
______	______	Stubborn	______
______	______	Conventional	______
______	______	Progressive	______
______	______	Sly	______
______	______	Tradition-loving	______
______	______	Pleasure-loving	______
______	______	Competitive	______
______	______	Honest	______
______	______	Modern	______
______	______	Emotional	______
______	______	Logical	______
______	______	Sincere	______
______	______	______	______
______	______	______	______

The adjectives you checked constitute the content of your stereotypes. To find out how favorable the stereotypes are add the numbers next to the adjectives you checked and divide by the number of adjectives you checked for that group. Compute separate favorableness scores for the stereotype of your group and the other group. Scores range from 1 to 5. The higher the score, the more favorable your stereotype.

your stereotypes. To complete this assessment, you need to think of one of your ingroups (such as your ethnicity or sex) and an outgroup (such as another ethnic group or the opposite sex). You can fill this assessment out for several different groups if you use different marks or ink colors. (*Note:* Do not erase your original marks; you will want to be able to compare the content of your different stereotypes.) Take a few minutes to complete the assessment now.

You completed Assessment 7.1 for two groups. In order to understand how stereotypes fit into your implicit theory of communication, it would be a good idea to complete this assessment for several different groups (including age groups, disabilities, and so forth). This will tell you the content of the categories you use to communicate with members of other groups. You can then use this information in your communication with members of other groups. When we have negative stereotypes, for example, it creates negative expectations for our interactions with members of other groups.

The important thing to keep in mind about your stereotypes is that the content of your stereotypes and the favorability you assign to the traits in your stereotypes create expectations for your own and other people's behavior. It is critical that we remember that, although some people—possibly even a majority of the people—in a category may share a trait, the trait will *never* apply to all, or even most, members of a category.

Our stereotypes create expectations for how people in a category will behave. Our expectations also are affected by our attitudes toward other groups. Let's begin by looking at the most general attitude that influences our interactions with others: ethnocentrism.

Ethnocentrism

Ethnocentrism is the view that "one's own group is the center of everything, and all others are scaled and rated with reference to it. . . . the most important fact is that ethnocentrism leads people to exaggerate and intensify everything in their own folkways which is peculiar and which differentiates them from others" (Sumner, 1940, p. 13). In other words, ethnocentrism is our tendency to identify with our ingroups, such as our ethnic group, culture, gender, age group, family or social class, and to evaluate outgroups and their members according to our ingroup's standards. We can be ethnocentric with respect to any of our ingroups.

We are all ethnocentric to some degree. This is unavoidable. Because of our ethnocentrism, we tend to view our ingroup's values and ways of doing things as the "right" and natural values and ways of doing things. As a major consequence of this, our ingroup's values and ways of doing things are seen as superior to outgroups' values and ways of doing things. When we are highly ethnocentric, we divide the world into "us" and "them."

Cultural relativism is the opposite of ethnocentrism. Being *culturally relative* involves recognizing that we can only understand the behavior of members of other groups in the context of their group. If we try to understand the behavior of members of other groups

Businesses today know that catering to a variety of customer types is good for business. The use of bilingual signs decreases the psychological distance between the business and its customers.

JUMP START reprinted by permission of UFS, Inc.

using our own group's standards, we will inevitably misinterpret their behavior. If we are very high in ethnocentrism, we are very low in cultural relativism; if we are very low in ethnocentrism, we are very high in cultural relativism.

High levels of ethnocentrism lead to anxiety when we communicate with members of other groups (Stephan & Stephan, 1985). High levels of ethnocentrism also lead us to make inaccurate predictions and explanations for the behavior of members of other groups. The reason for this is that highly ethnocentric people use their own group's perspective for interpreting the behavior of members of other groups.

Assessing your Ethnocentrism. Assessment 7.2 is designed to assess your ethnocentrism. Take a few minutes to complete it now.

The higher your score on Assessment 7.2, the greater your ethnocentrism. There is nothing wrong with a high score, but it is important to remember that people who are highly ethnocentric will interpret other people's behavior using their group's standards. This may lead to misunderstandings. Even if we are highly ethnocentric, we can choose to interpret other people's behavior in a culturally relativistic way when we are mindful of our communication. High levels of ethnocentrism also will lead us to use ethnocentric speech.

Ethnocentric Speech. The attitudes we hold influence the way we speak to other people. We use the way we speak to other people to increase or decrease the psychological distance between us. We may, for example, select specific words or ways of talking to increase or decrease the psychological distance between us and members of other groups. The psychological distance we establish by the way we communicate affects the degree to which we keep other people "at arm's length" or allow them to get close to us. Our ethnocentrism influences the psychological distance we establish with members of different groups (Lukens, 1978). Five psychological distances can be isolated, based on different levels of ethnocentrism and cultural relativism.[1] Figure 7.1 isolates the psychological distances as five positions on a continuum from very low cultural relativism/very high ethnocentrism to very high cultural relativism/very low ethnocentrism.

The *distance of disparagement* involves very high levels of ethnocentrism and very low levels of cultural relativism (Lukens, 1978). Communication at this distance reflects animosity of the ingroup toward the outgroup and occurs when the two groups are in com-

Assessment 7.2 *Assessing Your Ethnocentrism*

The purpose of this questionnaire is to assess your ethnocentrism. Respond to each statement by indicating the degree to which the statement is true regarding the way you typically think about yourself. When you think about yourself, is the statement "Always False" (answer 1), "Mostly False" (answer 2), "Sometimes True and Sometimes False" (answer 3), "Mostly True" (answer 4), or "Always True" (answer 5)? Answer honestly, not how you think you should be.

_______ 1. I do not apply my values when judging people who are different.

_______ 2. I see people who are similar to me as virtuous.

_______ 3. I cooperate with people who are different.

_______ 4. I prefer to associate with people who are like me.

_______ 5. I trust people who are different.

_______ 6. I am obedient to authorities.

_______ 7. I do not fear members of other groups.

_______ 8. I try to maintain distance from members of other groups.

_______ 9. I blame other groups for troubles I have.

_______ 10. I believe that my values are universal values.

To find your score, first reverse the responses for the *odd numbered* items (i.e., if you wrote 1, make it 5; if you wrote 2, make it 4; if you wrote 3, leave it as 3; if you wrote 4, make it 2; if you wrote 5, make it 1). Next, add the numbers next to each of the statements. Scores range from 10 to 50. The higher the score, the more ethnocentric you are.

petition for the same resources. It is characterized by the use of pejorative (negative) expressions about the outgroup and the use of ethnophaulisms (name calling). The important thing to keep in mind about pejorative expressions is that it is how other people perceive the expression that makes it pejorative, not our intent. At the distance of disparagement, imitation and mockery of speech styles are used (Lukens, 1978). The use of "baby talk" with elderly people is one example of language that is perceived as mockery. Communicating at the distance of disparagement is a form of aggressive communication (see Chapter 3) because it involves attacking other people's self-concepts (specifically their social identities).

The *distance of avoidance* is established in order to avoid or minimize contact with members of an outgroup (Lukens, 1978). One technique commonly used to accomplish this is the use of an ingroup dialect. Using the

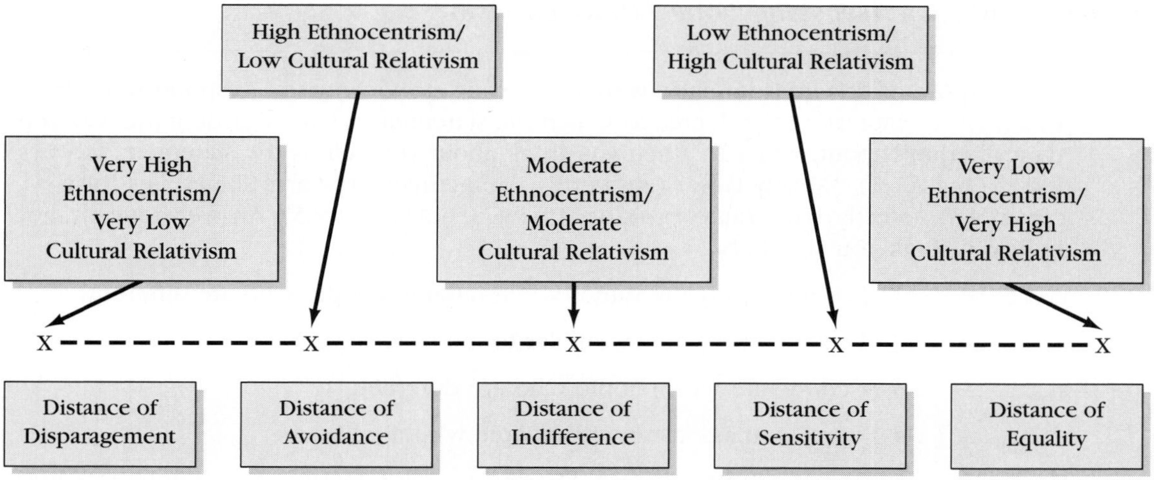

FIGURE 7.1 Psychological Distances

ingroup dialect can make ingroup members appear unapproachable to outgroup members. The use of jargon common to an ingroup, such as computer experts' use of "computerese," can have the same effect as the use of dialects. At this distance, members of the ingroup also may use terms of solidarity. Feelings of ingroup pride and solidarity are increased through the use of such expressions as *Viva La Raza.* Another way that people establish a distance of avoidance is through the use of high-context messages or restricted codes. When high-context messages are used, listeners must understand the context to understand what is said. If listeners do not understand the context, they cannot participate in the ongoing interaction.

The *distance of indifference* is the speech form used when group differences are not recognized and there is an insensitivity to other groups' perspectives (Lukens, 1978). One example of the speech used at this distance is "foreigner talk," the form of speech used when talking to people who are not native speakers of a language. It usually takes the form of loud and slow speech patterns, exaggerated pronunciation, and simplification such as deletion of articles. We often assume that, "if we speak slowly enough or loudly enough, anyone can understand us" (Downs, 1971, p. 19). This style of speech, however, tends to be perceived by others as patronizing and condescending. The use of idiomatic expressions—such as "black sheep," "black list," "black magic," "low person on the totem pole," "Indian giver," "Jew them down," "Mexican standoff," and "the blind leading the blind"—suggest indifference to other groups' points of view.

The *distance of sensitivity* reveals a sensitivity to group differences (Gudykunst & Kim, 1984). Speech at this level reflects a desire to decrease the psychological distance between ourselves and members of other groups. Speech at this distance reflects a sensitivity to group differences, but the groups are not necessarily viewed as equal. When speaking at this level with members of different ethnic groups, for example, we would use the term for the ethnic group that its members prefer, even if it is different from the one we typically use, in order to demonstrate sensitivity to their feelings. When a man is speaking with a woman at this distance he avoids using the terms "lady" or "girl" if they cause offense to her.

The *distance of equality* reflects our desire to minimize the distance between ourselves and others (Gudykunst & Kim, 1984). This distance involves an attitude of equality, one in which we demonstrate that we are interpreting the language and behavior of others in terms of their groups' standards. Speech at this distance avoids evaluations of other groups. The use of "he" or "she" instead of "he" as a generic pronoun, for example, would reflect equality between men and women (sexist language is discussed below).

Ethnocentric speech can occur between members of any type of social groups. Sexist communication (discussed below), for example, is a form of ethnocentric speech between men and women. Ethnocentric speech can also occur when members of fraternities and sororities are communicating with nonmembers on campus. Many of us tend to use the distances of disparagement, avoidance, or indifference when we communicate on automatic pilot, but it is important to keep in mind that we can choose to use the distances of sensitivity or equality when we are mindful of our communication.

Prejudice

Another attitude closely related to ethnocentrism is prejudice. *Prejudice* involves "a judgment based on previous decisions and experiences" (Allport, 1954, p. 7). Our prejudices are our preconceived judgments of whom we like and whom we do not like. While prejudice can be positive or negative, there is a tendency for most of us to think of it as negative. Before proceeding, think about your prejudices. Answer the following questions:

Toward which groups are you negatively biased? (List specific groups.) ________

____

____

Toward which groups are you positively biased? (List specific groups.) ________

____

____

Your answers to these questions should provide some insight into the role of prejudice in your implicit personal theory of communication. Keep your answers to these questions in mind as you read the remainder of this section.

Negative prejudice is "an antipathy based on a faulty and unflexible generalization. It may be felt or expressed. It may be directed toward a group as a whole, or toward an individual because he [or she] is a member of that group" (Allport, 1954, p. 10). Our negative prejudices often are based on our stereotypes. To illustrate, if our mental picture of another group includes only negative traits (such as lazy or nasty), we would have negative prejudice toward the group. We can have negative prejudice toward any social group, including cultural groups, ethnic groups, gender groups, age groups, fraternities/sororities, professors, students, and so forth. When the negative prejudice is based on gender, the attitude is called sexism; when it is based on age, it is called ageism; when it is based on race, it is called racism; when it is based on gender orientation, it is called homophobia (sexism and ageism are discussed later in this chapter). Our negative prejudices usually are directed toward outgroups, but they can be directed toward our ingroups. Negative prejudice creates anxiety about interacting with members of the group against which we are prejudiced negatively. Negative prejudice also leads to inaccurate predictions and explanations of other people's behavior.

We tend to think of prejudice in terms of a dichotomy; either we are prejudiced or we are not. Prejudice, however, varies along a continuum from low to high. **We are all prejudiced to some degree.** As with ethnocentrism, this is natural and unavoidable. It is the result of our being socialized as members of our ingroups. Even people with low levels of prejudice prefer to interact with people who are similar to themselves because such interactions are more comfortable and less stressful than interactions with members of other groups.

As indicated earlier, we also can think of prejudice as varying along a continuum ranging from very positive to very negative. We tend to be positively prejudiced toward our ingroup and negatively prejudiced toward outgroups. It is possible, however, to be positively prejudiced toward outgroups and negatively prejudiced toward our ingroup. Whether our prejudices are positive or negative must be taken into consideration in trying to understand our reactions to violations of our expectations. As noted earlier, we can be prejudiced for or against many different types of people. If we are not aware of our prejudices and we do not mindfully manage them, they can have a tremendous influence on the people with whom we interact.

Assessing your Prejudice. Assessment 7.3 is designed to help you assess your level of prejudice. Take a few minutes to complete it now.

The higher your score on this Assessment 7.3, the greater your prejudice. High levels of prejudice lead us to misinterpret other people's behavior.

As indicated earlier, we are all prejudiced to some degree, and our prejudices influence our communication when we communicate on automatic pilot. The important point to keep in mind is that we can choose *not* to react in a prejudiced fashion when we are mindful of our communication. Conscious control of our reactions when our stereotypes are activated is necessary to control our prejudiced responses. Responding in a nonprejudiced fashion requires "a conscious decision to behave in a nonprejudiced fashion. In addition, new responses must be learned and well practiced before they can serve as competitive responses to the automatically activated stereotype-congruent response" (Devine, 1989, p. 15). Stated differently, mindfulness is necessary to decrease the likelihood that we will discriminate against members of other groups (Langer, 1989). To illustrate, if a store clerk's stereotype of a group involves members of the group being dishonest, the clerk might follow members of this group around the store to make sure they do not steal anything. This is a prejudiced response. If the clerk is mindful, he or she can recognize the stereotype and choose not to follow members of the group around the store unless they do something suspicious.

Prejudice and Communication. Prejudice is an attitude, a predisposition to behave in a certain way. We often express ambivalent attitudes when we talk about or communicate with members of other groups (Billig et al., 1988). Even people who are highly prejudiced (and hold negative views of other groups) tend to talk about other groups in such a way that they appear reasonable. If people are going to make a negative comment about other groups, for example, they preface their comment with a claim of not being prejudiced. To illustrate:

[INTERVIEWER]: Did you ever have any unpleasant experiences [with foreigners]?

[INTERVIEWEE]: I have nothing against foreigners. But their attitude, their ag-

Assessment 7.3 *Assessing Your Prejudice*

The purpose of this questionnaire is to assess your prejudice. Respond to each statement by indicating the degree to which the statement is true regarding the way you typically think about other groups. When you think about other groups, is the statement "Always False" (answer 1), "Mostly False" (answer 2), "Sometimes True and Sometimes False" (answer 3), "Mostly True" (answer 4), or "Always True" (answer 5)? Answer honestly, not how you think you should be.

_______ 1. Affirmative action programs discriminate against whites.

_______ 2. Members of other groups have not received as much support as they deserve, to make up for past discrimination.

_______ 3. Members of other groups have received more attention in the media than they deserve.

_______ 4. I understand why members of other groups are angry at my group.

_______ 5. Members of other groups should not push themselves where they are not wanted.

_______ 6. Members of other groups are cooperative.

_______ 7. Members of other groups are too demanding in their push for equal rights.

_______ 8. Discrimination against members of other groups is a problem today.

_______ 9. Members of other groups are receiving unfair privileges in society today.

_______ 10. I have positive feelings about members of other groups.

To find your score, first reverse the responses for the *even numbered* items (i.e., if you wrote 1, make it 5; if you wrote 2, make it 4; if you wrote 3, leave it as 3; if you wrote 4, make it 2; if you wrote 5, make it 1). Next, add the numbers next to each statement. Scores range from 10 to 50. The higher your score, the greater your prejudice.

> gression is scaring. We are no longer free here. You have to be careful. (van Dijk, 1984, p. 65)

Prejudiced talk falls into four categories: (1) "they are different (culture, mentality)"; (2) "they do not adapt themselves"; (3) "they are involved in negative acts (nuisance, crime)"; and (4) "they threaten our (social, economic) interests" (van Dijk, 1984, p. 70).

The way we talk about people who are different from us is, in large part, a function of how we want to be seen by our ingroup (van Dijk, 1984). We try to be seen in a positive light by members of our ingroups. The complaints that we verbalize about members of other groups, therefore, are likely to be ones that we think members of our ingroups share.

We all engage in prejudiced talk to some degree. It is inevitable. We can, however, reduce the degree to which we engage in prejudiced talk if we are mindful of our communication, by recognizing that not all members of other groups fit our stereotype or by reducing our prejudice.

We can also influence the amount of prejudiced talk in which others engage. When we express antiprejudiced sentiments, others are less likely to make prejudiced comments in our presence (Blanchard, Lilly, & Vaughn, 1991). Reading 7.2 presents a discussion of the effects of our comments on others.[2] When

Reading 7.2 COMBATTING INTENTIONAL BIGOTRY AND INADVERTENTLY RACIST ACTS/Fletcher A. Blanchard

What you say about racial discrimination matters: Your vocal opinions affect what others think and say. A series of experiments that I and my students and colleagues conducted demonstrate that racial prejudice is much more malleable than many researchers, policy makers, and educational leaders believe. In the wake of the verdict in the case of four Los Angeles policemen accused of beating Rodney King and the violence that followed it, the search for ways to lessen the devastating consequences of racism in America has intensified. If we understand that simply overhearing others condemn or condone racial harassment dramatically affects people's reactions to racism, we may be able to help find solutions to tensions and bigotry—both on campuses and in the larger society.

In the experiments we conducted, the first two of which are described in an article in *Psychological Science* (March, 1991), we briefly interviewed students as they walked between classes. In some portions of the experiment, the interviewer also stopped a second person, ostensibly another student but in reality a member of the research team, who offered her programmed opinions first. After hearing someone else condemn racism, college students expressed anti-racist sentiments much more strongly than those who heard someone express equivocal views. However, students who first heard someone condone racism then voiced views that reflected strong acceptance of racism.

The large differences that we observed appeared both when research participants spoke their views publicly and when we measured their opinions more anonymously by asking them to complete a questionnaire and return it to the researcher in a sealed envelope.

The research that I described at the outset suggests that each of us can affect others' concern for eliminating racism by taking strong public stands condemning bigotry on campuses. Just as anti-smoking attitudes among non-smokers eventually led to regulations banning smoking in public places, a broad consensus that eschews bigotry surely can reduce the display of intentional bias and inadvertent discriminatory behavior on campuses.

Our research suggests that no one need wait for administrators to take the lead. Each of us can influence each other by criticizing the willful bigotry of the mean-spirited few and gently guiding the well-intentioned efforts of the inexperienced many.

Blanchard, Fletcher "Combatting Intentional Bigotry and Inadvertently Racist Acts", *Chronicle of Higher Education,* May 13, 1992, p. 81–82. Reprinted by permission of the author.

we are bystanders, we "can define the meaning of events and move others toward empathy and indifference. [We] can promote values and norms of caring, or by passivity or participation in the system [we] can affirm the perpetrators" (Staub, 1989, p. 87). As bystanders, it is important that we speak out when we see other people expressing prejudice. A Protestant minister who was imprisoned in Dachau, a concentration camp in Germany in 1938, said:

> In Germany, the Nazis first came for the communists, and I didn't speak up because I wasn't a communist. Then they came for the Jews, and I didn't speak up because I wasn't a Jew. Then they came for the trade unionists, and I didn't speak up because I wasn't a trade unionist. Then they came for the Catholics, but I didn't speak up because I was a Protestant. Then they came for me, and by that time there was no one left to speak for me. (Reverend Martin Niemoeller).

If we speak out, others will too.

If we find that other people are making prejudiced remarks in our presence, we need to point out that this type of speech is not acceptable to us. If we do not, we are being morally exclusive. We could say something like, "I'd prefer that you didn't put down other groups in my presence." By simply stating our opinion in this way, we decrease the likelihood that others will continue to make prejudiced remarks in our presence. **If we do not speak out when other people make prejudiced comments or behave in a discriminatory manner, we are partially responsible for the consequences of the remarks or behavior.**

Reducing our Prejudice. If we interact on automatic pilot with members of other groups against which we are prejudiced, our interactions will tend to reinforce our prejudices. When we meet a person from a group toward which we are negatively prejudiced who does *not* conform to our stereotype of that group, we tend to see this person as "an exception to the rule." Our interactions with people we see as exceptions to the rule do not reduce our prejudice or change our stereotypes. There are, however, ways that we can reduce our negative prejudices.

One way that we can reduce our prejudices is by changing our attitude toward other groups as a whole. This tends to occur unconsciously if we have extensive contact with members of other groups under *favorable* conditions (Stephan, 1985). Favorable conditions for reducing prejudice include interacting with members of the other group who have the same or higher status than we do, working cooperatively with members of the other group, finding similarities between ourselves and members of other groups, having rewarding contact with members of other groups, having nonsuperficial contact with members of other groups, having positive outcomes from the contact, and having the norms and rules support contact with the other group.

Another way that we can reduce our negative prejudices is to increase the complexity of our views of other groups (Brewer & Miller, 1988). As we increase the complexity of our views of other groups, we recognize that not all members of the groups are alike. Our views toward the groups as wholes may not be altered, but we will recognize "subtypes" within the groups. This will stop us from automatically applying our general stereotype to all group members.

We also can reduce our negative prejudice by not using the particular group membership to categorize other people (Brewer & Miller, 1988). This is probably the most difficult way to change our attitudes because we learned most of the categories we use to divide people when we were children. We can, however, mindfully stop ourselves when we find ourselves categorizing other people and mindfully choose not to use the category to predict their behavior.

Sexism

Sexism occurs when we prejudge others based on their biological sex (Nilsen et al., 1977). Although we can be sexist toward either males or females, sexism usually is viewed as prejudice against women. There are several different ways in which sexism is expressed, including viewing women as genetically inferior, supporting discriminatory practices against women, engaging in hostility toward women who do not fulfill traditional sex roles, using derogatory names to refer to women or negatively stereotyping women, and treating women as sexual objects (Benson & Vincent, 1980).

Although both men and women are sexist, men tend to be more sexist than women. If we look at individuals' psychological sex roles, however, it appears that **highly masculine men and highly feminine women are more sexist than men and women who are androgynous or have an undifferentiated sex role** (Faulkender, 1985). People who have positive stereotypes of women tend to hold positive attitudes toward women (Eagly & Mladinic, 1989). High levels of sexism lead to anxiety and inaccurate predictions of other people's behavior in male-female interactions.

Sexism in Language Usage. Sexism is expressed mainly through our language. Sexism in language occurs when women are ignored, in the ways that women are defined, and in the deprecation of women (Henley, Hamilton, & Thorne, 1985). One of the ways in which our language usage ignores women is through the use of masculine words to include both males and females (Schmidt, 1991). There are many words in the English language, for example, that include the word "man" which traditionally have been used to include women. Examples of these words include "chairman," "mailman," "spokesman," and "mankind." Another way women are ignored in language usage is through using the generic pronoun "he." Many of us learned that, when we write or talk, pronouns for males can be used to refer to both males and females. This, however, is not how we actually process the information. When we use male pronouns, it elicits a vision of a male for the reader or listener (Schneider & Hacker, 1973).

Another way that language usage can be sexist is in how women are defined. Some people, for example, have a tendency to address women by their first names in situations in which men would be addressed by their titles (Mr., Dr.) and last names (McConnell-Ginet, 1978). Women also are devalued when terms "such as honey, cutie, and sweetie" are used to refer to them (Schmidt, 1991, p. 30).

Our language also is sexist in the ways women are deprecated. In English, for example, there are over 200 terms to call a woman sexually promiscuous, but fewer than 25 to call a man sexually promiscuous (Stanley, 1977). Although there are more masculine terms (more than 350) in the English language than feminine (fewer than 150), there are more negative feminine terms than masculine (Nilsen, 1977).

Using Language to Describe Males and Females. Our language describes women and men differently, which affects our behavior in interpersonal relationships. The following comparisons, which might be used to talk about the same behavior, illustrate this process (adapted in part from Eakins & Eakins, 1978, p. 131):

She	**He**
chattered	discussed
nagged	reminded
gossiped	networked
bitched	complained
is an airhead	is forgetful
is picky	is fastidious
is talkative	is articulate
has wrinkles	has character lines
is pushy	is assertive
is stubborn	is firm
is secretive	is discreet

Our language describes men and women in terms of sex role stereotypes. Because language usage is a reflection of the society in which we live, as long as society defines men and women in terms of sex role stereotypes, differences in language usage will persist.

To illustrate the way we use language, take a moment to complete the following sentences:

> As the construction worker surveyed the building site, ________________________
>
> ______________________________________
>
> The nurse who works on the fifth floor is very helpful. In fact, yesterday ______
>
> ______________________________________
>
> ______________________________________
>
> When someone wins the lottery, ______
>
> ______________________________________
>
> After a judge instructs the jury, ______
>
> ______________________________________

You probably did not have any difficulty adding a pronoun to each of these sentences. For most of us, our choice of pronoun is determined by traditional stereotypes. We are likely to use he when considering traditionally male roles, such as judge and construction worker, and she when considering traditional female roles, such as nurse and secretary (Wheeless, Berryman-Fink, & Serafini, 1982). Neutral roles (such as winners in the lottery) are identified as either he or they, even though they may not be grammatically correct in a particular context. These are examples of how traditional sex role stereotypes affect our language choice.

When we read or hear sentences containing *generic pronouns,* such as "Everyone deserves his right to a fair trial," we are likely to believe that the sentences refer more to men than to women. There are no feminine generics in English; that is, feminine words used to represent both the feminine and the masculine forms (Smith, 1985). This is problematic because people perceive "man"-linked words (such as "chairman" or "spokesman") as more likely to refer to men than to women, while non-"man"-linked words (such as chairperson or spokesperson) are seen as equally likely to refer to men or to women (Todd-Mancillas, 1981).

Assessing your Sexism. Assessment 7.4 is designed to help you assess your sexism. Take a few minutes to complete it now.

The higher your score on Assessment 7.4, the more sexist you are. If your score is higher than you would like it to be, keep in mind that you can choose to behave in a nonsexist fashion and to use nonsexist language when you are mindful of your communication. Suggestions on how this can be accomplished are provided in the following section.

Avoiding Sexist Language. To include everyone in our language usage, we can use several alternatives to conventional "man"-

Assessment 7.4 *Assessing Your Sexism*

The purpose of this questionnaire is to assess your sexism. Respond to each statement by indicating the degree to which the statement is true regarding the way you typically think about men and women. When you think about women and men, is the statement "Always False" (answer 1), "Mostly False" (answer 2), "Sometimes True and Sometimes False" (answer 3), "Mostly True" (answer 4), or "Always True" (answer 5)? Answer honestly, not how you think you should be.

_______ 1. Husbands should make decisions in the family.

_______ 2. Women and men are equal in all respects.

_______ 3. Men are more courageous than women.

_______ 4. Men and women can handle pressure equally well.

_______ 5. Women are more emotional than men.

_______ 6. Women can lead as effectively as men.

_______ 7. Men should be the dominant sex.

_______ 8. Women and men are equal in intelligence.

_______ 9. Women are influenced by others more than men.

_______ 10. Men and women should have the same rights.

To find your score, first reverse the responses for the *even numbered* items (i.e., if you wrote 1, make it 5; if you wrote 2, make it 4; if you wrote 3, leave it as 3; if you wrote 4, make it 2; if you wrote 5, make it 1). Next, add the numbers next to each statement. Scores range from 10 to 50. The higher your score, the greater your sexism.

linked and third-person singular, masculine generic pronouns (Todd-Mancillas, 1981). Existing language options can be used instead of "man"-linked words and masculine pronouns. Sentences can be pluralized ("Students are expected to type their papers" instead of "A student is expected to type his paper"), or words like people or human beings can be substituted for "man" or "mankind." Grammatical constructions that call specific attention to both males and females also can be used, such as he or she, women and men, or his or her. In addition, neutral words, such as server (instead of waiter and waitress) or worker (instead of "workman"), or mail carrier (instead of "mailman"), can be used.

Most of us learned sexist language as children, and modifying our language requires that we mindfully decide to change. There are several guidelines we can use to avoid sexist language when we mindfully try to modify our language usage:

1. Commit yourself to remove sexist language from all of your communication.
2. Practice and reinforce nonsexist communication patterns until they become habitual. The ultimate test is your ability to carry on a nonsexist private conversation and to think in nonsexist terms.
3. Set a nonsexist communication example and direct or persuade others to adopt your example.
4. Use familiar idioms whenever possible, but if you must choose between sexist and the unfamiliar, use the unfamiliar until it becomes the familiar.
5. Take care not to arouse negativism in the [listener or reader] by using awkward, cumbersome, highly repetitious, or glaring [language]. . . .
6. Use the full range of techniques for correction of sexist communication, including reconstruction, substitution, and omission.
7. Check roots and meanings of words to be sure that the words need to be changed before changing them.
8. Check every outgoing message—whether written, oral, or nonverbal—for sexism before sending it. (Sorrels, 1983, p. 17)

Following these guidelines requires that we be mindful of our communication. After consciously following the guidelines for some period of time, however, the use of nonsexist language will become automatic.

Ageism

When our prejudice is based on other people's age, ageism is involved. *Ageism* is based on negative attitudes toward people who are older than we are (usually people we consider "old"). Teenagers, for example, may be prejudiced against people over thirty, while people in their thirties may be prejudiced against people who are retired. Ageism is based on "a deep-seated uneasiness on the part of the young and middle-aged—a personal revulsion to and distaste for growing older" (Butler, 1969, p. 243). It also can emerge from competition between the groups (young and old) over scarce resources and jobs (Levin & Levin, 1980). Overall, attitudes toward aging tend to be negative in the United States (Palmore, 1982). These negative attitudes are reinforced in the popular media, including magazines (Nussbaum & Robinson, 1984). Negative attitudes toward members of other age groups leads to anxiety and inaccurate predictions of the behavior of members of other age groups.

Ageism in Language Usage. Ageism may be expressed in our language usage. Although the term "old" has connotations of experience, skill, and wisdom, it also is used in derogatory terms, such as "old hag" or "old fogey" (Covey, 1988). In the English language, there is a wide variety of terms referring to old people which have negative overtones, such as "battleaxe" or "geezer." Many of the attributes used to talk about the elderly, such as cantankerous or grumpy, also have negative connotations (Nuessel, 1984). More than half the jokes in English about aging reflect a negative view of old people, with a greater portion of negative jokes about women than about men. Terms like aged and elderly are perceived to be negative, while terms like senior citizen and retired person are evaluated more positively by people of all age groups (Barbato & Feezel, 1987).

Older people's use of language tends to be evaluated negatively and is processed in a stereotypical fashion by younger people (Giles et al., 1992). Older speakers, for example, often are seen as "doddering," "vague," and "rambling." How older people act with younger people is partly a function of younger people's stereotypes of older people. Young people's negative stereotypes of older people may effectively frustrate many older people's positive adaptive attempts, "creating and reinforcing communication barriers to successful aging" (Giles et al., 1992, p. 281).

Assessing your Ageism. Assessment 7.5 is designed to help you assess your ageism. Take a few minutes to complete it now.

Scores on Assessment 7.5 range from 10 to 50. The higher your score, the greater your ageism. The higher your score, the greater the possibility of misunderstandings when you are communicating with someone older or younger than you. If you have a high score,

Assessment 7.5 *Assessing Your Ageism*

The purpose of this questionnaire is to assess your ageism. Respond to each statement by indicating the degree to which the statement is true regarding the way you typically think about others' age. When you think about someone's age, is the statement "Always False" (answer 1), "Mostly False" (answer 2), "Sometimes True and Sometimes False" (answer 3), "Mostly True" (answer 4), or "Always True" (answer 5)? Answer honestly, not how you think you should be.

_______ 1. I find it more difficult to communicate with an old person than with a young person.

_______ 2. I am not afraid of growing old.

_______ 3. I see old people as cantankerous.

_______ 4. I learn a lot when I communicate with elderly people.

_______ 5. I prefer to interact with people my own age.

_______ 6. I do not see all old people as alike.

_______ 7. I see old people as a group.

_______ 8. My communication with people older than me is as effective as my communication with people my own age.

_______ 9. I have to speak loudly and slowly for old people to understand me.

_______ 10. I look forward to growing old.

To find your score, first reverse the responses for the *even numbered* items (i.e., if you wrote 1, make it 5; if you wrote 2, make it 4; if you wrote 3, leave it as 3; if you wrote 4, make it 2; if you wrote 5, make it 1). Next, add the numbers next to each statement. Scores range from 10 to 50. The higher your score, the greater your ageism.

you can choose to stop your negative reaction toward people of a different age when you are mindful of your communication.

Summary

Our perceptions of other people's behavior are a function of the person engaging in the behavior and the situation in which the behavior occurs. Since we cannot take in all of the stimuli occurring, our perceptions are biased. We tend to assume, however, that our perceptions of other people's behavior are accurate, especially when we communicate on automatic pilot. The more rigid the categories we use to interpret other people's behavior, the more likely we are to misinterpret their behavior. When we think there is a possibility that our interpretations may not be accurate, we need to become cognitively flexible; that is, not hold rigid categories. In addition, we need to use the perception checking skill to check our understanding of other people's thoughts and feelings.

Our perceptions are influenced by our expectations for other people's behavior. Our expectations for other people's behavior are based in part on our stereotypes of the groups in which we categorize them, as well as our attitudes, such as ethnocentrism, prejudice, sexism, and ageism. When we communicate on automatic pilot, our stereotypes and attitudes create expectations for other people's behavior, and we assume they are behaving consistently with our expectations. Our attitudes also influence the distance we set up between ourselves and other people when we communicate with them. If we rigidly hold our stereotypes and attitudes and are not willing to question them, we can never reach the point where we know other people as individuals.

Notes

1. Lukens (1978) isolated the first three distances, Gudykunst and Kim (1984) isolated the final two.
2. Blanchard, Lilly, and Vaughn actually use the term racism. We believe that their results will extend to any form of prejudice.

Journal Reflections

1. *Identifying Your Expectations.* We all have expectations for how others will communicate. Some of these expectations are learned from our culture and ethnic group, and some are a function of our stereotypes and prejudices. In at least four interactions this week, reflect on how your expectations (both conscious and unconscious) influenced how you communicated with others. To isolate "unconscious" expectations (including stereotypes and prejudices), you will have to stop after an interaction and ask yourself what expectations you had for the encounter without realizing they were there. Of the four interactions, two should involve a person of the same sex (or ethnic group) as yourself and two should involve people of the opposite sex (or a different ethnic group).
2. *Perception Checking.* Perception checking is appropriate only in certain situations. In at least two situations this week in which you think perception checking is appropriate, try this skill. In your journal, describe the situations, discuss why you thought perception checking was appropriate in those situations, and reflect on how perception checking influenced the quality of your communication.
3. *Observing Your Use of Sexist and Ageist Language.* In the next two days, carefully observe your use of sexist and ageist language. What effect does this type of language have on you and the people with whom you are communicating? After observing your use of sexist language for two days, try to consciously follow the guidelines for avoiding sexist language for

one day. What effect does this have on your communication?

12. How does ageism influence the way young and older people communicate?

Study Questions

1. What is involved when we perceive other people's behavior?
2. How are our perceptions biased?
3. What is the role of categorizations in the perceptual process?
4. How does perception checking increase the quality of our communication?
5. How do our expectations influence our perceptions?
6. What happens when our expectations are violated?
7. What do stereotypes, ethnocentrism, prejudice, and sexism have in common?
8. How do stereotypes influence communication?
9. How is prejudice manifested in communication?
10. How does our ethnocentrism lead us to create communicative distances?
11. How does sexist language influence the quality of our communication with members of the opposite sex?

Suggested Readings

Coupland, N., & Nussbaum, J. (Eds.). (1993). *Discourse and lifespan identity.* Newbury Park, CA: Sage. The contributors to this volume examine how age affects everyday talk and how social rituals are involved in "acting our age."

de Bono, E. (1991). *I am right, you are wrong.* New York: Viking. In this book, Edward de Bono discusses processes that can help us increase the accuracy of our perceptions. He suggests that we try to move from using "rock logic" (rigid categories) to "water logic" (fluid categories).

Fisher, G. (1988). *Mindsets.* Yarmouth, ME: Intercultural Press. Glen Fisher examines how culture influences our perceptions of people from other cultures. He discusses how to improve the accuracy of our perceptions in international business and diplomacy.

van Dijk, T. (1984). *Prejudice in discourse.* Philadelphia: Benjamins. Tuen van Dijk examines the ways that our prejudices are expressed in the ways we talk. He explains the contexts in which we express prejudice, the topics on which we express prejudice, and the types of stories we tell about members of other groups.

8

LISTENING AND FEEDBACK

The Process of Listening

Hearing Versus Listening

Why We Do Not Listen Effectively

Responsive Listening

Readiness to Listen

Following Skills

Comprehending

Skill Practice

Speakers Can Help Others Listen Effectively

Giving and Receiving Feedback

Giving Feedback

Receiving Feedback

Effective listening is important in all aspects of our lives. Average college students, for example, spend 53 percent of the time they are awake listening, 17 percent of their time reading, 16 percent speaking, and 14 percent writing (Barker et al., 1980). Most of us, however, take listening for granted when we are communicating. We usually are not aware of our listening behavior.

Effective listening does not mean that we necessarily agree with the opinions of the people with whom we talk. Rather, it means trying to understand other people's verbal and nonverbal messages before responding to or evaluating what they say. Effective listening is an important interpersonal communication skill. Effective listening helps us to reduce uncertainty and minimize misunderstandings in interactions and to maximize mutual understanding of the messages that are being exchanged. By taking the time to listen to others, we display respect for other people and their opinions and feelings.

Part of effective listening involves providing feedback to the people speaking. Feedback involves the messages we transmit to others when they are speaking. When others are talking, we give them feedback on how we are reacting to what they are saying by the look on our face, the direction of our gaze, our body posture, and the words of encouragement we provide.

To understand what is involved in effective listening, we must begin by recognizing the differences between hearing and listening, and the reasons why we do not listen effectively. Once we understand why we do not listen effectively, we can learn the specific skills involved in responsive listening. To listen effectively, we also need to know how to give feedback to others and to be able to receive their feedback without becoming defensive. Let's begin by looking at the general process of listening.

The Process of Listening

There are many reasons why we do not always listen effectively. Before reading further, think about the role of listening in your implicit theory of interpersonal communication. To accomplish this, take a moment to answer the following questions:

How do you know when someone is not listening to you? List the signals that suggest that other people are not listening.

____

____

____

How do you usually react when someone does not appear to be listening when you speak? ______________

____

____

____

What are some of the reasons why you do not listen when other people are speaking? List as many specific reasons as you can. ______________

____

____

____

Your answers to these questions should provide some insight into the role of listening in your implicit personal theory of communication. Look over the reasons you listed for not listening, and cross-check them with the reasons identified below. We usually do not listen because of a combination of factors. To place these reasons in context, we'll distinguish between hearing and listening.

Hearing Versus Listening

Hearing is the physical process of taking in auditory sensations without deliberate

Hearing is an automatic process whereas listening involves taking in what we hear and organizing it so it makes sense.

thoughtful attention. When we watch television and read a magazine at the same time, for example, we hear all kinds of noises around us. We may not, however, pay attention to these noises. We may hear the melody of a song over and over again, but we may not be able to recall the words we heard. We hear the music, but we may not be motivated to listen to the words attentively. Hearing is an automatic process of absorbing auditory stimuli; it does *not* require a high degree of attentiveness. The fact that we can hear without being attentive plays an important role in our ability to cope with information overload in our environment. It helps us tune out information that we have no great desire to understand. It helps us relax. It allows our mind to roam freely in our own imagination and fantasy. Hearing is a physical process of reacting to sounds without concentrating. Of course, we have to hear before we can listen.

Listening is more than hearing. ***Listening* is the process of taking in what we hear, and mentally organizing it so that we can make sense of it** (Goss, 1982). Our listening ability, therefore, is related to our ability to process information. The more complex our information processing, the more effective our listening (Beatty & Payne, 1984). Effective listening demands attentiveness and concentration. Hearing demands only the physiological operation of our ears.

In Chinese characters, the character for "hearing" (*wen*) denotes only "opening the doors to your ears" so you can absorb the sounds in the environment. The character for "listening" (*ting*), in contrast, means "listening with your ears, eyes, and a concentrated heart." *Ting* implies listening responsively. *Responsive listening* is a mindful process in which we focus on the meanings of other people's verbal and nonverbal messages and clearly indicate to them that we are paying attention. Responsive listening takes time, energy, and interpersonal commitment. Responsive listening helps us to comprehend the content and the relational meanings of other people's messages. Responsive listening is critical when we want to understand others.

Why We Do Not Listen Effectively

Effective listening involves attending, interpreting, responding, understanding, and remembering. Effective listening is influenced by the people with whom we are communicating, the types of messages we are exchanging, and the situation in which we are interacting. While we typically play both the speaker and

HAGAR THE HORRIBLE. Reprinted with special permission of King Features Syndicate.

the listener roles when communicating interpersonally, the terms "speakers" and "listeners" are used throughout this chapter for the sake of clarity when explaining the basic concepts of effective listening.

There are many reasons why we do not listen effectively: external noises and distractions, preoccupation, wandering mind, assumptions, personality, listening apprehension, ego-involvement, information overload, and lack of training. More than one of these reasons may prevent us from listening effectively in a particular situation. Let's begin with external noises and distractions.

External Noises and Distractions. External noises, such as those in a crowded restaurant or a small classroom, are distracting for listeners and speakers. When everyone is speaking at the same time in a crowded room, it is physically impossible to concentrate on listening to other people. The only thing we can do in such situations is to move to a quieter setting or to signal other people that we are not hearing the message clearly. Speakers may have to raise their voices louder than usual, and listeners may have to move physically closer to speakers. Speakers and listeners may also agree to postpone their discussion until they can find a quieter time to talk.

It is not only noises that we hear that inhibit our ability to listen. Physical distractions in the environment also get in the way of effective listening. Having a television playing, for example, even with the sound turned down, can distract us from listening to others. Similarly, some screen savers on personal computers are very entertaining, but they can distract listeners who look at them from paying attention when conversations take place in the office.

Preoccupation. We often are preoccupied with our own problems or feelings when we communicate with others. **When we are distracted by our own problems, we cannot focus attentively on other people's messages.** Though we may engage in pseudolistening behavior, such as nodding our head

Sometimes environmental noises are not so distracting that we cannot maintain our attention on our conversations.

or maintaining eye contact, we are really not listening. We may be thinking of an upcoming exam or a date that evening while someone is talking. Often, we are just too busy with our own activities and schedules to have time to listen attentively to other people. Many of us juggle different jobs and conflicting role demands. We need time to shift from one role to another before we can listen responsively when someone else is speaking.

Wandering Mind. Another thing that inhibits our effective listening is the fact that we are capable of understanding 600 words per minute, while a speaker's average verbal rate is 150 to 200 words per minute (Wolvin & Coakley, 1992). In an average conversation, there is plenty of time for our mind to wander off and then come back to the ongoing interaction. Our mind may wander off because we are thinking of something else or because of something that the speaker says. Unfortunately, once we drift off, we often have a hard time returning to the conversation taking place.

When our mind wanders, we already have missed important points in the conversation. We tend to make irrelevant responses or unrelated comments when our mind wanders. When we are mentally and physically exhausted, our mind may easily wander from the main points of the conversation. Since listening effectively is an energy-consuming activity, it is easier to drift off than to pay close attention to what other people are saying.

Assumptions. Another reason why we do not listen effectively is the assumptions we have concerning the speaker or the content of the messages being transmitted. Our assumptions cause us to block out incoming information or to listen selectively. We may assume that the speaker will be boring and that therefore it is not worth listening. We might assume that the content of the message is too difficult to understand and that therefore it is a waste of time to listen. We also may assume that there is nothing new to learn from the speaker and mentally drift away. Finally, our negative stereotypes and prejudices concerning the speaker can inhibit us from fully concentrating when we are listening.

Our assumptions can lead us to selectively focus on those aspects of a conversation that validate our preconceived viewpoints. Our biases lead to *selective listening.* When we listen selectively, we have not given ourselves or the speaker a fair chance to advance genuine understanding. Our stereotypes and prejudices about the speaker often act as mental blinders to effective listening. We may hear the words, but we are not listening for the meaning of the message. In such situations, we need to become mindful and listen responsively. We need to suspend our own biased attitudes and prejudices.

Personality. Our personalities influence the way we respond to other people, and the way we respond to others affects the way we listen (Burleson, 1985). Some people consistently affirm or acknowledge other people's feelings when listening to them. These people tend to be sensitive to others when listening to them. Other people are not sensitive to other people's feelings when listening. **The more sensitive we are when we listen to other people, the more effectively we can listen.**

Our personality affects our preferences for the ways to listen. When we listen, we tend to be people-oriented, content-oriented, action-oriented, or time-oriented (Watson, Barker, & Weaver, 1992). People-oriented listeners demonstrate concern for speakers' feelings and emotional states. Content-oriented listeners focus on evaluating speakers' facts and evidence and prefer to listen to technical information. Action-oriented listeners are impatient with disorganized or rambling speakers and often finish speakers' thoughts. Time-oriented listeners emphasize the time they have to listen to others. We tend to emphasize one orientation or another, but we can use more than one orientation. Of those people who use mainly one orientation, women tend to be more people-oriented than men, and men tend to be more action-oriented than women.

Listening Apprehension. Listening apprehension, "the fear of processing or psychologically adjusting to messages" sent by others (Preiss & Wheeless, 1989, p. 75), also influences our ability to listen effectively. Our anxiety can stem from a fear of encountering new information, new people, or unfamiliar situations. When interviewing for a job, for example, we may be so nervous that we do not listen carefully to the questions the interviewer asks us. No matter what the source, listening apprehension leads to inefficient processing of information and results in a backlog of unassimilated facts (Fitch-Hauser, Barker, & Hughes, 1990). Our unfamiliarity with other people's style of speaking, accent, or different nonverbal gestures often can cause listening apprehension. When we experience high levels of listening anxiety, our listening behavior tends to be defensive or distracting. Too little apprehension also can inhibit effective listening. Having a moderate amount of apprehensiveness leads to an ability to listen effectively.

Having an open-minded, inquiring attitude helps alleviate listening apprehension. In addition, using cues such as head nods or responsive facial expressions from speakers also may help to reduce listening apprehension.

Ego-involvement. When the issues being discussed by other people are important to us, we often do not listen attentively. In these situations, we are often eager to express our own viewpoints or to refute other people's viewpoints. We put our opinions or ideas above the speaker's ideas or feelings. We are self-focused in the listening process rather than other-directed. When this happens, we are more interested in what we have to say than in what the speaker has to offer. When we are ego-involved, we may grasp some of the main points proposed by the speaker, but we do not have a genuine understanding of the speaker's position. In this situation, we engage in selective listening for the purpose of presenting our own arguments.

When we notice that we are feeling impatient for other people to stop speaking or find ourselves interrupting, we are ego-involved. **To decrease our ego-involvement, we must become mindful and consciously choose to try to understand other people's points of view.** When we are mindful, we need to focus on other people's messages and not focus on our own messages.

Information Overload. Many college students encounter information overload after they have attended three or four classes in a row. There is just too much information to synthesize and remember. When we experience information overload, our minds raise protective shields to handle the onslaught of information by automatically tuning out new information.

Prolonged responsive listening can cause psychological and emotional burnout. In professional service fields, counselors, therapists, nurses, and lawyers often have a high burnout rate because they must listen to the self-disclosures and complaints of their clients and patients every day. It is critical that listeners who experience information burnout give themselves some quiet time to engage in activities that do not require attentive listening. Reading for fun or meditating daily may help to refresh our mental and psychological energy. Exercises such as yoga, daily walks, or running may also help to rejuvenate us when we experience information overload. Alternatively, listening for the sake of pure enjoyment, such as listening to the sounds of rustling leaves, children playing, the ocean, our favorite music, or the tranquil silence in our sacred places may help to refresh us when we experience information overload.

Lack of Training. Most of us think that we comprehend what others are saying when we try to understand them. This, however, is not necessarily the case. Although we think that we remember 75 to 80 percent of the information we hear, we actually remember only about 25 percent when listening normally (Roach & Wyatt, 1988). We have not been taught to listen effectively. **We do not think about our listening behavior very much, even though we spend the majority of our personal and professional lives listening to others.**

Listening is one of the most important communication skills in an organization, but few employees are trained in listening. Listening effectively is critical in business, because "a good manager needs to listen as much as he [or she] needs to talk. Too many people fail to realize that real communication goes in both directions. . . . You have to be able to listen well if you're going to motivate people who work for you. Right there, that's the difference between a mediocre company and a great company" (Iacocca, 1984, pp. 54–55).

Assessing Your Listening Behavior. Assessment 8.1 offers you an opportunity to assess your listening behavior. Take a few minutes to complete it now.

The higher your score on Assessment 8.1, the more effective your listening. It is important to keep in mind, however, that we can teach ourselves to be more effective listeners. Some specific suggestions for how to engage in responsive listening are provided in the next section. These skills, nevertheless, should not be viewed as a prescriptive formula for effective listening. Effective listening is highly dependent on our goals, the situation, and the people with whom we are communicating.

Responsive Listening

The way that we listen influences other people's talkativeness. To illustrate, the more we reflect other people's feelings by being empathic or supportive when we are listening, the longer other people will talk. The more we give advice, ask questions, or try to help other people solve problems when we are listening, in contrast, the less other people are likely to talk (D'Augelli et al., 1978). The way we listen also influences whether other people see us as helpful or unhelpful. When talking with bereaved parents or spouses, for example, we will be perceived as helpful if we express our concern, if we provide an opportunity for them to express their feelings, or if we are simply quiet and available to listen. If we encourage recovery, give advice, or force cheerfulness, we will be perceived as unhelpful (Lehman, Ellard, & Wortman, 1986).

Our listening behavior also influences our moods and attitudes. Trying to help other people solve their problems or giving advice when listening to them, for example, can lead to our being in a negative mood after the interaction. Being supportive of other people by using the responsive listening skills discussed in this section, in contrast, does not lead to negative moods after listening (Notarius & Herrick, 1988).

There are three objectives in responsive listening: understanding the content meaning of other people's messages, understanding the relational meaning of other people's messages,

Assessment 8.1 *Assessing Your Listening Behavior*

The purpose of this questionnaire is to assess your listening behavior. Respond to each statement indicating the degree to which it is true regarding the way you generally listen: "Always False" (answer 1), "Usually False" (answer 2), "Sometimes False and Sometimes True" (answer 3), "Usually True" (answer 4), and "Always True" (answer 5).

_______ 1. I have a difficult time separating important and unimportant ideas when I listen to others.

_______ 2. I check new information against what I already know when I listen to others.

_______ 3. I have an idea what others will say when I listen to them.

_______ 4. I am sensitive to others' feelings when I listen to them.

_______ 5. I think about what I am going to say next when I listen to others.

_______ 6. I focus on the process of communication that is occurring between me and others when I listen to them.

_______ 7. I cannot wait for others to finish talking so I can take my turn.

_______ 8. I try to understand the meanings that are being created when I communicate with others.

_______ 9. I focus on determining whether others understand what I said when they are talking.

_______ 10. I ask others to elaborate when I am not sure what they mean.

To find your score, first reverse your responses for the *odd-numbered* items (if you wrote 1, make it 5; if you wrote 2, make it 4; if you wrote 3, leave it as 3; if you wrote 4, make it 2; if you wrote 5, make it 1). Next, add the numbers next to each statement. Scores range from 10 to 50. The higher your score, the better your listening behavior.

and holistically understanding the people who are delivering the verbal and nonverbal messages. *Content meaning* refers to the specific information content of the message, such as the basic story line, the facts, the evidence, the examples, and the metaphors being used by the speaker. Content meaning typically is delivered through verbal messages. Understanding the content meaning of other people's messages helps us better predict and explain their behavior.

Sometimes when we listen to other people we think that the content of what they tell us is biased. When this occurs, we may engage in *second-guessing*. We second-guess others when we think their messages are biased and try to correct the biases (Hewes & Planalp, 1982). When we second-guess others, we are trying to develop a "truer" account of what other people are saying. Consider the following example:

> Your sister (the source) tells you that she saw your dating partner flirt with members of the desired sex at a bar last night (the message). Your first reaction is jealousy, but you want [to] be sure that there is a reason to feel this way since jealousy can damage a relationship. You might second-guess the message based on your knowledge of your dating partner's typical behavior (he or she is innocently flirtatious), the state of your relationship (secure), your sister's ability to identify flirtation when she sees it (she sees sexual implications in everything). In short, you may use information about source or target to reconstruct what "really" happened last night. (Hewes & Graham, 1989, p. 215)

In this example, second-guessing would decrease the chances that you would feel jealous about what happened last night. Second guessing can be combined with perception checking (discussed in last chapter) to ensure our perceptions are accurate.

Relational meaning refers to the relationship aspect of the messages. It involves the emotional undertone that accompanies the verbal message. This emotional undertone can be expressed through tone of voice, facial expressions, eye movements, hand gestures, body postures, and a mixture of many other nonverbal movements. When we pay attention to the relational meaning, we are trying to understand how other people are defining the ongoing interpersonal relationship between us. Understanding other people's relational meanings can help us manage our anxiety about interacting with them.

We also want to listen for the sake of understanding other people holistically. Understanding other people holistically means that we are motivated to understand the context that frames their point of view. The context can include their cultural and ethnic values, family socialization, past experiences, and present moods that affect the person at that particular moment.

Responsive listening has many benefits. By paying close attention to other people's messages, for example, we confirm them. *Confirmation* expresses recognition of other people's existence, acknowledges a relationship of affiliation with them, expresses awareness of their significance or worth, and accepts or "endorses" other people's self-experiences (particularly emotional experience; Cissna & Sieburg, 1981). Responsive listening affirms and validates the intrinsic worth of other people; it indicates that other people's opinions or ideas are valued (confirmation is discussed in detail in Chapter 14). It promotes interpersonal trust and rapport in our relationships with others. It opens the door for a collaborative dialogue, even in conflict situations. Responsive listening allows us to clarify misattributions and misunderstandings. It helps us to build quality interpersonal relationships.

Before proceeding, think about the situations in which other people have listened to you responsively. Take a few minutes to answer the following questions:

> How do you know when someone is listening to you responsively? List the specific verbal and nonverbal behaviors that signal someone is listening to you responsively. ______________________
> ________________________________
> ________________________________

What are some of your typical reactions when someone listens to you responsively? ______________________________

____

____

Identify people who consistently listen to you responsively. What do you think are some of the reasons they listen to you responsively? ______________________________

____

____

Your answers to these questions should provide some insight into the role of responsive listening in your implicit personal theory of communication. Keep your answers to these questions in mind as you read the remainder of this section.

It is important to recognize that we should *not* use responsive listening all of the time. This would be too time consuming. We do need to improve our listening in everyday conversations, but we do not need to use all of the responsive listening skills in every conversation:

> Listening to self-absorbed, confused, or selfish talk should be a matter of choice. I might *choose* to give my attention . . . to someone whose talk is disordered, overdetailed, or self-concerned due to distress, but I might not choose to listen to someone in the habit of flooding others with trivial and redundant disclosures designed only to entertain themselves. Sometimes "good listening" may be hazardous to your communication health. (Goodman & Esterly, 1988, p. 173)

In most conversations, our listening will improve if we selectively use the skills associated with responsive listening discussed in this section. When it is important that we fully understand the other person, however, using all of the skills discussed in this section will improve the quality of our communication. As you read the remainder of this section, try to think of specific situations in which the skills would be useful.

Responsive listening involves checking the accuracy of our understanding of the content and relational meaning of other people's messages. There are three types of responsive listening skills: readiness, following, and comprehending. As you read the remainder of this section, remember that the focus is on listening. To explain responsive listening, the process of listening is discussed in isolation. As you will recall from Chapter 1, however, this is not what happens when we communicate. When we communicate, we transmit and interpret messages simultaneously.

Readiness to Listen

When we want to understand other people's messages, we have to mindfully choose to be ready and willing to listen. We must be willing to modify our ineffective listening habits and work at attending and responding to other people's messages. The commitment to listen includes our physical preparation to listen, as well as our cognitive and affective readiness to listen.

Our *physical readiness* includes our readiness to use our ears, eyes, face, voice, body, mind, and heart to listen in a nondistracting environment. For effective listening to be possible, we need to make sure that we are in a nondistracting environment. If it is important that we listen effectively, we should turn the television or stereo off and make sure there are no other distractions. Removing physical barriers also can help us to improve our listening. When one person sits behind a desk and the other person sits in front of the desk, the desk can be a barrier to effective listening. Both people would be able to listen more effectively if they sat in chairs facing each other, without the desk between them. Physical preparation also means that we set aside our own work or activities temporarily and engage fully in listening to another person.

Our *cognitive readiness* includes a willing suspension of our preoccupations with our thoughts or emotional problems. It requires that we focus on the present moment and remain open to alternative viewpoints or ideas. We need to focus our cognitive abilities on understanding and remembering what is said. For most of us, cognitive preparation means being mindful of our communication. When we communicate on automatic pilot, we are not likely to listen responsively.

Affective readiness requires that we be emotionally "present" with other people. In doing this, we focus on the emotional meanings of other people's messages rather than on the content meaning alone. It means being sensitive to the emotional nuances of the messages and being aware of other people's emotional states. Affective readiness requires that we pay attention to other people's changing emotions.

When we first try to increase our readiness to listen and start being attentive to others, it may seem unnatural and awkward. Being ready to listen, however, has a tremendous influence on the way we attune to others:

> Individuals may sometimes begin attending in an artificial, deliberate manner. However, once attending has been initiated, the person to whom one is listening tends to become more animated, and this in turn reinforces the attender who very quickly forgets about attending deliberately and soon attends naturally. . . . [People] have engaged in conscious attending behavior only to find themselves . . . interested in the person with whom they are talking. (Ivey, 1975, quoted by Bolton, 1979, p. 39)

Being ready and willing to listen to others, therefore, provides the foundation for making connections with others.

Following Skills

In addition to being ready to listen, we need to show other people that we are following their messages closely (Bolton, 1979). When we are listening responsively, we need to observe other people's verbal styles, such as their tone of voice, rate of speech, intonations, verbal pauses, or hesitations. We should also observe nonverbal behaviors, such as facial expressions, hand gestures, body postures, leg movements, touch behavior, and the use of physical props, such as tapping a pencil on the desk. Our observations, however, should not cause discomfort to others. We also need to signal behaviorally that we are listening attentively. **We use the following skills to implicitly send the relational message "I am paying attention, I care about you, and I respect what you have to say."**

One way we tell other people that we are ready to listen is by being silent (Bolton, 1979). We need to allow other people time to collect their thoughts and decide what they want to say. Since many of us have a low tolerance for silence, we must mindfully choose to be quiet and allow other people to speak. To begin listening responsively, we can invite other people to talk by saying something like "I'm interested in what you have to say" or "Would you like to talk about it?"

It is important to recognize that different people may have different orientations toward silence in conversations. Some of us have a high tolerance for silence, and some of us have

We need to be aware of the cultural and ethnic differences in orientations toward silence. If we were not aware, for example, that Native Americans value silence more than European Americans, we might inadvertently insult someone involved in our conversation.

a low tolerance. If someone with a low tolerance for silence is communicating with someone with a high tolerance for silence, he or she will have to mindfully remain silent longer than usual to give the other person time to talk. Also, there are cultural and ethnic differences in orientations toward silence. Native Americans, for example, tend to use longer silences in conversations than European Americans.

An appropriate body posture also is important in signaling that we are listening. If we are leaning back with our arms crossed, for example, other people probably will interpret our nonverbal cues as signaling that we are not interested in what they have to say. If we lean forward facing other people, in contrast, they will probably assume that we are interested in what they have to say. If we are totally still, other people may not think we are listening to them. If we remain still, others will perceive that we are cold and aloof (Bolton, 1979). When we listen responsively, we move our bodies. In moving our bodies, however, we want to avoid motions that distract the speaker.

Appropriate eye contact also is important in signaling that we are following what other people are saying. Appropriate eye contact indicates that we are interested in other people and their messages. Appropriate eye contact does *not* mean staring in other people's eyes or repeatedly looking away from them. Rather, appropriate eye contact in the European American subculture means making eye contact, holding the contact for a short length of time, and then briefly shifting our gaze from other people's eyes to another part of their body or around the room. The appropriate length of time to hold eye contact depends on our relationship with other people and our cultural background.

Vocalizations like "mm-hmm" and "uh-huh" tend to serve as encouraging signals for other people to continue to express their ideas and feelings. Verbally, short words and phrases like "I see," "I hear you," "That's very interesting," "Tell me some more," "Go on," and "Really?" can also indicate to other people that we are paying attention to what they are saying.

Another way we can let other people know that we are listening and understanding what they are saying is by using reflections. *Reflections* "mirror back" the main part of

Elaine learns to be a good listener.

SINGLE SLICES © Peter Kohlsaat, October 16, 1992, Los Angeles Times Syndicate. Reprinted with permission.

other people's messages. Reflections do *not* involve analyzing a message. Rather, they "simply show that meaning has been registered. They reveal an act of empathy. They tell the [other person] he or she has been heard" (Goodman & Esterly, 1988, p. 38). We often use reflections naturally when others tell us something that makes them happy, sad, excited, or angry; for example,

SHE: This letter says I didn't get the job. Damn, they didn't even interview me. It's not right! They never gave me a real chance.

HE: I can't believe it. That's really not right. It's so unfair. Without even giving you an interview! (Goodman & Esterly, 1988, p. 224)

Reflections are *not* restatements of what other people say, but rather clearly telling other people we understand what they say. Reflections are a simple way that we can indicate to others that we hear them and empathize with their feelings.

We often can use reflections as a way to start responsive listening, even when other people ask us for advice. Imagine a conversation between Sean and Morris. Sean says to Morris, "I've thought about this a lot and I just don't know how to handle this situation. What would you do if you were in my shoes?" (Bolton, 1979, p. 98). Most of us would tend to respond by giving advice when communicating on automatic pilot. There is, however, another alternative. Morris could say, "This one's really got you stumped!" (p. 98). This response reflects Sean's feelings back to him and allows Sean to begin working out a solution for himself, because "when the listener accurately reflects the feeling or meaning that lies behind the question, the speaker often forgets that he [or she] even asked a question and usually plunges into a deeper discussion of the matter and begins to grope toward a solution" (p. 98). If speakers recognize that their questions have not been answered, listeners can indicate that their job as listeners is to help the speaker solve the problem, not give advice.

Comprehending

Comprehending involves interpreting, clarifying, and understanding. When we *comprehend,* we cross-check our understanding of both the content and the relational meanings of the message. We also expand and extend our understanding of the original message by encouraging other people to provide us with more details or information. There are four skills we can use to increase comprehension: paraphrasing, perception checking, probing/clarifying responses, and encouraging elaboration.

Paraphrasing is one way to make sure we are interpreting the content of other people's verbal messages accurately. *Paraphrasing* involves verbally restating our interpretation of the *content meaning* of other people's messages in our own words. Paraphrasing is *not* repeating other people's messages in their words. Rather, it is interpreting the meaning of other people's messages and restating them in our own words. The restatement should reflect our understanding of other people's meaning. Phrases such as "It sounds like to me that . . ." and "In other words, you're saying that . . ." can serve as ways to begin paraphrasing. In some cases, paraphrasing should be preceded by a qualifying response. Statements like "I'm not sure whether this is what you mean, but this is how I interpret what you have just said . . ." and "I'm not sure whether I'm following you accurately, but let me try to summarize your point of view . . . ," for example, can signal tentativeness in understanding and readiness for more information.

Paraphrasing is different from reflection. The goal of using reflections is to demonstrate that we heard what was said and empathize with what happened. The goal of paraphrasing, in contrast, is to make sure that we understand the *content* of other people's messages.

Perception checking, as discussed in Chapter 7, is designed to help us make sure we are perceiving other people's thoughts or feelings accurately. It is a skill that can be used any time we are unsure that we understand other people's thoughts or feelings. As you will recall, perception checking involves describing other people's behavior, giving our interpretation of the thoughts or feelings behind the behavior, and then asking whether our perceptions are correct. Statements such as "Your facial expression suggests that you are very tense right now. Are you?" and "You look like you're having a great time. Are you?" are examples of perception checking statements.

Paraphrasing and perception checking can be combined. We can restate what we think other people's content meaning is and then check our perceptions of the speaker's thoughts or feelings. To illustrate, suppose a woman friend says, "I had a date with my boyfriend last night and he didn't show up" in what we think is an angry tone of voice. We can paraphrase the content of her message by saying something like "Your boyfriend stood you up and didn't call?" She would probably respond by saying "yes." We could stop there, but we would only understand the con-

BALLARD STREET by Jerry Van Amerongen. By permission of Jerry Van Amerongen and Creators Syndicate.

tent of her message, not her feelings. We interpreted her tone of voice as anger, but we could be wrong. To make sure we are perceiving her feelings correctly, we can use perception checking. We might say something like "The tone of your voice tells me that you're angry. Are you?"

Paraphrasing and perception checking allow us to make sure we understand others. Once we know that our perceptions are correct, we can probe for more information or ask clarifying questions. *Probing* involves looking for an extension of the content of what is being said or the relational meaning being expressed. Verbal probes seek more detail through open-ended questions (who, what, when, where, why, how). Specific *clarifying questions* help us gather more content and emotional data from the other person. Examples of clarifying questions include "I'm not sure what you mean by an analytical paper, can you define it for me?" and "You sounded confused, but I'm not sure what you are confused about. Can you tell me what is bothering you?" We need to be careful, however, in asking others questions. If we ask too many questions, we may begin to work on our own agenda rather than trying to understand the other person. Any questions we ask should facilitate our understanding of the speaker.

Encouraging responses, such as "This is really interesting. I want to hear more about what influences your thinking" and "I've never thought of our relationship as a merry-go-round until this very moment. Can you tell me something more about this merry-go-round feeling?" can help build a supportive interaction climate between people. Questions such as "Can you tell me some more about your family? I think it'll really help me to understand you better" and "I really want to learn more about your culture. Do you mind telling me about your culture?" used in situationally appropriate contexts and in a timely manner will help us to improve the quality of our understanding of other people and the context that frames their behavior.

In sum, responsive listeners are trying to understand other people and the content and relational messages they are transmitting. **By using responsive listening, we are saying implicitly, "We want to understand the meaning of your message with accuracy, and we are also eager to understand the person behind the message."**

Skill Practice

Most of us do not have scripts for responsive listening. Rather, we tend to think about what we wanted to say while others are talking, not listen responsively. We therefore need to develop new scripts for listening. Before proceeding, think about how you might use responsive listening in specific situations. Take a few minutes to complete Skill Exercise 8.1.

Many people's typical responses to the situations in Skill Exercise 8.1 are to give advice or judge other people. Giving advice or judging, however, are *not* part of responsive listening. The goal of responsive listening is to understand other people and their points of view, not telling them what to do. Of course, if other people ask us for our advice, we are free to give it *after* we are sure we understand their point of view.

Responsive listening is one of the most important skills you can add to your communication resources. It will feel awkward the first few times you use this skill. Any time we do something new, it feels awkward at first. This is natural and to be expected, because you do not have a responsive listening script. Using responsive listening *when appropriate* can improve the quality of communication in any particular encounter. When responsive listening is used regularly in a relationship, it also can improve the quality of

Skill Exercise 8.1 *Responsive Listening*

Responsive listening involves listening to understand what the other person is saying from his or her perspective. For each of the messages listed below, indicate how you would typically respond and how you might respond using responsive listening.

1. Jim says, "I got a D on my exam in interpersonal communication. I have to get a C for the course to count toward my general education credit."

   How would you typically respond? ______

   How would you respond to Jim using responsive listening? ______

2. Sue says, "I don't think that my boss likes me. I don't know how to approach the boss to talk about it."

   How would you typically respond? ______

   How would you respond to Sue using responsive listening? ______

3. Lisa says, "I just heard that the guy I've been dating is seeing someone else. I don't know what to do."

   How would you typically respond? ______

   How would you respond to Lisa using responsive listening? ______

the relationship. The benefits of listening are outlined in Reading 8.1.

As indicated earlier, **we do not necessarily want to use all of the responsive listening skills in every situation.** The various skills discussed in this chapter are resources we can use when we need them. To illustrate, if you find yourself in a work setting and it is important that you understand the information your boss is telling you, you would *not* want to use *all* of the responsive listening skills presented. When you need to recall information you are being told, it is important to make sure that you are listening in a nondistracting environment, stop your internal monologue, be silent so your boss can talk, avoid premature judgments about what your boss is saying, and listen for the main points when your boss is speaking. Do perception checking to improve your understanding. Ask clarifying or probing questions as needed. Once your boss has finished speaking, you

Reading 8.1 THE ART OF LISTENING/LEO F. BUSCAGLIA

It seems that few people listen anymore. Everyone seems to be too busy speaking. Some of us have forgotten that we learn by listening to others, not by listening to ourselves.

It is a mistake to believe that the more we say the more we impress. Unless we have something of import to contribute, nothing can be further from the truth. The fact is, everyone loves a listener. I'm beginning to wonder if they are a vanishing breed.

Listening, of course, is not simply the act of being quiet or hearing someone. It is far more subtle than that. It involves many other skills. It is based upon the proposition that we are interested in others. We want to know their point of view, their feelings and, on a deeper level, what they mean by what they cannot verbalize easily.

Listening is the only way we can understand other people and bridge those gaps that are responsible for our loneliness. It is said that, because of their personal nature, the most significant statements humans utter are often spoken in whispers. They therefore run the risk of never being heard, or if heard, being misinterpreted.

Every person we encounter is a specialist of sorts with a wealth of knowledge and history that, if shared, would make us richer, more human and understanding. Unless we accept this, we will continue to indulge ourselves in selective listening—learning and relearning what we already know, effectively keeping us from change and growth, confirming our ignorance and lack of sensitivity.

It is only when we have convinced others that we are genuinely interested in them that conversation can rise above the vain, petty and vapid and become real communication.

When we value every human being, we become open to their potential to teach us. I recall that many years ago, walking along the river in St. Louis, I encountered an elderly man who greeted me with a toothless smile. He might easily have been dismissed as a derelict had it not been for his dancing eyes and pleasant greeting.

I was immediately taken with his positive, joyful attitude and acceptance of life. I could not resist asking him if he had a philosophy to share. Without hesitation he replied, "If you want to be happy and lead a good life, always keep your mind full and your bowels empty. With too many people the opposite is true." I've never forgotten that little piece of wisdom.

Listening is a vital part of communication. It encourages others to reveal themselves, to share their knowledge and romance. It sets the tone for the vital connections that give life meaning and purpose.

When others ask us to listen to them, they are not implying that they want our advice or solutions to their problems. They are most often simply requesting a caring ear. When we are silent and listen, it is a way of showing them that we believe in them, that we trust in their finding their own solutions.

Listening is an art and, like all arts, requires sensitivity and patience before it can be mastered. But when the art is mastered, it affords us one of the most useful skills possible for cementing relationships and assuring our love.

Perhaps it is true that no one can ever completely know what another person is saying—there are such strong barriers between people's thoughts and feelings. This, it seems to me, challenges us even more to make the most of our listening skills. Perhaps a good rule of thumb to start with is to keep in mind the old New England proverb: "Don't talk unless you can improve the silence."

might paraphrase the main points in your own words to make sure you understand.

Speakers Can Help Others Listen Effectively

Effective communication is not only the responsibility of listeners. Speakers can help other people listen more effectively (Weaver, 1972). When we are speaking, we need to empathize with listeners so that we understand how they are interpreting our messages. If we assume that listeners are interpreting our messages in the same way we mean them, we are likely to have misunderstandings. When possible, we need to adapt our messages to the specific people listening to us, so that they can interpret our messages as accurately as possible. We can only do this if we are aware of our own biases.

When we are speaking, we also can help others listen effectively if we prepare them for our messages (Weaver, 1972). We might, for example, tell listeners the general issue we want to talk about before we talk about specific details. When we give specifics, they need to be presented in a way that listeners can understand them. We can accomplish this by using language with which listeners are familiar and avoid jargon and slang unless listeners share our meanings for these words. Our goal is to minimize the number of inferences listeners must make and minimize the listeners' misinterpretations of our messages.

We also need to keep our messages interesting so listeners do not get too involved in their own internal monologues (Weaver, 1972). Others are more likely to listen responsively when they are interested than when they are bored. If it appears that listeners are drifting away while we are talking, we can help them refocus their attention or decide to continue at a later time.

When we are speaking and we are not sure that the person listening is comprehending what we are saying, we can ask her or him to paraphrase what we said. The important thing to keep in mind is that we do not want to make the other person defensive. One way we can do this is to say something like, "I'm not sure I'm being clear. Would you mind telling me what you heard me say so I can tell you if I'm being clear?" By putting it this way we are taking responsibility for the clarity of communication and the other person probably will not become defensive.

To summarize, effective communication is a two-way street. Both speakers and listeners must share responsibility. Just because one person does not live up to his or her responsibility, it does not relieve the other person of her or his responsibility. Speakers are responsible for making their messages as clear as possible; listeners are responsible for listening responsively so that they can understand the speaker.

Giving and Receiving Feedback

When we listen responsively to other people, we often give them feedback on their messages. *Feedback* is information we transmit to others in reaction to the verbal and nonverbal messages we have received from them. There are times when we want to go further than being responsive and talk with other people about how their behavior affects us. The goal of giving feedback to others, therefore, is different from that of responsive listening. Our goal when we listen responsively is to understand other people. Our goal when we give feedback to others is to tell them how their behavior affects us. This can help other people manage their uncertainty about us.

Our feedback to others allows them to understand how their behavior affects

us. We can give feedback to encourage, to give advice, to disagree or agree, to show appreciation, to assert our point of view, and to evaluate critically. Most people's tendency, however, is only to give feedback when something goes wrong. When we receive feedback from others, it allows us an opportunity to mindfully think about our behavior so we can decide if we want to modify our behavior to achieve our goals. When we use feedback effectively in our relationships, we are likely to achieve understanding and shared meanings. Feedback, therefore, is a major resource we can use for effective communication with others.

Giving Feedback

We often give feedback to others without thinking about it. Think about how you typically give other people feedback on how their behavior affects you. Answer the following questions:

> Think of a situation in which you gave feedback and other people got upset with you or did not change their behavior. How did you give the feedback? (Describe the comments you made.) ____________
>
> ______________________________
>
> ______________________________
>
> What was the other people's reaction?
>
> ______________________________
>
> ______________________________
>
> ______________________________
>
> What characteristics of the messages you sent made them ineffective? ________
>
> ______________________________
>
> ______________________________
>
> Think of a situation in which you gave feedback to other people and it was successful. How did you give the feedback? (Describe specific messages.) ________
>
> ______________________________
>
> ______________________________
>
> ______________________________
>
> What was the other people's reaction?
>
> ______________________________
>
> ______________________________
>
> ______________________________
>
> What made your feedback effective? ___
>
> ______________________________
>
> ______________________________
>
> ______________________________

Your answers to these questions should provide some insight into the role of giving feedback in your implicit personal theory of communication. Keep you answers to these questions in mind as you read the remainder of this section.

Prior to giving feedback, we have to understand the people who are going to listen to our feedback. We need to understand their expectations regarding feedback, as well as their motivations and goals in receiving the feedback. This will allow us to figure out the most effective way to present the information to them so that they can use it in a constructive manner. To give effective feedback, we have to be sensitive to other people's needs and interests.

There are several areas where people tend to give feedback to others: their performance of a skill, their appearance, relational issues, their character, and their decisions/attitudes (Tracy, Dusen, & Robinson, 1987). The type of relationship we have with others influences the types of feedback they give us. Peers and parents are most likely to give us feedback on our appearance, while bosses and teachers are most likely to comment on our performance of skills. People with whom we have a close relationship, such as a friend or romantic partner, are most likely to give us feedback on relational issues and our character.

Some general guidelines on giving feedback are provided below (these guidelines are adapted, in part, from those developed by Haslett & Ogilvie, 1988). Keep in mind, however, that these are general guidelines and that they must be adapted to the specific situation in which we give feedback to other people and our relationship with them. The main thing to keep in mind is that we want to give feedback in a way that helps other people *not* become defensive. Well-given feedback produces positive consequences for our relationships with others. Poorly given feedback, in contrast, is perceived as "off the mark" or produces negative reactions (Tracy et al., 1987).

Timing. We need to give feedback close to the occurrence of the behavior on which we are giving feedback, but it needs to be at a time when other people are receptive. **In giving feedback, we have to make sure that other people are available to listen to our feedback.** When other people are physiologically or emotionally exhausted, for example, it is the wrong situation or the wrong time to give feedback. In this situation, other people are not psychologically available to listen. To illustrate, it is not a good time to give your roommate feedback about not doing the dishes after she or he has been up all night writing a paper. In situations like these, we may need to schedule a special time and place to discuss our feedback with other people.

Specificity. Feedback needs to be clear, direct, specific, and supported by evidence. The use of impersonal responses, such as "One should always be on time" and "There seems to be a procrastinator among us," for example, are too vague and impersonal to have any direct effect on the listener. To be effective, feedback also needs to be specific to a particular situation and supported by evidence. Providing evidence means describing the data on which we based our feedback. It also is critical that we identify the reason for our interpretations when giving feedback. After explaining our interpretations, we can invite other people to respond to our interpretations.

Effective feedback also can involve providing details about how other people can change if they are ready to listen to suggestions or if they ask for suggestions. To illustrate, if an employee has been late coming back from lunch, the boss might say something like "You've been late from lunch three times this week. Other employees have asked me to find someone else to cover their stations when they go to lunch because they have to wait for you to return. You're usually prompt. What's the problem?" This message is direct, specific, and provides the data on which the feedback is based.

Nonevaluative. Effective feedback requires that we separate the person from the issue on which we are giving feedback. **We need to avoid judging the person to whom we are giving feedback.** The use of responses like "That's really stupid" and "What a crazy idea" do not help to correct the existing situation in a constructive manner. If we are evaluative when we give feedback to others, they will become defensive and will not be able to listen to our feedback. When giving feedback, we need to describe other people's behavior and give our interpretation of the behavior, *not* evaluate them. (See Chapter 4 for a discussion of the differences between description, interpretation, and evaluation.)

Mutual Problem. To be effective, feedback needs to be presented in a way that

suggests that the issue on which feedback is being given is a mutual problem. If an employee is consistently late, for example, the boss might say, "We seem to have a problem—you've been late several times the past week. Let's talk about what we can do to solve the problem." If the boss presented the issue as the employee's problem by saying something like "You're late again. What are you going to do about it?" the employee could become defensive, which would make solving the problem more difficult.

When giving feedback, we must avoid blaming other people. We need to recognize that other people's perceptions may be different from ours. Since the problems on which we are giving feedback in an interpersonal relationship are mutual problems that need to be solved, we can improve the effectiveness of our feedback by offering to help other people deal with the issue. Offering to help is particularly important if we are giving feedback on the performance of a skill or a relational issue. To illustrate, we could say to our romantic partner, "It really bothers me when you let irritation build until you blow up. Would it help if we sat down once a week to discuss things that are bothering us?"

Assertive Manner. Feedback needs to be given in an assertive, not an aggressive, manner. The use of "I messages," such as "This is where I see our relationship is going," "This is how I interpret what happened," or "I am disappointed because . . . ," signal clear ownership of perceptions and feelings. "I messages" create a clear sense of accountability in terms of where our interpretations and emotions are derived. When giving feedback, we need to limit what we say to our own observations, *not* what others have told us. We cannot use "I messages" when we report second-hand information from others. Skill Exercise 8.2 provides an opportunity for you to practice creating "I messages." Take a few minutes to complete it now.

A critical aspect of being assertive is the language we use. If we use offensive or obscene language, we are being aggressive, not assertive (see Chapter 3). A harsh manner of speaking, like raising your voice or yelling, also should be avoided if feedback is to be effective.

For feedback to be assertive, there needs to be an opportunity for other people to respond. We can invite other people to enter a collaborative dialogue with us in the feedback process. We can ask other people to paraphrase what we have just said (if appropriate to the situation) and ask for their reflections and interpretations concerning our behavior. For feedback to be effective, we should always give other people an opportunity to clarify and express their interpretations and reactions. If other people are not allowed to respond, our feedback will appear to be aggressive, not assertive.

Fairness. For feedback to be effective, we need to be fair and allow other people to maintain their public images when we give them feedback. If other people think that we are not being fair, it will cause them to become defensive and not listen to our feedback. Similarly, if we threaten other people's public self-images by criticizing them in front of bystanders when giving feedback, they will become defensive, and our feedback will be ineffective. Feedback can be clear and at the same time display concern and respect for other people.

When giving feedback, we should also display sensitivity to nuances of our ongoing relationships with others. We can use explicit relationship reminders like "I have enjoyed working with you for a long time" to let other people know that we value them as special people. We should also use relationship re-

Skill Exercise 8.2 *Using "I Messages"*

We often use "you" or "we" when we communicate with others, and it appears that we are blaming or accusing others. To illustrate, saying, "You make me angry" places blame on the other person. A more accurate statement is "I am angry." In this type of statement, the person takes responsibility for his or her own feelings of anger. For each of the statements below, suggest how they could be reworded as "I messages" that do not blame the other person.

1. You never tell me you love me.

 ____

2. Our relationship would be stronger if we talked more.

 ____

3. You don't do your fair share of work around here.

 ____

4. You're making too much noise for me to study.

 ____

5. You're always late.

 ____

minders such as "I value our relationship above all things" to indicate to other people that we care about our relationships with them.

Balance. We can increase the effectiveness of our feedback if we balance positive and negative feedback. If we give other people only negative feedback, it can threaten their self-images. By balancing positive and negative feedback, we can help other people maintain their self-images, thereby increasing the effectiveness of our feedback. To help people accept our negative feedback we may want to begin with positive feedback. After giving negative feedback we can help others feel good about themselves if we end with more positive feedback.

Here and Now. When we give feedback to others, we need to focus on the present. If we drag up the past (the there and then), we decrease the effectiveness of our feedback. When we bring up the past, we may overload other people and they will feel like we are "dumping" on them.

Verbal/Nonverbal Consistency. Nonverbal behavior plays a critical role in displaying our attitude toward other people. Inattentive facial expressions or body movements and inconsistent nonverbal and verbal messages signal to other people that we are really not interested in them. Attentive nonverbal facial expressions and body postures need to accompany our verbal feedback. **Our verbal and nonverbal behaviors should be congruent and signal to other people that "I care for you as a person even though I'm conveying negative information about your behavior."**

Concluding Feedback Sessions. Feedback sessions should end with a clear statement of mutual understanding of the situation and a statement of the specific actions that will be taken in the future. If there is not a clear summary statement of future expectations, there may be a need to repeat the process in the future. Effective feedback can help us to develop better insights into our own behavior, and it can increase the quality of our relationship with the other person.

Skill Exercise. Skill Exercise 8.3 provides an opportunity for you to practice giving feedback. Take a few minutes to complete it now.

When you practice giving feedback, it is important to remember several things. It is important to recognize that, when you first start using this skill, you will have to be mindful, and it will seem awkward. The reason for this is *not* that the skill is ineffective, but rather that you do not have a script for giving feedback. It is not something your parents, peers, or teachers taught you when you were learning to communicate. The more you practice giving feedback, the easier it will become and the more effective you will become at it.

It also is important to recognize that the guidelines on giving feedback are based on an individualistic, direct form of communication. If you are an individualist and you are going to give feedback to collectivists who use indirect forms of communication, direct feedback may not be effective. Rather, it may be necessary to adapt your feedback to other people's communication styles to be effective. It may be necessary, for example, to give feedback in an indirect manner.

Receiving Feedback

In addition to giving feedback, we also receive it from others. Before proceeding, think about how you typically respond to the feedback you receive from others. Take a few moments to answer the following questions:

> Think of a situation in which you wanted feedback from another person. The person gave you feedback, but you did not find it useful. What specific characteristics of the message made the feedback ineffective? ______________________
>
> ______________________
>
> ______________________
>
> ______________________
>
> How do you typically react to ineffective feedback? ______________________
>
> ______________________
>
> ______________________
>
> ______________________
>
> Think of a situation in which you wanted feedback from another person. The person gave you feedback, and you found the feedback very useful. What specific characteristics of the message made the feedback effective? ______________________
>
> ______________________
>
> ______________________
>
> ______________________
>
> How do you typically react to effective feedback? ______________________
>
> ______________________
>
> ______________________
>
> ______________________

Your answers to these questions should provide some insight into the role of receiving feedback in your implicit personal theory of communication. Keep your answers to these questions in mind as you read the remainder of this section.

Receiving feedback from others can increase our anxiety and uncertainty. We often react defensively or aggressively when receiv-

Skill Exercise 8.3 *Giving Feedback*

Being able to give positive and negative feedback is important to effective interpersonal communication. Indicate how you might typically respond in each of the situations when you are on automatic pilot *and* how you might give positive or negative feedback when you are mindful of your communication.

1. You are working on a group project in class, and one group member did an excellent job that helped improve the group's grade on the project.

   How would you typically respond? ____

   How could you give this person positive feedback? ____

2. Your romantic partner planned a special evening for the two of you, and you really enjoyed it.

   How would you typically respond? ____

   How could you give your partner positive feedback? ____

3. You are working on a group project in class, and one group member has not done his or her fair share of the work. You think this person's performance will lower the group's grade on the project. You want the person to do his or her share of the work before the project is due.

   How would you typically respond? ____

   How could you give this person negative feedback? ____

4. Your friend is always late when you make plans to get together. You want your friend to be on time in the future.

   How would you typically respond? ____

   How could you give your friend negative feedback? ____

ing feedback from other people. We can easily slip into defensive or aggressive reactions when other people do not have the skills to provide feedback responsively and sensitively, or when we are not mindful of our communication. There are two general conditions under which we receive feedback: when we request it from others and when others give feedback without our requesting it. Let's begin by looking at what we can do when we request feedback.

Preparing to Receive Requested Feedback. There are several specific things that we need to keep in mind when we ask other people for feedback on our behavior. **By requesting feedback from other people, we are indicating that we are ready to listen and that we are ready to learn from them.** When we request feedback, we have to assume that other people are providing feedback based on good intentions. Even though other people may not be skillful at giving us feedback, we should respect their intention to serve as a mirror to our behavior.

Our request for feedback should be specific and to the point. We should indicate to other people why we are soliciting feedback and how we intend to use the feedback to promote change. We should encourage other people to provide constructive feedback in areas that we want to change and that we are capable of changing. It should be noted that problems will arise later in the relationship if we ask for feedback in an area and then do not make an attempt to change. We need to find a comfortable physical setting in which to receive feedback from others. We will not feel inhibited in communicating and we will be ready to receive feedback in a private, comfortable, and nondistracting setting.

Responses to Receiving Unrequested Feedback. When others provide feedback without our requesting it, we are not necessarily in control of the situation, and we must therefore mindfully manage our reactions. Most of us have a fear of receiving feedback, but feedback is critical to improving our communication in our interpersonal relationships and to improving our performance on the job. Reading 8.2 contains a discussion of the advantages of feedback we receive from others, even when it is not requested.

When we receive feedback from others, we have three different responses that we can use when responding to criticism (Burns, 1980). Consider the example of a boss saying, "You've been doing sloppy work and goofing off lately."

Our first possible response to this feedback is "I'm no good" (Burns, 1980). If we have this response, we might think that "I'm always goofing up. I'm worthless." This thought might lead us to feel anxious or sad. These feelings may lead us to isolate ourselves from our boss and our co-workers. We often respond this way when our self-esteem is low and/or when we are not mindful of our communication.

The second possible response to this feedback is "You're no good" (Burns, 1980). If we respond in this way, we might think, "That stupid jerk is on my back again." These thoughts might lead us to feel angry or frustrated. Based on our anger, we might say something to our boss that we will regret later. Again, we are likely to respond this way when our self-esteem is low and/or when we are on automatic pilot.

The third, and preferable, response to this criticism is a "self-esteem response" (Burns, 1980). If we respond in this fashion, we consciously think, "Here's a chance to learn something." This thought would lead us to feel more prepared to respond to feedback, and we therefore might ask our boss for specific information; for example, we might ask, "In what ways have I been goofing off?" Responding in this fashion requires that we are mindful of

Reading 8.2 FEAR OF FEEDBACK/ROBERT MCGARVEY

Imagine the boss shows up at your desk and says he [or she] has some feedback for you. "Great!" you respond. "I love hearing how I've goofed. Fire away!" Maybe that's how it goes in another solar system, but not here. We don't seek out feedback, and when it comes our way, we duck and shuffle and give our best imitation of Muhammad Ali floating like a butterfly and just waiting for an opportunity to sting like a bee.

There are exceptions, however. Bill Marriott, the hotel magnate, annually dispatches his top executives for a daylong retreat at which their sole assignment is to write down their criticisms of how the boss is doing. Marriott's no masochist, either. He says hearing these reviews enables him to do his job better. "It doesn't make me feel good," he admits, "but I need it."

Then there's Dr. Hendrie Weisinger. By training, he's a psychologist, but to spread his findings on the nature of criticism, Weisinger's branched out into writing. When his latest book, *The Critical Edge,* was in manuscript form, his editor frequently offered detailed critiques. "Hearing that is not always fun or easy, but I would have to be crazy to not hear it, " says Weisinger. "My editor is telling me how she thinks the book could be made better, and that is valuable information. Even if it hurts my feelings, I want to hear it because the results, the end product, will make it worthwhile.

"Accept that criticism will hurt your feelings," Weisinger goes on. "Nobody can tell you otherwise. But I can also tell you this: Our success—in the workplace and in life—is directly correlated with our ability to hear criticism. That is how we learn. We all go into occasional plateaus where our growth halts. How do we get off a plateau? Often it's the criticism we hear from others."

Easy for them to say: They do not have a fire-breathing boss who makes Darth Vader look like a cream puff. Granted, most bosses are inept critics. We all are. We're brusque and brutal, and leave the hurt and wounded in our wake. Even so, "There may be a nugget of truth in that feedback, no matter how it is delivered," says Dr. Bob Abramms, a senior associate with Amherst, Massachusetts-based ODT Inc., a management consulting firm specializing in upward appraisal and feedback. "Feedback tells us if we're on course or off course. And the least powerful position in the world is to keep doing the same thing over and over without knowing what its impact is. You've got to learn how to take feedback."

"The goal of learning to hear feedback is to move away from the emotional response and into an intellectual one," adds Weisinger. "Time will cure any hurt to our feelings, but it won't cure our failings. That's why we must learn to put our feelings aside and coolly assess the truth of the criticism we get."

our communication. When we hear our boss's criticism, we would have to immediately recognize any increase in our anger or anxiety, and immediately manage them so that we can be open to learning something. Being able to use a self-esteem response to unrequested feedback is a valuable resource for effective communication and improving the quality of our interpersonal relationships.

Skill Exercise. Skill Exercise 8.4 is designed to provide you with an opportunity to think about how you would respond to critical feedback. Take a few minutes to complete it now.

It is important to recognize that we typically respond to critical feedback in a defensive fashion. To change this response pattern, we must mindfully manage our emotional reac-

Skill Exercise 8.4 *Responding to Critical Feedback*

We often receive critical feedback from others. If we respond defensively, it will create a defensive climate in the relationship. We therefore need to learn how to respond nondefensively. For each of the following questions, indicate how you might typically respond and how you could respond nondefensively.

1. Your boss tells you that the report you submitted was not acceptable.

   How would you typically respond? ____

   ____

   ____

   ____

   ____

   How might you respond nondefensively? ____________________

   ____

   ____

   ____

   ____

2. A friend tells you that she or he is upset that you are always late when the two of you plan to get together.

   How would you typically respond? ____

   ____

   ____

   ____

   How might you respond nondefensively? ____________________

   ____

   ____

   ____

3. Your romantic partner tells you that lately you have not been as attentive as usual.

   How would you typically respond? ____

   ____

   ____

   ____

   How might you respond nondefensively?

   ____

   ____

   ____

tions to criticism and learn a new script for responding to negative feedback.

Summary

We generally do not listen effectively. Our ineffective listening may be due to external noises and distractions, preoccupation, wandering mind, assumptions, our personality, listening apprehension, ego-involvement, information overload, and because we lack training in effective listening. We can, however, learn to listen more effectively.

Responsive listening is designed to help us understand other people. It involves three clusters of skills: readiness, following, and comprehending. To listen effectively, we must be physically, psychologically, and emotionally ready to listen. Listening effectively also requires that we pay attention to what other people are saying. This involves the following skills of being silent, indicating nonverbally we are listening (such as by leaning forward and making appropriate eye contact), verbally indicating we are listening (such as by saying "I see"), and by reflecting what we hear others saying. To increase our comprehension, we can paraphrase what other people say, check our perceptions, and use probing or clarifying questions. Any questions we ask should be aimed at better understanding the speakers and their positions on the issues being discussed.

When we listen to other people, we often provide feedback on their messages. At times, we also want to tell other people how their behavior affects us. This involves giving them feedback on their behavior. Effective feedback should be timed appropriately, be specific, be nonevaluative, be presented as a mutual problem, be assertive, be fair, be balanced, that is, give both positive and negative feedback, focus on the present, and have verbal/nonverbal consistency. When we receive feedback from other people, we need to be mindful, not become defensive, and focus on what we can learn from their feedback.

Journal Reflections

1. *Responsive Listening.* Responsive listening is not appropriate in all communication situations. In at least two conversations when you think responsive listening is appropriate and might increase the quality of your communication, use this skill. In your journal, describe when you used the skill and why you thought it was appropriate in this situation, and reflect on how it affected the quality of your communication.
2. *Giving Feedback.* The use of feedback depends on the situation (for instance, is the other person ready to receive feedback?). In at least two situations in which you think giving feedback to another person would improve the quality of your communication with that person, try to use the skill. In your journal, describe when you used the skill and why you thought it was appropriate in this situation, and reflect on how it influenced the quality of your communication.
3. *Responding to Critical Feedback.* When we perceive (consciously or unconsciously) that others are "attacking" our self-concept, we tend to respond defensively. Our defensiveness, however, will decrease the quality of communication that takes place. When you find yourself feeling defensive, stop and consciously decide to respond nondefensively. In your journal, describe the situations in which you tried to respond nondefensively and what you did to be nondefensive, and analyze the influence of your use of this skill on the quality of the communication that occurred.

Study Questions

1. What are the differences between hearing and listening?
2. Why do we usually not listen effectively?

3. How can we indicate to others that we are paying attention to (following) them when they are talking?
4. What is the difference between paraphrasing and perception checking?
5. What is the goal of responsive listening?
6. What types of feedback do we generally give others?
7. What factors do we need to take into consideration when giving feedback?
8. Why are we generally afraid of receiving feedback?
9. What are the different ways we can respond when receiving feedback?

Suggested Readings

Roach, C., & Wyatt, N. (1988). *Successful listening.* New York: Harper & Row. Carol Roach and Nancy Wyatt discuss myths about our listening behavior. They also provide suggestions for improving our ability to listen effectively.

Weaver, C. H. (1972). *Human listening.* Indianapolis: Bobbs-Merrill. Carl Weaver examines cognitive factors that lead us to engage in selective attention when we are listening. He also examines sex differences in listening behavior and provides suggestions for improving listening behavior.

Wolff, F. I., & Marsnik, N. C. (1992). *Perceptive listening* (2nd ed.), New York: Harcourt, Brace, Jovanovich. Florence Wolff and Nadine Marsnik examine methods to enhance listening comprehension, maintain emotional control when listening, and provide suggestions for retraining ourselves to be better listeners.

9

LANGUAGE AND VERBAL INTERACTIONS

Language is the most important communication resource we possess. People in every society use a language, and it is the language that allows people in a society to share their humanity. Without language, there would be no literature, no conversations, no singing, and no street signs. Language is critical to our ability to hold conversations. Our ability to use language allows us to open, take turns in, manage topics in, make repairs of, and close conversations. Our conversations, in turn, are critical to the relationships we establish with others.

Our cultural and ethnic identities influence how we use language. People in some cultures use a direct style of communicating, while people in other cultures use an indirect style. People in some cultures use an elaborate style of communication, and people in other cultures use an understated style of communicating. Our gender identity also affects our verbal interaction styles. Men tend to use a more controlling style than women, while women tend to use a more affiliative style than men. Men also tend to use a more competitive style than women; women tend to use a more cooperative style than men.

Understanding our language use and verbal interaction styles is critical to improving the quality of our communication. If we do not understand how our language and verbal interaction styles influence our communication when we communicate on automatic pilot, we cannot choose alternative styles when we are mindful of our communication. Let's begin our analysis of message transmission by looking at language.

Language

All human languages contain both cultural-universal and cultural-specific dimensions. All languages, for example, possess "pronouns, methods of counting, ways to deal with time and space, a vocabulary that includes abstract words, and the capacity for full aesthetic and intellectual expression" (Farb, 1973, p. 11). The written symbols, the grammatical forms, the sounds, the meaning emphasis of different words, and the nonverbal nuances that surround different verbal expressions, in contrast, vary across cultures.

Native speakers of a language have the ability to make up new words, use old words in new ways, compose sentences they have never heard before, and combine sentences in new ways (Chaika, 1989). By the time children with normal speech development patterns reach their fourth birthday, they already have internalized the basic structures of their native language.

Using language is such a familiar feature of daily life that we rarely stop to think about it. Language is a purely human method of communicating. It is the major link between individuals and the society in which they live. Language makes it possible for people to form basic human bonds and to live together in society. We'll begin our discussion of language by looking at its structure and functions.

Language is Rule Governed

All languages are constructed of words or symbols that are arranged in patterned ways; that is, they are *rule governed.* All human languages have three interrelated rule systems: phonological rules, grammatical rules, and semantic rules. *Phonological rules* guide the set of sounds that makes up a language. The phonological rules of a language determine how words are formed and pronounced. English and Chinese, for example, sound very different because of their phonological systems.

The *grammatical rules* determine the possible combination of the elements. All languages have a grammatical system that tells speakers the appropriate order in which to put words to form sentences or how to make a verb past tense. In English, for example, sentences generally are arranged in a subject-verb-object order (for example, "I ate lunch"). In German, the verb often is found at the end of the sentence. This pattern varies from language to language, but most languages use either a subject-verb-object, a subject-object-verb, or a verb-subject-object pattern (O'Grady, Dobrovolsky, & Aronoff, 1989).

The *semantic rules* tell us the meanings that are expressible in a language. In every language there is some relationship between a word and the thing to which it refers. This relationship involves semantic meanings.

The rules of language are different in different speech communities. *Speech communities* are groups of people who share knowledge of the rules for the conduct and interpretation of speech (Hymes, 1974). People in a speech community share at least one form of speech and know its pattern of use. Within a speech community there are many *speech situations,* or occasions when people speak to each other. These consist of ceremonies like weddings or graduations, meals, fights, or even parties. Each of these situations is characterized by a different type of speech.

Speech events are activities that have rules or norms governing the use of speech. A conversation during a party and a speech at a political event, for example, require very different types of speech. Of course, the same type of speech event may occur in different speech situations. To illustrate, we could pass a note to someone in church or in a classroom. Speech events can be described by formal rules specifying their occurrence and characteristics.

The smallest unit in this analysis is the *speech act* that occurs within a speech event. A joke is a speech act that occurs in a conversation during a party (a speech situation). The same type of speech act can occur in various events and situations. We can tell a joke in a public speech, in a meeting, or in a conversation with one other person.

Functions of Language

Language serves three basic functions in communication: informative, expressive, and directive. As the name implies, the *informative function* of language is to communicate information and knowledge. When we are using language to fulfill the informative function, we may be answering a question, telling someone a story about our job interview, or writing an answer to an essay question.

The *expressive function* of language allows us to communicate feelings, attitudes, and emotions. Describing how a particular type of music gives us a headache is an example of using language to accomplish an expressive function. The expressive function of language can be used to communicate our own feelings (telling ourself to stay calm before we go into a job interview) or to evoke feelings in others (describing our feelings when a friend had a car accident after drinking at a party in order to make other friends feel concerned enough to change their behavior).

The *directive function* of language occurs when language is used to cause or prevent overt action. This may consist of asking questions, giving orders, or making requests. Of course, language often is used to serve more than one function at a time.

Characteristics of Language

Several characteristics of language are critical to understanding interpersonal communication. *Productivity* is the capacity to combine elements of the language into new meaningful utterances (Hockett, 1958). We are able to combine words into sentences that are immediately understandable to others, even though they have never heard this particular combination of words before.

Duality means that, although the number of distinct sounds in any language is rather small, usually under fifty, these sound units can

Speech events require different types of speech. Toasting the bride and groom is an event that has norms governing the use of speech.

be combined into thousands and thousands of meaningful units (Hockett, 1958). Language as we know it would not exist without this property. If every word we used consisted of a separate sound, we would have to learn to distinguish thousands of sounds.

Our language exhibits *discreteness* because we are able to perceive sounds as meaningfully distinct or discrete. We are able to distinguish between the sound at the beginning of the word *pin,* for example, and the sound at the beginning of the word *fin.* This one difference in sound changes the meaning. If we could not perceive discrete sounds, we would not be able to combine them into meaningful units (words and phrases), and our vocabulary would be severely limited.

Language is distinct from other forms of communication because it is *self-reflexive.* Language can be used to refer to itself, and we use language to critically examine it. In order to describe language, we have to use language. When you are writing a paper for a class, for example, you might read a particular sentence and say to yourself, "That's a very confusing sentence. I'd better rewrite it." In this instance, you are using language to talk about language.

Language is also distinct from other communication systems because of *displacement,* or the ability to refer to something that is not present in the immediate environment or even to something that does not exist. We can use language to describe our commute to work after it has happened. In addition, we are able to talk about imaginary beings (like unicorns) or to propose hypothetical situations ("What would happen if . . . ?"). Because of displacement, we can easily talk about the past or the future.

Arbitrariness means that neither words nor sounds have a direct connection with the meaning or function being performed (Hockett, 1958). All languages are systems of *arbitrary symbols* used to represent things or ideas about things. Words are symbolic because they *represent* objects, ideas, relationships, people, places, emotions, and many other concepts. Your name represents you, for example, but it is not you. Your name can't go to class, read a book, or talk with a friend. Only you can do these things. When other people speak about you in a conversation, they nevertheless use your name to represent you.

The words or symbols we use to represent the things about which we are communicating are arbitrary. In English, the word "table" is understood to represent a flat surface supported by legs. We could communicate just as effectively if we all had learned that type of object should be called "xymrff." Misunderstandings often occur when we forget that symbols are arbitrary.

Languages are not static entities; they are *constantly changing.* English grammar, for example, has changed over the centuries from that in Shakespearean English to that in modern English. Individual words, in contrast, change more rapidly. We are constantly adding new words to our language, losing some words, and combining others. Words like astronaut and Watergate are recent inventions, while words like uptight and aviatrix have faded from usage. In recent years, we have added many words to our language to reflect the technologies available to us. Many of these words are combinations of other words, such as compact disk player, satellite dish, and disk drive.

Language and Perceptions

Our language reflects our basic beliefs about the nature of the world. Our everyday language usage serves as a prism or kaleidoscope through which we interpret what we perceive to be "out there." In other words, our language influences our perceptions of the important

If we still spoke Shakespearean English, our lives would sound a lot more interesting.

features in our interactions with others and how we structure information in our environment.

Our everyday language usage influences, but does not determine, our thought processes. The language we speak affects the way we categorize the phenomena we encounter and shapes our thought processes (Sapir, 1925; Whorf, 1952). This is known as the *Sapir-Whorf hypothesis.* People who speak different languages tend to view the world differently and process cognitive information differently. The language we speak, for example, influences how we process information about other people (Hoffman, Lau, & Johnson, 1986). We tend to recall information that is consistent with the personality labels used in our language, such as "artistic."

To illustrate the influence of language on thought, let's compare Hopi speakers and English speakers. The Hopi language does not possess a discrete past-present-future grammatical system, as do most European languages (Whorf, 1952). Instead, it has a wide range of present tenses that concern the relationship of verbal statements to the knowledge of the event held by the person who is talking. Consider the example of talking about someone who is running. An English speaker might say something like "He (or she) is running" or "She (or he) ran earlier today." The verb focuses on the time when the running occurred. A Hopi speaker, in contrast, might say something like "I know that he (or she) is running at this very moment" or "I am told that he (or she) is running" (Farb, 1979, p. 495).

The differences in grammatical structure between Hopi and English influence the way time is viewed in the two cultures. English speakers emphasize the importance of time and Hopi speakers do not. Being "on time," for example, is not considered as important in the Hopi subculture as it is in the European American subculture.[1] The focus on the present tense in speaking also can be used to explain the absence of clocks and calendars in traditional Hopi culture (Farb, 1979).

Language Usage in Conversations

One of the major reasons we use language is to hold conversations with others. Our conversations with others provide the basis for forming and maintaining our relationships with them. The extent to which we are able to coordinate our verbal messages with others plays a large role in whether we will develop relationships with them and whether these relationships will continue after they are formed. Conversational participants, however, perceive what is going on in conversations differently. Two people can actually engage in a conversation, talk about different things, and not even know it. The Zen parable in Reading 9.1 provides an extreme example of two people discussing different topics and not realizing that they are misunderstanding each other. Although our everyday conversations are not as extreme as this parable, we often fail to cooperate with others when we hold conversations with them.

The main principle guiding conversations in individualistic cultures like the United States is the *cooperative principle.* This principle states that our contributions to conversations should meet the requirements of the conversation at the time we make it and take into consideration the purpose of the conversation (Grice, 1975). If someone asks us a question and we do not answer the question, for example, we have not met this requirement for holding conversations. If we are talking with our boss about developing a plan for a meeting, we are not cooperative if we try to change the conversation to our boss helping us solve a personal problem.

There are four *conversational maxims*

Reading 9.1 A Zen Parable/P. Reps

In a temple in the northern part of Japan two brother monks were dwelling together. The elder one was learned, but the younger one was stupid and had but one eye.

A wandering monk came and asked for lodging, properly challenging them to a debate about the sublime teaching. The elder brother, tired that day from much studying, told the younger one to take his place. "Go and request the dialogue in silence," he cautioned.

So the young monk and the stranger went to the shrine and sat down.

Shortly afterward the traveler rose and went in to the elder brother and said: "Your young brother is a wonderful fellow. He defeated me."

"Relate the dialogue to me," said the elder one.

"Well," explained the traveler, "first I held up one finger, representing Buddha, the enlightened one. So he held up two fingers, signifying Buddha and his teachings. I held up three fingers, representing Buddha, his teachings and his followers, living the harmonious life. Then he shook his clenched fist in my face, indicating that all three come from one realization. Thus he won. . . ." With this, the traveler left.

"Where is that fellow?" asked the younger one, running in to his elder brother.

"I understand you won the debate."

"Won nothing, I'm going to beat him up."

"Tell me the subject of the debate," asked the elder one.

"Why, the minute he saw me he held up one finger, insulting me by insinuating that I have only one eye. Since he was a stranger I thought I would be polite to him, so I held up two fingers, congratulating him that he has two eyes. Then the impolite wretch held up three fingers, suggesting that between us we only have three eyes. So I got mad and started to punch him, but he ran out and that ended it!"

that we must follow for our contributions to conversations to be viewed as cooperative in individualistic cultures like the United States (Grice, 1975). If we consistently fail to follow the conversational maxims, other people will see us as uncooperative and not want to talk with us.

First, the *maxim of quantity* suggests that our contributions to conversations should be as informative as is necessary, but that we should not give more information than is required (Grice, 1975). We violate this conversational maxim when we give other people too little or too much information. If someone asks what we thought of the movie we just saw, for example, and we answer, "It was okay," we are not giving sufficient information. If someone asks us what we do for a living and we give a detailed description of the tasks we do at work, we are giving too much information.

Second, the *maxim of quality* states that our contributions to conversations should be true (Grice, 1975). We should not say anything we think is false, and we should not say anything for which we do not have evidence. When we lie or deceive other people, we violate this conversational maxim. We also violate this maxim when we make claims we cannot support.

Third, the *maxim of relevance* suggests that our contributions to conversations should be relevant to what others say before us (Grice, 1975). This maxim deals with turn taking and topic management in conversations, discussed in detail below. For now it is sufficient to recognize that, if we want to be viewed as cooperative, our contributions to conversations must be related in some way to what the person who speaks before us says.

Fourth, the *maxim of manner* requires that our contributions to conversations be brief, orderly, not obscure, and not ambiguous (Grice, 1975). Of course, there are times when we may choose to violate the maxims to accomplish our goals. As indicated later in this chapter, for example, there are times when ambiguity is useful in conversations. If we use obscure words that other people are not likely to know, we violate this maxim. We also violate this maxim if we yell at other people, because our contribution then is not orderly.

Generally, we follow the four conversational maxims when we open conversations, cooperate in conversations, repair conversations when problems arise, and close conversations. Let's begin by looking at opening conversations.

Opening Conversations

There are three aspects to opening conversations (Clark, 1985). First, contact must be initiated. Second, the individuals must greet each other. Third, the initial topic of conversation must be selected. When these activities are carried out successfully, it helps us manage our anxiety and uncertainty about the interaction. The initiation of contact involves sighting other people, getting their attention, such as by waving if the person is known or dipping the head, and approaching them (usually involving gazing at each other).

Many different forms of verbal greetings can be used to start conversations (Knapp & Vangelisti, 1992). We can use "verbal salutes," such as "Good morning" or "Hello." Another way to greet others is by using direct references to their name or nickname, such as "Hi, Sandy." We can make inquiries of other people, like "How ya' doin'?" Compliments such as "You look very nice today" or references to the situation also can be used. In a grocery store, for example, we might say, "Do you know anything about selecting a ripe melon?" References to things outside the immediate situation ("How do you like the weather?") and references to ourselves ("Hi, I'm . . .") are potential ways we can greet others. In

DENNIS THE MENACE used by permission of Hank Ketcham and c by North America Syndicate.

addition, we can use apologies, such as "Excuse me, but . . . ," or we can tell other people the topic we want to discuss with them ("The reason I want to talk with you is . . ."). These examples are not necessarily complete. If you think about it for a few minutes, you can probably come up with other options. Obviously, we also can use combinations of these different types of greetings.

Once greetings have taken place, the initial topic of conversation has to be introduced. Usually the person who initiates contact introduces the first topic. A typical opening sequence might go something like this:

LIZ: Hi, Sunny, how are you?

SUNNY: Hi. I'm fine. How are you?

LIZ: I'm great! I just got a job.

SUNNY: Congratulations. What kind of job is it?

In this situation, Liz introduced the first topic in her second turn.

It is also possible to start a conversation without a greeting. To illustrate,

POLLY: Professor. (making eye contact)

RON: Yes, what can I do for you?

Ron's question returns the conversation to Polly to introduce the first topic. Once the initial topic is introduced, the participants need to coordinate their messages by turn taking and topic management.

Coordinating Messages in Conversations

Once we have greeted others, we need to coordinate the exchange of messages with them. There are two related processes involved in coordinating our messages in conversations. Somehow we have to coordinate our taking turns at talking, and we also have to manage the topics that we discuss with others. Let's begin by looking at turn taking.

Turn Taking. In our conversations with others, we have to coordinate our turn taking; "that is, who speaks when and for how long. . . . Coordination is accomplished by a system that allows or obligates certain parties to talk at certain times" (Clark, 1985, p. 181). In addition to focusing on the need for coordination, how we take turns reflects who controls the conversation (Wiemann, 1985). Turns must be managed sequentially in conversations, on a moment-by-moment basis (Sacks, Schegloff, & Jefferson, 1974).

There are several properties of conversations that are important in understanding turn taking (Sacks et al., 1974). Generally, one person talks at a time, and when one speaker is finished, another talks. Although it is common for two (or more) people to be speaking at the same time in conversations, the overlaps do not last long. Generally, there is no gap, or only a small gap, between when one person finishes speaking and another person begins. The order and length of turns in conversations are not fixed. The relative distribution of turns in conversations also is not fixed. Turn allocation techniques are used in conversations. In conversations with more than two people, the speaker can determine who speaks next by asking the person a question, or the person who speaks next can self-select. There also are repair mechanisms that can be used when problems in turn taking arise. To illustrate, if two people are talking at the same time, one can stop talking to repair the problem.

Conversations are mutually constructed by the participants. The person speaking and the people listening have an equal responsibility for managing who talks when and what is discussed (see the discussion of topic management below). Our conversations are "constructed on an utterance-by-utterance basis, with each subsequent utterance to some extent dependent on preceding ones for its sensibility and appropriateness" (Wiemann, 1985, p. 93).

We signal that we are ready to give up our speaking turn in several ways (Wiemann, 1985). How we do this depends on the content of the conversation and the context in which it occurs. Context can include the physical setting in which the conversation is held, our relationship with the other person, and the reasons we have for holding the conversation. Depending on the context, we might interpret cues such as verbally completing a thought, changes in intonation, using gestures, or changing the direction of gaze, as signals that other people are ready to give up their turn speaking. We may also use cues like this to signal to other people that we are ready to give up our turn. These cues, however, also can have other meanings and therefore must be interpreted within the framework of the ongoing conversation (Wiemann, 1985).

We define our relationships with others by the way we communicate with them. **How we hold conversations with people lays the foundation for our future relationships with them.** If we want to develop a relationship with another person, we want to get off on the right foot. This is accomplished, at least in part, by how we negotiate turn taking in our initial conversations. The way we take turns in conversations influences how cooperation will develop in the relationship; it also has implications for how control will be managed in the relationship. By making choices about when to change speakers, we define who is in control of our conversations and the relationship at that time (Wiemann, 1985).

In dealing with turn taking in conversations, we often deal with control issues in the relationship before we are consciously aware of them. To illustrate, consider the issues of simultaneous speech (two or more people talking at the same time) and interrupting other people when they speak. Simultaneous speech occurs frequently in conversations. Sometimes it indicates that people are highly involved in the conversation and at other times it means that the person who has not been speaking wants to speak. Interruptions can be viewed as problems in conversations because people interrupting others often are viewed as rude. Interruptions, however, also can be viewed as conversational resources we can use. From this viewpoint, interruptions are tactics "available for interactants to use to accomplish some conversational or relational goal—e.g., to dominate a conversation, to establish dominance in a relationship, to show enthusiasm for a topic, to show interest in one's partner, etc." (Wiemann, 1985, p. 97).

Interruptions can confirm the other person or perform empathic and supportive functions within the relationship. To understand the meaning of interruptions, we must look at the content of what is said, not just the fact that an interruption occurred.

Topic Management. Successfully managing topics in conversations has positive consequences for us as individuals and for our relationships with other people (Tracy, 1985). If we talk about the topic other people introduce, it gives them the freedom to define what we talk about and shows them deference. It also demonstrates that we are cooperative and interested in them. If we change the topic of conversation, it establishes our importance and demonstrates that we have a right to define topics of conversation. When we change the topic appropriately, we may be viewed as "self-confident, assertive, [and] full of interesting things to say." When we change topics inappropriately, in contrast, we may be seen as "overly dominant, rude, or stupid" (Tracy, 1985, p. 31).

How we manage topics in conversations also has consequences for our relationships with other people. Even though we tend to communicate on automatic pilot, other people often assume that we consciously choose what to say next. **Because we are viewed as making conscious choices about the topics we discuss in conversations, the way we handle topic management in conversations is viewed as an indicator of how we will act in interpersonal relationships.** To illustrate, if we change topics when it seems like other people are ready to talk about something else, it suggests to them that we are cooperative and friendly. This will increase the chance that other people will want to communicate with us again. If we do not manage topics in conversations successfully, there will be awkward silences and our conversations will not flow smoothly. If other people perceive that this is due to our behavior, they may not want to form relationships with us.

To successfully manage topics within conversations, we have to establish a context within which other people can interpret our remarks. There are three different types of contexts we can use when we respond to what other people say (Tracy, 1985). First, we can use the conversation itself as the context for what we say. One way we can do this is to comment on what other people said just prior to our talking. We also can refer to something said earlier in the conversation. Second, we can respond to what other people say based on the general environment in which our conversation is taking place. We can, for example, comment on someone walking past us. Third, we can base our comments on the general cultural knowledge we share with other people. This might involve invoking our "getting to know you" script if we do not know the people with whom we are communicating.

Other people expect us to comment on what they have just said, and it is the easiest for them to comprehend (Tracy, 1985). Commenting on something said earlier in the conversation often is difficult for other people to comprehend because they have to search their memory for the earlier referent before they can respond. If we comment on the environment or use general cultural knowledge, our comments may be difficult for other people to understand, because they have to search for a specific context in which to interpret our remarks. We can, of course, make it easier by explicitly telling other people how to interpret our comments. We might, for example, say something like "Going back to . . ." or "Not to change the subject, but. . . ."

When we attempt to extend what others say, we often have a choice in terms of talking about an issue or an event in what they said. To illustrate the difference, consider the following message:

> (1) Reading *Time* is just like the advertisements say. I find it interesting—it's a good way to pass time and I learn something. Last week I learned about those sets of separated twins who grew up not knowing each other and yet are very similar. (Tracy, 1985, p. 41)

The issue being discussed is that reading *Time* is a worthwhile activity; the event being discussed is the story of twins who grew up apart.

Given this distinction, how do we respond? Which of the following two alternative responses do you think the speaker in this example would see as most appropriate?

> (2) It's good to get a weekly magazine but I like *Newsweek* better than *Time*.
> (3) Were there two women twins who both wore seven rings on their hands? (Tracy, 1985, p. 41)

Response (2) builds on the issue being discussed, while response (3) builds on the event being discussed. The speaker would probably perceive our response as more appropriate if we used response (2) (Tracy, 1985). Extending issues is preferred if there is a choice between extending an issue or an event.

If we want to change the topic of conversation, there are several strategies we can use (Tracy, 1985). One way we can change the topic is to forget about extending what the speaker is saying and just change the topic. When we do this, we usually give other people an explicit indication that we are changing topics, by saying something like "Let's talk about something else." Changing topics without recognizing what other people say, however, may be perceived negatively.

There are several ways we can build on what other people say and also change the topic (Tracy, 1985). First, we can use our knowledge of other people's issues to change the topic. In the earlier example, we might say something like "I also enjoy reading the cinema section of *Time* . . ." (p. 43). By doing this, we would change the topic to movies. We could mention a particular review we read if we wanted to talk about a particular movie. Second, we can use a direct link to an idea in other people's messages. In the earlier example, we could use the idea of learning and say something like "Yeah, there are a lot of ways we can learn. I sometimes learn by watching people." Third, we can show how the issue other people are discussing is an example of a broader issue. To illustrate, "Reading *Time* is one way to spend time. I prefer to spend my time. . . ." Fourth, we can suggest a link between what other people say and what we want to say, when there actually may not be a link. Many of us use phrases like "I know exactly what you mean" and "That reminds me of" (Tracy, 1985, p. 44) to accomplish topic changes. This strategy, however, really does not extend the previous speaker's topic; it only appears to on the surface.

Cultural Differences. The ways we take turns and manage topics in conversations differ across cultures. Individualism-collectivism influences topic management and turn distribution in conversations.[2] **Collectivists tend to organize topics interdependently, while individualists tend to organize topics independently.** Japanese (collectivists), for example, "take short turns, distribute their turns relatively evenly, and continue to distribute their turns evenly regardless of who initiates a topic" (Yamada, 1990, p. 291). North Americans (individualists), in contrast, "take long monologic turns, distribute their turns unevenly, and the participant who initiates a topic characteristically takes the highest proportion of turns in that topic" (p. 291).

The way we manage conversations also is affected by individualism-collectivism. Collectivists use verbal and nonverbal expressions and repetition to support other people when they speak and to maintain negotiations. Individualists, in contrast, use less synchronizing behaviors and repetition than collectivists. Individualists tend to use feedback devices, such as questions or comments, to indicate that they are attentive, while collectivists tend to use back channeling (brief utterances that make conversation flow smoothly) to accomplish this purpose. To illustrate, when North American "speakers orient attention, they focus on the specific topical content. Japanese speakers only value the empathic interactional behavior and tend to consider the message exchange secondary" (Hayashi, 1990, p. 188).

Conversational Repairs

Repairs help us fix problems that emerge in conversations. Generally, **it is expected that the people who create problems in conversations will take responsibility for repairing the problems** (McLaughlin, 1984). If we recognize that we made an error, we can repair it while we are still speaking. We might, for example, say something like "Everyone feels . . . well, *most* people feel. . . ." In this example, we would have repaired our initial exaggeration.

Repairs are necessary when one of the four conversational maxims (quantity, quality, relevance, and manner) are violated or when there are problems in turn taking or topic management. When we initiate a repair sequence in conversations because of a problem that was created by other people, three steps are necessary. First, we have to make a request for a repair; we have to tell other people that something is wrong. Second, other people have to provide a remedy. Third, we need to acknowledge the repair.

Consider the following example of how these steps are followed when one person says something that the other does not comprehend:

> In the conversational excerpt below, which is addressed to a violation of the maxim of quantity (**A** doesn't say enough for **B** to establish a unique antecedent), the repairable is at line 5, the request for repair at line 6, the remedy at lines 7-9, and the acknowledgement at line 10.
>
> 1 **B**: How can you say that?
> 2 **A**: Because it's a proven fact. I mean like
> 3 I read it.
> 4 **B**: Well, what do you base this on?
> 5 **A**: On this magazine.
> 6 **B**: What magazine?
> 7 **A**: Uh, *D*.
> 8 **B**: *Big D,* the Dallas magazine.
> 9 **A**: Yeah, *D* magazine.
> 10 **B**: Yeah, yeah. Huh.
> 11 **A**: They said not now, but a few—many years ago—
> 12 five years ago.
> 13 **B**: Yeah, maybe. Yeah. (McLaughlin, 1984, p. 212)

Violations of other conversational maxims will differ in content, but the same three steps are followed.

The general guideline concerning repairs in conversations is that "if a statement is made and is followed by a demonstration/assertion that a hearer did not understand, then the one who made the statement may/must provide a clarification" (Jefferson, 1972, p. 305). The "may/must" component of this guideline suggests that we can choose whether to correct errors we make if others do not understand. Whether and how we make the repair influences other people's perceptions of our competence as a conversational partner.

Closing Conversations

Closing conversations typically involves three steps (Clark, 1985). First, we must terminate the topic of conversation. Second, we must begin leave-taking behavior. Third, we need to terminate contact. Terminating the topic of conversation usually requires the agreement of both parties in the conversation. When it appears that the topic has run its course, one of the participants will suggest an ending by saying something like "Okay" or "I don't have anything else to say about this." This allows the other person to introduce a new topic or begin the leave-taking. About 45 percent of the time, one person ends a conversation without the other person's consent (Reynolds, 1991). When this happens, the person must provide some sort of justification for ending the conversation (Kellermann, Reynolds, & Chen, 1991).

The most critical aspect of closing conversations is leave-taking. There are three functions of leave-taking: summarizing the conversation, signaling to others that we are breaking contact for now, and being supportive of the other person (Knapp et al., 1973). In leave-taking we try to reassure each other that our break in contact is only temporary and that we will see each other again (Goffman, 1971). Leave-taking usually also includes promising future contact with the other person and wishing the other person well. This often is ritualized in terms of the way we break contact by saying "good-bye," "see you," or "good night" (Clark, 1985).

To conclude, the ways that we initiate conversations, take turns, change topics, repair problems, and conclude conversations affect whether other people want to get to know us or develop relationships with us. How other people interpret our verbal messages depends in large part on the verbal interaction style we use. Our verbal interaction style is affected by our culture, ethnicity, and gender. We'll look at culture and ethnic influences first.

Cultural and Ethnic Verbal Interaction Styles

Language and verbal interaction styles differ across cultures and ethnic groups. Two important differences are particularly important in recognizing how misunderstandings occur when we communicate with members of different groups: direct versus indirect styles (the degree of revealed intent in verbal interaction, gestures, and postures) and elaborate versus understated styles (the degree to which expressive language is used). Each of these styles can be thought of as a continuum. The following discussion of the styles, however, is focused on the end points of the continua in order to demonstrate the differences. Let's begin by looking at the direct versus indirect styles.

Direct Versus Indirect Styles

The direct-indirect interaction styles refer to the degree to which we reveal our intentions through the use of explicit statements and direct tones of voice (Gudykunst & Ting-Toomey, 1988). In a *direct verbal style,* verbal statements clearly reveal a speaker's intent. In the *indirect verbal style,* in contrast, verbal statements camouflage and conceal a speaker's actual intent. In the United States, the direct verbal interaction style is reflected in phrases such as "be honest," "say what you mean," "don't beat around the bush," and "get to the point." Recall from Chapter 2 that direct messages are characteristic of low-context communication, while indirect mes-

Speaking styles differ across cultures and ethnic groups. We must be aware of the differences so we can recognize how misunderstandings occur when we communicate with members of different groups.

sages are characteristic of high-context communication.

Cultural differences in direct and indirect forms of communication can be illustrated by comparing individualists in the United States and collectivists in Japan. **In the United States, individualists use explicit words and directly express opinions when they communicate.** Categorical words like "absolutely," "certainly," "always," and "never" are used frequently (Okabe, 1983). English also requires that the subject of a sentence be clear. "I" or "you," therefore, often are used as subjects of sentences. Individualistic values require that individuals clearly state their opinions when asked.

To maintain harmony in the ingroup in Japan, collectivists tend to use implicit language and avoid expressing direct opinions. Direct statements of opinions might cause conflict, which would destroy the ingroup harmony. Japanese use qualifying words like "maybe" and "perhaps" frequently in conversation (Okabe, 1983). Also, the Japanese language does not require that subjects of sentences be stated explicitly. Whose opinion is being discussed, therefore, often is ambiguous.

Koreans also prefer not to make direct, negative responses such as "no," "I cannot do it," and "I disagree with you." Rather, they prefer to use indirect expressions, such as "[I] kind of agree with you in principle" and "[I] kind of understand your situation, but [I also] have my own difficulties" (Park, 1979). The "I"s are in brackets because the subject of the sentence often is omitted in Korean, and it needs to be inserted for the English translations to make sense.

The indirect style is not limited to Asian cultures like Japan and Korea. Language use in Puerto Rico (a collectivistic culture) shares many commonalities with Asian cultures (Morris, 1981). Puerto Ricans take care not to put themselves or others in situations where conflict might occur. This often is accomplished by being indirect and blurring meanings when they speak. Because of their indirect language usage, Puerto Ricans constantly have to try to figure out what other people mean when they speak. These attempts, however, are indirect rather than direct. Puerto Ricans are able to figure out what other people mean when they speak because the information they need comes from their relationships with others. Understanding relationships with others is critical to interpreting indirect messages. Since indirect messages predominate, Puerto Ricans judge themselves and others by what they do, not what they say.

Although directness predominates in individualistic cultures like the United States, indirectness also occurs. The reasons for the use of indirectness in individualistic cultures, however, appear to be different from those in collectivistic cultures. In interpersonal relationships in individualistic cultures, for example, ambiguity can promote relationship development (Eisenberg, 1984). When messages are ambiguous, other people can "fill in" meanings. We tend to fill in meanings in a way that is consistent with our prior beliefs about the person speaking. This often leads to our perceiving similarity between ourselves and others. Perceived similarity, in turn, leads to attraction. The use of ambiguity also facilitates the development of a restricted code unique to the specific interpersonal relationship. This also leads to relationship development.

Assessment 9.1 provides an opportunity to assess your direct or indirect communication style. Take a few minutes to complete it now.

Scores on Assessment 9.1 range from 10 to 50. The higher your score, the more you value directness in communication. If your score is very low or very high, you'll want to keep this in mind when you communicate with people who use a different style than you do. Effective communication in these situations requires mindfulness; one or both of the people involved must consciously change their style for effective communication to occur.

Elaborate Versus Understated Interaction Styles

The elaborate versus understated dimension focuses on the degree to which talk is used (Gudykunst & Ting-Toomey, 1988).[3] An *elaborate style* refers to the use of expressive language in everyday conversation. Expressive language can involve the use of exaggeration or animation. An *understated verbal style,* in contrast, involves extensive use of silence, pauses, and understatements in conversation. The French, Arabs, Latin Americans, and Africans tend to use an elaborate interaction style, while the Chinese, Japanese, Korean, and Thai tend to use an understated interaction style. Individualists in the United States tend to fall somewhere in the middle of the continuum. To understand this dimension with respect to the communication style used by individualists in the United States, we need to make two types of comparisons: comparing the elaborate style with that used by individualists in the United States, and comparing the understated style with that used by individualists in the United States. Let's start by looking at the elaborate end of the continuum.

Elaborate Style. As indicated earlier, the elaborate style can be based on either exaggeration or animation. The verbal communication style used in the Arabic language is an example of the exaggerated style:

> An Arab feels compelled to overassert in almost all types of communication because others expect him [or her] to. If an Arab says exactly what he [or she] means without the expected assertion, other Arabs may still think that he [or she] means the opposite. For example, a simple "No" by a [male] guest to the host's request to eat more or drink more will not suffice. To convey the meaning that

Assessment 9.1 *Assessing Your Direct and Indirect Communication Style*

The purpose of this questionnaire is to help you assess your tendency to be direct or indirect when you communicate. Respond to each statement regarding the degree to which you agree or disagree. If you strongly disagree with the statement, answer 1; if you disagree, answer 2; if you neither agree nor disagree, answer 3; if you agree, answer 4; if you strongly agree, answer 5.

_______ 1. I hint at what I want when I communicate.

_______ 2. I can talk about personal information with most people.

_______ 3. I am able to recognize subtle and indirect messages easily.

_______ 4. I often try to persuade others when I communicate with them.

_______ 5. I qualify my language (use "maybe," "perhaps") when I communicate.

_______ 6. I avoid ritualistic forms of communication when I talk with others.

_______ 7. I focus on what others are not saying more than what they are saying when we communicate.

_______ 8. I openly disagree with others when I communicate.

_______ 9. I expect others to infer my opinion when we communicate.

_______ 10. I am not ambiguous when I communicate with others.

To obtain your score, first reverse the answers you gave to the *odd numbered* items (i.e., if you answered 1, make it a 5; if you answered 2, make it a 4; if you answered 3, leave it a 3; if you answered 4, make it a 2; if you answered 5, make it a 1). Once you have reversed the odd numbered items, add the responses for the items. Your score will range from 10 to 50. The higher your score, the more you are direct when you communicate; the lower your score, the more indirect you tend to be.

> he is actually full, the [male] guest must keep repeating "No" several times, coupling it with an oath such as "By God" or "I swear to God." . . . an Arab often fails to realize that others, particularly foreigners, may mean exactly what they say even though their language is simple. (Almaney & Alwan, 1982, p. 84)

The Arab proclivity to use verbal exaggerations is probably responsible for more diplomatic misunderstandings between the United States and Arab countries than any other single factor (Cohen, 1987).

The French also use an elaborate style in conversations with people close to them. The French style, however, is expressive in terms of animation, not exaggeration. For the French, a conversation must be "engaged, sustained, fueled, and revived if it is 'dragging.' Once we [the French] permit a conversation to begin, we owe it to ourselves to keep it from dying, to care for it, to guide it, to nourish it, and to watch over its development as if it were a living creature" (Carroll, 1988, p. 24). French conversations are like a spider's web, "we can see the exchanging words as playing the role of the spider, generating the threads which bind the participants. The ideal French conversation would resemble a perfect spider's web: delicate, fragile, elegant, brilliant, of harmonious proportions, a work of art" (Carroll, 1988, p. 25). This animated interaction style, however, is reserved for close relationships, and it is used in informal situations. In "serious conversations," long, uninterrupted responses and attentive listening are used.

There also are ethnic differences within the United States in the use of animated interaction styles. There are, for example, differences between the European American and African American verbal interaction styles (Kochman, 1990). African Americans' verbal interaction style tends to be emotionally animated and expressive, while European Americans' verbal interaction style tends to be restrained and subdued. These style differences often lead to misunderstandings in intergroup encounters. Interethnic miscommunication arises when African Americans perceive European Americans as verbally detached and distant, and conversely, European Americans interpret the verbal style and tone of African Americans as emotionally threatening and intimidating. Even routine conversations can escalate to conflict because of the basic stylistic conversational differences when people communicate on automatic pilot. Recognizing and dealing with differences in verbal styles requires mindfulness.

Understated Style. Up to this point, the elaborate end of the continuum has been compared with the middle—individualists in the United States. Let's now turn to a comparison of the understated end of the continuum with the middle. Recall that the understated style involves the use of understatements, pauses, and silences in conversations (Gudykunst & Ting-Toomey, 1988). More generally, this style involves *not* emphasizing talk in interactions.

European Americans see talk as more important and enjoyable than native-born Chinese or Chinese Americans (Wiemann, Chen, & Giles, 1986). European Americans are more likely than the other two groups to initiate conversations with others and to engage in conversations when opportunities present themselves. Chinese Americans are more likely to engage in these activities than native-born Chinese. European Americans also see talk as a means of social control, while native-born Chinese see silence as a control strategy. The differences in beliefs about talk between Chinese and European Americans are due to individualism-collectivism:

> Individualists have a choice among many groups . . . to which they do belong, and usually belong to these groups because they volunteer. Collectivists . . . are born into a few groups and are more or less stuck with them. So, the collectivists do not have to go out of their way and exert themselves to be accepted, while individualists have to work hard to be accepted. Hence, the individualists often speak more, try to control the situation verbally, and do not value silence. (Triandis quoted in Giles et al., 1992, p. 11)

This should not be taken to suggest that collectivists do not engage in small talk or gossip, because they do. Collectivists, however, do not see that talk is as important as individualists do in developing relationships with others.

Cultures that do not value talk tend to value silence. **Silence tends to be valued more in collectivistic cultures than in individualistic cultures.** There are, for example, four meanings of silence in Japan: truthfulness, social discretion, embarrassment, and defiance (Lebra, 1987). Japanese view truth as occurring only inside the person. Activities of the outer self do not involve an individual's true feelings and, therefore, frequently involve distortion, deception, or "moral falsity." A person who speaks little is trusted more than a person who speaks a great deal. In Japan, truthfulness emerges from silences, not from words. Silence also allows Japanese to be socially discreet and "to gain social acceptance or to avoid social penalty" (Lebra, 1987, p. 347). At times, talking may be dangerous in that it may require a person to tell the truth. In these instances, silence allows the person to avoid social disapproval. Silence also saves Japanese from embarrassment. Verbally expressing emotions to each other, for example, may cause a traditional married couple in Japan to become embarrassed. Japanese also may indicate disagreement or anger with someone else by being silent.

Silence is valued by some groups within the United States. Asian Americans who hold collectivistic values, for example, will value silence in conversations. Silence also is valued by many Native Americans. To illustrate, Apache Indians see silence as appropriate in contexts where social relations between individuals are unpredictable and involve high levels of uncertainty. They also prefer silence over talk in situations in which role expectations are unclear (Basso, 1970).

Stylistic differences with respect to understatement and silence can create problems in interethnic communication in North America. To illustrate, Native Americans in Canada and Alaska prefer more silence in conversations than European Americans (Scollon & Wong-Scollon, 1990). For Native Americans, conversations are seen as threatening because other people may try to change them. Conversations therefore are avoided unless everyone's opinions are known in advance. European Americans, in contrast, "feel that the main way to get to know the point of view of people is through conversation with them" (Scollon & Wong-Scollon, 1990, p. 263). The conversational paradox in this case also lies in the fact that one of the primary functions of talk for European Americans is to bridge relational distance. European Americans tend to reserve silence for intimate relationships. For Native Americans, silence is used to protect the self from strangers, while talk is used when the relationship becomes more intimate.

Assessing Your Beliefs About Talk. Assessment 9.2 provides an opportunity to assess your beliefs about the importance of talk and silence in conversations. Take a few minutes to complete it now.

Scores on Assessment 9.2 range from 10 to 50. The higher your score, the more you value talk. If your score is very high or very low, you'll want to keep this in mind. When you communicate with people who use a different style, you'll want to be mindful of your communication so you can try to accurately interpret their messages and minimize misunderstandings.

Gender and Verbal Interaction Styles

Like our cultural and ethnic identities, our gender identities affect the way we communicate. Before proceeding, think about how your gender identity influences your communication. Answer the following questions:

How do males and females typically communicate in the *same* ways? ____________

____

____

____

Assessment 9.2 *Assessing Your Beliefs About Talk*

The purpose of this questionnaire is to help you assess your beliefs about talk. Respond to each statement regarding the degree to which you agree or disagree with the statement. If you strongly disagree with the statement, answer 1; if you disagree, answer 2; if you neither agree nor disagree, answer 3; if you agree, answer 4; if you strongly agree, answer 5.

_______ 1. I enjoy talking when I find myself in social situations.

_______ 2. I do not enjoy small talk.

_______ 3. I try to break the ice by talking when I first meet others.

_______ 4. I view people who are reticent positively.

_______ 5. I could talk for hours at a time.

_______ 6. I do not enjoy talking with others.

_______ 7. I think that untalkative people are boring.

_______ 8. I do not trust the words people use when they talk.

_______ 9. I judge people by how well they speak.

_______ 10. I do not talk when I have nothing important to say.

To obtain your score, first reverse the answers you gave to the even numbered items (i.e., if you answered 1, make it a 5; if you answered 2, make it a 4; if you answered 3, leave it a 3; if you answered 4, make it a 2; if you answered 5, make it a 1). Once you have reversed the even numbered items, add the responses for the items. Your score will range from 10 to 50. The higher your score, the more you value talk as a way of communicating.

How do males and females typically communicate *differently*? ____________________

____

____

____

Why do differences in male and female styles of communication exist? __________

____

____

____

How is your communication similar to and different from that of other members of your sex? ____________________

____

____

____

Your answers to these questions should provide some insight into the role of gender identity in your implicit personal theory of communication. Keep your answers to these questions in mind as you read the remainder of this section.

Ways of Explaining Gender Differences

There are three general ways of explaining gender differences in conversational styles: gender as deficit, gender as culture, and gender as power (Henley & Kramarae, 1991). These different explanations provide insight into differences in gender styles of communication.

Gender often is viewed as a *deficit,* or shortcoming (Henley & Kramarae, 1991). One side of this view suggests that people evaluate the ways males and females talk differently and tend to think that the ways that females talk need improvement. Women, for example, are seen by people who hold this view as using less powerful language than men (Lakoff, 1975). In order to overcome the deficit, women are expected to be able to talk like men or to be "bilingual" (be able to talk like men and like women). In this view, women tend to be seen as responsible both for the problems of miscommunication in male-female interaction and for the solutions to those problems (because women are expected to be bilingual, whereas men are not).

There is another side to the gender-as-deficit perspective. In this view, men are viewed as having a deficit (Henley & Kramarae, 1991). To illustrate, people who hold this view see males as lacking the ability to disclose their emotions to their intimate partners (McGill, 1986). Men also are seen as having more problems interpreting other people's nonverbal expression of emotions than women (Noller, 1980). In this view, men are seen as responsible for problems in female-male interaction. They also are expected to create the solution by learning how to self-disclose their feelings and how to establish intimate relationships with women.

Another way that male-female differences are viewed is in terms of *cultural differences.* In this view, men and women are seen as being socialized into different subcultures with dif-

A conversation between women differs from a conversation between men because of the inherent gender differences. Women view communications important to developing and maintaining relationships; men tend to see talk as weakening intimate relationships.

ferent beliefs about the nature of communication and different rules for communication (Maltz & Borker, 1982; Tannen, 1990). Men and women are viewed as coming from different "subcultures which have different conceptions of what constitutes friendly conversation, different rules for engaging in such conversations and different rules for interpreting interaction behavior" (Henley & Kramarae, 1991, p. 24).

From the cultural differences perspective, women are viewed as being socialized to develop close relationships with others (Maltz & Borker, 1982) and to be involved with others (Tannen, 1990). Women are socialized to view talk as important to developing and maintaining relationships (Tannen, 1990). Men, in contrast, learn to assert their dominance (Maltz & Borker, 1982) and to be independent (Tannen, 1990). Men learn to see talk as a way of establishing their dominance and therefore do not see talk as central to intimate relationships because dominance is not important in these relationships. Men tend to see talk as weakening intimate relationships (Tannen, 1990). Misunderstandings between women and men, according to the cultural differences perspective, are due to interpreting cues from the other group using one's own group's rules (Maltz & Borker, 1982).

The third view suggests that gender differences in communication are due to differences in *power* (Henley & Kramarae, 1991). Because men have greater power in society than women, men use more powerful and dominating language than women, while women use more powerless and submissive language than men. Men also pay less attention to women in conversations than women pay to men (Henley & Kramarae, 1991). In this view, the way men communicate with women is explained by the power differences between the two groups in society. If there were no power differences, for example, men would pay the same attention to other men and to women in conversations.

There are patterns of communication consistent with the power perspective. To illustrate, "men are seen as trying to control interactions even to the point of ignoring the contributions of others and changing the topic to suit themselves, as using every opportunity to act as experts or problem solvers and ignoring what could be considered the basic rules of conversation" (Noller, 1993, p. 139). The power perspective suggests that these patterns of communication are possible only because men have more power than women in society. The cultural differences perspective, in contrast, would suggest that these patterns of communication are due to the way men and women are socialized.

Most of us use one of these three explanations when we try to understand female-male differences in communication. The perspective we use influences the way we interpret gender differences in communication and how we expect these gender differences to be handled in conversations and relationships. If a male, for example, uses a female deficit perspective, he will expect females to adapt to him when they communicate. If a woman uses a power perspective, she may see herself as a victim when communicating with men. It is therefore important that we understand how we explain gender differences in our implicit theories of communication.

Given this brief overview of the various ways that gender differences in communication are explained, let's look at specific patterns of communication. Two of the major ways that male and female communication styles differ is in terms of control versus affiliation and cooperative versus competitive styles of communication. Keep in mind as you read the following sections that there are different ways that the patterns described can be explained. Let's begin by looking at control versus affiliation.

Control Versus Affiliation

The psychological sex roles of "femininity and masculinity encourage women and men to construe communication situations and the goals of interaction somewhat differently" (Smith, 1985, p. 135). The traditional masculine sex role is associated with control, the extent to which a person can exert active control over the process and outcomes of an interaction. Affiliation, the tendency to elicit warmth and approach, is associated with the traditional feminine sex role. Thus, men may be more concerned with control than women while women are more concerned with the goal of affiliation than men. It must be noted, however, that "men are not 'dominant' and women 'muted' " (Smith, 1985, p. 136). Rather, men are taught to be masculine and therefore focus on the control-related aspects of their interactions with women, while women are taught to be feminine and therefore focus on affiliation in their interactions with men.

Men are likely to use direct control tactics, such as directives ("Why don't you write down our answers?"), and to maintain their speaking turns by using fillers ("And another thing . . .") to begin sentences in conversations (Mulac et al., 1988). Women, in contrast, are likely to use indirect control strategies, such as questions ("What next?"), and to express interest in others through the use of personal pronouns like "we."

To illustrate differences in men's and women's conversational styles, consider the following:

> Imagine that you are at a restaurant observing a couple having dinner together. For a while, they read their menus and she asks him, "What are you going to order?" He responds, "The bacon and cheddar burger." She says, "That sounds good. I think I'll have the chicken salad." After the server takes their order, there is a moment of silence. Then she says, "I went to the mall today to look for a dress for my sister's wedding." He replies, "Yeah." She continues, "but I couldn't find anything I liked. I guess I'll have to keep looking around." He remains silent. She says, "Did you hear about what happened to Angela today? She had a big fight with Bob about spending so much money on a present for Allison's wedding." "Uh, huh," he responds. She tries again by asking "Did you get the new tires for your car?" He says, "No, they didn't have time to balance them today so I have to go back tomorrow." Then she says, "Are they a good deal? Should I get some for my car?" He replies, "You don't really need new tires. Wait until they wear some more." She says, "Okay. I talked to your mother today. She invited us over for dinner on Tuesday." He looks over her shoulder and says, "Oh." (Adapted from Stewart et al., 1990)

This example illustrates one way that men may inhibit conversations when speaking with women, by giving minimal responses, such as "yeah" or "oh," to topics introduced by women. This type of minimal response violates the turn-taking rules for conversation. When topics initiated by women receive only minimal responses, the conversation breaks down (Parlee, 1979). Thus, men control conversations with little effort, when they fail to respond to topics initiated by women and have the topics they bring up accepted (Fishman, 1978). Women work harder than men in conversations because they initiate more topics, as well as respond to topics initiated by men (Parlee, 1979).

Deferential language is another area of speech in which the norms of control and affiliation appear. *Deferential language* is characterized by the use of tag questions (such as "That is important, isn't it?"), qualifiers (such as "probably"), hedges (such as "I'm not sure if this is correct, but. . ."), and other forms of speech traditionally associated with "women's language." We evaluate speakers who use deferential language as more submissive, less assertive, and less willing to take a stand than speakers who use nondeferential language (Liska, Mechling, & Stathas, 1981). In addition, deferential language users are more likely to be perceived as conforming to a traditional feminine sex role. In general, we are more likely to perceive users of deferential language as having less power and more personal warmth than users of nondeferential language (Liska et al., 1981). Thus, the deferential style of communication is associated closely with traditional concepts of femininity.

For the most part, men use a variety of communication behaviors to develop control in their relationships with others (Mulac et al., 1988). Because the control dimension of communication is strong for males, males use more verbally aggressive, persuasive message strategies than females; to use fewer of these messages would violate sex role expectations and would weaken male persuasive impact. Females are less verbally aggressive and use message strategies oriented toward others, and they tend to be penalized for deviating from this expected strategy.

Cooperative Versus Competitive Styles

Speech accommodation theory (Giles et al., 1987) suggests that, because of their traditionally lower status in society, women are especially aware of the communication behavior of others and adapt to these behaviors. Because of their heightened awareness of the effects of interaction, women tend to accommodate (adapt) their speech to others, especially to men. Although all of us use both feminine and masculine language forms, those of us who identify ourselves in terms of the traditionally masculine or feminine sex roles differ in the amount of conversational accommodation we use. Individuals using feminine sex roles are more accommodating than individuals using masculine sex roles (Wheeless,

CATHY © Cathy Guisewite. Reprinted with permission of UNIVERSAL PRESS SYNDICATE. All rights reserved.

1984). In other words, people who conform to a traditionally feminine sex role use speech that is more considerate, cooperative, helpful, sensitive, sincere, submissive, and sympathetic than do people who are traditionally masculine.

Men tend to adopt a competitive style in conversation, while women tend to adopt a cooperative mode. Although women sometimes adopt the male mode in female-male conversations, they are likely to use a less assertive, more cooperative style when interacting with other women (Coates, 1986). This difference even appears in children. To illustrate, boys on a Philadelphia street are more likely to use commands ("Gimme the pliers," "Get off my step"), while girls are more likely to use modal auxiliaries such as "can" and "could" ("We *could* go around looking for more bottles") (Goodwin, 1980). Girls' groups are more likely to be nonhierarchically structured in a cooperative form. Boys' groups are hierarchically structured and based on competition (Goodwin, 1980).

In general, males are more likely to pursue a style of interaction based on *power,* while females are more likely to use a style based on *solidarity and support* (Coates, 1986). These norms are effective when they are followed by all members of a group, but they can cause difficulties in communication in mixed-sex interaction.

Problem Areas in Male—Female Interaction

There are several specific problem areas in conversations between males and females (Coates, 1986). To illustrate, *questions* appear to have a different meaning for males and females. Women use questions more than men, and they tend to use them as a conversational maintenance strategy—to keep the conversation going. Men are more likely to interpret a question as a simple request for information. They answer the question and feel that they have completed their task. Women then have to ask another question to continue the conversation. Both parties may feel frustrated because they do not understand the intent of the other person's behavior.

Links between speaker turns also cause problems in male-female conversation (Coates, 1986). Women are more likely to start a speaking turn by directly acknowledging the contribution of the previous speaker and then talking about the previous topic ("I think Stephen is right. Let's all contribute five dollars for a gift."). Conversely, men are more likely than women not to acknowledge what has gone on before and to make their own point ("I'm going for pizza. Anybody want some?"). Because of these differing styles, women may feel that their comments are being ignored, while men may feel that switching the topic implicitly expresses agreement ("If I disagreed, I would have said so.").

Topic shifts may be very abrupt in all-male conversations (Coates, 1986). Women typically shift topics gradually. Both sexes may be frustrated in a female-male interaction that they feel is dragging on too long or is moving too fast.

All-male groups commonly engage in loud, aggressive arguments. These arguments may focus on seemingly trivial topics and are enjoyed for their own sake. They may include shouting, name-calling, and other insults. Many women, on the other hand, try to avoid displays of verbal aggressiveness. They think these displays are unpleasant and interpret them personally, because "such displays represent a disruption of conversation, whereas for men they are part of the conventional structure of conversation" (Coates, 1986, p. 153). These differences once again reinforce the observation that women tend to organize their talk cooperatively, while men are more likely to organize their talk competitively.

Gender differences in conversational styles can create misunderstandings in male-female communication. The advantages of understanding these differences is illustrated in Reading 9.2.

We tend to use a particular perspective (deficit, cultural, or power) for interpreting male-female differences and communicate in particular ways when we communicate on automatic pilot. We can, however, mindfully choose to interpret gender differences from an alternative perspective. We also can mindfully choose to communicate using different conversational styles. Changing our style will feel awkward at first. After using the new style for a period of time, it will become habitual.

Reading 9.2 OPENING LINES OF COMMUNICATION/DEBORAH TANNEN

Many experts tell us we are doing things wrong and should change our behavior—which usually sounds easier than it turns out to be. Sensitivity training judges men by women's standards, trying to get them to talk more like women. Assertiveness training judges women by men's standards and tries to get them to talk more like men. No doubt, many people can be helped by learning to be more sensitive or more assertive. But few people are helped by being told they are doing everything all wrong. And there may be little wrong with what people are doing, even if they are winding up in arguments. The problem may be that each partner is operating within a different system, speaking a different genderlect.

An obvious question is, Can genderlect be taught? Can people change their conversational styles? If they want to, yes, they can—to an extent. But those who ask this question rarely want to change their own styles. Usually, what they have in mind is sending their partners for repair: They'd like to get him or her to change. Changing one's own style is far less appealing, because it is not just how you act but who you feel yourself to be. Therefore a more realistic approach is to learn how to interpret each other's messages and explain your own in a way your partner can understand and accept.

Understanding genderlects makes it possible to change—to try speaking differently—when you want to. But even if no one changes, understanding genderlect improves relationships. Once people realize that their partners have different conversational styles, they are inclined to accept differences without blaming themselves, their partners, or their relationships. The biggest mistake is believing there is one right way to listen, to talk, to have a conversation—or a relationship. Nothing hurts more than being told your intentions are bad when you know they are good, or being told you are doing something wrong when you know you're just doing it your way.

Not seeing style differences for what they are, people draw conclusions about personality ("you're illogical," "you're insecure," "you're self-centered") or intentions ("you don't listen," "you put me down"). Understanding style differences for what they are takes the sting out of them. Believing that "you're not interested in me," "you don't care about me as much as I care about you," or "you want to take away my freedom" feels awful. Believing that "you have a different way of showing you're listening" or "showing you care" allows for no-fault negotiation: You can ask or make adjustments without casting or taking blame.

Source: "Opening Lines of Communication" from *You Just Don't Understand* by Deborah Tannen. Copyright © 1991, pp. 297–298.

SUMMARY

Language is the most important resource we have for communication. Language allows us to use symbols to communicate. Languages are rule governed, but the rules differ across speech communities. The language we speak influences the way we look at the world. Our use of language makes holding conversations possible.

When we interact with other people, we need to be able to open conversations, know how to take turns and change topics, repair problems when they arise, and close conversations. The way we manage individual conversations influences the way we act in relationships. If we are cooperative in the way we manage conversations, we are likely to be cooperative in our relationships with other people.

Interaction styles differ across cultures. People in individualistic cultures tend to use direct styles of communication (low-context), while people in collectivistic cultures tend to use indirect styles of communication (high-context). A direct style involves directly expressing opinions and saying what we mean. An indirect style involves the use of implicit and ambiguous language and not directly stating opinions. Interactional styles also differ in terms of whether they are elaborate or understated. An elaborate style involves the use of exaggeration and/or animation to overstate the points being made. An understated style, in contrast, involves *not* emphasizing talk when communicating.

Gender identity affects our communication. We tend to view gender differences in communication from one of three perspectives: one gender is viewed as having a deficit in communication skills, gender differences are viewed as due to cultural differences, and gender differences are viewed as due to differences in power. Individuals who use masculine sex roles tend to use controlling and competitive interactional styles, while individuals who use feminine sex roles tend to use affiliative and cooperative interactional styles.

Notes

1. The view of the Sapir-Whorf hypothesis we are presenting is known as the "weak" version of the hypothesis. The "strong" version states that language *determines* the way we view the world. Research supports the weak, but not the strong, version (see Steinfatt, 1989, for a review).
2. The examples presented are drawn from Japanese–North American conversations, but we believe these patterns generalize to other collectivistic and individualistic cultures.
3. Gudykunst and Ting-Toomey used *succinct* where we are using *understated.*

Journal Reflections

1. *Observing Your Turn Taking and Topic Management in Conversations.* In the next two days, observe your turn taking and topic management in conversations. Are you cooperative in the way you manage conversations? Is there any aspect of the way you handle turn taking or topic management that you would like to change? How can you change these patterns?
2. *Observing Your Use of Direct and Indirect Language Usage.* Over the next two days, observe your use of direct and indirect forms of communication. In what situations are you direct? In what situations are you indirect? Write your answers to these questions in your journal. Also write out a plan for how you can deal more effectively in the future with people who use a different style.
3. *Observing Your Use of Silence.* Over two days, observe your use of silence. When are you silent? Under what circumstances do you tolerate silences in conversations? Write your answers to these questions in your journal. Also write out a plan for how you can deal more

effectively in the future with people who use a different style.

Study Questions

1. How is language rule governed?
2. What are the major functions of language?
3. Why is it important to understand the characteristics of language?
4. What is the Sapir-Whorf hypothesis?
5. How does turn taking in conversations reflect issues of control in our relationships?
6. How can we change topics in conversations and be viewed positively by others?
7. How do the direct and indirect styles of communication differ?
8. How do the elaborate and understated styles of communication differ?
9. How do we use the deficit, culture, and power perspectives when we communicate with members of the opposite sex?
10. What differentiates male and female interactional styles?

Suggested Readings

Giles, H., & Coupland, N. (1991). *Language: Contexts and consequences.* Pacific Grove, CA: Brooks/Cole. Howard Giles and Nicholas Coupland examine the social psychological functions of language. This book is particularly useful in understanding language usage in intergroup encounters.

Gumperz, J. (Ed.). (1982). *Language and social identity.* New York: Cambridge University Press. This is an edited volume containing numerous studies of how our social identities influence our language usage. The authors examine numerous different ethnic groups in the United States and England, as well as male-female differences in communication styles.

McLaughlin, M. (1984). *Conversation: How talk is organized.* Newbury Park, CA: Sage. Margaret McLaughlin provides a complete introduction to how talk is organized. Her discussion is more detailed and complete than Nofsinger's, and is excellent follow-up reading to Nofsinger's book (see below). It is an excellent source if you want to study conversations.

Nofsinger, R. (1991). *Everyday conversations.* Newbury Park, CA: Sage. Robert Nofsinger provides a short introduction to conversation in everyday life. He helps the reader understand what is taking place in conversations from saying hello to saying good-bye. This is an excellent introduction to how to understand conversations.

Tannen, D. (1990). *You just don't understand: Women and men in conversation.* New York: Morrow. Deborah Tannen summarizes research on male and female differences in conversational styles. It provides numerous interesting examples of the material summarized in this chapter.

10

VERBAL MESSAGES IN EVERYDAY CONVERSATIONS

The previous chapter focuses on how language and verbal interaction styles are important components of interpersonal communication. In everyday conversations, we use language and verbal messages to coordinate our interactions and to define the nature of our relationships with others. The way we use language and verbal messages in initial interactions can determine whether others want to get to know us or never see us again.

One of the major ways that we use verbal messages in conversations is in exchanging information. We have to gather information about other people and they have to gather information about us in order to decide whether we want to form or continue a relationship with each other. We also use verbal messages to try to get others to like us. The way we talk may lead others to be attracted to us, or it may lead them to want to avoid us. We not only use verbal messages to attract other people, we use verbal messages to try to influence other people. The verbal messages we use to try to influence others affects whether we are able to get what we want from them. We'll begin our discussion of verbal messages by looking at how we exchange information in conversations.

Exchanging Information in Conversations

As indicated in Chapter 4, we use three interactive strategies to reduce our uncertainty about others: asking questions, self-disclosure, and detecting deception. These strategies also are the major ways we exchange information with others in conversations. Let's start by looking at asking questions.

We engage in conversations possibly dozens of times a day. We use verbal messages used in these conversations to influence others.

Asking Questions

Asking questions is one of the ways we keep conversations going and reduce our uncertainty about other people. Before proceeding, think about when you ask questions of other people. Answer the following questions:

Under what circumstances do you typically ask other people questions about themselves? ______________________

____

____

Under what conditions do you typically avoid asking other people questions about themselves? ______________________

____

____

What types of questions about themselves do you typically ask other people? ______

____

____

What types of questions about themselves do you typically avoid asking other people? ______________________

____

____

Your answers to these questions should provide some insight into the role of asking questions in your implicit personal theory of communication. Keep your answers to these questions in mind as you read the remainder of this section.

The more effectively we can ask questions, the smoother our interactions will be and the more information we will learn about others. There are, however, relatively clear expectations for the types of questions we can ask other people and they can ask us. One reason for this is that we have scripts for asking questions.

Scripts for Asking Questions. As we grow up and watch other people communicate, we learn cultural scripts for asking questions in different situations. The scripts we learn are part of our memory organization packets (discussed in Chapter 6). When we first meet someone, for example, we tend to ask questions about the other person's well-being, such as "How are you?" We also ask questions about why others are in the situation in which we are talking, such as "How do you know Dave and Tina [the host and hostess for the party]?" or about where they live, such as "Where do you live?" Assuming that the people with whom we are talking are members of our culture, they probably have learned similar scripts and they will provide answers that meet our expectations.

If we ask other people "How are you?" we expect that they will respond with something like "I'm fine, and you?" We are not really asking about other people's state of being with this question; we are recognizing their existence. If other people follow our script and meet our expectations, we can continue with our "getting to know you" script. If other people say something like "I'm not doing well. I just found out that my aunt is in the hospital," in contrast, we would have to stop and think about what to say next. When other people violate our expectations in answering our questions, we tend to become mindful of our communication.

When we are first getting to know other people, our questions tend to be impersonal and about things external to our relationship with them (Berger & Bradac, 1982). We generally do not ask personal questions of people we do not know, questions that require them to tell us intimate information about themselves. We also do not ask other people questions that are about our relationship with them. John's questions in the following dialogue would be inappropriate if John and Mary were meeting for the first time:

JOHN: Do you like me a lot?

MARY: What?

JOHN: Are you really attracted to the way my face looks?

MARY: I think you are very strange. (Berger & Bradac, 1982, p. 82)

While we tend to avoid asking personal questions when we first get to know others, there are exceptions. There are situations in which we feel a close connection with a person and feel that it is okay to ask many personal questions.

As we get to know others, it is expected that we will ask personal questions and questions about our relationship with them. In any relationship, however, there may be topics that are taboo. If one partner, for example, "is concerned about ageing, the other partner may not feel free to ask: 'How does it feel to be getting up there?' " (Berger & Bradac, 1982 p. 83). If we are dating someone who just came out of a bad relationship, asking questions about that relationship may be taboo. As we get to know other people and our relationships become more personalized, we do not have to follow cultural scripts for asking questions, and we can negotiate the specific types of questions that we can ask (Pearce, 1976). These negotiations, however, do not necessarily take place consciously.

Rules for Asking Questions. There are cultural rules guiding the questions we can ask other people. In initial interactions and early stages of getting to know others, the questions we ask others should seek information in a polite way, and we should not repeatedly try to get others to answer questions they do not want to answer (Berger & Bradac, 1982).

The form of our questions influences the degree to which we are able to get the information we want. We can, for example, make requests in different ways. To illustrate, assume that we are trying to collect money for the

American Cancer Society (Cantor, 1979). When approaching others, we could use (1) polite imperatives, such as "Please contribute to the American Cancer Society"; (2) agreement questions, such as "Won't you contribute to the American Cancer Society?" (3) information questions, such as "Would you like to contribute to the American Cancer Society?" or (4) statements, such as "I would like you to contribute to the American Cancer Society." Polite imperatives are the most effective strategies, while information questions are the least effective (Cantor, 1979). Similar patterns should emerge when we ask other people questions about themselves (Berger & Bradac, 1982). We therefore can obtain information about others by saying something like "Please tell me about . . ." rather than by saying, "Would you like to tell me about yourself?"

Loaded Questions. About 25 percent of the things we say in conversations involve asking questions (Goodman & Esterly, 1988). Not all of these questions, however, are aimed at gathering information from others. Many of the questions we ask are loaded questions. *Loaded questions* are questions we ask that implicitly give advice to other people or interpret other people's behavior:

> Loaded questions aren't difficult to spot in conversations. They often start with mild opposition and words like wouldn't, couldn't, aren't, doesn't, and shouldn't. "Wouldn't it be better if? . . ." "Why don't you? . . ." Shouldn't we try to? . . ." "Aren't you being? . . ." Doesn't that make you? . . ." (Goodman & Esterly, 1988, p. 121)

Loaded questions are not used to gather information, but rather to give opinions in an indirect manner.

Loaded questions generally are thought to be a negative way to communicate. They can be "slightly sneaky to downright menacing" depending on the motives of the person asking the question. Loaded questions, however, also can be used to increase the effectiveness of our communication, because they allow us to soften our advice to other people and to give advice in an indirect fashion (Goodman & Esterly, 1988). If we are going to use loaded questions to give advice to other people, we need to make sure that they are in a receptive mood, that we have the information necessary to give good advice, and that we are empathic when we give the advice (Goodman & Esterly, 1988).

SALLY FORTH. Reprinted with special permission of King Features Syndicate.

Loaded questions also allow us to check out our interpretations of other people's behavior indirectly. To illustrate, if we thought our romantic partner was angry with someone, we could check our perceptions by asking a loaded question like "Wouldn't it be better if you waited to talk to the person until you are not angry?" Implicit in this question is advice (to wait to talk), but our romantic partner's response also would tell us if our perceptions are correct. This can be an effective strategy as long as we make sure that our loaded questions do not evaluate other people.

Open versus Closed Questions. The questions we ask also can be open or closed (Goodman & Esterly, 1988). *Closed questions* are questions that other people can answer with a "yes" or a "no" or some other short answer. If we meet other people for the first time and ask them, "How long have you lived here?" we are asking a closed question. *Open questions,* in contrast, are designed to obtain more information than closed questions. Open questions are asked in such a way that other people cannot give a one-word answer, as with "what," "how," or "why." Asking other people, "What type of experiences have you had since you moved here?" would gain more information than a closed question like "Do you like your new school?"

One problem in our conversations with others involves using the wrong type of question (Goodman & Esterly, 1988). Both open and closed questions are useful in gaining information from other people. Short answers to closed questions does not mean that the information is trivial. Long answers to open questions can provide information we do not need or want to know. Asking the wrong question can make us feel frustrated with other people's responses. When we communicate on automatic pilot, we may "blame" our frustration on other people. The problem, however, may really be a function of the type of question we asked.

We often use open questions when we want a direct answer, but at the same time, we want to be polite and not put pressure on other people (Goodman & Esterly, 1988). If we really want a direct answer to our question, we should ask a closed question. To illustrate, if we want to know if our romantic partner wants to go to a movie tonight, we might indirectly ask, "When's the last time we went to the movies?" The answer to this question may or may not lead our romantic partner to suggest that we go to the movies. If we really want to go to the movies that night, a closed question like "Would you like to go to a movie tonight?" would be more effective.

We often ask closed questions when we want a great deal of information. Asking several closed questions instead of one good open question can make a small problem seem like a big one (Goodman & Esterly, 1988). To illustrate, suppose you are having a conflict with your roommate. You have just explained your position on the conflict. You want to know how your roommate responds to what you said. In this situation, many of us might ask something like "Is what I said okay with you?" The roommate's response to this closed question will not tell us much about his or her opinions. If you ask many closed questions, your roommate will feel like she or he is being interrogated. To gain more information, you could ask an open question like "What do think about what I just said?"

Frequency of Questions. Although questions are a useful way to gather information about others, we can easily ask too many questions. When our anxiety is above our maximum threshold, for example, we may ask others too many questions because we are anxious and do not know what to say. We may also ask many questions of people who do not open up with us. Asking too many questions usually backfires, and we do not end up with useful information about other people (Goodman & Esterly, 1988). Asking too many questions does not allow our conversations to flow smoothly. Also, others may perceive our questions as insincere or intrusive, and they may try to stop the conversation.

When we see that others are not responding to our questions, or when we recognize that we are barraging others with questions, we need to mindfully recognize this pattern. If we are asking too many questions because we are anxious, we need to manage our anxiety (see Chapter 5). If we are asking too many questions because others are not opening up, we need to mindfully choose an alternative strategy for communicating with them. In selecting another strategy, we need to think about whether we are violating other people's privacy. If we are, backing off may be the best strategy. If we do not think we are violating other people's privacy, then we can select another way to gather information. We could, for example, decide to self-disclose information about ourselves and see if they reciprocate.

Self-Disclosure and Privacy Regulation

As indicated in Chapter 4, *self-disclosure* involves telling other people information of a personal nature about ourselves that they do not already know. Before proceeding, think about when you self-disclose to others. Answer the following questions:

> Under what conditions do you typically avoid self-disclosing to others? ________
>
> ________________________________
>
> ________________________________

> Under what conditions do you typically self-disclose to others? ________
>
> ________________________________
>
> ________________________________

> What information do you typically disclose to others? ________
>
> ________________________________

> What information do you typically avoid telling others? ________
>
> ________________________________
>
> ________________________________

Your answers to these questions should provide some insight into the role of self-disclosure in your implicit personal theory of communication. Keep your answers to these questions in mind as you read the remainder of this section.

Any time we self-disclose information to other people, we make ourselves vulnerable. A certain amount of self-disclosure, however, is necessary for our relationships with other people to become close. If we avoid self-disclosing to other people, they cannot get to know us as individuals. If we self-disclose too much, we are not able to maintain our privacy. We constantly have to balance openness and closedness in our relationships with others. Let's begin by looking at how self-disclosure tends to change as our relationships become more intimate.

Social Penetration. One of the major theories designed to explain how our relationships become more intimate, social penetration theory (Altman & Taylor, 1973), focuses on the concept of self-disclosure. Social penetration theory suggests that, when we first meet new people, the information we tell them about ourselves is superficial and involves a limited number of topics. We select from the possible topics of self-disclosure, which can include our background, our attitude toward different things, such as politics, what we value, our past behavior, or any other information we can tell people about ourselves. As we get to know others, we begin to tell them more intimate information on the topics we already have discussed and we also open new topics for discussion, such as our feelings about ourselves and others or our relationships with them. The more intimate our relationships become, the more topics we discuss and the more intimate our self-disclosures are on these topics.

As our relationships become more intimate, our communication with our partners becomes more personalized and synchronized, and we experience less difficulty in communicating (Knapp, Ellis, & Williams, 1980). *Personalized* refers to our tendency to disclose personal information about ourselves. *Synchronized* involves the degree to which our communication is coordinated with other people and there is rhythm to our interaction. *Difficulty* refers to the problems, such as misunderstandings, we have communicating with others. The trend for increases in personalization and synchronization and for decreases in difficulty as relationships becomes more intimate is consistent across cultures (Gudykunst & Nishida, 1986b), and the same pattern occurs in relationships between people from different groups (Gudykunst, Nishida, & Chua, 1987).

Rules of Self-Disclosure in the European American Subculture. Self-disclosure varies from person to person, but there are patterns in the way we tend to self-disclose to others. There are rules for self-disclosure in any culture. Nine rules of self-disclosure in the United States can be isolated:

1. Do not disclose intimate information to new acquaintances.
2. Do disclose nonintimate information to new acquaintances.
3. Do disclose intimate information to intimate friends.
4. Do not disclose non-intimate information to intimates.
5. Disclose positive . . . (non-intimate) information to new acquaintances.
6. Do not disclose negative . . . information to new acquaintances.
7. Do not disclose excessively.
8. Do disclose moderately.
9. Disclose honestly and accurately. (Berger & Bradac, 1982, pp. 86–87)

Violation of these rules in initial interactions can end a relationship before it has a chance to begin. Of course, the rules for self-disclosure are not always followed. Sometimes, for example, we meet someone with whom we connect, and we tell this person intimate information about ourselves when we first meet. There also are times when we self-disclose intimate information about ourselves to total strangers on planes, trains, or buses (see Reading 10.1).

The rules outlined here are limited to European Americans in the United States. There are cultural, as well as ethnic and gender, differences in the rules guiding self-disclosure (some of these are discussed below).

Self-Disclosure in Everyday Conversations. It was pointed out in Chapter 4 that self-disclosure is one of the ways we gather information about other people to reduce our uncertainty about them. Self-disclosure, however, is an inefficient way to gather information about other people (Berger & Kellermann, 1983). Self-disclosure provides information about others because we follow the *reciprocity norm* (Gouldner, 1960). If one person tells another person something about her

Reading 10.1 WHY DO WE CONFIDE IN COMPLETE STRANGERS?/SUSAN JACQUES

Psychologists get paid for it. For airline passengers, who do it for free, it can make a six-hour flight fly by or inspire you to push your seatmate out the emergency exit. . . .

It's happened to you. Or maybe, just *maybe* you've done it yourself. You know . . . total strangers who confide in total strangers. Exchanging intimate details in cabs, planes and taverns before exchanging names.

Experts agree that bending anonymous ears has a certain advantage over bending the ears of those we know. It's a kind of therapy, born of a basic human need to minimize tension and fear. . . .

According to USC psychologist Chaytor Mason, being among strangers makes all of us more apprehensive and triggers a series of physiological changes. This "general activation symptom" makes our heart beat harder, muscles tighten and sweat glands go to work, leading us to more active behavior.

"On an airplane, train or bus where people are captive, they can't get up and walk away. The tension needs resolution, and that often comes in the form of talking," Mason says. . . .

Those on the receiving end do not always welcome such conversations, especially people who either feel used or responsible for solving others' problems. Surprise confidences also can trigger in the listener feelings of guilt about tuning out and shame about not caring.

"Most people are glad to get an audience and reduce tension but [won't] allow the other person to do the same," Mason adds. "If the person doesn't want to give and take, just take, the listener will quickly become resentful. . . ."

or himself, the other person tends to disclose similar information. The reciprocity norm operates when we communicate with new people and acquaintances. Reciprocity operates differently in our close relationships. Once our relationships become close, there needs to be a general balance in the things we tell each other, but we do not necessarily reciprocate self-disclosures at the same time. If one person tells a close friend about a problem with his or her romantic partner, for example, the person receiving the self-disclosure is not necessarily expected to talk about problems with her or his romantic partner at that time. The person engaging in self-disclosure might expect, however, that his or her friend would talk about personal problems when they occurred.

Intimate self-disclosure does not take place frequently. We do not self-disclose intimate information at high levels in our everyday conversations (Duck et al., 1991). When we do self-disclose in our close relationships, we tend to talk about our relationships with romantic partners, friends, or family (Schmidt & Cornelius, 1987). Self-disclosures in our close relationships allow us to share our thoughts, release our feelings, seek advice and reassurance, and strengthen our relationship with the person to whom we are self-disclosing.

One type of interaction in which self-disclosure is an important issue is when nondisabled and disabled people communicate. Nondisabled people, for example, react more positively to disabled people who self-disclose than to those who do not self-disclose, especially when the self-disclosure is about the disability (Thompson, 1982). Self-disclosure does not necessarily reduce tension, but it does increase the nondisabled people's acceptance of disabled people (Thompson & Siebold, 1978).

Disabled people tend to disclose about their disability in response to nondisabled people's questions about their disabilities—if they perceive that the disclosure is appropriate to the relationship and the context in which they are communicating (Braithwaite, 1991). Disabled people, however, prefer to have nondisabled people get to know them as individuals before answering questions about their disabilities. To accomplish this, disabled people may try to direct the conversation and suggest topics for conversation other than their disabilities. If disabled people perceive that a nondisabled person with whom they are communicating is experiencing great discomfort, they may choose to disclose about their disabilities to make the other person more comfortable (Braithwaite, 1991).

The age of the communicators also affects self-disclosure. Older people tend to disclose more than younger people, especially with respect to negative feelings (Dickson-Markman, 1986). Self-disclosure in intergenerational encounters does not necessarily follow the same patterns as it does in encounters with members of the same generation (Giles et al., 1992). When older people interact with younger people, they tend to self-disclose more than younger people, especially about painful information such as accidents, deaths in the family, and medical problems. When older people self-disclose to younger people they do not know, the younger people do not necessarily reciprocate self-disclosures at the same rate as when communicating with other younger people. When young people self-disclose, in contrast, older people tend to reciprocate.

Openness with other people does not always lead to better communication and increases in the intimacy of our relationships. Self-disclosing inappropriate information or self-disclosing at the wrong time can inhibit relationship development. Also, we all have many relationships, such as those with acquaintances and co-workers, in which we do not self-disclose at high levels. We cannot self-disclose at high levels with everyone. We need to consciously choose with whom we will self-disclose.

Group Differences in Self-Disclosure. Often we assume that women are more likely to disclose intimate information about themselves than men.[1] To a certain extent this is true (Cline, 1989). Females, however, self-disclose more intimate information about themselves to other women than to

Self-disclosure is made of choices: who do we self-disclose to? what do we say? what do we not *say? Our choices are based on gender, culture, nationality, among many other criteria.*

men. Both men and women appear to prefer to self-disclose personal information to women, and therefore there is more intimate self-disclosure in female-female and male-female interactions than in male-male interactions.

One explanation for male-female differences in the intimacy of self-disclosure has to do with their orientations toward vulnerability and power. Women, for example, may not disclose personal information to others in order to avoid being hurt or creating relational problems (Rosenfeld, 1979). Men, in contrast, avoid self-disclosing information to maintain control. Since self-disclosure involves making them vulnerable, men assume that they will lose control if they disclose intimate information about themselves.

There are both similarities and differences in how self-disclosure is viewed across cultures. Table 10.1 illustrates the topics that Japanese and North American students generally would and would not discuss in the first thirty minutes of an initial interaction with people they meet for the first time (Nishida, 1991). As you can see from the table, there are similarities in the topics that members of the two cultures discuss. These include weather, names, arrangements to meet again, recent movies, music, and college life. Generally, Japanese and North Americans prefer to talk about their tastes and opinions and prefer to avoid discussing their physical attributes and personalities (Barnlund, 1975).

There also are important cultural differences in the topics of discussion in initial interactions. Some of the topics that North Americans discuss that Japanese do not include telephone numbers, life goals, friends, mutual friends, and after-graduation plans. These topics tend to be individualistic in that they involve getting to know the other person as a unique person. The topics that the Japanese discuss that North Americans do not include universities, ages, and club activities. These topics are collectivistic in that they present information about the other person's status or ingroup memberships.[2] This information is necessary to reduce uncertainty in collectivistic cultures.

Overall, **members of individualistic cultures are expected to self-disclose personal information about themselves more than members of collectivistic cultures.**[3] One reason for this is that the main ways people get to know others in individualistic cultures like the United States is by gathering personal information about them. This type of information is not critical in the early stages of relationship development in collectivistic cultures. In collectivistic cultures, individuals need to know information about other people's ingroup memberships and status in order to predict their behavior. In best friendships, however, members of collectivistic cultures self-disclose personal information at rates similar to those in individualistic cultures.

Understanding Your Self-Disclosure. All of us must decide for ourselves when to disclose information about ourselves based on the situation in which we find ourselves and the person with whom we are communicating. Skill Exercise 10.1 is designed to help you understand how self-disclosure fits into your implicit theory of interpersonal communication. Take a few minutes to complete it now.

After completing Skill Exercise 10.1, you should understand to whom you self-disclose and to whom you do not self-disclose. This knowledge should help you better understand the role of self-disclosure in your implicit theory of interpersonal communication. As suggested earlier, although there are some general guidelines for self-disclosure in the United States, each of us must decide on a case-by-case basis whether we want to disclose information about ourselves to another person. We

Table 10.1

TOPICS DISCUSSED IN FIRST THIRTY MINUTES OF CONVERSATIONS WITH STRANGERS

United States	Japan
Topics That Would be Discussed	
weather (5)	weather (5)
names (5)	names (5)
academic majors (5)	universities (5)
immediate surroundings (5)	ages (5)
recent movies (6–15)	club activities (6–15)
recent events (6–15)	music (6–15)
friends (6–15)	college life (6–15)
college life (6–15)	arrangements to meet again (16–30)
music (6–15)	recent movies (16–30)
mutual friends (6–15)	travel (16–30)
arrangements to meet again (16–30)	
telephone numbers (16–30)	
life goals (16–30)	
after-graduation plans (16–30)	
Topics Never Discussed	
personal savings	personal savings
religion	religion
sex lives	sex lives
drugs	drugs
authors read	authors read
	politics
	marriage
	boy/girl friend
	life goals
	telephone numbers
	gossip
	personalities
	after-graduation plans

Adapted from Nishida (1991). Topics listed were reported by at least 40 percent of the respondents. Numbers in parentheses indicate the time period in which the topic would be discussed (for example, 5 = first five minutes) of a thirty-minute conversation with a stranger.

use our implicit theories to guide us in making these decisions when we communicate on automatic pilot. We may decide not to self-disclose in order to maintain our privacy.

Maintaining Privacy. When we self-disclose information about ourselves, we are being open and making ourselves accessible to others. When we do not tell others about

Skill Exercise 10.1 *Self-Disclosure*

We self-disclose different information to different people. The purpose of this exercise is to help you understand what you choose to self-disclose in different relationships.

1. Initial interactions with strangers:
   What type of information do you generally tell strangers? ____________________

   What type of information do you definitely not tell strangers? ____________________

2. Acquaintances:
   What type of information do you generally tell acquaintances? ____________________

   What type of information do you definitely not tell acquaintances? ____________________

3. Friends (not close or best friends):
   What type of information do you generally tell friends? ____________________

   What type of information do you definitely not tell friends? ____________________

4. Close friends:
   What type of information do you generally tell close friends? ____________________

   What type of information do you definitely not tell close friends? ____________________

5. Romantic partners:
   What type of information do you generally tell romantic partners? ____________________

   What type of information do you definitely not tell romantic partners? ____________________

ourselves, we are being closed and making ourselves inaccessible. *Privacy,* therefore, involves the "selective control of access to the self or to one's group" (Altman, 1975, p. 18). We desire different amounts of privacy in our interactions with others. We may or may not achieve the amount of privacy we desire. To the extent we are able to actually achieve the amount of privacy we want, we have controlled our interaction with others (Altman, 1975).

Our desire for openness and closedness varies with the person with whom we are communicating, our moods, and the situations in which we find ourselves. The degree to which we are open and closed also varies within a particular relationship. As our relationships with other people become more intimate, there is a general tendency for us to be more open with them. Also, as our relationships with other people begin to deteriorate, we tend to become more closed. Even though we tend to be more open as our relationships become more intimate, at any particular time we may need privacy and we may be closed with others. The extent to which we are open and closed, therefore, is a dialectic (see Chapter 3 for characteristics of dialectics). Figure 10.1 illustrates one potential way openness and closedness might change as a relationship develops over time.[4]

The pattern of openness and closedness illustrated in Figure 10.1 is only one of the possible patterns that might occur in our relationships. The general tendency is for short cycles of openness and closedness to occur within conversations and for larger cycles to occur across conversations (Vanlear, 1991). We try to time our openness and closedness so that they coincide with our partners' need for openness and closedness.

The way openness and closedness are handled in a relationship depends on the individuals involved and their needs for openness and closedness. It also depends on what is happening in each person's life and in the relationship

FIGURE 10.1 Openness-Closedness and Relationship Development

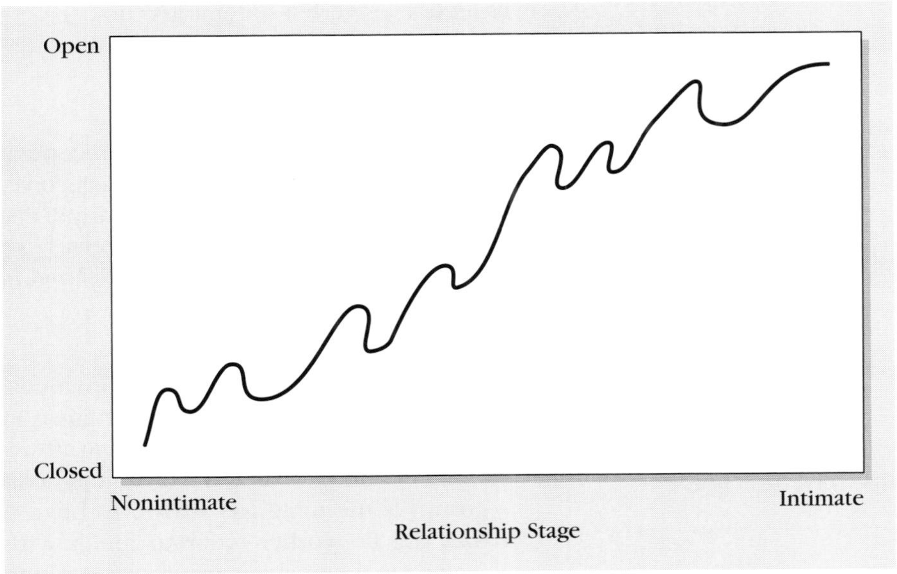

at the particular time. We use several general strategies for managing the openness and closedness in our relationships (Hoppe, 1993). We can alternate the topics we discuss by avoiding topics that create problems and discussing topics that create good feelings. We also can alternate the times that we are open so that they coincide with times when our partner is open. If we are getting more openness than we want, we can withdraw, and we can ask questions if we are not getting sufficient openness. Another strategy that people use to manage the openness and closedness in their relationships is being deceptive.

Deception

Being deceptive is one way to manage the openness-closedness dialectic (Hoppe, 1993), and detecting deception in other people's messages is a way to reduce uncertainty about others (Berger, 1979). The degree to which others deceive us, lie to us, or are honest with us influences whether we want to have a relationship with them. Before proceeding, think about your use of deception when you communicate. Answer the following questions:

> Under what conditions do you deceive or lie to other people? ________________
>
> ____
>
> ____

> Under what conditions do you definitely *not* deceive or lie to other people? ____
>
> ____
>
> ____

> How do other people react when they find out that you deceived or lied to them? ________________________
>
> ____
>
> ____

> How do you react when you find out that other people deceived or lied to you? __
>
> ____
>
> ____

Your answers to these questions should provide insight into the role of deception in your implicit personal theory of communication. Keep your answers to these questions in mind as you read the remainder of this section.

There are several interrelated ideas that need to be differentiated here. *Deception* involves leading others to false conclusions. *Deceptive communication* refers to "message distortion resulting from deliberate falsification or omission of information by a communicator with the intent of stimulating in another, or others, a belief that the communicator himself or herself does not believe" (Miller, Mongeau, & Sleight, 1986, p. 497). In addition to deceptive communication messages, deception can involve being purposefully ambiguous to mislead others or even telling the truth to lead others to a false conclusion (Hopper & Bell, 1984). *Lying* in everyday usage implies making untrue verbal statements (Bok, 1978). Let's begin by looking at deceptive communication.

Deceptive Communication. Deceptive communication involves the *intent* to deceive. Sometimes in interpersonal relationships, disagreement over the intent to deceive can cause major problems. Consider the following example:

> When recounting the day's happenings, [a] spouse may suffer an honest lapse in memory and fail to mention that an attractive co-worker was part of a luncheon group. If the mate has reason to believe that the co-worker went to lunch with the group, he or she may infer or attribute deceptive intent because of the omission.

> Indeed, if the mate suspects a relationship between the spouse and co-worker, he or she may inquire whether the co-worker was at lunch even though there was no specific evidence to suggest it. Having been cued about the omission, a subsequent denial by the spouse would qualify as an instance of deceptive communication, rather than an honest memory lapse. (Miller et al., 1986, p. 498)

Not mentioning the co-worker the first time could be a lapse of memory. After being specifically asked, however, the spouse should recall the co-worker's presence. If he or she then said the co-worker was not present, she or he would be engaged in deceptive communication and also lying.

To discuss deceptive communication, the two individuals communicating must be differentiated. For simplicity's sake, the people doing the deceiving are called "deceivers," and the people being deceived are called "receivers." Deceivers monitor their communication to determine how successful they are being by watching the receivers' reactions to their messages (Buller, Strzyzewski, & Comstock, 1991).

Deceivers usually are not totally successful in hiding the fact that they are being deceptive. Deceivers often unconsciously give off cues that receivers interpret as indicating the deceivers are lying (Zuckerman et al., 1975). These are referred to as *leakage cues.* Deceivers are least likely to display leakage cues in nonverbal areas they can easily control, such as their facial expressions. Rather, leakage cues are most likely to emerge in body motions such as nervous twitches and in the eyes (pupil dilation, eye blinking). Other behaviors associated with lying include few smiles, large numbers of hesitations when speaking, speech errors, and a high pitch (Knapp & Hall, 1992). There is, however, no simple rule for determining whether people are lying; "there is no sign of deceit itself—no gesture, facial expression, or muscle twitch that in and of itself means that a person is lying" (Ekman, 1985, p. 90).

Once receivers think that deceivers may be deceiving them, they try to find out if they are correct (Buller et al., 1991). In doing this, receivers also give off cues that they are suspicious. Receivers may speak slowly, not be clear in their messages, and pause before they speak. When deceivers perceive that receivers are suspicious, they also try to manage their behavior. Deceivers may, for example, try to avoid giving off cues that would suggest they are nervous and take longer than usual to respond to receivers' questions. The amount of positive affect, such as smiles and laughter, that the deceivers transmit to the receivers also decreases when they think receivers are suspicious.

We generally are not very accurate at detecting deceptive communication when we do not know the people involved. When we think we detect that people we do not know are deceiving us, however, we tend to be confident in our judgments (Miller et al., 1986). When we are trying to determine if people we do not know are deceiving us, we must rely on our stereotyped notion of how liars behave. We may base our decision on the extent to which other people appear nervous or on the way they speak. We may also look at whether what other people say is logically structured and consistent. The problem is that there can be other causes for the symptoms we associate with lying. People who are highly communication apprehensive (see Chapter 3), for example, may appear to be deceivers when they are telling the truth because of the cues they emit, such as appearing nervous.

When we are communicating with people we know reasonably well, we do not have to rely on our stereotype of how liars behave, because we know how they usually behave (Miller et al., 1986). We can use other people's past behavior as a comparison to judge whether they are lying in any particular interaction. We often assume that changes in the behavior of people we know, such as their eye contact or the length of their messages, are cues that they are deceiving us. We also can use our observations of the person being judged when they deceived other people in the past. We may, for example, have heard our romantic partner tell a friend that a meal he or she served was delicious when our partner actually thought the meal was terrible.

Deceptive communication has different consequences for our close relationships than for our less intimate relationships. Being caught in a lie by a person with whom we have a close relationship can "cast a pall over the relationship itself," and "being lied to by a close friend or romantic partner is personally devastating" (Miller et al., 1986, pp. 508–509). Some lies in close relationships may be intended to preserve and protect the relationship, but they may not have this effect (see the section on lying below). In general, people perceive little deception in their close relationships, but they also tend to believe that "some deception is necessary to keep the relationships on an even keel" (Miller et al., 1986, p. 509). Deception, however, is *not* necessary to keep relationships on an even keel.

Lying. As indicated earlier, lying involves making untrue verbal statements (Bok, 1978).[5] Usually lies are made verbally or in writing, but they also can be made in Morse code, smoke signals, sign language, and so forth.

Lying is dysfunctional in our relationships with others. Our behavior needs to be based on the *principle of veracity,* or truthfulness, because "trust in some degree of veracity functions as the *foundation* of relations among humans" (Bok, 1978, p. 33). More specifically,

> the function of the principle of veracity as a foundation is evident when we think of trust. I can have different kinds of trust: that you will treat me fairly, that you will have my interests at heart, that you will do me no harm. But if I do not trust your word, can I have genuine trust in the first three? If there is no confidence in the truthfulness of others, is there any way to assess their fairness, their intentions to help, or to harm? How, then, can they be trusted? *Whatever* matters to human beings, trust is the atmosphere in which it thrives. (Bok, 1978, p. 33)

Trust is necessary for our relationships to grow and develop, and trust is based on truthfulness.

Small lies, which often are viewed as harmless, are not necessary (Bok, 1978). There is always a truthful alternative. In any situation in which lying is a possible choice of how to respond, we should always look for a truthful alternative. To illustrate, suppose that our romantic partner just bought a new shirt and is very happy with the purchase. We do not like the shirt. What should we do? One option is to lie and say that we like the shirt. The rationale for lying in this situation might be that whether or not we like the shirt is trivial, not telling our partner the truth will not hurt the relationship, and telling the truth might hurt our romantic partner's feelings. Our underlying motivation for lying, however, probably is to avoid conflict (LaFollette & Graham, 1986).

The rationale provided (telling the truth might hurt our partner's feelings) is not sufficient justification for lying. Part of the problem with lying in this situation is that we cannot stop at one lie. We will have to compliment our partner when we see the shirt in the future. Also, lying so that we won't hurt our partner's feelings is problematic:

> Persistent fear of hurting other's frail constitution would greatly limit discussion and create an uneasy atmosphere. More generally, since everyone will be annoyed by several features of their intimates, similar reasoning will lead them to lie about other "trivial" aspects of their intimates, e.g., their hair or shoes or mannerisms etc.—all on the grounds that such sharing will hurt their feelings. Thus, they will have to advance and protect a network of lies. There is no way, however, to be comfortable with another if one is constantly on guard about what one says and does. Under such circumstances, one could not have an intimate relationship. (LaFollette & Graham, 1986, p. 9)

For these reasons, a lie should only be considered as a last resort. When we do consider lying, we must go a step further and decide whether it is morally justified. Even if we can morally justify a lie as our only alternative, we must keep in mind that any lie diminishes us—we lose dignity and integrity when we lie. How we can deal with lies is examined in Reading 10.2.

Before proceeding, it is important to recognize that there are many ways that we can tell the truth or lie. Our messages to others can be clear or ambiguous. It is possible to use ambiguous messages to tell the truth or to lie (Bavelas et al., 1990). Ambiguous messages are not necessarily "lies of omission." If we are selling a car that is basically safe, but we know that it needs some repairs, for example, we would be telling the truth if we said, "The car is in fairly good but not perfect condition" (Bavelas et al., 1990, p. 183). How this statement is interpreted depends on the receiver's experience with cars. It also is important to recognize that ambiguous messages are the preferred method of communication used in collectivistic cultures.

Attracting and Influencing Others in Conversations

When we communicate with others, we often use *strategies,* or broad categories of behaviors, to accomplish our goals. Within each strategy, there are specific behaviors we use to enact the strategy. These specific behaviors are called *tactics* (Bell & Daly, 1984). Self-disclosure, asking questions, and deception detection are strategies we use to gain information about others. Two other important types of strategies involve getting oth-

Reading 10.2 LYING/SISSELA BOK

Individuals, without a doubt, have the power to influence the amount of duplicity in their lives and to shape their speech and action. They can decide to rule out deception wherever honest alternatives exist, and become much more adept at thinking up honest ways to deal with problems. They can learn to look with much greater care at the remaining choices where deception seems the only way out. They can make use of the test of publicity to help them set standards to govern their participation in deceptive practices. Finally, they can learn to beware of efforts to dupe them, and make clear their preference for honesty even in small things.

But individuals differ greatly in their ability to carry through such changes. They differ in their knowledge of deception and its alternatives; in their desire to bring about changes; and in their understanding of what lying can do to them, either as deceiver or as deceived. Many who might be able to change the patterns of duplicity in their own lives lack any awareness of the presence of a moral problem in the first place, and thus feel no need to examine their behavior and explore the alternatives carefully. Others are beyond caring.

Still another difference among individuals cuts sharply into the capacity of many to make changes: the difference in the power to carry through a change and in the freedom and security from repercussions should they challenge deeply rooted habits of duplicity. The lack of power and freedom to cope with the consequences of battling deceptive practices reinforces the lack of awareness or concern wherever it exists; it puts great pressure even on those least comfortable with deceit.

ers to like us (affinity-seeking strategies) and influencing others. Let's begin by looking at how we get others to like us.

Affinity Seeking

We devote a lot of time and energy in our interactions with others trying to get them to like us (Bell & Daly, 1984). Before proceeding, think about how you try to get other people to like you. Answer the following questions:

How do you communicate with other people if you want them to like you?

____

____

____

How do you find out if other people actually like you? ______________________________

____

____

Your answers to these questions should provide some insight into the role of affinity in your implicit personal theory of communication. Keep your answers to these questions in mind as you read the remainder of this section.

Affinity seeking is the "process by which individuals attempt to get others to like and feel positive toward them" (Bell & Daly, 1984, p. 91). There are certain strategies we can use to get others to like us. There are also ways we can test whether or not others like us. Let's begin by looking at what leads us to want to get others to like us.

There may be no group to which affinity seeking is more important than teenagers. Commonality is one of the affinity-seeking strategies.

Nature of Affinity Seeking. We often have the conscious or unconscious goals of wanting other people to like us when we interact with them. We may want other people to like us because it will help us meet other goals, such as accomplishing a task at work, or we may want other people to like us so that they will see us as polite, nice people. We also may want other people to like us so that we can develop an interpersonal relationship with them (Bell & Daly, 1984). We may not be highly aware of our attempts to get others to like us, because we have affinity-seeking scripts that we use when we communicate on automatic pilot. Alternatively, we may consciously decide to try to get other people to like us when we are mindful of our communication.

Several factors influence our ability to get other people to like us. Our social and personal identities influence our attempts. If we are highly communication apprehensive, for example, it inhibits our attempts to get other

people to like us. Our communication skills also influence our ability to accomplish our goals. The context in which we are interacting with other people also influences our ability to seek affinity. To illustrate, we will have a better chance to get people to like us in informal situations than in formal situations, where our behavior is guided by our roles. Other people's characteristics also influence our ability to get them to like us; for instance, it may be easier to get extroverts to like us than introverts.

Affinity Seeking Strategies. The strategies we use to get other people to like us fall into the seven categories (Bell & Daly, 1984) shown in Table 10.2. First, we use strategies that involve *control and visibility* when we make ourselves stand out from other people. These strategies include establishing our autonomy, assuming control, and trying to look physically attractive. Second, we use strategies to establish *mutual trust* by showing other people that we are trustworthy and open. Third, we use strategies to demonstrate our

Table 10.2

A Typology of Affinity-Seeking Strategies

Control and Visibility

1. *Personal autonomy.* The person presents him or herself an independent, free-thinking person.
2. *Reward association.* The person presents her or himself in such a way that the other person thinks she or he will be rewarded for the association.
3. *Assume control.* The person presents her or himself as a person who has control over what is going on.
4. *Dynamism.* The person presents him or herself as an active, enthusiastic person.
5. *Present interesting self.* The person presents him or herself as a person who would be interesting to know.
6. *Physical attractiveness.* The person tries to look and dress as attractively as possible.

Mutual Trust

1. *Trustworthiness.* The person presents her or himself as an honest, reliable person.
2. *Openness.* The person discloses personal information about her or himself.

Politeness

1. *Conversational rule-keeping.* The person adheres closely to the rules for polite, cooperative interaction.
2. *Concede control.* The person allows the other person to take charge of relational activities.

Concern and Caring

1. *Self-concept confirmation.* The person demonstrates respect for the other person and helps the other person feel good about him or herself.
2. *Elicit other's disclosures.* The person encourages the other to talk by reinforcing his or her contributions to the conversation.
3. *Listening.* The person listens responsively to the other person.
4. *Supportiveness.* The person supports the other person in her or his social encounters.
5. *Sensitivity.* The person acts in a warm, empathic way toward the other person.
6. *Altruism.* The person tries to help the other person in whatever he or she is doing.

Table 10.2
CONTINUED

Other Involvement
1. *Facilitate enjoyment.* The person tries to maximize the positiveness of the encounters with the other person.
2. *Inclusion of other.* The person includes the other person in his or her social groups.
3. *Nonverbal immediacy.* The person signals interest to the other person nonverbally (e.g., smiling).

Self-involvement
1. *Self-inclusion.* The person arranges the environment so that he or she has frequent contact with the other person.
2. *Influence perception of closeness.* The person engages in behavior that makes the other person think the relationship is closer than it actually is.

Commonalities
1. *Similarities.* The person tries to convince the other person that they share commonalities.
2. *Assuming equality.* The person demonstrates that he or she thinks he or she is equal to the other person.
3. *Comfortable self:* The person acts comfortable in the other person's presence.

Adapted from Bell and Daly (1984).

politeness by following the rules of conversation in a particular situation and not controlling other people. Fourth, we use strategies that involve *concern and caring* when we support other people's self-concepts, listen, and generally are supportive. Fifth, we use strategies to increase *other involvement* when we draw other people out in conversations or try to maximize the positive aspects of our interactions with others. Sixth, we use strategies to increase *self-involvement* when we tell other people that we want to have a relationship with them. Finally, we use strategies designed to demonstrate *commonalities* by showing other people that we are similar and equal.

The use of affinity-seeking strategies has positive consequences for our relationships with others. The more we use affinity-seeking strategies, for example, the more others like us, the more our romantic partners say they love us, and the more others see us as being effective (Bell & Daly, 1984).

We choose different strategies depending on the situation in which we find ourselves (specific tactics are defined in Table 10.2). We are likely to use altruism, inclusion of other, and self-inclusion, for example, in social situations more than in task situations. We are likely to use listening, physical attractiveness, and supportiveness more in task situations than in social situations (Bell & Daly, 1984). Further, we tend to use conversational rule-keeping, facilitate enjoyment, and engage in self-inclusion more in interactions with equals than in interactions with people of higher status. We are likely to use autonomy and trustworthiness tactics more with people of higher status than with people of equal status.

Understanding the Affinity-Seeking Strategies You Use. Skill Exercise 10.2 is designed to help you understand the strategies you use to get others to like you. Take a few minutes to complete it now.

The answers you gave regarding how you would get others to like you when you are not consciously thinking about what you do are part of your implicit theory of interpersonal communication. By labeling these strategies using the types in Table 10.2 and reviewing the discussion of when the various strategies tend to be used, you can begin to get an idea if the strategies you use when you communicate on automatic pilot are effective. You might also find it useful to think about how you would use the other strategies described in Table 10.2 in these situations. This will help you to begin to develop new affinity-seeking scripts.

Strategies to Test Other People's Affinity For Us. When we interact with others, we make a decision about whether we like them and want to get to know them better. Since developing a relationship requires mu-

---

Skill Exercise 10.2 ***Understanding Your Affinity-Seeking Strategies***

We all try to get others to like us. For each of the following situations, think about what you do to get people to like you and want to continue a relationship. You may not be highly aware of many of the things you do. Therefore, think of the things you do without thinking about it, and the things you consciously decide to do.

1. You meet a person at a social gathering who you think might be a potential romantic partner.

   What do you do *without thinking about it* to get this person to be attracted to you? ______________________________

   ____

   ____

   What do you *consciously* try to do to get the other person to like you or want to see you again? ______________________________

   ____

   ____

2. You just started working at a new job. One of your co-workers seems very interesting to you, and you would like to see more of this person outside of work. (If it makes it easier, assume that you have just moved to a new city and do not know anyone else in the city.)

   What do you do *without thinking about it* to get this person to like you? ______________________________

   ____

   ____

   ____

   What do you *consciously* try to do to get the other person to like you and want to see you outside of work? ______________________________

   ____

   ____

   ____

After completing both scenarios, look at Table 10.2, which describes the various types of affinity-seeking strategies we use. Try to classify the responses you gave in this exercise into the types described in the table.

tual liking, we also need to have an idea of whether other people like us. To determine this, we sometimes use *affinity-testing* strategies.

There are eight types of strategies we use to find out if others like us (Douglas, 1987). First, we use *confronting* strategies when we ask other people to give direct evidence of their liking for us. This could be accomplished by directly asking other people whether they like us. Second, we use *withdrawing* to see if other people will maintain their interaction with us. We might, for example, be silent to see if they will carry on the conversation or leave. Third, we use *sustaining* strategies when we do something to keep the interaction going, such as asking other people a lot of questions. Fourth, we use *hazing* strategies by getting other people to perform a service for us. Asking other people for a ride home is an example of this strategy. Fifth, we use *diminishing* when we put ourselves down. If we ask other people if we are keeping them from doing something, we are diminishing ourselves. Sixth, we use *approaching* strategies when we try to increase the intimacy of our encounters with others. To illustrate, moving physically closer to other people increases the intimacy of the encounter. Seventh, we use *offering* strategies when we generate conditions favorable for other people to approach us. Helping other people carry something to their cars is one tactic illustrating this strategy. Eighth, we use *networking* strategies when we involve third parties. Telling one person that we like another person is an illustration of this strategy.

These strategies differ in terms of the degree to which we perceive them as efficient and socially appropriate (Douglas, 1987). In the United States, networking, approaching, offering, and sustaining are viewed as efficient and socially appropriate. Confronting, in contrast, is viewed as efficient, but socially inappropriate. Withdrawing, hazing, and diminishing the self are viewed as inefficient and socially inappropriate. These strategies probably increase other people's uncertainty about our behavior and, therefore, decrease their liking for us. The perceived appropriateness of these strategies, however, varies across cultures. Diminishing the self and withdrawing, for example, are viewed as efficient and socially appropriate strategies in many collectivistic cultures.

Compare the strategies for finding out if other people like you that you listed in the question at the beginning of this section with the strategies listed here. Which do you use most frequently?

Interpersonal Influence

In addition to trying to get other people to like us, we try to influence other people when we communicate with them. Before proceeding, think about how you try to influence other people. Answer the following questions:

How do you typically communicate when you want someone to do something for you? ______________________

____

____

____

How do other people typically respond when you communicate in this way?

____

____

____

When other people want you to do something for them, how do they communicate that leads you to want to comply?

____

____

____

When other people want you to do something for them, how do they communicate that leads you to not want to comply?

____

____

____

Your answers to these questions should provide some insight into the role of influence in your implicit personal theory of communication. Keep your answers to these questions in mind as you read the remainder of this section.

Our attempts to influence other people are affected by the goals we have in the particular situation, the plans we have to reach our goals, and the strategies we use in trying to influence them. To place the process of influence in context, the goals and plans we have when we are trying to influence others are examined first.

Influencing Other People. When we try to influence other people, we base our influence attempts on our goals. *Goals* are future states of affairs that we are committed to achieving (Dillard, 1990). Our goals influence the way we interpret our actions and our interactions with other people. There are at least six types of goals we might have when we are trying to influence someone in an interpersonal relationship (Dillard, 1989). First, we can give *lifestyle advice* to others by trying to convince our roommate to take music lessons. Second, we can try to *gain assistance* from other people, such as trying to get a friend to help us with a paper that is due the next day. Third, we can try to get other people to *share activities* with us. Convincing our romantic partner to go to the restaurant of our choice for dinner is an example of this strategy. Fourth, we can try to *change political stances,* like trying to get a friend to vote in a particular way. Fifth, we can *give health advice* to others; for example, trying to get our friend to exercise. Sixth, we can try to *change relationships (or people).* Trying to get our romantic partner to "dress up" more than usual is one tactic illustrating this strategy.

Our goals influence the types of messages we use to influence other people (Dillard, 1989). If our goal is to change our relationship or to give health advice, we transmit messages that involve directness, positivity, and logic. If our goal is to gain assistance, change political views, or share activities, we use messages that are not direct, positive, or logical. Messages used to accomplish these goals tend be indirect, such as hinting.

There are three basic types of responses other people can have to our attempts to influence them: they can comply with our attempt, they can resist our attempt to influence, or they can exit (Dillard, 1990). If other people comply with our attempt to influence them, the process of influencing them is over. If they physically exit the situation, the process of influence also is over. If others exit by changing the topic of conversation, we have to reevaluate what we want to do. We could try to change the topic of the conversation back to what we were discussing or go along with the other person's topic change. The option we select depends on our other goals for the interaction and our relationship with the other person. If other people resist our attempt to influence them, we might continue to try to influence them using alternative plans, or we might decide to stop our attempts to influence them. Again, the option we select depends on our other goals for the interaction, the relationship we have with the other person, and how the other person responds. If the other person responds in an unfriendly manner or in a strong manner, however, we are likely to become verbally aggressive, too (Lim, 1990).

Compliance-Gaining Strategies. When we try to influence others, we construct our messages in a way that we think will gain their compliance. There are at least 16 different strategies we can use to gain compliance from others (Marwell & Schmitt, 1967). The example used to illustrate the various strategies in Table 10.3 involves trying to get a friend to repay money owed you.

The compliance-gaining strategies presented in Table 10.3 are based on different ways that we can use social power to influence others. The strategies vary in the degree to which they involve instrumental verbal aggressiveness (Burgoon, Dillard, & Doran, 1983). To illustrate, the use of threats, aversive stimulation, negative expertise, and debt involve high levels of verbal aggressiveness, while the use of promise, pregiving, positive moral appeal, altruism, and liking are not verbally aggressive.

The extent to which the various compliance-gaining strategies are effective depends on how others expect us to use language. Expectancy theory (Burgoon & Miller, 1985) suggests that, **when we use language that is viewed as socially or culturally inappropriate, it will negatively violate other people's expectations and inhibit our ability to influence them.** Our ability to influence other people depends on our using socially appropriate language or positively violating other people's expectations. We can positively violate other people's expectations in two ways. First, other people might expect us to deviate from expected behavior in a negative way and we do not. To illustrate, other people might expect us to raise our voice and yell, but we speak in a calm voice. Second, we can positively violate other people's expectations by performing better than expected. If other people expect us to be an average speaker, for example, and we speak eloquently, then we have positively violated their expectations.

Other people use four types of strategies to resist our attempts to influence them (O'Hair, Cody, & O'Hair, 1991). First, they can use *negative relational strategies,* such as pointing out that they have not made such requests of us, saying that no reasonable person would try to get them to do this, telling us that they do not want to discuss it, or simply refusing to go along. Second, they can use *negotiation* strategies, such as telling us that we need to talk to work it out, offering a concession, or asking us the reason for our request. Third, they can use *justifications.* Explaining why we would benefit if they do not comply or explaining the negative consequences if they do comply are examples of justifications. Fourth, they can use *positive identity management* strategies, such as trying to get us to feel good about ourselves so they will not have to go along, or appealing to our affection for them.

Understanding Your Influence Strategies. Skill Exercise 10.3 provides an opportunity for you to better understand the strategies you use to try to influence others. Take a few minutes to complete it now.

The strategies you typically use to try to get other people to do what you want them to do are part of your implicit theory of interpersonal communication. You can compare your strategies to those in Table 10.3 to see where they fall in terms of the general strategies you use to gain compliance. If the strategies you consistently use when communicating on automatic pilot are highly verbally aggressive, you might want to mindfully think about alternative strategies. Highly verbally aggressive strategies are not always effective, because, like other forms of aggression, only the interests of the person using the strategies are taken into consideration. They do not take into consideration the interests of the person being influenced. Thinking about alternative

Table 10.3
TYPES OF COMPLIANCE-GAINING STRATEGIES

1. *Promise.* If you comply, I will reward you. ("You tell your friend that you will do something for him or her if the money is repaid.")
2. *Threat.* If you do not comply, I will punish you. ("You tell your friend that if she or he does not repay the money you will do something she or he does not like.")
3. *Expertise (Positive).* If you comply, you will be rewarded because of "the nature of things." ("You tell your friend that if he or she repays the money, he or she will be able to borrow more in the future.")
4. *Expertise (Negative).* If you do not comply, you will be punished because of "the nature of things." ("You tell your friend that if he or she does not repay the money, he or she will not be able to borrow more in the future.")
5. *Liking.* Actor [or actress] is friendly and helpful to get target in "good frame of mind" so that he [or she] will comply with the request. ("You help your friend do something, then ask her or him to repay the money.")
6. *Pre-Giving.* Actor [or actress] rewards target before requesting compliance. ("You fix your friend dinner, then ask him or her to repay money.")
7. *Aversive Stimulation.* Actor [or actress] continuously punishes target making cessation contingent on compliance. ("You refuse to speak to your friend until she or he repays the money.")
8. *Debt.* You owe me compliance because of past favors. ("You tell your friend that you've always helped her or him in the past, so she or he should repay the money.")
9. *Moral Appeal.* You are immoral if you do not comply. ("You tell your friend that he or she is immoral if he or she does not repay the money.")
10. *Self-Feeling (Positive).* You will feel better about yourself if you comply. ("You tell your friend that she or he will feel better about her or himself if she or he repays the money.")
11. *Self-Feeling (Negative).* You will feel worse about yourself if you do not comply. ("You tell your friend that he or she will not feel good about him or herself if he or she does not repay the money.")
12. *Altercasting (Positive).* A person with "good qualities" would comply. ("You tell your friend that a responsible person would repay the money.")
13. *Altercasting (Negative).* Only a person with "bad" qualities would not comply. ("You tell your friend that only an irresponsible person would not repay the money.")
14. *Altruism.* I need your compliance very badly, so do it for me. ("You tell your friend that you need the money badly.")
15. *Esteem (Positive).* People you value will think better of you if you comply. ("You tell your friend that you will be proud of him or her if he or she repays the money.")
16. *Esteem (Negative).* People you value will think worse of you if you do not comply. ("You tell your friend that you will not think highly of her or him if she or he does not repay the money.")

Adapted from Marwell and Schmitt (1967, pp. 350–364).

Skill Exercise 10.3 ***Understanding How You Try to Influence Others***

At times, we all try to influence others. For each of the situations described below, think about how you would normally try to influence the other person. Describe the approach you would use in the space provided.

1. You have made plans to go to a movie with a friend. You want to see a particular movie, but your friend indicates that he or she wants to see another movie, one you do not want to see.

   How would you typically try to get your friend to go to the movie you want to see? ______________________________

   ____

   ____

   ____

   If your typical strategies do not work, what other strategies would you use to try to convince your friend? ______________________________

   ____

   ____

   ____

2. You receive a paper back in your interpersonal communication course, and you think that your instructor graded you unfairly. You want to try to convince your instructor to raise your grade.

   How would you typically try to get your instructor to change your grade? ______________________________

   ____

   ____

   ____

   ____

   If your typical strategies do not work, what other strategies would you use to try to convince your instructor? ______________________________

   ____

   ____

   ____

   ____

After answering the questions, look at the strategies for gaining compliance in Table 10.3. Which types of strategies did you use when answering the questions?

strategies can help you begin to develop new influence scripts before you need to use them. To use these scripts, however, you will have to be mindful of your communication.

Group Differences in Compliance-Gaining. There are cultural differences in the use of compliance-gaining strategies (Gudykunst & Ting-Toomey, 1988). Members of collectivistic cultures take the context and their relationship with the person they are trying to influence into consideration more than members of individualistic cultures do. Members of collectivistic cultures tend to use altruistic strategies and strategies that are considered socially appropriate more than members of individualistic cultures. Members of individualistic cultures, in contrast, are more likely to use strategies that are direct and strategies perceived as socially inappropriate, such as verbally aggressive strategies, than do members of collectivistic cultures.

In addition to cultural differences, there are differences by age group in the United States (Dillard et al., 1990). People over seventy, for example, are more willing to apply pressure when they are trying to gain compliance than are younger people (in their early twenties). Both younger and older people, however, are more likely to be direct when they are trying to gain compliance from a person in the other age group than when trying to gain compliance with members of their own age group.

To conclude, we use information exchange, affinity-seeking, or influence strategies in all conversations we have with others. To be able to modify how we use these strategies, we need to understand the dynamics that guide our conversations with others.

Summary

When we interact with other people, we exchange information. This is accomplished by asking questions, self-disclosing, and detecting deception. We follow cultural rules and have scripts for asking questions with people we do not know well. We use both open and closed questions to gather information about other people, but problems may arise if we ask the wrong type of question.

Like asking questions, there are rules for self-disclosure when we interact with other people. Even though we self-disclose frequently in our everyday conversations, intimate self-disclosure does not take place frequently. Openness does not always lead to better communication and increases in the intimacy of our relationships.

Deception involves leading others to false conclusions. When we deceive other people, we give off cues (leakage cues) that lead them to think we are deceiving them. We are, however, generally not very effective in determining when other people are deceiving us. We often think that some deception is needed to keep our relationships on an even keel. This, nevertheless, is not the case.

When we interact with other people, we use affinity-seeking strategies to get them to like us. Our use of affinity-seeking strategies generally has positive consequences for our relationships with other people. The more we use affinity-seeking strategies, the more other people tend to like us. In addition to using strategies to get other people to like us, we use strategies to test whether others like us.

We also use strategies to influence other people when we communicate with them. The strategies we use vary in terms of the degree to which they involve instrumental verbal aggressiveness. Our ability to influence other people is decreased when we use language that is viewed as socially inappropriate.

Notes

1. The relationship between gender and self-disclosure is complicated. We attempt to summarize major trends in the research findings, but those interested in this area should examine specific studies. Cline's (1989) summary is a good beginning and many of the conclusions we present are drawn from this work.
2. Nishida's results are similar to those reported by Berger et al. (1976) for the United States and by Barnlund (1989) for Japan and the United States.
3. Also, see the discussion of topics of conversation in our discussion of situational influences on communication in Chapter 6.
4. The idea for Figure 10.1 is adapted from Altman, Vinsel, & Brown (1981).
5. It is possible to talk about verbal statements as varying along a continuum from totally false

to totally true (see Bavelas et al., 1990). This conceptualization, however, makes the ethical argument we are making more complicated than necessary. We therefore discuss lies and truth telling as a dichotomy.

Journal Reflections

1. *Self-disclosure.* Self-disclosure is necessary in intimate relationships, and it can facilitate relationship development. Self-disclosure, however, is not appropriate in all relationships. There are two issues with respect to self-disclosure: (1) deciding when and to whom to self-disclose, and (2) disclosing information appropriate to the relationship. In the next week, try self-disclosing with two different people. In order to examine the appropriateness of self-disclosure, self-disclose to one person at a time and place where you think it is appropriate, and self-disclose something to someone else at a time and place where you think it may be inappropriate. In your journal, discuss the two situations (why you thought one was appropriate and the other inappropriate) and analyze the influence of your self-disclosures on your communication with the two people involved.
2. *Asking Questions.* In the next week, observe your use of questions in your interactions with others. To what extent do you use questions? How frequently do you use loaded questions? Do you use both open and closed questions? After you get a feeling for how you use questions, try other alternatives in your everyday conversations. If you typically ask a lot of questions, try asking fewer. If you typically use loaded questions, try to stop using them. Try to mix your open and closed questions to maximize the information you gather from others.
3. *Observing Your Use of Deception.* Over the next week, observe when you deceive or lie to others. Are there particular circumstances in which you engage in these behaviors? What are they? Why do you lie or deceive others in these situations? How do you want to change your behavior in the future?
4. *Observing Your Use of Affinity-Seeking Strategies.* Over the next week, observe how you try to get other people to like you. How do the strategies you use compare with those discussed in this chapter? Are there any strategies you use that you want to change? How can you change them?
5. *Observing Your Use of Compliance-Gaining Strategies.* Over the next week, observe how you try to gain other people's compliance. How do the strategies you use compare with those discussed in this chapter? Are there any strategies you use that you want to change? How can you change them?

Study Questions

1. What are the rules guiding the questions we ask others?
2. When are open questions more useful than closed? When are closed questions more useful than open?
3. What are loaded questions, and what functions do they perform in conversations?
4. How does self-disclosure generally progress over the course of the development of interpersonal relationships?
5. Why does self-disclosure differ in individualistic and collectivistic cultures?
6. How do we maintain privacy in our interpersonal relationships?
7. What are the differences among deception, deceptive communication, and lying?
8. Why is truthfulness necessary in an interpersonal relationship?
9. How does the way we detect deceptive communication in close and nonclose (with strangers) relationships differ?
10. How do we get others to like us (affinity-seeking strategies)?
11. How do we try to influence others?

Suggested Readings

Bok, S. (1978). *Lying: Moral choice in public and private life.* New York: Vintage Books. Sissela Bok examines all aspects of lying. Her discussions of the role of lying in building trust and the consequences of lying are especially useful in understanding the importance of honesty in our interpersonal relationships.

Bok, S. (1983). *Secrets: On the ethics of concealment and revelation.* New York: Vintage Books. Sissela Bok addresses issues of when holding secrets is appropriate and when it is inappropriate. She talks about the advantages and disadvantages of holding secrets and when we should consider breaking a promise of secrecy that we made to others.

Miller, G. R., & Stiff, J. (1993). *Deceptive communication.* Newbury Park, CA: Sage. Gerald Miller and James Stiff examine why people engage in deceptive communication. They explain the verbal and nonverbal indicators that people use to decide if others are deceiving them.

11

NONVERBAL COMMUNICATION

Other people's nonverbal communication can have a powerful effect on our perceptions of them. The nonverbal cues of appearance and touch, for example, have a significant effect on the way we perceive other people. Other nonverbal cues, such as tone of voice, pitch, gestures, and facial expressions, play a major role in interpersonal communication as well. We use nonverbal communication to reveal our emotions, our attitudes, our personalities, and the nature of our relationships with others.

Nonverbal communication consists of "all human communication events which transcend spoken or written words" (Knapp, 1978, p. 38). It includes all of the visual cues we use when we communicate, including facial expression, eye contact, gestures, posture, physical appearance, and clothing. Vocal characteristics that surround our verbal messages—characteristics such as vocal range, pitch, inflection, vocal quality, speech rate, and pauses—also are part of nonverbal communication. In addition, nonverbal communication involves touch, our use of space, the environment, and our use of time. Together, these sets of cues comprise all communication except that which is coded through words.

Nonverbal communication has been called a relationship code because nonverbal cues are often the primary means of signaling the nature of our interpersonal relationships with others. We use nonverbal cues to communicate things that are too direct or potentially too embarrassing to be stated in words. As a romantic relationship develops between two people, for example, they stand closer together, maintain more eye contact, and touch each other more frequently. These cues communicate affection without using words.

There are many different ways that we communicate nonverbally. The ways that we structure our environment (such as decorating our homes), our physical appearance, the way we use space, the way we use our bodies, the ways we touch, the ways we use our voice,

One of the most visible forms of nonverbal communication is visual cues. We can communicate with others through our appearance, our interior decorating touches, even how we design our homes. Each of these aspects describes a bit of our personality to those who see our cues.

and the way we use time all can be used to communicate nonverbally. Our cultural and gender identities affect the way we transmit and interpret these nonverbal cues. We'll begin our discussion by looking at the nature of nonverbal communication.

The Nature of Nonverbal Communication

Although people all over the world experience feelings like happiness, sadness, and anger, the way they communicate these emotions nonverbally is generally different. Most nonverbal behavior is learned and varies from culture to culture. Nonverbal behavior also varies considerably within cultures. Within a culture, such " 'people' factors as gender, age, socioeconomic status, [ethnicity], and personality make a difference [in our use of nonverbal cues]. So do contextual factors such as the type of occupation in work settings and environmental constraints" (Burgoon, 1985, p. 360). Although the focus in this chapter is primarily on the United States and thus applies mainly to people raised in this culture, examples from other cultures are provided to demonstrate the variability in nonverbal behavior. While members of different cultures may engage in similar types of nonverbal behaviors, the interpretations, the functions, and the end goals of each nonverbal cue may vary from one culture to the next. To understand nonverbal cues, it is necessary to recognize how they are different from verbal cues.

Verbal and Nonverbal Cues

Nonverbal cues and language share some characteristics and are different in some respects (Burgoon et al., 1989). Like language, nonverbal cues are discrete and can be divided into separate units. We can, for example, separate a smile from a frown. Some nonverbal cues are created by agreement among members of a group and therefore are arbitrary, like words or symbols. In the United States, people generally agree that "the finger" is an obscene gesture, but people in some other cultures do not recognize this gesture as having the same meaning. Other nonverbal cues, in contrast, are not arbitrary. Some nonverbal cues are iconic; that is, they directly resemble their referent. To illustrate, holding up five fingers to indicate that we did something five times is an iconic cue, which closely represents the referent.

While language is characterized by displacement (talking about things that are not present in space and time), nonverbal cues generally do not involve displacement. In using nonverbal cues, we are limited to referring to things in the present. Similarly, nonverbal cues are not reflexive like language (we can use language to refer to itself). Although language does not have universal meaning, there appear to be some nonverbal cues that have universal meaning (see the discussion of culture later in this chapter).

Verbal and nonverbal cues also differ in the relative weight we give them in determining social meaning when we communicate (Burgoon et al., 1989). In general, "adults place more reliance on nonverbal cues than verbal ones in determining verbal meaning" (Burgoon et al., 1989, p. 155). Children, however, tend to rely on verbal more than nonverbal cues. One estimate is that children are five times more likely to pay attention to verbal cues than to nonverbal cues (Philpott, 1983). Our tendency to rely on nonverbal more than on verbal cues is most prominent when the verbal and nonverbal cues are not congruent. If we say we are happy and have a frown on our face, other people tend to believe our nonverbal cue. Whether we focus on verbal or nonverbal cues to determine meaning depends on the context of our communication. To illustrate, if we are judging emotions or attitudes, we tend to focus on nonverbal cues; if we are dealing with factual or cognitive functions, we rely on verbal cues.

Functions of Nonverbal Communication

Nonverbal communication serves many functions when we communicate (Argyle, 1979). Nonverbal cues, such as facial expressions and body movements, help us to *express attitudes* like approval or disgust. We *express emotional states* like happiness or despondency in gestures, in smiles or frowns, even through the clothes we choose to wear. Nodding our head or breaking eye contact helps us *manage turn taking* in conversations. Kissing at the end of a wedding ceremony is a nonverbal *ritual* used to signify public commitment. Our physical appearance and artifacts, such as clothing and jewelry, serve as *signs of our self-presentation.*

Nonverbal cues also serve important functions in relation to our verbal cues, in synchronizing our behavior with others and in establishing relationships with others. Let's begin by looking at how nonverbal cues are related to verbal cues.

Functions of Nonverbal Cues in Relation to Verbal Cues. Nonverbal cues may be used independently or in conjunction with a verbal message. When nonverbal cues are used with verbal messages, they relate to verbal cues in six primary ways. Nonverbal cues repeat, contradict, substitute, complement, or accent a verbal message, and/or regulate interaction (Knapp & Hall, 1992).

First, nonverbal cues may simply *repeat* the verbal message. When people in a car stop to ask us directions to a nearby store, we may give them verbal directions followed by a nonverbal gesture that points in the direction we have told them to drive. In this instance, our nonverbal gesture (pointing north) repeats the verbal message ("Go north").

Second, nonverbal cues may *contradict* the verbal message. The comment "I'm never nervous when giving a public speech" may be contradicted by sweaty palms, quavering voice, and shaking hands. Adults rely more heavily on nonverbal cues for indications of feelings and on verbal cues for information about other people's beliefs or intentions (Friedman, 1978).

Third, nonverbal cues may *substitute* for

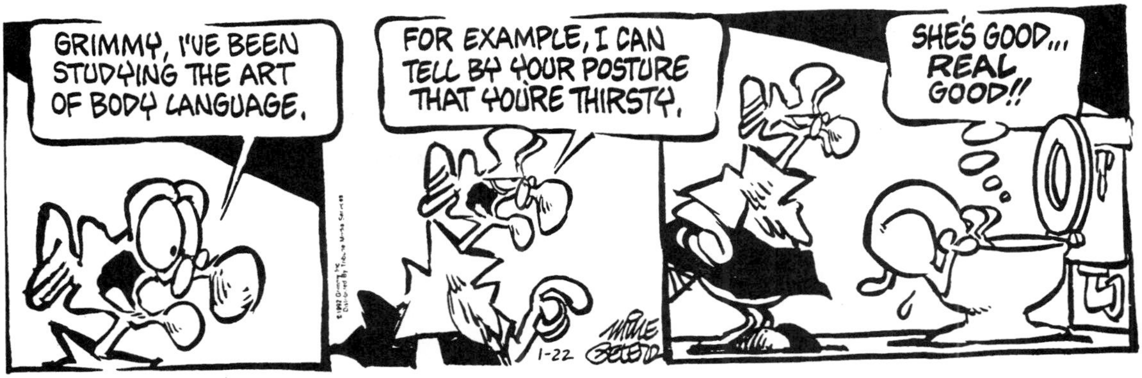

MOTHER GOOSE AND GRIMM © *Grimmy Inc., distributed by Tribune Media Services. Reprinted by permission.*

the verbal message altogether. Workers at airports who guide airplanes on the ground use hand gestures to tell the pilot how to maneuver the airplane. Smiling at someone at a party signals that we want to start a conversation. The nonverbal message is clear, and no verbal message is necessary in order for communication to occur.

Fourth, nonverbal cues may *complement* the verbal message. A pat on the back accompanying our boss' verbal message "You did a good job today," for example, complements the words that are spoken and lets us know that our boss thought we did a really good job. The look in our parents' eyes when they tell us that they are disappointed in us for doing something inappropriate accompanies the verbal message and underscores their disappointment.

Fifth, nonverbal cues may *accent* parts of a verbal message, much as italics are used in writing to accent parts of a sentence. Holding up two fingers while telling someone that the third verse of a song gets repeated twice accents the importance of repeating the verse two times.

Finally, nonverbal cues may *regulate* the back-and-forth flow of communication between people. Nonverbal cues can signal the initiation, maintenance, yielding, and termination of conversation. Nodding our heads up and down slowly encourages a speaker to continue speaking. Nodding our heads up and down more quickly indicates that we want to break in and begin speaking. If we look off into space, other people may interpret our behavior as a sign that we want to end the conversation.

We learn how to use nonverbal communication at a very early age. Although there are many similarities in these communicative functions across groups, some people learn that different cues are appropriate in different circumstances. Skill Exercise 11.1 is designed to help you better understand your use of nonverbal communication. Take a few minutes to complete it now.

Skill Exercise 11.1 should provide you with an indication of how you use nonverbal communication. It is important to be mindful about your nonverbal communication and your perception of other people's nonverbal communication if you want to communicate effectively.

Function of Nonverbal Cues in Providing Rhythm to Interactions. **Nonverbal cues are critical to providing rhythm**

Skill Exercise 11.1 *Identifying the Functions of Nonverbal Communication*

Nonverbal communication relates to verbal messages in six ways: (1) repeating, (2) contradicting, (3) substituting, (4) complementing, (5) accenting, and/or (6) regulating. Think about all of the interactions you were involved in today. What role did nonverbal communication play in these interactions? Identify two examples in specific communication situations. One example should be of your own use of nonverbal cues; the other example should be your observation of someone else's use of nonverbal cues.

Function	*Your Behavior*	*Someone Else's Behavior*
Repeating	________	________
Contradicting	________	________
Substituting	________	________
Complementing	________	________
Accenting	________	________
Regulating	________	________

Were the nonverbal cues used in each of these situations effective? Why or why not?

____

____

If you could relive these situations, how would you change your behavior to be more mindful?

____

____

to our interactions with others. Without rhythm in our interactions, we could not synchronize our behavior with others. *Interpersonal synchronization* refers to convergent rhythmic movements between two people on both verbal and nonverbal levels (Hall, 1983). Every facet of human behavior is involved in this rhythmic process. When synchronization occurs, our behavior is rhythmic and we are locked together in a "dance" that functions almost totally out of awareness. A sense of synchronization in our interactions with others plays "a crucial role in our ability to talk to each other, to work with each other, and to fall and stay in love" (Douglis, 1987, p. 37).

Interpersonal synchrony or convergence is achieved when the nonverbal behavior between two individuals is unique to the dyad (two people), flexible, smooth, and spontaneous (Knapp, 1983). Interpersonal misalignment, or divergence, occurs when the nonverbal behavior between two individuals is stylized, rigid, awkward, and hesitant (Knapp, 1983). Interpersonal synchrony is related to liking, rapport, and attention, while interpersonal misalignment is related to disliking and indifference.

Interpersonal synchronization is most evident when we watch two lovers talk:

> Without realizing it, after awhile they actually begin to mirror each other's movements. She, facing him, leans on her right elbow as he leans on his left. They shift postures at the same time. They reach for their wine glasses, raise them and drink simultaneously, an unthinking toast to their closeness.
>
> Rhythms may even betray love at first sight to a careful observer before the lovers themselves realize what is happening. Over the course of an evening, a newly acquainted but smitten couple will begin to synchronize first head and arm movements. Then more body parts will join the

> mating dance, until the two are dancing as one. (Douglis, 1987, p. 42)

Observing that other people's behavior is synchronized is a good predictor of their mutual involvement (Douglis, 1987).

It is important to recognize that the rhythms we expect in our interactions are learned in our culture, ethnic group, and the region of the country in which we live. Many problems that occur when people from different groups communicate can be traced to different rhythms of interaction. Nonnative speakers of English, for example, may stress the wrong words in a sentence or fail to stress words when they should. This misalignment in the vocal nonverbal behavior throws off the rhythm of a conversation. People from other cultures also might expect to stand closer than we expect. When they stand close, we move back without thinking about it. When we move back, they will move closer without thinking about it. Again, these differences make coordinating behavior difficult. Some of the major group differences in nonverbal communication are discussed later in this chapter.

Function of Nonverbal Communication in Indicating Liking. One important function of nonverbal communication is to signal psychological closeness to other people. This is referred to as immediacy. *Immediacy behaviors* reflect sensory stimulation, indicate attentiveness, and communicate liking (Mehrabian, 1981). The behaviors associated with immediacy are "(a) close conversational distance, (b) direct body and facial orientation, (c) forward lean, (d) increased and direct gaze, (e) positive reinforcers such as smiling, head nods, and pleasant facial expressions, (f) postural openness, (g) frequent gesturing, and (h) touch" (Burgoon et al., 1989, p. 315). In combination, these behaviors suggest immediacy. Taken individually, however, these behaviors may only indicate the intensity of interaction. To illustrate, when we are angry with other people, we may engage in the same amount of eye contact as we do when we are attracted to them. When we are attracted to someone, we also will lean forward and have a pleasant look on our face.

The nonverbal immediacy behaviors are highly interrelated. Increases in one of the behaviors may be associated with decreases in another in order to keep the message balanced (Burgoon et al., 1989). To illustrate, if we move closer to someone, we may decrease our eye contact to maintain the same degree of psychological closeness to the other person. When the various immediacy behaviors are combined, the psychological closeness is increased. It is important to recognize that the immediacy behaviors described here apply in the United States, especially the European American subculture. Immediacy behaviors differ across cultures and across ethnic groups in the United States.

Assessment 11.1 provides an opportunity for you to assess your general tendency to use immediacy behaviors. Take a minute to complete it.

Scores on Assessment 11.1 range from 10 to 50. The higher your score, the more you generally use immediacy behaviors in your interactions with other people. If your score is lower than you would like, keep in mind that you can consciously choose to use more immediacy behaviors. To accomplish this, you will have to be mindful and consciously change your interpersonal distance, facial expressions, and so forth.

Forms of Nonverbal Communication

To fully understand the significance of nonverbal communication for our communication behavior, we need to examine the types of nonverbal behaviors used by people in every-

Assessment 11.1 *Assessing Your Immediacy*

The purpose of this questionnaire is to help you assess your general use of immediacy behaviors. Respond to each statement by indicating the degree to which it is true about your behavior in general: "Always False" (answer 1), "Usually False" (answer 2), "Sometimes True, Sometimes False" (answer 3), "Usually True" (answer 4), and "Always True" (answer 5).

_______ 1. I lean forward when I talk with other people.

_______ 2. I avoid making eye contact when I talk with other people.

_______ 3. I stand as close as is socially appropriate when I talk to other people.

_______ 4. My posture is stiff when I talk with other people.

_______ 5. I smile when I talk with other people.

_______ 6. I do not gesture much when talking with other people.

_______ 7. I touch other people when I talk with them.

_______ 8. I am not attentive when I talk with others.

_______ 9. I face people when I talk with them.

_______ 10. I do not nod my head much when other people are talking to me.

To find your score, first reverse the responses for the *even numbered* items (i.e., if you wrote 1, make it a 5; if you wrote 2, make it a 4; if you wrote 3, leave it as a 3; if you wrote 4, make it a 2; if you wrote 5, make it a 1). Next, add the numbers next to each statement. Scores range from 10 to 50. The higher your score, the immediacy behaviors you tend to use.

day life. There are seven different forms of nonverbal communication: the communication environment, the communicator's physical appearance, proxemics (use of space), body motion or kinesic behavior, paralanguage, touch, and chronemics (use of time). Let's begin by looking at the environment.

Environment. The *communication environment* includes "those elements that impinge on the human relationship, but are not 'directly' a part of it" (Knapp & Hall, 1992, p. 13). These factors include furniture, architectural style, decorating, lighting, temperature, noises, and other factors in the communication environment. Imagine how your communication with a professor changes if you are in the professor's office cluttered with books, file folders piled on the desk, and papers stacked on the floor, as opposed to when you meet the same professor shopping in the mall. You probably feel more comfortable talking with the professor in the office than in the mall. Obviously, what you talk about will be different in the two locations.

There are fixed and semi-fixed features of the environment (Hall, 1966). *Fixed features* are the relatively permanent aspects of the environment, including floors, walls, the way space is arranged, and the amount of space. One important fixed feature is the way lines and angles are used. In the United States, for example, right angles and straight lines predominate in constructing buildings. Many other cultures, however, emphasize curved lines in their construction of buildings.

Semi-fixed features include those elements that can be moved around. In the United States, furniture tends to be placed along the walls. Other semi-fixed features of the environment include the way light and color are used, the temperature, and noise level. All of these features can influence the way we communicate. To illustrate, think about how you communicate differently with other people in noisy and in quiet, tranquil environments. The objects we use to decorate our homes also are semi-fixed features. In the United States, people select objects to express their individuality. In collectivistic cultures, in contrast, people tend to select objects to demonstrate their commonalities with others (Gudykunst & Ting-Toomey, 1988).

Physical Appearance. The communicator's physical characteristics affect our interactions. *Physical characteristics* include body type, general attractiveness, height, weight, and hair and skin color. The traditional classification of body type divides people into three categories: the tall and thin ectomorph, the muscular and athletic mesomorph, and the short endomorph. In the United States, the mesomorph body type is the most desired, especially for males. Of course, the perception of ideal body type is culture-specific and has changed over time within cultures.

Our physical appearance transmits a great deal of information about us. We may consciously or unconsciously decide to transmit information to others by our physical appearance. The clothes we select and the way we cut our hair, for example, can be used to express an identity. It also can be a function of our desire to be accepted by our peers or to conform to a dress code at work. Other people's physical appearance influences the opinions we form of them. To illustrate, clerks in department stores often ignore people dressed in cutoffs because the clerks assume they will not spend a lot of money, while the clerks bend over backwards to help people dressed in suits.

Proxemics. *Proxemics* involves the distances between people in their daily interactions and the arrangements of space in places such as homes, offices, buildings, and even

"How would you feel about your personal space if you were walking on this street?"

towns. **The use of interpersonal space or distance helps individuals regulate intimacy by controlling sensory exposure** (Hall, 1966). Our use of space can be divided into four territories: intimate, personal, social, and public distance.

In the United States, *intimate distance* includes touching to approximately 18 inches from another person. Closer intimate distances are used for intimate behavior, grooming, and comforting. Intimate distance often is referred to as our personal bubble. In general, we respond with defensiveness when strangers intrude into this territory. We feel more comfortable with strangers approaching us at this distance at our sides or backs. People in crowded elevators tend to line up "facing the numbers" to help alleviate the feeling of discomfort caused when strangers enter each other's intimate space.

Personal distance ranges from 18 inches to 4 feet. This distance is usually reserved for close friends, spouses, and relatives. Entrance into the personal zone is usually by "invitation only."

Social distance is 4 to 12 feet and used for business meetings and impersonal social gatherings. This distance allows business to be conducted with a minimum of emotional involvement.

Public distance ranges from 12 to 15 feet but may extend up to 25 feet or more. This distance is outside the circle of involvement and nearly always involves one-way communication from a speaker to an audience. It is difficult to carry on a personal conversation when you are standing 15 feet away from someone.

The specific distances listed in the preceding paragraph apply in the United States. In some cultures, such as Middle Eastern and Latin cultures, the distances for each territory will be smaller than those given. In other cultures, such as most Asian cultures, the distances associated with each territory will be larger than those used in the United States.

The study of personal space also includes the concept of *territory.* In the United States, higher-status people have larger and better spaces than lower-status people. Executive suites, for example, are often on the top floors of office buildings and are much larger and more lavishly decorated than managerial-level offices. Higher-status people also have territory that is more protected. To illustrate, bosses can often protect their territory by closing their office doors, whereas secretaries often have desks that are visible to everyone who passes. The concept of territory extends to our homes. In the United States, people commonly invite other people to their homes or to their dorm rooms to visit, to have a party, and perhaps to share a meal. Having someone visit your home is a sign of friendship or of fulfilling a social obligation.

Of course, issues of territory like interpersonal distance are culture-specific. People from other cultures maintain different interpersonal spaces than people in the United States. In Japanese organizations, for example, workers at all levels share space in a common room. In some countries, it is rare to invite someone into your home. Entertaining, even with very close friends, is done in restaurants. The experience of spaciousness or crowdedness and the perception of space violation vary from one culture to the next.

Body Motion. Body motion is called *kinesic behavior* and includes posture, gestures, and movements of the body, head, hands, arms, legs, and feet. When we approach a group of our friends sitting around a table, the overall movement of their bodies gives us a good idea of their mood. If they are sitting slumped over their books with their heads in their hands and there is little discussion, we probably assume that they are studying intensely. If they are shifting in their seats, looking at each other, and gesturing actively, we know that a good conversation is taking place.

There are five types of body motion: emblems, illustrators, affect displays, regulators, and adaptors (Ekman & Friesen, 1969). *Emblems* are nonverbal cues with a direct verbal translation about which there is high agreement among members of a culture on the definition. Most emblems are culture-specific. The "V for victory" sign used by speakers of English in the United States has quite a different meaning in other cultures. It is the equivalent of "the finger" in the United States. Emblems are not just hand gestures, however. They include shrugging our shoulders to indicate "I don't know," holding our nose to indicate "something smells," and hand or arm signals used by television directors to cue the talent. Emblems are nonverbal cues that are purposely used to communicate a particular idea.

Illustrators, the second type of body motion, are nonverbal cues that directly accompany speech. These behaviors nonverbally illustrate what is being said verbally. Illustrators may accent or emphasize a word, draw a picture of a referent, or repeat a word or phrase. Illustrators are more spontaneous than emblems but are generally used intentionally. One indication of the intentional nature of illustrators is that people are more likely to use illustrators in face-to-face conversations than when they are talking on the telephone and can't see the other person. We all, nevertheless, nod our heads in agreement occasionally while listening to someone on the telephone. People in difficult communication situations, such as explaining how hard they have been working while asking for a raise or giving someone complicated directions, are likely to use illustrators as they try to convey their ideas to another person.

Affect displays are facial expressions that display affective or emotional states. Smiling, frowning, and pouting are examples of affect displays. Affect displays are often unintentional and can repeat, contradict, or be unrelated to the verbal expression of affect. People with "poker faces" have learned to control their affect displays and not to indicate either happiness or disappointment when they see the type of cards in their hand. Computer mail users have symbols to indicate affect displays in electronic mail; a smile is indicated by :-) and a frown by :-(. This is one of the few forms of nonverbal communication incorporated into electronic mail.

Regulators are body motions that maintain and regulate the back-and-forth nature of speaking and listening. Speakers within a culture learn how to nonverbally indicate interest or disinterest in a conversation. One way regulators are used is to manage turn taking in conversations. The most familiar turn-taking cues are head nods and eye behavior. As indicated earlier, a slow head nod tells the other person to continue talking, while rapid head nods might tell the other person that we want to talk. In the European American subculture in the United States, it is appropriate to look at a speaker when listening and to look away while talking. Look/listen behavior indicates that we are willing to let the other person continue speaking, while look/talk behavior signals that we want our speaking turn (Ellyson, Dovidio & Fehr, 1984). Prolonged lack of eye contact often means "let's end this conversation."

Adaptors are the body motions we use to express discomfort or nervousness. Adaptors can be self-directed, object-directed, or alter-directed. *Self-directed* adaptors are the manipulation of one's own body, including holding, scratching, pinching, and stroking. The use of self-directed adaptors, such as stroking a strand of hair or biting your fingernails, often increases as your anxiety level increases. *Alter-*

directed adaptors include leg movements and foot tapping. These behaviors are unconscious responses to the desire to flee a difficult situation. *Object-directed* adaptors, as their name suggests, are the manipulation of objects, such as playing with a pencil, rearranging the objects on a desk, or doodling.

Skill Exercise 11.2 is designed to help you identify different types of body motion. Next time you watch television, take a few minutes to complete it.

Skill Exercise 11.2 *Identifying Types of Body Motion*

Watch two different types of television shows (for example, a daytime drama and a situation comedy, or a sports event and an action/adventure series). List all of the types of body motions that you observed.

	Show #1	*Show #2*
Emblems	______	______
Illustrators	______	______
Affect Displays	______	______
Regulators	______	______
Adaptors	______	______

How are nonverbal behaviors used on television?

____

____

Are these behaviors comparable to those you observe in everyday life?

____

____

Paralanguage. *Paralanguage* consists of the nonverbal vocal cues that surround speech behavior or, very simply, *how* something is said, not *what* is said. Paralanguage can be divided into two components: voice qualities and vocalizations (Trager, 1958). *Voice qualities* include pitch, range, rhythm, tempo, and resonance. The way our intonation rises or falls tells other people whether we are asking a question, making a statement, or planning on stopping or continuing to talk. To illustrate, saying, "I should visit my parents" with a rising intonation at the end would suggest a question; saying it with a falling intonation at the end would indicate a statement, expecting a reply; saying it with no change in intonation at the end would indicate that the person plans to continue speaking.

Vocalizations include vocal characteristics (such as laughing, crying, sighing, whispering), vocal qualifiers (such as intensity), and vocal segregates (such as "uh-huh," "um," "ah"). We often use vocal segregates to fill pauses in conversations. They indicate that we want to continue speaking, but that the words have eluded us or that we are thinking. The more thought that we need in order to say what we are trying to say, the more "ums" and "ahs" we tend to use.

We often judge how other people feel by their paralanguage. If someone approaches us laughing while saying "What a day!" we perceive a very different meaning that if the person says the same words while sighing or frowning.

Another aspect of vocal characteristics that is important in interpersonal communication is the dialect we speak. In the United States, the standard dialect is similar to what is spoken in the Midwest. It is the dialect that is used by most people who read the news on national broadcasts. The standard dialect is rated as more prestigious, even by people who do not speak the standard dialect, than nonstandard dialects, such as regional or ethnic dialects (Ryan, Hewstone, & Giles, 1984). People who speak the standard dialect are

CALVIN AND HOBBES © Watterson. Reprinted with permission of UNIVERSAL PRESS SYNDICATE.

rated as having more status than people who speak nonstandard dialects. People who speak nonstandard dialects, however, are rated as displaying more solidarity with others than people who speak the standard dialect. People speaking regional or ethnic dialects, for example, are viewed as more friendly than people using the standard dialect.

Touch. Being touched is essential for being human. Lack of touch in childhood is associated with violent behavior in adulthood (Prescott, 1975). The amount that we touch others changes across the life span (Morris, 1971). Infants and their parents, for example, engage in extensive touching behavior, but this decreases during adolescence. The amount of touching behavior increases after adolescence as young people begin to establish romantic relationships. No matter how much we are touched, however, most of us want to be touched more than we are (Mosby, 1978).

There are different types of touches: positive affective touches, playful touches, control touches, ritualistic touches, and task-related touches (Jones & Yarbrough, 1985). *Positive affective touches* transmit messages of support, appreciation, affection, or sexual intent. *Playful touches* lighten our interactions with others. *Control touches* are used to get other people's attention and to gain their compliance. *Ritualistic touches* are those we use during communication rituals such as greeting others and saying good-bye. *Task-related touches* are those that are necessary for us to complete tasks on which we are working. Touches also can fit into more than one category at a time. We can, for example, touch others as part of a ritual to express positive affection.

The United States is generally a noncontact culture. People do not engage in a great deal of touching. There are, however, situations in which people are likely to touch (Henley, 1977). People are more likely to touch, for example, when giving information or advice than when receiving information or advice. People are more likely to touch others when giving orders than when receiving orders, when asking for a favor than when granting a favor, or when trying to persuade others than when being persuaded.

Communicator characteristics such as age, sex, and region of the country also influence the amount people touch. To illustrate, people between eighteen and twenty-five and between thirty and forty report the most touching, while old people report the least (Mosby, 1978). Women find touching more pleasant than men, as long as the other person is not a stranger (Heslin, 1978). Finally, people who live in the South touch more than people who live in the North (Howard, 1985). Reading 11.1 provides an opportunity for you to test your knowledge of touch.

Chronemics. The last important form of nonverbal communication is *chronemics,* or the use of time. Beyond the use of space and touch, time is reflective of the psychological environment in which communication occurs. Time flies when we are enjoying ourselves and having a good time. Time crawls when we stare at other people and have nothing to say to them.

Two patterns of time can be distinguished: monochronic time schedule (M-time) and polychronic time schedule (P-time) (Hall, 1983). M-time and P-time are very different:

> Each has its strengths as well as its weaknesses. . . . P-time stresses involvement

Reading 11.1 DON'T UNDERESTIMATE POWER OF LOVING TOUCH/DR. JOYCE BROTHERS

How powerful is loving touch? Is it important in life? Here's an opportunity to compare your views on the subject with those of some experts. [Answer true or false.]. . .

1. The child who seems normal in other ways but hates to be touched or cuddled probably has emotional problems and needs professional counseling.
2. Americans are among the biggest touchers in the world.
3. Hugging and touching are more important to women than to men.
4. Violence is frequently related to a lack of affectionate touch.

ANSWERS:

. . .

1. FALSE. Such a child is not necessarily in emotional trouble. Some children have more sensitive skins and some simply need less cuddling and touching than others. However, if somebody makes fun of physical affection in front of a child, he might withdraw even though he doesn't wish to.

2. FALSE. Americans tend to shrink from touching. Males, especially, are frequently afraid of being touched, often viewing it as not masculine. But soldiers in many other countries—Turkey, Italy and India, to name a few—can be seen holding hands or walking arm in arm.

3. TRUE. This might, however, be something that has been learned by both sexes. Marc Hollender, chief of psychiatry at Vanderbilt University, reports that his research indicates women have a far greater psychological need for hugging than men. When they don't get enough, they often sublimate by overeating or other compulsive behavior.

4. TRUE. James Prescott, who has studied the effects of physical affection, says most violence occurs in societies where there isn't enough fondling or caressing in the family. Children who have lots of loving touch are more likely to grow up into nonviolent adults, partly because they will have inner strength and be more secure.

SALLY FORTH. Reprinted with special permission of King Features Syndicate.

> of people and completion of transactions rather than adherence to preset schedules. Appointments are not taken as seriously and, as a consequence, are frequently broken. P-time is treated as less tangible than M-time. For polychronic people, time is seldom experienced as "wasted," and is apt to be considered a point rather than a ribbon or a road, but that point is often sacred. (Hall, 1983, p. 46)

M-time and P-time patterns are different; "like oil and water," they "don't mix" (Hall, 1983, pp. 45–46).

People who follow M-time patterns usually engage in one activity at a time, compartmentalize time schedules to serve self-needs, and tend to separate task-oriented time from social time. People who follow P-time tend to do multiple tasks at the same time, tend to hold more fluid attitudes toward time schedules, and tend to integrate task need with social needs. A person using a P-time orientation, for example, will stop a conversation with one person to take a phone call from another, especially a friend or relative. People who follow M-time schedules tend to emphasize individual privacy, schedules, and appointments. People who follow P-time schedules, in contrast, tend to emphasize the connection between people, fluidity, and the flexible nature of time.

Assessment 11.2 provides an opportunity for you to determine your general time orientation. Take a few minutes to complete it.

Scores on Assessment 11.2 range from 10 to 50. The higher your score, the more monochronic you tend to be. The main thing to keep in mind is that, whatever your orientation is, problems may arise in your interactions with people who have the opposite orientation, especially when it involves making appointments.

Time is an important variable in terms of keeping appointments. In an M-time orientation, five time intervals for arriving late for an appointment can be isolated: (1) mumble something time, (2) slight apology time, (3) mildly insulting time, (4) rude time, and (5) downright insulting time (Hall, 1959). If people who follow M-time schedules are five minutes late for an appointment, they mumble something. If they are ten to fifteen minutes late, they probably make a slight apology. Being thirty minutes late is considered rude. It is not unusual for a person who follows a P-time schedule to be forty-five or sixty minutes late and express only a slight apology or

Assessment 11.2 *Assessing Your Orientation Toward Time*

The purpose of this questionnaire is to help you assess your general orientation toward time. Respond to each statement by indicating the degree to which it is true about your behavior in general: "Always False" (answer 1), "Usually False" (answer 2), "Sometimes True, Sometimes False" (answer 3), "Usually True" (answer 4), and "Always True" (answer 5).

_______ 1. I do many things at the same time.

_______ 2. I stick to my daily schedule as much as possible.

_______ 3. I prefer to finish one activity before starting another one.

_______ 4. I feel like I waste time.

_______ 5 I would take time out of a business meeting to talk with a relative or friend who called on the phone.

_______ 6. I separate work time and social time.

_______ 7. I break appointments with others.

_______ 8. It is important that events in my life occur in an orderly fashion.

_______ 9. I schedule more than one activity at a time.

_______ 10. Being on time for appointments is important to me.

To find your score, first reverse the responses for the *odd numbered* items (i.e., if you wrote 1, make it a 5; if you wrote 2, make it a 4; if you wrote 3, leave it as a 3; if you wrote 4, make it a 2; if you wrote 5, make it a 1). Next, add the numbers next to each statement. Scores range from 10 to 50. The higher your score, the more monochronic you are.

not even "mumble something." This behavior obviously annoys a person who follows M-time.

The forms and functions of daily nonverbal communication discussed so far in this chapter create expectations for how other people will nonverbally communicate with us. Other people, however, do not always meet our expectations; sometimes they violate them. To communicate effectively, we need to understand how we tend to respond when others violate our expectations.

Violations of Nonverbal Expectations

We have expectations for how other people will behave nonverbally. In the United States, for example, people expect that nonintimates will stand at least an arm's length away when they talk. The manner in which we react to other people's nonverbal violations of our expectations depends on the characteristics of the person violating our expectations and the degree of the violation (Burgoon, 1992). We are not usually aware of this process. In other words, we are not necessarily mindful of our interpretations and evaluations of violations of our nonverbal expectations.

Factors Affecting How We Evaluate Violations of Our Expectations

When we interact with others, we want to approach some things and avoid some things, and these needs often conflict (Burgoon, 1992). We want to approach other people, for example, when their behavior is consistent with our expectations. We often want to avoid others, in contrast, when they violate our expectations.

The way we react to other people is influenced by whether we think we will receive rewards, such as affection or prestige, from them. We judge the likelihood that we will get positive reinforcements or other rewards from people with whom we communicate (Burgoon, 1992). We enjoy communicating with people who seem friendly, for example, because they reward us with kind words and supportive behaviors. Attractive people are often seen as having a higher reward potential than less attractive people.

We expect others to react nonverbally in particular ways (Burgoon, 1992). We do not expect someone who has heard tragic news, for example, to smile or laugh. We expect that business associates to shake our right hand in greeting.

We perceive other people's nonverbal behaviors on a continuum from very favorable to very unfavorable (Burgoon, 1992). We prefer to have people smile at us instead of frown, touch us lightly on the shoulder instead of grab our arm, and stand at a distance that is comfortable for us to talk.

Our desire to approach rather than to avoid others, the likelihood that we will receive rewards from others, our expectations for other people's nonverbal behavior, the favorableness of other people's nonverbal behavior, and the meaning that we attach to other people's nonverbal behavior all affect how we respond to other people's violations of our expectations. With this in mind, let's look at how we respond when other people violate our expectations.

Evaluation of Violations

When other people violate our expectations, we become aroused and distracted. Noticing that other people have violated our expectations leads us to think about the people committing the violation and our relationship with them (Burgoon, 1992). In other words, when someone violates our expectations for nonverbal behavior, we begin to think about the communicator or our relationship with the communicator instead of about the messages being transmitted. We pay attention to communicator characteristics, such as gender or age, and to the implicit meaning of the nonverbal behavior more when our expectations are violated than when they are not. We may not, however, be highly aware of what has aroused us and shifted our attention.

The extent to which other people can provide us with rewards "moderates the interpretation of ambiguous or multi-meaning nonverbal behaviors" (Burgoon, 1992, p. 61). When communicators who can provide us with rewards violate our expectations regarding nonverbal behaviors, we interpret their violations positively. When people who cannot provide us with rewards violate our expectations, we interpret their violations negatively. This explains why we put up with actions from our good friends that we would not accept from others. We put up with friends who are always late because they provide rewards for us, but we are not likely to accept this behavior from someone who is not a friend. We may get mildly annoyed at our friend, but furious at an acquaintance who agreed to meet us and is an hour late.

The way we evaluate violations of our expectations is a function of how large the violation is and whether it is a positive or a negative violation. We compare individuals' nonverbal behavior with our expectations. If the actual nonverbal behaviors are viewed more positively than expected behaviors, this would lead to positive violations. When actual behaviors are viewed more negatively than expected behaviors, negative violations occur. If you turn a paper in to a professor past the deadline, for example, you expect a negative facial expression, a harsh tone of voice, and perhaps even a negative body movement, such as quickly taking the paper and putting it away. If instead the professor smiles when taking the paper from you and responds with a positive tone of voice, your expectation has been violated in a positive manner. If the professor turns extremely red, waves the paper around, and mutters something about irresponsible students who have no place in college, your expectations have been violated in a negative manner.

When we perceive that other people positively violated our expectations, there tend to be favorable outcomes, while when we perceive that other people negatively violated our expectations, there tend to be negative outcomes (Burgoon, 1992). Positive violations of expectations can lead to increases in "credibility, attraction, persuasion, and comprehension" (p. 63). In the above example, you obviously feel better if the professor graciously accepts your late paper than if the professor harshly reprimands you for your tardiness.

In general, we consciously recognize major violations of our nonverbal expectations. When we recognize these violations we try to make sense out of them. We rarely stop and think, however, when minor violations of our expectations for nonverbal behavior occur. Rather, we interpret the violation from our own frame of reference. To increase the likelihood of positive outcomes, like effective communication, we must become mindful of our communication. We must stop and think about what the behavior that violated our expectations means to the people committing the violation. In other words, we need to reduce our uncertainty. We cannot do this if we are highly anxious, however. When we become mindful, we must cognitively manage our emotional reaction to the behavior. Cognitively managing our emotional reaction and understanding what the behavior means to other people are necessary for effective communication to occur.

Cultural Identity and Nonverbal Behavior

As indicated earlier in this chapter, the interpretation of nonverbal cues varies from culture to culture. Culture influences the forms of nonverbal communication we learn as children. To illustrate the variety of nonverbal differences throughout the world, proxemics, touch, use of time, and affect displays are examined. Let's begin with proxemics.

Proxemics

The use of interpersonal distance differs across cultures. To illustrate, consider the use of space in Japan, Venezuela, and North America (Sussman & Rosenfeld, 1982). When speaking their native languages, Japanese sit farther apart than Venezuelans, and North Americans sit at an intermediate distance. When speaking English, however, Japanese and Venezuelans use personal distances closely approximating North American conversational distance norms. Thus, it seems that, when individuals converse in their native language, the use of this language also triggers a wider array of culturally appropriate nonverbal behaviors, and when people speak another language, different nonverbal behaviors are triggered. This indicates that verbal and nonverbal cues are interlinked.

Japanese prefer greater interaction distances with a friend, father, or professor than Japanese Americans or European Americans do (Engebretson & Fullmer, 1970). Members of Southern European cultures, such as Greeks and southern Italians, prefer closer distances than do northern Europeans (Little, 1968). Argentineans adjust their use of personal distance depending on the person with whom they are interacting, while Iraqis make few adjustments (LaFrance & Mayo, 1978). Members of individualistic cultures tend to take an active, aggressive stance when their space is violated, while members of collectivistic cultures tend to take a passive, withdrawn stance when their personal space is intruded (Gudykunst & Ting-Toomey, 1988).

People from cultures that value contact with others, such as Latin American or Arab cultures, stand closer than European Americans expect. Since people from other cultures generally are not seen as providing rewards, standing closer than expected tends to be interpreted negatively, and the people from the other culture are viewed as "pushy." If European Americans are interacting with their boss, their reaction would be different. Since the boss provides rewards, his or her standing closer than expected is likely be interpreted as the boss showing that she or he likes the subordinate.

Touch

People from different cultures interpret touch behavior in different ways. To illustrate, for Arabs "to be able to smell a friend is reassuring. Smelling is a way of being involved with another, and to deny a friend his [or her] breath would be to act ashamed. . . . In contrast, the [North] Americans seem to maintain their distance and suppress their sense of smell." (Almaney & Alwan, 1982, p. 17). Arabs, therefore, typically feel a strong sense of "sensory deprivation" and alienation at the lack of close, intimate contact when they communicate with North Americans, while North Americans find Arabs' need for close personal space anxiety-provoking and disturbing. Thus, the tendency for North Americans to stand farther away than Arabs desire often leads Arabs to suspect North Americans' intentions. The close contact Arabs want, in contrast, often constitutes a violation of the personal space and privacy of North Americans.

Similarly, people in Latin American cultures engage in more frequent touching than European Americans (Engebretson & Fullmer, 1970). While Japanese females tend to touch more than Japanese males (Barnlund, 1975), in Mediterranean cultures, male-male touch behavior is used more frequently than female-female touch behavior (LaFrance & Mayo, 1978).

Chronemics

People in Denmark, Finland, Germany, Norway, and the United States tend to follow the M-time pattern, while people in France, Greece, Iran, Japan, Turkey, the Philippines, and Thailand tend to follow the P-time pattern (Hall, 1983). Generally, M-time patterns predominate in individualistic cultures, and P-time patterns predominate in collectivistic cultures.

People from individualistic cultures tend to be clock bound. Time is viewed in a linear fashion. One thing should be scheduled at a time, and events should be scheduled in an orderly fashion. Individualists tend to view time as something that can be possessed, killed, and wasted.

Members of collectivistic cultures tend to see time holistically. Many events may be scheduled at a time. The emphasis is on the activities in which people are engaged, not the time it takes. Collectivists tend to view time as contextually based and relationally oriented.

Affect Displays

People in different cultures share many similarities in how they express their emotions. The similarities can be seen as characteristics that are inborn in all humans (Darwin, 1872). To illustrate, everyone uses the same muscles in their face to form facial expressions. It appears that **there is consistency across cultures in people's ability to recognize at least seven emotions in other people's facial expressions—anger, contempt, disgust, fear, happiness, sadness, and surprise** (Matsumoto, Wallbott, & Scherer, 1989). People are able to recognize not only the emotion, but also the intensity of the emotion and often the secondary emotion being experienced.

While there is consistency across cultures in people's ability to recognize emotions on the face, there are cultural differences in the display rules we use for expressing emotions. Cultural *display rules* are the procedures we learn for managing the way we express emotions (Ekman, 1971). They tell us when it is acceptable and when it is not acceptable to express our emotions. When it is acceptable to display "negative" emotions is different in individualistic and collectivistic cultures (Gudykunst & Ting-Toomey, 1988). In individualistic cultures like the United States, for example, it is acceptable to express negative emotions when alone or in the presence of others. In collectivistic cultures, in contrast, negative emotions are not expressed in public, especially to people higher in status. To illustrate, in the collectivistic culture of Indonesia, people will keep quiet and hide their feelings if they are angry with their boss, while in the individualistic culture of Australia, people will express their anger toward their boss (Noesjirwan, 1978). Reading 11.2 provides a comparison of emotion expression in Sumatra and the United States.

Gender Identity and Nonverbal Behavior

Like cultural identity, our gender identity influences our interpretation of nonverbal behavior. Gender identity influences sensitivity to nonverbal cues and the forms of nonverbal behavior we use. Let's begin by looking at sensitivity to nonverbal cues.

Interpreting Nonverbal Cues of Emotion

Women are better at accurately interpreting other people's facial expressions than men (Zuckerman et al., 1975). Men are better at interpreting facial expressions of people they know well than people they do not know. Overall, however, women tend to be more sensitive than men to other people's nonverbal cues (Rosenthal et al., 1979).

Reading 11.2 SMILES OF A SUMATRA NIGHT

In the longest-running debate on human behavior, nature and nurture have been duking it out for over a century, with nature getting an awful lot of decisions in the past decade or two. Now comes evidence delineating just how much nature shapes our emotional reactions.

When Americans create the expressions associated with anger and fear, the autonomic nervous system swings into gear and puts the body on alert, raising heart rate and altering skin temperature. To determine whether these changes are specific to Americans, and thus learned, or are part of a common inheritance, Robert Levenson, Ph.D., of Berkeley, and Paul Ekman, Ph.D., of San Francisco, headed off to West Sumatra. There they looked at people as different from us as you can get: the Minangkabau, a matrilineal, Moslem, agrarian culture that discourages displays of negative emotion.

Yet, when the Minangkabau were taught facial muscle contraction in order to mimic angry or fearful expressions, they registered the same physiologic changes—though they didn't feel the same way. No matter how different we seem, deep down we're all alike, observes the team in the *Journal of Personality and Social Psychology* (Vol. 62, No.6).

But if biological events turn out to be the same, subjective emotional experience is altogether different. "In our culture, we focus on the physiological sensations that happen when we feel emotions. This is in fact one of the most important aspects of emotion for us," reports Levenson. Ask an American what anger is and he'll tell you what he physically experiences when he is angry. But the Minangkabau didn't feel any emotions when they made the negative facial expressions.

"In their culture, the people are more entwined. Emotions define their relationships, not bodily sensations," explains Levenson. To them, anger is when a friend is mad at you, not how your body responds.

"Physiological responses to emotions are hard-wired into us; they're common for all people," says Levenson. "But what we do with that information is culturally variable."

Women are especially proficient at interpreting nonverbal cues that facilitate relationship maintenance—empathic facial expression, head nods that indicate agreement and support, and touch to seek affiliative responses (Rosenthal & DePaulo, 1979). Because women traditionally are socialized to maintain smooth relationships, they may be more likely than men to be sensitive to nonverbal cues that facilitate and reinforce a close, supportive relationship.

Gender Differences in Forms of Nonverbal Behavior

Nonverbal cues can be divided into two general areas—those cues that signify emotional warmth and concern and those cues that communicate dominance or high status. Many sex differences in nonverbal behavior can be found in these two sets of cues. Women are more likely than men to use cues of emotional warmth, such as head nods, smiling, eye con-

Men are less likely to use cues of emotional warmth, such as touch. On the playing fields though, men are less restricted in their use of nonverbal cues, even touch.

tact, and laughter (Hall, 1984). Men are more likely than women to use dominance cues, such as speaking louder, violating someone else's personal space or territory, and taking up more space.

As noted earlier in this chapter, higher-status people in the United States tend to have larger and better spaces than low-status people. In general, women have less territory and take up less physical space than men. In the home, a mother's space is often the kitchen, while a father has his study, his workbench, or his desk. All family members have access to the kitchen and frequently use it as a gathering place. Father's study is often his private space and can only be entered when he permits access to it.

There are interesting proxemic differences between women and men in the United States. Women tend to be approached more closely than men, for example, and men tend to maintain greater distance from others when talking to them than women (Hall, 1984). In addition, women are more likely to face each other when talking, while men are more likely to maintain a less direct body position (Tannen, 1990). This difference remains constant across age groups. When best friends enter a room to hold a conversation, girls (from the ages of five to fifteen) generally face toward each other to talk, often leaning close together. Boys, in contrast, sit side by side and tend to talk while looking straight ahead, not at each other. The friends discuss similar, often highly intimate topics, but the girls look directly at each other and the boys do not. This difference in nonverbal behavior may lead to women's feelings that men are not listening to them because they are not looking at them and to men's frustration at being accused of not listening when they are (Tannen, 1990).

In addition to differences in their use of space, women are more comfortable than men with the nonverbal cues that signify emotional warmth, such as touch (Fromme et al., 1989). Women are more likely to touch other women than men are to touch other men (Major, 1984). Sports is the one area in the United States in which men are permitted almost unrestricted access to touching each other in public.

Summary

Nonverbal communication is an important element in the communication process. Nonverbal cues share some similarities with language, such as being discrete and divided into separate units. There are also important differences between language and nonverbal cues. Language, for example, is characterized by displacement and reflexivity; nonverbal cues are not.

Nonverbal communication allows us to convey interpersonal attitudes, express emotional states, manage conversations, exchange rituals, and regulate self-presentation. Nonverbal cues are critical for developing interpersonal synchronization with others and in indicating liking for others. We indicate physical closeness to others by using immediacy nonverbal behaviors, such as smiling and leaning forward.

Nonverbal cues may repeat, contradict, substitute for, complement, accent, and/or regulate a verbal message. The major forms of nonverbal communication are the communication environment, the communicator's physical characteristics, the study of proxemics, body motion or kinesic behavior, paralanguage, touch, and chronemics, or the use of time.

We have expectations for how other people will behave nonverbally. We react when other people violate these expectations. In general, we react favorably to positive violations of our nonverbal expectations and unfavorably to negative violations of our nonverbal expectations.

Our cultural and gender identities affect our use of nonverbal behavior. Generally, members of collectivistic cultures are more sensitive to other people's nonverbal behavior than members of individualistic cultures. Members of collectivistic cultures need to use nonverbal cues to know how to interpret people's indirect language usage. Similarly, females tend to be more sensitive to other people's nonverbal behavior than males.

Journal Reflections

1. *Identifying Your Nonverbal Expectations.* We all have expectations for how others will communicate nonverbally. Consider the interactions with others that you had today. Were any of your expectations for nonverbal communication violated? How did you respond? How would you have responded if someone seriously violated your expectations in either a positive or a negative manner?
2. *Changing Your Nonverbal Communication.* Many of us have areas of nonverbal communication that we feel need improvement or at least that we wish we could change. Some of us smile too much when we are nervous. Some of us fidget too much when we are bored by what someone else is saying. In your journal, discuss any areas of nonverbal communication that you think you would like to change. Discuss some strategies that you could use to change. If you feel comfortable, discuss this entry with someone in your class or with a friend. Does this person agree with your assessment?
3. *Understanding Other People's Nonverbal Communication.* Many cultural, ethnic, and gender differences in nonverbal communication have been discussed in this chapter. In your interactions with others, identify some of the differences you have observed. How have you reacted to these differences? Were you always mindful? If not, how could you change your reactions to be more mindful in the future?

Study Questions

1. Define nonverbal communication.
2. What are the five basic functions of nonverbal communication?

3. What are the six ways in which nonverbal cues relate to verbal messages? Give an example of each.
4. What are the seven major forms of nonverbal communication? Give an example of each.
5. How can you explain the differences in how you react when a friend stands closer to you than you expect and your reactions when a person you do not like engages in the same behavior?
6. How does culture influence nonverbal communication?
7. How do males and females differ in the use of nonverbal cues of emotional warmth versus dominance and status?

Suggested Readings

Burgoon, J. K., Buller, D. B., & Woodall, W. G. (1989). *Nonverbal communication: The unspoken dialogue.* New York: Harper & Row. This is a widely used nonverbal communication text. It provides an extensive overview of nonverbal communication in interpersonal relationships.

Hall, E. T. (1976). *Dance of life.* New York: Doubleday. Edward T. Hall examines how nonverbal communication contributes to the rhythm of our lives. He examines the process of interpersonal synchronization and how it differs across cultures. Hall also provides an extensive discussion of how P-time and M-time influence our lives.

Jones, S. (1993). *The right touch.* Cresskill, NJ: Hampton. Stanley Jones examines the messages conveyed by touch, the "taboos" of touch, rules of touch in the workplace, and the ways that touch is used to exhibit power. Jones also examines gender differences in touch.

Morris, D., Collett, P., Marsh, P., & O'Shaughnessy, M. (1979). *Gestures.* New York: Stein and Day. Desmond Morris and his associates examine how twenty gestures are used in forty different locations in northern and southern Europe. They examine gestures such as fingertip kiss, forearm jerk, ear touch, nose tap, V-sign, and head toss, to name only a few.

Part Three

Relational Processes and Outcomes

12

Relationship Development and Termination

Up to this point, the focus of discussion has been on the nature of interpersonal communication. It is important to recognize, however, that interpersonal communication takes place in a relational context. We need to understand how communication influences the escalation and deescalation of relational intimacy, as well as how communication skills can be used to maintain and transform relationships and manage conflicts in relationships.

To understand how our interpersonal relationships develop and deteriorate, we need to recognize the factors that influence whether we form interpersonal relationships with others in the first place. Understanding the general patterns that describe how our relationships develop and deteriorate over time, as well as the paradoxes, inconsistencies, and contradictions inherent in our interpersonal relationships can help us improve their quality. How our cultural and ethnic identities influence the development of relationships also needs to be considered. Let's begin by looking at the factors that contribute to the formation of relationships.

Factors Contributing to the Formation of Interpersonal Relationships

There are many factors that contribute to the formation of interpersonal relationships. Some of the most important factors that affect whether we form relationships with others are the extent to which they support our self-concepts, the degree of similarity we perceive that we share with them, the predictability of their behavior, the degree to which we can manage our anxiety when we communicate with them, the degree to which others are involved with us when we interact, and whether we develop a relational culture with them. Let's begin with self-concept support.

Self-concept Support

As indicated in Chapter 2, our self-concept influences all of our communication behavior. It guides and regulates our "thoughts, feelings, and actions. . . . It influences how information is perceived, processed, and recalled" (Schlenker, 1986, p. 24). Our self-conceptions influence how we communicate with others and our choices (conscious or unconscious) of those with whom we form interpersonal relations.

Perceived self-concept support is critical in the formation of close relationships (Cushman, Valentinsen, & Dietrich, 1982). The more we think other people will support our self-concepts, the more likely we are to communicate with them. The more other people support our self-concepts, the more we think they want to be friends with us. **Our desire to form close relationships with others is a result of perceiving their messages to us as positively supporting our identities.** The greatest likelihood of close relationship formation occurs when there is reciprocal self-concept support; that is, we support other people's self-concepts, and they support our self-concepts.

Perceived Similarity

One of the reasons that perceived self-concept support leads to a desire to establish close relationships is because perceived similarity of self-concepts influences our attraction to others. Actual similarities in our self-concepts and others are *not* related to our attraction to them (Wylie, 1979). Rather, **we are attracted to others we perceive to be similar to ourselves.**

In addition to perceived similarity in self-concepts, we are also attracted to others if we perceive similarities in attitudes, values, and communication styles. Before proceeding, think about the similarities you and your close friends share. Answer the following questions:

> When you are getting to know others, what similarities are necessary for you to develop a close relationship with another person? ____________________
>
> ________________________________
>
> When you are getting to know others, what dissimilarities facilitate your developing a relationship with them? __________
>
> ________________________________
>
> ________________________________

Your answers to these questions should provide some insight into the role of similarity in your implicit personal theory of communication. Keep your answer to this question in mind as you read the remainder of this section.

If we perceive that our attitudes are similar to other people's attitudes, we will be attracted to them because the perceived similarity in attitudes validates our view of the world (Byrne, 1971). We filter potential relational partners on the extent to which we perceive that they are similar to us in terms of attitudes, beliefs, values, and so forth (Duck, 1977). In the initial stages of getting to know other people, we focus on general attitudes and opinions that we hold. As we get to know others, we search for similarities in central aspects of our world views or our core values.

One of the most important similarities we search for in potential relational partners is similarity in our orientations toward interpersonal interactions (Sunnafrank, 1991). If we perceive similarities in our orientations toward communication, we are likely to form interpersonal relationships with others.

Friends tend to have similar orientations toward five specific communication activities: conflict management, ways to comfort each other, ways to persuade each other, ways to support each other's self-concepts, and ways to tell stories and jokes (Burleson, Samter, & Lucchetti, 1992).

Perceived similarity is not only important in predicting the development of close relationships between people from the same group, it also is important in predicting the development of close relationships between people from different groups. When we meet people from different groups, one of the main factors inhibiting the development of relationships is the group differences. Although it is important to recognize genuine differences, it also is necessary to go beyond looking at group differences. In order to go beyond recognizing group differences to develop relationships with members of other groups, we must talk with them to discover whether we are similar in other areas.[1] Perceived similarities in attitudes, lifestyles, and world views facilitate the development of close relationships between members of different groups (Sudweeks et al., 1990).

Assessment 12.1 is designed to help you assess the degree of perceived similarity in different relationships. Take a few minutes to complete it now.

Scores on the three scales in Assessment 12.1 range from 10 to 50. The higher your score, the more similarities you perceive in the relationship. In general, you probably perceive more similarities with your acquaintance than with a stranger. You probably also perceive more similarities with your close friend than with your acquaintance.

Predictability of Behavior

As indicated in Chapter 3, one of our basic needs is for our interactions with other people is for their behavior to be predictable (Turner, 1988). The predictability of other people's behavior gives our interactions rhythm. If our interactions do not have rhythm, we experience anxiety. Experiencing anxiety above our maximum threshold leads us to avoid interacting with other people.

Predictability of other people's behavior is based on several factors. Other people's behavior is predictable to the extent that they follow the scripts we use to communicate with them. We only use scripts to guide our behavior, however, in nonclose relationships. Our close relationships are not guided by scripts or cultural norms (Wright, 1978). Rather, they are based on rules that are unique to the specific relationship (Miller & Steinberg, 1975). We do not communicate the same way, for example, with our various close friends. Each of our close friendships has a unique set of rules that are used to guide behavior in the specific relationship.

Given that close relationships are unique and guided by different rules, we have to reduce our uncertainty (lack of predictability) about other people's behavior if we are to develop a close relationship with them. As we get to know others, our uncertainty regarding their behavior generally decreases (Gudykunst & Nishida, 1986a). This does not mean, however, that we want to totally reduce our uncertainty or that, once it is reduced, our uncertainty stays at a lower level. As indicated in Chapter 4, we have minimum and maximum thresholds for uncertainty. If uncertainty is too high, we cannot predict other people's behavior. If it is too low, we become bored and overconfident in our ability to predict other people's behavior.

At any particular moment, our uncertainty may increase or decrease based on what other people do. If other people engage in behavior we do not expect, our uncertainty about their behavior increases. Depending on what other people do and how it is handled

Assessment 12.1 *Assessing Perceived Similarity When Communicating in Different Relationships*

The purpose of this questionnaire is to help you assess the amount of similarity you perceive when you communicate in different relationships. Respond to each statement by indicating the frequency that the statement applies in the particular relationship. If you "Never" have the experience, answer 1 in the space provided; if you "Almost Never" have the experience, answer 2; if you "Sometimes" have the experiences and sometimes do not, answer 3; if you "Almost Always" have the experience, answer 4; if you "Always" have the experience, answer 5. Space is provided for you to complete the questionnaire three times: once for your interactions with strangers, once for your interactions with acquaintances, and once for your interactions with close friends. Answer all questions for strangers (STR) first. Next, think of a particular acquaintance (ACQ) and answer the questions a second time. Finally, think of a specific close friend (CLFR) and answer the questions again.

STR	ACQ	CLFR	
______	______	______	1. I perceive that ______ and I have similar opinions.
______	______	______	2. I do not think that ______ and I have similar values.
______	______	______	3. I think that ______ and I have similar attitudes.
______	______	______	4. I do not think that ______ and I have similar ways of communicating.
______	______	______	5. I perceive that ______ and I have similar lifestyles.
______	______	______	6. I do not think that ______ and I have similar ways of telling stories and jokes.
______	______	______	7. I think that ______ and I have similar ways of managing conflict.
______	______	______	8. I do not think that ______ and I have similar ways of comforting each other.
______	______	______	9. I perceive that ______ and I have similar ways of persuading each other.
______	______	______	10. I do not think that ______ and I have similar ways of supporting each other's self-concepts.

To find your scores, first reverse the responses for the *even numbered* items (i.e., if you wrote 1, make it 5; if you wrote 2, make it 4; if you wrote 3, leave it as 3; if you wrote 4, make it 2; if you wrote 5, make it 1). Next, add the numbers next to each of the items. Scores range from 10 to 50. The higher your scores, the more similarity you perceive when interacting in the different relationships.

within the relationship, it can lead to increases in the intimacy of the relationship or to the end of the relationship (Planalp, Rutherford, & Honneycutt, 1988). Conversations with people we know well, nevertheless, rarely lead to new insights that are not related to our prior expectations about them (Sillars, 1985). The role of the predictability-novelty dialectic in relationship development is discussed in detail later in this chapter.

Assessment 12.2 is designed to help you assess your uncertainty in different relationships. Take a few minutes to complete it now.

Scores on the scales in Assessment 12.2 range from 10 to 50. The higher your score, the greater your uncertainty. In general, your uncertainty should be lower when communicating with acquaintances than when communicating with strangers. It also should be lower when communicating with close friends than when communicating with acquaintances.

Managing Anxiety

As indicated in Chapter 5, if we experience too much or too little anxiety when we meet others, we will not be motivated to interact with them. If we experience too little anxiety, we will not have sufficient interest in other people to want to get to know them. If we experience too much anxiety, we will be so concerned with trying to reduce our anxiety that we will not be able to get to know other people. For close relationships to develop, our anxiety about interacting with other people needs to be between our minimum and maximum thresholds.

Managing anxiety is associated closely with developing trust. Trust is "confidence that one will find what is desired from another, rather than what is feared" (Deutsch, 1973, p. 149). **When we trust others, we expect positive outcomes from our interactions with them; when we have anxiety about interacting with others, we fear negative outcomes from our interactions with them.** When we first meet someone, "trust is often little more than a naive expression of hope" (Holmes & Rempel, 1989, p. 192). For us to have hope about the relationship, our anxiety must be below our maximum threshold. For relationships to form,

> most people need to act *as if* a sense of [trust] were justified, and set their doubts aside. To do so requires a "leap of faith" in the face of evidence that can never be conclusive. Thus trust becomes . . . an emotionally charged sense of closure. It permits an illusion of control . . . where one can plan ahead without anxiety. (Holmes & Rempel, 1989, p. 204)

Without some minimal degree of trust, relationships cannot develop.

Assessment 12.3 is designed to help you assess your anxiety in relationships. Take a few minutes to complete it now.

Scores on the three scales in Assessment 12.3 range from 10 to 50. The higher your score, the greater your anxiety. In general, your anxiety should be lower when communicating with acquaintances than when communicating with strangers. It also should be lower when communicating with close friends than when communicating with acquaintances. To determine how the other person's group memberships influences your anxiety, you can answer the questionnaire once more, thinking of a stranger from a different group. If you are like most people, your score will be higher than when you were thinking of a stranger from one of your own groups.

Before proceeding, it is important to recall (from Chapter 5) that one of the things that differentiates our initial interactions with members of our own groups and members of other groups is the amount of anxiety we experience. The anxiety we experience when we interact with members of other groups often is above our maximum threshold. If we

Assessment 12.2 *Assessing Your Uncertainty When Communicating in Different Relationships*

The purpose of this questionnaire is to help you assess the amount of uncertainty you experience when you communicate in different relationships. Respond to each statement by indicating the frequency that the statements occur when you communicate in different relationships. If you "Never" have the experience, answer 1 in the space provided; if you "Almost Never" have the experience, answer 2; if you "Sometimes" have the experiences and sometimes do not, answer 3; if you "Almost Always" have the experience, answer 4; if you "Always" have the experience, answer 5. Space is provided for you to complete the questionnaire three times: once for your interactions with strangers, once for your interactions with acquaintances, and once for your interactions with close friends. Answer all questions for strangers (STR) first. Next, think of a particular acquaintance (ACQ) and answer the questions a second time. Finally, think of a specific close friend (CLFR) and answer the questions again.

STR	ACQ	CLFR	
_____	_____	_____	1. I am not confident when I communicate with _____.
_____	_____	_____	2. I can interpret _____'s behavior when we communicate.
_____	_____	_____	3. I am indecisive when I communicate with _____.
_____	_____	_____	4. I can explain _____'s behavior when we communicate.
_____	_____	_____	5. I am not able to understand _____ when we communicate.
_____	_____	_____	6. I know what to do when I communicate with _____.
_____	_____	_____	7. I am uncertain about how to behave when I communicate with _____.
_____	_____	_____	8. I can comprehend _____'s behavior when we communicate.
_____	_____	_____	9. I am not able to predict _____'s behavior when we communicate.
_____	_____	_____	10. I can describe _____'s behavior when we communicate.

To find your scores, first reverse the responses for the *even numbered* items (i.e., if you wrote 1, make it 5; if you wrote 2, make it 4; if you wrote 3, leave it as 3; if you wrote 4, make it 2; if you wrote 5, make it 1). Next, add the numbers next to each of the items. Scores range from 10 to 50. The higher your scores, the more uncertainty you experience when interacting in the different relationships.

Assessment 12.3 *Assessing Your Anxiety When Communicating in Different Relationships*

The purpose of this questionnaire is to help you assess the amount of anxiety you experience when you communicate in different relationships. Respond to each statement by indicating the frequency that the statement applies in the particular relationship. If you "Never" have the experience, answer 1 in the space provided; if you "Almost Never" have the experience, answer 2; if you "Sometimes" have the experiences and sometimes do not, answer 3; if you "Almost Always" have the experience, answer 4; if you "Always" have the experience, answer 5. Space is provided for you to complete the questionnaire three times: once for your interactions with strangers, once for your interactions with acquaintances, and once for your interactions with close friends. Answer all questions for strangers (STR) first. Next, think of a particular acquaintance (ACQ) and answer the questions a second time. Finally, think of a specific close friend (CLFR) and answer the questions again.

STR	ACQ	CLFR	
______	______	______	1. I feel calm when I communicate with ______.
______	______	______	2. I get frustrated when I communicate with ______.
______	______	______	3. I do not get ruffled when I communicate with ______.
______	______	______	4. I am insecure when I communicate with ______.
______	______	______	5. I feel composed when I communicate with ______.
______	______	______	6. I feel anxious when I communicate with ______.
______	______	______	7. I do not get excited when I have to communicate with ______.
______	______	______	8. I feel stress when I communicate with ______.
______	______	______	9. I feel relaxed when I communicate with ______.
______	______	______	10. I am worried when I communicate with ______.

To find your scores, first reverse the responses for the *odd numbered* items (i.e., if you wrote 1, make it 5; if you wrote 2, make it 4; if you wrote 3, leave it as 3; if you wrote 4, make it 2; if you wrote 5, make it 1). Next, add the numbers next to each of the items. Scores range from 10 to 50. The higher your scores, the more anxiety you experience when interacting in the different relationships.

Adapted from Stephan and Stephan (1985).

are going to develop relationships with members of other groups, we must consciously manage our anxiety when we first meet them if it is above our maximum threshold, so that we will be open to the possibility of getting to know them.

Interaction Involvement

Interaction involvement "is the extent to which an individual participates with another in conversation" (Cegala et al., 1982, p. 229). People who are involved highly in interaction integrate their thoughts, feelings, and prior experiences with their ongoing interactions. They focus on themselves, other people, and the topic of conversation when interacting with others. People who are not highly involved in interactions, in contrast, are psychologically removed (such as appearing remote) from the interactions in which they engage. Individuals who are low in interaction involvement "may appear preoccupied with other thoughts or goals, distracted, uncertain, and/or withdrawn from the immediate social context. Their speech may be marked by vagueness, ambivalence, inconsistency, or misunderstanding" (Cegala et al., 1982, p. 229).

There are three dimensions of interaction involvement (Cegala et al., 1982). *Attentiveness* is the extent to which we pay attention to the cues in our immediate environment. This includes paying close attention to what others say, listening carefully, knowing what is expected of us in particular situations, and not allowing our mind to wander off when others are talking. *Responsiveness* involves the "tendency to react mentally to one's social circumstances and adapt by knowing what to say and when to say it" (Cegala et al., 1982, p. 233). This means knowing what to do, knowing what to say, knowing our role in the situation, knowing what others are saying, and feeling involved in the situation. *Perceptiveness* involves the extent to which we understand the meanings others are attributing to messages and how to interpret other people's behavior accurately. This means accurately perceiving other people's intentions, being aware of how others perceive us, observing how others respond to us, being sensitive to hidden meanings in conversations, and paying close attention to others in order to gather information needed to interact effectively.

Generally, we prefer to form relationships with others who are involved in an interaction rather than with people who are not involved in an interaction. **Others are most likely to want to form relationships with us if we demonstrate high levels of attentiveness, responsiveness, and perceptiveness in our early interactions with them.**

Developing Relational Cultures

As two people get to know each other over time, they have unique experiences and a unique relational culture develops. Our definitions of our relationships with other people are established through the way we talk with them, but we rarely explicitly talk about how we define our relationships (Sillars, 1985). We, therefore, often are not consciously aware of the relational culture that has developed. One way we develop a relational culture in the United States involves our use of humor and play. Play provides a psychological way that we can integrate our internal needs and the external demands placed on us by our relationships with other people (Betcher, 1987).

Humor and Play. Humor performs important functions in the development of interpersonal relationships. It influences the degree to which we are attracted to others, and it helps us decrease interpersonal distance

MARMADUKE reprinted by permission of UFS, Inc.

between ourselves and others. Its effect depends on the type of humor we use.

There are at least three different types of humor we use in interpersonal relationships (Graham, Papa, & Brooks, 1992). First, humor is used to express *positive affect*; for example, to make light of situations, be playful, and help friendships develop. Second, humor is used as a form of *expressiveness*; for example, to disclose difficult information about ourselves, to let others know our likes and dislikes, and to avoid telling others information about ourselves. Third, humor is used to express *negative affect*; for example, to demean others, to say negative things about others, or to put others in their place. Only the use of humor to express positive affect leads to the formation of positive impressions. **The use of humor to put others down is never justified.**

Play performs a number of important functions in our relationships with others (Baxter, 1992). First, play is an index of intimacy in our relationships because it indicates the degree to which people are in synchrony. Play not only reflects relational intimacy, it promotes it. Second, play helps us moderate tension in our relationships. Third, play allows us to engage in behavior that might otherwise be embarrassing. Fourth, play provides us with a creative outlet in our relationships. Fifth, play provides us with alternative ways to communicate with our partners in close relationships.

Play is particularly important in romantic relationships. It is important to recognize that

> in any relationship that involves commitment, two people are simultaneously relating in dynamic ways on many levels, only some of which are conscious. Inevitably, tensions arise, not only because we are two separate individuals with different needs, but also because each of us struggles with our emotional contradictions. We wish to be independent, yet we yearn for closeness; we seek a reassuring sense of sameness and security, but we also want to keep the spark of romance alive. . . . successful coping requires a balancing act, a blending of the two psychological forces or needs rather than rigid opting for either extreme. Intimate play is ideally suited to the holding together of apparently mutually exclusive alternatives. It embodies the flexibility and humor that couples must cultivate in order to reconcile conflicting needs. (Betcher, 1987, pp. 27–28)

Play can perform the same function in friendships as well.

Like self-disclosure, play involves a risk. When we engage in play, we are showing others parts of us that they may not otherwise have seen. The risk comes in that they may not like what they see. Deciding to engage in play with someone, therefore, is a decision to be open to some degree.

We take a risk when we show our humorous side to other people because they may not appreciate that side of us. The people involved in the relationship have to gauge how much they are willing to show their partner.

We use several different types of play in our close relationships (Baxter, 1992), as shown in Table 12.1. The most frequently used forms of play are private verbal codes, role playing, verbal teasing, prosocial physical play, and antisocial physical play. Games, gossiping, and public performances are used least frequently. The amount of play is associated with relationship closeness in same-sex friendships, but not in romantic relationships (Baxter, 1992). In romantic relationships, the type of play is more important than the amount of play.

The different types of play perform special functions in our close personal relationships (Baxter, 1992). Private verbal codes, for example, are indicators of the intimacy of our relationships. Public performances, role-playing, and gossiping allow us to engage in behaviors and not be embarrassed by them or have major consequences for our relationships. By gossiping, for instance, "partners could signal to one another the qualities they value (and not value) in others while distancing themselves from any offense taken by the partner" (Baxter, 1992, p. 359). Prosocial physical play and private verbal codes are the most useful forms of play in managing conflict.

Idioms. One of the major forms of play we use in our close friendships and romantic relationships is developing relational idioms—"words, phrases, gestures that have unique meaning within a specific relationship" (Bell, Buerkel-Rothfuss, & Gore, 1987, p. 48). The development of idioms appears to take place at the same time as intimacy (Hopper, Knapp, & Scott, 1981). The use of idioms builds cohesion and solidifies commitments within the relationship. Although we use idioms when we play, not all idioms involve play. Some idioms, for example, help us to manage conflict.

We use a variety of idioms in close friendships and romantic relationships (Bell & Healey, 1992), as shown in Table 12.2. We can use idioms to refer to activities, to express affection, to confront, to express emotions, to

Table 12.1

A TYPOLOGY OF PLAY IN CLOSE INTERPERSONAL RELATIONSHIPS

1. *Private verbal codes.* Private verbal codes involve idiomatic expressions. (One couple uses "bleach" to indicate that they want to be alone when others are present.)
2. *Role playing.* One or both parties in a relationship take play roles (someone other than themselves). (Pretending to be a cartoon character or a rock star.)
3. *Verbal teasing.* One-sided or two-sided exchanges designed to tease the other person. (A person might tease a friend by telling the friend that a potential romantic partner is watching when the person is not present.)
4. *Prosocial physical play.* Transforming a typically prosocial act into play. (Greeting someone by waltzing down the hallway.)
5. *Antisocial physical play.* Transforming an act that is usually antisocial into play. ("Mock" fighting.)
6. *Games.* Play in which there are explicit rules and a winner is named. (Counting the number of puns that are used in a conversation.)
7. *Gossiping.* Talking about others in their absence. (Using Disney character names for friends and talking about others "in character.")
8. *Public performances.* Engaging in some sort of public behavior in order to observe others' reactions. (A romantic couple might pretend to have an argument in public to see how others react.)

Adapted from Baxter (1992).

greet or say good-bye, to label others, to refer to objects, to make requests, to make sexual references, to tease, to refer to ourselves or others, and to refer to places we have been (Bell & Healey, 1992). The most frequently used idioms in romantic relationships include nicknames, teasing insults, sexual invitations, affection, and labels for others, while requests and confrontation are not used frequently (Bell et al., 1987). In close friendships, labels for others, affection, and nicknames are the idioms used the most frequently (Bell & Healey, 1992).

Most idioms tend to be verbal. In romantic relationships, the male partners tend to invent a slightly higher percentage of the idioms than the female partners (Bell et al., 1987). In friendships, idioms are used predominantly in public rather in private (Bell & Healey, 1992). In romantic relationships, idioms are used slightly more frequently in public than in private (Bell et al., 1987). The use of idioms in public allows romantic couples or friends to project themselves as a social unit. The use of idioms in public, for example, leads others to see a romantic couple as a "couple." The use of idioms in public also allows the couple to coordinate their actions without letting others know what they are doing (Bell et al., 1987). To illustrate, couples may have idioms to tell their partner not to talk about certain subjects or to let them know when it is time to leave a social gathering.

Using idioms influences our relationships with others. In romantic relationships, for example, the more idioms the couple uses, the

Table 12.2

A Typology of Idioms Used in Close Relationships

1. *Activities.* Idioms referring to activities in which the person was engaged. (Using "PP" [pee pause] to indicate that the person was going to the bathroom.)
2. *Express affection.* Idioms to uniquely express positive feelings for the other person. (Saying, "God, I hate you" to tell a friend that you like him or her.)
3. *Confrontation.* Idioms used to manage conflicts or make the other person aware that you are upset. (Saying "slow down" to tell a friend to mellow out during a conflict.)
4. *Emotions.* Using unique words to talk about emotions. (Using "dead bunnies" to indicate sadness.)
5. *Greetings and good-byes.* Special ways of saying hello or good-bye. (Using "olla" for both comings and goings.)
6. *Labels for others.* Idioms referring to people outside relationship; either a specific person or a group. (Calling a vegetarian woman "rabbit woman" or referring to potential formal dates as "PFDs.")
7. *Objects.* Special names for objects. (Calling a computer a "confuser.")
8. *Requests.* Special ways to make requests. (Saying, "Let's make like a tree" when you want to leave a social event.)
9. *Sexual reference.* Code words for sexual encounters. (A friend might tell a friend that she or he was making out by saying "pout"; one couple indicated they wanted sex by saying, "Let's do the laundry.")
10. *Teasing insults.* Idioms used to tease the partner in the spirit of play. (Calling a friend "King Clash" to make fun of the way he dresses.)
11. *Nicknames for self.* Names used to refer to self. (Calling yourself "the King.")
12. *Nicknames for other.* Names used to refer to romantic partner or friend. (Calling your romantic partner "Pookers.")
13. *Places.* Idioms used to refer to special places. (Referring to a quiet place that you go to rest as "the old mill pond.")

Adapted from Bell and Healey (1992). Examples also are drawn from Bell et. al. (1987).

closer the couple is, the more intimacy is expressed in the relationship, and the more committed the partners are to each other (Bell et al., 1987). In friendships, the use of idioms is associated with the degree to which the friends like and trust each other. Friends see their use of idioms as having a positive effect on their relationship.

To summarize, many factors influence whether we develop relationships with others. We tend to develop relationships with others when we perceive that they support our self-concept, when we perceive similarities between ourselves, when we see other people's behavior as predictable, when we trust them, when we see them as involved in interactions with us, and when we develop a relational culture. As we get to know others, our relationships progress through stages of development.

Stages of Relationship Development and Deescalation

The development and deterioration of interpersonal relationships can be *described* as a series of stages (Knapp & Vangelisti, 1992).[2] These stages are illustrated in Figure 12.1. Although the stages are divided into those involving "coming together" and "coming apart," there is nothing inherently good about coming together, and there is nothing inherently bad about coming apart. The stages, therefore, should be viewed as "descriptive of what seems to happen—not what should happen" (Knapp & Vangelisti, 1992, p. 32).

The stages are not totally distinct from one another. Each stage includes some behaviors that might take place in the adjacent stages, so identifying the stages of our relationships is a matter of emphasis. Although most of our relationships tend to go from one stage to the next in a systematic manner, some relationships can skip stages. Also, our relationships tend to move forward, but they also can move backward. With these preliminary considerations in mind, let's look at the stages of coming together.

Stages of Coming Together

The stages of coming together describe how we develop relationships with others. There are five stages: initiating, experimenting, intensifying, integrating, and bonding. Let's begin by looking at the initiating stage.

Initiating. When we first interact with people we do not know, we are potentially initiating a relationship. When we first meet new people, we try to display ourselves as people who are "pleasant, likable, understanding, and socially adept" (Knapp & Vangelisti, 1992, p. 35). In the initiating stage, we tend to follow the scripts we have learned for initial interactions. Following these scripts allows us to interact with others without knowing a lot about them. To illustrate, after being introduced at a party, two people might say something like "It's nice to meet you. Do you know anyone else here?" "Nice to meet you, too.

FIGURE 12.1 The Stage Model of Relationship Development

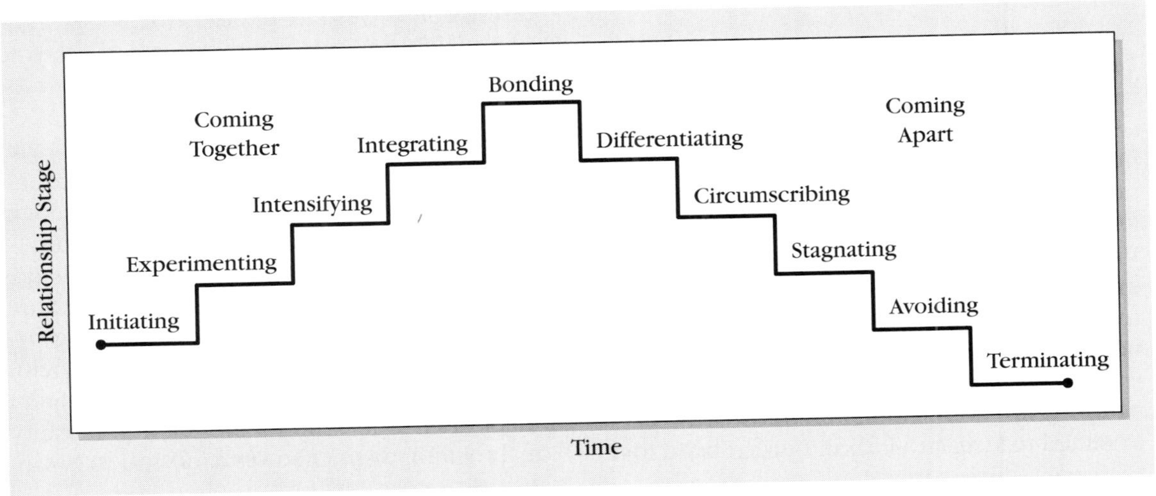

Yeah, I know. . . ." During this stage, we make initial judgments about other people's competence, and they make judgments about ours.

Experimenting. Experimenting involves reducing our uncertainty about others (Knapp & Vangelisti, 1992). Small talk is the predominant form of communication during this stage of a relationship. Small talk is superficial and conventional talk about a wide variety of topics. When we engage in small talk, we discuss the weather, the news, books we've read, and so forth (several topics discussed were presented in Table 10.1). Two people might say something like "Did you hear that our tuition might be raised?" and "Yeah, I'm attending a rally to protest the increase tomorrow."

Small talk can be seen as an "audition for friendship" (Knapp & Vangelisti, 1992). Small talk helps us isolate topics we can talk about in later stages of relationship development. Small talk also helps us identify similarities between ourselves and others, and it helps us and the other person reduce our uncertainty about each other. When others perceive our small talk as inappropriate, the relationship may not go any further than this stage. Relationships at this stage are casual, and commitment is very limited.

Intensifying. During this stage, we increase the information we disclose about ourselves to others (Knapp & Vangelisti, 1992). Our disclosures at this stage may include secrets (such as our frustrations, fears, or imperfections) that others do not know about us. We may disclose information about a variety of topics during this stage, but our disclosures regarding the development of a relationship with other people are most important because they make us vulnerable to them. In a dating relationship, one person might say, "I'm really attracted to you, and I think I might be in love with you" during this stage.

At the party, Mark dishes up a little small talk.

SINGLE SLICES © Peter Kohlsaat, February 11, 1992, Los Angeles Times Syndicate. Reprinted with permission.

In the intensifying stage, the way we address others becomes more informal, and nicknames or terms of endearment may be used. The use of "we" or "us" also increases during this stage. Private codes also develop during this stage of relationship development (see the discussion of idioms earlier in this chapter). Overall during this stage, we are displaying our uniqueness to others.

Integrating. During the integrating stage, we begin to arrange our everyday lives around our partners' everyday lives, and we become involved in each others' social networks. A jointly constructed view of the world begins to emerge. Also during this stage, our interdependence with our partners begins to be visible to others. Romantic partners start being treated as couples during this stage. Integration does not mean a loss of individuality; maintaining distinct selves is critical to having a healthy relationship.

Conversations in close friendships, as in the integrating stage, are distinguished from conversations in acquaintance relationships, as in the experimenting stage, by the presence of mutual knowledge, intimacy of self-disclosure, and relaxation (Planalp & Benson, 1992). There also is greater frequency of interaction, interaction occurs in a greater number of settings, the interactions are more exclusive, and interactions provide more benefits in close friendships than in acquaintance relationships (Planalp & Benson, 1992). The most important factors that seem to differentiate friends' and acquaintances' conversations are mutual knowledge and references to the continuity of the relationship, such as references to past conversations and to the future (Planalp, 1993).

Bonding. Bonding often involves "a public ritual that announces to the world that commitments have been formally contracted" (Knapp & Vangelisti, 1992, p. 39). In a romantic relationship, bonding may involve going steady and getting engaged or married. Romantic partners might propose and get married or decide to live together during this stage.

When we become bonded, it changes the nature of our relationships. Interpretations of our partners' communication behavior is based on the nature of the relationship we have with them. If in the integrating stage we are not sure that our partners are committed to our relationships this influences the way we interpret their behavior. Once our relationships reach the bonding stage, in contrast, we recognize that our partners are committed, and our interpretation of their behavior will be based on recognizing this commitment. To illustrate, if our partners said that they needed to spend some time alone during the integrating phase, we might assume that there is a problem with the relationship. In the bonding phase, in contrast, the same statement would not necessarily lead to the same interpretation because we would know that our partners are committed to our relationships.

Stages of Coming Apart

The stages of coming apart describe what happens when our relationships are terminating. Assuming that the relationship reaches the

Terminating a relationship can be difficult and painful. Most relationships go through the five stages of coming apart though some may skip stages.

bonding stage, there are five stages of coming apart: differentiating, circumscribing, stagnating, avoiding, and terminating. Let's begin by looking at differentiating.

Differentiating. Differentiating involves becoming different or distinct. During this stage, we begin to recognize that we are different from our partners. Conversations during this stage may focus on the differences between the partners. One person might say something like "You're not as talkative as I am. Why don't you talk more?" The other person might reply, "You're right, I don't talk as much as you do."

Differences become the central focus of our attention, and these differences lead to greater interpersonal distance between us and our partners in the differentiating stage. The "we" orientation begins to be replaced by a "my" orientation. The most obvious aspect of communication in "differentiating, or affirming individuality, is fighting or conflict" (Knapp & Vangelisti, 1992, p. 41).

Circumscribing. Circumscribing involves constricted communication. During this stage, we restrict our communication with our partners to "safe" areas. Touchy topics of conversation are avoided in this stage. Our communication with our partners takes place with low frequency, and there is little depth to the topics we discuss. When we do talk, our communication usually is limited to superficial topics. To illustrate, one person might ask the other, "How was your day?" and the other person might respond, "It was fine," without giving any additional information.

We exchange little information about our personal opinions or the relationships during the circumscribing stage. When our relationships are in this stage of development, we may, however, present a civil image to others. To illustrate, we might drive to a party with our partners in silence, but be very talkative at the party.

Stagnating. Stagnating involves inactivity. In this stage, an expectation of unpleasant conversations and the feeling that we have little to say to our partners emerge (Knapp & Vangelisti, 1992). If our relationships are at this stage, we may think about our interactions with our partners and become convinced that we know what the outcome will be, and since we know the outcome, there is no need to talk. To illustrate, one person might say, "There's nothing to talk about, is there?" and the other person might respond by saying only "no."

During the stagnating stage, we avoid talking about the relationships. Our communication is awkward, scripted, and often similar to the way we talk to strangers. There also is a tendency during this stage to hold imagined conversations, like "If I say this, she'll say. . . ."

Avoiding. If our relationships are in this stage, we rearrange our lives so that there is little need to interact with our partners (Knapp & Vangelisti, 1992). Conversations at this stage often involve telling the other person that we are not available. One person, for example, might say, "I've been too busy to call lately. Can I call you when things calm down?" The other person might respond by saying, "Yeah, But I may not be home. I've been busy, too."

The relationship component of the messages being exchanged during the avoiding stage often are interpreted as involving antagonism or unfriendliness. When we get together with our partners at this stage, one of us might be consistently late or indicate that we can only stay a short period of time. There also may be direct verbal statements, such as "I don't want to talk to you anymore."

Terminating. This stage involves physically and psychologically leaving relationships (Knapp & Vangelisti, 1992). Terminating our relationships may take a long time, or it may occur very quickly. We may terminate relation-

DRABBLE reprinted by permission of UFS, Inc.

ships we have had for only a short period of time or terminate relationships we have had for many years. Relationships can terminate when partners stop contacting each other, or they can terminate when one person decides to end it and leaves.

Communication that occurs when we terminate relationships tends to be characterized by messages that create a distance between us and our partners, such as saying something like "Don't call me, I'll call you." Distance also can be communicated nonverbally using a "cold" tone of voice, little eye contact, and so forth. We also transmit messages that help prepare our partners for life without us. To illustrate, we might use single-person pronouns like "I" or "me" in situations in which we had used "we." Our communication at this stage will be awkward, difficult, and hesitant.

Factors Influencing Movement Through the Stages

Our movement through the stages of relationship development and dissolution tends to be systematic and sequential (Knapp & Vangelisti, 1992). When we are coming together and coming apart, we tend to go through the stages presented. Our relationships do not, however, go through a series of fixed movements; they are always in a state of flux. When our relationships are developing or dissolving, we can skip stages. Two people may, for example, meet at a party (initiating) and, if mutually attracted, jump to the intensifying stage (skipping the experimenting stage). Relationships that are coming apart also may skip stages. To illustrate, a married couple could jump from bonding to terminating if one spouse moved to another city without telling the other person. Generally, movement is vertical or horizontal, as the stages are depicted in Figure 12.1 (Knapp & Vangelisti, 1992). If two people are in the integrating stage and have not bonded, when they start to come apart, they move to the differentiating stage (which is on the same horizontal level in Figure 12.1).

Movement through the stages may be *forward* toward greater intimacy or *backward* toward less intimacy. There also will be movement within stages, since "we constantly try to arrest possible disintegration by achieving some steady state or equilibrium" (Knapp & Vangelisti, 1992, p. 54). Our relationships may stabilize at the beginning of one stage and then move toward the next stage and stabilize again within that stage.

Several factors influence the rate at which our relationships move through the stages (Knapp & Vangelisti, 1992). When we have little time to get to know others, for example, our movement through the stages of coming together may be very fast. The more frequently we see others, the more quickly our relationships can develop with them. Our needs also influence our movement through the stages. If our need for inclusion has not been met, for example, we will move through the stages faster than people whose need for inclusion has been met. Movement through the stages depends on whether both people want it to change. If we are in a relationship and both of us want it to be more intimate, it will change faster than if both of us are not sure how intimate we want the relationship to be.

Paradoxes, Contradictions, and Inconsistencies in Relationships

The stage model of relationship development and deterioration focuses on the consistent patterns that occur as our relationships with others develop and deteriorate over time. Our relationships, however, are not always consistent and patterned. Our relationships also involve paradoxes, inconsistencies, and contradictions. The focus on contradictions and paradoxes provides an alternative approach to understanding our relationships with others. The dialectical perspective introduced in Chapter 3 focuses on explaining the contradictions, inconsistencies, and paradoxes in our relationships. Let's begin by looking at the primary dialectics that operate in our relationships.

Primary Relational Dialectics

Three primary dialectics influence how our relationships develop and change over time: autonomy-connection, novelty-predictability, and openness-closedness (Baxter, 1988).[3] *Autonomy* refers to our desire to be differentiated or separate from others. *Connection,* in contrast, refers to our need to feel included (see the discussion of our need for inclusion in Chapter 3). Autonomy involves recognizing that we are independent people and differentiating ourselves from others. Connection involves being interconnected and doing things together if we are going to sustain a relationship.

The autonomy-connection dialectic is the primary contradiction that influences the development and deterioration of our relationships with others. We cannot form relationships with others unless we give up some of our autonomy. If we emphasize our need for autonomy in our relationships with others to the exclusion of our need for connection, we will form only shallow relationships with others. Similarly, if we emphasize our need for connection with others to the exclusion of our need for autonomy, we will not develop quality relationships because our individual identities will get lost. **Developing quality relationships requires balancing our needs for autonomy and connection and being aware of our partners' need for autonomy and connection.** The poem in Reading 12.1 expresses how autonomy and connection coexist in our relationships.

It is important to recognize that men and women have different ways of expressing their needs for autonomy and connection in romantic relationships (Noller, 1993). In marital relationships, men tend to focus on sex and giving practical advice as ways to express connection, while women emphasize affection and expressing emotions. The differences in styles can create problems. To illustrate, consider a couple, Maxwell and Samantha. "MAXWELL wants to be left alone and SAMANTHA wants attention; so HE LEAVES HER ALONE and SHE

Reading 12.1 The Whole Is More Than The Sum of Its Parts/Natasha Josefowitz

Of course I love you
and I love me too
but most of all
I love "us"

I love the "we"
the you *and* me,
the relationship,
the way each one
is enriched
by the other

I am smarter
when you're around
you are braver
when I am there

We find each other
beautiful, brilliant
and great fun

Each of us is the other's parent
each, the other's child
each is the other's partner, colleague
friend, consultant, lover
and accomplice

You tend to be serious
I'm rather spontaneous
you make me think more
I make you laugh more

Of course I love you
and I love me too
but most of all
I love "us."

GIVES HIM ATTENTION" (Tannen, 1986, p. 27). To meet each other's needs for autonomy and connection, males and females often have to behave in ways that are different from the way they have been socialized, and different from the way they prefer to be treated (Tannen, 1990).

Predictability is a basic need in relationships because it allows us to coordinate our interactions with others. As noted in Chapter 3, however, some degree of *novelty* also is necessary to keep our relationships interesting and for us not to become overconfident that we totally understand the other person. **Developing quality relationships requires that we recognize our needs for predictability and for novelty.**

Openness with others is necessary to develop intimacy with them. When we are open with others, however, we make ourselves vulnerable. Protecting ourselves, therefore, requires some degree of *closedness.* This dialectic operates at two levels (Baxter, 1988). First, it operates within the relationship. Second, it operates in terms of how the people in the relationship interact with others. When we are establishing a relationship with another person, we need privacy (being closed to people not involved in the relationship) in order to establish intimacy. For relationships to develop they also must be recognized by outsiders, and this requires openness. **Developing quality relationships requires that we are able to balance our needs and our partners' needs for openness and closedness in our relationships.**

The three primary dialectics are always operating in our relationships with others. The ways that we deal with the dialectics are a function of the people in the relationship, what is happening in each of their lives, and what is happening in the relationship. As we get to know others, the ways that the dialectics are managed can be viewed as going through phases. These dialectical phases are different from the linear stages in the stage model. We do not, for example, resolve the autonomy-connection dialectic once in our relationship and then it remains stable. Rather, since change is inevitable, we always have to deal with autonomy and connection issues throughout the course of our relationships. Our relationships may go through some of the phases many times, depending on how the dialectical contradictions are resolved and depending on the events happening in the relationship. Going through a series of phases is referred to as a cycle. The cycles are illustrated in Figures 12.2 and 12.3 (the figures are discussed below).

Since the autonomy-connection dialectic is primary, it can be used to define the phases of relational paradoxes and contradictions: autonomy to connection, autonomy and connection, autonomy-connection synthesis, connection to autonomy. The openness-closedness and the predictability-novelty dialectics operate differently within the phases defined by the autonomy-connection dialectic. The phases are described in terms of what happens initially as we get to know others (the initial cycle), and how the dialectics operate in subsequent cycles are illustrated. Let's begin by looking at the initial phase of getting to know others.

Autonomy to Connection

In this phase, we are getting to know other people and deciding whether we want to form a relationship with them (Baxter, 1988). There are two aspects of the novelty-predictability dialectic occurring during this phase: individual and interaction episodes. At the individual level, we experience novelty during this phase because we do not have much information about other people, and this novelty creates uncertainty. We therefore use uncertainty reduction strategies to gather information about others (see Chapter 4). Even though we do not know much about others during this phase, their behavior is relatively predictable. We can predict other people's behavior during this phase because of our initial interaction scripts.

There is a tension between the individual and interaction levels. If others follow all of our initial interaction scripts, we will not gather much information about them. If they violate our initial interaction scripts, in contrast, we will gather a great deal of information about them. At the same time, however, these violations of our initial interaction scripts may lead us to decide that we do not want to get to know them because they are not meeting our expectations.

If others engage in a high degree of openness during this phase of a relationship, it helps us reduce our uncertainty. At the same time, this openness violates our initial interaction scripts. We tend to be somewhat closed and to engage in superficial self-disclosures during initial interactions with strangers, because this demonstrates that we are willing to be open and does not violate our initial interaction scripts (Baxter, 1988). Our initial interaction scripts allow us to talk openly about certain topics and to avoid other topics (see the rules of self-disclosure discussed in Chapter 10).

Autonomy and Connection

In this phase, we work out the details of how we will be connected to others, particularly in how we will be autonomous in our relationships (Baxter, 1988). As noted earlier, however, it is important to keep in mind that we do not work out the details of how we are connected to others once and then it remains stable throughout the relationship. Rather, we have to work out new ways to be connected when things change in our relationships. Because we are working out details of our relationships, this phase of relationship development often is characterized by ambivalence, conflict, and instability.

The ambivalence, conflict, and instability that occur during this phase lead us to focus on our need for predictability. We are not necessarily concerned with the predictability of other people's behavior, but rather the predictability of the relationship. We want to know what the state of our relationship is. During this phase, we use a variety of symbols and rituals to develop relational predictability. We might, for example, develop private codes such as nicknames, sexual code words, and private jokes that we use with our relational partners (see the discussion of idioms earlier in this chapter). Partners in romantic relationships also may use special places or songs to mark the relationship. The symbols and rituals we develop during this phase tell us what is valued and expected in our relationships, and this helps us to establish relational predictability (Baxter, 1988).

While we have a need for relational predictability during this phase, we also have a need for novelty (Baxter, 1988). For us to develop close relationships with others, we have to engage in nonscripted interaction. Often, relational partners may recall a "unique, nonscripted interaction" as a *turning point* in the relationship.

The conflict that occurs during the autonomy and connection phase threatens the relational predictability, but it also provides novelty in the relationship. During this phase, we do not attribute the conflicts that occur to other people's faults or to the incompatibilities between us. Since we do not blame others, we are able to use solution-oriented strategies to manage the conflict that arises during this phase.

In this phase, we avoid discussing our relationship with our partners; the relationship is a *taboo topic* (Baxter, 1988). We fear that discussing the relationship will put it in jeopardy. When our relationships are in this phase, we use secret tests to gain information about them. We might use *endurance tests,* such as making the other person work hard to maintain the relationship to find out if the other person is committed to the relationship. Alternatively, we might use *separation tests,* such as spending time apart to determine if the relationship will survive our being separated from our partner, or we might use *indirect hints* to find out if our relational partner is sensitive to our needs. Presenting the relationship in public might be a secret test to see how the partner reacts. These secret tests are all indirect ways of gathering information about the relationship and thereby reducing our uncertainty.

During the autonomy and connection phase, relational partners are working out how they will be connected. Assuming the partners work out a satisfactory resolution, the partners move to the third phase, autonomy-connection synthesis. If the partners do not work out a satisfactory resolution in the autonomy and connection phase, the relationship could remain in this phase, return to the autonomy to connection phase, or move to the connection to autonomy phase.

Autonomy-Connection Synthesis

In this phase, we no longer view autonomy and connection as opposites. We have worked out a way to synthesize these two different needs within our relationships (Baxter, 1988). The exact way this is worked out, however, may differ tremendously across relationships. The major issue with which we are struggling in this phase is how we can maintain our autonomy-connection synthesis in the presence of pressure for change. Recall from Chapter 3 that the dialectical perspective assumes constant change within relationships.

There are two sources of predictability in our relationships that also can lead to change during this phase (Baxter, 1988). First, the daily routines that take place in our relationships can become boring and reduce the emotional arousal we experience in our relationships. Second, when we think we know our partners very well, we may become overconfident. It is important to recognize that our relationships with others require work if we are going to keep them from becoming too predictable and, at the same time, make sure there is some degree of stability. We can use *preventative strategies,* such as planning exciting trips, calling our partner in the middle of the day, and so forth, or we can use *repair strategies,* such as being especially attentive to our partners or doing them favors. These strategies are discussed in detail in the next chapter.

During this phase of our relationship, we assume that we know each other rather well, and we do not see a need for openness (Baxter, 1988). Also, we see openness about our relationships as work, and therefore we tend to discuss the relationship only when it is absolutely necessary. We tend to use indirect, rather than direct, strategies to work on our relationships during this phase.

No relationship can sustain the same autonomy-connection synthesis for the life of the relationship. Inevitably something happens in a relationship, and the synthesis the partners worked out no longer works well for them. In a marriage, for example, the autonomy-connection synthesis needs to be renegotiated when a child is born. Changes in relationships require that a new autonomy-connection synthesis be negotiated.

The length of time that a relationship remains in the autonomy-connection phase can vary tremendously. The synthesis romantic partners initially work out, for example, lasts until they get married or begin living together. The change in living arrangements is a sufficient change to require a new autonomy-connection synthesis to be negotiated. The synthesis worked out after marriage may last until one of the partners changes jobs or a child is born; then a new synthesis will be needed. Some relationships may remain in the same autonomy-connection synthesis for years, while others may stay in this phase only for short periods of time.

When changes in relationships occur, the next phase depends on the people involved and what they want from their relationships. Assuming that both partners want to continue the relationship, a new autonomy-connection cycle must be initiated (see Figure 12.2). If the changes that occur in a relationship are relatively minor, the new cycle may begin with the autonomy and connection phase. If massive changes occur, such as one of the partners taking a job in another city, the partners may have to return to the autonomy to connection phase to begin working out a new synthesis. Returning to earlier phases to start a new cycle does not always happen. If things are not going well in the relationship, the partners may move to the connection to autonomy phase (see Figure 12.3).

Figure 12.2 presents an example of the possible dialectical cycles in an ongoing relationship. The initial dialectical tensions are resolved in this example, and an initial autonomy-connection synthesis is achieved. After a period of time, something happens in the relationship, such as one person changing jobs with the new job requiring more work than the old one. This requires that the partners work out a new autonomy-connection synthesis. Since the change is relatively minor, they return to the autonomy and connection phase. A new synthesis is achieved, and the synthesis lasts longer than the first. At some point something else happens which upsets the synthesis, such as a baby being born. This is a major change, so the couple returns to the autonomy to connection phase. Over time, a new autonomy-connection synthesis is negotiated.

Figure 12.3 illustrates the cycles that might occur in a relationship that moves to

FIGURE 12.2 An Example of Possible Dialectical Cycles in Ongoing Relationships

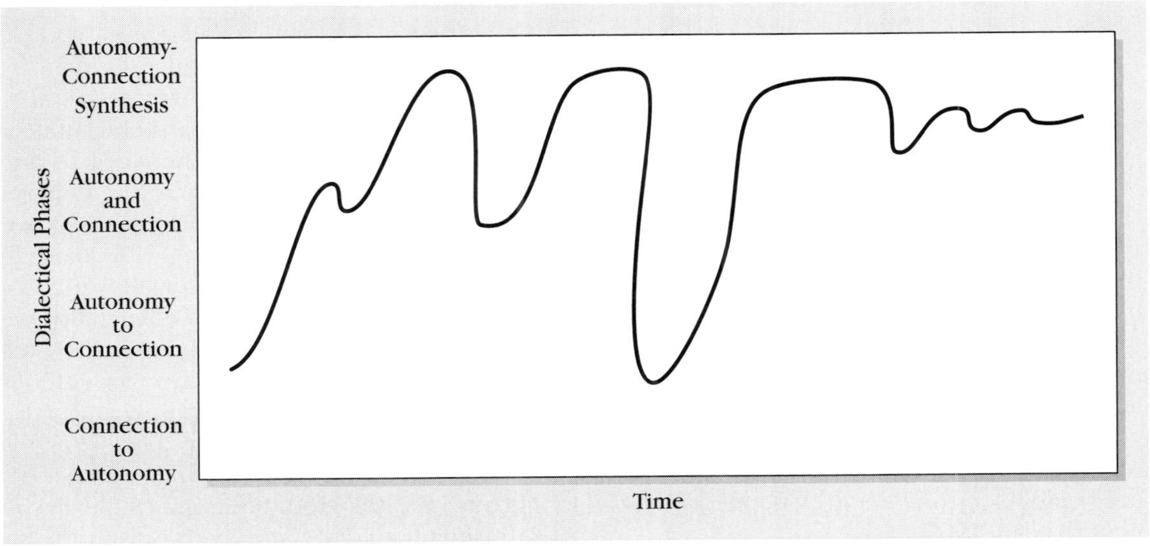

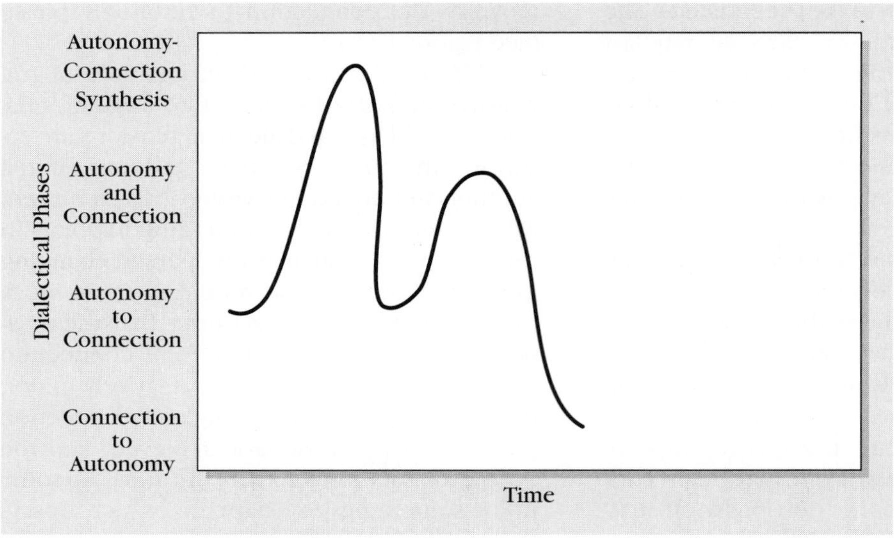

FIGURE 12.3 An Example of Possible Dialectical Cycles in Terminated Relationships

the next dialectical phase, connection to autonomy. In this example, the partners are able to work out an initial autonomy-connection synthesis. When change occurs in the relationship, however, they are not able to work out a new synthesis, which eventually leads to the couple entering the connection to autonomy phase.

Connection to Autonomy

When partners in a relationship cannot sustain the autonomy-connection synthesis they worked out, they evolve into the fourth phase. In the stage model of relationship development and deterioration presented earlier, coming apart is seen as the reverse of coming together (Knapp & Vangelisti, 1992). The dialectical view of relationships, however, suggests that there are differences that can be seen in how the relational partners handle predictability-novelty and openness-closedness (Baxter, 1988).

In this phase of our relationships, we have ambivalent feelings (Baxter, 1988). Our ambivalent feelings, however, are different from those in the autonomy and connection phase. Here we are concerned with whether we should end our relationships or try to fix them. Our ambivalence during this phase leads to an increase in the conflict that occurs, and we make fewer attempts to manage the conflict when it arises. During this phase, we tend to attribute the conflict to our partners' faults or to irreconcilable differences between us and our partners. Since we attribute the conflict to our partners or differences between us, we tend to use controlling strategies to manage the conflict. When our relationships are dissolving, the one source of predictability we may have is that conflict will occur. This undermines our desire to be connected with our partners, stay in our relationships, and work toward fixing them. The source of novelty is that the established routines are no longer occurring, and this, too, undermines our desire to maintain a connection with our partners.

With a reduction in our connection during this phase, we are less open with our partners (Baxter, 1988). The closedness between us and our partners contributes to our desire to terminate our relationships. The main source of openness during this phase is the conflict that occurs. This openness is hurtful, however, which also contributes to our desire to leave our relationships.

Comparing Stages and Phases

The dialectical and stage models are alternative ways to explain how our relationships develop and change over time. The stage model is based on the assumption that relationships are characterized by patterns and regularities that are relatively consistent across relationships. The dialectical perspective, in contrast, is based on the assumption that relationships are constantly changing and that partners in relationships must manage the contradictions and paradoxes inherent in relationships.

Although there are distinct differences between the two perspectives, both are useful in understanding how our relationships with others operate. The stage model helps us understand the general patterns of developing intimacy with others. The dialectical perspective is useful in understanding the everyday communication that occurs in our relationships with others. Understanding our relationships requires both understanding general patterns and recognizing the contradictions and inconsistencies that take place in our unique relationships.

Understanding our relationships with others also requires that we recognize how people from different groups form relationships and what happens when we form relationships with members of different groups. Let's therefore turn our attention to group differences in relationships.

Group Membership and the Development of Close Relationships

Our culture and our ethnicity influence the types of relationships we form, the rules that influence how we communicate in nonclose relationships, and the way our relationships develop. Let's begin by looking at how culture influences our perceptions of the intimacy of our relationships.

Culture and Perceived Intimacy of Relationships

There are both similarities and differences in how relationships are perceived across cultures. To illustrate, Table 12.3 presents ratings

Table 12.3
Perceived Intimacy of Relationship Terms in Japan and the United States

	U.S.	Japan
Interpersonal Relationships		
Stranger	8.35	7.99
Acquaintance	6.79	4.95
Friend	3.67	3.42
Best friend	2.51	1.73
Boy/girlfriend	1.70	3.32
Lover	1.25	2.81
Ingroup Relationships		
Co-worker	5.76	5.27
Colleague	5.33	4.76
Classmate	5.72	3.84

Based on Gudykunst and Nishida (1986b). Scores range from 1 = very intimate to 9 = nonintimate.

of the intimacy of several terms used for interpersonal relationships in Japan and the United States (Gudykunst & Nishida, 1986b).[4] The relationships are divided into interpersonal and ingroup relationships. The intimacy ratings range from 1 (very intimate) to 9 (nonintimate), so the lower the score, the more intimate the relationships are perceived to be.

Let's begin by looking at the similarities in the ratings in Table 12.3. If we look at the first four interpersonal relationships listed, we can see that strangers are perceived as the least intimate relationship in *both* cultures. Acquaintance relationships are perceived as more intimate than relationships with strangers, and less intimate than relationships with friends in *both* cultures. Similarly, best friend relationships are perceived as more intimate than friend relationships in *both* cultures. These patterns suggest that the stages of relationship development discussed earlier in this chapter generalize across cultures.

You probably noticed that, in discussing the interpersonal relationships, boy/girlfriend and lover were not mentioned. The reason for this is that there are cultural differences in this area. In the United States, both boy/girlfriend and lover are perceived as more intimate relationships than best friend relationships. In Japan, on the other hand, best friend relationships are perceived as more intimate than either boy/girlfriend or lover relationships. One explanation for this is that, in Japan, individuals interact most frequently with members of the same sex, and there is little interaction between members of the opposite sex. Opposite-sex relationships, therefore, are perceived as less intimate than same-sex relationships. In the United States, in contrast, there is more interaction between members of the opposite sex than in Japan, so opposite-sex relationships are perceived as intimate.

If you look at the ingroup relationships in Table 12.3, you will see that the Japanese perceive all three relationships to be more intimate than the North Americans. This can be explained by recognizing that the United States is an individualistic culture and Japan is a collectivistic culture. Ingroup relationships are perceived as more intimate in collectivistic cultures than in individualistic cultures.

Intergroup Relationship Development

Most of our close interpersonal relationships are with people who are relatively similar to us. We tend to develop close relationships with members of our own groups, such as our culture, ethnic group, age group, social class, and disability status (Pogrebin, 1987). Nondisabled people, for example, generally "do not want to enter unpredictable, and therefore, stressful interactions with visibly disabled people, and they avoid doing so by extending only 'fictional acceptance' which does not go beyond a polite, inhibited, and overcontrolled interaction" (Safilios-Rothschild, 1982, p. 44). Class differences also hinder members of different social classes from developing close relationships (Fussell, 1983). With respect to intergenerational interactions, age segregation in society "has hampered the opportunity for young and old to come to know one another. Hence, when they do come into contact, well-worn and often detrimental stereotypes may persist, and participants must make an active effort to dispel these preconceptions for a healthy dialogue to take place" (Tamir, 1984, p. 39).

One reason why we do not have close relationships with members of other groups is that we do not have much contact with them. Another reason is that our initial interactions and superficial contacts with members of other groups often result in ineffective communication. Since our communication with members of other groups often is not as effective and satisfying as we would like, we do not necessarily *try* to develop intimate relationships with them. If we understand the pro-

Cultural stereotype is broken down in intimate areas. If the stereotypes are broken, the group from which the other comes will have less of an impact on the relationship.

cess of relationship development, however, we can make an informed, conscious decision as to whether or not we want to have intimate relationships with members of other groups. In making such a decision, it is important to keep in mind that the more we know about members of other groups, the more accurately we can predict their behavior (Honeycutt, Knapp, & Powers, 1983).

Group differences often are problematic in the early stages of our relationships. **For our relationships with members of other groups to get past the early stages of development, we need to recognize genuine group differences.** If we ignore these differences, we will never be able to get close. **We also must recognize individual similarities that we can use as a foundation on which to build a relationship.** The similarities we have with members of other groups can be based on our attitudes, beliefs, values, lifestyles, or ways of communicating. If we do not perceive individual similarities, it is not likely that our relationships with members of other groups will develop beyond the experimenting stage.

Once we develop close relationships with people from other groups, the influence of group memberships on the relationship decreases dramatically. Communication in close friendships, for example, is characterized by "freewheeling and loose" exchange and "facile switching from one mode of communication to another" (Altman & Taylor, 1973, p. 139). This appears to be true across cultures (see the discussion of friendships in the next chapter). In close friendships, "the dyad has moved to the point where interaction is relatively free in both peripheral and in more central areas of the personality. Cultural stereotypy is broken down in these more intimate areas and there is a willingness to move freely in and out of such exchanges" (pp. 139–140). If stereotypes are broken down, the groups from which others come will not be a major factor influencing the interaction, because predictions are based on psychological information about the other person. Close relationships between people from the same group, therefore, should not be expected to differ dramatically from those between people from different groups. The differences that exist among close relationships are due to the unique relational cultures that develop.

The ways in which ethnicity is friendship enhancing is outlined in Reading 12.2. The position in Reading 12.2 can be extended to all forms of group differences, such as those based on culture, disability, age, or social class.

SUMMARY

We tend to form relationships with people who we perceive support our self-concepts and whose behavior we see as predictable. Whether we perceive other people to be similar to us and whether we trust them also affects our desire to develop relationships with them. We also tend to develop relationships with people who are actively involved in the interactions we have with them, including those who use humor and play.

Our relationships with other people can be described as going through a series of stages. The stages of coming together include initiating, experimenting, intensifying, integrating, and bonding. The stages of coming apart include differentiating, circumscribing, stagnating, avoiding, and terminating. Even though our relationships tend to move through the stages in a sequential manner, they can skip stages.

Reading 12.2 PLURALISTIC FRIENDSHIP/LETTY COTTIN POGREBIN

The United States is home to more than 100 nationalities. About 188 million of us identify as white, 27 million as Black, 15 million as Hispanic, and 7 million as "other races." Almost a third of all Americans are of mixed ancestry. Fourteen million of us are foreign-born.

Even these bare demographic facts suggest that humanity is a smorgasbord, not a stew. Rather than boil down this marvelous diversity in a "melting pot," rather than subsume our various friendships in the bland togetherness of a UNICEF card or a soft-drink commercial, I'd like to see us aspire to a "pluralistic friendship" ideal that celebrates *genuine* differences arising out of life experience and culture that rejects *socially constructed* differences resulting from stereotypes or discrimination. . . .

Ethnicity is friendship-enhancing when it is not oppressive to anyone.

Ethnicity is friendship-enhancing when it does not make another group into an "Other" group.

Ethnicity is friendship-enhancing when we make it an "and," not a "but." The difference is palpable: "She's my friend *and* she's Jewish" allows me the pride of difference that a "but" would destroy.

Group identity spawns both pride *and* prejudice. What makes a group special also makes it different. For some people, "different" must mean "better" or it is experienced as "worse." But people who do not need ethnic supremacy to feel ethnic pride find comfort and cultural regeneration among their "own kind" and also are able to make friends across racial and ethnic boundaries.

Our relationships also can be described as going through phases that involves managing the contradictions inherent in relationships: autonomy-connection, predictability-novelty, and openness-closedness. The first phase involves moving from autonomy to connection. In the second phase, we work out the details of how we will be connected to others. The third phase involves balancing our needs for autonomy and connection within the particular relationship. The final phase involves moving from connection to autonomy.

Our group memberships affect the nature of relationships we form with others. Group differences generally affect communication in early stages of relationship development because communication in these stages is guided by cultural norms. If we perceive similarities between ourselves and members of different groups, we will develop relationships with them. Group differences do not have a major affect on our relationships when they become close because close relationships are not guided by cultural norms.

Notes

1. Sunnafrank and Miller's (1981) research clearly indicates that communication can lead to perceptions of similarity when we initially thought there was only dissimilarity.
2. Our discussion of stages of relationship development is drawn from Knapp and Vangelisti (1992). We have tried to keep citations to a minimum to make reading easier, but the ideas presented in this section are Knapp and Vangelisti's.
3. The ideas presented in this section are drawn from Baxter (1988). We extend her analysis by including the idea of cycles through which the phases pass. Baxter (1988) draws upon several of her research studies to develop her argument. To keep citations to a minimum, we cite these references only when absolutely necessary. Readers interested in this line of work are encouraged to review Baxter's work.
4. This study was an extension of Knapp, Ellis, and Williams' (1980) study conducted in the United States.

Journal Reflections

1. *Tracing Your Relationships.* Select one of your close relationships. Imagine that you were going to write a novel about this relationship. Describe the chapter titles in your novel. Explain why you selected the titles you did. How do your chapter titles compare to the stages and/or the contradictions outlined in this chapter?
2. *Ingroup and Outgroup Relationships.* Think of a relationship that you have with a person from a different culture or ethnic group. Think of a relationship that is at about the same level of intimacy with a person from your own culture or ethnic group. Compare and contrast how these two relationships developed and changed over time. What factors attracted you to the other person? What factors contributed to the development (or lack of development) in these relationships?

Study Questions

1. How does self-concept support contribute to the development of our relationships with others?
2. Why are perceived similarities necessary for relationships to become close?
3. How do we make other people's behavior predictable?
4. Why is trust necessary for relationships to develop?
5. How does interaction involvement contribute to relationship development?
6. Why is play important in the development of interpersonal relationships?
7. How does using idioms help us build relational cultures?
8. How are the stages of coming together and coming apart similar?

9. What factors influence the ways that our relationships move through the stages of coming together and coming apart?
10. Why is it necessary to understand relationship dialectics if there are general stages through which our relationships develop?
11. How do the dialectics operate in our relationships?
12. How are relationships with members of the same culture or ethnic group similar to and different from relationships with members of other cultures or ethnic groups?

Suggested Readings

Betcher, W. (1987). *Intimate play.* New York: Penguin Books. William Betcher examines play in romantic relationships. He discusses the role of play in making a commitment, the role of play in developing a relational culture, using play to cope with parents and the past, and using play with children. He also provides suggestions on how to learn to play more.

Knapp, M. L., & Vangelisti, A. L. (1992). *Interpersonal communication and human relationships.* Boston: Allyn & Bacon. This is an upper-division text for courses in relationship development. It provides a solid overview of the role of communication in relationship development.

Scarf, M. (1987). *Intimate partners.* New York: Ballantine Books. Maggie Scarf examines patterns of interaction in love and marriage. She presents excellent illustrations of how couples deal with the autonomy-connection dialectic and provides suggestions for how we can manage this dialectic in our relationships.

White. M. (1993). *The material child: Coming of age in Japan and America.* New York: Free Press. Merry White examines the lives of teenagers in Japan and the United States. She discusses how family life, school, friendships, and sexuality differ in the two cultures.

13

Communication in Close Relationships

When we meet new people, some form of relationship develops. Our interactions with the vast majority of people we meet lead to the development of nonclose relationships, such as those between acquaintances. Our interactions with a limited number of people, however, lead to the development of close relationships. Understanding our communication in close relationships can help us increase the quality of these relationships.

Close relationships are critical to our survival. Our close relationships with others provide us with the intimacy we need to be human and the support we need in times of crisis. In order to improve the quality of our communication in our close relationships, we need to understand the nature of these relationships and our communication in them.

Closeness is not a quality of the type of relationship, but rather of the interaction between the people in a relationship. Some, but not all, friendships, for example, are close. Similarly, some, but not all, romantic relationships, marital relationships, and family relationships are close. To understand our communication in such relationships, it is necessary to begin by looking at what is meant by a close relationship.

Defining Close Relationships

How do we differentiate our close relationships from our nonclose relationships? What is it that makes a relationship close? How do we communicate differently with people in close and nonclose relationships? Before proceeding, think about how you define a close relationship. Take a few minutes to answer the following questions:

> Think of the people with whom you have close relationships. What characteristics

do these relationships have in common? ______________________________
____
____

How is your communication in close relationships similar to your communication in nonclose relationships? ______________________________
____
____

How is your communication in close relationships different from your communication in nonclose relationships? ______________________________
____
____

Your answers to these questions will help you understand the role of closeness in your implicit theory of interpersonal communication. Keep your answers in mind as you read the remainder of this chapter.

Ways We Typically Define Closeness

There are several ways that we typically define close relationships (Berscheid, Snyder, & Omoto, 1989). Many of us, for example, define closeness in terms of the type of relationship we have with another person. To illustrate, friendships and romantic relationships often are assumed to be close relationships. We also may assume that family relationships, such as husband-wife or parent-child, are close relationships. This, however, is not necessarily the case. Consider the different types of marital couples (Fitzpatrick, 1988; these are discussed in more detail later in this chapter). In *traditional marriages,* the partners are highly interdependent; partners in *independent marriages* are moderately interdependent; and *separates* are not highly interdependent. Although these are all marital relationships, they are not necessarily equally close because of the differences within the relationships.

Another way we might try to define the closeness of a relationship is in terms of the words we use to think about it (Berscheid et al., 1989). We frequently use words like attachment, caring, commitment, love, meaningful, significant, and trust when we think about our close relationships. These words, however, can have very different meanings to different people. Because these words can have such different meanings, they are not very useful in differentiating close from nonclose relationships.

A third way we can define closeness is by the satisfaction or positive feelings in our relationships with others. We often think that close relationships are loving relationships characterized by "positively toned emotional events of various kinds and infrequently marred by negative events" (Berscheid et al., 1989, p. 68). It is possible, however, for us to have positive emotional experiences in our relationships and not be close. It also is possible for our relationships with frequent negative events to be close. To discuss close relationships in this chapter, a more precise definition is needed. The amount of interdependence in our relationships is one way that close and nonclose relationships can be differentiated.

Interdependence

Closeness can be assessed by looking at the activities in which we engage in our relationships with others (Kelley et al., 1983). Three criteria are critical to *interdependence* in our relationships: we have to interact frequently, we need to engage in a variety of activities together, and we need to influence each other's behavior (Berscheid et al., 1989). The length of our relationships is not critical to their closeness (Berscheid et al., 1989). Close relationships can be of short duration, at least in the United States. This is not necessarily true, however, in collectivistic cultures like Japan. Close relationships in collectivistic cultures tend to be of long duration.

There are differences in the type of relationship we view as our closest relationship. North Americans, for example, tend to see their romantic partners as closer than their friends (Berscheid et al., 1989). They are more likely to see friends as their closest relationships other than spouses—even closer than other family members. Few North Americans see a work relationship as their closest relationship. Japanese, in contrast, tend to see their friends as closer than their romantic partners (Gudykunst & Nishida, 1993).

Before proceeding, consider the following questions designed to help you think of the amount of interdependence in your relationships with others. For each question, think of a specific relationship you consider to be very close and another specific relationship that is friendly but not close. Take a few minutes to answer the questions now.

> In an average week, how many hours do you spend with the person with whom you have a close relationship? ________
>
> In an average week, how many hours do you spend with the person with whom you have a nonclose relationship? _____
>
> In an average week, how many different types of activities do you do with the person with whom you have a close relationship? (each different thing you do together is an activity)? ____________
>
> In an average week, how many different types of activities do you do with the person with whom you have a nonclose relationship? (each different thing you do together is an activity)? ____________
>
> To what extent does the person with whom you have a close relationship influence your behavior across situations (0 = no influence, 9 = tremendous influence)? ____________________
>
> To what extent does the person with whom you have a nonclose relationship influence your behavior across situations (0 = no influence, 9 = tremendous influence)? ________________

If you are more interdependent in your close relationship than in your nonclose relationship, you probably spend more time and do more activities with this person, and this person probably has more influence on you.

Keeping in mind the factors that influence our closeness to others, we can look at how we communicate in specific close relationships. Let's begin by looking at friendships.

FRIENDSHIPS

Friendship is hard to define. The criteria each of us uses for determining whether someone is a friend are slightly different. Although there are differences in how we define friends, generally "friends are people who are liked, whose company is enjoyed, who share interests and activities, who are helpful and understanding, who can be trusted, with whom one feels comfortable, and who will be emotionally supportive" (Argyle & Henderson, 1985,

p. 64). Before continuing, think about how you communicate with your friends. Answer the following questions:

> How does your communication with people you call friends differ from your communication with people you call acquaintances? ______________________
> ______________________
> ______________________
> ______________________

> How does your communication with people you consider your close friends differ from that with people you do not consider close friends? ______________________
> ______________________
> ______________________
> ______________________

Your answers to these questions should provide some insight into the role of friendship in your implicit personal theory of communication. Keep your answers in mind as you read the remainder of this section.

We form many different types of close relationships. Friendships are the broadest type of close relationship we form. We also form close romantic and marital relationships, and we may also have close relationships with members of our families. Let's begin our discussion of friendship by looking at the characteristics of friendships.

Characteristics of Friendships

***Friendships* are voluntary, informal, personal relationships involving equality among the participants, that are concerned mainly with sociability** (Allan, 1989). To begin, our friendships with others are voluntary. We are not forced to become friends with others. We choose when to become friends with others, and we choose when to end our friendships. Friendships are also informal in that there are no cultural rules telling us how to be close friends with others. The rules that develop in friendships are developed within the relationship and are unique to the particular relationship.

For us to become friends with others, our communication must take a personal focus. That is, we need to use personal information about other people to predict their behavior (Miller & Steinberg, 1975). Friendships also are relationships in which hierarchy and authority are irrelevant (Allan, 1989); friends are equal within the relationship. Friendships are concerned mainly with sociability. In other words, friends get together because they enjoy being with each other. Friends are central to our well-being in part because "above all we need friends to do things with, especially leisure activities, going out, and having fun" (Argyle & Henderson, 1985, p. 84). Friends also do favors for each other, but this is not the main purpose of the relationship. Individuals may engage in different activities and talk about different things with different friends.

Another characteristic of friendships is that they provide us with social support (Argyle & Henderson, 1985). Friends provide us with a sense of attachment and people with whom we can confide intimate information about ourselves. Friends provide the major source of social support for unmarried people, married people whose spouses are not supportive, adolescents, and older people who do not have relatives living in the area (Argyle & Henderson, 1985). The importance of friends as a source of social support is especially critical during life crises, such as a death in the family, and during life transitions, such as getting married or divorced. The characteristics of friendships are illustrated by the poem in Reading 13.1.

Reading 13.1 WILL YOU BE MY FRIEND?/JAMES KAVANAUGH

Will you be my friend?
There are so many reasons why you never should:
I'm sometimes sullen, often shy, acutely sensitive,
My fear erupts as anger, I find it hard to give,
I talk about myself when I'm afraid
And often spend a day without anything to say.
    But I will make you laugh
    And love you quite a bit
    And hold you when you're sad.
I cry a little almost every day
Because I'm more caring than the strangers ever know,
And, if at times, I show my tender side
(The soft and warmer part I hide)
    I wonder,
    Will you be my friend?
A friend
    Who far beyond the feebleness of any vow or tie
    Will touch the secret place where I am really I,
    To know the pain of lips that plead and eyes that weep,
    Who will not run away when you find me in the street
    Alone and lying mangled by my quota of defeats
    But will stop and stay—to tell me of another day
    When I was beautiful.

Will you be my friend?
There are so many reasons why you never should:
Often I'm too serious, seldom predictably the same,
Sometimes cold and distant, probably I'll always change.
I bluster and brag, seek attention like a child,
I brood and pout, my anger can be wild,
    But I will make you laugh
    And love you quite a bit
    And be near when you're afraid.
I shake a little almost every day
Because I'm more frightened than the strangers ever know
And if at times I show my trembling side
(The anxious, fearful part I hide)
    I wonder,
    Will you be my friend?

Reading 13.1 CONTINUED

A friend
    Who, when I fear your closeness, feels me push away
    And stubbornly will stay to share what's left on such a day,
    Who, when no one knows my name or calls me on the phone,
    When there's no concern for me—what I have or haven't done—
    And those I've helped and counted on have, oh so deftly, run,
Who, when there's nothing left but me, stripped of charm and subtlety,
Will nonetheless remain.

Will you be my friend?
    For no reason that I know
    Except I want you so.

Psychological Processes Underlying Friendships

The factors contributing to the formation of relationships discussed in the previous chapter all apply to the formation of friendships. To illustrate, we tend to form friendships with people who support our self-concepts and whose behavior is predictable. There are different explanations for why we remain friends with other people once our friendships are formed, however, that were not discussed in the previous chapter.

One explanation is based on the notion of social exchange (Thibaut & Kelley, 1959). In this view, we remain friends with people because our exchange of resources with them is equitable. The resources we exchange include services, social support, information, status, affection, and so forth. We provide resources to friends with the expectation that we will get something in return. We may, for example, help friends move and take care of their pets when they go on vacation. In exchange, they help us with our work and take us to interesting social gatherings. As long as the exchange of resources with others remains relatively equitable, our friendship continues.

An alternative explanation is based on the idea that friendships are communal relationships (Clark & Mills, 1979). From this perspective, friends do *not* do things for each other with the expectation of getting something in return. Rather, they do things for each other because they are concerned about each other's welfare. Friends, in this view, act unselfishly. People do not expect friends to reciprocate and do things for them. The things friends do for each other are noncomparable, and friends provide each other with benefits based on their perception of each other's needs.

Although the exchange and communal perspectives are different, we probably use both approaches in our friendships with others. Some of our friendships are based on exchange and some, on communal principles. Also, we differ as individuals. Some of us may tend to use exchange principles more than communal principles in our friendships, while

HAGAR THE HORRIBLE. Reprinted with special permission of King Features Syndicate.

others of us use communal principles more than exchange principles.

Communication in Close Friendships

Communication in interpersonal relationships involves various themes, such as immediacy/affection, depth, receptivity, composure, formality, task orientation, dominance, and equality (Burgoon & Hale, 1987).[1] These themes can be used to describe communication in close friendships.

Communication in our close friendships is characterized by a high degree of immediacy/affection. *Immediacy/affection* describes the extent to which we are involved in conversations, find our conversations stimulating, show enthusiasm and interest in our conversations, and are attracted to the other person. Close friendships also involve depth of communication. *Depth* refers to the extent we try to move our conversations to a deep level, indicate that we like the other person, and act like good friends. We also demonstrate a high degree of receptivity in close friendships. *Receptivity* occurs when we are sincere, show we are interested in talking, demonstrate that we are willing to listen, and indicate that we are open to the other person's ideas. We are composed in our interactions with close friends. *Composure* involves not feeling tense, being calm and poised, feeling relaxed when talking, and generally being comfortable in talking with the other person.

Our communication in close friendships also involves low levels of formality. Lack of *formality* involves focusing on informal, casual topics of conversation. Communication in close friendships is not *task oriented.* That is, we engage mostly in social conversations and are not highly task oriented with our friends. We do not try to *dominate* others in close friendships. We do not, for example, try to persuade others all of the time, try to gain our friends' approval, or try to get the upper hand in conversations. Finally, our close friend-

We turn to our friends in good and difficult times. By providing us with support and a sense of attachment, friendships central to our well-being.

ships involve *equality.* We consider each other as equals and cooperate with each other in close friendships.

Gender and Friendship

Gender differences in communication styles, discussed in Chapter 9, influence the ways that men and women communicate in friendships. Women tend to have a few intimate friends, while men tend to have larger, but less intense, friendship networks (Hendrick & Hendrick, 1992). Women tend to talk a great deal with their friends about their feelings and problems (Sherrod, 1989). Women's "talk with their close friends creates a mosaic of noncritical listening, mutual support, enhancement of self-worth, relationship exclusiveness, and personal growth and self-discovery" (Johnson & Aries, 1983, p. 353).

In contrast to women, men tend to engage in a large number of activities with their friends (Hendrick & Hendrick, 1992). The talk that men focus on in their friendships tends to revolve around sports, politics, and business (Sherrod, 1989). Men prefer less intimacy in their same-sex friendships than women, and "when the typical male does achieve a high level of intimacy with another man, he usually follows a different path than a woman, one that emphasizes activities and companionship over self-disclosure and expressiveness" (Sherrod, 1989, p. 175).

Romantic Relationships

Romantic relationships are close relationships involving love between the participants. Let's begin our discussion of romantic relationships by looking at how we conceive of our ideal romantic relationships.

Ideal Romantic Relationships

What we want from our ideal romantic relationships can be described by two dimensions: intimate versus superficial and romantic-traditional versus practical-nontraditional (Rusbult, Onizuka, & Lipkus, 1993). *Intimacy* in romantic relationships is associated with friendship, altruism, devotion, a shared life, mutual respect/admiration, and strong commitment. One woman describes her ideal relationship this way: "We'd be friends first and always. Our love would grow from knowing each other's faults, and being able to accept them. We would grow together. . . . We'd have arguments, but we'd be able to work them out by talking about them . . . we'd know one another so well" (Rusbult et al., 1993, p. 504). *Superficial* romantic relationships, in contrast, are nonegalitarian, not based on friendship, self-centered, and uncommitted. One man describes his preference for superficial romantic relations this way: "I really don't want a 'romantic' relationship. I'd prefer one-night stands myself" (p. 504).

The *romantic-traditional* ideal of romantic relationships emphasizes shared values, marriage, and the family (Rusbult et al., 1993). One woman describes her preferences like this: "We'd begin to spend more time together, and would have romantic dinners, go dancing, walk along quiet moonlit beaches. . . . We'd get married. . . . I'd continue my career until we had a child" (p. 507). *Practical-nontraditional* preferences, on the other hand, recognize that values will not be totally shared and emphasize "realistic" views. One woman puts it this way: "We would be able to talk about our problems together and still remain rational. We would wait until we completed our education before we got too involved. If the relationship were to end . . . we would be able to leave each other and still be friends" (p. 507).

By combining the two dimensions, four types of ideal romantic relationships can be isolated (Rusbult et al., 1993). In *superficial and romantic-traditional* ideal relationships, the relationship develops quickly and involves little intimacy, partners tend to follow traditional sex roles, friendship is not important, and the relationship is not based on respect/admiration. People who want this type of relationship are looking for passion, an exciting life, and glamorous activities. *Intimate and romantic-traditional* ideal relationships emphasize marriage and the family, traditional sex roles, a shared life, high intimacy, and strong commitment; sex is not a major factor in the relationship. *Superficial and practical-nontraditional* ideal relationships are characterized by little intimacy, little sharing, little commitment, and little family orientation; sex is a major factor in the relationship. The emphasis in these relationships is on attractiveness and possessions. *Intimate and practical-nontraditional* ideal relationships involve friendship, equality between partners, and respect and admiration between partners; the partners have a practical orientation toward each other.

There are sex differences in our preferences for different types of romantic relationships (Rusbult et al., 1993). Women tend to prefer more intimacy, shared lives, commitment, devotion, friendship, and emphasis on marriage and the family than men. The only factor that men emphasize more than women is sex.

Types of Love in Romantic Relationships

Friendships tend to be based on liking, while romantic relationships tend to be based on love (Berscheid & Walster, 1974). When our relationships are based on liking, we are aware that the actual rewards we receive from the other person are important. In our love relationships, on the other hand, we often think that we are receiving rewards out of proportion to their actual occurrence. Liking tends to increase over time, but love appears to become diluted over time. While we associate liking with positive outcomes, we associate love with conflicting outcomes. Love often involves both pleasure and pain, ecstasy and despair. One reason for this is that there are two types of love.

Passionate love involves the intense emotions we experience when we "fall in love." It includes the physical symptoms we may have when we are with the person we love: pounding heart, dry mouth, and so forth. Two conditions must be met for us to see ourselves as having passionate love for another person (Berscheid & Walster, 1974). First, we must be aroused physiologically. Second, we must think that passionate love is an appropriate label for our feelings in the situation. Although passionate love is important in our initial attraction to others, it cannot sustain a relationship over a long period of time.

Companionate love is "the affection we feel for those with whom our lives are deeply intertwined" (Walster & Walster, 1978, p. 9). If we have a sufficient number of positive experiences and shared activities with our romantic partners, companionate love can provide the foundation for the long-term success of our relationship. The development of companionate love requires that other people's behavior be predictable and that our uncertainty is below our maximum threshold. Engaged couples tend to define love in terms of companionate love; that is, they define it in terms of affection, companionship, mutual support, sharing, and understanding (Baum, 1972).

For North American romantic relationships to be enjoyable, interesting, and able to survive over long periods of time, some combination of passionate and companionate love is necessary:

> The secret that each couple needs to discover is (1) how to steadily build the solid virtues of companionship (2) without the loss of the ability to periodically refuel the fires of passion. The secret is far from easily discovered. There is no answer to this dilemma at present other than common sense suggestions, such as varying routines, seeking out exciting environments together, programming in ample romance time, and so on. (Hendrick & Hendrick, 1992, p. 93)

A wide range of factors in how couples structure their day-to-day behavior influences the outcomes of marriages (Whyte, 1990). Sharing power and decision making, enjoying similar leisure activities, and having mutual friends, for example, tend to be associated with successful marriages. Reading 13.2 provides an opportunity for you to test your knowledge of love and romance. Take a moment to read it before continuing.

The Triangular Theory of Love

The triangular theory of love is based on three components: intimacy, passion, and commit-

Reading 13.2 On Love, Romance and the Sexes/Dr. Joyce Brothers

How alike are men and women when it comes to love and romance? Here's a chance to test your views with those of some experts. [Answer true or false.]

1. Women today are just as likely to be adulterous as men.
2. Females are basically much more romantic than males.
3. The more secure a person is, the more likely the individual is to fall in love quickly and often.
4. Those who are relatively poor are much more likely to have sex for money.
5. It's easier for people to fall in love when they feel the attraction is reciprocal.
6. Passionate love brings with it intimacy and strong commitment.
7. Most males don't enjoy caressing and could do without foreplay, so in this sense, they're much less romantic than females.
8. Women, unlike men, seem to feel more confident and secure when they value and have intimacy in their lives.

ANSWERS:

1. FALSE. Although women are more apt to have extramarital affairs today than in the past, men are still much more likely to engage in infidelity.
2. FALSE. Males fall in love faster. Whereas females are likely to be more pragmatic, it's the male who is more romantic and starry-eyed about love.
3. FALSE. Those who are insecure, anxious and lonely tend to fall in love faster than those who are secure and self-confident; however, secure, self-confident people tend to have happier, longer-lasting relationships once they do fall in love.
4. FALSE. In their book, "The Janus Report on Sexual Behavior," Drs. Samuel and Cynthia Janus write that it's the middle-income group that is most likely to exchange money for sex.
5. TRUE. According to Arthur Aron, professor of psychology at UC Santa Cruz, the perception of being liked ranked just as high as the partner's having desirable characteristics.
6. FALSE. Not necessarily. Yale University psychologist Robert Sternberg says that although the fullest love requires passion, intimacy and commitment, those elements don't necessarily come at the same time. Passion, he adds, is the quickest to develop and the quickest to fade. Intimacy develops much more slowly, and commitment even more slowly.
7. FALSE. Studies show that males also enjoy caressing, kissing, hugging, tender touch and foreplay.
8. FALSE. Dan McAdams, a psychologist at Loyola University, says that "men who value and have intimacy more feel a secure emotional base in life." Women, too, he points out, tend to feel more confident when they have a secure relationship, but the effect tends to be stronger for men.

If you answered six of the eight questions correctly, you're better informed than most.

ment (Sternberg, 1986). *Intimacy* involves the feelings of closeness and support that we receive from our romantic partners. There are two types of intimacy: manifest and latent. Manifest intimacy involves talking about intimate things, while latent intimacy refers to nonverbal forms of intimacy. *Passion* refers to our physiological arousal and desire to be united with our romantic partner. *Commitment* includes a short-term decision to love our romantic partner and a long-term decision to maintain the relationship.

Based on these three components, eight types of relationships can be formed (Sternberg, 1986). *Nonlove* is a relationship in which the three components are low or totally absent. This combination characterizes the vast majority of our relationships with others. *Liking* occurs when intimacy is high, while commitment and passion are low or absent. This occurs in relationships when people are just getting to know each other. *Infatuation* involves high levels of passion, while commitment and intimacy are low or absent. This type of love may take place in "one-night stands." *Empty love* occurs when commitment is high, while passion and intimacy are low or absent. This form of love occurs in marriages in which the couple decides to stay together for the sake of the children. *Romantic love* involves high levels of intimacy and passion, but commitment is low or absent. Short-term dating relationships and brief affairs often involve this type of love. *Fatuous love* occurs when there are high levels of commitment and passion, but intimacy is low or absent. This form of love might occur when people meet and get married in a very short period so that intimacy has not had a chance to develop. *Companionate love* involves high levels of commitment and intimacy, but passion is low or absent. A romantic relationship in which the partners have lost their attraction for each other is an example of this type of love. A long-term friendship also could be based on companionate love. *Consummate love* involves high levels of passion, intimacy, and commitment. This type is the ideal toward which many romantic couples strive. It is, however, both difficult to achieve and difficult to maintain over time.

You'll note that, while this is a theory of "love," other types of relationships can be explained using the three dimensions (intimacy, passion, and commitment). Often, we may not recognize love being present when we think of the other person as a friend. As romantic relationships become closer, there is a general tendency for commitment to increase and for passion and manifest intimacy to decrease (latent intimacy, however, will increase) (Sternberg, 1986).

The triangular theory of love has been examined in China. Generally, the theory appears to generalize across cultures, but there are some cultural differences (Gao, 1993). There is more passion in romantic relationships in the United States than in China, but levels of commitment and intimacy are similar in the two cultures. One explanation for this is that attraction and passion are not the main criteria for the selection of romantic partners in collectivistic cultures, while they are critical for the selection of romantic partners in individualistic cultures like the United States (Dion & Dion, 1988). Attraction in collectivistic cultures often is based on how well the other person will fit into individuals' ingroups, such as families.

Marital Relationships

One of the major tasks with which couples must deal when they get married is redefining the views of the world they bring with them and constructing a new, jointly shared view of the world (Berger & Kellner, 1964). The

An ideal romantic relationships is also an equal partnership. A successful marriage in the United States includes sharing power and decision making, enjoying similar leisure activities, and having mutual friends.

way couples develop this new view of the world is affected by how they communicate. Developing a shared view of the world has become more difficult for marital partners in recent years because there are additional demands on marital relationships that were not present in earlier times. Because of these demands, "spouses are now asked to be lovers, friends, mutual therapists in a society which is forcing the marital bond to become the closest, deepest, most important and most enduring relationship of one's life" (Slater, 1968, p. 99). The societal demands affect couples differently, so couples do not use the same approaches to developing joint views of the world. Let's begin the discussion of marital relationships by looking at the various ways couples can develop a jointly shared view of their relationship.

Types of Couples

Marital couples can be divided into three broad types with respect to views of their relationships: traditionals, independents, and separates (Fitzpatrick, 1988).[2] Spouses in *traditional* marriages hold conventional values about relationships. These conventional values focus on stability in the relationship (as opposed to spontaneity), the idea that the wife should take the husband's name after marriage, and that infidelity is always wrong. Spouses in traditional marriages are highly interdependent. They engage in a high degree of sharing and view companionship as important. They also tend to follow regular daily schedules. Although spouses in traditional couples are not highly assertive, they do not avoid conflict.

Spouses in *independent* marriages hold nonconventional values regarding relationships. They tend to believe that marriage should not constrain the individual spouse's autonomy. While spouses in independent marriages engage in sharing and companionship, they also maintain independent space to control access. People in independent relationships do not follow regular daily schedules. Like spouses in traditional marriages, spouses in independent marriages do not avoid conflict.

Spouses in *separate* marriages hold opposing values with respect to relationships. Like traditionals, separates hold conventional values regarding marriage and the family. Also, like independents, separates believe that individual freedom is more important than maintaining the marriage. Separates may state one set of values in public and behave differently in private. There is less sharing and companionship in separate couples than in either traditional or independent couples. Separates are interdependent by maintaining regular daily schedules. Although spouses in separate marriages try to persuade their partners, they avoid conflict.

Spouses in a marriage can see their relationship in the same way or differently. When they see the marriage in the same way, the couple falls into one of the three types described here. *None* of the types of marriage is better than the others. They are just different ways of viewing marriage. When spouses do not see their relationship in the same way, they are a "mixed type." To illustrate, a traditional husband and a separate wife are a mixed couple. Spouses in mixed couples disagree on major issues in their relationships. The disagreement can cause problems in marriages, especially when children are born.

Spouses in the three different types of couples differ in their gender attitudes (Fitzpatrick, 1988). Those in traditional, separate, and mixed traditional/separate marriages hold conventional gender attitudes, such as a division of labor in the home. Spouses in independent marriages, in contrast, hold attitudes of male and female equality.

Couple type affects the communication that occurs within a marriage (Fitzpatrick, 1988). Traditional couples, for example, engage in a moderate amount of self-disclosure and balance openness with protecting themselves. Traditionalists focus on both their emotions and their thoughts/opinions during marital conversations. They also tend to interpret their spouses' experiences, such as "You've been too busy lately," in their conversations. Independents, in contrast, engage in high levels of self-disclosure. They are expressive and open in their conversations. Independents also tend to use messages that confirm and acknowledge their spouses in everyday conversations. Separates do not engage in high levels of self-disclosure and are not likely to express their feelings. Rather, they tend to use questions, statements of opinion, and giving their spouses advice when they communicate.

Marital Satisfaction and Communication

The degree to which marital partners are satisfied with their relationships is partially a function of the rewards they receive from the marriage. There are many different types of rewards that can contribute to marital satisfaction. Spousal warmth, for example, provides rewards and leads to marital satisfaction (Lorenz et al., 1991). Perceiving that there is equity in the rewards that are exchanged is necessary for partners to be satisfied (Adams, 1965).

Many other factors also contribute to marital satisfaction. Feeling understood by their spouse, for example, facilitates partners' marital satisfaction (Allen & Thompson, 1984). Perceiving that their partners are emotionally expressive (King, 1993) and receiving companionship from their spouse (Berry & Williams, 1987) also lead to marital satisfaction. Similarly, people who are personally committed to their partners are more satisfied with their marriages than people who are not committed to their partners (Rusbult, 1983).

The communication that takes place within a marital relationship affects the degree of satisfaction. The ability to reduce uncertainty about each other's behavior, for example, is related to marital satisfaction (Gottman, 1979). Self-disclosure also is related to marital satisfaction (Gilbert, 1976). Negative and rigid communication patterns (Gilbert, 1976), and dominating communication messages (Millar & Rogers, 1987) are associated with marital dissatisfaction.

Violations of relational expectations are related to marital satisfaction (Kelley & Burgoon, 1991). Partners who perceive that their spouses positively violate their relational expectations are more satisfied than those who perceive that their spouses negatively violate their expectations. To illustrate, partners who perceive that their spouses are more intimate than they expect them to be are more satisfied than partners who perceive that their spouses are less intimate than they expect them to be.

The amount of satisfaction in marital relationships also affects the nature of communication that takes place between the spouses. People in distressed marriages, for example, have more trouble interpreting their spouses' nonverbal behavior than they have interpreting the nonverbal behavior of people they do not know (Noller, 1984). Partners in unhappy marriages are more direct and more intense in communicating negative information to their spouses than partners in happy marriages (Noller, 1985). Partners in unhappy marriages use more redundant communication messages than partners in happy marriages (Ting-Toomey, 1983). Partners in unhappy marriages attack their partners more and are more defensive than partners in happy marriages. Partners in happy marriages, in contrast, transmit more concerning messages and are more flexible than partners in unhappy marriages.

Spouses in distressed marriages reciprocate each other's negative feelings more than partners in nondistressed marriages (Gottman, Markman, & Notarius, 1977). Partners in nondistressed marriages, in contrast, do not necessarily reciprocate negative affect when they receive these types of messages from their spouses. Partners in distressed marriages are more likely to escalate conflict that occurs than are partners in nondistressed marriages. Further, when explaining their spouses' behavior, partners in distressed marriages tend to focus on perceived personality defects of their spouses and overlook situational explanations for their spouses' behavior (Orvis, Kelley, & Butler, 1976).

The nonverbal communication between couples also is affected by satisfaction. To illustrate, in comparison to couples with high levels of disagreement, couples with low levels of disagreement "sat closer together, looked at each other more frequently and for a longer period of time, touched each other more often, touched themselves less often and held their legs in a more open position" (Beier & Sternberg, 1977, p. 96). The ability to encode and decode messages also affects satisfaction. Husbands who can easily understand their wives' nonverbal cues, for example, are satisfied with their marriages (Sabatelli, Buck, & Dreyer, 1982). Wives who are skilled at interpreting their husbands' nonverbal messages also are satisfied with their relationships.

Themes in Marital Communication

The verbal communication that takes place in marital relationships falls into three general themes: communal, individual, and impersonal (Sillars et al., 1987). The first theme, the *communal* aspects of the relationship, involves the exchange of messages reflecting that the marriage is a product of the interdependent qualities of the spouses. Communality is indicated when people talk about togetherness ("We enjoy being together"), cooperation ("We need to cooperate to get things done"), the nature of their communication ("I feel better when we talk things out"), and their mutual influence on each other ("It makes things worse if I get upset when you're upset").

The second theme in marital conversations involves *individuality* (Sillars et al., 1987). Communication based on this theme expresses the idea that the marriage is a function of the spouses' separate roles or identities. This theme is expressed when spouses talk about their separateness ("I need to spend time being alone"), their individual personalities ("I'm quiet and you're talkative"), or their roles ("You have your jobs around the house and I have mine").

The third theme in marital communication involves the discussion of *impersonal* topics (Sillars et al., 1987). Impersonal topics deal with how the relationship is affected by forces outside the control of the individual partners. The forces may be qualities intrinsic to people in general ("Women are more affectionate than men"), external stress or responsibilities ("I have to get this book done this week"), and indifference to pleasure or pain ("We just don't worry about the future").

The themes that predominate between marital couples is a function of the level of satisfaction and the couple type. Couples who are more interdependent (traditionals) and who are satisfied with their relationship tend to devote more of their communication to communal themes than to individuality and impersonal themes (Sillars et al., 1987). Autonomous types (independents, separates) and couples who are dissatisfied, in contrast, tend to focus on individuality and impersonal themes when they communicate (Sillars et al., 1992).

Family Relationships

Communication with family members is different in at least one major way from communication in other types of interpersonal relationships—family relationships are not voluntary. Families are systems (see Chapter 1) in which each member's communication influences all other family members' communication. The way our families communicate influences how we communicate with people outside of our families. We learn much of our communication in our family of origin. It is in the family of origin that a child

> observes the environment he [or she] inhabits, partakes of its ambiance. He [or she] forms values and beliefs; develops assumptions about how marriages and families are and should be; learns about life cycle, including how to handle changes of maturation and of aging and death. He [or she] learns about power and control and about the consequences of emotions, both his [or her] own and others. He [or she] is schooled in patterns of communication; what role to take in triangles; how to handle secrets; how to respond to pressure. (Kramer, 1985, p. 9)

In our families, we learn about things that are acceptable to discuss, how we can talk about these things, and to whom we can talk about these things (Satir, 1988). How we communicate in our families depends on the type of family we have. Let's therefore begin by looking at the types of families that exist.

Types of Families

There are two primary functions of any family: developing some degree of family cohesion and developing some degree of adaptability. Functions, in this sense, are the things systems need to do in order not to break down (Galvin & Brommel, 1991). *Family cohesion* is "the emotional bonding that family members have toward one another" (Olson & McCubbin, 1983, p. 48). *Family adaptability* is "the ability of a marital or family system to change its power structure, role relationships, and relationship rules in response to situational and developmental stress" (p. 48). These two functions can be used to define various family types. Prior to defining the family types, however, it is necessary to look at cohesion and adaptability in more detail.

There are four levels of cohesion that can exist in a family: disengaged (very low cohesion), separated (low to moderate cohesion), connected (moderate to high cohesion), and enmeshed (very high cohesion). Neither very high levels nor very low levels of cohesion are highly functional for family communication (Olson & McCubbin, 1983). When cohesion is very high, there is overidentification with the family, and individual family members' autonomy is severely restricted. When cohesion is very low, family members "do their own thing," and there is little sense of family.

The idea that neither extremely high nor extremely low levels of cohesion are desirable is consistent with the discussion of the autonomy-connection dialectic in Chapter 12. For relationships to develop, some balance must be found between autonomy and connection. The balance in a family comes when cohesion is in the middle range (separated and connected in Figure 13.1 below). Although extreme levels of family cohesion are not functional on a day-to-day basis, they occur

FIGURE 13.1 Types of Families. Source: Reprinted from Olson, D., & McCubbin, H., *Families: What makes them work.* Copyright © 1983 Sage Publications. Used with permission.

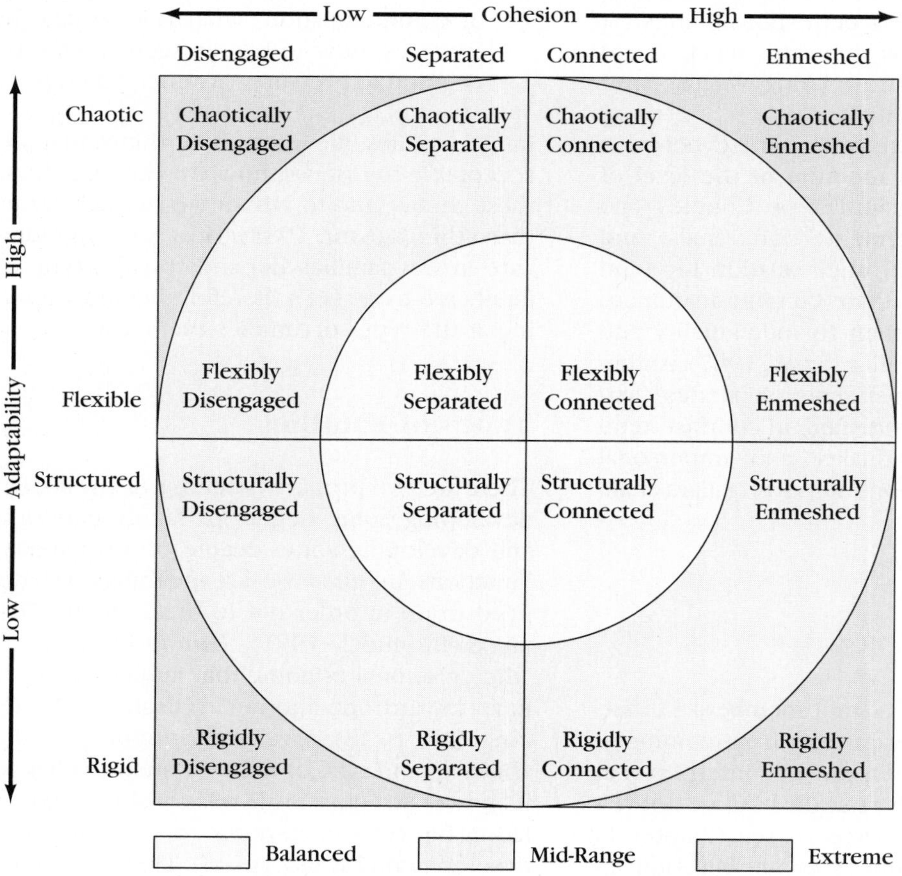

naturally when there is a need. To illustrate, families with moderate cohesiveness tend to become highly cohesive when a family member dies but return to their normal level after the crisis is over.

Four levels of adaptability are possible in families: rigid (very low adaptability), structured (low to moderate adaptability), flexible (moderate to high adaptability), and chaotic (very high adaptability). Like cohesion, neither high nor low levels of adaptability are desirable. When adaptability is very low, families cannot adapt to stress or to changes in the environment. As children grow from infancy to adolescence, for example, the families need to be able to adapt to the children's changing needs. When adaptability is too high, family members are not sure how they are expected to behave. When families are always adapting, life is chaotic.

Although the extremes of adaptability are not functional on a day-to-day basis, families that are in the middle may shift to the extreme from time to time. When families move from one city to another, for example, high levels of adaptability are needed. Families with a moderate level of adaptability may become highly adaptable after the move and then return to their normal level after they have adapted to the new place.

Communication is critical to movement along the two dimensions. Cohesion develops through communication, and the nature of the messages being transmitted affects the level of cohesion in the family. If family members never talk about personal feelings, for example, it is impossible to develop high levels of cohesion. Communication also is critical if families are going to adapt, because "any effective adaptation relies on shared meanings gained through the family message system. Through communication, families make it clear to their members how much adaptation is allowed within the system" (Galvin & Brommel, 1991, p. 22).

When the four types of cohesion and the four types of adaptability are combined, 16 different family types are possible. These types are diagrammed in Figure 13.1. The sixteen types can be combined into three broad clusters. Balanced families are those that fall in the middle on both cohesion and adaptability. Mid-range families fall in the middle on one dimension, but are extreme on the other dimension. Extreme families are extreme on both dimensions.

Before proceeding, think about where your family falls in Figure 13.1. You can get a rough idea by asking yourself two questions: How cohesive is your family: very low cohesion, low to moderate cohesion, moderate to high cohesion, or very highly cohesive? and How adaptive is your family?: very low adaptability, low to moderate adaptability, moderate to high adaptability, or very highly adaptable? Combine your two answers to see where your family falls on Figure 13.1.

In comparison to the other family types, balanced families function better and have more resources for dealing with stress (Olson & McCubbin, 1983). **Balanced families function well in day-to-day life and are able to respond to stressful situations by becoming more adaptable and cohesive when necessary.** Extreme families, in contrast, may not function well in day-to-day life, because extremely high or extremely low levels of cohesiveness and adaptability inhibit effective communication. Members of balanced families are more satisfied with their marriages, families, and lives in general than are members of the other types of families. Members of balanced families also use more effective communication and fewer ineffective communication skills than members of other family types. Effective communication skills include "sending clear congruent messages, empathy, supportive statements, and effective problem-solving skills" (Olson & McCubbin, 1983, p. 68). Ineffective communication skills, in contrast, include "sending incongruent and disqualifying messages, lack of empathy, nonsupportive (negative) statements, poor problem-solving skills, and paradoxical and double-binding messages" (p. 68).

The way we communicate influences the type of family we have. One person can change the type of communication that occurs in a relationship. This suggests that, if we begin to communicate with members of our families in ways that facilitate the development of balanced family structures, such as using the effective communication skills discussed earlier and using the communication resources presented in this book, other members of our family will change the way they communicate with us. This will not happen overnight, but if we change the way we communicate, it will affect the way our family members communicate with us. We also can use this model to guide the way we structure our new families when we leave our families of origin (the families in which we were raised).

Family Systems

As pointed out in Chapters 1 and 6, families are communication systems. Like all communication systems, families are interdependent, form a whole that is different from its parts, are open to some degree, and adapt to their environments. This is true whether or not the members of the family are related by marriage. In order to understand our interdependence with other family members, we have to understand how our behavior is intertwined with other family members and is a function of our family history. A family, for example, can be viewed as a mobile hanging from a hook; when one part moves, all other parts have to move and adjust to the first part's movement (Satir, 1988). Changes in the family lead to changes in the individual members.

To understand the behavior of any particular family member, we must understand the whole family, because "communication patterns between or among family members emerge as a result of this 'wholeness.' Conflict or affection may become an inherent part of communication between various members. A certain cue may trigger patterns of behavior without members' awareness" (Galvin & Brommel, 1991, p. 37). Families also are open and adapt to their environments. The environments to which families must adapt include

Family cohesion is "the emotional bonding that family members have toward one another." The family should exist with a moderate level of cohesion to be highly functional.

DRABBLE reprinted by permission of UFS, Inc.

the community in which they live and educational, legal, political, and economic systems, to name only a few.

Recognizing that families are systems is critical for understanding the communication that occurs and for improving communication in families. Recognizing the systemic nature of families forces us to recognize that no family member's behavior occurs in a vacuum, that our relationships with other family members both cause and affect our behavior, and that communication in our families is guided by rules of which we may not be aware (see next section; Galvin & Brommel, 1991). Recognizing that family communication is a system also provides us with a way to improve our communication in our families:

> Becoming aware of their system usually opens the way for family members to become searchers and to stop berating themselves and others when things go wrong. People can ask "how" questions instead of "why" questions. Generally speaking "how" questions lead to information and understanding, and "why" questions imply blame and so produce defensiveness. (Satir, 1988, p. 136)

Recognizing how our behavior is part of a family system, therefore, can help us understand our interaction with family members and thereby improve the quality of our communication.

Family Communication Rules

We learn the communication rules in our families in the same way we learn the communication rules of our culture: through repeated interactions (Galvin & Brommel, 1991). We can, however, negotiate specific rules with members of our families. Many of the rules in our families can be traced back to our parents' families of origin. The rules in our parents' families of origin, however, may have been different. Our father, for example, may have come from a family that used the rule "When you are angry, be quiet and do not say anything," while our mother might have come from a family that used the rule "When you are angry, yell at the person with whom you are angry." These different rules may create problems in our parents' marriage unless they recognize the different rules and negotiate a new rule that they use in their own marriage. If our parents negotiate a new rule, we learn that rule as we are raised in the family. If our parents do not negotiate new rules, we probably learn the rule that the same-sex parent uses.

As indicated earlier, there are three types of rules about communication in our families: what things are acceptable for us to discuss, how we can talk about these things, and to whom we can talk about them (Satir, 1988). The communication rules in our families tell us whether it is okay to talk about feelings, money, drugs, health problems, sex, a family member's weird behavior, and so forth. Most families have rules about what can and cannot be discussed (Galvin & Brommel, 1991). There also are rules about how we talk about the various topics we can discuss. These rules tell us whether we should be direct or indirect, how we should tell others bad news, how we should express our anger, and when we can talk to whom (when it is okay to talk to father). Finally, there are rules for whom we can tell what. Children, for example, may not be told about a parent's health problems. There may be topics that are limited to only family members, or some topics from which specific family members may be excluded.

There are a large number of rules in any family. Consider the following rules one woman isolated in her family:

> Don't talk back to Dad unless he's in a good mood.
>
> When Mother is hassled, don't discuss school problems.
>
> Tell the truth at all times unless it involves a happy surprise.
>
> Do not fight except with Mom about your appearance.
>
> Don't talk about the family's worth outside the family.
>
> Do not discuss politics or religion.
>
> Do not discuss sex.
>
> Don't ask Sally about her boyfriend.
>
> Kiss Mom when coming and going. Kiss Dad at night.
>
> Share feelings with Mom.
>
> Don't talk about Granddad's two remarriages.
>
> Never mention Aunt Bea's cancer.
>
> Tim's hearing problem is not to be discussed.
>
> Family deaths are discussed only in terms of religion.
>
> Mother's pregnancy at marriage is not admitted. (Galvin & Brommel, 1991, p. 65)

When we do not understand the rules used in our families, we follow them when we communicate on automatic pilot. To the extent that we understand the rules of our families, we can choose whether to follow them.

Before proceeding, think about the rules used in your family. Keep in mind that you know the rules because you follow them, but you may not be highly aware of what they are. Try to list as many rules as you can:

____

____

____

____

____

These rules are part of your implicit theory of communication.

Are there any of the rules you listed that you do not like following or that you think create communication problems in your family? Is there something you can do to renegotiate the rules in your family? It is important to keep in mind that you will carry these rules on to your next family when you marry or live with a romantic partner. If you are mindful, however, you can choose which rules you want to use in your new family and which rules you want to modify.

SUMMARY

The closeness of our relationships with others is a function of the amount of interdependence we have with them. We are interdependendent with other people when we interact with them frequently, when we do a variety of activities with them, and when we influence each other.

Friendships are voluntary relationships that involve informal personalized interaction among equals. Women tend to have a few intimate friends, while men tend to have large networks with low levels of intimacy. Friendships often involve companionate love, the affection we have for people with whom we are close.

Romantic relationships differ from friendships in that they are formed on the basis of passionate love. Passionate love, however, is not a sufficient base on which to build healthy, long term relationships. For high quality romantic relationships in the United States to exist for a long period of time both companionate and passionate love are needed.

Marital relationships can be characterized as one of three types: traditionals, separates, and independents. Partners in traditional marriages are highly interdependent, while partners in independent and separate marriages are not highly interdependent. The type of marriage a couple has affects the ways that they communicate. The way marital partners communicate affects their satisfaction with the marriage. Three themes tend to explain couples communication: communal, individual, and impersonal. Partners who are satisfied with their marriages tend to discuss communal themes more than partners who are not satisfied.

Relationships with members of our families differ from other interpersonal relationships in that they are not voluntary. Families are systems and the interdependence among the family members affects their communication within the system. All families have rules guiding how members communicate, when they communicate, where they communicate, with whom they communicate, and what they communicate.

Journal Reflections

1. *Communication in Close Friendships.* Over the next week, monitor your communication in your close friendships. What do you discuss with your friends? Do you talk about different things with different close friends (or do different things with different friends)? Are you satisfied with the way you communicate with your friends? Why or why not? If you're not satisfied, what do you want to do to improve the quality of your communication? Write your responses to these questions in your journal.
2. *Communication in Romantic, Marital, or Family Relationships.* Over the next week, monitor your communication in a romantic, marital, or family relationship. What do you discuss with this person? Do you talk about different things (or do different things) with this person than you do with other people? Are you satisfied with the way you communicate in this relationship? Why or why not? If you're not satisfied, what do you want to do to improve the quality of your communication? Write your responses to these questions in your journal.

Notes

1. The dimensions discussed in this section are derived from Burgoon and Hale (1987), but the conclusions regarding communication in close friendships are ours.
2. The research presented in this section on the various couple types was conducted by Fitzpatrick and her associates. It is reported in Fitzpatrick (1988), which contains the original citations.

Study Questions

1. Why is interdependence a useful way of defining the closeness of our relationships?
2. What are the characteristics of friendships?

3. How does communication in close friendships differ for males and females?
4. How can we explain the differences in our ideal romantic relationships?
5. What is the difference between passionate and companionate love?
6. What are the components of the triangular theory of love? How does the combination of these components lead to different types of relationships?
7. Why is communication different in the different types of marital relationships (traditional, independent, and separate)?
8. How does communication affect marital satisfaction?
9. How does marital satisfaction influence couple communication?
10. What are the major themes of communication in marital relationships?
11. How does the family system influence the way you communicate?
12. How do the rules of communication in your family of origin influence your communication with your current (or a past) romantic partner?
13. Why are cohesion and adaptability important in explaining family communication?

Suggested Readings

Allan, G. (1989). *Friendship.* Boulder: Westview. Graham Allan provides an overview of friendships. He examines factors that contribute to the development of friendships, gender differences in friendships, friendship in old age, and the role of friendships when we experience crises.

Blumstein, P., & Schwartz, P. (1983). *American couples.* New York: William Morrow. Philip Blumstein and Pepper Schwartz report a nationwide survey of American couples. The focus of the book is on the way couples deal with money, work, and sex. The authors include data from all different types of couples, including heterosexual and homosexual couples, as well as cohabiting and married couples.

Fitzpatrick, M. A. (1988). *Between husbands and wives.* Newbury Park, CA: Sage. Mary Ann Fitzpatrick summarizes the research she has conducted on the different types of married couples. She describes the couple types in detail and analyzes how partners in the various types of marriages communicate differently.

Galvin, K., & Brommel, B. (1991). *Family communication: Cohesion and change* (3rd ed.), New York: Harper Collins. This is a widely used introduction to family communication. Kathleen Galvin and Bernard Brommel discuss family dynamics, how meaning is created in the family, how intimacy is created in the family, family decision making, family conflict, and family stress.

Hendrick, S., & Hendrick, C. (1992). *Liking, loving, and relating* (2nd ed.), Belmont, CA: Brooks/Cole. In this book, Susan Hendrick and Clyde Hendrick discuss how we relate to each other in close relationships. They provide an excellent overview of the love, courtship, and marital interactions.

14

Maintaining and Rejuvenating Relationships

Communication is central to maintaining and rejuvenating our relationships with others. There are at least two ways that our communication with our romantic partners, friends, or co-workers influences the maintenance and rejuvenation of our relationships (Duck, in press). First, we engage in strategic planning regarding our relationships. Our strategic planning, however, tends to focus on how to change and transform our relationships with others, not maintain them. Second, our routine everyday communication with our relational partners makes our relationships what they are. The way we communicate with our partners defines the nature of the relationships and creates our reality within the relationships.

Communicating effectively in our everyday encounters can help us maintain quality relationships. If there are problems in our relationships, there are things we can do strategically to transform and rejuvenate our relationships with others. Let's begin by looking at general issues of what is involved in maintaining our relationships.

Maintaining Interpersonal Relationships

There are four ways we tend to think about relationship maintenance (Dindia & Canary, 1993). First, we may view the maintenance of our relationships as "sustaining the existence of the relationship" (Duck, 1988). If we take this view, the relationship is maintained as long as it continues to exist. Second, we may define maintaining our relationships as keeping them in a particular condition. Generally, this means maintaining a certain level of intimacy (Ayres, 1983). Third, we may view maintaining our relationships as keeping them in a satisfactory condition. In this view, we are maintaining our relationships if we are satisfied with them. Fourth, we may define maintaining our relationships as keeping them in "repair." Repair, however, has slightly different connotations than the other views of maintenance in that it suggests that we want to change or fix the state of the relationship. Repair of relationships, therefore, is discussed in the next section of this chapter. The first three ways of defining the maintenance of our relationships are examined in this section. Let's begin by looking at the role of communication in sustaining our relationships.

The Role of Communication in Sustaining Relationships

Different people tend to make different assumptions about how their relationships with others are held together (Duck, 1992). Before proceeding, think about the role communication plays in how you maintain your relationships with others. Answer the following questions:

> Why is communication important or unimportant in maintaining your interpersonal relationships? ______________________
> ____________________________________
> ____________________________________

> When there are problems in your relationships, what is the role of communication in dealing with these problems? ________
> ____________________________________
> ____________________________________

Your answers to these questions should provide insight into the role of relationship maintenance in your implicit personal theory of communication. Keep your answers to these questions in mind as you read the remainder of this section.

Some people assume that their relationships will fall apart unless they do something to hold them together. Other people assume that their relationships will be held together naturally unless something pulls them apart. There is probably some truth in each of these assumptions, but there is more that unconsciously keeps our relationships together than most people tend to think there is (Duck, in press). **The routine behaviors in which we engage every day bind us to others and create the reality of our relationships** (Berger & Kellner, 1964). Once our relationships are established, we tend to take them for granted.

Our conversations with others create meaning for us, and this meaning sustains our relationships with them (Duck, in press). The meaning created through our verbal and nonverbal communication with others indicates

Effective communication in our relationships helps us maintain our relationships.

to us that we have a relationship. The act of communicating is more important than the specific topics of our conversations with others in terms of maintaining a relationship (Duck et al., 1991). While much of our everyday conversation is trivial, it is still important to maintaining our relationships. The trivial talk in which we engage in our interpersonal relationships reinforces our relationships with others and allows us to maintain our relationships with them (Duck, in press).

We do not necessarily maintain our relationships in a state of equilibrium or balance. We may want to maintain a steady state in our relationships with others and ignore information from our partners suggesting change, but there are tensions for change in any relationship. As you will recall from Chapter 12, for example, as we move closer to others and make connections with them, we must also deal with our need for autonomy. As we try to balance the autonomy-connection, openness-closedness, and predictability-novelty dialectics in our everyday communication, there is pressure on the relationship to change.

Our everyday communication is critical to maintaining our relationships with others. There are many aspects of our everyday communication that we can change to increase the quality of our relationships. Let's begin by looking at what contributes to our communication satisfaction in our relationships.

Communication Satisfaction

The third view of maintaining relationships discussed earlier involves the degree to which we are satisfied with other people's communication with us and the degree to which others are satisfied with our communication with them. *Satisfying communication* is our emotional reaction to our communication that "is both successful and expectation fulfilling" (Hecht, 1984, p. 201). Before continuing, think about what factors influence your satisfaction with communication in interpersonal relationships. Take a few minutes to answer the following questions before you read further:

> What do you do or say in conversations that leads you to be satisfied with your communication? ______________________
> ______________________________________
> ______________________________________

> What do you do or say in conversations that leads you to be dissatisfied with your communication with others? ____________
> ______________________________________
> ______________________________________

> What do others do or say in conversations that leads you to be satisfied with your communication with them? ____________
> ______________________________________
> ______________________________________

> What do others do or say in conversations that leads you to be dissatisfied with your communication with them? ____________
> ______________________________________
> ______________________________________

Your answers to these questions should provide insight into the role of satisfaction in your implicit personal theory of communication. Keep your answers to these questions in mind as you read the remainder of this section.

Communication Satisfaction in Interpersonal Relationships. The way we communicate and the way other people communicate with us affects our satisfaction

The routine behaviors in which we engage every day bind us to others and create the reality of our relationships.

(Hecht, 1978).[1] In satisfying conversations, other people express interest in what we have to say, indicate that they want to get to know us, indicate that they understand what we say, and let us know we are communicating effectively. In satisfying conversations, we are able to present ourselves to other people as we want other people to view us, we get to say what we want to say, and we talk about things in which we are interested. In addition, in satisfying conversations, we enjoy the interaction, the interaction flows smoothly, and other people contribute a lot to the interaction. Our expectations for how we accomplish these outcomes in conversations depends on the person with whom we are communicating. To illustrate, we have different expectations for communication in our interactions with our lovers, family members, friends, acquaintances, and strangers. We also have different criteria for successful communication in these different types of relationships.

Assessment 14.1 contains a questionnaire designed to help you assess your satisfaction with communication in a particular relationship. Take a few minutes to complete it now.

Scores on Assessment 14.1 range from 10 to 50. The higher your score, the greater your satisfaction with your communication in this relationship. You can complete the questionnaire for any relationship. You may want to complete it for your most important relationships before you continue reading. If you are not satisfied with your communication in your relationships, you can use the suggestions provided throughout this chapter to improve the quality of your communication.

Communication Satisfaction in Intergroup Relationships. Many of the factors that lead to satisfaction in our communication with members of our own group also lead to communication satisfaction with members of other groups. The more communication in a relationship is personalized and synchronized, and the less difficulty people have communicating with their partner, for example, the more satisfied they are with the communication in the relationship (Gudykunst, Nishida, & Chua, 1986). Also, the more partners self-disclose to each other, the more they are attracted to each other, the more similarities they perceive, and the more uncertainty they reduce about each other, the more satisfied they are (Gudykunst, Nishida, & Chua, 1986). Further, the more effective the partners judge each other's communication to be, the more satisfied they are.

There are some factors that appear to be especially important to satisfaction in interethnic encounters. Several factors contribute to African Americans' satisfaction with their conversations with European Americans (Hecht, Ribeau, & Alberts, 1989). To be satisfied, Afri-

Assessment 14.1 *Assessing Your Communication Satisfaction with Others*

The purpose of this questionnaire is to help you assess your satisfaction with your communication in a specific relationship. Please think of a relationship with a specific person when you answer the questions. Respond to each statement by indicating the degree to which it is true of your communication with a particular person: "Always False" (answer 1), "Usually False" (answer 2), "Sometimes True and Sometimes False" (answer 3), "Usually True" (answer 4), or "Always True" (answer 5).

_______ 1. I am satisfied with my communication with this person.

_______ 2. This person is evasive when we communicate.

_______ 3. I enjoy communicating with this person.

_______ 4. I do not feel confirmed when I communicate with this person.

_______ 5. I feel accepted when I communicate with this person.

_______ 6. I do not get to say what I want to say when I communicate with this person.

_______ 7. I am able to present myself as I want to when I communicate with this person.

_______ 8. This person does not understand me when we communicate.

_______ 9. Conversations flow smoothly when I communicate with this person.

_______ 10. I do not accomplish my goals when I communicate with this person.

To find your score, first reverse the responses for the even numbered items (i.e., if you wrote 1, make it 5; if you wrote 2, make it 4; if you wrote 3, leave it as 3; if you wrote 4, make it 2; if you wrote 5, make it 1). Next, add the numbers next to each statement. Scores range from 10 to 50. The higher your score, the greater your satisfaction in communicating with this person.

can Americans need to feel that they are respected, confirmed, and accepted by the European Americans with whom they communicate. Satisfying conversations with European Americans also include emotional expression and the European Americans being authentic, genuine, and not evasive. African Americans also perceive that there is understanding and goal attainment in satisfying conversations, while they perceive negative stereotyping and feel powerless or manipulated and controlled in dissatisfying conversations.

Similarly, several factors are associated with Mexican Americans' satisfying and dissatisfying conversations with European Americans (Hecht, Ribeau, & Sedano, 1990). Similar to African Americans, Mexican Americans see acceptance as an important aspect of satisfying conversations. Satisfying conversations with European Americans also include the expression of feelings and behaving rationally. The presence of self-expression and relational solidarity also contribute to satisfaction in conversations. Negative stereotyping and the absence of perceived similarities emerge as important factors in dissatisfying conversations.

To summarize, **European Americans need to communicate acceptance, express emotions, and avoid negative stereotyping in order for non-European Americans to be satisfied with interethnic conversations.** European Americans need to perceive similar factors in their communication with non-European Americans to be satisfied. Communicating acceptance and avoiding negative stereotyping are important in developing relationships across class, age, and disability lines as well (Pogrebin, 1987).

Creating Supportive Communication Climates

In maintaining relationships with others, it is important that we maintain a supportive climate (Gibb, 1961). Supportive climates facilitate effective communication, while defensive climates inhibit effective communication in our relationships with others.

Before proceeding, think about when you become defensive and when you feel supported. Take a few minutes to answer the following questions:

In what ways do others communicate with you that make you feel defensive?

____

____

____

____

In what ways do others communicate with you that make you feel supported?

____

____

____

Your answers to these questions should provide some insight into the role of supportiveness in your implicit personal theory of communication. Keep your answers to these questions in mind as you read the remainder of this section.

Characteristics of Supportive Communication Climates. *Defensiveness* is "that behavior which occurs when an individual perceives threat or anticipates threat" (Gibb, 1961, p. 141). The way we communicate creates either a defensive or a supportive communication climate in our relationships. There are six characteristics that differentiate the two types of climates (see Table 14.1).

The first characteristic of a supportive climate is *description* rather than evaluation. We cannot understand others if we evaluate them before we understand their positions. Evaluative speech can threaten other people's self-concepts, and it may cause them to become

Table 14.1
CHARACTERISTICS OF SUPPORTIVE AND DEFENSIVE CLIMATES

Supportive	Defensive
Description	Evolution
Problem Orientation	Control
Being Spontaneous	Being Strategic
Empathy	Neutrality
Equality	Superiority
Provisionalism	Certainty

Adapted from Gibbs (1961).

defensive. Descriptive speech, in contrast, does not make other people uneasy. If we tell other people, for example, that "Your behavior was insensitive," they will become defensive. If we describe the behavior that led us to think other people were insensitive, they will not become defensive; in addition, it gives them an opportunity to tell us what they intended.

Taking a *problem orientation* is the second characteristic of a supportive climate. Defining a mutual problem and expressing a willingness to collaborate in finding a solution implies that we have no predetermined outcome in mind. This leads to a cooperative climate with others. If we have a predetermined outcome in mind and try to force this outcome on others, we are trying to control them. Attempts to control others are inevitably met with resistance. Not controlling others is important to maintaining supportive relationships with them. To illustrate, if we want to talk with a friend about being late when we get together, our friend will become defensive if we try to control his or her behavior by saying something like "You've got to stop being late!" If we present the issue as a mutual problem, in contrast, by saying something like "I get bored waiting for you when we get together. Is there some way we can work it out so that you don't feel pressured and I don't feel bored?" the friend should not become defensive.

Being spontaneous, as opposed to being strategic, is the third characteristic of a supportive climate. If we appear to have a hidden motive, lie, manipulate others, or act in what appears to be a strategic way, it will arouse defensiveness in others. If we appear spontaneous and not strategic, on the other hand, others will not get defensive. Spontaneous messages suggest that we are open to other people's ideas and open to being persuaded. To illustrate, if we wanted to watch a slapstick movie and our friend said, "I don't like slapstick comedy," we would be spontaneous if we said something like "I didn't know that. Why?" We would appear strategic if we said something like "This movie is different. You'll enjoy it." This message would be perceived as strategic because it does not take our friend's comment into consideration.

Empathy also is important in establishing a supportive environment. If we convey empathy in our communication with others, they will know that we want to understand them and are concerned with their welfare. If we appear neutral toward others, they will become defensive. Neutrality is disconfirming (see the discussion of confirmation below) because it emphasizes the content of a discussion over the relationship between the people. If a friend is explaining her or his feelings about a problem he or she is having and we say something like "There is no reason to feel that way," we are being neutral toward the friend. If we respond by saying something like "That's terrible. Tell me more about it," we are responding with empathy.

The fifth characteristic of a supportive climate is communicating that we are *equal.* When we communicate equality, we do not talk down to others and we do not treat them as though they are superior to us. If we talk in a way that others perceive as sounding superior or condescending, they will become defensive. Any time we say something like "I know more about this than you do," we are acting superior. If we truly want to create supportive climates with others, we must communicate with others as though we are equal and respect their ideas or opinions.

The final characteristic of a supportive climate is *provisionalism.* If we communicate to others that we are open to their viewpoints and willing to experiment with our behavior (try to change it if needed), they will not become defensive. If, on the other hand, we communicate in such a way that indicates that we think we are right and certain of our attitudes and behavior, they will become defensive. If we say something like "I know this won't work," we are communicating certainty. Thinking that we are right and others are wrong polarizes communication. As indicated throughout the book, flexibility and openness are critical to effective communication (see Reading 14.1).

Learning Supportive Communication Scripts. Most of the scripts for communication that we learned as children include messages that cause others to become defensive. Skill Exercise 14.1 provides an opportunity for you to begin to develop a script for supportive communication. Take a few minutes to complete it now.

In the skill exercise, you indicated how you would typically respond in the situation, as well as how you might respond using defensive and supportive messages. If your typical response is closer to the defensive response, then this is an area where you might want to mindfully try to change your style of communication. If we want to maintain satisfying, close relationships with others, we need to establish supportive communication climates in our relationships. This requires that our messages be descriptive, problem-oriented, spontaneous, empathic, equal, and provisional. For most of us, creating a supportive climate in our relationships requires that we be mindful, because we may not have learned supportive communication scripts when we were children.

Confirming and Disconfirming Communication

Confirmation is the most fundamental human need (Buber, 1958). Confirmation is related

Reading 14.1 YOUR TREASURED OPINIONS NEVER MADE ANYONE HAPPY

PLANET: Sauv[10]

TRANSLATION: The primary industry on Sauv[10] is the codification of all mortal knowledge. Their encyclopedias, dictionaries, and other reference books are widely used in several galaxies. The long-term effect of this occupation on the Sauvits themselves has been to develop a deep neutrality regarding all intellectual issues. **"Facts are fashion,"** they say. And when someone is overheard insisting doggedly on his or her point of view, the typical Sauvit retort is, **"About even this, you will change your mind."**

MEANING: You cannot insist on being right and at the same moment extend the gift of love. The only punishable crime on Sauv[10] is narrow-mindedness, the penalty for which is to be a foster parent to a two-year-old and a parrot. The parrot is trained to say "I'm right" in a firm but cheerful voice forty-eight times a day, and the two-year-old is not trained to, but nevertheless does, say "No" in a firm but uncheerful voice to all attempts at communication. Despite their apparent skepticism regarding opinions, knowledge, and facts, Sauvits have cultivated an unreasonable love for all living things. Language is used carefully, not to achieve accuracy but to achieve compassion. Or, as the Sauvits themselves would put it: **An unloving question has no answer.**

Skill Exercise 14.1 *Creating Supportive Climates*

Imagine that you are having a discussion with your romantic partner over where to spend the holidays. Answer each of the following questions.

1. It is obvious that you cannot spend time with both your family and your partner's family. How can you address this with your partner?

   How would you typically respond?

   ____

   ____

   ____

   How might you respond using a control orientation? ______________

   ____

   How might you respond using a problem orientation? ______________

   ____

   ____

2. Your partner says that he or she wants to spend the holidays with his or her family. You don't think this is a good idea.

   How would you typically respond?

   ____

   ____

   ____

   What would you respond using an evaluative response? ______________

   ____

   What would you respond using a descriptive response? ______________

   ____

   ____

3. Your partner asks you why you do not want to spend the holidays with her or his family.

   How would you typically respond?

   ____

   ____

   ____

   How would you respond strategically?

   ____

   ____

   How would you respond being spontaneous? ______________

   ____

   ____

4. Your parents have not met your partner, but you have met your partner's parents. Your partner points out that he or she did not spend the holidays with his or her family last year.

   How would you typically respond? ____

   ____

   ____

   ____

   How would you respond using a neutral orientation?______________

   ____

   ____

Skill Exercise 14.1 *Continued*

How would you respond using an empathic orientation? ______________________

____

____

____

5. Your partner says that you are in a better position to make a decision since you have met her or his parents (you liked her or his parents).

How would you typically respond?

____

____

____

____

How would you use a response using a superiority orientation? ______________________

____

____

____

How would you respond using an equality response? ______________________

____

____

6. Your partner indicates that he or she thinks that you have already made up your mind and are not open to making a mutual decision.

How would you typically respond?

____

____

____

How would you respond using a certainty orientation? ______________________

____

How would you respond using a provisional response? ______________________

____

____

____

closely to the idea of supporting other people's self-concepts, as discussed in Chapter 2. Before reading further, take a few minutes to think about how others confirm or disconfirm you and how you confirm or disconfirm others, by answering the following questions:

How do others communicate with you that makes you feel confirmed or acknowledged as a person? ______________________

____

____

How do others communicate with you that makes you feel disconfirmed or insignificant? ______________________

____

____

How do you typically confirm others when you communicate with them?

____

____

____

How do you typically disconfirm others when you communicate? ____________

____

____

Your answers to these questions should provide some insight into the role of confirmation in your implicit personal theory of communication. Keep your answers to these questions in mind as you read the remainder of this section.

Characteristics of Confirming and Disconfirming Messages. *Confirmation* is "the process through which individuals are recognized, acknowledged, and endorsed" (Laing, 1961, p. 83). Confirming communication involves recognizing others, responding to other people's messages to us, accepting other people's experiences as real, and indicating to others that we are willing to be involved with them (Cissna & Sieburg, 1981). The relationship component of confirming messages implies several meanings: "To me, you exist," "We are relating," "To me, you are significant," and "Your way of experiencing the world is valid" (Cissna & Sieburg, 1981, p. 232).

We typically use three types of confirming responses in our conversations with others:

> *Recognition.* A verbal or nonverbal recognition of other's presence, e.g., eye contact, touch, or a facilitating verbal response, e.g., "un huh."
> *Acknowledgement.* A verbal acknowledgement that one is in a relationship with the other; acknowledgement of the other's perceptions, statements, or questions, e.g., agreement in reply to a question or request for clarification. A different but relevant topic could be introduced only if the previous speaker's content was verbally acknowledged.
> *Endorsement.* A verbal endorsement of the other's way of experiencing, especially the other's feelings, e.g., appreciation of the other's feelings or experiences. (Garvin & Kennedy, 1986, pp. 8–9)

Recognition is expressed when we say things like "I'm interested in what you think" or "I respect you." Acknowledging occurs when we say things like "I understand that you see the situation differently than I do" or "I'm not sure I understand your question. Could you ask it differently?" Endorsement is expressed when we say things like "I understand you're angry with me" or "You have a right to be upset." The problem is that we use confirming responses less than we think we do when we communicate on automatic pilot.

Disconfirmation occurs when others, their experiences, or their significance is denied (Cissna & Sieburg, 1981). Disconfirming communication involves not recognizing others, not acknowledging that we have a relationship with others, not accepting others' experiences, and denying the validity of others' experiences (Cissna & Sieburg, 1981). The relationship component of disconfirming messages sends the relational meanings "To me, you do not exist," "We are not relating," "To me, you are not significant," and "Your way of experiencing the world is invalid" (Cissna & Sieburg, 1981, p. 232).

We use three types of disconfirming responses in our conversations with others:

> *Indifference.* A response which fails to acknowledge the other's attempt to communicate, e.g., silence, use of impersonal language, monologue, interruption, or change of topic. Indifference conveys the message that the speaker simply does not matter, or does not exist.
> *Disqualification.* A response which indicates the other person, the message, or the self are disqualified, e.g., name calling,

> blaming, laughter at the speaker, tangential response, or an incomplete, qualified or ambiguous response.
>
> *Impervious.* A response which indicates the existence of the other, but fails to respond to the other's experience, e.g., denies the other's feelings, offers false reassurance, or challenges the other's rights to have feelings. (Garvin & Kennedy, 1986, p. 9)

We express indifference when we do not respond when other people talk to us or say something like "Your point of view doesn't matter." We disqualify others when we call them names or say something like "Can't you do anything right?" We are impervious when we deny other people's feelings when we say something like "You shouldn't be angry" or "You don't really mean. . . ." We disconfirm other people's experiences when we say something like "No matter what you do, I know you love me." We all use disconfirming messages more than we think we do when we communicate on automatic pilot.

We confirm or disconfirm others by the words we choose to use when we talk to them and the way that we say what we do. We often talk in judgmental ways that are disconfirming when we communicate on automatic pilot. To illustrate, saying something like "You jerk" or "That's a stupid idea" is judgmental and disqualifies others. All forms of hate speech, such as racist, sexist, ageist, or homophobic language, also disconfirm members of other groups. To overcome our tendency to speak in these ways, we need to be mindful of our communication.

Our relational messages define the relationships between us and others. We often are not aware of how others interpret our relational messages. We may not intend to transmit a disconfirming message, but others may interpret what or how we say something to be disconfirming. This can be especially problematic in our communication with members of other groups, because they may interpret the relational component of our messages differently than we intend. We need to make sure that our messages are interpreted as confirming by others. This requires that we be mindful of our communication and watch for signs that others may be interpreting our messages as disconfirming. If this occurs, we need to check our perceptions to correct any misperceptions.

Confirming Members of Other Groups. As indicated in the previous section, the words we use can disconfirm others.

BEETLE BAILEY. Reprinted with special permission of King Features Syndicate.

The words we use also influence how we think about members of other groups, and they influence whether they interpret our messages as confirming or disconfirming. If we consistently use male pronouns ("he, him") to refer to people in different occupations, for example, it affects the way we think about the occupations to which we refer.[2] To illustrate, if we use the term "mailman," we will think of all people who deliver the mail as men. This obviously is not the case. Women deliver the mail, too. The inclusive term we can use instead of "mailman" is "mail carrier." By inclusive language we refer to language that makes everyone feel included and confirmed. This may seem like a small thing, but our language usage clearly influences our attitudes toward and thoughts about particular groups (see Chapter 7).

Consistently using male pronouns or man-linked words disconfirms women. There are many idioms referring to ethnic groups we use in our everyday language, such as "Jew them down" or "black magic," which disconfirm members of the ethnic groups involved. There also are idioms referring to disabilities, such as "the blind leading the blind," which disconfirm disabled people. To be confirming when we communicate with members of different groups, we need to avoid the use of these terms and idioms. We all use noninclusive language in our everyday interactions when we communicate on automatic pilot. To the extent that we can minimize our use of noninclusive language, we can be more confirming to others. To the extent that we use inclusive language, we can decrease the influence of our stereotypes on our communication. We must be mindful of our communication in order to change our use of noninclusive language.

Skill Exercise 14.2 provides an opportunity for you to practice using inclusive language. Take a few minutes to complete it now.

Being inclusive also involves referring to members of other groups in a way that they want to be called (see Chapter 2). Sometimes we try to avoid group labels when we talk about or to members of other ethnic groups. One reason for this is that we may want to downplay group

Skill Exercise 14.2 *Creating Nonstereotyped, Inclusive Messages*

Using stereotyped language and/or noninclusive words can create communicative distance between ourselves and others. Rewrite each of the messages below so that they do not involve stereotypes and are inclusive.

1. Policemen have a difficult job.

   ____

2. We have a gentleman's agreement.

   ____

3. The mailman delivered an express package.

   ____

4. Martin Luther King, Jr., was a black leader of the civil rights movement.

   ____

5. Chris told a white lie.

   ____

differences. This strategy may work well when we are interacting with members of other groups who do not identify strongly with their groups. Playing down group differences, however, does not work well when we are interacting with members of other groups who do identify strongly with their groups. Another reason we may try to avoid the use of group labels is that we may want to focus on similarities rather than differences. This strategy never works well. **To communicate effectively with others, we must understand both the differences and the similarities.** If we focus exclusively on the similarities, the differences become all the more problematic when they arise.

Rather than ignore group labels, it is important for us to understand how members of other groups want us to refer to them. We must support other people's self-concepts if we want to develop closer relationships with them. Calling others what they want to be called and recognizing group memberships that are important to them are part of supporting their self-concepts.

Strategies for Rejuvenating and Transforming Relationships

Problems in interpersonal relationships arise for many reasons (Beck, 1988). One reason problems arise is that our expectations are not fulfilled. One partner in a marriage, for example, may expect his or her spouse to provide support when the partner feels low. When the spouse does not fulfill his or her expectations, the partner becomes disappointed with the relationship. Another reason problems arise is that we may break our promises to each other. Broken promises often are viewed as indicating that the other person does not care about us. Problems may also arise in relationships because we have different perspectives. One may be a romantic who seeks out novelty, while the other may be a person who values a predictable life. Problems may arise because of our styles of communication, such as being vague when directness is needed. Any time problems arise in our relationships, our anxiety and uncertainty in-

We tend to forget about the things that make our relationships run smoothly when we are having a problem.

crease, even to the point of rising above our maximum threshold. When this happens, we have to manage our anxiety before we try to reduce our uncertainty.

Ideally, partners in relationships will sit down and discuss the issues mindfully when problems arise. Sometimes, however, problems lead individuals to stop communicating with each other. If this occurs, the relationship cannot be rejuvenated unless one of the individuals takes the first step toward reconciliation (see Reading 14.2). Most problems in

Reading 14.2 Take Steps Toward Reconciliation/Ann Landers

DEAR ANN: I have suddenly become aware that the years are flying by. Time somehow seems more precious.

My parents suddenly seem old. My aunts and uncles are sick, and I fear they don't have many years left. I haven't seen some of my cousins for several years. I really love my family, Ann, but we have grown apart.

I am also thinking of my friends, some I've known since childhood. Those friendships become more precious as the years pass.

Nothing warms the heart like sharing a laugh with someone you've known for a long time.

Then my thoughts turn to the dark side. I remember the feelings I've hurt, and I recall my own hurt feelings—the misunderstandings and unmended fences that separated us and set up barriers.

I have a close friend in New York I haven't spoken to in three years. Another 28-year relationship in Seattle is on the rocks. We're both 41 now, and time is marching on.

I think of my mother and her sister, who haven't spoken to each other in five years. As a result of that argument, my cousin and I haven't spoken either. I don't know if she has children. Neither of us has met the other's husband.

What a waste of precious time. I'm sure there are millions of people in your reading audience who could tell similar stories.

Wouldn't it be terrific if a special day could be set aside to reach out and make amends? We could call it "Reconciliation Day." Everyone would vow to write a letter or make a phone call and mend a strained or broken relationship.

It could also be the day on which we would all agree to accept the olive branch extended by a former friend. This day could be the starting place. We could go from there to heal the wounds in our hearts and rejoice in a new beginning

—VAN NUYS

DEAR VAN NUYS: What a beautiful idea. In the absence of a national holiday, it would be wonderful if every person who sees your letter picked up the phone and called someone with whom he or she has had a falling out.

Are you game, folks? I'll guarantee some heartwarming results. Go ahead and do it. And please write and tell me all about it.

interpersonal relationships do not lead to a dissolution of the relationship. Many problems in interpersonal relationships can be traced to miscommunication between the partners (Beck, 1988). Interpersonal relationships are interrelated systems. In interpersonal systems, the individuals are interdependent. What one person in an interpersonal relationship does influences the other person and the way the other person behaves. When problems arise in a relationship, "no one owns the problem. Both people are involved in the relationship patterns, and both contribute to the development and maintenance of problems in the relationship" (Duncan & Rock, 1991, p. 44). If one person is doing something that bothers the other person, it is a problem for both people in the relationship.

Ideally, relationship problems will be resolved by the partners discussing the issues and coming to a joint solution. This can be accomplished by following the suggestions for managing conflict discussed in the next chapter and by using the various communication skills discussed throughout the book, such as responsive listening, feedback, perception checking, and so forth. Often, however, one partner will see an issue as a problem and the other will not. In these circumstances, trying to find a joint solution may not be the best strategy. This does *not* mean that the situation is hopeless, however. The person who perceives the problem and experiences the most discomfort can choose to deal with the problem. As pointed out earlier in this chapter, one person can change a relationship. By focusing on his or her own behavior, one partner can influence the other person's behavior. The strategies discussed in this section can be used by both partners jointly or by one person in a relationship. Let's begin by looking at the advantage of focusing on what works when there are problems in our relationships.

Focus on What Works

When we have problems in our interpersonal relationships, we usually focus on the problem (Weiner-Davis, 1992). Our relationships, however, are *not* always dominated by these problems. Often our relationships run smoothly or are smoother than when we are having the problems. We forget about these times when we focus on problems. When we have problems, our perceptions are biased in the direction of the problems (see Chapter 7). To begin to deal with the problem, we need to be able to describe what happens differently when the relationship is going smoothly. In other words, we need to find exceptions to the problem, because "once a single exception is acknowledged . . . either/or thinking is eliminated. People realize that their problems aren't as all-encompassing as they thought" (Weiner-Davis, 1992, pp. 124–125). To illustrate, when partners are not communicating much, it often appears that they never communicate. If the partners look for exceptions, however, they will begin to recognize that they do communicate effectively at certain times. Once the partners recognize that there are exceptions, their view that they can't communicate changes to "sometimes we have an easier time talking than other times" (Weiner-Davis, 1992, p. 125). By focusing on the times when we do communicate effectively, we can increase these occurrences in our relationships.

When we do not see exceptions, we tend to assume that our partners are not changeable. Once we recognize exceptions in our relationships, we also see that our partners are changeable (Weiner-Davis, 1992). We begin to recognize that our own behavior and our partners' behavior "are triggered by specific conditions or contexts rather than the result of deeply ingrained personality characteristics" (p. 125). Once

JUMP START reprinted by permission of UFS, Inc.

we recognize the exceptions, we can begin to see solutions to the problems.

When we see solutions to the problems we are having, we may not like them, particularly if the solution involves doing something we think we should not have to do (Weiner-Davis, 1992). We may think, for example, that we should not have to control ourselves or modify our behavior; rather, the other person should change. We cannot, however, force the other person to change. **The only person whose behavior we can control is our own.** We need to "do what works, even if '[we] shouldn't have to' " (Weiner-Davis, 1992, p. 125). The more we try to understand and accept other people and *not* try to change them, the more likely they are to change (Rogers, 1961).

To find solutions to relationship problems, we need to break our bad habits. This requires that we be mindful of our communication. When we communicate on automatic pilot, we will continue our bad habits. If we find ourselves doing something that does not work, we should do something different (Weiner-Davis, 1992). Breaking bad habits requires that we find new, novel ways to respond. When we engage in novel responses, it leads the other person to be attentive and become more mindful. Novel behavior interrupts negative sequences of behaviors and allow us to explore options.

To illustrate the influence of novel responses, consider the following example (provided by Weiner-Davis, 1992). The wife gets upset with her husband when he is late for dinner. The wife "pouts" until her husband asks, "What's wrong?" and then she "lets him have it." Things generally go downhill from there. One evening the husband is late, and when he sits down at the table, he does not ask the wife, "What's wrong." Instead, the husband sits down, begins to eat, and starts a conversation with the daughter about her day. Although the wife is upset with her husband for ignoring her, she finds herself becoming involved in the conversation between her husband and daughter, and the remainder of the evening is pleasant. The husband's novel response, therefore, defuses a problematic situation. This example is *not* designed to suggest that it is acceptable to be late for dinner as long as we behave differently. Rather, it illustrates that we can defuse problematic situations with novel behavior.

Not Becoming Defensive

Focusing on what works is not the only way we can rejuvenate our relationships. We also can mindfully decide not to become defensive. There are four characteristics of defensiveness: it is based on flaws we perceive in ourselves that we refuse to admit, we are sensitive to the flaws, we perceive we are attacked by others, and we assume that others are attacking our flaws (Stamp, Vangelisti, & Daly, 1992). Defensiveness emerges out of our interaction with others. When one in a relationship becomes defensive, the other also tends to become defensive.

We can deal with problems in our relationships by focusing on our own behavior and not becoming defensive (Duncan & Rock, 1991).[3] When we become defensive, we explain, justify, defend, and apologize for our behavior.

> When people *explain,* they describe motives for and reasoning behind certain actions. *Justification* involves pointing out the reasons that a course of action was the correct or proper one. *Defending* is justification that occurs when an "attack" or hostile questioning is perceived. Occasionally, this pattern involves *apologizing,* which is an admission of wrongdoing accompanied by an expression of regret for doing so. (Duncan & Rock, 1991, p. 145)

While there is nothing wrong with any of these behaviors in isolation, when one person consistently engages in these behaviors over time, there is a problem in the relationship.

When we consistently explain, justify, defend, or apologize, we give up power in our relationships. To balance the power and *not* become defensive, we need to stop explaining, justifying, defending, and apologizing. Instead of being defensive, we can be silent. Many European Americans, however, may find it difficult to be silent. In this case, people can simply give a one-sentence explanation and repeat it if necessary.

Instead of being silent or giving a one-sentence explanation when we would normally be defensive, there is another alternative. We also can agree verbally but not change our behavior (Duncan & Rock, 1991). Since it takes two people to be in a power struggle, if one person refuses to participate, the power struggle is effectively over. Many of us are reluctant to use this strategy because we see it as giving in or losing. Others may think they have won, but it is up to us, if we are agreeing, to decide whether we want to change our behavior. Our words and our behavior do *not* have to be consistent. Consider the following example:

> WIFE: "I thought you were going to cut the grass."
>
> HUSBAND: "I am."
>
> WIFE: "But I thought you were going to do it today."
>
> HUSBAND: "You're right. I probably should. But you know how I procrastinate sometimes." (Duncan & Rock, 1991, p. 125)

In this case, the husband clearly maintains his freedom to choose whether to cut the grass that day without getting defensive about his wife's response.

There is a side benefit to giving in verbally and not necessarily changing our behavior (Duncan & Rock, 1991). Since we do not get defensive, we are better able to listen to others because we do not have to prepare our response while they are talking. The more we listen, the more likely we are to understand other people's points of view.

Before proceeding, it is important to point out that using this strategy does not involve lying. When we go along with other people, we need to be honest, and we do not agree to change our behavior. If we say we will change our behavior, we should. There also

ANDY CAPP. Reprinted with special permission of North America Syndicate.

are times when we would not want to use the strategy of agreeing verbally, but not complying behaviorally. This strategy works between peers, where there is a relative balance of power in the relationship. It does not work well, however, in relationships where there are real imbalances in power; for example, boss-employee, parent-child, or teacher-student.

Creative Interpretations

Another strategy for dealing with problems in our relationships is creatively interpreting other people's behavior. **When we creatively interpret other people's behavior, we recognize that there is more than one way to interpret any event or behavior.** As indicated in Chapter 7, our perceptions are biased, but we tend to assume that our perceptions are accurate when we communicate on automatic pilot. When we use creative interpretations, we perceive "a problem circumstance in an entirely different light," and we verbalize our "new perceptions to the other person involved" (Duncan & Rock, 1991, p. 161). To illustrate, assume that our romantic partners do not talk to us as much as we would like. When we communicate on automatic pilot, we might assume that this is a problem with our partners such as they do not know how to communicate. We could try to get our partners to talk more by asking questions, but they may see the questions as intrusions and become more reluctant to talk. Rather than trying to change our partners, we can focus on changing our own behavior by reinterpreting our partners' behavior. We could interpret our partners' behavior as their not wanting to burden us with their problems, for example, or their being comfortable and not feeling a need to talk (Duncan & Rock, 1991). By telling our partners our new interpretations, we can reassure ourselves about the relationships.

We should seek out positive interpretations for other people's behavior (Duncan & Rock, 1991). Our positive interpretations will affect the way we view others, which in turn will influence how we behave toward them. Imagine how the following redefined perceptions would influence your relationships with others:

> Arguing: sharing emotional intensity
> Controlling: structuring one's environment, taking charge
> Defiance: having one's way of doing things . . .
> Reclusiveness, withdrawn: introspection, contemplation . . .
> Rigidity: steadfast purpose (Duncan & Rock, 1991, p. 162)

The new perceptions allow for solutions to be found more easily than the original perceptions of the behavior. It is easier for others to change their behavior when we see their current behavior positively than when we see their current behavior negatively.

Going with the Flow

As indicated earlier, when we find ourselves in a rut when dealing with problems in our relationships, we need to try something different. **When we are on automatic pilot, we tend to follow our old patterns and cannot see alternatives.** When we are mindful, however, we can choose to go with the flow.

Going with the flow involves listening to others, accepting what they say, and *avoiding* taking a position in opposition to them (Duncan & Rock, 1991). To do this, we have to overcome our natural tendency to want to reason or argue with others. Going with the flow works particularly well when we have been trying to get others to change. Trying to change others never works well. It creates a power struggle, and others will resist our attempts to change them. As stated earlier, we can only change ourselves. Rather than trying to change others, we need to genuinely accept them as they are (see the discussion of self-concept support in Chapter 3). Obviously, this does not apply if the other person's behavior is unacceptable, such as being verbally or physically abusive.

Once we accept others and stop trying to change them, the power struggle is over. Since the pressure to change is off others, they can think about the situation and what their options are. When examining their behavior, others may decide to change of their own free will.

Modifying Our Expectations

It was pointed out in Chapter 7 that all expectations involve a "should" component. We believe that others should behave in a particular way when they interact with us. **All expectations involve judgments** (Prather, 1986). The problem is that we usually are not highly aware of our expectations for other people's behavior in interpersonal relationships; our expectations are implicit, not explicit. When our implicit expectations are violated, we make judgments about other people. These judgments, in turn, lead us to communicate in a defensive, rather than a supportive, way.

Consider a telephone conversation that illustrates the problems that expectations create in communication. Max, a medical researcher, is calling home from a medical convention:

MAX: [*Sybil will be glad that I'm getting on so well, meeting a lot of people, learning a lot.*] I'm having a great time. How are you?

SYBIL: [*He's having a great time while I have two sick kids on my hands.*] Joan and Freddie are sick.

MAX: [*Oh no, she's going to lay something on me.*] What's the matter with them?

SYBIL: [*Will he respond? Show a sense of responsibility?*] They have chicken pox. They're running a fever.

MAX: [*Chicken pox is not serious. She's exaggerating the problem.*] You don't have to worry. They'll be all right.

SYBIL: [*Why doesn't he offer to come home.*] All right.

MAX: [*I hope she's reassured.*] I'll call tomorrow.

SYBIL: [*He's never around when I need him.*] You do that! [sarcastically] (Beck, 1988, p. 53)

The problems in communication illustrated in this conversation can be traced to the implicit expectations that Max and Sybil had for each other's behavior before they got married (Beck, 1988). Sybil expected that Max would always put her and the children before his career, that she would not have to ask him directly for help, that her needs would be apparent to him, and that he would make sacrifices to help her. Max, in contrast, expected Sybil to respect and identify with his career and take care of the children and house.

When we are not aware of our expectations in relationships, we assume that others share our view of what is expected. We create *rules* for our relationships based on our expectations. Sybil, for example, probably created the rule that "my spouse should put me and the children first." When we form rules, we see them as rights, and once we define an expectation as a right, it can evolve into a demand very easily (Beck, 1988). In the conversation, Sybil expected that Max would offer to come home if he cared for her and the children, but she did not tell Max this. Hidden or implicit expectations can disrupt a relationship.

Shared expectations provide partners in a relationship with a sense of stability in their relationship because they know what is expected of them. Becoming aware of our expectations and/or making them explicit to our partner, therefore, is critical to improving the quality of our interpersonal relationships.

Skill Exercise 14.3 provides an opportunity for you to think about your expectations in a particular relationship. Take a few minutes to complete it now.

In completing Skill Exercise 14.3, you had to think of a particular relationship. You can complete this exercise for many different relationships. You may want to think about your expectations in your important interpersonal relationships before reading further.

If, after completing the exercise, you recognize that you have expectations for other people's behavior of which they are not aware, you have two options. You can tell others about your expectations. If others are not aware of your expectations, they might not fulfill them. If you tell others about your expectations and they are *not* willing to meet your expectations, you will need to be prepared to negotiate your expectations if you want to maintain the relationship.

Alternatively, you can change or give up your expectation for others without discussing your expectations with them. **Letting go of our expectations for others is one way to improve the quality of our interpersonal relationships** (Prather, 1986). Expectations lead us to focus on the past or on the future of our relationships. If we let go of our expectations, we are able to be mindful and focus on the process of communication that is taking place in the present.

Modifying Our Styles of Communication

The way that we communicate, our *style* of communication, often leads to misunderstandings in our relationships with others. Our style of communication is a function of the culture in which we were raised, our ethnic group, our gender, our social class, our age, the area of the country in which we live, our family upbringing, and our unique communication experiences. While we tend to form relationships with people who are similar to us in terms of culture, ethnicity, age, and social class, our communication style is never a perfect match with the people with whom we form relationships. We make adjustments for other people's styles of communication, but often the differences in our communication styles create problems in our communication with others.

To illustrate potential problems created by style of communication, consider indirectness or ambiguity. The following conversation

Skill Exercise 14.3 ***Understanding Your Expectations***

The purpose of this exercise is to help you isolate your expectations in a particular interpersonal relationship. Think of a particular relationship and answer the following questions.

1. If the other person cares for me, he or she will ________________________

   ____

   ____

2. If I am in distress, I expect that she or he will ________________________

   ____

   ____

3. If the other person disagrees with something I say in public, she or he will

   ____

   ____

   ____

4. If the other person does something that upsets me, I expect that he or she will

   ____

   ____

   ____

5. If the other person is upset with me, I expect that he or she will ____________

   ____

   ____

   ____

illustrates how indirectness can create problems in communication in interpersonal relationships in the United States, where low-context communication predominates:

SALLY: The Scotts said something about dropping over to their house on Thursday.

TOM: [hurt] They invited *you*? [meaning: *Only you and not me*?]

SALLY: [testily] I just told you. [*He's challenging my veracity.*]

TOM: [hurt] How come they invited *you*? [meaning: *You and not me also.*]

SALLY: [hurt] Obviously they like me. [*He doesn't think I'm likeable enough to be invited on my own.*]

TOM: Well, go. I'm sure you'll have a wonderful time. [*I hope you have a terrible time.*]

SALLY: [bitter] I'm sure I will. [*He doesn't want to go because they issued the invitation to me.*] (Beck, 1988, pp. 70–71)

Clearly, there is miscommunication between Sally and Tom. Each of them is being vague in the way they express themselves to the other person.

When our close relationships with others are going well, vagueness and ambiguity can be effective ways of communicating. We often express our emotions to others through hints and indirect messages, and this is effective if we are getting along with the other person. When we are not getting along well with others, or when other people expect us to be direct, however, indirect messages inhibit effective communication. To communicate effectively in these situations requires that we be direct and honest with our partners.

Assessment 14.2 provides a means for you

Assessment 14.2 *Problems in the Style of Communication*

Below is a list of behaviors that may cause problems. In the left-hand column, rate the behaviors your partner uses with you. Use the following numbers to indicate frequency: (0) does not apply, (1) rarely, (2) sometimes, (3) frequently, (4) all the time. In the middle column, indicate how much the problem bothers you: (0) not at all, (1) slightly, (2) moderately, (3) a great deal. In the right-hand column, rate the behaviors you use with your partner. Your partner should also complete this questionnaire.

	Communication Style		
	Your Partner with You	This Bothers Me	You with Your Partner
1. Doesn't listen	______	______	______
2. Talks too much	______	______	______
3. Doesn't talk enough	______	______	______
4. Interrupts	______	______	______
5. Too vague	______	______	______
6. Never gets to the point	______	______	______
7. Doesn't nod or indicate agreement	______	______	______
8. Doesn't utter listening signals (for example, "mm-hmm")	______	______	______
9. Doesn't give partner a chance to talk	______	______	______
10. Won't discuss touchy subjects	______	______	______
11. Talks too much about touchy subjects	______	______	______
12. Asks too many questions	______	______	______
13. Doesn't ask enough questions	______	______	______
14. Shuts partner up	______	______	______
15. Withdraws when upset	______	______	______

Note: There is no absolute score that indicates when you need to be concerned about communication. However, if you are aware of difficulties in this area, this checklist will enable you and your partner to pinpoint them and start to improve them. Keep in mind that your perception of your partner's behavior may be incorrect or exaggerated.

to assess potential problems with style of communication in a particular relationship. You can use this self-assessment in any close relationship. Take a few minutes to complete it for a close friend or romantic partner now.

There is no score for Assessment 14.2. Any areas you checked are areas of potential problems.

How can we best deal with problems created by differences in communication styles? One way to deal with these problems in our interpersonal relationships is to sit down with our partner (friend, romantic partner, family member, co-worker) and discuss the issue. If we choose this option, the discussion needs to take place in a noncritical, supportive way. The goal is *not* to change our partner, but to negotiate ways that we can *both* be satisfied with each other's styles of communication in the relationship. An alternative way to deal with different styles of communication is to focus on our own style. As indicated earlier, if we change our own behavior, other people are likely to change their behavior. Many of the suggestions discussed earlier in this section can be used to modify your own styles of communication.

Summary

Maintaining our relationships can be seen as sustaining the existence of the relationship, keeping our relationships in a particular condition, keeping our relationships in a satisfactory condition, or as keeping them in "repair." No matter how we conceive of maintaining our relationships, it is important we recognize that our routine, everyday communication with other people binds us with them and defines our relationship with them.

Once we have formed relationships with other people, there are strategies we can use to maintain and rejuvenate these relationships. To maintain quality relationships, we want to create supportive communication climates by being descriptive, taking a problem orientation, being spontaneous, being empathic, treating others as equals, and being provisional. If the communication in our relationship tends to be defensive, we can choose to change the communication climate and communicate in a supportive fashion. We also want to confirm our relational partners by sending messages that involve recognizing, acknowledging, and endorsing them as people.

We also can rejuvenate relationships when there are problems. Ideally, we work with our relational partners to solve the problems that exist. If our partners are not interested in working on the problems, there are many things that we can do on our own that will help solve problems in our relationships.

Focusing on the problems is not a constructive way to manage relationship problems when they occur because we tend to focus on the problems and not see the solutions. One way we can begin to solve problems that exist is to focus on what works by recognizing the communication patterns that occur when our relationships are going well. We can stop negative cycles in our relationships by consciously deciding that we will not become defensive. We also can rejuvenate relationships by not negatively interpreting our partners' behavior, and using creative interpretations of our partners' behavior to see them in a positive light. Further, we can go with the flow, modify our expectations, or modify our styles of communication to improve the quality of communication taking place in our relationships.

Notes

1. This discussion is based on Hecht's (1978) measure of communication satisfaction. We do not list all items on the measure, however.

2. See the references in Chapter 7 in our discussion of sexism.
3. We refer to only three of Duncan and Rock's suggestions here. A complete list of their suggestions is provided in the Suggested Readings.

Journal Reflections

1. *Responding Nondefensively.* When we perceive (consciously or unconsciously) that others are "attacking" our self-concept, we tend to respond defensively. Our defensiveness, however, will decrease the quality of communication that takes place. In the next week, when you find yourself feeling defensive, stop and consciously decide to respond nondefensively. In your journal, describe the situations in which you tried to respond nondefensively and what you did to be nondefensive, and analyze the influence of your use of this skill on the quality of the communication that occurred.
2. *Creating Confirming Messages.* We often unconsciously put others down when we communicate with them. Supporting others' self-conceptions can improve the quality of our communication and lead to increases in the intimacy of a relationship. In the next week, try using confirming messages in at least two relationships: (1) a relationship in which you feel that you have put the other person down in the past, and (2) a relationship with a friend or romantic partner. In your journal, describe the two relationships, the messages you used, and why these messages were confirming, and analyze the influence the messages had on your communication.
3. *Rejuvenating a Relationship.* Several skills for rejuvenating relationships were discussed in this chapter. Select one of these skills to use in the next week in an ongoing relationship in which you have had problems communicating. In your journal, describe the relationship, the problems you have been having, the situation in which you used the skill, and the effect of using the skill. If the skill was not successful, explain why.

Study Questions

1. What are the different ways that we can define relationship maintenance?
2. How does our everyday communication define our relationships with others?
3. What are the differences in supportive and defensive communication climates?
4. How are our messages to others confirming and disconfirming?
5. Why is a problem that one person perceives in a relationship a problem for both people?
6. Why is behaving in a novel fashion an effective way to deal with problems in relationships?
7. Why is recognizing exceptions critical to resolving relational problems?
8. How does focusing on what works help us manage relational problems?
9. How does using creative interpretations help us manage relational problems?
10. How does going with the flow help us manage relational problems?
11. How does recognizing our expectations help us manage relational problems?
12. How does recognizing our communication style help us manage relational problems?

Suggested Readings

Beck, A. (1988). *Love is never enough.* New York: Harper & Row. Aaron Beck is one of the top cognitive therapists in the United States. In this book, he explains how our cognitive distortions and cognitive processing influence our relationships with others. He provides suggestions for dealing with problems that arise.

Duncan, B. L., & Rock, J. W. (1991). *Overcoming relational impasses.* New York: Insight Books. Barry Duncan and Joseph Rock use a systems perspective to deal with problems in relationships. They suggest strategies for dealing with relationship problems that individuals can use alone. These strategies include giving up power to be more effective, staying off the defensive, using creative interpretations, shifting the focus, and going with the flow.

Prather, H. (1986). *Notes on how to live in the world . . . and still be happy.* Garden City, NY: Doubleday. Hugh Prather provides suggestions on how to function effectively in interpersonal relationships. His discussion of letting go of expectations is especially useful in the context of this chapter.

Weiner-Davis, M. (1992). *Divorce busting.* New York: Summit Books. Michelle Weiner-Davis provides suggestions for how individuals can deal with problems in their relationships alone or with their partners. As indicated in the text, her suggestions focus on finding exceptions, doing what works, and engaging in novel responses.

15

MANAGING CONFLICT

In the previous chapter, suggestions for dealing with communication problems in our relationships were provided. If problems are not addressed, they can lead to major conflicts. *Conflict* "exists whenever incompatible activities occur" (Deutsch, 1973, p. 10). When one person's actions are incompatible with another person's actions, this obstructs or interferes with one or both people accomplishing their goals. This involves a wide range of situations. Conflicts can range from minor disagreements, such as a difference of opinion with someone with whom we have an ongoing relationship, to war. Knowing how to manage conflict is critical to maintaining and rejuvenating our relationships. This chapter, therefore, is a continuation of the previous chapter.

Conflict is inevitable in any relationship; it is going to happen whether we want it to or not. Conflict arises from several sources (Roloff, 1987). It occurs when people misinterpret each other's behavior. Misinterpreting other people's intent, for example, is one of the major causes of discontent in marriages (Gottman et al., 1976). Conflict also can arise from perceptions of incompatibility, such as perceiving that personality characteristics are not compatible. Conflict also arises when people disagree on the causes of their own or other people's behavior. As indicated in Chapter 7, we tend to explain our own positive behavior based on personal characteristics, and other people's positive behavior is attributed to situational demands. We tend to attribute our own negative behavior to situational demands and other people's negative behavior to their personal characteristics.

Conflict in relationships can be overt and out in the open (manifest conflict) or it can be out of sight (latent conflict). When conflict is out of sight, we can easily avoid addressing the conflict. In fact, avoidance is probably the most widely used strategy for dealing with conflict. It has been estimated that we avoid 50 percent of our conflicts with others (Sillars et al., 1982). One reason we avoid conflict is that many of us view conflict negatively. **Conflict itself, however, is not positive or negative. How we manage the conflicts we have, in contrast, can have positive or negative consequences for our relationships with others.**

Our conflicts often seem to get out of control without our realizing it. There are four aspects of conflict development that contribute to this (Donohue, 1993). First, once conflicts start, they tend to perpetuate themselves, especially if there are already problems between the people involved. Conflict breeds conflict, unless it is successfully managed. Second, conflicts always take place within a context, but we often are not aware of how the context contributes to our conflicts with others. To manage conflicts, we have to understand the contexts in which they occur. Third, our conflicts always have implications for our relationships with others. When conflicts are over, our relationships change in some way, but we often do not recognize that it is how we manage the conflict that is critical to how it will affect our relationship. Fourth, conflict gets out of control because we do not recognize that manifest conflict actually serves many positive functions in our lives. If two people have conflict with a common enemy, for example, it brings them closer. Our conflict with others also helps define our roles, understand our feelings about others, and make the conflict issues clearer.

In this chapter, different strategies for managing conflict are examined, and suggestions for how to communicate effectively in conflict situations are provided. Before proceeding, think about how you tend to deal with conflict. Answer the following questions:

What is your attitude toward conflict? Is it inherently negative or positive? Why? ______

______

______

Under what conditions do you typically try to avoid conflicts that arise? Why do you try to avoid conflicts in these situations? ______

______

______

Under what conditions do you typically try to address conflicts that arise? Why do you try to address conflicts in these situations? ______

______

______

Do you react the same way toward conflict in all situations? How does your reaction differ in various situations? ______

______

______

How successful is the way you usually deal with conflict? What could you do to improve the way you manage conflict?

______

______

______

Your answers to these questions should provide insight into the role of conflict in your implicit personal theory of communication. Keep your answers to these questions in mind as you read the remainder of this section.

Conflict and Communication

Conflicts with other people are recognized, defined, expressed, and managed through communication. When interpersonal conflict occurs, we engage in strategic interaction to manage it. We make choices about how effective our alternative behaviors will be, given our goals and our perceptions of other people's goals (Putnam & Wilson, 1982). We are not highly aware of the strategies we use to deal with conflict on automatic pilot. When we communicate on automatic pilot, for example, we may tend to choose one strategy without thinking about it. When we are mindful, however, we can consciously choose the strategy we want to use to manage conflict in the particular situation. Let's begin the discussion of conflict and communication by looking at the strategies we use for dealing with conflict.

Strategies for Managing Conflict

Conflict strategies are the "behavioral choices" we make when we are confronted with a conflict (Putnam & Wilson, 1982). In other words, conflict strategies involve the way we choose to communicate with other people when we are engaged in a conflict. We use three major strategies in conflict situations (Putnam & Wilson, 1982).[1] A *solution orientation* to conflict refers to "direct confrontation, open discussion of alternatives, and acceptance of compromises" (p. 638). This strategy involves using low-context messages (see Chapter 2) and speaking directly with other people about the conflict. The focus is on integrating the needs of both parties and finding a solution that works for both individuals involved in the conflict. The "For Better or for Worse" cartoon illustrates how both people can win when compromise occurs.

A *nonconfrontation strategy* toward conflict emphasizes "avoidance and smoothing as indirect strategies for dealing with conflict" (Putnam & Wilson, 1982, p. 638). This strategy involves the use of high-context messages and indirect methods of managing the conflict (including silence) and *not* confronting other people. When this strategy is used, ill feelings are concealed and differences are glossed over.

Every relationship has conflicts. A solution orientation to conflict refers to directly confronting the conflict. Couples may seek counseling to help them open up their communication lines again.

FOR BETTER OR FOR WORSE © Lynn Johnston Prod., Inc. Reprinted with permission of UNIVERSAL PRESS SYNDICATE. All rights reserved.

A *control strategy* toward "direct confrontation . . . leads to persistent argument and nonverbal forcing" when dealing with conflict (Putnam & Wilson, 1982, p. 638). Like the solution-orientation strategy, the control strategy involves directly confronting other people. The difference is that, in the solution-orientation strategy, other people's positions are taken into consideration, while in the control strategy, other people's positions are ignored or taken into consideration when it does not get in the way of meeting goals.

The solution-orientation strategy appears to be the most effective and constructive strategy for managing conflict among European Americans in the United States (ethnic differences are discussed in the last section of this chapter). The nonconfrontation strategy tends to be perceived as a desirable way to handle conflict, but it is not perceived to be effective because it may hinder goal achievement, especially in organizations. The solution-orientation and nonconfrontation strategies, however, may be constructive strategies in different situations. "Confrontation . . . may not be a beneficial strategy when the conflict is trivial and when quick decisions are required. Avoidance may be quite effective for handling less important and highly volatile conflicts" (Putnam & Wilson, 1982, p. 633).

The control strategy is perceived to be an effective strategy for managing conflicts among European Americans, but people tend to see it as an undesirable way to manage conflict. People who use a control strategy are *not* perceived as constructive in their handling of conflict (Burke, 1970). As a communication strategy, control has many of the disadvantages of aggressiveness (discussed in Chapter 3). Using a control strategy for dealing with conflict, for example, leads to not taking other people's feelings into consideration and frequently involves attacking other people's self-concepts.

The nature of the relationship people have and their expectations regarding communication also affect the conflict strategies that work best (Pike & Sillars, 1985). To illustrate, consider the three different types of marriages introduced in Chapter 13 (Fitzpatrick, 1988). Traditional couples follow traditional gender roles, share their time together, and prefer stability over change. These couples prefer to confront rather than to avoid conflict (Pike & Sillars, 1985). Independent couples reject traditional roles and prefer novelty and change to stability. Like traditional couples, independent couples' orientation toward conflict is confrontation. Separate couples, in contrast, emphasize their individual autonomy and emotional distance. These couples tend to avoid conflict. Separate couples, however, can be very satisfied with their relationships when conflict issues are avoided (Pike & Sillars, 1985).

Assessing Your Conflict Strategies

Assessment 15.1 contains a questionnaire to help you assess the conflict strategies you use in a particular relationship. Take a few minutes to complete the questionnaire now.

You should have computed three scores for Assessment 15.1: solution orientation, nonconfrontation, and control. The higher your score on each of these scales, the more you tend to use this strategy in the specific relationship on which you based your responses. Keep in mind that you may use different strategies in different relationships and in different situations. You can choose to use any strategy you want when you are mindful of your communication. The important thing to keep in mind is that we tend to communicate on automatic pilot in conflict situations, and we tend to use the strategy on which we score the highest.

Constructive Conflict Management

Conflicts can arise from instrumental sources, such as differences in goals or practices, and from expressive sources, such as tension generated from hostile feelings (Olsen, 1978). Ongoing or recurring conflicts often are indicators of unresolved issues in our relationships (Donohue, 1993). In this case, conflicts may appear instrumental, such as a conflict over the family budget, but may actually be expressive, such as a struggle for control in the marriage. Managing conflict constructively can help us maintain and improve the quality of our relationships with others. Let's begin our discussion of constructive conflict by looking at how it differs from destructive conflict.

Constructive Versus Destructive Conflict Management

When we try to manage conflict, our goal is to "reach agreement" and "enhance the relationship" (Hocker & Wilmot, 1991, p. 64). These goals can be accomplished only if we manage conflict constructively. Conflicts can be classified as constructive or destructive based on the process used in managing them and the outcomes of the conflict (Johnson & Johnson, 1982).

With respect to the *process,* the management of conflicts is *constructive* if the conflict is defined as a mutual problem and if it is defined as a "win-win" situation in which both parties gain. For conflict to be managed constructively, participants must express their ideas openly and honestly, and all parties must be viewed as equal, with their positions taken seriously, valued, and respected. In constructive conflict management, the participants use effective communication skills, such as responsive listening and perception checking, so that differences in opinions can be clarified and understood. Participants must express their assumptions and perspectives on the problem and not take disagreements as rejection. Finally, similarities in participants' positions on the conflict must be understood and integrated so that they can work toward a mutually satisfying solution.

The *processes* involved in the *destructive* management of conflict are the opposite of those involved in the constructive management of conflict (Johnson & Johnson, 1982).

Assessment 15.1 *Assessing Your Conflict Strategies*

The purpose of this questionnaire is to help you assess the strategies you use for managing conflict. Since your strategies may be different with different people and in different situations, you will need to select a specific relationship and then keep the person and situation you select in mind when responding to the statements listed. Respond to each statement indicating the degree to which you agree or disagree: "Strongly Disagree" (answer 1), "Disagree" (answer 2), "Sometimes Disagree and Sometimes Agree" (answer 3), "Agree" (answer 4), and "Strongly Agree" (answer 5).

Select a person with whom you have a relationship. To illustrate, you could select a friend, lover, parent, or supervisor at work. Think about this person and your relationship when you complete this assessment.

_______ 1. I blend my ideas with others to create new alternatives for resolving a conflict.

_______ 2. I shy away from topics that are sources of disputes.

_______ 3. I insist my position be accepted during a conflict.

_______ 4. I suggest solutions that combine a variety of viewpoints.

_______ 5. I steer clear of disagreeable situations.

_______ 6. I give in a little on my ideas when the other person also gives in.

_______ 7. I avoid a person I suspect of wanting to discuss a disagreement.

_______ 8. I integrate arguments into a new solution from issues raised in a dispute.

_______ 9. I stress my point by hitting my fist on the table.

_______ 10. I will go fifty-fifty to reach a settlement.

_______ 11. I raise my voice when trying to get another person to accept my position.

_______ 12. I offer creative solutions in discussions of disagreements.

_______ 13. I keep quiet about my views in order to avoid disagreements.

_______ 14. I frequently give in a little if the other person will meet me halfway.

_______ 15. I downplay the importance of a disagreement.

_______ 16. I reduce disagreements by saying they are insignificant.

_______ 17. I meet the opposition at a midpoint of our differences.

_______ 18. I assert my opinion forcefully.

_______ 19. I dominate arguments until the other person understands my position.

_______ 20. I suggest we work together to create solutions to disagreements.

_______ 21. I try to use everyone's ideas to generate solutions to problems.

_______ 22. I offer tradeoffs to reach solutions in a disagreement.

_______ 23. I argue insistently for my stance.

_______ 24. I withdraw when someone confronts me about a controversial issue.

_______ 25. I sidestep disagreements when they arise.

_______ 26. I try to smooth over disagreements by making them appear unimportant.

_______ 27. I stand firm in my views during a conflict.

_______ 28. I make our differences seem less serious.

_______ 29. I hold my tongue rather than argue.

_______ 30. I ease conflict by claiming our differences are trivial.

There are three scores to be computed. To compute your scores for the scales, add your responses for the items listed for each scale. Solution-orientation: Add your responses to items 1, 4, 6, 8, 10, 12, 14, 17, 20, 21, and 22; Nonconfrontation: 2, 5, 7, 13, 15, 16, 24, 25, 26, 28, 29, and 30; Control: 3, 9, 11, 18, 19, 23, and 27.

Conflicts are *destructive* when the conflict is *not* defined as a mutual problem and when it is defined as a "win-lose" situation in which one person gains and the other loses. When conflict is managed destructively, participants are not open or are deceitful, and they do not view each other as equal or respect others' ideas. In destructive conflict management, participants do not use effective communication skills, and differences in opinions are suppressed or ignored. Participants do not clarify their assumptions or perspectives on the problem, and they take disagreements as rejection. Finally, when conflict is managed destructively, participants do not understand similarities in their positions or try to integrate them, and they do not work toward a mutually satisfying solution.

With respect to *outcomes,* conflicts are *constructive* when the participants feel understood, think they influenced others, are committed to the solution, are satisfied with the decision, feel accepted by the other person, and grow in their ability to manage future conflicts (Johnson & Johnson, 1982). Conflicts have *destructive outcomes* when participants do *not* feel understood, think they had little influence on others, are *not* committed to the solution, are *not* satisfied with the solution, do *not* feel accepted, and the ability to manage future conflicts is decreased.

When we communicate on automatic pilot, many of us tend to manage conflict destructively. We can, however, change the way we manage conflict when we are mindful. One of the guiding principles we need to follow when we are mindful is to be unconditionally constructive.

Be Unconditionally Constructive

One person can change a relationship (Fisher & Brown, 1988). If we change the way we react to other people, they will change the way they react to us. The objective of change is developing "a relationship that can deal with differences" (p. 3). Achieving change requires that we separate the relationship and substantive issues and pursue goals in each arena separately.

When we are trying to manage conflicts, we should **always be unconditionally constructive.** We should:

> Do only those things that are both good for the relationship and good for us, whether or not [other people] reciprocate.
>
> 1. *Rationality.* Even if [other people] are acting emotionally, balance emotion with reason.
> 2. *Understanding.* Even if [other people] misunderstand us, try to understand them.
> 3. *Communication.* Even if [other people] are not listening, consult them before deciding on matters that affect them.
> 4. *Reliability.* Even if [other people] are trying to deceive us, neither trust nor deceive them; be reliable.
> 5. *Noncoercive modes of influence.* Even if [other people] are trying to coerce us, neither yield to that coercion nor try to coerce them; be open to persuasion and try to persuade them.
> 6. *Acceptance.* Even if [other people] reject us and our concerns as unworthy of their consideration, accept them as worthy of our consideration, care about them, and be open to learning from them. (Fisher & Brown, 1988, p. 38)

Few, if any, of us follow these six guidelines in our everyday communication with other people. In order to apply these guidelines, we must be mindful. When we are mindful, one of the major issues we need to examine is how power is distributed in the relationship because imbalances in power make it difficult to manage conflict constructively.

Power and Constructive Conflict Management

Power is "the **ability to influence or control events**" (Folger, Poole, & Stutman, 1993, p. 99). We can use a wide variety of resources to influence others or events. Potential resources include our knowledge of the subject being discussed, our skills related to the task being completed, our ability to reward or punish others, our ability to persuade others, our attractiveness, and so forth. In order for us to be able to influence others, they have to give some credence to our use of the resources. Others, therefore, allow us to exert power.

There are many different ways that we can use power in conflict situations (Folger et al., 1993). We can, for example, make threats or promises. A *threat* is "an individual's expressed intention to behave in a way that appears detrimental to the interests of another, if that other does not comply with the individual's request or terms" (p. 112). A *promise,* in contrast, is "an individual's expressed intention to behave in a way that appears beneficial to another, if the other complies with the individual's request or terms" (p. 112). The extent to which our threats or promises work in conflict situations depends on whether we can control the relevant resources. To illustrate, if we threaten to dock someone's pay, the threat works only if we have the authority to do this. Similarly, if we promise to take our romantic partner on vacation, the promise works only if she or he thinks we have the resources to do this.

We often exert power by *relational control.* We can use the relational component of our messages to define or control our relationships with others when we engage in conflicts (Folger et al., 1993). The way we transmit messages to other people by using the tone of our voice, for example, can lead other people to think we are superior to them. If other people respond in a way that suggests that they have accepted our definition of the relationship, our use of power has been successful. For relational control to be an effective power strategy in conflicts, it needs to be undetected by other people in the conflict. If other people recognize that we are trying to control the relationship, they can stop us. In the preceding example, if other people recognize our power move and say something like "Why are you talking like you're superior to me?" our use of power will not be successful.

We also can use power to control the issues involved in the conflict. *Issue control* may involve redirecting other people's attention away from the conflict or suppressing conflicts by making people afraid to raise the conflict issues (Folger et al., 1993). If other people recognize that we have power, for example, they may not discuss the conflict issues with us.

As indicated earlier, imbalances in power in relationships make constructive conflict management difficult (Folger et al., 1993). When power imbalances exist, we may accidentally escalate the conflict by using our power (assuming we have more power than the other person). When we use power and the other person does not think we should have, it leads to destructive conflict management. To constructively manage conflict, we must try to balance power in our relationship with the other person. We can do this by not exerting our power if we have more than the other person or by empowering the other person so that the power is equal.

Assessing Your Management of Conflict

Assessment 15.2 is designed to help you assess how you manage conflict. Take a few minutes to complete it now.

Scores on Assessment 15.2 range from 10 to 50. The higher your score, the greater your potential for constructively managing conflict with others. If your score is low, remember that managing conflict constructively requires that you be mindful of the *process* of your communication. When you are mindful, you may want to keep in mind the material discussed in the remainder of this section when you try to manage conflicts.

Communicating to Manage Conflict

The way we approach others regarding conflicts and how we can negotiate solutions to conflicts affect the outcomes. To constructively manage conflicts, we must be mindful of our communication and be concerned with both ourselves and the other person. While the focus of this section is on constructively managing conflicts, a decision tree for selecting alternative strategies is presented at the end of this section.

Approaching Others

The first step in managing conflicts is to *approach* others regarding the conflict (Johnson,

Assessment 15.2 *Assessing Your Management of Conflict*

The purpose of this questionnaire is to help you assess your ability to successfully manage conflict. Respond to each statement by indicating the degree to which it is true regarding how you manage conflict with strangers: "Always False" (answer 1), "Usually False" (answer 2), "Sometimes True and Sometimes False" (answer 3), "Usually True" (answer 4), or "Always True" (answer 5).

_______ 1. I respond emotionally when I have conflict with others.

_______ 2. I try to understand others with whom I am having a conflict.

_______ 3. If someone rejects my ideas during a conflict, I also reject theirs.

_______ 4. I act reliably (i.e., consistently) when trying to manage conflicts with others.

_______ 5. I try to get others to agree with me when we have a conflict.

_______ 6. I balance emotion with reason when trying to manage conflicts with others.

_______ 7. I am not open to being persuaded when I have conflicts with others.

_______ 8. I consult others before deciding on matters that affect them.

_______ 9. I am not as constructive as I could be when I have conflicts with others.

_______ 10. I try to do what is best for the relationship, even if the person with whom I am having a conflict does not reciprocate.

To find you score, first reverse the responses for the *odd-numbered* items (if you wrote 1, make it 5; if you wrote 2, make it 4; if you wrote 3, leave it as 3; if you wrote 4, make it 2; if you wrote 5, make it 1). Next, add the numbers next to each statement. Scores range from 10 to 50. The higher your score, the greater your potential to successfully manage conflicts with strangers.

1986). **We need to approach other people when we are sure that they are available and emotionally capable of discussing the conflict** (they are not upset and they have time to talk). When we approach other people, we need to express our thoughts and feelings about the conflict and ask them to do the same.

The goal of approaching other people about the conflict is to clarify and explore the issues surrounding the conflict (Johnson, 1986). We want to try to define the problem, establish a cooperative environment, and schedule a negotiation session. Unless the conflict is very minor, we should *not* try to manage the conflict when we approach other people, but rather schedule a time later when we can negotiate a solution. Other people need time to think about their goals and the solutions that are acceptable to them before they can negotiate a solution to the conflict with us.

To be effective, **our approach needs to be done in a way that does not increase other people's anxiety or defensiveness, and in a way that allows them to maintain their self-concepts.** This involves using the communication resources discussed throughout this book. We must, for example, use our communication resources to establish a supportive communication climate, we must listen responsively, be empathic, and so forth. Since most of us do not have scripts in these areas, we have to be mindful of our communication in order to focus on the interaction taking place, and not get distracted by thinking about the outcome of the conflict.

Defining Conflicts

When we approach other people, we need to define the conflict as we see it and ask them to do the same. To successfully manage conflicts, we need to be *cooperative,* not competitive (Deutsch, 1973). We need to define the conflict as a *mutual problem* that needs to be solved. When we communicate on automatic pilot, we tend to define conflicts in a way that they are one person's problem. When conflicts are defined in this way, only one person can win. **When conflicts are defined as a mutual problem to be solved, both parties can win, instead of one party having to win and the other lose.** Remember, interpersonal relationships are communication systems. What each person does influences the other. As indicated in Chapter 13, there is no problem in an interpersonal relationship that is a problem for only one of the people involved.

We tend to blame other people for conflicts when we view the conflict issues as important, when conflicts occur frequently, and when we are not satisfied with our relationship with the other person (Sillars, 1980). We tend to be willing to accept responsibility for conflicts when the topic is not important to us, when conflicts are not frequent, and when we are satisfied with our relationships. It therefore is important for us to be mindful when we are engaged in conflict. If we blame the other person, we cannot define the conflict as a mutual problem.

In addition to defining conflict as a mutual problem, we need to look for a *common definition of the problem.* If we do not agree on the definition of the problem, we cannot solve it. Many conflicts are due to the parties involved perceiving that their goals are different or even incompatible. Often people involved in conflicts discover they actually want the same thing. In this case, when they define the problem underlying the conflict, common goals emerge. When the goals are actually different or incompatible, it is necessary to agree on the problem in order to actually solve it. This may mean that the individuals define the problem as "Person A wants *X* and Person B wants *Y.*"

We need to define conflicts in the most limited way possible (Johnson, 1986). The reason for focusing on limited issues is that it increases the likelihood of successful conflict management. If we have a big problem to address, we can break it down into smaller ones and deal with each smaller problem one at a time.

In order to define a conflict problem successfully, we must know what our goals are (Hocker & Wilmot, 1991). We cannot find solutions if we do not know what we want. We can alter and accomplish our goals more easily if they are clear than if they are vague, and only clear goals can be shared. Before approaching other people with whom we have a conflict, we need to take time to clarify our goals. After we approach other people, it is important to remember that they may need time to clarify their own goals.

Negotiating Solutions

We have three basic options when it comes to managing conflicts (Hocker & Wilmot, 1991). First, we can try to change others. This is a somewhat natural response, but it usually is not very successful. If we try to change others and they try to change us, we will both appear rigid and unreasonable to each other. Second, we can try to alter the conditions underlying the conflict. If we "can increase scarce resources, alter the nature of problematic interdependence, change perceptions or incompatible goals, or make some other alteration in the conflict elements," we can change the nature of the conflict and find solutions (Hocker & Wilmot, 1991, p. 180). Third, we can change our own behavior. Although we may perceive this to be the most difficult and least desirable way to manage a conflict, it often is the most successful. If we change our orientation toward the other person or our interpretation of the issues, or try to communicate more effectively, we can alter the outcome of the conflict. By changing our orientation, we can change a win-lose conflict into a win-win. This process is illustrated in Reading 15.1.

In managing conflicts, we need to try to communicate as effectively as possible. There are two sides to effective communication: adapting our messages and understanding others. We must *adapt our messages* so that others can accurately interpret them. This means using language to create a supportive communication environment (as opposed to a destructive environment). It also means using language with which other people are familiar. We need to make sure that we avoid putting other people down or calling them names if we want to constructively manage the conflict. Since conflict produces stress, however, we may not adapt our messages when we are on automatic pilot. To be able to adapt our messages, we have to manage our anxiety.

A large part of adapting our messages involves using concrete, as opposed to abstract, language. Abstract language is open to interpretation, and other people's interpretations of abstract language often are different from our own. To illustrate, if one partner in a romantic relationship says, "You don't love me

Resentment can flare up, even in a playful way, when couples do not have enough time together. This is a mutual problem and both partners need to win in order to solve the conflict.

Reading 15.1 FROM ZERO SUM TO THE NEW MATH/WILLIAM BETCHER

During drawn-out disagreements couples tend to become more and more committed to their points of view and unwilling to consider alternatives because it feels like conceding. A situation that each sees as having only a "zero sum" outcome, in terms of one winning and the other losing, will only create resentment. Play can help change this no-win situation into one in which both can win and are changed in the process. Play provides an atmosphere in which partners can feel safe to explore options rather than asserting rigid positions. The next couple illustrates how playful exaggeration can change a couple from being adversaries to problem solvers.

"My wife says I'm compulsive. We still argue about it, but over the years I've mellowed a bit. For example, whenever we fly I'm a nervous wreck until I'm actually at the departure gate. My palms start getting sweaty the night before our flight. I'm at my worst in foreign countries—I'm sure that the way to every airport is a jungle of police checkpoints, dirt roads, and seven-car accidents. It's amazing to me that anyone makes it to the airport on time.

"Recently we were in Milan, where the airport is a good distance from the city, just the situation where my fertile imagination could run wild. The desk clerk suggested we allow three hours to get there. Since our flight left at two P.M., that meant leaving by at least eleven. My wife was pleased that she could get a little shopping done in the morning.

"I awoke at six and shaved and showered by six thirty. I went into the bedroom where my wife was just waking up. 'I've been thinking about our flight,' I said. 'Maybe we should leave now.' She looked as if she was about to have a fit until she saw that I was grinning. We left at ten thirty, which gave her a chance to do some shopping and gave me a little reassurance on the way to the airport."

The goal is to devise creative solutions, not necessarily to win a partner over to your point of view. For even were you to manage agreement on content, there can be lingering resentment if the solution is felt to be imposed.

anymore," the other partner is likely to respond by saying, "Yes, I do!" The first person will then respond, "No, you don't!" The problem may be that they mean different things by the word *love*. Love may mean being together, sharing household chores, and talking together to the first person, but it may mean having romantic feelings to the second person. Since love is an abstract term, the two people will not be able to manage the conflict successfully unless they use more concrete language. Skill Exercise 15.1 is designed to help you use more concrete language. Take a few minutes to complete it.

The critical thing in Skill Exercise 15.1 is clarifying abstract language. In the first scenario, for example, the word fun can be problematic. One person may mean laughing and joking by the word "fun" and the other person may mean doing enjoyable activities. If the two people do not clarify what they mean by the abstract word "fun," they will never understand each other.

The second aspect of effective communi-

Skill Exercise 15.1 ***Using Concrete Language***

Misunderstandings often occur when we use abstract language (very general words). We tend to use global, abstract terms when we communicate on automatic pilot. Our communication often is more effective when we use concrete (specific words) language. This requires that we be mindful of our communication and of the words we are using. For each of the situations listed below, indicate the concrete language you could use to increase communication effectiveness.

1. Your romantic partner says, "We never have any fun." You say, "Yes we do. We have fun all the time." What concrete words could you use to clarify to your partner what you mean by "fun"?
   ____
   ____

2. You meet with your instructor and say, "Your grading system is not fair!" The instructor responds, "I think my grading system is fair." What concrete words could you use to explain to your instructor why you think that her or his grading system is "unfair"? ____________
   ____
   ____
   ____

3. You and a friend are discussing Pat, another person you both know. You say, "Pat is a nasty person." Your friend says, "I don't think Pat is nasty." What concrete language could you use to explain why you think Pat is nasty? ____________
   ____
   ____
   ____

cation during conflicts involves making sure that we *understand others.* This requires that our perceptions be as accurate as possible. **Conflict causes anxiety and stress, and our anxiety in turn causes us to process information more simply than we usually do.** Simple information processing does not allow us to see other people's points of view. We therefore are likely to misinterpret other people's behavior in conflict situations. We can decrease the distortions and biases in our perceptions by mindfully using the perception checking skill, responsive listening skills, and empathy discussed earlier in this book.

When our perceptions are distorted, we may perceive that other people have negative and hostile feelings toward us and not perceive the positive feelings they have. This can lead to a self-fulfilling prophecy, if we communicate on automatic pilot. To minimize distortions in our perceptions, we need to adopt a conciliatory orientation toward others (Stuart, 1980). This involves mindfully trying to see other people's behavior in the most positive way possible and trying to resolve the conflict equitably. We have to make it clear to other people that we are interested in finding a solution that is fair to them. If other people perceive that we care only about ourselves, it decreases our chance to manage the conflict constructively.

If we do not understand other people's positions and they do not understand our position, there is no way we can find a solution

SALLY FORTH. Reprinted with special permission of King Features Syndicate.

acceptable to both of us. To successfully manage conflict, we must be able to predict and explain other people's behavior as accurately as possible. To accomplish this, we need to focus on the present situation, not on the past or the future (Stuart, 1980). Searching for the cause of the conflict by asking why it occurred is not highly productive. Rather, we need to focus on solutions in the present and ask how can we manage the conflict constructively.

To manage any conflict, **we must understand the differences between ourselves and others** (Johnson, 1986). Rather than ignoring differences, we need to seek out differences in opinions and ideas regarding the conflict. We must be able to disagree with others and, at the same time, *confirm* them and their views of themselves. If we treat other people as though they are not valued, they will become defensive, and their anxiety will increase. Conflicts cannot be managed constructively when either party is highly anxious or defensive.

Once we understand other people's positions and they understand ours, we may find that there are irreconcilable differences. If we suspect irreconcilable differences and we want to continue our relationship, we need to find an alternative to directly confronting the issues involved. This may be a situation in which indirectly dealing with the conflict or avoiding it altogether is the best strategy.

Recognizing similarities and not just focusing on differences also is necessary to successfully manage conflict (Johnson, 1986). If we focus only on differences between our position and other people's positions, we will never be able to manage the conflict. **Finding a solution that will work for us and other people requires that we see similarities in our positions and then build on these similarities.** To successfully manage conflicts, both parties must understand and see similarities in each other's positions and feelings.

In trying to find a solution for the problem, we need to recognize how our behavior contributed to creating the problem, not just focus on other people's behavior. Both parties to a conflict contribute to the formation of the conflict. We cannot manage a conflict constructively, if we do not understand our contribution to it. We also cannot manage a conflict constructively by trying to label a winner. For constructive conflict management, both parties have to win.

To manage a conflict successfully, we may have to coordinate our motivations to manage the conflict (Johnson, 1986). We may be ready to manage the conflict today, but other people

SALLY FORTH. Reprinted with special permission of King Features Syndicate.

may not be. Tomorrow other people may be ready and we will not be. We can, however, consciously change our own motivation if we choose. As indicated earlier, we can choose to change our own behavior, but we cannot successfully change other people's behavior.

Reaching an agreement occurs when we have a joint solution with which all parties are satisfied. Our agreement should specify how each person will act differently in the future, including both new things that the person will do in the future and things that will be avoided, such as criticizing.

Reading 15.2 provides a *negative* summary of the points made in this section. It is negative because the rules for how to *ruin* a discussion are summarized. The *reverse* of these rules are reasonable guidelines for constructively managing conflicts.

Selecting Appropriate Strategies

Throughout this section, the focus has been on how to constructively manage conflicts. We may not, however, always want to constructively manage conflicts. When our relationships with other people are not important, for example, we may prefer to use another approach to dealing with a conflict. A decision tree can be used to select specific conflict strategies in particular situations (Folger et al., 1993), as in Figure 15.1. Before looking at the decision tree, however, the questions in the decision tree and the specific strategies from which we can select must be discussed.

Questions We Must Address. Our decisions about how to manage conflict can be made by answering five questions (Folger et al., 1993): How important are the issues involved in the conflict to us? How important are the issues to the other person? How important is maintaining a positive relationship with the other person? How much time pressure is there? How much can we trust the other person?

The first question we have to address is the importance of the conflict issue to us. If the issue is important to us, we want to use strategies that help us accomplish our objectives more than if the issue is not important to us. If the issue is not important to us, we can use flexible strategies for managing the conflict because they require less time and energy (Folger et al., 1993).

The second question we must address is the importance of the conflict issue to the other person. If the issue is important to the other person, it is to their advantage *and* to

Reading 15.2 THE MAGIC RULES FOR RUINING ANY DISCUSSION/HUGH PRATHER AND GAYLE PRATHER

1. *Bring the matter up when at least one of you is angry.*
   Variations: Bring it up when nothing can be done about it (in the middle of the night; right before guests are due; when one of you is in the shower.)
   Bring it up when concentration is impossible (while driving to a meeting with the IRS; while watching the one TV program you both agree on; while your spouse is balancing the checkbook.)
2. *Be as personal as possible when setting forth the problem.*
   Variations: Know the answer before you ask the question.
   While describing the issue, use an accusatory tone. Begin by implying who, as usual, is to blame.
3. *Concentrate on getting what you want.*
   Variations: Overwhelm your partner's position before he or she can muster a defense (be very emotional; call in past favors; be impeccably reasonable).
   Impress on your partner what you need and what he or she must do without.
   If you begin losing ground, jockey for position.
4. *Instead of listening, think only of what you will say next.*
   Variations: Do other things while your partner is talking. Forget where your partner left off.
   In other words, listen with all the interest you would give a bathroom exhaust fan.
5. *Correct anything your partner says about you.*
   Variations: Each time your partner gives an example of your behavior, cite a worse example of his or hers.
   Repeat "That's not what I said" often.
   Do not accept anything your partner says at face value (point out exceptions; point out inaccuracies in facts and in grammar).
6. *Mention anything from the past that has a chance of making your partner defensive.*
   Variations: Make allusions to your partner's sexual performance.
   Remind your husband of his mother's faults.
   Compare what your wife does to what other women do, and after she complains, say, "I didn't mean it that way."
7. *End by saying something that will never be forgotten.*
   Variations: Do something that proves you are a madman [or madwoman].
   Let your parting display proclaim that no exposure of your partner could be amply revealing, no characterization too profane, no consequence sufficiently wretched.
   At least leave the impression you are a little put out.

our advantage if we select strategies that take the other person into consideration (Folger et al., 1993). If the issue is not important to the other person, we can select strategies that do not take the other person into consideration.

The third question we must address focuses on the importance of the relationship with the other person. How we manage conflicts with other people depends on the importance of our long-term relationship with them (Folger et al., 1993). If it is important that we maintain a long-term relationship with other people, then we want to select strategies that take them and their viewpoints into consideration. If we do not care if we maintain a good relationship with other people or if we see this as an impossible goal, we can select strategies that do not take the other people into consideration.

The fourth question involves the amount of time pressure there is to manage the conflict. If there is a great deal of time pressure, we need to select strategies that will force a resolution to the conflict (Folger et al., 1993). If, on the other hand, there is little time pressure, we can select strategies that require a longer time to manage the conflict.

The final question we have to address deals with the degree we can trust the person with whom we are having a conflict (Folger et al., 1993). If we think we can trust the other person, we can use strategies that empower the other person. When we do not trust the other person, we need to select strategies that protect our own power.

Alternative Tactics. Earlier in this chapter, three general strategies for managing conflicts were introduced: solution orientation, nonconfrontation, and control. The specific conflict tactics listed in Figure 15.1 are subsumed under the three broader strategies introduced earlier. The solution-orientation strategy includes three specific tactics: problem solving, firm compromise, and flexible compromise. The nonconfrontation strategy includes five specific tactics: smoothing, yielding, conceding, protecting, and withdrawing. Control can be divided into two tactics: contending and forcing. It is not necessary to memorize the specific tactics, but they do need to be defined so that you can understand the options available to you. Let's look at the specific tactics.

Problem solving is the first solution-oriented tactic. Problem solving is designed to meet the needs of both parties involved in the conflict (Folger et al., 1993). In using this tactic, we are committed to our goals and unwilling to sacrifice them. At the same time, however, we are concerned with the other person's need. We are looking for a win-win solution, a solution with which both parties in the conflict are happy. We are flexible in our approach to managing conflicts when we use this tactic.

The second solution-oriented tactic is *firm compromise.* When we use this tactic, we are willing to engage in tradeoffs, but we are not very flexible in terms of our willingness to change our position (Folger et al., 1993). Our position is well defined, and we do not want to change it. In using this tactic, we take the lead in working out a compromise, and we may push others to get them to cooperate with us.

Flexible compromise is the third solution-oriented tactic. This tactic differs from firm compromise in that our position is not necessarily well defined (Folger et al., 1993). In using this tactic, we are willing to follow the other person's lead in reaching a compromise. We will self-disclose to provide information the other person needs to know about us and our position in order to work out a compromise.

The first nonconfrontation tactic is *smoothing.* Smoothing involves playing down

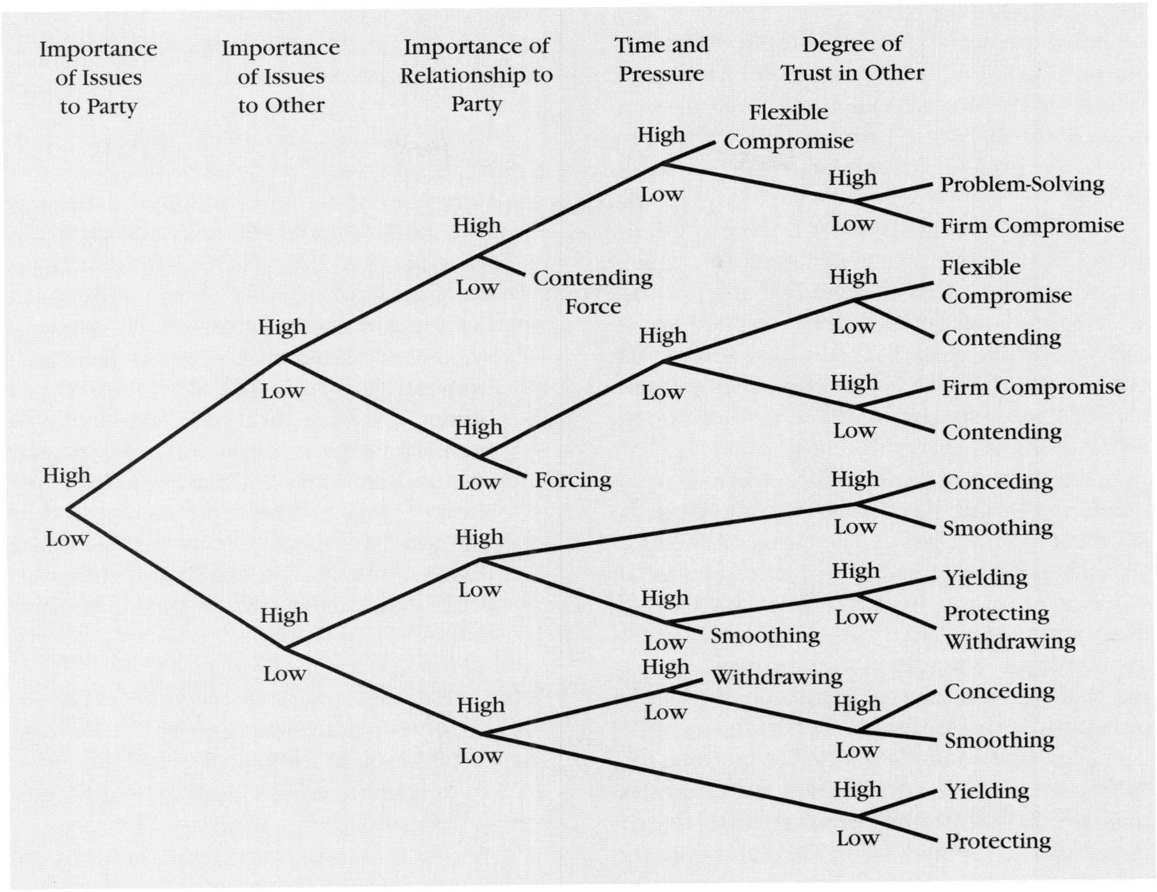

FIGURE 15.1 A Decision Tree for Selecting Conflict Strategies. Source: From *Working Through Conflict,* 2nd Edition by Joseph P. Floger, Marshall Scott Poole and Randall K. Stutman. Copyright © 1993 by HarperCollins College Publishers. Reprinted by permission.

the differences between ourselves and the other person (Folger et al., 1993). We emphasize positive parts of the interactions and the commonalities between ourselves and the other person. In using this tactic, we avoid talking about issues that would hurt the person's feelings or make the other person angry. When talking to the other person, we try to keep the conversation focused on topics other than on the conflict.

Yielding is the second type of nonconfrontation tactic. When we yield, we have apathy toward the conflict, and we are not concerned with our own needs (Folger et al., 1993). We accommodate to the other person and allow the other person to control the conflict.

The third nonconfrontation tactic is *conceding.* When we use a conceding tactic, we are more involved in the conflict than when we use a yielding strategy (Folger et al., 1993). We still accommodate to the other person, but our motivation is different than when we yield. When we use a conceding tactic, we are concerned for the other person, and we accommodate to build a better relationship with him or her.

Protecting is the fourth nonconfrontation tactic. In using a protecting tactic, our goal is to protect ourselves by avoiding the conflict at all costs (Folger et al., 1993). To accomplish this, we build a shell around ourselves. We are not highly attentive to the other person, especially when the conflict is mentioned, when using a protecting tactic.

The final nonconfrontation tactic is *withdrawing.* When we withdraw, we work to keep the conflict below the surface (Folger et al., 1993). We are, however, more flexible than when we use a protecting tactic. We may address some issues involved in the conflict but avoid others. When issues are brought up that we want to avoid, we try to change the subject or withdraw from the conversation.

The first control tactic is *contending.* When we use this strategy, we are interested mainly in accomplishing our own goals (Folger et al., 1993). We may be flexible and take the other person's goals into consideration, but only if meeting the other person's goals does *not* get in the way of accomplishing our goals. When using this tactic, we may express *sympathy* for the other person's feelings because we are concerned with the future of our relationship with the other person.

Forcing is the second control tactic. Forcing involves trying to get the other person to go along with what we want (Folger et al., 1993). When we use this tactic, we do not express any concern for the other person or the other person's position. When using this tactic, we obviously are *not* concerned with preserving our relationship with the other person.

Using the Decision Tree. To illustrate the use of the decision tree in Figure 15.1, consider the following conflict scenario:

> Robin and Joe have been going together for three years. They often disagree over where to spend the holidays. This year they both want to spend Thanksgiving at their parents' house. The parents live far enough apart so that they cannot visit both sets of parents. Robin really wants to see her parents because she hasn't been home in a long time. Joe also has not been home in a long time and would like to see his parents, but his main goal is for the two of them to have a good time together. Robin brings up the topic of where they are going to spend Thanksgiving, and a decision needs to be made at this time so they can finalize their travel arrangements.

What tactic for managing this conflict should Joe use when talking with Robin? Before reading further, look at the decision tree in Figure 15.1 to determine which tactic would be best for Joe to use.

The issue is important to Joe, so he would take the top branch (High) at the first decision point in Figure 15.1. The issue also is important to Robin, so Joe would take the top branch (High) at the second decision point. The relationship is important to Joe, so he would take the top branch (High) at the third decision point. There is time pressure to make the decision, so Joe would take the top branch (High) at the fourth decision point. This leads to a flexible compromise tactic.

To make sure you understand how to use the decision tree, try another example:

> You are working in a task group in a class. Getting a good grade is important to you. You did not know any of the people in

> your group prior to the class and do not expect to see any of them again after the class. The other members of your group feel the same way. One of the members of the group has not done his or her share of the work by the agreed-upon deadline. There is still time for this person to do her or his work before the project must be submitted to your professor, but there is only a limited amount of time to complete the task. You do not have time to do the other person's work, nor do any of the other members of the group.

You plan to tell the other person today that he or she must complete her or his work. What tactic should you use? Use the decision tree to select a tactic before reading further.

Since the issue is important to you, you would take the top branch (High) at the first decision point in Figure 15.1. You would probably assume that the issue is not important to the other person, so you would take the bottom branch (Low) at the second decision point. The relationship is not important to you, so you would take the bottom branch (Low) at the third decision point. This would lead to a forcing tactic.

It is important to keep in mind that our answers to the questions posed in the decision tree may change over the course of a conflict (Folger et al., 1993). We therefore have to monitor the changing conditions of our conflicts to make sure that the tactic we initially selected is still appropriate. The decision tree in Figure 15.1 is very general and therefore can be used with a wide variety of conflicts.

Developing New Scripts for Managing Conflicts

Most of our everyday scripts for managing conflicts do not follow the principles for managing conflict constructively outlined here. Skill Exercise 15.2 provides an opportunity for you to better understand your typical approach to managing conflict and to begin to develop new scripts for more constructive conflict management. Take a few minutes now to complete the skill exercise.

As suggested throughout this section, most of us have *not* been taught how to constructively manage conflicts. To successfully manage conflicts, we need to learn new scripts and develop new attitudes toward conflict. This exercise provides practice in developing new scripts, but we must also develop new attitudes. If we enter conflicts with the attitude that we have to win and others have to lose, we cannot constructively manage the conflicts. To constructively manage conflicts, we must find solutions acceptable to both parties; both parties must be able to win.

Cultural and Ethnic Issues in Managing Conflict

Our culture and our ethnicity influence what we perceive to be a conflict and how we prefer to deal with conflicts. In this section, cultural and ethnic differences in conflict are overviewed and suggestions for how to manage intergroup conflicts are provided. Let's begin by looking at group differences in how conflict is managed.

Group Differences in Managing Conflict

There are group differences in how conflict is managed. Understanding cultural and ethnic differences is necessary to manage intergroup conflicts constructively. We'll begin with cultural differences.

Skill Exercise 15.2 *Managing Conflict Constructively*

To manage conflicts constructively, we need to define the issue involved in the conflict as a mutual problem to be solved. The purpose of this exercise is to think about how you can confront conflict issues, how conflict issues can be defined as mutual problems, and how conflict issues can be managed constructively.

Consider the following scenario: You and your romantic partner are at a party. While at the party, you see your romantic partner spending a lot of time talking to another person (a potential rival for your partner's affection). They seem to enjoy each other's company and you begin to feel jealous. You observed your partner engaging in similar behavior at the last party the two of you attended. At that time you let it go and tried to forget about it. You can't do that this time. Answer the following questions regarding how you might handle this conflict. Try to be as specific as possible (write a specific statement you might make in this situation).

1. How would you typically respond in this situation? ______________________
____
____
____

2. Assuming that you want to manage this conflict constructively, how might you confront your partner? ______________________
____
____
____

3. How could you and your partner define this as a mutual problem that needs to be solved? ______________________
____
____
____

4. How would you communicate your position and feelings to your partner? ______
____
____
____
____

5. How would you communicate your cooperative intentions to your partner?
____
____
____
____

6. How would you make sure that you understand your partner's perspective?
____
____
____
____

7. Outline an agreement that you think would be acceptable to you and your partner if you had this disagreement.
____
____
____
____

Cultural Differences. People in individualistic cultures prefer direct strategies for dealing with conflict, such as controlling or solution orientation (Ting-Toomey, 1988). People in collectivistic cultures, on the other hand, prefer indirect strategies of dealing with conflict that allow all parties to preserve face. *Face* is the image we project to others in our relationships with them (Ting-Toomey, 1988). Collectivists tend to use smoothing strategies of conflict resolution or avoid the conflict altogether (nonconfrontation strategies) because these strategies do not threaten anyone's face and help maintain ingroup harmony.

These differences are consistent with descriptions of conflict strategies in Japan and the United States. People in the United States, for example, "prefer to defend themselves actively, employing or developing the rationale for positions they have taken. When pushed they may resort to still more aggressive forms that utilize humor, sarcasm, or denunciation. Among Japanese, . . . defenses tend to be more passive, permit withdrawal, and allow greater concealment" (Barnlund, 1975, p. 423). Japanese avoid conflicts to protect harmony in the ingroup and to avoid losing face or a person's public image.

Avoiding conflict in order to preserve face is not limited to the Japanese culture. Chinese, for example, would advise an executive to meet separately with a person who insulted someone else and with the target of the insult, so that conflict between the two could be avoided. People in the United States, in contrast, would advise an executive to have a joint meeting so that the problem between the insulter and the target of the insult could be resolved (Bond et al., 1985). Similar differences emerge when people in the United States and Mexico are compared. Specifically, Mexicans tend to avoid or deny that conflict exists, while people in the United States tend to use direct strategies to deal with it (McGinn, Harburg, & Ginsburg, 1973).[2]

Ethnic Differences. There also are differences across ethnic groups in the United States.[3] African Americans, for example, prefer a controlling conflict resolution style, while European Americans prefer a solution-oriented style (Ting-Toomey, 1986). Where European Americans "use the relatively detached and unemotional *discussion* mode to engage an issue, [African Americans] use the more emotionally intense and involving mode of *argument.* Where [European Americans] tend to *underestimate* their exceptional talents and abilities, [African Americans] tend to *boast* about theirs" (Kochman, 1981, p. 106). African Americans favor forceful outputs, such as high volume, while European Americans prefer subdued outputs. African Americans interpret European Americans' subdued responses as lifeless, and European Americans interpret African Americans' responses as in bad taste (Kochman, 1981).

There are several other areas where European American and African American styles of communication may differ when they communicate with each other, particularly in a conflict situation. One area of importance for dealing with conflict is how members of the two groups view their responsibilities to other people's sensibilities and feelings. Differences in reactions to an assignment in an interpersonal communication class where students were told to confront each other and comment on their perceptions of the other person's style of communication illustrate the two approaches (Kochman, 1981). The student responses to the assignment divided basically along ethnic lines:

> Twelve of the fourteen [European American] students argued for the right of students *not* to hear what others might want to say about them—thus giving priority to the protection of individual sensibilities, those of others as well as their own, even if this might result in forfeiting their own

> chance to say what they felt. . . . The eight [African American] students and the remaining two [European American] students, on the other hand, argued for the rights of those students to express what they had to say about others even if the protection of all individual sensibilities would be forfeited in the process. On this last point, one [African American] woman said: "I don't know about others, but if someone has something to say to me, I want to hear it." (Kochman, 1981, pp. 122–123)

Withdrawing the protection of sensibilities is seen as insensitive or cruel by European Americans, while African Americans see European Americans failing to say what they think as lack of concern for African American real selves.

One of the major implications of these differences is what happens when African Americans and European Americans are involved in an interethnic conflict situation. African Americans have a tendency to express themselves more forcefully than European Americans. The tendency "to receive and manipulate the forceful assertions of others gives them greater leverage in interracial encounters" (Kochman, 1981, p. 126). When African Americans offend European Americans' social sensibilities, European Americans demand an apology. African Americans see this demand as weak and inappropriate. Part of the difference is in who is considered responsible when people are upset. When European Americans are upset, they tend to see the cause as the other person. African Americans, in contrast, see themselves as responsible for their feelings. African Americans "will commonly say to those who have become angry, '*Others* did not make you angry'; rather, 'You *let yourself* become angry' " (Kochman, 1981, p. 127).

The preceding examples are designed only to illustrate some of the cultural and ethnic approaches to conflict. It is important to keep in mind, however, that there are differences within ethnic groups. Responses to the class assignment discussed earlier, for example, illustrated that some European Americans share the approach of African Americans. In conflict situations, it is important to be aware of *potential* cultural or ethnic differences in the approach to conflict, but the focus in resolving the conflict has to be on being mindful of our communication and dealing with the other person as an individual.

Adaptations Needed to Manage Intergroup Conflicts

In many ways, managing intergroup conflict is similar to managing conflict with members of our own groups. To successfully manage intergroup conflicts, however, requires that we adapt our behavior in at least two ways (Gudykunst, 1994). First, we must take other people's group memberships into consideration. If others are collectivist, for example, they may prefer to avoid the conflict. If we are an individualist and think it is important to address the conflict, we need to adapt our style of communication to accommodate to collectivists by being more indirect than we usually are. We also must take other people's group memberships into consideration in interpreting their messages. Second, we must be aware of how our expectations for members of other groups influence our communication. Our expectations, such as those based on our ethnocentrism, prejudice, or stereotypes, influence how we interpret other people's messages when we are on automatic pilot. **To successfully manage conflict, we must set our group-based expectations aside, understand real group differences, and focus on understanding other people's perspectives on the conflict.** To do this, we must be mindful.

Individualists and collectivists can adapt their behavior to increase their effectiveness when they have a conflict (Ting-Toomey, 1994). Individualists can make several adaptations that will increase the likelihood of success in managing conflicts with collectivists. First, individualists need to remember that collectivists use an interdependent self-construal. Their actions reflect on their ingroups, and they have to take their ingroups into consideration in managing conflicts. Second, individualists should try to deal with conflicts when they are small, rather than allow them to become large issues, and recognize that collectivists may want to use a third party to mediate the conflict. Third, individualists need to help collectivists maintain face (public image) during the conflict. This means not humiliating or embarrassing collectivists in public. Fourth, individualists need to pay attention to collectivists' nonverbal behavior and implicit messages. Fifth, individualists need to actively listen when collectivists talk. Sixth, individualists need to use indirect messages more than they typically do. This means using qualifier words, such as *maybe* or *possibly,* being more tentative, and avoiding bluntly saying "no." Seventh, individualists need to let go of conflict if collectivists do not want to deal with it (recall that avoiding is the preferred collectivist strategy).

Collectivists also need to make adaptations when dealing with individualists (Ting-Toomey, 1994). First, collectivists need to recognize that individualists often separate the conflict from the person with whom they are having conflict. Second, collectivists need to focus on the substantive issues involved in the conflict. Third, collectivists need to use an assertive, rather than a nonassertive, style when dealing with conflict. Fourth, collectivists need to be more direct than they usually are. This involves using "I messages" and directly stating their opinions and feelings more than they usually do. Fifth, collectivists need to provide verbal feedback to individualists and focus on the verbal aspects of communication more than they typically do. Sixth, collectivists need to recognize that individualists do not value silence in conversations. Seventh, collectivists need to try to manage conflicts when they arise, rather than avoiding them.

SUMMARY

Conflict is inevitable in any relationship. Most of us tend to view conflict negatively and try to avoid it whenever we can. Conflict is not positive or negative, but how we manage conflicts has positive or negative consequences for our relationships.

We tend to use one of three general strategies when we manage conflicts: solution-oriented, control, or nonconfrontation strategies. Solution-oriented strategies are designed to allow both parties to win. Control-oriented strategies involve one person getting what she or he wants and the other person not getting what he or she wants. Nonconfrontation involves avoiding or smoothing over the conflict.

Constructive conflict management is the preferred way to manage conflict. When we manage conflict constructively, we seek a solution in which both parties can win. We need to be cooperative with others and seek a common definition of the problem. Additionally, we need to understand both our differences and similarities with the other person. To constructively manage conflicts, we need to mindfully draw on all of the communication resources discussed throughout the book. To illustrate, we need to listen responsively, be empathic, check our perceptions, be assertive, not aggressive, and so forth.

When we are not mindful, we tend to use our preferred strategy for managing conflict. Our preferred strategy, however, may not always be effective. When we are mindful, we can consciously choose to use other strategies. Different strategies are appropriate depending on the importance of the conflict issue to ourselves and the other person, the importance of our relationship with the other person, the time we have to manage the conflict, and whether we trust the other person.

Culture and ethnicity affect how people manage conflicts. Individualists, for example, tend to use solution-oriented and controlling strategies more than collectivists. Collectivists, in contrast, tend to use nonconfrontation more than individualists. When we have conflicts with members of other groups, we need to adjust the way we try to manage conflicts if we want to be successful.

Conclusion: Becoming a More Effective Communicator

When we do not think about our communication behavior, our behavior is guided by our implicit personal theories of communication. We do not make a conscious decision to base our communication on our implicit theories; rather, it is unconscious. When we communicate on automatic pilot, we use our implicit theories to predict other people's behavior and to interpret their behavior. Our implicit theories are sufficiently accurate for us to communicate relatively successfully under many conditions. When we communicate on automatic pilot, however, our resources for effective communication are limited to the communication skills we learned when we were growing up.

When we communicate on automatic pilot, we have only a limited number of ways that we can transmit messages to other people. To illustrate, we may have only one way to deal with anger when we communicate on automatic pilot. Our implicit theories of communication lead us to assume that other people are interpreting our messages in the way that we intended. This often is not the case. We all use our own frames of reference to interpret other people's messages. When our implicit theories guide our behavior, we also have only a limited number of ways of interpreting the messages other people transmit to us. When we are on automatic pilot, we interpret other people's behavior from our own frame of reference, and our expectations (including our stereotypes and our attitudes) for their behavior affect how we interpret their behavior. This often leads to misunderstandings, especially in intergroup encounters, even though we may not recognize that the misunderstandings occurred.

To increase our resources for effective communication, we need to consciously decide to think about our communication behavior. Stated differently, we need to become mindful. When we are mindful of our communication, the first thing we need to do is to manage our anxiety, if it is above our maximum threshold. Once we have managed our anxiety, we need to pay attention to the process of communication occurring between ourselves and others. Focusing on the process means paying attention to our own and other people's verbal and nonverbal messages, and making sure that we understand their messages and they understand our messages. When we are mindful of our communication, we need to gather the information needed to increase the accuracy of our predictions and interpretations of other people's behavior. Improving the accuracy of our predictions and interpretations requires that we listen responsively to others and use perception checking any time we are not sure that we understand their thoughts or feelings.

Our implicit theories not only influence

our communication in everyday conversations, they affect how we form interpersonal relationships and the way we communicate in these relationships. Communicating on automatic pilot with our relational partners often leads to misunderstandings. Once we know others fairly well, we assume that we can accurately predict and interpret their behavior. Our predictions and interpretations, however, are often in error. Not recognizing that we are misinterpreting other people's behavior or that we are inaccurately predicting their behavior leads to problems or conflicts in our relationships. When problems or conflicts occur in our relationships, we need to be mindful of our communication to find the best solutions to the problems or to successfully manage the conflicts. When we are mindful, we can consciously decide what we need to do to solve problems, manage conflicts, or to communicate effectively. When we communicate on automatic pilot, we will not recognize all of the options that we have to solve problems and to manage conflicts, and our communication will not be as effective as it could be.

Mindfulness is the major resource we have available to improve the effectiveness of our communication. When we are mindful, we can choose to use the other communication resources available to us, such as those discussed throughout the book. These include, but are not limited to, listening responsively, checking our perceptions, overcoming cognitive distortions, processing information in a complex fashion, tolerating ambiguity, managing our goal-incongruent emotions (anger, anxiety, and so forth), forgiving others, developing supportive communication climates, confirming others, focusing on what works (rather than the problems), using creative interpretations of other people's behavior, changing our expectations or communication styles, and managing conflict constructively.

Being mindful is necessary to increase our communication effectiveness. Each of us has to decide for her- or himself how much of the time we want to be mindful. Some people might believe that consciously thinking about their communication takes away spontaneity. This, however, is not the case. Mindfulness does not take away spontaneity. Optimal experiences are only possible when we consciously pay attention to what we are doing. When we pay attention to what we are doing, we will not rule out members of other groups as potential relational partners, just because they are members of other groups. Being mindful and consciously thinking about our behavior allows us to engage in dialogue with others and ensures that we will behave morally. It is impossible to be morally exclusive, for example, when we are mindful of our behavior.

Most of us will not be mindful all of the time. We can, however, make a concerted effort to be mindful in those situations in which misunderstandings might occur and in those situations in which understanding other people is important. The more we are mindful in these situations, the more effective our communication with others will be and the more we can improve the quality of our relationships with others.

Notes

1. Although there are other approaches on which we could have focused, we have selected Putnam and Wilson's because they emphasize the idea of choices.
2. We have cited only representative studies here. For a more detailed discussion, see Gudykunst and Ting-Toomey (1988).
3. Our focus below is on African American–European American differences. Japanese American, Chinese American, and Mexican American patterns are similar to the cultural differences cited earlier. For other examples, see Boucher, Landis, and Clark (1987) and

Strobe, Kruglanski, Bar-Tal, and Hewstone (1988).

Journal Reflections

1. *Monitor Your Conflicts.* We have more conflicts with others than we think we do. Over the next week, keep track of your disagreements with others. When did the conflicts occur? With whom did you have the conflicts? Try to isolate any patterns you can in terms of your patterns of conflict.
2. *Managing Conflicts Constructively.* In the next week, consciously try to use the skills for managing conflict constructively in at least one conflict situation that you encounter. In your journal, describe the situation, how you tried to manage it constructively, and the influence your use of the skill had on the quality of your communication.

Study Questions

1. Why is conflict inevitable in any relationship?
2. How do the solution-orientation, nonconfrontation, and control strategies for dealing with conflict differ? Under what conditions is each the best strategy to use?
3. How are constructive and destructive approaches to managing conflict different?
4. Why does the advice "Be unconditionally constructive" work in managing conflicts?
5. How is power related to constructive conflict management?
6. Under what conditions should we approach others regarding conflicts? What should we try to accomplish when we approach others?
7. What do we need to do to manage conflict successfully?
8. How do people with individualistic cultural identities deal with conflict differently than people with collectivistic cultural identities?
9. What do we need to do to constructively manage conflicts with members of other groups?

Suggested Readings

Deutsch, M. (1973). *The resolution of conflict.* New Haven, CT: Yale University Press. Morton Deutsch summarizes his research on constructive and destructive aspects of conflict. He examines the role of cooperation and competition on conflict, as well as the role of threats, promises, trust, and suspicion in resolving conflict.

Donohue, W., with Kolt, R. (1993). *Managing interpersonal conflict.* Newbury Park, CA: Sage. William Donohue presents an overview of managing interpersonal conflict. One of the major strengths of this book is that it focuses on issues of bargaining and negotiation more than similar books.

Folger, J. P., Poole, M. S., & Stutman, R. K. (1993). *Working through conflict* (2nd ed.). New York: HarperCollins. Joseph Folger, Marshall Scott Poole, and Randall Stutman present a comprehensive overview of managing conflict. They overview the major theories that can be used to explain conflict, as well as present specific suggestions for managing conflict constructively. Conflict in groups and organizations is addressed in this book.

Hocker, J. L., & Wilmot, W. W. (1991). *Interpersonal conflict* (3rd ed.). Dubuque, IA: Wm. C. Brown. Joyce Hocker and William Wilmot present a sound overview of interpersonal conflict. They discuss conflict strategies, methods of assessing conflicts, and ways to manage conflicts.

Glossary

Active strategies for reducing uncertainty Doing something more than merely observing other people to acquire information about them. They require us to actively seek out information about others without actually interacting with them (Berger, 1979).

Adaptors The body motions we use to express discomfort or nervousness.

Affect displays Facial expressions that display affective or emotional states.

Affective resources The emotional responses and ways of managing our emotions that help us communicate effectively with others. Some affective resources include the abilities to tolerate ambiguity, manage anxiety, manage anger, and forgiving others.

Affinity seeking The "process by which individuals attempt to get others to like and feel positive toward them" (Bell & Daly, 1984, p. 91).

Ageism Negative attitudes toward people who are older than we are (usually people we consider "old").

Anger The emotion we experience when we perceive that someone has committed a demeaning offense against us or people close to us (Lazarus, 1991).

Anxiety An affective response involving the feeling of being uneasy, tense, worried, or apprehensive about what might happen. "Anxiety stems from the anticipation of negative consequences" (Stephan & Stephan, 1985, p. 159).

Assertiveness Communicating in a way that indicates that we are standing up for our rights but at the same time respecting the rights of others.

Attitudes Learned predispositions "to respond in an evaluative (from extremely favorable to extremely unfavorable) manner toward some attitude object" (Davidson & Thompson, 1980, p. 27).

Attributions Our explanations for why other people behave the way they do.

Autonomy Our desire to be differentiated or separate from others (Baxter, 1988).

Behavioral resources for communication The behavioral skills we can use to improve the quality of our communication with others. Some of these skills include the ability to gather information, check our perceptions, listen responsively, and display empathy.

Certainty orientation Not being interested in seeking information to reduce the uncertainty experienced (Sorrentino & Short, 1986).

Chronemics The use of time.

Closed questions Questions that can be answered with a "yes" or a "no" or some other short answer.

Cognitive complexity The use of a large number of constructs to understand other people's behavior. Cognitive simplicity, in contrast, involves the use of a small number of constructs to understand other people's behavior.

Cognitive distortions Ways we process information that lead us to misinterpret our own or other people's feelings or behavior.

Cognitive resources The ways we think about others that can help us improve the quality of our communication. Some of the cognitive resources include managing our uncertainty, having open and complex stereotypes of other groups, being cognitively complex, uncertainty orientation, and being able to understand how other people are interpreting our messages.

Collective self-esteem The degree to which we generally evaluate our social groups positively (Crocker & Luhtanen, 1990).

Communication Process of using symbols to exchange messages and create meanings.

Communication apprehension "A relatively stable predisposition toward experiencing fear and/or anxiety in a variety of communication contexts" (McCroskey & Richmond, 1987, p. 143).

Communication environment "Those elements that impinge on the human relationship, but are not 'directly' a part of it" (Knapp & Hall, 1992, p. 13).

Communication networks Our personal ties with others, through which we exchange information, express affect, and help each other (Albrecht & Adelman, 1984).

Companionate love "The affection we feel for those with whom our lives are deeply intertwined" (Walster & Walster, 1978, p. 9).

Compassion The emotion experienced when we are moved by other people's suffering and want to help them (Lazarus, 1991).

Compliance-gaining strategies The strategies we use to try to influence others.

Confirmation "The process through which individuals are recognized, acknowledged, and endorsed" (Laing, 1961, p. 83).

Conflict "Exists whenever incompatible activities occur" (Deutsch, 1973, p. 10).

Conflict strategies The "behavioral choices" we make when we are confronted with a conflict (Putnam & Wilson, 1982).

Connection Our need to feel included with others (Baxter, 1988).

Control strategy toward conflict "Direct confrontation that leads to persistent argument and nonverbal forcing" when dealing with conflict (Putnam & Wilson, 1982, p. 638).

Cooperation "Acting together, in a coordinated way at work, leisure, or in social relationships, in the pursuit of shared goals, the enjoyment of the joint activity, or simply furthering the relationship" (Argyle, 1991, p. 4).

Culture Our theory of the "game being played" in our society (Keesing, 1974). Our knowledge of our culture tends to be unconscious; we tend to follow the rules of our culture without thinking about it.

Cultural identity The social identity associated with being a member of our culture.

Deception Leading others to false conclusions.

Deceptive communication "Message distortion resulting from deliberate falsification or omission of information by a communicator with the intent of stimulating in another, or others, a belief that the communicator himself or herself does not believe" (Miller, Mongeau, & Sleight, 1986, p. 497).

Deception detection The process of trying to find out if others are deceiving us. An interactive strategy for reducing uncertainty.

Defensiveness "Behavior which occurs when an individual perceives threat or anticipates threat" (Gibb, 1961, p. 141).

Description An actual report of what we have observed, with a minimum of distortion and without attributing social significance to the behavior.

Dialogues Conversations in which other people are not treated as objects and communication is adjusted to what other people say and do.

Differentiation Making ourselves stand out from others.

Dignity A minimal level of self-respect (Pritchard, 1991). It refers to feeling worthy, honored, or respected as a person.

Direct verbal style Style in which verbal statements clearly reveal a speaker's intent.

Disconfirmation When others, their experiences, or their significance is denied (Cissna & Sieburg, 1981).

Disgust The emotion experienced when we want to avoid or get away from something we find offensive (Lazarus, 1991).

Dispositions Our enduring tendencies or inclinations to think, feel, or behave in a particular way (Daly, 1987).

Egocentric bias The tendency to see our own behavior as normal, and compare other people's behavior to our own.

Elaborate verbal style The use of expressive language in everyday conversation. Expressive language can involve the use of exaggeration or animation.

Emblems Nonverbal cues with a direct verbal translation about which there is high agreement among members of a culture on the definition.

Emotions Our affective responses to changing relationships between ourselves and our environment (Lazarus, 1991).

Empathy "The imaginative intellectual and emotional participation in another person's experience" (Bennett, 1979, p. 418).

Envy The emotion experienced when we want something that someone else has (Lazarus, 1991).

Ethical resources for communication Our moral orientations which help us communicate effectively and develop quality relationships with others. Examples include integrity, dignity, moral inclusion, and walking a narrow ridge.

Ethnic identity "A person's subjective orientation toward his or her ethnic origins" (Alba, 1990, p. 25).

Ethnocentrism The view that "one's own group is the center of everything, and all others are scaled and rated with reference to it. . . . the most important fact is that ethnocentrism leads people to exaggerate and intensify everything in their own folkways which is peculiar and which differentiates them from others" (Sumner, 1940, p. 13).

Expectations Anticipations of future events or anticipations of other people's future behavior.

Feedback Information we transmit to others in reaction to the verbal and nonverbal messages we have received from them.

Forgiveness Letting go of the strong emotions attached to past experiences with others.

Friendships Voluntary, informal, personal relationships involving equality among the participants, and concerned mainly with sociability (Allan, 1989).

Fright The emotion that occurs when we face an immediate physical danger (Lazarus, 1991).

Fundamental attribution error Our tendency to overestimate the influence of personal characteristics and to underestimate the influence of situational factors when we explain other people's behavior.

Grammatical system The set of elements and rules that determine the possible combination of the elements.

Guilt The emotion that occurs when we have done something or want to do something that we find morally wrong (Lazarus, 1991).

Goals Future states of affairs that we are committed to achieving (Dillard, 1990).

Hearing The physical process of taking in auditory sensations without deliberate thoughtful attention.

High-context message Message in which "most of the information is either in the physical context or internalized in the person, while very little is in the coded, explicit, transmitted part of the message (Hall, 1976, p. 79).

Human identity Those views of ourselves that we believe we share with all other humans.

"I messages" Messages where we take responsibility for our own feelings rather than blaming our emotions on others.

Identity The way we view ourselves in a situation. The combination of all our identities is our self-concept.

Illustrators Nonverbal cues that directly accompany speech. These behaviors nonverbally illustrate what is being said verbally.

Immediacy behaviors Behaviors that reflect sensory stimulation, indicate attentiveness, and communicate liking (Mehrabian, 1981).

Implicit personal theories of interpersonal communication Our unconscious, taken-for-granted assumptions about communication. Our implicit theories guide our communication when we communicate on automatic pilot.

Inclusion The degree to which we fit in with others.

Independent construal of self Viewing ourselves as unique individuals with clear boundaries that separate us from others (Markus & Kitayama, 1991).

Interdependent construal of self Viewing ourselves as part of a social relationship and not separate from others (Markus & Kitayama, 1991).

Indirect verbal style Style in which verbal statements camouflage and conceal a speaker's actual intent.

Ingroups "Groups of people about whose welfare [we are] concerned, with whom [we are] willing to cooperate without demanding equitable returns, and separation from whom leads to discomfort or even pain" (Triandis, 1988, p. 75).

Intentions Instructions we give ourselves about how to behave in a specific situation (Triandis, 1977).

Interaction involvement "The extent to which an individual participates with another in conversation" (Cegala et al., 1982, p. 229).

Interactive strategies for reducing uncertainty Strategies used when we communicate directly with the person about whom we are trying to gather information (Berger, 1979).

Interdependence Occurs in our relationships when we interact frequently, engage in a variety of activities together, and influence each other's behavior (Berscheid et al., 1989).

Intergroup communication Communication in which the majority of the predictions we make about other people's behavior are based on the categories in which we place them. Our social identities guide our behavior when we engage in intergroup communication.

Interpersonal communication Communication in which the majority of the predictions we make about other people's behavior are based on personal information we have about them. Our personal identities guide our behavior when we communicate interpersonally. Interpersonal and intergroup communication tend to occur at the same time.

Interpersonal synchronization Convergent rhythmic movements between two people on both verbal and nonverbal levels (Hall, 1983).

Interpreting messages The process of perceiving messages using our senses (seeing, hearing, touching, smelling, and tasting) and attaching meaning to them.

Interrogation Asking others questions to gather information about them. An interactive uncertainty reduction strategy.

Kinesics The body motions we use to communicate nonverbally.

Language A system of rules regarding how sounds are combined to form words, how meanings are assigned to words or combinations of words, and how sentences are formed.

Leakage cues The nonverbal cues people give off without being aware of it that lead others to think they are lying.

Listening The process of taking in what we hear and mentally organizing it so that we can make sense of it (Goss, 1982).

Loaded questions Questions we ask that implicitly give advice to other people or interpret other people's behavior.

Low-context message Message in which "the mass of information is vested in the explicit code" (Hall, 1976, p. 70).

Lying Making untrue verbal statements.

Meaning The significance we attach to the message or our translation of the message.

Mindfulness Being aware of our behavior. It involves three processes: "(1) creation of new categories; (2) openness to new information; and (3) awareness of more than one perspective" (Langer, 1989, p. 62).

Monologues Self-centered conversations in which other people are treated as objects.

Moral exclusion Seeing individuals or groups "as outside the boundary in which moral values, rules, and considerations of fairness apply. Those who are morally excluded are perceived as nonentities, expendable, or undeserving; consequently, harming them appears acceptable, appropriate, or just" (Optow, 1990, p. 1).

Needs "Fundamental states of being that create feelings of deprivation and that mobilize [people] to act on their environment in ways to eliminate this sense of deprivation" (Turner, 1988, p. 59).

Nonconfrontation strategy toward conflict Use of "avoidance and smoothing as indirect strategies for dealing with conflict" (Putnam & Wilson, 1982, p. 638).

Nonverbal communication "All human communication events which transcend spoken or written words" (Knapp, 1978, p. 38).

Norms Socially shared guidelines for expected and accepted behaviors, violation of which leads to some form of sanction (Gibbs, 1965). The sanctions can vary from a disapproving look to ostracism from a group or even to death. Norms are based in our moral codes.

Open questions Questions that cannot be answered with a one-word response.

Paralanguage The nonverbal vocal cues that surround speech behavior or, very simply, *how* something is said, not *what* is said.

Paraphrasing Verbally restating our interpretation of the content meaning of other people's messages in our own words.

Passionate love The intense emotions we experience when we "fall in love."

Passive strategies for reducing uncertainty Strategies that involve taking the role of unobtrusive observers and not participating in the situation we are observing (Berger, 1979).

Perception The process of selecting cues from the environment, organizing these cues into some coherent pattern, and interpreting the pattern.

Perception checking A skill used to make sure that we understand other people's feelings or thoughts. It involves three processes: (1) describing other people's behavior; (2) giving our interpretation of other people's thoughts and/or feelings; and (3) asking other people if our perceptions are accurate.

Personal identities Those views of ourselves that differentiate us from other members of our ingroups—those characteristics that define us as unique individuals.

Personal integrity Upholding of a set of principles for the right reasons, even under adverse circumstances (McFall, 1987).

Phonological system The set of sounds that makes up a language.

Plans Cognitive thoughts which tell us the actions we need to do to accomplish our influence goals (Berger, 1988).

Power "The ability to influence or control events" (Folger et al., 1993, p. 99).

Prejudice "A judgment based on previous decisions and experiences" (Allport, 1954, p. 7).

Pride Enhancing our self-esteem by taking credit for something that we did or something we obtained (Lazarus, 1991).

Privacy The "selective control of access to the self or to one's group" (Altman, 1975, p. 18).

Promise "An individual's expressed intention to behave in a way that appears beneficial to another, if the other complies with the individual's request or terms" (Folger et al., 1993, p. 112).

Proxemics The distances between people in their daily interactions and the arrangements of space in places such as homes, offices, buildings, and even towns.

Psychological sex roles The traits and behaviors that traditionally are called masculine or feminine.

Regulators Body motions that maintain and regulate the back-and-forth nature of speaking and listening.

Relational idioms "Words, phrases, gestures that have unique meaning within a specific relationship" (Bell, Buerkel-Rothfuss, & Gore, 1987, p. 48).

Responsive listening A mindful process in which we focus on the meanings of other people's verbal and nonverbal messages and clearly indicate to them that we are paying attention.

Role The set of behavioral expectations attached to any position we hold in society. Examples of positions are professor, student, wife, husband, child, clerk, judge, and so forth.

Role conflict The conflict that occurs when we are expected to behave one way based on one of our roles and differently based on another role in a particular situation.

Role-set conflict The conflict that occurs when we are expected to engage in contradictory behavior in the same role.

Rules Guidelines for the ways we are expected to communicate, that are not based in morality.

Sapir-Whorf hypothesis The view that our everyday language usage influences, but does not determine, our thought processes. Our thought processes, in turn, define our experiences with others (Sapir, 1925; Whorf, 1952).

Satisfying communication Our emotional reaction to our communication that "is both successful and expectation fulfilling" (Hecht, 1984, p. 201).

Scripts Habitual patterns of communication that are shared by a group of people (Abelson, 1976, p. 33).

Self Ourselves as we really are (Westin, 1991).

Self-concepts Our views of ourselves when we think about ourselves (Westen, 1991).

Self-disclosure Telling other people information about ourselves that they do not already know; an interactive uncertainty reduction strategy.

Self-esteem Our positive or negative orientations toward ourselves (Rosenberg, 1979).

Semantic system The set of meanings that are expressible in a language.

Sexism Prejudging others based on their biological sex (Nilsen et al., 1977).

Shame The emotion that we experience when we perceive that we fail to live up to our expectations in someone else's eyes (Lazarus, 1991).

Social categorization Ordering our social environment and the people with whom we come in contact by grouping people in a way that makes sense to us (Tajfel & Turner, 1979).

Social cognition Our thought processes that are focused on human interaction. It involves how our knowledge about people is acquired and processed.

Social group Two or more people who define themselves as sharing a common bond (Turner, 1982).

Social identities Those views of ourselves that we assume we share with other members of our ingroups (Tajfel & Turner, 1979).

Social situation "Two or more individuals interacting within a physical setting, in which the interaction has an observable beginning and ending" (Cody & McLaughlin, 1985, p. 264).

Solution orientation toward conflict A "direct confrontation, open discussion of alternatives, and acceptance of compromises" (Putnam & Wilson, 1982, p. 638).

Speech communities Groups of people who share knowledge of the rules for the conduct and interpretation of speech (Hymes, 1974).

Stereotypes "Pictures in our heads" of people in a particular social category (Lippman, 1936).

Subcultures Groups within a culture whose members share many of the values of the culture but that also have some values that differ from those of the larger culture.

Symbol A thing conventionally used to represent something else.

Sympathy "The imaginative placing of ourselves in another person's position" (Bennett, 1979, p. 411).

System An interdependent set of elements that constitute a whole.

Threat "An individual's expressed intention to behave in a way that appears detrimental to the interests of another, if that other does not comply with the individual's request or terms" (Folger et al., 1993, p. 112).

Tolerance for ambiguity The ability to deal successfully with situations, even when a great deal of information needed to interact effectively is unknown.

Transmitting messages Putting our thoughts, feelings, emotions, and/or attitudes into a form recognizable by others.

Uncertainty Cognitive inability to predict and/or explain our own and other people's attitudes, feelings, values, and behavior (Berger & Calabrese, 1975).

Uncertainty orientation Orientation involving an interest in seeking out information to reduce uncertainty when they experience it (Sorrentino & Short, 1986).

Understated verbal style Extensive use of silence, pauses, and understatements in conversation.

Values "Modes of conduct and end-states of existence. To say that a person 'has a value' is to say that he [or she] has an enduring belief that a specific mode of conduct or end-state of existence is personally and socially preferable to alternative modes of conduct or end-states of existence" (Rokeach, 1972, pp. 159–160).

Verbal aggressiveness "The tendency to attack the self-concepts of individuals instead of, or in addition to, their positions on topics of communication" (Infante, 1987, p. 164).

Walking a narrow ridge Taking both our own and other people's viewpoints into consideration in our dealings with others.

References

Abelson, R. (1976). Script processing in attitude formation and decision making. In J. Carroll & J. Payne (Eds.), *Cognition and social behavior.* Hillsdale, NJ: Erlbaum.

Adams, J. (1965). Inequality in social exchange. In L. Berkowitz (Ed.), *Advances in experimental social psychology* (Vol. 2). New York: Academic Press.

Adelman, M., Parks, M., & Albrecht, T. (1987). Supporting friends in need. In T. Albrecht & M. Adelman (Eds.), *Communicating social support.* Beverly Hills, CA: Sage.

Alba, R. (1990). *Ethnic identity: The transformation of white America.* New Haven, CT: Yale University Press.

Alberti, R., & Emmons, M. (1990). *Your perfect right* (6th ed.). San Luis Obispo, CA: Impact.

Albrecht, T., & Adelman, M. (1984). Social support and life stress. *Human Communication Research, 11,* 3–32.

Allan, G. (1989). *Friendship.* Boulder, CO: Westview.

Allen, A., & Thompson, T. (1984). Agreement, understanding, realization, and feeling understood as predictors of communication satisfaction in marital dyads. *Journal of Marriage and the Family, 46,* 915–921.

Allport, G. (1954). *The nature of prejudice.* New York: Macmillan.

Almaney, A., & Alwan, A. (1982). *Communicating with the Arabs.* Prospect Heights, IL: Waveland.

Altman, I. (1975). *The environment and social behavior.* Monterey, CA: Brooks/Cole.

Altman, I, & Taylor, D. (1973). *Social penetration.* New York: Holt, Rinehart and Winston.

Altman, I., Vinsel, A., & Brown, B. (1981). Dialectical conceptions in social psychology. In L. Berkowitz (Ed.), *Advances in experimental social psychology* (Vol. 14). New York: Academic Press.

Applegate, J., & Sypher, H. (1983). A constructivist perspective. In W. Gudykunst (Ed.), *Intercultural communication theory.* Beverly Hills, CA: Sage.

Argyle, M. (1979). New developments in the analysis of social skills. In A. Wolfgang (Ed.), *Nonverbal behavior.* New York: Academic Press.

Argyle, M. (1991). *Cooperation.* London: Routledge.

Argyle, M., & Henderson, M. (1984). The rules of relationships. In S. Duck & D. Perlman (Eds.), *Understanding personal relationships.* Newbury Park, CA: Sage.

Argyle, M., & Henderson, M. (1985). *The anatomy of relationships.* London: Heinemann.

Argyle, M., Henderson, M., Bond, M., Iizuka, Y., & Contarelo, A. (1986). Cross-cultural variations in relationship rules. *International Journal of Psychology, 21,* 287–315.

Arnett, R. C. (1986). *Communication and community.* Carbondale: Southern Illinois University Press.

Arnoff, C. (1974). Old age in prime time. *Journal of Communication, 24,* 86–87.

Ashford, S., & Cummings, L. (1983). Feedback as an individual resource. Organizational Behavior and Human Performance, 32, 370–398.

Averill, J., & Nunley, E. (1992). *Voyages of the heart.* New York: Basic Books.

Ayres, J. (1983). Strategies to maintain relationships. *Communication Quarterly, 31,* 62–67.

Ball-Rokeach, S. (1973). From pervasive ambiguity to definition of the situation. *Sociometry, 36,* 378–389.

Barbato, C., & Feezel, J. (1987). The language of aging in different age-groups. *Gerontological Society of America, 27,* 527–531.

Barker, L., Edwards, R., Gains, C., Gladney, K., & Holley, F. (1980). An investigation of proportional time spent in various communication activities. *Journal of Applied Communication Research, 8,* 101–109.

Barnlund, D. (1962). Toward a meaning centered philosophy of communication. *Journal of Communication, 2,* 197–211.

Barnlund, D. (1975). *Public and private self in Japan and the United States.* Tokyo: Simul.

Barnlund, D. (1989). *Communicative styles of Japanese and Americans.* Belmont, CA: Wadsworth.

Barnsley, J. (1972). *The social reality of ethics.* London: Routledge.

Barringer, F. (1993, May 16). Pride in a soundless world. *New York Times,* pp. 1, 14.

Barth, F. (1969). *Ethnic groups and boundaries.* London: Allen and Unwin.

Basso, K. (1970). To give up on words: Silence in western Apache culture. *Southern Journal of Anthropology, 26,* 213–230.

Bateson, G. (1979). *Mind and nature.* New York: Dutton.

Baum, M. (1972). Love, marriage and the division of labor. In H. Dreitzel (Ed.), *Family, marriage and the struggle of the sexes.* New York: Macmillan.

Bavelas, J., Black, A., Chovil, N., & Mullett, J. (1990). *Equivocal communication.* Newbury Park, CA: Sage.

Baxter, L. (1988). A dialectical perspective on communication strategies in relationship development. In S. Duck (Ed.), *Handbook of personal relationships.* New York: Wiley.

Baxter, L. (1992). Forms and functions of intimate play in personal relationships. *Human Communication Research, 18,* 336–365.

Beatty, M., & Payne, S. (1984). Listening comprehension as a function of cognitive complexity. *Communication Monographs, 51,* 85–89.

Beck, A. (1976). *Cognitive therapy and the emotional disorders.* New York: International Universities Press.

Beck, A. (1988). *Love is never enough.* New York: Harper & Row.

Beier, E., & Sternberg, D. (1977). Marital communication. *Journal of Communication, 27,* 92–103.

Bell, R. (1987). Social involvement. In J. McCroskey & J. Daly (Eds.), *Personality and interpersonal communication.* Beverly Hills, CA: Sage.

Bell, R., Buerkel-Rothfuss, B., & Gore, K. (1987). "Did you bring the yarmulke for the cabbage patch kid?" The idiomatic communication of young lovers. *Human Communication Research, 14,* 47–67.

Bell, R., & Daly, J. (1984). The affinity-seeking function of communication. *Communication Monographs, 51,* 91–115.

Bell, R., & Healey, J. (1992). Idiomatic communication and interpersonal solidarity in friends' relational cultures. *Human Communication Research, 18,* 307–335.

Bellah, R. N., Madsen, R., Sullivan, W. M., Swidler, A., & Tipton, S. M. (1985). *Habits of the heart: Individualism and commitment in American life.* Berkeley: University of California Press.

Bem, S. (1970). Case study of non-conscious ideology. In D. Bem (Ed.), *Beliefs, attitudes, and human affairs.* Belmont, CA: Brooks/Cole.

Bem, S. (1974). The measurement of psychological androgyny. *Journal of Consulting and Clinical Psychology, 42,* 155–162.

Bem, S. (1993). *The lenses of gender.* New Haven, CT: Yale University Press.

Bennett, M. (1979). Overcoming the Golden Rule: Sympathy and empathy. In D. Nimmo (Ed.), *Communication yearbook 3.* New Brunswick, NJ: Transaction.

Benson, P., & Vincent, S. (1980). Development and validation of the sexist attitude toward women scale. *Psychology of Women Quarterly, 5,* 276–291.

Berger, C. R. (1979). Beyond initial interactions. In H. Giles & R. St. Clair (Eds.), *Language and social psychology.* Oxford: Blackwell.

Berger, C. R. (1988). Planning, affect, and social action generation. In R. Donohue, H. Sypher, & E. T. Higgins (Eds.), *Communication. social cognition, and affect.* Hillsdale, NJ: Erlbaum.

Berger, C. R., & Bell, R. (1988). Plans and the initiation of social relationships. *Human Communication Research, 15,* 217–235.

Berger, C. R., & Bradac, J. (1982). *Language and social knowledge.* London: Edward Arnold.

Berger, C. R., & Calabrese, R. (1975). Some explorations in initial interactions and beyond: Toward a developmental theory of interpersonal communication. *Human Communication Research, 1,* 99–112.

Berger, C. R., & Douglas, W. (1982). Thought and talk. In F. Dance (Ed.), *Human communication theory.* New York: Harper & Row.

Berger, C. R., Gardner, R., Parks, M., Shulman, L., & Miller, G. (1976). Interpersonal epistemology and interpersonal communication. In G. Miller (Ed.), *Explorations in interpersonal communication.* Beverly Hills, CA: Sage.

Berger, C. R., & Kellermann, R. (1983). To ask or not to ask. In R. Bostrom (Ed.), Communication yearbook 7. Beverly Hills, CA: Sage.

Berger, P., & Kellner, H. (1964). Marriage and the construction of reality. *Diogenes, 46,* 1–24.

Berlo, D. (1960). *The process of communication.* New York: Holt.

Bernstein, B. (1973). *Class, codes, and control* (Vol. 1). London: Routledge and Kegan Paul.

Berry, R., & Williams, F. (1987). Assessing the relationship between quality of life and marital and income satisfaction. *Journal of Marriage and the Family, 49,* 107–116.

Berscheid, E., Snyder, M., & Omoto, A. (1989). Issues in studying close relationships. In C. Hendrick (Ed.), *Close relationships.* Newbury Park, CA: Sage.

Berscheid, E., & Walster, E. (1974). A little bit about love. In T. Huston (Ed.), *Foundations of interpersonal attraction.* New York: Academic Press.

Betcher, W. (1987). *Intimate play.* New York: Penguin.

Bidney, D. (1968). Cultural relativism. In D. Sills (Ed.), *International encyclopedia of the social sciences* (Vol. 3). New York: Free Press.

Billig, M. (1987). *Arguing and thinking.* Cambridge: Cambridge University Press.

Billig, M., Condor, S., Edwards, D., Gane, M., Middleton, D., & Radley, A. (1988). *Ideological dilemmas.* London: Sage.

Birenbaum, A., & Sagarin, E. (1976). *Norms and human behavior.* New York: Praeger.

Blanchard, F., Lilly, T., & Vaughn, L. (1991). Reducing the expression of racial prejudice. *Psychological Science, 2,* 101–105.

Blau, P., & Schwartz, B. (1984). *Cross-cutting social circles.* New York: Academic Press.

Bloom, L., Coburn, K., & Pearlman, J. (1975). *The new assertive woman.* New York: Dell.

Bodenhaugen, G., Gaelick, L., & Wyer, R. (1987). Affective and cognitive factors in intragroup and intergroup communication. In C. Hendrick (Ed.), *Group processes and intergroup relations.* Newbury Park, CA: Sage.

Bok, S. (1978). *Lying: Moral choice in public and private life.* New York: Vintage Books.

Bok, S. (1983). *Secrets: On the ethics of concealment and revelation.* New York: Vintage Books.

Bok, S. (1989). *A strategy for peace: Human values and the threat of war.* New York: Pantheon.

Bolton, R. (1979). *People skills.* New York: Simon & Schuster.

Bond, M. H., Wan, K., Leung, K., & Giacalone, R. (1985). How are the responses to verbal insults related to cultural collectivism and power distance? *Journal of Cross-Cultural Psychology, 16,* 111–127.

Boomer, D. (1978). The phonemic clause. In A. Siegman & S. Feldstein (Eds.), *Nonverbal behavior and communication.* Hillsdale, NJ: Erlbaum.

Boucher, K., Landis, D., & Clark, K. (Eds.). (1987). *Ethnic conflict.* Beverly Hills, CA: Sage.

Boulding, E. (1988). *Building a global civic culture.* Syracuse, NY: Syracuse University Press.

Boyer, E. (1990, June 20). Letter to the editor. *Chronicle of Higher Education,* p. B4.

Bradac, J. (1990). Language attitudes and impression formation. In H. Giles & P. Robinson (Eds.), *Handbook of language and social psychology.* London: Wiley.

Braithwaite, D. (1991). "Just how much did that wheelchair cost?" Management of privacy boundaries by persons with disabilities. *Western Journal of Speech Communication, 55,* 254-274.

Branden, N. (1992). *The power of self-esteem.* New York: Health Communications.

Breakwell, G. (1979). Women: Group and identity. *Women's Studies International Quarterly, 2,* 9-17.

Brewer, M. B. (1981). Ethnocentrism and its role in interpersonal trust. In M. Brewer & B. Collins (Eds.), *Scientific inquiry and the social sciences.* San Francisco: Jossey-Bass.

Brewer, M. B. (1991). The social self. *Personality and Social Psychology Bulletin, 17,* 475-482.

Brewer, M. B., & Miller, N. (1988). Contact and cooperation: When do they work? In P. Katz & D. Taylor (Eds.), *Eliminating racism.* New York: Plenum.

Brislin, R. W., Cushner, K., Cherrie, C., & Yong, M. (1986). *Intercultural interactions: A practical guide.* Beverly Hills, CA: Sage.

Brodie, H. K. (1989, September 9). No we're not taught to hate, but we can overcome instinct to fear 'the other.' *Los Angeles Times,* Part II, p. 16.

Brown, P., & Fraser, C. (1979). Speech as a marker of situation. In K. Scherer & H. Giles (Eds.), *Social markers in speech.* Cambridge: Cambridge University Press.

Bruner, J. (1958). Social psychology and perception. In E. Maccoby, T. Newcomb, & E. Hartley (Eds.), *Readings in social psychology* (3rd. ed.). New York: Holt, Rinehart and Winston.

Buber, M. (1958). *I and thou.* New York: Scribner.

Buber, M. (1965). *Between man and man.* New York: Macmillan.

Buller, D., Strzyzewski, K., & Comstock, J. (1991). Interpersonal deception I: Deceivers' reactions to receivers' suspicions and probes. *Communication Monographs, 58,* 1-24.

Burgoon, J. (1985). Nonverbal signals. In M. Knapp & G. R. Miller (Eds.), *Handbook of interpersonal communication.* Beverly Hills, CA: Sage.

Burgoon, J. (1992). Applying a comparative approach to nonverbal expectancy violations theory. In J. Blumler, K. Rosengren,, & J. McLeod (Eds.), *Comparatively speaking.* Newbury Park, CA: Sage.

Burgoon, J., Birk, T., & Pfau, M. (1990). Nonverbal behaviors, persuasion, and credibility. *Human Communication Research, 17,* 140-169.

Burgoon, J., Buller, D., & Woodall, W. (1989). *Nonverbal communication: The unspoken dialogue.* New York: Harper & Row.

Burgoon, J., & Hale, J. (1987). Validation and measurement of the fundamental themes of relational communication. *Communication Monographs, 54,* 19-41.

Burgoon, J., & Hale, J. (1988). Nonverbal expectancy violations. *Communication Monographs, 55,* 58-79.

Burgoon, J., & LePoire, B. (1993). Effects of communication expectancies, actual communication, and expectancy disconfirmation on evaluations of communicators and their communication behavior. *Human Communication Research, 20,* 67-96.

Burgoon, J., Parrott, R., LePoire, B., Kelley, D., Walther, J., & Perry, D. (1989). Maintaining and restoring privacy through communication in different types of relationships. *Journal of Social and Personal Relationships, 6,* 131-158.

Burgoon, M., Dillard, J., & Doran, N. (1983). Friendly and unfriendly persuasion. *Human Communication Research, 10,* 283-294.

Burgoon, M., & Miller, G. R. (1985). An expectancy interpretation of language and persuasion. In

H. Giles & R. St. Clair (Eds.), *Recent advances in language, communication, and social psychology.* London: Erlbaum.

Burke, P., & Franzoi, S. (1988). Studying situations and identities using experimental sampling methodology. *American Sociological Review, 53,* 559–568.

Burke, R. (1970). Methods of resolving superior-subordinate conflict. *Organizational Behavior and Human Performance, 5,* 393–411.

Burleson, B. (1985). The production of comforting messages. *Journal of Language and Social Psychology, 4,* 253–273.

Burleson, B., Samter, W., & Lucchetti, A. (1992). Similarity in communication values as predictors of friendship choices. *The Southern Communication Journal, 57,* 260–276.

Burns, D. (1980). *Feeling good: The new mood therapy.* New York: Morrow.

Burns, D. (1989). *The feeling good handbook.* New York: William Morrow.

Buscaglia, L. (1984). *Loving each other.* New York: Fawcett.

Butler, R. (1969). Age-ism: Another form of bigotry. *Gerontologist, 9,* 243–246.

Byrne, D. (1971). *The attraction paradigm.* New York: Academic Press.

Byrne, D., & Kelley, K. (1981). *An introduction to personality* (3rd ed.). Englewood Cliffs, NJ: Prentice-Hall.

Campbell, A. (1993). *Men, women and aggression.* New York: Basic Books.

Cantor, J. (1979). Grammatical variations in persuasion. *Communication Monographs, 46,* 296–305.

Cantor, N., Mischel, W., & Schwartz, J. (1982). Social knowledge. In A. Isen & A. Hastorf (Eds.), *Cognitive social psychology.* New York: Elsevier.

Carroll, R. (1988). *Cultural misunderstanding: The French-American experience.* Chicago: University of Chicago Press.

Cegala, D., Savage, G., Brunner, C., & Conrad, A. (1982). An elaboration of the meaning of interaction involvement. *Communication Monographs, 49,* 229–248.

Cegala, D., & Waldron, V. (1992). A study of the relationship between communicative performance and conversational participants' thoughts. *Communication Studies, 43,* 105–123.

Chaika, E. (1989). *Language: The social mirror* (2nd ed.). Rowley, MA: Newbury House.

Chinese Culture Connection. (1987). Chinese values and the search for culture-free dimensions of culture. *Journal of Cross-Cultural Psychology, 18,* 143–164.

Cissna, K., Garvin, B., & Kennedy, C. (1990). Reliability in coding social interaction: A study of confirmation. *Communication Reports, 3,* 58–69.

Cissna, K., & Sieburg, E. (1981). Patterns of interactional confirmation and disconfirmation. In C. Wilder-Mott & J. Weakland (Edg.), *Rigor and imagination.* New York: Praeger.

Clark, H. (1985). Language use and language users. In G. Lindzey & E. Aronson (Eds.), *The handbook of social psychology* (3rd ed., Vol. II). New York: Random House.

Clark, H., & Marshall, C. (1981). Definite reference and mutual knowledge. In A. Joshi, B. Webber, & I. Sag (Edg.), *Elements of discourse understanding.* New York: Cambridge University Press.

Clark, M., & Mills, J. (1979). Interpersonal attraction in exchange and communal relationships. *Journal of Personality and Social Psychology, 37,* 1224.

Clark, R., & Delia, J. (1977). Cognitive complexity, social perspective-taking and functional persuasive skills in second-to-ninth-grade children. *Human Communication Research, 3,* 128–134.

Clark, R., & Delia, J. (1979). *Topoi* and rhetorical competence. *Quarterly Journal of Speech, 65,* 187–206.

Cline, R. (1989). The politics of intimacy. *Journal of Social and Personal Relationships, 6,* 5–20.

Coates, J. (1986). *Women. men, and language.* New York: Longman.

Cody, M., & McLaughlin, M. (1985). The situation as a construct in interpersonal communication. In M. Knapp & G. Miller (Eds.), *Handbook of interpersonal communication.* Beverly Hills, CA: Sage.

Cofer, C., & Appley, M. (1964). *Motivation.* New York: Wiley.

Cohen, R. (1987). Problems in intercultural communication in Egyptian-American diplomatic relations. *International Journal of Intercultural Relations, 11,* 29–47.

Coleman, L., & DePaulo, B. (1991). Uncovering the human spirit: Moving beyond disability and "missed" communication. In N. Coupland, H. Giles, & J. Wiemann (Eds.), *"Miscommunication" and problematic talk.* Newbury Park, CA: Sage.

Collier, M. (1986). Culture and gender. In M. McLaughlin (Ed.), *Communication Yearbook 9.* Beverly Hills, CA: Sage.

Collier, M., Ribeau, S., & Hecht, M. (1986). Intracultural communication rules and outcomes within three domestic cultures. *International Journal of Intercultural Relations, 10,* 439–458.

Condon, J. (1984). *With respect to the Japanese.* Yarmouth, ME: Intercultural Press.

Condor, S. (1986). Sex role beliefs and "traditional" women. In S. Wilkenson (Ed.), *Feminist social psychology.* Milton Keynes: Open University Press.

Coupland, J., Nussbaum, J., & Coupland, N. (1991). The reproduction of aging and ageism in intergenerational talk. In N. Coupland, H. Giles, & J. Wisemann (Eds.), *"Miscommunication" and problematic talk.* Newbury Park, CA: Sage.

Coupland, N., Coupland, J., Giles, H., & Henwood, K. (1988). Accommodating the elderly. *Language in Society, 17,* 1–42.

Covey, H. (1988). Historical terminology used to represent older people. *Gerontologist, 28,* 291–297.

Crocker, J., & Luhtanen, R. (1990). Collective self-esteem and ingroup bias. *Journal of Personality and Social Psychology, 58,* 60–67.

Crockett, W., & Friedman, P. (1980). Theoretical explorations in the process of initial interactions. *Western Journal of Speech Communication, 44,* 86–92.

Crosby, F., Bromley, S., & Saxe, L. (1980). Recent unobtrusive studies of black and white discrimination and prejudice. *Psychological Bulletin, 87,* 546–563.

Csikszentmihalyi, M. (1990). *Flow: The psychology of optimal experience.* New York: Harper & Row.

Cushman, D. P., & Cahn, D. (1985). *Interpersonal communication.* Albany: State University of New York Press.

Cushman, D. P., Valentinsen, B., & Dietrich, D. (1982). A rules theory of interpersonal relationships. In F. Dance (Ed.), *Human communication theory.* New York: Harper & Row.

Dahnke, G. (1983). Communication between handicapped and nonhandicapped. In M. McLaughlin (Ed.), *Communication yearbook 6.* Beverly Hills, CA: Sage.

Daly, J. (1987). Personality and interpersonal communication: Issues and directions. In J. McCroskey & J. Daly (Eds.), *Personality and interpersonal communication.* Beverly Hills, CA; Sage.

Dance, F. (1982). A speech theory of human communication. In F. Dance (Ed.), *Human communication theory.* New York: Harper & Row.

Darwin, C. (1872). *The expression of emotions in man and animals.* London: John Murray.

D'Augelli, A., Handis, M., Brumbaugh, L., Illig, V., Searer, R., Turner, D., & D'Augelli, J. (1978). The verbal helping behavior of experienced and novice telephone counselors. *Journal of Community Psychology, 6,* 222–228.

Davidson, A. (1975). Cognitive differentiation and culture training. In R. Brislin, S. Bochner, & W. Lonner (Eds.), *Cross-cultural perspectives on learning.* Beverly Hills, CA; Sage.

Davidson, A., & Thompson, E. (1980). Cross-cultural studies of attitudes and beliefs. In H. Triandis & R. Brislin (Eds.), *Handbook of cross-cultural psychology* (Vol. 5). Boston: Allyn & Bacon.

Davis, F. (1977). Deviance disavowal. In J. Stubbins (Ed.), *Social and psychological aspects of disability.* Baltimore, MD: University Park Press.

Deaux, K. (1991). Social identities. In R. Curtis (Ed.), *The relational self.* New York: Guilford.

Deaux, K. (1993). Reconstructing social identity. *Personality and Social Psychology Bulletin, 19,* 4-12.

Deaux, K., & Ethier, K. (1990). [Dimensions of social identity.] Unpublished raw data reported in Deaux (1991).

Derber, C. (1979). *The pursuit of attention: Power and individualism in everyday life.* Boston: G. K. Hall.

Detweiler, R. (1975). On inferring the intentions of a person from another culture. *Journal of Personality, 43,* 591-611.

Detweiler, R. (1978). Culture, category width, and attributions. *Journal of Cross-Cultural Psychology, 11,* 101-124.

Deutsch, K. (1968). Toward a cybernetic model of man and society. In W. Buckley (Ed.), *Modern systems theory for the behavioral scientist.* Chicago: Aldine.

Deutsch, M. (1973). *The resolution of conflict.* New Haven, CT: Yale University Press.

Devine, P. (1989). Stereotypes and prejudice. *Journal of Personality and Social Psychology, 56,* 5-18.

Dickson-Markman, F. (1986). Self-disclosure with friends across the life cycles. *Journal of Social and Personal Relationships, 3,* 259-264.

Dillard, J. (1989). Type of influence goals in personal relationships. *Journal of Social and Personal Relationships, 6,* 293-308.

Dillard, J. (1990). A goal-driven model of interpersonal influence. In J. Dillard (Ed.), *Seeking compliance.* Scottsdale, AZ: Gorsuch Scarisbrick.

Dillard, J., Henwood, K., Giles, H., Coupland, N., & Coupland, J. (1990). Compliance gaining, young and old. *Communication Reports, 3,* 84-91.

Dindia, K., & Canary, D. (1993). Definitions and theoretical perspectives on maintaining relationships. *Journal of Social and Personal Relationships, 10,* 163-173.

Dion, K. L., & Dion, K. K. (1988). Romantic love: Individual and cultural perspectives. In R. Sternberg & M. Barnes (Eds.), *The psychology of love.* New Haven, CT: Yale University Press.

Donohue, W., with Kolt, R. (1993). *Managing interpersonal conflict.* Newbury Park, CA: Sage.

Douglas, M. (1986). *How institutions think.* Syracuse, NY: Syracuse University Press.

Douglas, W. (1987). Affinity-testing in initial interactions. *Journal of Social and Personal Relationships, 4,* 3-16.

Douglis, C. (1987, November). The beat goes on. *Psychology Today,* pp. 37-42.

Downs, J. (1971). *Cultures in crisis.* Chicago: Glencoe Press.

Duck, S. (1977). *The study of acquaintance.* Farnborough, UK: Saxon House.

Duck, S. (1988). *Relating to others.* Monterey, CA: Brooks/Cole.

Duck, S. (1992). *Human relationships* (2nd ed.). London: Sage.

Duck, S. (in press). Steady as (s)he goes: Relational maintenance as a shared meaning system. In D. Canary & L. Stafford (Eds.), *Communication and relationship maintenance.* New York: Academic Press.

Duck, S., Rutt, D., Hurst, M., G Strejc, H. (1991). Some evident truths about conversations in everyday relationships. *Human Communication Research, 18,* 228-267.

Duncan, B. (1976). Differential social perception and attribution of intergroup violence. *Journal of Personality and Social Psychology, 34,* 590-598.

Duncan, B. L., & Rock, J. (1991). *Overcoming relationship impasses.* New York: Insight Books.

Duran, R. L. (1983). Communicative adaptability. *Communication Quarterly,* 31, 320-326.

Eagly, A., & Mladimic, A. (1989). Gender, stereotypes and attitudes toward men and women. *Personality and Social Psychology Bulletin, 15,* 543-558.

Eakins, B., & Eakins, R. (1978). *Sex differences in human communication.* Boston: Houghton Mifflin.

Edelman, R. (1987). *The psychology of embarrassment.* New York: Wiley.

Edwards, J. (1985). *Language, society, and identity.* Oxford: Blackwell.

Ehrenhaus, P. (1983). Culture and the attribution process. In W. Gudykunst (Ed.), *Intercultural communication theory.* Beverly Hills, CA: Sage.

Eisenberg, E. (1984). Ambiguity as a strategy in organizational communication. *Communication Monographs, 51,* 227–242.

Ekman, P. (1971). Universals and cultural differences in facial expression of emotions. In J. Cole (Ed.), *Nebraska symposium on motivation.* Lincoln: University of Nebraska Press.

Ekman, P. (1985). *Telling lies.* New York: Norton.

Ekman, P., & Friesen, W. (1969). Nonverbal leakage cues to deception. *Psychiatry, 32,* 88–106.

Elliot, S., Scott, M., Jensen, A., & McDonald, M. (1982). Perceptions of reticence. In M. Burgoon (Ed.), *Communication yearbook 5.* New Brunswick, NJ: Transaction.

Ellyson, S., Dovidio, J., & Fehr, B. (1981). Visual behavior and dominance in women and men. In C. Mayo & N. Henley (Eds.), *Gender and nonverbal behavior.* New York: Springer-Verlag.

Engebretson, D., & Fullmer, D. (1970). Cross-cultural differences in territoriality. *Journal of Cross-Cultural Psychology, 1,* 261–269.

Erickson, F. (1981). *Anecdote, rhapsody, and rhetoric.* Paper presented at the Georgetown University Roundtable on Language and Linguistics, Washington, DC.

Essed, P. (1991). *Understanding everyday racism.* Newbury Park, CA: Sage.

Eshleman, J. R. (1991). *The family* (6th ed.). Boston: Allyn & Bacon.

Etzioni, A. (1993). *The spirit of community.* New York: Crown.

Farb, P. (1973). *Word play: What happens when people talk.* New York: Bantam.

Farb, P. (1979). Man at the mercy of language. In D. Mortenson (Ed.), *Basic readings in communication theory.* New York: Harper & Row.

Faulkender, P. (1985). Relationships between Bem sex-role inventory and attitudes of sexism. *Psychological Reports, 57,* 227–235.

Fields, R. (1984). *Chop wood, carry water.* New York: St. Martin's Press.

Fisher, B. A. (1978). *Perspectives on human communication.* New York: Macmillan.

Fisher, B. A. (1982). The pragmatic perspective of human communication. In F. Dance (Ed.), *Human communication theory.* New York: Harper & Row.

Fisher, C., Jackson, R., Stueve, C., Gerson, K., & Jones, L. (1977). *Networks and places.* New York: Free Press.

Fisher, R., & Brown, S. (1988). *Getting together: Building relationships as we negotiate.* New York: Houghton Mifflin.

Fishman, P. (1978). Interaction: The work women do. *Social Problems, 25,* 397406.

Fitch-Haoser, M., Barker, B., & Hughes, A. (1990). Receiver apprehension and listening comprehension. *Southern Journal of Communication, 56,* 62–71.

Fitzgerald, T. (1993). *Metaphors of identity.* Albany: State University of New York Press.

Fitzpatrick, M. A. (1988). *Between husbands and wives.* Beverly Hills, CA: Sage.

Folger, J., Poole, M., & Stutman, R. (1993). *Working through conflict* (2nd ed.). New York: HarperCollins.

Forgas, J., & Bond, M. (1985). Cultural influences on perceptions of interaction episodes. *Personality and Social Psychology Bulletin, 11,* 75–88.

Friedman, H. (1978). The relative strength of verbal and nonverbal cues. *Personality and Social Psychology Bulletin, 4,* 147–150.

Fromme, D., Jaynes, W., Taylor, D., Hanold, E., Danielle, J., Roundtree, R., & Fromme, M. (1989). Nonverbal behavior and attitude toward touch. *Journal of Nonverbal Behavior, 13,* 3–13.

Fuentes, C. (1992). *The buried mirror.* Boston: Houghton Mifflin.

Furnham, A. (1986). Situational determinants of intergroup communication. In W. B. Gudykunst (Ed.), *Intergroup communication.* London: Edward Arnold.

Fussell, P. (1983). *Class.* New York: Summit Books.

Gaertner, S., & Bickman, L. (1971). Effects of race on the elicitation of helping behavior. *Journal of Personality and Social Psychology, 20,* 218–222.

Galston, W. (1991). Rights do not equal rightness. *Responsive Community, 1,* 78.

Galvin, K., & Brommel, B. (1991). *Family communication* (3rd ed.). New York: HarperCollins.

Gandhi, M. K. (1948). *Nonviolence in peace and war.* Ahmedabad, India: Garland.

Gans, H. (1979). Symbolic ethnicity. *Ethnic and Racial Studies, 2,* 1–20.

Gao, G. (1993). *A test of the triangular theory of love in Chinese and EuroAmerican romantic relationships.* Paper presented at the International Communication Association convention, Washington, DC.

Gao, G., & Gudykunst, W. B. (1990). Uncertainty, anxiety, and adaptation. *International Journal of Intercultural Relations.*

Gardner, R. (1985). *Social psychology and second language learning.* London: Edward Arnold.

Garreau, J. (1981). *The nine nations of North America.* New York: Houghton Mifflin.

Garrett, P., Giles, H., & Coupland, N. (1989). The contexts of language learning. In S. Ting-Toomey & F. Korzenny (Eds.), *Language, communication, and culture.* Newbury Park, CA: Sage.

Garvin, B., & Kennedy, C. (1986). Confirmation and disconfirmation in nurse-physician communication. *Journal of Applied Communication Research, 14,* 1–19.

Geertz, C. (1966). *Person, time and conduct in Bali.* New Haven, CT: Yale Southeast Asia Studies Program.

Geertz, C. (1973). *The interpretation of cultures.* New York: Basic Books.

Gerbner, G. (1978). The dynamics of cultural resistance. In G. Tuchman et al. (Eds.), *Health and home.* New York: Oxford University Press.

Gerbner, G., Gross, L., Morgan, M., & Signorielli, N. (1980). The "mainstreaming" of America. *Journal of Communication, 30,* 10 29.

Gibb, J. (1961). Defensive communication. *Journal of Communication, 11,* 141–148.

Gibbs, J. (1965). Norms. *American Journal of Sociology, 70,* 586–594.

Giddens, A. (1984). *The constitution of society.* Berkeley: University of California Press.

Gilbert, S. (1976). Self-disclosure, intimacy and communication in families. *Family Coordinator, 25,* 221–229.

Giles, H. (1973). Accent mobility. *Anthropological Linguistics, 15,* 87–105.

Giles, H., Bourhis, R., & Taylor, D. (1977). Towards a theory of language in ethnic group relations. In H. Giles (Ed.), *Language, ethnicity, and intergroup relations.* London: Academic Press.

Giles, H., & Byrne, J. (1982). The intergroup theory of second language acquisition. *Journal of Multilingual and Multicultural Development, 3,* 17–40.

Giles, H., Coupland, N., Coupland, J., Williams, A., & Nussbaum, J. (1992). Intergenerational talk and communication with older people. *International Journal of Aging and Human Development, 34,* 271–297.

Giles, H., Coupland, N., & Wiemann, J. (1992). "Talk is cheap. . ." but "my word is my bond." In R. Bolton & H. Kwok (Eds.), *Sociolinguistics today.* London: Routledge.

Giles, H., & Hewstone, M. (1982). Cognitive structures, speech, and social situations. *Language Sciences, 4,* 181–219.

Giles, H., & Johnson, P. (1981). The role of language in ethnic group relations. In J. Turner & H. Giles (Eds.), *Intergroup behavior.* Chicago: University of Chicago Press.

Giles, H., & Johnson, P. (1987). Ethnolinguistic identity theory. *International Journal of the Sociology of Language, 68,* 69–90.

Giles, H., Mulac, A., Bradac, J., & Johnson, P. (1987). Speech accommodation theory. In M. McLaughlin (Ed.), *Communication yearbook 10.* Beverly Hills, CA: Sage.

Giles, H., & Smith, P. (1979). Accommodation theory. In H. Giles & R. St. Clair (Eds.), *Language and social psychology.* Oxford: Blackwell.

Gilligan, C. (1982). *In a different voice.* Cambridge: Harvard University Press.

Glazer, N., & Moynihan, D. (1975). *Ethnicity.* Cambridge: Harvard University Press.

Goffman, E. (1959). *The presentation of self in everyday life.* Hammondsworth: Penguin.

Goffman, E. (1963). *Stigma.* Englewood Cliffs, NJ: Prentice-Hall.

Goffman, E. (1971). *Relations in public.* Hammondsworth: Penguin.

Gonzalez, D. (1992, November 15). What's the problem with Hispanic? Just ask a Latino. *Los Angeles Times,* p. E6.

Goodman, G., & Esterly, G. (1988). *The talk book.* Emmaus, PA: Rodale Press.

Goodwin, M. (1980). Directive response speech sequences in girls' and boys' task activities. In S. McConnel-Ginet, R. Borker, & N. Furnan (Eds.), *Women and language in literature and society.* New York: Praeger.

Gordon, M. (1964). *Assimilation in American life.* Oxford: Oxford University Press.

Goss, B. (1982). Listening as information processing. *Communication Quarterly,* 30, 304-307.

Gotanda, P. K. (1991). Interview with Philip Kan Gotanda. *Los Angeles Performing Arts, 25(1),* p-10, p-11.

Gottman, J. (1979). *Marital interaction.* New York: Academic Press.

Gottman, J., Markman, H., & Notarius, C. (1977). The topography of marital conflict. *Journal of Marriage and the Family, 39,* 461-478.

Gottman, J., Notarius, C., Markman, H., Bank, S., Yoppi, B., & Rubin, M. (1976). Behavioral exchange theory and marital decision making. *Journal of Personality and Social Psychology, 34,* 14-23.

Gouldner, A. (1960). The norm of reciprocity. *American Sociological Review, 25,* 161-179.

Graham, E., Papa, M., & Brooks, G. (1992). Functions of humor in conversation. *Western Journal of Communication, 56,* 161-183.

Granovetter, M. (1973). The strength of weak ties. *American Journal of Sociology, 78,* 1360-1380.

Greeley, A. (1989). Protestant and Catholic: Is the analogical imagination extinct? *American Sociological Review, 54,* 485-502.

Greenberg, J., Pyszczynski, T., & Solomon, S. (1986). The causes and consequences of a need for self-esteem. In R. Baumeister (Ed.), *Public self and private self.* New York: Springer-Verlag.

Grice, H. (1975). Logic and conversation. In P. Cole & J. Morgan (Eds.), *Syntax and semantics* (Vol. 3). New York: Academic Press.

Grove, T., & Werkman, D. (1991). Communication with able-bodied and visually disabled strangers. *Human Communication Research, 17,* 507-534.

Gudykunst, W. B. (1988). Uncertainty and anxiety. In Y. Kim & W. Gudykunst (Eds.), *Theories in intercultural communication.* Newbury Park, CA: Sage.

Gudykunst, W. B. (1991). *Bridging differences.* Newbury Park, CA: Sage.

Gudykunst, W. B. (1993). Toward a theory of interpersonal and intergroup communication: An anxiety/uncertainty management (AUM) perspective. In R. Wiseman & J. Koester (Eds.), *Intercultural communication competence.* Newbury Park, CA: Sage.

Gudykunst, W. B. (1994). *Bridging differences* (2nd ed.). Newbury Park, CA: Sage.

Gudykunst, W. B., Gao, G., Schmidt, K., Nishida, T., Bond, M. H., Leung, K., Wang, G., & Barraclough, R. A. (1992). The influence of individualism-collectivism on communication in ingroup and outgroup relationships. *Journal of Cross-Cultural Psychology, 23,* 196-213.

Gudykunst, W. B., Gao, G., Sudweeks, S., Ting-Toomey, S., & Nishida, T. (1991). Themes in opposite-sex Japanese-North American relationships. In S. Ting-Toomey & F. Korzenny (Eds.), *Cross-cultural interpersonal communication.* Newbury Park, CA: Sage.

Gudykunst, W. B., & Hammer, M. R. (1988). The influence of social identity and intimacy of interethnic relationships on uncertainty reduction processes. *Human Communication Research, 14,* 569-601.

Gudykunst, W. B., & Kim, Y. Y. (1984). *Communicating with strangers: An approach to intercultural communication.* New York: McGraw-Hill.

Gudykunst, W. B., & Lim, T. S. (1985). Ethnicity, sex, and self-perceptions of communicator style. *Communication Research Reports, 2 (1),* 68-75.

Gudykunst, W. B., & Nishida, T. (1986a). Attributional confidence in low- and high-context cultures. *Human Communication Research, 12,* 525-549.

Gudykunst, W. B., & Nishida, T. (1986b). The influence of cultural variability on perceptions of communication behavior associated with relationship terms. *Human Communication Research, 13,* 147-166.

Gudykunst, W. B., & Nishida, T. (1993). Closeness in interpersonal relationships in Japan and the United States. *Research in Social Psychology, 8,* 76-84.

Gudykunst, W. B., & Nishida, T. (in press). *Bridging Japanese/North American differences.* Newbury Park, CA: Sage.

Gudykunst, W. B., Nishida, T., & Chua, E. (1986). Uncertainty reduction processes in Japanese-North American relationships. *Communication Research Reports, 3,* 39-46.

Gudykunst, W. B., Nishida, T., & Chua, E. (1987). Perceptions of social penetration in Japanese-North American relationships. *International Journal of Intercultural Relations, 11,* 171-190.

Gudykunst, W. B., & Ting-Toomey, S., with Chua, E. (1988). *Culture and interpersonal communication.* Newbury Park, CA: Sage.

Guilford, J. (1959). *Personality.* New York: McGraw-Hill.

Gumperz, J. (1982). *Discourse strategies.* Cambridge: Cambridge University Press.

Gumperz, J., & Hernandez-Chavez, E. (1972). Bilingualism, bidialectism and classroom interaction. In C. Cazden, V. John, & D. Hymes (Eds.), *Functions of language in the classroom.* New York: Teacher's College Press.

Gurin, P., & Townsend, A. (1986). Properties of gender identity and their implications for gender consciousness. *British Journal of Social Psychology, 25,* 139-148.

Gutmann, A. (1992). Introduction. In A. Gutmann (Ed.), *Multiculturalism and the politics of recognition.* Princeton, NJ: Princeton University Press.

Hall, E. T. (1959). *The silent language.* New York: Doubleday.

Hall, E. T. (1966). *The hidden dimension.* New York: Doubleday.

Hall, E. T. (1976). *Beyond culture.* New York: Doubleday.

Hall, E. T. (1983). *The dance of time.* New York: Doubleday.

Hall, J. A. (1984). *Nonverbal sex differences.* Baltimore, MD: Johns Hopkins University Press.

Hamilton, D., Sherman, S., & Ruvolo, C. (1992). Stereotyped based expectancies. In W. B. Gudykunst & Y. Y. Kim (Eds.), *Readings on communicating with strangers.* New York: McGraw-Hill (Originally published in *Journal of Social Issues,* 1990, *46(2),* 35-60).

Hampshire, S. (1989). *Innocence and experience.* Cambridge, MA: Harvard University Press.

Hanh, T. N. (1991). *Peace in every step.* New York: Bantam.

Hargie, O. (1986). *A handbook of communication skills.* New York: New York University Press.

Haslett, B. (1990). Social class, social status and communicative behavior. In H. Giles & W. Robinson (Eds.), *Handbook of language and social psychology.* Chichester, England: Wiley.

Haslett, B., & Ogilvie, J. (1988). Feedback processes in small groups. In R. Cathcart & L. Samovar (Eds.), *Small group communication: A reader* (5th ed.). Dubuque, IA: William C. Brown.

Hass, R., Katz, I., Rizzo, N., Bailey, J., & Moore, L.

(1992). When racial ambivalence evokes negative affect. *Personality and Social Psychology Bulletin, 18,* 786–797.

Hayashi, R. (1990). Rhythmicity, sequence and synchrony of English and Japanese face-to-face conversations. *Language Sciences, 12,* 155–195.

Hecht, M. (1978). The conceptualization and measurement of communication satisfaction. *Human Communication Research, 4,* 253–264.

Hecht, M. (1984). Satisfying communication and relationship labels. *Western Journal of Speech Communication, 48,* 201–216.

Hecht, M., & Ribeau, S. (1991). Sociocultural roots of ethnic identity. *Journal of Black Studies, 21,* 501–513.

Hecht, M., Ribeau, S., & Alberts, J. (1989). An Afro-American perspective on interethnic communication. *Communication Monographs, 56,* 385–410.

Hecht, M., Ribeau, S., & Sedano, M. (1990). A Mexican-American perspective on interethnic communication. *International Journal of Intercultural Relations ,14,* 31–55.

Heider, F. (1958). *The psychology of interpersonal relations.* New York: Wiley.

Heimberg, R., Montgomery, P., Madsen, C., & Heimberg, J. (1977). Assertion training. *Behavior Therapy, 8,* 953–971.

Hendrick, S., & Hendrick, C. (1992). *Liking, loving, and relating* (2nd ed.). Belmont, CA: Brooks/Cole.

Henley, N. (1977). *Body politics.* Englewood Cliffs, NJ: Prentice-Hall.

Henley, N., Hamilton, M., & Thorne, B. (1985). Womanspeak and manspeak. In A. Sargent (Ed.), *Beyond sex roles.* New York: West.

Henley, N., & Kramarae, C. (1991). Gender, power, and miscommunication. In N. Coupland, H. Giles, & J. Wiemann (Eds.), *"Miscommunications" and problematic talk.* Newbury Park, CA: Sage.

Henry, W. (1990, April 9). Beyond the melting pot. *Time,* pp. 28–31.

Herman, S., & Schield, E. (1961). The stranger group in a cross-cultural situation. *Sociometry, 24,* 165–176.

Herskovits, M. (1950). *Man and his works.* New York: Knopf.

Herskovits, M. (1955). *Cultural anthropology.* New York: Knopf.

Heslin, R. (1978). *Responses to touching as an index of sex roles norms and attitudes.* Paper presented at the American Psychological Association convention.

Hewes, D., & Graham, M. (1989). Second-guessing theory. In J. Andersen (Ed.), *Communication Yearbook 12.* Newbury Park, CA: Sage.

Hewes, D., & Planalp, S. (1982). There is nothing as useful as a good theory . . . In M. Roloff & C. Berger (Eds.), *Social cognition and communication.* Beverly Hills, CA: Sage.

Hewstone, M., & Brown, R. (1986). Contact is not enough. In M. Hewstone & R. Brown (Eds.), *Contact and conflict in intergroup encounters.* Oxford: Blackwell.

Hewstone, M., & Giles, H. (1986). Stereotypes and intergroup communication. In W. Gudykunst (Ed.), *Intergroup communication.* London: Edward Arnold.

Hewstone, M., & Jaspars, J. (1984). Social dimensions of attributions. In H. Tajfel (Ed.), *The social dimension* (Vol. 2). Cambridge: Cambridge University Press.

Hirokawa, R., & Miyahara, A. (1986). A comparison of influence strategies utilized by managers in American and Japanese organizations. *Communication Quarterly, 34,* 250–265.

Hocker, J., & Wilmot, W. (1991). *Interpersonal conflict* (3rd ed.). Dubuque, IA: William C. Brown.

Hockett, C. (1958). *A course in modern linguistics.* New York: Macmillan.

Hodges, H. (1964). *Social stratification.* Cambridge, MA: Schenkman.

Hoffman, C., Lau, I., & Johnson, R. (1986). The linguistic relativity of person cognition. *Journal of Personality and Social Psychology, 51,* 1097–1105.

Hoffman, M. (1983). Affective and cognitive process in moral internalization. In E. T. Higgins, D. Ruble, & W. Hartup (Eds.), *Social cognition and moral development.* New York: Cambridge University Press.

Hofman, T. (1985). Arabs and Jews, Blacks and Whites: Identity and group relations. *Journal of Multilingual and Multicultural Development, 6,* 217 237.

Hofstede, G. (1979). Value systems in forty countries. In L. Eckensberger, W. Lonner, & Y. Poortinga (Eds.), *Cross-cultural contributions to psychology.* Lisse, Netherlands: Swets & Zeitlinger.

Hofstede, G. (1980). *Culture's consequences.* Beverly Hills, CA: Sage.

Hofstede, G. (1991). *Cultures and organizations.* London: McGraw-Hill.

Hofstede, G., & Bond, M. (1984). Hofstede's culture dimensions. *Journal of Cross-Cultural Psychology, 15,* 417–433.

Holmes, J., & Rempel, J. (1989). Trust in close relationships. In C. Hendrick (Ed.), *Close relationships.* Newbury Park, CA: Sage.

Honess, T. (1976). Cognitive complexity and social prediction. *British Journal of Social and Clinical Psychology, 15,* 22–31.

Honeycutt, J. M., Knapp, M. L., & Powers, W. G. (1983). On knowing others and predicting what they say. *Western Journal of Speech Communication, 47,* 157–174.

Hoppe, A. (1993). Marital commitment and dialectical contradictions. M.A. thesis, California State University, Fullerton.

Hopper, R., & Bell, R. (1984). Broadening the deception construct. *Quarterly Journal of Speech, 70,* 288–302.

Hopper, R., Knapp, M., & Scott, L. (1981). Couples' personal idioms. *Journal of Communication, 31,* 23–33.

Howard, L. (1985, May 31-June 2). Embraceable USA—by region. *USA today,* p. A1.

Howell, W. S. (1982). *The empathic communicator.* Belmont, CA: Wadsworth.

Hoyle, R., Pinkley, R., & Insko, C. (1989). Perceptions of social behavior: Evidence of differing expectations for interpersonal and intergroup behavior. *Personality and Social Psychology Bulletin, 15,* 365–376.

Hraba, J., & Hoiberg, E. (1983). Origins of modern theories of ethnicity. *Sociological Quarterly, 24,* 381–391.

Hwang, J., Chase, L., & Kelly, C. (1980). An intercultural examination of communication competence. *Communication, 9,* 70–79.

Hymes, D. (1974). Ways of speaking. In R. Bauman & J. Sherzer (Eds.), *Explorations in the ethnography of speaking.* Cambridge: Cambridge University Press.

Iacocca, L. (1984). *Iacocca: An autobiography.* New York: Bantam.

Infante, D. (1987). Aggressiveness. In J. McCroskey & J. Daly (Eds.), *Personality and interpersonal communication.* Beverly Hills, CA: Sage.

Infante, D. (1988). *Arguing constructively.* Prospect Heights, IL: Waveland.

Inkeles, A. (1974). *Becoming modern.* Cambridge: Harvard University Press.

Ittelson, W., & Cantril, H. (1954). *Perception, a transactional approach.* Garden City, NY: Doubleday.

Ivey, A. (1975). *Microcounseling.* Springfield, IL: Thomas.

Jackman, M., & Jackman, R. (1983). *Class awareness in the United States.* Berkeley: University of California Press.

Jackson, J. (1964). The normative regulation of authoritative behavior. In W. Grove & J. Dyson (Eds.), *The making of decisions.* New York: Free Press.

Jampolsky, G. (1989). *Out of darkness into the light.* New York: Bantam.

Janis, I., & Mann, L. (1977). *Decision making.* New York: Free Press.

Jaspars, J., & Warnaen, S. (1982). Intergroup relations, social identity, and self-evaluation in India. In H. Tajfel (Ed.), *Social identity and intergroup relations.* Cambridge: Cambridge University Press.

Jefferson, G. (1972). Side sequences. In D. Sudnow (Ed.), *Studies in social interaction.* New York: Free Press.

Johnson, D. (1986). *Reaching out* (3rd ed.). Englewood Cliffs, NJ: Prentice-Hall.

Johnson, D., & Johnson, F. (1982). *Joining together* (2nd ed.). Englewood Cliffs, NJ: Prentice Hall.

Johnson, F., & Aries, E. (1983). The talk of women friends. *Women's Studies International Forum, 6,* 353–361.

Johnstone, L., & Hewstone, M. (1991). Intergroup contact. In D. Abrams & M. Hogg (Eds.), *Social identity theory.* New York: Springer-Verlag.

Jones, E., & Nisbett, R. (1972). The actor and the observer. In E. Jones, D. Kanouse, H. Kelley, R. Nisbett, S. Valins, & B. Weiner (Eds.), *Attribution: Perceiving the causes of behavior.* Morristown, NJ: General Learning.

Jones, S., & Yarbrough, A. (1985). A naturalistic study of the meanings of touch. *Communication Monographs, 52,* 19–56.

Josephs, L. (1991). Character structure, self-esteem regulation, and the principle of identity maintenance. In R. Curtis (Ed.), *The relational self.* New York: Guilford.

Jussim, L., Coleman, L., & Lerch, L. (1987). The nature of stereotypes. *Journal of Personality and Social Psychology, 52,* 536–546.

Kanouse, D., & Hanson, L. (1972). Negativity in evaluations. In E. Jones, D. Kanouse, H. Kelley, R. Nisbett, S. Valins, & L. Petrullo (Eds.), *Attribution.* Morristown, NJ: General Learning Press.

Kanter, R. (1977). *Men and women in the corporation.* New York: Basic Books.

Karniol, R. (1990). Reading people's minds. In M. Zanna (Ed.), *Advances in experimental social psychology* (Vol. 23). New York: Academic Press.

Katriel, T. (1986). *Talking straight.* Cambridge: Cambridge University Press.

Katz, D., & Braly, K. (1933). Racial stereotypes of 100 college students. *Journal of Abnormal and Social Psychology, 28,* 280–290.

Keefe, S, & Padilla, A. (1987). *Chicano Ethnicity:* Albuquerque, NM: University of New Mexico Press.

Keesing, R. (1974). Theories of culture. *Annual Review of Anthropology, 3,* 73–97.

Kellermann, K. (1986). Anticipation of future interaction and information exchange in initial interactions. *Human Communication Research, 13,* 41–65.

Kellermann, K. (1991). The conversational MOP II. *Human Communication Research, 17,* 385–414.

Kellermann, K. (1993). Extrapolating beyond: Processes of uncertainty reduction. In S. Deetz (Ed.), *Communication yearbook 16.* Newbury Park, CA: Sage.

Kellermann, K., & Reynolds, R. (1990). When ignorance is bliss: The role of motivation to reduce uncertainty in uncertainty reduction theory. *Human Communication Research, 17,* 5–75.

Kellermann, K., Reynolds, R., & Chen, J. (1991). Strategies of conversational retreat. *Communication Monographs, 58,* 362–383.

Kelley, D., & Burgoon, J. (1991). Understanding marital satisfaction and couple types as functions of relational expectations. *Human Communication Research, 18,* 40–69.

Kelley, H., Cunningham, J., Grisham, J., Lefebure, L., Sink, C., & Yablon, G. (1978). Sex differences in comments during conflict with close heterosexual pairs. *Sex Roles, 4,* 473–492.

Kelley, H. H. (1967). Attribution theory in social psychology. *Nebraska Symposium on Motivation, 15,* 192–238.

Kelley, H. H. (1972). Causal schemata and the attribution process. In E. Jones, D. Kanouse, H. Kelley, R. Nisbett, S. Valins, L B. Weiner (Eds.), *Attribution: Perceiving the causes of behavior.* Morristown, NJ: General Learning Press.

Kelley, H. H., Berscheid, E., Christensen, A., Harvey, J., Huston, T., Levinger, G., McClintock, E., Peplau, L., & Peterson, D. (1983). *Close relationships.* New York: Freeman.

Kelly, G. (1955). *The psychology of personal constructs.* New York: Norton.

Kennerley, H. (1990). *Managing anxiety: A training manual.* New York: Oxford University Press.

Kim, H. J., & Stiff, J. (1991). Social networks and the development of close relationships. *Human Communication Research, 18,* 70–91.

King, L. A. (1993). Emotional expression, ambivalence over expression, and marital satisfaction. *Journal of Social and Personal Relationships, 10,* 601608.

King, M. L., Jr. (1958). *Stride toward freedom.* New York: Harper & Row.

King, M. L., Jr. (1963). Letter from Birmingham jail. In *Why we can't wait.* New York: Harper & Row.

Kitayama, S., & Burnstein, E. (1988). Automaticity in conversations. *Journal of Personality and Social Psychology, 54,* 219–224.

Klass, E. (1990). Guilt, shame, and embarrassment. In H. Leitenberg (Ed.), *Handbook of social and evaluation anxiety.* New York: Plenum.

Kleinke, C. (1975). *First impressions.* Englewood Cliffs, NJ: Prentice-Hall.

Kluckhohn, F., & Strodtbeck, F. (1961). *Variations in value orientations.* New York: Row, Peterson.

Knapp, M. (1978). *Nonverbal communication in human interaction* (2nd ed.). New York: Holt, Rinehart and Winston.

Knapp, M. (1983). Dyadic relationship development. In J. Wiemann & R. Harrison (Eds.), *Nonverbal interaction.* Beverly Hills, CA: Sage.

Knapp, M., Ellis, D., & Williams, B. (1980). Perceptions of communication behavior associated with relationship terms. *Communication Monographs, 47,* 262–278.

Knapp, M., & Hall, J. (1992). *Nonverbal communication in human interaction* (3rd ed.). New York: Harcourt Brace.

Knapp, M., Hart, R., Friederich, G., & Shulman, G. (1973). The rhetoric of goodbye. *Speech Monographs, 40,* 182–198.

Knapp, M., & Vangelisti, A. (1992). *Interpersonal communication and human relationships* (2nd ed.). Boston: Allyn & Bacon.

Kochman, T. (1981). *Black and white: Styles in conflict.* Chicago: University of Chicago Press.

Kochman, T. (1990). Force fields in black and white communication. In D. Carbaugh (Ed.), *Cultural communication and intercultural contact.* Hillsdale, NJ: Erlbaum.

Kohn, M. (1969). *Class and conformity.* Homewood, IL: Dorsey.

Kramer, J. (1985). *Family interfaces.* New York: Brunner/Mazel.

Krauss, R., & Fussell, S. (1991). Constructing shared communicative environments. In L. Resnick, J. Levine, & S. Behrend (Eds.), *Perspectives on socially shared cognition.* Washington, DC: American Psychological Association.

Krishnamurti, J. (1975). *The first and last freedom.* New York: Harper & Row.

Kraut, R., & Higgins, E. (1984). Communication and social cognition. In R. Wyer & T. Srull (Eds.), *Handbook of social cognition* (Vol. 3). Hillsdale, NJ: Erlbaum.

LaFollette, H., & Graham, G. (1986). Honesty and intimacy. *Journal of Social and Personal Relationships, 3,* 3–18.

LaFrance, M., & Mayo, C. (1978). Cultural aspects of nonverbal behavior. *International Journal of Intercultural Relations, 2,* 71–89.

Laing, D. (1961). *The self and others.* New York: Pantheon.

Lakoff, R. (1975). *Language and women's place.* New York: Harper & Row.

Lakoff, R. (1990). *Talking power.* New York: Basic Books.

Lamke, L. (1982). The impact of sexual orientation on self-esteem in early adolescence. *Child Development, 53,* 1531–1535.

Langer, E. (1978). Rethinking the role of thought in social interaction. In J. Harvey, W. Ickes, & R. Kidd (Eds.), *New directions in attribution research* (Vol. 2). Hillsdale, NJ: Erlbaum.

Langer, E. (1989). *Mindfulness.* Reading, MA: Addison-Wesley.

Larkey, L., Hecht, M., & Martin, J. (1993). What's in a name? African-American ethnic labels and self-distinctions. *Journal of Language and Social Psychology, 12,* 302–317.

Lazarus, R. (1991). *Emotion and adaptation.* New York: Oxford University Press.

Leary, M., Kowalski, R., & Bergen, D. (1988). Interpersonal information acquisition and confidence in first encounters. *Personality and Social Psychology Bulletin, 14,* 68–77.

Lebra, T. S. (1987). The cultural significance of silence in Japanese communication. *Multilingua, 6,* 343–357.

Lee, H., & Boster, F. (1991). Social information for uncertainty reduction during initial interactions. In S. Ting-Toomey & F. Korzenny (Eds.), *Cross-cultural interpersonal communication.* Newbury Park, CA: Sage.

Lee, S. (1990, July 12). Interview on *48 Hours.* CBS Television.

Lehman, D., Ellard, J., & Wortman, C. (1986). Social support for the bereaved. *Journal of Consulting and Clinical Psychology, 54,* 438–446.

Lennox, R., & Wolfe, R. (1984). Revision of the self-monitoring scale. *Journal of Personality and Social Psychology, 46,* 1349–1364.

Levin, J., & Levin, W. (1980). *Ageism: Predujice and discrimination.* Belmont, CA: Wadsworth.

Levine, D. (1979). Simmel at a distance. In W. Shack & E. Skinner (Edg.), *Strangers in African societies.* Berkeley: University of California Press.

Levine, D. (1985). *The flight from ambiguity.* Chicago: University of Chicago Press.

LeVine, R. A., & Campbell, D. T. (1972). *Ethnocentrism: Theories of conflict, ethnic attitudes, and group behavior.* New York: Wiley.

Lieberson, S. (1985). Unhyphenated whites in the United States. *Ethnic and Racial Studies, 8,* 158–180.

Lim, T. S. (1990). The influence of receivers' resistance on persuaders' verbal aggressiveness. *Communication Quarterly, 38,* 170–186.

Linville, P., Fisher, G., & Salovey, P. (1989). Perceived distributions of the characteristics of in-group and out-group members. *Journal of Personality and Social Psychology, 57,* 165–188.

Lippman, W. (1936). *Public opinion.* New York: Macmillan.

Liska, J., Mechling, E., & Stathas, S. (1981). Differences in subjects' perceptions of gender and believability between users of deferential and nondeferential language. *Communication Quarterly, 29,* 40–48.

Little, K. (1968). Cultural variations in social schemata. *Journal of Personality and Social Psychology, 10,* 1–7.

LoCastro, V. (1987). *Aizuchi:* A Japanese conversational routine. In L. Smith (Ed.), *Discourse across cultures.* Englewood Cliffs, NJ: Prentice-Hall.

Loewy, E. (1993). *Freedom and community.* Albany: State University of New York Press.

Longmore, P. (1987). Screening stereotypes. In A. Gartner & T. Jol (Eds.), *Images of the disabled, disabling images.* New York: Praeger.

Lorenz, F., Conger, R., Simon, R., Whibeck, L., & Elder, G. (1991). Economic pressure and marital satisfaction. *Journal of Marriage and the Family, 53,* 375–388.

Loveday, L. (1982). Communicative interference. *International Review of Applied Linguistics in Language Teaching, 20,* 1–16.

Lukens, J. (1978). Ethnocentric speech. *Ethnic Groups, 2,* 35–53.

Lynberg, M. (1989). *The path with heart.* New York: Fawcett.

Major, B. (1984). Gender patterns in touching behavior. In C. Mayo & N. Henley (Eds.), *Gender and nonverbal behavior.* New York: Springer-Verlag.

Maltz, D., & Borker, R. (1982). A cultural approach to male-female miscommunication. In J. Gumperz (Ed.), *Language and social identity.* New York: Cambridge University Press.

Markus, H., Crane, M., Bernstein, S., & Siladi, M. (1982). Self-schemata and gender. *Journal of Personality and Social Psychology, 42,* 38–50.

Markus, H., & Kitayama, S. (1991). Culture and the

self: Implications for cognition, emotion, and motivation. *Psychological Review, 98,* 224–253.

Marwell, G., & Schmitt, D. (1967). Dimensions of compliance-gaining behavior. *Sociometry, 30,* 350–364.

Mascheter, C., & Harris, L. (1986). From divorce to friendship. *Journal of Social and Personal Relationships, 3,* 177–189.

Matsumoto, D., Wallbott, H., & Scherer, K. (1989). Emotions in intercultural communication. In M. Asante & W. B. Gudykunst (Eds.), *Handbook of international and intercultural communication.* Newbury Park, CA: Sage.

May, R. (1977). *The meaning of anxiety.* New York: Washington Square Press.

McArthur, L. (1982). Judging a book by its cover. In A. Hastorf & A. Isen (Eds.), *Cognitive social psychology.* New York: Elsevier.

McConahay, J. B. (1986). Modern racism, ambivalence, and the modern racism scale. In J. Dovidio & S. Gaertner (Eds.), *Prejudice, discrimination, and racism.* New York: Academic Press.

McConnell-Ginet, S. (1978). Address forms in sexual politics. In D. Butturff & E. Epstein (Eds.), *Women's language and styles.* Akron: L&S Books.

McCornack, S., & Levine, T. (1990). When lovers become leery. *Communication Monographs, 57,* 219–230.

McCornack, S., & Parks, M. (1986). Deception detection and relationship development. In M. McLaughlin (Ed.), *Communication yearbook 9.* Beverly Hills, CA: Sage.

McCroskey, J., & Richmond, V. (1987). Willingness to communicate. In J. McCroskey & J. Daly (Eds.), *Personality and interpersonal communication.* Beverly Hills, CA; Sage.

McFall, L. (1987). Integrity. *Ethics, 98,* 5–20.

McFall, R. (1982). A review and reformulation of the concept of social skills. *Behavioral Assessment, 4,* 1–33.

McGill, M. (1986). *The McGill report on male intimacy.* New York: Harper & Row.

McGinn, N., Harburg, E., L Ginsburg, G. (1973). Responses to interpersonal conflict by middle class males in Guadalajara and Michigan. In F. Jandt (Ed.), *Conflict resolution through communication.* New York: Harper & Row.

McLaughlin, M. (1984). *Conversation: How talk is organized.* Beverly Hills, CA: Sage.

McLeod, J., & Chaffee, S. (1973). Interpersonal approach to communication research. *American Behavioral Scientist, 16,* 469–499.

McPherson, K. (1983). Opinion-related information seeking. *Personality and Social Psychology Bulletin, 9,* 116–124.

Mehrabian, A. (1971). *Silent messages.* Belmont, CA: Wadsworth.

Mehrabian, A. (1981). *Silent messages* (2nd ed.). Belmont, CA: Wadsworth.

Mehrabian, A. (1972). *Nonverbal communication.* Chicago: Aldine.

Merton, R. (1957). *Social theory and social structure.* New York: Free Press.

Messick, D., & Mackie, D. (1989). Intergroup relations. *Annual Review of Psychology, 40,* 45–81.

Milardo, R. (1982). Friendship networks in developing relationships. *Social Psychology Quarterly, 45,* 162–172.

Milardo, R. (1986). Personal choice and social constraint in close relationships. In V. Deregla & B. Winstead (Eds.), *Friendship and social interaction.* New York: Springer-Verlag.

Millar, F., & Rogers, L. (1987). Relational dimensions and interpersonal dynamics. In M. Roloff & G. Miller (Eds.), *Interpersonal processes.* Newbury Park, CA: Sage.

Miller, G., Mongeau, P., & Sleight, C. (1986). Fudging with friends and lying to lovers. *Journal of Social and Personal Relationships, 3,* 495–512.

Miller, G., & Steinberg, M. (1975). *Between people.* Chicago: Science Research Associates.

Miller, G., & Sunnafrank, M. (1982). All is for one but one is not for all. In F. Dance (Ed.), *Human communication theory.* New York: Harper & Row.

Mintz, N. (1956). Effects of aesthetic surroundings II. *Journal of Personality, 41,* 459–466.

Molnar, A., & Lindquist, B. (1989). *Changing problem behavior in schools.* San Francisco: Jossey-Bass.

Morris, D. (1971). *Intimate behavior.* New York: Random House.

Morris, M. L. (1981). *Saying and meaning in Puerto Rico.* Elmsford, NY: Pergamon.

Morrow, A. (1969). *The practical theorist: The life and work of Kurt Lewin.* New York: Basic Books.

Mosby, K. (1978). An analysis of actual and ideal touch behavior as reported by a modified version of the body accessibility questionnaire. Ph.D. dissertation, Virginia Commonwealth University.

Mulac, A., Studley, L., Wiemann, J., & Bradac, J. (1988). Male/female gaze in same-sex and mixed-sex dyads. *Human Communication Research, 13,* 323–343.

Mullen, B. (1991). Group composition, salience, and cognitive representations. *Journal of Experimental Social Psychology, 27,* 297–323.

Mullen, B., & Johnson, C. (1993). Cognitive representations in ethnophaulisms as a function of group size. *Personality and Social Psychology Bulletin, 19,* 296–304.

Nakane, C. (1970). *Japanese society.* Berkeley: University of California Press.

Nakane, C. (1974). The social system reflected in interpersonal communication. In J. Condon & M. Saito (Eds.), *Intercultural encounters with Japan.* Tokyo: Simul Press.

Neuberg, S. (1989). The goal of forming accurate impressions during initial interactions. *Journal of Personality and Social Psychology, 56,* 374–386.

Nichols, R., & Stevens, L. (1957). *Are you listening?* New York: McGraw-Hill.

Nilsen, A. (1977). Sexism as shown through the English vocabulary. In A. Nilsen, H. Bosmajian, H. Gershuny, & J. Stanley (Eds.), *Sexism and language.* Urbana, IL: National Council of Teachers of English.

Nilsen, A., Bosmajian, H., Gershuny, H., & Stanley, J. (Eds.). (1977). *Sexism and language.* Urbana, IL: National Council of Teachers of English.

Nishida, T. (1991). *Sequence patterns of self-disclosure among Japanese and North American students.* Paper presented at the Conference on Communication in Japan and the United States, California State University, Fullerton.

Noesjirwan, J. (1978). A rule-based analysis of cultural differences in social behavior. *International Journal of Psychology, 13,* 305–316.

Noller, P. (1980). Misunderstandings in marital communication. *Journal of Personality and Social Psychology, 39,* 1135–1148.

Noller, P. (1984). *Nonverbal communication in marital interaction.* Oxford: Pergamon.

Noller, P. (1985). Negative communication in marriage. *Journal of Social and Personal Relationships, 2,* 289–302.

Noller, P. (1993). Gender and emotional communication in marriage. *Journal of Language and Social Psychology, 12,* 132–152.

Notarius, C., & Herrick, L. (1988). Listener response styles to a distressed other. *Journal of Social and Personal Relationships, 5,* 97–108.

Nozick, R. (1974). *Anarchy, state, and utopia.* New York: Basic Books.

Nozick, R. (1989). *The examined life.* New York: Simon & Schuster.

Nuessel, F. (1984). Ageist language. *Maledicta, 8,* 17–28.

Nussbaum, J. (1985). Successful aging: A communication model. *Communication Quarterly, 33,* 262–269.

Nussbaum, J., & Robinson, J. (1984). Attitudes toward aging. *Communication Research Reports, 1,* 21–27.

Ogden, C., & Richards, I. (1923). *The meaning of meaning.* New York: Harcourt Brace.

O'Grady, W., Dobrovolsky, M., & Aronoff, M. (1989). *Contemporary linguistics.* New York: St. Martin's.

O'Hair, M., Cody, M., & O'Hair, D. (1991). The impact of situational dimensions on compliance-resisting strategies. *Communication Quarterly, 39,* 226-240.

Okabe, R. (1983). Cultural assumptions of east and west. In W. B. Gudykunst (Ed.), *Intercultural communication theory.* Beverly Hills, CA: Sage.

O'Keefe, D., & Sypher, H. (1981). Cognitive complexity measures and the relationship of cognitive complexity to communication. *Human Communication Research, 8,* 72-92.

Olsen, M. (1978). *The process of social organization* (2nd ed.). New York: Holt, Rinehart and Winston.

Olson, D., & McCubbin, H. (1983). *Families: What makes them work.* Beverly Hills, CA: Sage.

Omi, M., & Winant, H. (1986). *Racial group formation in the United States.* New York: Routledge.

Optow, S. (1990). Moral exclusion and injustice: An introduction. *Journal of Social Issues, 46 (1),* 1-20.

Orvis, B., Kelley, H., & Butler, D. (1976). Attributional conflicts in young couples. In J. Harvey, W. Ickes, & R. Kidd (Eds.), *New directions in attributional research* (Vol. 1). Hillsdale, NJ: Erlbaum.

Palmore, E. (1971). Attitudes toward ageing as shown by humor. *The Gerontologist, 2,* 181-186.

Palmore, E. (1982). Attitudes toward the aged. *Research on Aging, 4,* 333-348.

Park, M. (1979). *Communication styles in two different cultures: Korean and American.* Seoul: Han Shin.

Park, R. E. (1950). Our racial frontier in the Pacific. In R. Park (Ed.), *Race and culture.* New York: Free Press.

Parks, M., & Adelman, M. (1983). Communication networks and the development of romantic relationships. *Human Communication Research, 10,* 55-80.

Parlee, M. (1979, May). Conversational politics. *Psychology Today,* pp. 48-56.

Pearce, W. B. (1976). The coordinated management of meaning. In G. R. Miller (Ed.), *Exploration in interpersonal communication.* Beverly Hills, CA: Sage.

Peck, M. S. (1978). *The road less traveled.* New York: Simon & Schuster.

Peck, M. S. (1987). *The different drum: Community making and peace.* New York: Simon & Schuster.

Peng, F. (1974). Communicative distances. *Language Sciences, 31,* 32-38.

Perrine, R. (1993). On being supportive. *Journal of Social and Personal Relationships, 10,* 371-384.

Pettigrew, T. F. (1958). The measurement and correlates of category width as a cognitive variable. *Journal of Personality, 26,* 532-544.

Pettigrew, T. F. (1978). Three issues in ethnicity. In Y. Yinger & S. Cutler (Eds.), *Major social issues.* New York: Free Press.

Pettigrew, T. F. (1979). The ultimate attribution error. *Personality and Social Psychology Bulletin, 5,* 461-476.

Pettigrew, T. F. (1982). Cognitive styles and social behavior. In L. Wheeler (Ed.), *Review of personality and social psychology* (Vol. 3). Beverly Hills, CA: Sage.

Philpott, J. (1983). The relative contributions to meaning of verbal and nonverbal channels of communication. M.A. thesis, University of Nebraska.

Pike, G., & Sillars, A. (1985). Reciprocity of marital communication. *Journal of Social and Personal Relationships, 2,* 303-324.

Planalp, S. (1993). Friends' and acquaintances' conversations II. *Journal of Social and Personal Relationships, 10,* 339-354.

Planalp, S., & Benson, A. (1992). Friends' and acquaintances' conversations I. *Journal of Social and Personal Relationships, 9,* 483-506.

Planalp, S., Rutherford, D., & Honeycutt, J. (1988). Events that increase uncertainty in relationships. *Human Communication Research, 14,* 516-547.

Pleck, J. (1977). The psychology of sex roles. *Journal of Communication, 26,* 193–200.

Pogrebin, L. C. (1987). *Among friends.* New York: McGraw-Hill.

Powell, J. (1969). *Why am I afraid to tell you who I am?* Chicago: Argus Communications.

Powers, W., & Lowry, D. (1984). Basic communication fidelity. In R. Bostrom (Ed.), *Competence in communication.* Beverly Hills, CA: Sage.

Prather, H. (1986). *Notes on how to live in the world . . . and still be happy.* Garden City, NY: Doubleday.

Preiss, R., & Wheeless, L. (1989). Affective responses in listening. *The Journal of the International Listening Association, 3,* 72–102.

Prescott, J. (1975). Body pleasure and the origins of violence. *Futurist, 9,* 164–174.

Pritchard, M. (1991). *On becoming responsible.* Lawrence: University of Kansas Press.

Putnam, L., & Wilson, C. (1982). Communication strategies in organizational conflicts. In M. Burgoon (Ed.), *Communication yearbook 6.* Beverly Hills, CA: Sage.

Pyszczynski, T., & Greenberg, J. (1981). Role of disconfirmed expectancies in the instigation of attributional processing. *Journal of Personality and Social Psychology, 40,* 31–38.

Ralston, D. (1985). Employee ingratiation. *Academy of Management Review, 10,* 447–487.

Raush, H., Barry, W., Hertel, R., & Swain, M. (1974). *Communication, conflict and marriage.* San Francisco: Jossey-Bass.

Rawlins, W. (1983). Negotiating close friendship. *Human Communication Research, 9,* 255–266.

Regan, T. (1983). *The case for animal rights.* Berkeley: University of California Press.

Renteln, A. (1988). Relativism and the search for human rights. *American Anthropologist, 90,* 56–72.

Reynolds, R. (1991). Beliefs about conversational abandonment. *Journal of Language and Social Psychology, 10,* 61–70.

Roach, C., & Wyatt, N. (1988). *Successful listening.* New York: Harper & Row.

Rodriguez, R. (1982). *The hunger of memory.* New York: Bantam Books.

Rogers, C. (1961). *On becoming a person.* Boston: Houghton Mifflin.

Rogers, C. (1975). Empathic: An unappreciated way of being. *The Counseling Psychologist, 2,* 2–10.

Rogers, C. (1980). *A way of being.* Boston: Houghton-Mifflin.

Rogers, E., & Bhowmik, D. (1971). Homophly-heterophily. *Public Opinion Research, 34,* 523–531.

Rogers, E., & Kincaid, D. L. (1981). *Communication networks.* New York: Free Press.

Rokeach, M. (1951). A method for studying individual differences in "narrowmindedness." *Journal of Personality, 20,* 219–233.

Rokeach, M. (1960). *The open and closed mind.* New York: Basic Books.

Rokeach, M. (1972). *Beliefs, attitudes, and values.* San Francisco: Jossey Bass.

Roloff, M. (1987). Communication and conflict. In C. Berger & S. Chaffe (Eds.), *Handbook of communication science.* Beverly Hills, CA: Sage.

Roosens, E. (1989). *Creating ethnicity.* Newbury Park, CA: Sage.

Rose, A. (1965). The subculture of aging. In A. Rose & W. Peterson (Eds.), *Older people and their social world.* Philadelphia: F. A. Davis.

Rose, T. (1981). Cognitive and dyadic processes in intergroup contact. In D. Hamilton (Ed.), *Cognitive processes in stereotyping and intergroup behavior.* Hillsdale, NJ: Erlbaum.

Rosenberg, M. (1979). *Conceiving the self.* New York: Basic Books.

Rosenfeld, L. (1979). Self-disclosure avoidance. *Communication Monographs, 46,* 63–74.

Rosenthal, R., & DePaulo, B. (1979). Sex differences in accommodation in nonverbal communication. In R. Rosenthal (Ed.), *Skill in nonverbal communication.* Cambridge, MA: Gunn & Hain.

Rosenthal, R., Hall, J., DiMatteo, M., Rogers, P., & Archer, D. (1979). *Sensitivity to nonverbal communication.* Baltimore, MD: Johns Hopkins University Press.

Ross, L. (1977). The intuitive psychologist and his shortcomings. *Advances in Experimental and Social Psychology, 10,* 174–220.

Ruben, B., & Kealey, D. (1979). Behavioral assessment of communication competency and the prediction of cross-cultural adaptation. *International Journal of Intercultural Relations, 3,* 15–48.

Rubin, R., Perse, E., & Barbato, C (1988). Conceptualization and measurement of interpersonal communication motives. *Human Communication Research, 14,* 602–627.

Rubin, T. I. (1990). *Anti-Semitism: A disease of the mind.* New York: Continuum.

Rusbult, C. (1983). A longitudinal test of the investment model. *Journal of Personality and Social Psychology, 45,* 101–117.

Rusbult, C., Onezuka, R., & Lipkus, I. (1993). What do we really want? Mental models of ideal romantic involvement expressed through multidimensional scaling. *Journal of Experimental Social Psychology, 24,* 493–527.

Ryan, E., Hewstone, M., & Giles, H. (1984). Language and intergroup attitudes. In J. Eiser (Ed.), *Attitudinal judgment.* New York: Springer-Verlag.

Sabetelli, R., Buck, R., & Dreyer, A. (1982). Nonverbal communication accuracy in marital couples. *Journal of Personality and Social Psychology, 43,* 1088–1097.

Sacks, H., Schegloff, E., & Jefferson, G. (1974). A simplest systematics for the organization of turn-taking in conversations. *Language, 50,* 696–735.

Safilios-Rothschild, C. (1982). Social and psychological parameters of friendship and intimacy for disabled people. In M. Eisenberg, C. Giggins, & R. Duval (Eds.), *Disabled people as second class citizens.* New York: Springer.

Saleh, S., & Gufwoli, P. (1982). The transfer of management techniques and practices: The Kenya case. In R. Rath et al. (Eds.), *Diversity and unity in cross-cultural psychology.* Lisse, The Netherlands: Swets & Zeitlinger.

Sapir, E. (1925). *Culture, language, and personality.* Berkeley: University of California Press.

Sarbin, T., & Allen, V. (1968). Role theory. In G. Lindzey & E. Aronson (Eds.), *Handbook of social psychology* (2nd ed.). Reading, MA: Addison-Wesley.

Satir, V. (1988). *The new peoplemaking.* Mountainview, CA: Science and Behavior Books.

Schearer, A. (1984). *Disability: Whose handicap?* Oxford: Blackwell.

Scheff, T. T. (1990). *Microsociology.* Chicago: University of Chicago Press.

Schegloff, E., Jefferson, G., & Sacks, H. (1977). The preference for self-correction in the organization of repair in conversation. *Language, 53,* 361–382.

Schlenker, B. R. (1986). Self-identification. In R. F. Baumeister (Ed.), *Public self and private self.* New York: Springer-Verlag.

Schmidt, K. L. (1991). Exit, voice, loyalty, and neglect: Responses to sexist communication in dating relationships. Unpublished Ph.D. dissertation, Arizona State University.

Schmidt, T., & Cornelius, R. (1987). Self-disclosure in everyday life. *Journal of Social and Personal Relationships, 4,* 365–374.

Schneider, J., & Hacker, S. (1973). Sex role imagery and the use of the generic "man" in introductory texts. *American Sociologist, 8,* 12–18.

Schutz, W. (1966). *The interpersonal underworld.* Palo Alto, CA: Science and Behavior Books.

Schwartz, J. (1980). The negotiation for meaning. In D. Larsen-Freeman (Ed.), *Discourse analysis in second language research.* Rowley, MA: Newbury House.

Schwartz, S. (1990). Individualism-collectivism: Critique and proposed refinements. *Journal of Cross-Cultural Psychology, 21,* 139–157.

Scollon, R., & Wong-Scollon, S. (1990). Athabaskan-

English interethnic communication. In D. Carbaugh (Ed.), *Cultural communication and intercultural contact.* Hillsdale, NJ: Erlbaum.

Scott, J. (1993, September 24). On-line, and maybe out of line. *Los Angeles Times,* pp. A1, 32–33.

Scotton, C. (1980). Explaining linguistic choices as identity negotiations. In H. Giles, P. Robinson, & P. Smith (Eds.), *Language: Social psychological perspectives.* Oxford: Pergamon.

Scotton, C. (1993). *Social motivations for code-switching.* New York: Oxford University Press.

Sherrod, D. (1989). The influence of gender on same sex friendships. In C. Hendrick (Ed.), *Close relationships.* Newbury Park, CA: Sage.

Sieburg, E. (1975). Interpersonal confirmation. ERIC document No. ED 098 634.

Sillars, A. (1980). Attribution and communication in roommate conflicts. *Communication Monographs, 47,* 180–200.

Sillars, A. (1982). Attribution and communication. In M. Roloff & C. Berger (Eds.), *Social cognition and communication.* Beverly Hills, CA: Sage.

Sillars, A. (1985). Interpersonal perception in relationships. In W. Ickes (Ed.), *Compatible and incompatible relationships.* New York: Springer-Verlag.

Sillars, A., Burggraf, C., Yost, S., & Zeitlow, P. (1992). Conversational themes and marital relationship definitions. *Human Communication Research, 19,* 124–154.

Sillars, A., Coletti, S., Parry, D., & Rogers, M. (1982). Coding verbal conflict tactics. *Human Communication Research, 9,* 83–95.

Sillars, A., & Parry, D. (1982). Stress, cognition, and communication in interpersonal conflicts. *Communication Research, 9,* 201–226.

Sillars, A., Weisberg, J., Burggraf, C., & Wilson, E. (1987). Content themes in marital conversations. *Human Communication Research, 13,* 495–528.

Simmel, G. (1950). The stranger. In K. Wolff (Ed. & Trans.), *The sociology of Georg Simmel.* New York: Free Press (originally published 1908).

Simon, S., & Simon, S. (1991). Forgiveness. *Lotus, Fall,* 3–9.

Simons, H., Berkowitz, N., & Moyer, R. (1970). Similarity, credibility, and attitude change. *Psychological Bulletin, 73,* 1–16.

Skevington, S. (1989). A place for emotion in social identity theory. In S. Skevington & D. Baker (Eds.), *The social identity of women.* London: Sage.

Skevington, S., & Baker, D. (Eds.). (1989). *The social identity of women.* London: Sage.

Slater, P. (1968). Some social consequences of temporary systems. In W. Bennis & P. Slater (Eds.), *The temporary society.* Boston: Little, Brown.

Smith, P. M. (1985). *Language. the sexes and society.* Oxford, UK: Blackwell.

Snyder, M. (1974). Self-monitoring of expressive behavior. *Journal of Personality and Social Psychology, 30,* 526–537.

Snyder, M., & Gangestad, S. (1982). Choosing social situations. *Journal of Personality and Social Psychology, 43,* 123–135.

Snyder, M., Gangestad, S., & Simpson, J. (1983). Choosing friends as activity partners. *Journal of Personality and Social Psychology, 45,* 1061–1075.

Sorrels, B. (1983). *The nonsexist communicator.* Englewood Cliffs, NJ: Prentice-Hall.

Sorrentino, R. M., & Short, J. A. (1986). Uncertainty orientation, motivation, and cognition. In R. M. Sorrentino & E. T. Higgins (Eds.), *Handbook of motivation and cognition.* New York: Guilford.

Spielberger, C. (1979). *Understanding stress in anxiety.* New York: Harper & Row.

Spitzberg, B., & Cupach, W. (1984). *Interpersonal communication competence.* Beverly Hills, CA: Sage.

Sprecher, S. (1987). The effects of self-disclosure given and received on affection for intimate partner and stability of the relationship. *Journal of Social and Personal Relationships, 4,* 115–128.

Stamp, G., Vangelisti, A., & Daly, J. (1992). The

creation of defensiveness in interaction. *Communication Quarterly, 40,* 177–190.

Stanley, J. (1977). Paradigmatic women. In D. Shores & C. Hines (Eds.), *Papers in language variation.* Tuscaloosa: University of Alabama Press.

Staub, E. (1989). *The roots of evil.* New York: Cambridge University Press.

Steinfatt, T. (1989). Linguistic relativity. In S. Ting-Toomey & F. Korzenny (Eds.), *Language, communication, and culture.* Newbury Park, CA: Sage.

Stephan, W. G. (1985). Intergroup relations. In G. Lindzey & E. Aronson (Eds.), *Handbook of social psychology* (3rd ed., Vol. II). New York: Random House.

Stephan, W. G., & Rosenfield, D. (1982). Racial and ethnic stereotyping. In A. Millar (Ed.), *In the eye of the beholder.* New York: Praeger.

Stephan, W. G., & Stephan, C. W. (1985). Intergroup anxiety. *Journal of Social Issues, 41,* 157–166.

Stephan, W. G., & Stephan, C. W. (1989). Antecedents of intergroup anxiety in Asian-Americans and Hispanic-Americans. *International Journal of Intercultural Relations, 13,* 203–219.

Sternberg, R. (1986). A triangular theory of love. *Psychological Review, 93,* 119–135.

Stewart, J. (1990). Interpersonal communication. In J. Stewart (Ed.), *Bridges not walls* (5th ed.). New York: McGraw-Hill.

Stewart, J., & Thomas, M. (1990). Dialogic listening. In J. Stewart (Ed.), *Bridges not walls* (5th ed.). New York: McGraw-Hill.

Stewart, L. P., Stewart, A.D., Friedley, S.A., & Cooper, P.J. (1990). *Communication between the sexes* (2nd ed.). Scottsdale, AZ: Gorsuch Scarisbrick.

Stone, A., Hedges, S., Neale, J., & Satin, M. (1985). Prospective and cross-sectional mood reports offer no evidence of a "Blue Monday" phenomenon. *Journal of Personality and Social Psychology, 49,* 129–134.

Stone, C. (1974). *Should trees have standing?* Los Altos, CA: Kaufmann.

Strobe, W., Kruglanski, A., Bar-Tal, D., & Hewstone, M. (Eds.). (1988). *The social psychology of intergroup conflict.* New York: Springer-Verlag.

Stryker, S. (1981). Symbolic interactionism. In M. Rosenberg & R. Turner (Edg.), *Social psychology.* New York: Basic Books.

Stryker, S. (1987). Identity theory. In K. Yardley & T. Honess (Eds.), *Self and society.* Chichester, UK: Wiley.

Stryker, S., & Statham, A. (1985). Symbolic interactionism and role theory. In G. Lindzey & E. Aronson (Eds.), *Handbook of social psychology* (3rd ed., Vol I). New York: Random House.

Stuart, R. (1980). *Helping couples change.* New York: Guilford.

Sudweeks, S., Gudykunst, W. B., Nishida, T., & Ting-Toomey, S. (1990). Relational themes in Japanese-North American relationships. *International Journal of Intercultural Relations, 14,* 207–233.

Sumner, W. G. (1940). *Folkways.* Boston: Ginn.

Sunnafrank, M. (1991). Interpersonal attraction and attitude similarity. In J. Anderson (Ed.), *Communication yearbook 14.* Newbury Park, CA: Sage.

Sunnafrank, M., & Miller, G. R. (1981). The role of initial conversation in determining attraction to similar and dissimilar others. *Human Communication Research, 8,* 16–25.

Sussman, N., & Rosenfeld, H. (1982). Influence of culture, language and sex on conversational distance. *Journal of Personality and Social Psychology, 42,* 66–74.

Swann, W. (1990). To be adored or to be known. In E. T. Higgins & R. Sorrentino (Eds.), *Handbook of motivation and cognition* (Vol. 2). New York: Guilford.

Tajfel, H. (1978). Social categorization, social identity, and social comparisons. In H. Tajfel (Ed.), *Differentiation between social groups.* London: Academic Press.

Tajfel, H. (1981). Social stereotypes and social groups. In J. Turner & H. Giles (Eds.), *In-*

tergroup behavior. Chicago: University of Chicago Press.

Tajfel, H., & Turner, J. (1979). An integrative theory of intergroup conflict. In W. Austin & S. Worchel (Eds.), *The social psychology of intergroup relations.* Monterey, CA: Brooks/Cole.

Tamir, L. (1984). The older person's communicative needs. In R. Dunkle, M. Haig, & M. Rosenberg (Eds.), *Communications technology and the elderly.* New York: Springer.

Tannen, D. (1975). Communication mix and mixup or how linguistics can ruin a marriage. *San Jose State Occasional Papers on Linguistics,* 205–211.

Tannen, D. (1979). Ethnicity as conversational style. In *Working papers in sociolinguistics* (No. 55). Austin, TX: Southwest Educational Development Laboratory.

Tannen, D. (1986). *That's not what I said.* New York: Ballantine.

Tannen, D. (1990). *You just don't understand.* New York: Morrow.

Tannen, D. (1993). Commencement address at State University of New York at Binghamton. Printed in *Chronicle of Higher Education,* June 9, 1993, p. B5.

Tavris, C. (1982). *Anger: The misunderstood emotion.* New York: Simon & Schuster.

Taylor, C. (1991). *The ethics of authenticity.* Cambridge: Harvard University Press.

Taylor, C. (1992). Multiculturalism and the politics of recognition. In A. Gutmann (Ed.), *Multiculturalism and the politics of recognition.* Princeton, NJ: Princeton University Press.

Taylor, S., & Fiske, S. (1978). Salience, attention, and attribution. In L. Berkowitz (Ed.), *Advances in experimental social psychology* (Vol. 11). New York: Academic Press.

Tempest, R. (1990, June 12). Hate survives a holocaust: Anti-Semitism resurfaces. *Los Angeles Times,* pp. H1, H7.

Thibaut, J., & Kelley, H. H. (1959). *The social psychology of groups.* New York: Wiley.

Thomas, K. (1983). Conflict and its management. In M. Dunnette (Ed.), *Handbook of industrial and organizational psychology.* New York: Wiley.

Thompson, T. (1982). Disclosure as a disability management strategy. *Communication Quarterly, 30,* 196–202.

Thompson, T., & Seibold, D. (1978). Stigma management in normal-stigmatized interaction. *Human Communication Research, 4,* 231–242.

Tinder, G. (1980). *Community: Reflections on a tragic ideal.* Baton Rouge: Louisiana State University Press.

Ting-Toomey, S. (1983). An analysis of verbal communication patterns in high and low marital adjustment groups. *Human Communication Research, 9,* 306–319.

Ting-Toomey, S. (1986). Conflict styles in black and white subjective cultures. In Y. Kim (Ed.), *Current research in interpersonal communication.* Beverly Hills, CA: Sage.

Ting-Toomey, S. (1988). A face negotiation theory. In Y. Kim & W. Gudykunst (Eds.), *Theories in intercultural communication.* Newbury Park, CA: Sage.

Ting-Toomey, S. (1994). Managing intercultural conflicts effectively. In L. Samovar & R. Porter (Eds.), *Intercultural communication: A reader* (7th ed.). Belmont, CA: Wadsworth.

Todd-Mancillas, W. (1981). Masculine generics = sexist language. *Communication Quarterly, 29,* 107–115.

Tracy, K. (1985). Conversational coherence. In R. Street & J. Cappella (Eds.), *Sequence and pattern in communicative behavior.* London: Edward Arnold.

Tracy, K., Dusen, D. V., & Robinson, S. (1987). "Good" and "bad" criticism. *Journal of Communication, 37,* 46–59.

Trafimow, D., Triandis, H. C., & Goto, S. (1991). Some tests of the distinction between the private self and the collective self. *Journal of Personality and Social Psychology, 60,* 649–655.

Trager, G. (1958). Paralanguage. *Studies in Linguistics, 13,* 1–12.

Triandis, H. C. (1975). Culture training, cognitive complexity, and interpersonal attitudes. In R. Brislin, S. Bochner, & W. Lonner (Eds.), *Cross-cultural perspectives on learning.* Beverly Hills, CA: Sage.

Triandis, H. C. (1977). *Interpersonal behavior.* Monterey, CA: Brooks/Cole.

Triandis, H. C. (1980). Values, attitudes, and interpersonal behavior. In M. Page (Ed.), *Nebraska symposium on motivation* (Vol. 27). Lincoln: University of Nebraska Press.

Triandis, H. C. (1983). Essentials of studying culture. In D. Landis & R. Brislin (Eds.), *Handbook of intercultural training* (Vol. I). Elmsford, NY: Pergamon.

Triandis, H. C. (1984). A theoretical framework for the more efficient construction of cultural assimilators. *International Journal of Intercultural Relations, 8,* 301–330.

Triandis, H. C. (1988). Collectivism vs. individualism. In G. Verma & C. Bagley (Eds.), *Cross-cultural studies of personality, attitudes, and cognition.* London: Macmillan.

Triandis, H. C., Brislin, R., & Hui, C. H. (1988). Cross-cultural training across the individualism-collectivism divide. *International Journal of Intercultural Relations, 12,* 269–289.

Triandis, H. C., Leung, K., Villareal, M., & Clack, F. (1985). Allocentric vs. idiocentric tendencies. *Journal of Research in Personality, 19,* 395–415.

Trilling, L. (1968). *Beyond culture.* New York: Viking Press.

Turner, J. C. (1982). Towards a cognitive redefinition of the social group. In H. Tajfel (Ed.), *Social identity and intergroup relations.* Cambridge: Cambridge University Press.

Turner, J. C. (1987). *Rediscovering the social group.* Oxford: Blackwell.

Turner, J. H. (1988). *A theory of social interaction.* Stanford, CA: Stanford University Press.

Turner, R. H. (1987). Articulating self and social structure. In K. Yardley & T. Honess (Eds.), *Self and society.* Chichester, UK: Wiley.

van Dijk, T. (1984). *Prejudice in discourse.* Philadelphia: Benjamins.

Vangelisti, A., Knapp, M., & Daly, J. (1990). Conversational narcissism. *Communication Monographs, 57,* 251–274.

Vanlear, A. (1991). Testing a cyclical model of communication openness in relationship development. *Communication Monographs, 58,* 337–361.

Vassiliou, V., Triandis, H. C., Vassiliou, G., & McGuire, H. (1972). Interpersonal contact and stereotyping. In H. Triandis, *Analysis of subjective culture.* New York: Wiley.

Vlastos, G. (1991). *Socrates, ironist and moral philosopher.* Ithaca, NY: Cornell University Press.

Wallace, A. (1952). Individual differences and cultural uniformities. *American Sociological Review, 17,* 747–750.

Walster, E., & Walster, G. (1978). *A new look at love.* Reading, MA: Addison-Wesley.

Waterman, A. (1984). *The psychology of individualism.* New York: Praeger.

Waters, M. (1990). *Ethnic options.* Berkeley: University of California Press.

Watson, K., Barker, L., & Weaver, J. (1992). *Development and validation of the listener preference profile.* Paper presented at the International Listening Association convention.

Watts, A. (1966). *The book: On the taboo against knowing who you are.* New York: Pantheon.

Watzlawick, P., Beavin, J., & Jackson, D. (1967). *The pragmatics of human communication.* New York: Norton.

Weaver, C. (1972). *Human listening.* Indianapolis: Bobbs-Merril.

Wegner, D., & Vallacher, R. (1977). *Implicit psychology.* New York: Oxford University Press.

Weiner-Davis, M. (1992). *Divorce busting.* New York: Summit Books.

Westen, D. (1991). Cultural, emotional, and unconscious aspects of self. In R. Curtis (Ed.), *The relational self.* New York: Guilford.

Wheeless, L., & Wheeless, V. (1982). Attributions, gender orientation, and adaptability. *Communication Quarterly, 30,* 56-66.

Wheeless, V. (1984). A test of the theory of speech accommodation using language and gender orientations. *Women's Studies in Communication, 7,* 13-22.

Wheeless, V., Berryman-Fink, C., & Sarafini, D. (1982). The use of gender specific pronouns in the 1980s. *The Encoder, 9(3-4),* 35-46.

White, S. (1989). Back channels across cultures. *Language in Society, 18,* 5976.

Whorf, B. (1952). *Collected papers on metalinguistics.* Washington, DC: Foreign Service Institute.

Whyte, M. (1990). *Dating, mating, and marriage.* New York: Aldine de Gruyter.

Wiemann, J. M. (1985). Interpersonal control and regulation in conversation. In R. Street & J. Cappella (Edg.), *Sequence and pattern in communicative behavior.* London: Edward Arnold.

Wiemann, J. M., & Backlund, P. (1980). Current theory and research in communication competence. *Review of Educational Research, 50,* 185-199.

Wiemann, J. M., & Bradac, J. (1989). Metatheoretical issues in the study of communicative competence. In B. Dervin (Ed.), *Progress in communication sciences* (Vol. 9). Norwood, NJ: Ablex.

Wiemann, J. M., Chen, V., & Giles, H. (1986). *Beliefs about talk and silence in cultural context.* Paper presented at the Speech Communication Association convention, Chicago.

Wiemann, J. M., & Kelly, C. (1981). Pragmatics of interpersonal competence. In C. Wilder-Mott & J. Weaklund (Eds.), *Rigor and imagination.* New York: Praeger.

Wilder, D. A., & Shapiro, P. (1989). Effects of anxiety on impression formation in a group context. *Journal of Experimental Social Psychology, 25,* 481-499.

Williams, J. (1984). Gender and intergroup behavior. *British Journal of Social Psychology, 23,* 311-316.

Wispe, L. (1986). The distinction between sympathy and empathy. *Journal of Personality and Social Psychology, 50,* 314-321.

Wolkin, A., & Coakley, C. (1992). *Listening* (5th ed.), Dubuque, IA: William C. Brown.

Worchel, S., & Norwell, N. (1980). Effect of perceived environmental conditions during cooperation on intergroup attraction. *Journal of Personality and Social Psychology, 38,* 764-772.

Wright, P. (1978). Toward a theory of friendship based on a conception of self. *Human Communication Research, 4,* 196-207.

Wylie, R. (1979). *The self-concept.* Lincoln: University of Nebraska Press.

Yamada, H. (1990). Topic management and turn distributions in business meetings: American versus Japanese strategies. *Text, 10,* 271-295.

Yankelovich, D. (1981). *New rules: Searching for self-fulfillment in a world turned upside down.* New York: Random House.

Yum, J. O. (1987). Korean philosophy and communication. In D. Kincaid (Ed.), *Communication theory from eastern and western perspectives.* New York: Academic Press.

Zajonc, R. (1980). Feeling and thinking. *American Psychologist, 35,* 151-175.

Zerubavel, E. (1991). *The fine line: Making distinctions in everyday life.* New York: Free Press.

Zoglin, R. (1993, June 21). All you need is hate. *Time,* p. 63.

Zuckerman, M., Lipets, M., Koivimakin, J., & Rosenthal, R. (1975). Encoding and decoding nonverbal cues of emotion. *Journal of Personality and Social Psychology, 32,* 1068-1076.

Photo Credits

P. 4, Owen Franken/Stock Boston; p. 16, Alan Carey/The Image Works; p. 19, Jean-Claude LeJeune/Stock Boston; p. 52, Mahoney/The Image Works; p. 58, Steven Burr Williams/The Image Bank; p. 63, Spencer Grant/Stock Boston; p. 74, Karen Kerckhove/Aurora Beacon News; p. 83, © Michael Newman/PhotoEdit; p. 104, Bob Sacha; p. 111, Dilip Mehta/ Contact Press Images; p. 116, © 1993 Bob Sacha; p. 136, Pascal le Segretain/Sygma; p. 139, Nicholas DeVore/Tony Stone Images; p. 151, Alon Reininger/Leo de Wys, Inc.; p. 167, © David W. Hamilton/The Image Bank; p. 175, © Chromosohm/Sohm/Stock Boston; p. 178, James Schnepf; p. 191, Steve Smith/Onyx; p. 196, PEOPLE WEEKLY © 1994 Matthew J. Atanian; p. 201, Barbara Rios/Photo Researchers; p. 219, Joseph Schuyler/Stock Boston; p. 221, Jennifer Waddell; p. 229, David Young-Wolff/PhotoEdit; p. 251, Hazel Hankin/Stock Boston; p. 262, Clark Jones/Impact Visuals; p. 268, Scott Robinson/Tony Stone Images; p. 278, Jean-Claude LeJeune; p. 285, David Hanson/Tony Stone Images; p. 295, Joe Sohm/The Image Works; p. 309, © M. Courtney-Clarke; p. 315, Bobbie Kingsley/Photo Researchers; p. 328, Bob Daemmrich Photography; p. 341, Stephanie Rausser/Impact Visuals; p. 347, Robert Brenner/PhotoEdit; p. 359, Alain McLaughlin/Impact Visuals; p. 371, Rhoda Sidney/Stock Boston; p. 376, Sharon Stewart/Impact Visuals; p. 382, Paul Conklin; p. 389, Frank Siteman/Stock Boston; p. 390, Tony Freeman/PhotoEdit; p. 402, © Catherine Karnow/ Woodfin Camp & Associates; p. 417, Bob Daemmrich Photography; p. 426, John Kaplan Photography.

Chapter Opening Credits

Chapter 1 "The Quilting Party." Artist Unidentified. Abby A. Rockefeller Folk Art Center, Williamsburg, VA.

Chapter 2 Russian Dolls. Photo by John Williamson.

Chapter 3 "Two Men Discussing Coming Hunt" by Kavavoa. Reproduced with the permission of the West Baffin Eskimo Co-operative Ltd. Photo Courtesy Canadian Museum of Civilization, Negative #J-19619-3.

Chapter 4 "Coney Island—Luna Park" by Vestie Davis. Collection of Joan and Darwin Bahm.

Chapter 5 "Conflict" by Katherine Knauer. Photo by Schecter Lee. Part of the Quilt National Collection. Transparency Courtesy The Taunton Press.

Chapter 6 "Duke and Duchess of Windsor on Their Wedding Day" by Jim Colclough. David L. Davies.

Chapter 7 "New York Lady" by Leslie L. Payne. Collection Chuck and Jan Rosenak.

Chapter 8 "Mother and Child in Mountain Landscape" attributed to Eunice Pinney. Abby A. Rockefeller Folk Art Center, Williamsburg, VA.

Chapter 9 "Cochiti Drummer-Storyteller" by Louis Naranjo. The Rainbow Man, Inc. Santa Fe, New Mexico.

Chapter 10 "Yard Sale" by Mattie Lou O'Kelley from *Mattie Lou O'Kelley: Folk Artist.* Copyright © 1989 by Mattie Lou O'Kelley. By permission Little, Brown and Company.

Chapter 11 "Cafe Bar" by Michiko Sonobe. Photo by Brian Blauser. Part of the Quilt National Collection.

Chapter 12 "Marriage Certificate for John Stover and Eliza Vonada Stover" attributed to Henry Young. Abby A. Rockefeller Folk Art Center, Williamsburg, VA.

Chapter 13 "Morgan Addressing His Friends." Artist unidentified. Abby A. Rockefeller Folk Art Center, Williamsburg, VA.

Chapter 14 "York Family at Home" atttributed to Joseph H. Davis. Abby A. Rockefeller Folk Art Center, Williamsburg, VA.

Chapter 15 "Accupuncture Pitchfork Style" by Uncle Jack Dey. Collection Chuck and Jan Rosenak.

Author Index

Subject Index